LIFE AND LEISURE
IN ANCIENT ROME

Dr J.P.V.D. Balsdon was a Fellow of Exeter College, Oxford, where he lectured in ancient history. He was President of the Society for the Promotion of Roman Studies, a Member of the Council of the British School in Rome, and a Fellow of the British Academy. Dr Balsdon died in 1977.

Other titles in the Phoenix Press Daily Life Series

Daily Life of the Etruscans by Jacques Heurgon
Daily Life in Ancient India by Jeannine Auboyer
Daily Life of the Aztecs by Jacques Soustelle
Daily Life in Greece at the Time of Pericles
by Robert Flacelière
Daily Life in Palestine at the Time of Christ
by Henri Daniel-Rops

LIFE AND LEISURE
IN ANCIENT ROME

J.P.V.D. Balsdon

PHOENIX
PRESS

5 UPPER SAINT MARTIN'S LANE
LONDON
WC2H 9EA

A PHOENIX PRESS PAPERBACK

First published in Great Britain
by The Bodley Head in 1969
This paperback edition published in 2002
by Phoenix Press,
a division of The Orion Publishing Group Ltd,
Orion House, 5 Upper St Martin's Lane,
London WC2H 9EA

A CIP catalogue record for this book is available
from the British Library.

Printed in Great Britain by Clays Ltd, St Ives plc

ISBN 1 84212 593 1

CONTENTS

6 CONTENTS

ILLUSTRATIONS

Supplementary notes on the illustrations will be found on page 349.

PREFACE

MY DEBTS to others are extensive and are appropriately acknowledged, I hope, in the notes. In two cases the debt is so great that it must be recorded here: to Professor A. Degrassi for his splendid publication of the *Fasti* in *Inscriptiones Italiae* xiii and to Mr. A. N. Sherwin-White for his admirable edition of the Letters of the younger Pliny. I have had invaluable assistance from both books. In the publishing world, Mr. Colin Haycraft persuaded me to write my *Roman Women* and was closely involved in the early stages of this present book. He has given me, and continues to give me, encouragement of a very rare kind for which I can never express sufficient thanks. Mr. James Michie has taken more trouble over this book than I could possibly have expected. What blemishes he has removed, only he and I know.

Two Oxford friends, Mr. Oswyn Murray of Balliol, my old pupil, and Mr. Fergus Millar of The Queen's College have generously helped me, and improved the book, by reading the proofs.

Translations from ancient authors are generally my own, but I have drawn heavily on William Arrowsmith's sparkling translation of Petronius' *Satyricon* and am grateful to him and to his publisher for permission to do this. I am extremely grateful, too, to those who have given me leave for the reproduction of illustrations; appropriate acknowledgements are made in the text.

As this book marks the end of my long teaching career at Oxford, my mind naturally goes back with affection and gratitude to my own teachers. To anybody who does not know Oxford—and to many who do—it will hardly seem credible that between 1920 and 1924 in a single Oxford College anybody could have had the fortune to be taught by four scholars of such outstanding distinction as Lewis R. Farnell, E. A. Barber, R. R. Marett and Bernard W. Henderson, to whom more than to anybody else I owe what pretensions I have to being a reputable historian.

In the last sentence of the preface to his last book, *Five Roman Emperors*, Henderson threw a bouquet to some of his old pupils, and there is no example of his that I would more willingly follow. My own intense interest in ancient history has been sharpened and stimulated over all these years by my own pupils in Greats and by the men and women who have patiently sat out my lectures. I often wonder if young people realize the degree to which they themselves determine the quality of the lectures to which they listen. If, as I am conceited enough to think, I lecture well, that is because I always seem to lecture to stimulating and exciting audiences. Whether or not this book falls into the hands of people whom I have taught or to whom I have lectured, I should like to think that each of them realizes the gratitude which I owe them all.

Oxford, 1969   J. P. V. D. Balsdon

IN THIS reprint, the bibliography is supplemented (p. 344) and mistakes and misprints are corrected, thanks to reviewers and friends who pointed them out to me, particularly M. L. Clarke, John H. D'Arms, Lily Ross Taylor, P. G. Walsh and Stefan Weinstock.

GREAT HASELEY, 1974   J.P.V.D.B.

INTRODUCTION

++

ANYBODY WHO is at all interested in the Romans is bound to ask what life was like in Roman times. The question could only be answered—if it could be answered at all—in a book several times as long as this.

What was life like—*for whom*? For an affluent upper-class Roman?* For the *bourgeoisie*? For manual workers in the cities? For agricultural workers? For freedmen? For slaves? For people living in Rome and Italy? For people living in the western provinces of the Empire, which Rome was civilizing? For those living in the eastern provinces from which so much of Roman civilization derived? For soldiers? For civilians? For those in the provinces who were Roman citizens or for those who were not? For men? For women? For children?

When you ask what life was like, what do you mean by *life*? What kind of pots people cooked with? How great was their fear of fire? Did Romans carry umbrellas? What did women do for handbags and shopping-bags? Were soldiers the only people who carried their money in their belts? Did other people, when they shopped, carry it in purses strung to their wrists or hung round their necks? What did the fold of the toga hold? Where did you keep your handkerchief?[2]

What of deeper, more intangible and yet more fundamental things? Did the Roman woman first aware of her pregnancy reflect that, if her child was born alive, there was a strong probability that it would not survive infancy and indeed a considerable possibility that she would herself die in childbirth? While the psalmist declared the days of man to be three-score years and modern insurance advertisements suggest, and their readers assume, a higher normal age than that, was the young adult Roman conscious of the fact that it was more likely than not that he would not survive his forties?[3] What of the dynamic of religion? For in a civilization that was so remarkably static through

* And what was affluence? What sized income? How much capital? And capital invested in what ways?[1]

the centuries,* religion was the one dynamic element. Traditional Roman religion withered with its lifeless, impersonal formality. Then came the excitement of the oriental cults and the sanguine belief which overlooked worrying facts—such as the astrologer who himself was shipwrecked†—that astrology could reveal, though it could not alter, the future. There was the horror of magic, increasingly pervasive. And in due course there was the challenge of Christianity, itself in several minds about itself.4 What of life and death? How many people were concerned by the prospects for good or ill of an afterlife? Did large numbers of people suffer from a profound anxiety-complex? Were the Romans by instinct an abnormally brutal, cruel people? How explain the ready courage with which so many people committed suicide? And what of sex, birth-control,5 homosexuality?

You have only to read Plautus, Terence and Petronius to realize that Romans laughed at the same sort of things as we laugh at. They cried— rather more uncontrollably, being Mediterranean people—at the kind of things that we cry over. They would have adored television and football matches, had they been available; there can be no doubt of it. But what about their watching gladiators killing one another?

A number of good books have been written about the material side of Roman life.6 A good book on what may be called the spiritual side of their civilization, about their outlook on living, has yet to be written. This book has a more modest scope. The questions which it seeks to answer are these. How did the Romans spend their time? What was the shape of a Roman day? Was the *nundinum* anything like a modern week? How did the seven-day week come into existence?

What were the features of family life? How much did people work and how much did they relax, and how did they relax? Were educated people bedevilled by their own principles? What games, indoors and outdoors, did people play? How much did they move about, in Italy and outside it? What were the public games and shows like, from the performers' and the victims' point of view as much as from the point of view of those for whom they made a Roman holiday?

Anybody who wants to know what kinds of lives Romans led has six different kinds of evidence at his disposal.

First there are the stray pieces of information which are dropped un-

---

* It is because it was so static that in a book like this, which concentrates on the first century B.C. and the first two centuries A.D., evidence can often be used from the second century B.C. at one extreme and the sixth century A.D. (Cassiodorus) at the other.

† Physician, heal thyself. Why did the astrologer not know it was going to happen?

wittingly by a wide range of ancient writers—playwrights, orators, historians, biographers, letter-writers. With little notion that anybody would ever want to scavenge for such scraps and use them, ancient writers from time to time revealed what at different times of the day and at different seasons of the year in a wide variety of places people were doing with their time. Suetonius, for instance, gave as an instance of the emperor Gaius' irresponsible cruelty that he woke his wife Caesonia to tell her that by a single sentence he had just condemned forty men who were before him on forty different charges.[7] From this we learn that while she was taking a siesta after lunch, the Emperor was busy in the courts.

Next there are the satirists and the epigrammatists, in the main Horace, Juvenal and Martial. Their evidence needs to be handled with extreme care. First of all they were, all three of them, idlers, leeches on the body of society. They were interested in a very particular and very limited world, in the things which society people gossiped about and the *bêtises* which, in society, ill-bred and ill-behaved people committed. They avoided, and avoided writing about, things and people that were tediously dull—about ordinary people, in fact. A satirist, like a cartoonist, must distort. Therefore within their limited field they are not to be treated as simple purveyors of the truth.

The evidence of the moralist, our third source, must be handled with greater caution still. Seneca has a great deal to tell us in his philosophical works and in his letters. But a man who has run away from many of the pleasures and enjoyments of ordinary human life, public entertainments, good eating and good drinking, a liking of beautiful material objects for their own sake, is no safe guide. He is in fact a bigot and sees life through badly distorted lenses. For, once you yourself cease to take pleasure in the common enjoyments of life, you hate the normal man who is so much more fortunate than yourself.[8]

Next there are inscriptions. Gravestones in their thousands give us what is almost our only contact with the bulk of Rome's population, with the ordinary man—the soldier, the trader, the shopkeeper, the artisan. There are all the *graffiti* at Pompeii. And there are important epigraphical documents, like the evidence of Marcus Aurelius' attempt to reduce the crippling expense which had to be shouldered by those whose position forced them to give public games.[9] Evidence of a similar kind to this last comes to us too, of course by a different and most valuable channel, Justinian's codification of Roman law, the *Corpus Iuris Civilis*.

Then, for Egypt, there is all the evidence of the wastepaper basket and of the rubbish dump, evidence in a class of its own for life in Egypt: account books, bills, receipts, private letters, school exercise-books and the rest. These have been used in a vivid account of life in Roman Egypt.[10] They often throw light on a wider field still.

Lastly, archaeology. Thanks to the archaeologist we know better than we could have known from any literary description the size and arrangement of the Roman private house, whether in the town or in the country. We know the dimensions and lay-out of baths, theatres, amphitheatres. We have numerous every-day objects, the furniture people sat on, the dice they played with. From Pompeii and Hercu-laneum we have all the evidence about life on the day when life stopped, in A.D. 79. There are numerous stone reliefs illustrating the hunt. And particularly for racing in the circus, the gladiatorial encounters and the wild beast hunts in the amphitheatre, we have a variety of startlingly good mosaics, from the Villa Borghesi in Rome, from Piazza Armerina in Sicily, from numerous sites in the Roman north-African provinces.

However, the archaeological evidence tells us more about the rich than about the poor. The owners of the excavated Pompeian houses were comfortably off and it is chiefly their not inexpensive possessions which have survived. The literary evidence is less representative still. Writers were educated and, generally, cultured men. They wrote for people like themselves, often patrons. In Rome particularly, writers on whom we depend heavily—Cicero, Horace, Seneca, the younger Pliny—give us marvellous information, but most of it concerns the upper crust of society. Household slaves and freedmen were an inti-mate part of such people's lives; without them they could not have lived as they did. So, apart from the fact that a slave was a good subject for a philosopher to moralize about, household slaves and the lives which such slaves led are better known to us than are the lives of simple Roman citizens who belonged to the lower social classes. Hence the unique value to us of Petronius' *Satyricon* and the funerary inscriptions, often with illustrative reliefs, of the lower *bourgeoisie*.

There are two monumental books on Roman social life, by Joachim Marquardt and by Ludwig Friedlaender. While there is very little indeed in the ancient literary sources which those scholars had not already noted, a historian today has the advantage of much epi-graphical and archaeological material, particularly published mosaics, which was not available when they wrote. If this book, a very slight book by comparison with theirs, proves to have interest, it will be because of its concentration on the lives which people actually led, in respect of work and leisure. In it an attempt is made to look at the Romans and their manner of living in the way in which sociologists and others are now concerning themselves with the significance of work and with the employment of leisure in the lives of present-day men and women.

Hours of the day in Rome,
expressed in modern terms (from Marquardt 1,257f.)

HOUR	MIDSUMMER	MIDWINTER
1	4.27–5.42	7.33–8.17
2	5.42–6.58	8.17–9.02
3	6.58–8.13	9.02–9.46
4	8.13–9.29	9.46–10.31
5	9.29–10.44	10.31–11.15
6	10.44–12.00	11.15–12.00
7	12.00–1.15	12.00–12.44
8	1.15–2.31	12.44–1.29
9	2.31–3.46	1.29–2.13
10	3.46–5.02	2.13–2.58
11	5.02–6.17	2.58–3.42
12	6.17–7.33	3.42–4.27

I

THE SHAPE OF THE DAY[1]

+++

1. Morning

THE ROMANS had a twenty-four-hour day and night, just as we do but, in a manner different from ours, daylight was divided into twelve hours and darkness into another twelve. Only at the equinox was each of the twenty-four hours of equal length. For the rest of the year an hour of daylight differed in length from an hour of night, and the length of an hour of daylight (and of night) differed from month to month. Noon, however, was always the sixth hour of the day and midnight the sixth hour of night. There were public sundials and water clocks[2] (these last adjusted to fit the current season of the year), sundials from the third century B.C., water-clocks from the second; they came to be found also in the baths and in private houses.[3] A plaguish modern invention, in the opinion of a parasite in a play of Plautus; things were better by far when your appetite told you that it was dinner time, and you had not to wait for the clock. '*Venter solarium*', 'My belly is my sundial'.[4]

So in Persia in the fourth century A.D. it continued to be, 'outside the King's tables'. It was more than a century after that when, in the northern kingdom of Burgundia, King Gundobad received from Theoderic, King of the Ostrogoths and Romans, the gift of a sundial and a water-clock, accompanied by a sententious letter drafted by Cassiodorus: 'Let Burgundia arrange her daily actions by the movements of God's great lights, let her nicely adjust the moments of each hour. In mere confusion passes the order of life when this accurate division of time is unknown. Men are like the beasts if they only know the passage of the hours by the pangs of hunger, and have no greater certainty as to the flight of time than such as is afforded them by their bellies'.[5]

Numerous private sundials have been found at Herculaneum and at Pompeii, and inscriptions from all over the empire record the gifts of public clocks. In public places (particularly in the baths) and in private houses slaves informed people of the time,[6] shouting the hours. To the burdensome afflictions of a house-bound old man might be added the misfortune, if he was deaf, of not knowing the time.[7]

While there was time, there was, in ordinary life, nothing like accurate time. 'Philosophers will agree sooner than clocks will.'[8]

In writing of the Roman day it is convenient to treat the first hour of day as lasting from six to seven o'clock in the morning and the twelfth as lasting from five to six in the evening.* In fact, however, a daylight 'hour' at the winter solstice in Rome was about forty-five minutes long, at the summer solstice about an hour and a quarter; and the first 'hour' in winter ended at about a quarter past eight in the morning, at midsummer at about a quarter to six.[9]

This system of reckoning time was an inconvenience which survived in Italy long past antiquity, long past the middle ages. De Brosses, visiting Rome in 1739, wrote as follows of the two clocks (whose vestiges can be seen today) on the towers of the church of Santa Trinità de' Monti above the Spanish Steps in Rome†: 'The face of the clock on one of the towers marks the hours in the Italian style, from sunrise to sunset; the face of the clock on the other marks them as in France, according to the passage of the sun to the meridian; this is the only clock in Rome of this kind. How can the Italians persist in their foolish custom which renders every day and hour unequal? It is of no use except to travellers, to whom it gives the little advantage of knowing how many hours of sunlight they have left. However, one soon gets accustomed to this.'

Figuratively the Romans described the successive periods of night and day as after-midnight, cockcrow (*gallicinium*), still-time (*conticinium*, when the cocks have stopped crowing, but men are still asleep), dawn, morning, afternoon, sunset, vesper (called from the evening star), lighting-up time (*prima fax*), bedtime (*concubium*), depth of night (*intempesta nox*).[10]

The Romans in general lived by day and slept by night and, as in summer days were very long (from 4.30 a.m. to 7.30 p.m., by our reckoning) and in winter they were very short (from 7.30 a.m. to

---

* 'Hora' in Latin can either mean the conclusion or the duration of an hour. 'Secunda hora', for instance, can mean 'at the end of the second hour' or 'during the second hour'. Care is necessary here; but even with care it is not always possible to be entirely certain as between the two possible meanings.

† Selections from the Letters of De Brosses, tr. Lord Ronald Sutherland Gower, London, 1897, 151. I owe this interesting reference to the late Mr. R. Wakeford.

4.30 p.m.), there must, apart from temperature and clothing, have been a profound difference between summer life and winter life. This was something which Roman writers took for granted and, except in the medical writers, it is not commonly emphasized. Only two differences are quite commonly noted: that the after-lunch siesta, so highly desirable in the long hot summer afternoon, was unnecessary in winter, and that there was something unusual about a serious and sober dinner party which did not break up until after dark in summer (when it would have lasted 3¾ hours by our reckoning), while in winter, after 2¼ hours, this was not remarkable.*

Bakeries in Rome† were busy, as they always must be, during the night and, bakers apart, a large section of the Roman population was up and at work at daybreak.[11] These were not only the artisans. Heavily occupied and responsible men, for whom the day was anyhow far too short, were up too. The elder Pliny, for instance, who combined the life of an administrator and a scholar, often rose soon after midnight in winter; and conscientious emperors, who were evidently the most hard-working of men, rose early—emperors like Vespasian, Marcus Aurelius, who reported once that he had overslept, but none the less was up at work at the eleventh hour of night,‡ Septimius Severus and Julian, 'who divided his night between rest, public business and the Muses'. It was not evidence of over-eating in Galba's case that he breakfasted before daybreak; it suggests rather that he started work at a very early hour. It was the mark of an imperial debauchee (Gaius Caligula) to stay in bed all morning and to wonder—as on the day when he was murdered, he wondered—whether he felt well enough to get up for lunch.[13]

In republican times it had been the habit in well-ordered families for the slaves and freedmen to enter and bid good morning to their master (as children said good morning to their parents) first thing in the morning and to bid him good night last thing in the evening, but the habit died out and Galba's was said to be the last Roman household in which the practice persisted.[14]

* See below, p. 51.
† Bakeries in Rome dated from the second century B.C. Before that, all baking was done privately (Plin., NH 18, 107).
‡ Even when on holiday in the country, M. Aurelius was sometimes up working all through the night. On days when he hunted (at 9 in the morning), he got up at 3 A.M., the ninth hour of night, and worked until 8.[12]

From the middle of the second century B.C.,* when Scipio Aemilianus (enemy though he was of unguents, mirrors, depilation and young people dancing) conformed to the then modern habit of shaving, until the second century A.D. when, with the emperor Hadrian setting the fashion, beards once again became popular, at some time or other during the day men needed to shave. But to what extent they were shaved at home by a slave or went to a barber's shop for the purpose (barbers' shops being notorious centres of male life and gossip), and whether they were shaved early in the day or, as often in the modern Mediterranean world, later, we do not know.[15]

People started the day with the lightest of meals,† the *ientaculum*,[16] just as many Italians today take no more than a small cup of black coffee and a bun or a piece of bread at home or in a bar on the way to work. 'Get up,' Martial wrote in an epigram, 'already the baker is selling schoolboys their breakfast.'[17] Only that gourmand of all time, the emperor Vitellius—who, thanks to emetics, wolfed down three or four good meals a day and was sometimes drunk and stuffed by lunch time—turned the *ientaculum* into a serious meal. On his way out to assume the post of commander of the army of Upper Germany in A.D. 68, 'at pothouses and inns (*per stabula ac deversoria*) he was un- usually affable to carters and travellers. Every morning he asked them if they had had breakfast, and gave a great belch to show that he had breakfasted himself.'[18]

The majority of Romans could evidently sustain a long and hard morning's work on an empty, or practically empty, stomach—but not all. It suited the constitution of very old people to eat three smallish rather than two larger meals a day, the first (of bread, with honey or olives) in the morning at the third or fourth hour. Galen had a patient, a teacher (*grammaticus*) who, if he was kept busy until midday, was apt to collapse in epilepsy; he was told to take 'elevenses', to eat a little bread soaked in wine in the middle of the morning, at the third or fourth hour. Men who would have to work through until the ninth or tenth hour might find it convenient to take a substantial snack in the middle of the morning since they would miss lunch at midday.

Other people too, particularly in summer, may have taken a mid- morning snack (just as the modern Italian often slips out for a coffee and a bun in the course of his morning's work) and this, and nothing

---

* According to Varro, there had been barbers in Rome since 300 B.C. (Plin., *NH* 7, 211).

† Bread and cheese, for example (Apul., *Met.* 1, 18).

more gross, may have been the indulgence for which L. Piso, the consul of 58 B.C. ('at the fifth hour, his breath stinking of a filthy snack-bar'*) and Antony ('drinking and vomiting from the third hour') were rated by Cicero. Unfriendly voices even asserted that the younger Cato drank after breakfast—but this was not true, Plutarch assures us.[19]

The shops opened early; and during the first and second hours of the day the doors of the Emperor's palace and of the houses of rich and important members of society in Rome, and also in the great country towns, were open to callers. This was the time of the morning levée, the *salutatio*. In the life of the upper crust of society this was an important daily ceremony, however tedious. Outside the Emperor's palace there was a chattering crowd waiting for the announcement, 'The Emperor is receiving'—'*Caesarem iam salutari*'. Lists of callers at imperial salutations were published. To be refused admission was ominous.[20]

In the households of the great at Rome, the morning call had been, in republican times, predominantly an occasion for the unofficial transaction of private and public business, the time when the client solicited the advice and assistance of his patron, when political manœuvres were devised by politicians, support was arranged for candidates at forthcoming elections, and when foreigners charged with diplomatic business in Rome sought to win the support and sympathy of important senators for their cause.[21]

In course of time, formalities were introduced, borrowed from the daily practices of the great Hellenistic monarchs. Callers were graded, and received different degrees of attention. The tribunes C. Gracchus and the younger Livius Drusus were said to have introduced this discrimination in Rome. First they received private callers, then callers in small groups; finally the public (in the main, no doubt, their clients) were admitted.[22]

Of the six ranks in the Ptolemaic court the fourth had been that of 'the King's first friends', the fifth that 'of the King's friends'. So the first to be received in a great man's house in the Roman Republic and after that at the Emperor's *salutatio* were his friends, his *amici*.[23]

At the end of the Republic a politician gained prestige from the number of his morning callers, but, as Cicero discovered when his political influence was on the wane, the call might be inspired by no feeling warmer than frigid politeness.[24] With the establishment of the Empire, the morning call—outside the imperial household—lost its official character and sank to the level of a tedious social chore. In

* On *popinae*, see pp. 152–4.

private houses, the wealthy (among women, especially the elderly childless widow) received their friends and clients.[25] There were some who called out of accepted courtesy, consuls even.[26] The bulk of callers, however, were in the Empire on the outer fringe or beyond the fringe of good society, unsuccessful men who, at the cost of whatever personal humiliation, hoped for gain, favour or advantage considerably greater than the *sportula**—the 25 asses (6¼ sesterces) a day, or the food which they received in lieu.[27] Only a few houses remained whose clients were what in the good republican days *clientes* had been, real dependants who came to their *dominus* with serious problems of their daily life, which he helped them to solve.† Paetus Thrasea (under Nero) still gave such service to his clients; so did that Piso, whose panegyric survives, whose clients were neither mocked, downtrodden nor despised. Conversely, when the clients of a candidate for office in a municipal town canvassed for their patron, as innumerable *graffiti* from Pompeii record, they were behaving in the way in which a client had always been expected to behave.[28] But as a general rule what had once been a useful feature of Roman life was now a degradation, 'an insulting form of charity', and there is no writer under the Empire who did not condemn it as such. The clients, conspicuous in the uncomfortable toga, a garment which was too hot at one moment and too cold the next, which few people wore unless they were forced to, had to pick their way through the muddy streets, often before daylight. They were received by the slaves of the household (whom they were often forced to tip heavily[29]) with that offensive contempt which in all countries at all times the servants of the rich have lavished on impoverished gentry.[30] The butler, as likely as not, had forgotten their names. The master of the house, in conversation with someone more important, failed to notice their greeting. Yet some of the callers were expected to remain and provide an escort and clear a path for him when he went out of the house into the street and to attend him to the baths and see him home afterwards; after which, if there was time, they had to try to snatch a bath themselves.[31] They might be called on to perform any one of a number of tedious services—to pack the audience, perhaps, and to lead the applause when their patron gave a public recitation of his frigid poems. They might be asked to dinner—to be

* *Sportula*, meaning a little basket, gave its name to the 'dole', whether in food or money, because it was in a little basket that the food was given.

† As nowadays in the South of Italy in the hall of a resident landowner who farms his own land, you will sometimes see peasants from the estate sitting in the evening, waiting to ask his help about their private problems.

placed in segregation, often fed with cheap unpalatable food, while the patron and his intimate friends ate a delicious and expensive meal.[32]

'Consider', Seneca wrote, 'the people who keep a whole programme of official calls, a nuisance to themselves and to everybody else, mad but quite resolute in their madness, doing their round of calls every day, never seeing a door open without going in. Now, when you consider the vast size and infinite distractions of the city, answer this question. After they have completed their stipendiary round of calls at a whole variety of mansions, just how many people will they in fact have succeeded in seeing? Several of them will be pushed out of the way because the patron is asleep or amusing himself—or out of sheer bad manners. Or, after teasing them for so long, he will pretend to be in a great hurry, and walk straight past them. Often when his hall is crammed full with his clients, he will avoid going out that way and will instead slip out of the house by an obscure back door. Would it not be better to exclude them altogether than to deceive them like that? They, poor creatures, have cut short their own sleep in order to attend somebody else's. The patron's name is whispered a thousand times; but he is drowsing, or still half drunk from the previous night's debauch—so in reply he scarcely raises his lips, but just gives an insolent yawn.'[33]

For those with social aspirations which their means could not satisfy, such servitude perhaps was tolerable. At least they could boast of consorting with 'Society'. But most clients, no doubt, were in search of material advantage. A poet like Martial needed patrons; as the great number of his epigrams on the subject testifies, he found plenty of 'material' in his experience as a client, the more degrading (for this purpose) the better.

A large *clientela* flattered the vanity of a patron. Yet on his side he had no illusions about his clients: they had no liking for him as a person. 'Not one is interested in you, only in what he can get out of you. Once clients wanted a powerful friend, now they want someone to rob. Let a lonely old man alter the terms of his will; next morning he will receive no callers.'[34]

The clients who found their way into the history books were such men as Iturius and Calvisius, 'who had run through the whole of their fortunes' and who—doubtless for a handsome fee—informed against Agrippina in A.D. 55; and P. Egnatius Celer, an elderly philosopher from Syria, who was prepared (again, no doubt, for an adequate fee) to produce the evidence which sent Barea Soranus to his doom. Un-lovable men.[35]

The client and the *sportula* are not the noblest features of Roman social life in the early Empire; but it would be a mistake, because of the attention given by Juvenal and by Martial to the rich man's reception of his clients, to think that any very substantial number of Romans passed the first two hours of day in this degrading manner. This is only one of the respects in which the satirist, the epigrammatist and the moralist may leave an altogether false impression of the general social life of their times.[36]

The courts sat early, from the third hour[37] or even earlier, for the trial of Milo in 52 B.C. started at the second hour,[38] and the provision in the charter of Julius Caesar's colony at Urso in Spain that the courts might not sit before the first or after the eleventh hour suggests an early start.[39] The Senate in Rome was bound by a similar regulation; it might not meet before daybreak or continue in session after dark.[40] We do not know what latitude consuls enjoyed in fixing the time of meeting; but it is clear that in urgent circumstances the House met at the earliest hour which the law allowed.[41] Meetings of the public assemblies in Rome also started early in the day.[42]

The third to the fifth were the active hours of the financier's day.[43] The Senate and courts at Rome might continue in session until the afternoon, and municipal magistrates were on call until the tenth hour (up to 4 p.m.). But in the upper social classes generally midday was the end of the active working day. Indeed anyone who worked through to midday without interruption had, on an average, six hours' work behind him ($7\frac{1}{2}$ at midsummer, $4\frac{1}{2}$ at midwinter)—a good day's work, in fact, a '*solidus dies*'. At midday work stopped and the shops closed, though they opened again later. 'Six hours are enough for work; after that, sample life', as an ingenious epigram in the Palatine Anthology advises.[44] If not the whole, certainly the main part of children's schooling took place in the morning.* The reason why libraries were built facing east, to get the morning light, was that the morning was the time when libraries were used.[45]

The Roman working day started early and, by our standards, it finished early; it was conditioned by the fact that, in the absence of good artificial light, daylight was a very precious thing.

Midday: time for lunch (*prandium*) and, in summer, a siesta.

The women of the household were ready for lunch, like the men.

* See below, p. 99.

Their morning had embraced a number of household duties, *domestica officia*—the apportioning of daily supplies from the household store (*penus*), of which the mistress of the house held the key and, in old-fashioned families down to the end of the Republic, spinning and weaving. Indeed the womenfolk of Augustus' household were by his insistence so employed. In places where there were no separate public baths for women but men and women took it in turn to use the same baths (as in the mining settlement in Portugal, some of the terms of whose contract, the *lex metalli Vipascensis*, survive), the men, whose priority was unquestioned, would need the baths in the afternoon; therefore the women's bathing hours were in the morning, from dawn to the seventh hour of the day.[46]

As a society develops, the main meal of the day is eaten later and later. At first the main Roman meal, *cena*, like English dinner in the seventeenth century, was at midday. In both cases as this meal moved forward, at one end of the day it dispossessed the evening meal (*vesperna* in Rome, supper in England), for which there was no longer any need, and at the other end it created a gap which required to be filled by a new meal, *prandium* in Rome, lunch in England.[47]

In the late Republic midday was the normal lunch hour. In the year 61 B.C. the spectators at the games rose of their own initiative and left, because they wanted their lunch, and after that there was a regular luncheon interval at midday.[48] When Caninius Rebilus was made consul at the seventh hour of the last day of the year, Cicero could say jokingly that he was the man in whose consulship nobody ate any lunch.[49]

Lunch might be a very light meal indeed. 'Dry bread, no need of a table, no need to wash my hands afterwards'; but Seneca was an old man of abnormally austere habits, more likely than not a victim of gastric neurasthenia.[50] Most people's lunch was more substantial than this; and though it was not on the scale of the *cena* which followed it at only three hours' interval, it was a meal of meat or fish and fruit, at which wine was drunk.[51] It was not a meal to which guests were frequently invited. Indeed within the household a father might feed in his own room rather than join the family at lunch. The emperor Domitian, therefore, was unusual in making it his main meal of the day.[52]

After lunch, in summer, came the siesta (*meridiatio*)—so normal a habit that the elder Pliny recorded it as a remarkable feature of life in Ceylon that nobody slept in the afternoon. Exceptionally busy men may have dispensed with the practice; Cicero, for instance, claims never to have taken a siesta as long as he was actively engaged in politics or at the bar. And in winter, the days being shorter, there was little need for sleep. In summer time, however, the siesta was an all but universal practice, and occupied the seventh hour of the day.[53] The streets were deserted. In camp the soldier needed his midday relaxation like anybody else, and even in war it was a stratagem which reeked a little of fraudulence and guile to launch an attack at such an hour.[54] The personal guard of the emperor Severus Alexander were asleep 'at about the seventh hour' (if the *Historia Augusta* is to be believed) on March 18th or 19th A.D. 235, except for the German who chose this suitable moment for his murder. Maximinus was Alexander's successor, and he and his son were murdered in camp at the same convenient hour. And on August 24th A.D. 410 Alaric took advantage of the fact that the defence of Rome was asleep at about midday to force the Porta Salaria and capture the city, just as in 49 B.C. the Massiliots had chosen this time for a treacherous sally after their pretended submission—a time when many soldiers of the beleaguering Roman army were asleep.[55]

After the siesta, exercise; and, after exercise, the bath.

By the end of the second century it is evident that a different routine could be followed. Septimius Severus took strenuous exercise and had a bath after his hard morning's work, before he ate lunch; so did Severus Alexander, who sometimes spent a whole hour in the *piscina* before lunch (though lunch was a meal which he sometimes skipped). After lunch and a siesta, Septimius Severus devoted himself to cultural relaxation and then, towards evening, had a second bath before he dined.[56]

2. The Baths

As a part of the Greek way of life which the Romans borrowed in the second century B.C., it was thought wise (and the view had the support of doctors like Galen[57]) to take exercise before a heavy meal. So the routine developed among the upper classes both in Rome and in the country of exercising—leisurely or strenuously, according to age and inclination—in the early afternoon, stripped and oiled and, after exercise,* of bathing.

* On athletic exercise and games, see below, pp. 159–68.

Luxurious bathing places, together with the habit of daily baths, were, in the view of the moralists, a Hellenistic contamination. In simpler and better days Romans had bathed rarely, and in surroundings of considerable squalor.

Seven palatial baths (*thermae*) were built at Rome under the Empire, the first by Agrippa in the Campus Martius, the second in the same part of Rome, near the Pantheon, by Nero. Titus' baths were near the Colosseum, within the precinct of Nero's golden house, and Trajan's baths were near them on the lower slopes of the Esquiline. Then came the baths of Caracalla (the *thermae Antoninianae*) beyond the Porta Capena and near the Via Appia, and Diocletian's baths on high ground north-east of the Viminal. The last great *thermae* were those of Constantine, on the Quirinal. The surviving shells of Caracalla's baths (large enough to dwarf even a production of *Aïda*) and of Diocletian's startle even the least imaginative by their size and splendour. These were no mere bathing establishments; but they included art-galleries and an assembly of halls and chambers in which people walked and sat, read—even recited[58]—and were refreshed and entertained. They were places to which people went to relax, people who had the time to spare.

These were the *thermae*. There were also the *balnea*,[59] already numerous by Cicero's time,[60] the private property or leaseholds of individuals who ran them for profit, charging quarter of an *as* to a man and twice as much to a woman.[61] Most of the baths in Italian and provincial towns were run for profit, their freeholds belonging either to private individuals or to the corporation. They were leased out to a *conductor*, who put in a bathman (*balneator*) to run them.* There is a *graffito* at Pompeii: *TO LET: for five years from August 13th next, on the estate of Iulia Felix, baths, shops, stalls and dining rooms.*[62] In some places there was no charge for bathing, thanks to the existence of an endowment, the legacy of a wealthy benefactor.[63]

In Rome there were 170 baths in the time of Augustus, 'an infinite number' in Pliny's time and, by the end of the Empire, over nine hundred.[64] Similarly in the towns of Italy and the western provinces the number was growing all the time, and the general standard of luxury in the best baths was rising. Maecenas is said to have given Rome its first heated swimming pool. A wealth of inscriptions survives to illustrate the gift of baths to a city by a wealthy benefactor,

---

* Buticosus, whose name and image survive on the mosaic floor of a bath-house in Ostia, may have been the *balneator*.

sometimes as an addition to baths already existing, sometimes as the complete reconstruction of baths which had been destroyed by fire (which, given the method of heating, must have been a frequent calamity) or by earthquake, or which had collapsed through not being kept in proper repair or which had mouldered through the interruption of the water supply.[65]

No rigid rule determined when a bath should be called *balneae* or *balnea* and when *thermae*. An inscription from the early third century A.D. from Lanuvium may, however, be typical. The community was able 'to build *thermae* to take the place of the *balneae*, which were very old and had gone out of use'.[66]

In Rome and in other towns baths varied in quality, from squalid establishments which were 'cover' for brothels at one extreme, to respectable and luxurious establishments at the other. It was probably only in establishments of doubtful character that men and women bathed together. Respectable women bathed (if they bathed out) in the separate women's baths, which were often adjacent to the men's, so that the same heating system could be used for both. Where there were no separate women's baths it is probable that (as we know to have been the case in the mining community in Portugal) the women used the baths in the morning, the men in the afternoon.[67]

Socially the baths were important meeting—and mixing—places, and in a town everyone had his favourite baths, where he met his friends, just as the Englishman has his favourite public house.[68] A veteran soldier might be addressed by the man next to him in the sweat chamber, and find himself talking to the Emperor.* Yet it is obvious that not all the bathing of the rich was done in public baths. The large town house had its own baths, and so had every luxurious villa. In bad weather or at odd hours—particularly after dark, when before Severus Alexander and after the emperor Tacitus the public baths in Rome were closed[69]—it was more convenient to bathe at home. As for the country, the younger Pliny puts the matter simply in respect of his Laurentine villa; if he arrived there unexpectedly or was staying for such a short time that it was not worth the expense of starting up his own baths, he went to one of the three public baths in the neighbouring village.[70]

While the main bathing hours for the leisurely were the eighth and

---

* See the story of Hadrian on p. 30. Severus Alexander bathed in the public baths, wearing a bathing costume (*Vita* 42, 1). There was Hellenistic precedent; see Polybius 26, 1, 12f. for the antics of Antiochus Epiphanes in the public baths.

ninth, the baths were in full use up to dark in Rome. Martial, who is often quoted for the statement that the tenth hour was a late hour for a bath, says nothing of the sort; he says that this was a late hour for a client to attend his patron to the baths, which is a different matter.[71] In some of the country towns the baths were open after dark.[72] But they were sometimes used also even before midday (the time at which the water was at its hottest) and at the end of the second century A.D. it was the mark of an undisciplined unit in Gaul that at midday its officers were all in the baths.[73] Once on a *festa* Juvenal suggested to a friend that he should bathe at the fifth hour.[74] Where men and women used the same baths at different times, as has been seen, the women had the use of the baths in the morning. And invalids and old people, it seems, might bathe in the morning too.

Bathing after dark, as a general rule, must have been in the private baths of houses and villas. An exceedingly busy man might not be free to bathe during the day, and might sometimes bathe at night (Augustus on occasion at the first hour of night). In a very different social world a host like Trimalchio might make for the baths with his tippling guests at a late hour in drunken pursuit of sobriety. And there were foolish men who bathed directly after a heavy dinner. The undigested peacock—it was an indiscretion which often a man did not live to repeat. There were intemperate bathers like the emperor Gordian I, who bathed four or five times a day in summer, twice a day in winter.[75]

'I oil myself,' the younger Pliny wrote; 'I take my exercise, I have my bath.'[76] This, in bare terms, was the strenuous athlete's programme. He stripped and oiled himself; he took his exercise, wearing a thick cloak (*endromis*) as athletes today wear track suits, to avoid chill when he was standing about.[77] Then he scraped off the oil and the dust and plunged into the *piscina* of the *palaestra* for a swim.[78]

Alternatively he came into the baths, like other men, when his exercise was finished. Here it seems that either of two different programmes could be followed. Normally you went from the *tepidarium* to the hot bath (*caldarium*) or to the hot sweat chamber (*laconicum*) and then, by way of the *tepidarium*, to the cold bath (*frigidarium*), after which you were towelled. On the other hand you might in the end return from the cold bath to the *caldarium* or *laconicum*, and then have your rub-down.[79] As for the oiling and strigilling, this—with the oil warmed for preference[80]—might be done in the *tepidarium* at the start, or, alternatively, before, during or after the sweat-bath or, thirdly, at the very end of the bath, as a precaution against catching a chill.[81]

The Roman arrived at the baths with all his paraphernalia—his oil flask* (*ampulla*), his strigil, his comb and his linen or woollen towels.[82] The rich man's kit was carried by his personal slaves, who would attend to his oiling and strigilling while he bathed, and to rubbing him down afterwards. It was an indication that a man had inherited money when he took to coming to the baths with five well-groomed slaves.[83] The elder Pliny even brought a secretary, so that he might dictate or be read to while the strigilling and the rubbing down took place. In the fourth century this was one of the aspects of Roman life by which Ammianus Marcellinus was shocked—the arrival in the baths of the blasé rich, attended each by an army of slaves. And Seneca mocked, as prize example of ineffective decadence, the man who, carried by his slaves from the bath to his sedan chair, asked, 'Am I on my seat now?' '*Iam sedeo?*'[84]

An emperor, whether in public or in private, was accompanied both in his exercise and afterwards in the bath by a freedman, one of his Grooms of the Bedchamber, a *cubicularius*.[85]

If a man was poor, he carried his own kit, and in the bath he did his own oiling and strigilling; despite the presence of a bath attendant— the 'sordidus unctor'—who could be hired for the purpose.[86] There is a famous story of Hadrian who, shocked to see an old soldier rubbing his body against the bath wall (because he could not afford to pay an attendant to strigil him down), gave the man slaves for the purpose, and money for their upkeep. The story spread; and on another occasion he found a number of old men in the baths rubbing themselves against the wall. He disappointed them by the suggestion that they should strigil one another.[87]

In good baths there were numerous attendants on whom you could call, at a price, for professional services—a doctor perhaps, certainly a masseur and an expert in the art of depilation.[88]

If you met a friend starting his bath, you might wish him a good bath—'*Bene lava*'—just as your waiter in Italy today, when he brings your food, will sometimes wish you '*Buon appetito*'. Afterwards, hoping that he had enjoyed his bath, you greeted him, '*Salve, lotus*'; and, when you bowed to acquaintances on arrival or departure, you might borrow an Alexandrian custom and say, '*Περίψημά σου*,' '*Peripsuma su*', which (as different as could be from the Italian '*Ciao*') meant, 'Your humble servant.'[89]

You dressed (here again was an opportunity for extravagance at

* Oils varied in quality and perfume, like modern soaps.

Rome gross enough to shock Ammianus Marcellinus),[90] walked round, watched other people at their games or exercise and perhaps ate a snack or had a drink.[91] The food and drink shops, run in association with the baths, were outside the main building, but slaves evidently walked round hawking food and drink, their cries as strident as those of the vendors of *aranciata, coca-cola* at Italian railway stations or of *caffè-cognac* at the open-air opera. Those with food offered, among other things, cakes and sausages[92]; and indeed a man could eat substantially—lettuce, eggs, lizard-fish: so substantially, indeed, as to invite comment. '"Oh, I shan't be having any dinner when I get home", he said,' and hoped to be believed.[93]

Some men drank heavily—so heavily that they were not sober when they reached the dining-room. Such men attracted the epigrammatist's and the moralist's attention. During the Empire, according to Quintilian, their number was on the increase.[94]

When the slave shouted the ninth hour, the fashionable world was already on the move, some going home to dine, some going to dinner parties. Often a man met a friend in the baths and invited him home; you might go back to dinner with Trimalchio even if you had never set eyes on the man before.[95]

'Having a bath', someone says coarsely in Petronius' *Satyricon*, 'is like sending your body to a cleaner. The bathman pulls you to pieces. So I don't bathe every day.' Once it had been thought sufficient to have a bath every eight days and, even in the imperial age of luxurious bathing, not everybody bathed regularly. Augustus did not bathe much in winter; he simply had an oiling, sweated in front of a fire and then had tepid water poured over him. Celsus recommended the healthy man sometimes to take a bath, at other times a cold plunge, and only to oil himself every now and then; and delicate persons were advised to have an occasional bath but as a rule simply to oil themselves, either in the sun or before a fire. Galen gives the example of a scholar who lived to the age of a hundred, who took two baths a month in winter, four in summer, and three at other times of the year, contenting himself on other days with an oiling and a brief rub-down.[96] Though the admission fee was small, oil cost money (until by an ordinance of Septimius Severus it was distributed free in Rome), and this must have been sufficient to deter poor people from frequent bathing, unless they were lucky enough to live near a baths where the supply of oil was subsidized by some benefaction. Farm hands, in Columella's opinion, should only be allowed to go to the baths on a *festa*.[97]

That in the Empire cleanliness was next to decadence was a view commonly expressed by the Romans themselves. Tacitus held that baths, porticoes and dinner parties represented the bad side of Romanization, by contrast with fine public and private building and sound education. A man like Seneca who held that the good life was a matter of waging continuous war on bodily pleasure was bound to disapprove of anything so enjoyable. He mocked the artificiality of the sweat-chamber; sweating should be the accompaniment of hard physical work—as in the great days of Scipio Africanus when, so far from enjoying the bright light of the windowed chambers of the imperial baths, a man bathed in the dark in a windowless cell.[98]

That there was considerable encouragement to moral delinquency in the less reputable bathing establishments is certain. But neither cleanliness nor exercise is a bad thing, and Roman bathing habits in general cannot be condemned unless it can be proved that they tempted large numbers of people to waste time which could have been more profitably employed, or that they really had a deleterious effect on people's health.

Everyone who has ever driven from Rome to Tivoli knows the stench of the sulphur baths at Acque Albule (Albulae). Galen has a nice story of a man who went there on business at the height of summer. He bathed there at the seventh hour, then dined and took a siesta, and after that returned to Rome, reaching the city after dark, when the baths were closed. Feeling exceedingly unwell, he summoned two doctors, who discovered that he had a high fever, and told him to remain in bed, drinking and eating nothing. Galen arrived after them, and made his own diagnosis—that the man had an allergy to sulphur, and that the pores of his body were clogged. So he got the man's slaves to give him a good oiling and a very hot bath; after which he recommended a cold bath, with a good meal to follow. The diagnosis was accurate and the next day the man was well again. Galen insisted on his staying in bed until the doctors came. The doctors arrived; finding that the fever had gone, they congratulated themselves and, to be on the safe side, advised the patient to abstain from food for one more day. 'The doctors left, and then everybody had a good laugh.'[100]

3. Dinner

Not every Roman dinner party was an orgy, and not every dinner was a dinner party. More often than not, whether in Rome or in the country, a family dined alone. If Horace was not dining out, he ate an extremely frugal meal at home and if spongers forced their company on him, this was the meal that they shared.[101] In Pliny's Tuscan villa there was a large dining room for parties (*triclinium*) and a small room (*cenatio*) which he used ordinarily, if he was dining alone with his wife or with a few friends.*[102]

Some dined at home alone from choice, others—unsuccessful parasites—from hard necessity. Theirs was the '*triste domicenium*'. All through the early afternoon they had haunted the baths and the public places, but in vain. Nobody had asked them to dinner.[103]

Often, too, men dined quietly because they had work to do when dinner was over. In early April 56 B.C. Cicero wanted to see Pompey before they both left Rome, Pompey for the North (in fact for Luca) and Cicero for the South. He had dinner with his prospective son-in-law Crassipes and after dinner was taken in a litter to Pompey's house: 'I had not been able to see him earlier in the day.' Seneca returned to work after dinner: 'I never end the day in idleness, and in fact I work into the night.' The elder Pliny left the table before dark in summer, within the first hour of night in winter, in order to work. And if the student took Quintilian's advice, he worked at night, when all was quiet and there was no distraction—as long as he did not exhaust himself by doing so. 'Busy men have no option; they *have* to work at night.'[104]

Though an informal dinner might be at the tenth hour (and, if you had a barrister to dinner, this was the earliest time at which it was safe to invite him), you were normally invited to a formal dinner party for the ninth hour, and invited some days beforehand—though in fourth-century Gaul Ausonius' luncheon guests seem to have been asked at about two hours' notice.[105]

You could accept (*promittere ad cenam*) or, if you had a good enough excuse, refuse (*se excusare*, or *exusare*). Ammianus Marcellinus found that in Rome of the fourth century A.D. a refusal was greatly resented. Having once reconciled himself to the idea of asking a stranger to dinner, a Roman host was so much annoyed by his refusal that 'it was better to murder a man's brother than to refuse his invitation to dine'.[106] As in any society, to accept and then not to come was a greater rudeness still; the host assumed that his guest had been tempted away by a more attractive invitation; but this was a society which did not know punctuality as the northern European knows it today, and

---

* See below, pp. 141f, for an anecdote concerning Lucullus dining alone.

there must have been long periods of waiting before it was certain that a guest would not appear.[107]

In such an event there was a last-minute effort to fill the empty place, and this was where clients had their uses. Someone like Horace, prepared to eat quietly at home, swallowed his pride and hurried off to his patron's—Maecenas'—table 'when it was already getting dark'— which means that Maecenas dined late, or had waited a long time for his defaulting guest and also perhaps that Horace had postponed the time of his own meal at home in the hope of such a last minute invitation. The client must not be offended if the invitation was singularly off-hand, as in Lucian's *Gallus*: 'Micyllus, I am having a party today in honour of my daughter's birthday and I have asked several of my friends. I hear that one of them is poorly and can't dine with us; so, after the bath, do come and take his place—unless, of course, I hear from him that he is coming after all, but that doesn't seem likely.'[108]

With greater informality (and clearly not for a set dinner party) a man might in any case be invited with very little notice. You invited a man to meet you in the baths and to dine with you afterwards; or you met a man in the baths, and invited him to take pot luck (*subitae ofellae*); or you felt indebted to some persistent sycophant and asked him home to dinner.[109] That prince of eccentrics, L. Marcius Philippus, consul in 91 B.C. and censor, returning home one day from the courts at the eighth hour, was so fascinated by the sight of a salesman (*praeco*) cleaning his nails in a barber's chair that he sent a slave to ask him to dinner. The man declined. So Philippus tracked him down at work the next morning early and asked him to dinner again, 'after the ninth hour'. However ungraciously and however unfortunately for his own future, the man accepted: '*Ut libet.*' 'I don't mind if I do.'[110]

By the late Republic and early Empire a man who moved in fashionable society 'dressed' when he attended a dinner party; he wore what was called a 'dinner suit' (*cenatoria* or *cubitoria*) or 'mixed dress' (*synthesis*). This latter consisted of a tunic and a smallish cloak (*palliolum*), both made of very light material for use in summer and of heavier stuff for use in winter. Both garments were of the same, usually very bright, colour,[111] and they might be worn also by women. Some men evidently were vain and ostentatious as peacocks; we know of a host who, on the excuse of the heat, changed his *synthesis* eleven times during the meal. Why, one of his less affluent guests, the poet Martial, wondered, possessing only one dinner suit, did he himself not feel hot at all?[112]

You arrived. At a full dinner party there would be nine people, three on the *summus lectus*, three on the *medius*, which was the most important, and three on the *imus*. But, instead of three couches, there might be one, larger and semicircular in shape, a *sigma*, and in this case the party was one of six (the ideal number, Ausonius thought), seven or eight persons; though some people had a prejudice against an even number, even if not as strong as the prejudice in other societies against the number thirteen. The party might be smaller—as small as three. In his satire 'Nobody knows what the late evening may have in store' M. Varro pronounced that the Muses made a nice large party, the Graces a nice small one; a host should not go above the one figure or below the other.*[113] Sometimes you knew in advance who your fellow-guests would be[114]; at other times you might receive a shock. In 46 B.C., arriving in the respectable company of his friends Atticus and Verrius to dine with Volumnius Eutrapelus in Rome, Cicero was startled to find his host's mistress, the actress Cytheris, a member of the party. This was not a cheerful period in his life, but he enjoyed the party greatly.[115]

When the vulgarian Nasidienus invited three men of letters to meet Maecenas, he buttressed himself with two of his own associates who, already familiar with the house, would be able to keep an eye with him on the serving of the dinner and, Maecenas having been invited to bring two 'shadows' (*umbrae*), the party was completed by two men who, in face of an embarrassing meal, showed that, though they might be Maecenas' friends, they had exceedingly bad manners.[116]

The limit of nine placed on any dinner given by a candidate for office in the colony of Urso shows that dinner parties were often larger. Larger dinners, indeed, there could be. In the provinces Julius Caesar usually entertained at two tables, his staff officers and Greek companions at one, Roman citizens and distinguished provincials at the other, nine people, presumably, reclining at each table. When Caesar was in Campania during the Saturnalia of 45 B.C., there was evidently more than one table when he dined with Philippus; and when he dined at Puteoli with Cicero, there were three—one for Caesar and his superior freedmen, one for less important freedmen and one for his slaves. In such cases two extra rooms, in addition to the dining room, were pressed into service. The evidence does not suggest that, apart from emperors and a few people of great wealth, many houses had a

---

* It is difficult to understand the 'well known saying', 'Seven makes a dinner, nine makes a brawl' ('*Septem convivium, novem vero convicium*') of SHA *L. Verus* 5, 1.

dining room large enough to hold more than one table; references to such rooms are extremely rare. On the other hand, large houses whether in Rome or in the country might have several dining-rooms, each, from its prospect, suited for use at a particular time of year. Lucullus' house in Rome had a number of dining rooms,* Trimalchio's at Puteoli had four dining rooms downstairs and one upstairs.[117]

The normal Roman's fondness for food is a historical fact which has to be faced. Fortunes were squandered on food by men 'who lived for their palate alone', men whom Seneca regarded as the most deplorable of all spendthrifts.[118] In extreme cases grossly expensive eating led in the end to bankruptcy; men unable even to afford the price of a rope to hang themselves with signed on as gladiators and, with no option, ate gladiators' rations.†[119] Apart from spectacular victims of sensational greed, men of all kinds—we know little about women—were fascinated by gourmandism. Crude ignoramuses posed pretentiously as *cognoscenti*.[120] Vulgarians boasted about the size, expense and origin of the dishes which they offered to their guests.[121]

Other men pontificated with knowledge. C. Matius (perhaps the son of the C. Matius whom we know from Cicero's letters as a sympathetic individual, an unashamed friend of Caesar in the weeks after Caesar was murdered) was the author of a work on cookery, whose three books were called 'The Cook', 'The Fishmonger' and 'The Pickle-Maker'. That uncrowned king of the culinary world M. Gavius Apicius, who lived in the time of Tiberius Caesar, was an evident *gourmet*, though his reputation was that of a wealthy glutton. He gave his name to a style of cooking, the *Apiciana coctura*. It was said that, after spending a hundred million sesterces on food, he checked his accounts and, finding himself left with a mere ten millions, committed suicide. He had written two works, one on cooking and one on sauces; and, for good or bad, his reputation did not die with him, for the manual on cooking which passes under his name, but which dates, probably, from the late fourth or early fifth century A.D., features recipes—for stuffed marrows, for instance, for a sauce to serve with ostrich, for seventeen different ways of cooking sucking pig—some of which were his.[122]

This pervasive interest in food was a feature of Roman city life by which Ammianus Marcellinus was shocked: 'Intent on stuffing themselves, they follow their noses and the shrieking women's voices to the

* See page 142.
† See below, p. 296.

kitchen, and like a flock of starving and screeching peacocks they stand on the tips of their toes biting their finger-nails waiting for the food to cool.'[123]

The satirists and the moralists handled the gourmand without mercy. It was terrible to waste money on a pleasure as ephemeral as eating. The world was scoured for delicacies, which were transported enormous distances to be eaten by people who were sick before they had even started to digest them.[124]

That enormous sums were spent on food by the rich is not to be doubted. An inaugural priestly dinner in the early Empire might cost (even with economies) a million sesterces, and Gaius Caligula once spent ten times that sum on a single dinner party. L. Verus' fantastic 'dinner for twelve' cost six million sesterces, largely because of the presents given to the guests. Elagabalus was said never to spend less than a hundred thousand sesterces on a dinner. In the late Republic the meal to which Lucullus entertained Pompey and Cicero should have cost 200,000 sesterces.* Yet Atticus lived well and entertained, and only spent 3,000 sesterces a month on housekeeping expenses.[125]

Cooking and eating, like everything else, had their history. The 'Trojan pig', *porcus Troianus*, went back to the second century B.C.—a porker which, when split open, revealed surprising contents (at Trimalchio's dinner, sausages and black puddings).[126] Among fish, a pike caught '*intra duos pontes*' at Rome, just above the Tiber island and below the influx of the *cloaca maxima*, was a *spécialité* already in the second century B.C.[127] The scientific culture of oysters in the Lucrine Lake was the achievement of Sergius Orata.[128] Fish was always an expensive luxury. Cato in the second century B.C. said that a fish might cost more than a cow; and in the early Empire a consular paid seven or eight thousand sesterces for a red mullet.†[129] By this time in Italy freshwater fish had gone out of fashion.

That sleek orator Q. Hortensius, who watered his plane trees with wine, was the first man to serve peacock at an augural dinner.[130] There was the goose and *foie gras*, which, according to the elder Pliny's researches, was the discovery of either Pompey's father-in-law, Metellus Scipio or of a possible forebear of Sejanus.[131] Once it had been enough to produce a third of a boar, 'a creature born for the table'; but the

* See pp. .141f
† This in Rome. Away from the Mediterranean, then as now, there were different, indeed in the northern Empire far better, fish. Cf. Ausonius, *Mosella* 85–149 on the best Moselle fish, including trout and salmon, and Symmachus' complaint (*Ep.* 1, 14) that Ausonius never produced such fish, when he dined with him.

father of P. Servilius Rullus, the tribune of 63 B.C., started the fashion of serving boars whole.[132] Sometimes a new fashion lasted, sometimes it was ephemeral. The *acipenser* was once a very popular and expensive fish; but by the elder Pliny's time it was held in no esteem at all. Yet, though fashions might change, standards were rising all the time.[133]

Much thought was given, naturally, to the selection of food for a dinner, and the host (or in households like that of Trimalchio, his wife) gave the cook instructions some days in advance. Varro in one of his satires observed that if a man devoted to philosophy even a twelfth part of the time which he spent on trying to get better bread out of his baker (a slave of the household, like the cook), he might find himself a morally good man.[134]

An austere man was one who lived chiefly on vegetables and, if given a hare or a sucking pig, made it last for three days. A disciple of good living was someone who fed on 'oysters, fattened birds and fish'.[135]

Even in this world of extravagance and over-eating, slight account had sometimes to be taken in republican days of the existing law; for every now and then a kind of public conscience expressed itself (together with conservative senatorial objection to business men profiteering in expensive commodities) and laws were passed to curb the excesses of gastronomic extravagance.

The elder Cato lived at the start and Augustus at the end of more than a century and a half of forlorn legislation, which Aulus Gellius thought fit to recapitulate, as did Macrobius.[136] Cato did not move a law himself, but he spoke, whether successfully or not,[137] in 181 B.C. to prevent the repeal of the *lex Orchia*, limiting the number of guests who might be entertained to a meal in Rome, which had been passed in the previous year. It will have been a nice irony if, in his hospitable old age, Cato was accused (and possibly he was) of breaking this law.[138]

In 161 B.C. a senatorial decree and a subsequent law of the consul C. Fannius Strabo fixed the sums which might be spent on dinners (120 or 100 asses on certain *feste*, 30 asses on ten other days in the month, ten asses on other days), forbade the serving of fattened hens (was this to encourage egg production?), and limited the number of guests from outside a family (five on *feste* and on *nundinae*,* three on other days). A steep rise in food prices encouraged a general disregard of the law. Later in the century only Rutilius Rufus and Aelius Tubero are said to have observed it, the one buying fish at his own price from his slaves who fished, the other buying birds from his own peasants. And quite

* On *nundinae*, see pp. 59–61.

generally when the fattened hen went off the market, the fattened *poussin* took its place.[139]

It is not easy to relate these measures to the vices of leading male society in Rome which, to judge by a speech made some years later in defence of the law by C. Titius, they were intended to reform: 'Dedicated dice-players, drenched in scent, the centre of a crowd of harlots . . . At the tenth hour* . . . they arrive in court and with looks of thunder order the case to start. They name the litigants; the judge calls the witnesses, and then retires to the lavatory. On returning, he says that he has heard everything and calls for the papers, which he scrutinizes, so drunk that he can hardly keep his eyes open. They retire to deliberate. The first man speaks, "What concern of mine are these time-wasters? Better to be drinking mead with Greek wine and eating fat thrush and good fish, genuine Roman pike, caught between the two bridges".'[140]

The *Lex Didia*, perhaps of 143 B.C., extended the operation of the law from the city of Rome to the whole of Italy, and made guests and hosts alike answerable for its violation. Legislation of M. Aemilius Scaurus, consul in 115 B.C., supported perhaps by the censors, prohibited dormice, shellfish and imported birds.[141] P. Licinius Crassus, austere father of the later triumvir, consul in 97 and censor in 89, re-enacted the last two laws without much variation, probably as aedile some time before 102 B.C., and in 89, with his colleague, fixed maximum prices for Greek and Picene wine.[142] Even Sulla followed suit with a *lex Cornelia sumptuaria*, which went further and fixed a maximum price for certain extravagant delicacies which were, in any case, outside an ordinary person's pocket.[143]

It is hard to understand how these laws can have been enforced at all. How, without forms and returns and ration cards and a great number of police and civil servants, could the aediles in Rome possibly have checked the family budget? The laws would only make economic sense if the previously uncontrolled demand for food by the rich had pushed prices up and had been responsible for starvation or under-nourishment of the poor, and if the enforced restriction of this demand threw supplies of food on to the open market and forced prices down to a figure which poorer people could afford to pay. Unless this happened, it could only be a bad thing, whether in the big ranching days of the *latifundia* or in the attempted revival of small-scale agriculture, to

* 4 p.m.

restrict demand for foodstuffs. No distinction was made except in 115 B.C. in the case of birds between Italian-grown and imported food.[144]

As for C. Titius' strictures on society, you were not likely to reform drunken judges by forbidding them to eat fattened hens.

The *lex Antia* of Antius Restio made sense, though it was evidently not observed. With a limited number of exceptions, it forbade magistrates or magistrates-elect to accept invitations to dinner in private houses. The law was concerned, presumably, with graft and corruption.[145]

Pompey and Crassus played with the idea of a sumptuary law, but thought better of it. Antony, who issued a laughable edict on the subject in the years after Caesar's death, would have been wise to follow their example.[146]

There remains Julius Caesar's law of 46 B.C., which, for some odd reason, neither Gellius nor Macrobius mentions, which forbade the sale of certain expensive foodstuffs and re-introduced a limit to the amount which a household might spend on food (a limit which Cicero found it easy to observe, though an exotic vegetarian dinner which he attended, vegetables not being controlled by the law, made him exceedingly ill). Being a dictator, Caesar imposed sanctions. Lictors and soldiers, detailed to supervise the observance of the law, were even given rights of entry to private houses while meals were in progress.[147] Finally there was Augustus' legislation of 22 B.C., amended whether by him or by Tiberius in a later edict, which fixed the maximum legitimate expenditure on food on a sliding scale, according to the day, from 300 to 2,000 sesterces. The law did not prove effective and when in A.D. 22 the aediles were anxious to make yet another attack on the problem, Tiberius told the Senate with blunt good sense that, though laws might be passed on this subject, experience showed that they could not be enforced. In the century between Actium and the civil wars of A.D. 69 extravagance was riotous and unchecked. After A.D. 70, for a number of different reasons, a more moderate standard of living became the fashion; for Vespasian believed in austerity and his new senators, representatives of the municipal *bourgeoisie*, preserved the simple habits to which they were accustomed.[148]

With no great punctuality the guests arrived. Even on a mule Martial once arrived for dinner an hour late a mile outside the city. The poor client excepted, they came with a slave or slaves (apart from the carriers who had brought them if they came by chair or by litter). There must be someone to carry and look after their shoes. For as in North America in winter the guest's first act is to discard his rubbers, the Roman on arrival for a party took off his outdoor shoes (*calcei*) and put on a pair of slippers (*soleae*) which in their turn he would discard as soon as he reclined at the dinner table.[149]

Drinking before dinner was a fairly modern fashion (dating from the principate of Tiberius) of which the elder Pliny disapproved. Guests might have been drinking already, perhaps heavily, in the baths. Juvenal's dreadful athlete hostess drank and was sick in front of her guests; so drink was presumably offered sometimes to guests on their arrival and before they lay down to dinner.[150]

At a certain point the host decided, if all the guests had not arrived, to wait no longer. In the disastrous dinner described in Lucian's *Convivium* one guest, a doctor, had been detained by his professional duties (a flute-player who had a brain storm in his surgery) and did not arrive until a late stage in the meal.[151]

The guests were given their places. There were normally three couches and three persons to a couch; but there were sometimes more than three on one or all of the couches. The host took the first place on the *imus lectus* and members of his family who were dining generally occupied the other places on that *lectus*. Next to him was placed the most distinguished guest (Maecenas, for instance, at Nasidienus' dinner), occupying the third place of the *lectus medius*. This was known as the *consularis locus*, perhaps because its occupant had plenty of room to deal with business (papers or individuals) which called for his urgent attention during the meal.[152] An unexpected guest might be asked by his host which place he would care to occupy.[153] It is to be assumed that hosts were not often embarrassed, as Brutus and Cassius were embarrassed at Sardis in 43 B.C., by a guest, and an uninvited guest at that, the Cynic boor M. Favonius, who destroyed the table plan by insisting on occupying a place on the *medius lectus*.[154]

Dinner was normally, as it is in Italy today, a three-course meal.[155] There seems to be no classical precedent for the *pastasciutta*, which is so often the first course today, for *polenta*, porridge, was a coarse and cheap food. Instead, the first course consisted of a variety of hors-d'œuvres, largely vegetables and herbs (for example lettuce, leek, mint). There were olives, of course. There could be sliced eggs, snails, shellfish (sea urchins, or oysters) and a kind of haggis. This was the *gustus* or *gustatio*.[156]

Then came the *cena* proper, the main course, when the guest took his choice from a variety of dishes which were brought round usually in three successive services (*cena prima, secunda, tertia*).[157] Young kid, before it had been weaned, was the kind of delicacy that *abbachio* is in early spring today. There might be fowl, perhaps pheasant or goose, ham, cutlets, hare and a variety of fish (lamprey and turbot in particular)—though the fish might have constituted a course of its own if the dinner was one of more than three courses. Often there were sow's udders and wild boar. There were vegetables too and often extremely rich and elaborate sauces.[158] The guest did not sample every dish; indeed a *cena dubia* was one where there was such a great variety of dishes that he found it hard to make his choice.[159]

Finally the dessert, *secundae mensae, bellaria*: apples, pears, grapes, nuts, figs. Grapes were kept fresh long after they were gathered. Apples from Picenum were good and especially delicious pears came from Segni (*Signina*) and Taranto (*Syria*).[160]

Unless impeded by gastric distemper, most Romans enjoyed food, and, if they could afford it, ate heavily. At the same time it is to be remembered that they ate only one large meal a day, whereas most modern Europeans eat two and some Northerners three.

'Men eat to vomit, and vomit to eat; their dishes are fetched from every corner of the earth, and then they do not even deign to digest them.' So, in a bilious mood, Seneca wrote. But the scholars who have made the closest study of the social habits of the Romans have rightly pointed out that occasional use of emetics was generally recommended by doctors in antiquity; that Caesar who, when he dined with Cicero, was taking emetics, was by all the evidence a most sparing eater and drinker; and that of Roman emperors, the sordid details of whose disordered private lives are all too well known, only Claudius and Vitellius, both abnormally greedy men even by the standards of their age, are known to have taken emetics as a frequent practice. There were Romans who were disgustingly greedy and for whom self-induced sickness was the only way of eating more when they had eaten too much already; and men who became exceedingly drunk were naturally exceedingly sick; but there is no reason to think of such men as typical Romans leading a normal daily life.[161]

When Cicero entertained Julius Caesar at Puteoli during the Saturnalia of 45 B.C. and the guests dined at three different tables, though he declared that all ate well, his language indicates that the guests both at the second and at the third tables ate less well than those above them—just as undergraduates at dinner in the hall of an Oxford or a Cambridge College eat a less good dinner than the dons at High Table. Frequently at dinner parties the guests were graded; some were the host's personal friends, others were his 'minor friends' (that is to say, his clients), while others were freedmen; and it was not uncommon for the members of the three classes to be given different food to eat, different wine to drink and even different table ware. This differentiation, it seems, could be made even between guests at the same table, and made in such a way that the client before whom an eel was placed could see that his host was gorging off a mullet or a lamprey. The host's smug explanation was that, while in his generosity he was prepared to entertain his clients to dinner, he could not afford the expense of entertaining them *au prince*. Though a client may well have known what humiliation was in store for him when he accepted an invitation, the humiliation (sharply described by Juvenal) was not in the event the less embarrassing on that account. However it is not to be thought that the younger Pliny was the only Roman who set his face firmly against the practice. If the more affluent guests who dined with Pliny found the menu dull—because that is how he got over the problem of expense—his humbler guests, presumably, enjoyed their dinner. When Hadrian entertained guests at a number of tables, he ordered food even from the bottom tables for himself to make sure that the catering contractors were not making a differentiation which he himself was not prepared to tolerate.[162]

Guests were evidently at liberty during dinner to occupy themselves in ways which in the modern world would not be thought goodmannered. They could, for instance, write or dictate letters at table.[163]

A good dinner deserved a good wine. Interest in good wines developed fast in the last century of the Republic, and 121 B.C., 'the consulship of Opimius', is the first famous vintage of which we know. At the end of the second century B.C., when Campania was exporting wine to Narbonese Gaul, Greek wine—Chian, in particular, was highly esteemed—was imported to Rome in very small quantities and was very sparingly drunk.* It was evidently an expensive luxury, and that is why in 89 B.C. a maximum price was fixed for it (as for Picene wine) by the censors. Falernian and Nomentanum were the most highly esteemed among Italian wines. Chian and Falernian were drunk at Caesar's triumphs and at a banquet given in 46 B.C. he offered

---

* The senatorial decree of 161 B.C. had forbidden the serving of foreign wine at certain dinners (AG 2, 24, 2).

Falernian, Chian, Lesbian and Mamertine; this was the first time that four different wines had been offered at a dinner.[164]

Heavy drinkers drank their wine neat; others, in the Greek manner, mixed it with water.

The commonest *vin ordinaire* was consumed before the following autumn. With increasingly refined tastes, there was more and more call on vintage wines. The best wines were kept for at least five years and were generally at their best about fifteen years after the vintage.[165]

Wine was drunk sparingly with the meal. After the meal was over, it continued to be drunk, in moderation or excess according to the nature of the party. This was the *comissatio*. If you were a light drinker, your cup was filled with three *cyathi* (quarter of a pint); if you were a hard drinker, with three times that quantity.[166]

The ingredients of a good dinner were good company, good talk, good wine and a good meal.[167]

The politer social manners of the Romans were derived from the Greeks. During dinner in a cultured household a party was entertained by readings, music and humorous recitations, these three varieties of diversion being collectively described by the Greek word *acroama*. For the reader the Romans often used not the Latin word *lector* but the Greek *anagnostes*.[168]

The cultured household possessed one or more readers among its freedmen or slaves, for whom a master had many valuable uses if his own eyesight gave trouble or if, like the elder Pliny, he wanted to be read to at a time when it was inconvenient to him to read himself, for instance in the bath.* Scholars like Cicero and the younger Pliny had good readers, cultured and well educated slaves to whom they were warmly attached.[169] A wealthy and pretentious ignoramus kept a number of such slaves, as you might possess a library, each knowing the text of some Greek author by heart, so as to stand by him at a party and to repair and, if he was smart enough, prevent the *gaffes* of his master's literary talk. It is no small achievement to read well and, when educated men were present, a slave will have taken pride in his skill; let him make a single mistake, and the critics were quick to pounce.[170]

If the poems to be read were of the host's own composition, he might do the reading himself. Martial illustrates the torture and tedium which, in such an event, the guests might suffer:

There is one reason, and one reason only, why you give a dinner

* See p. 30.

party, Ligurinus. You want an opportunity of reciting your dreadful poems. I have taken off my slippers, the lettuce and fish sauce is served—and here comes Book 1. The main course is held up so that we can hear Book 2—and, before the dessert, Book 3. Book 4. Book 5. If boar is served like this, course after course, it is revolting. Ligurinus, my friend, give those accursed poems of yours to fishmongers to wrap mackerel. Nobody will ever dine with you again if you don't.[171]

The younger Pliny, who wanted to read his own poems, had the wisdom to listen to those who told him that he read extremely badly. This did not save his guests. He used a reader and tortured himself with concern over the question of what was the proper deportment for a poet listening to the reading of his own poems. Martial once with elegant courtesy promised not to read his poems to a guest, but said that need not prevent the guest from reading his own works to him.[172]

In his 'You never know what the late evening has in store',* Varro stated that passages should be selected for reading at dinner which were both educational and entertaining. They were chosen by the host, no doubt with some thought of the guests whom he was entertaining. Passages of Greek and Roman history were read, lyric poems whether in Greek or in Latin, Homer or Virgil. A party with severe scholarly tastes might even listen to a work as austere as Gavius Bassus' *On the Origin of Words and Names*.[173]

At a polite dinner party, whether in Rome or in the country, there was music as well as reading, playing of the flute, the lyre or the cythera, sometimes as the accompaniment of a group of singers. (Martial hated such singing; it killed conversation.)[174] Sometimes there was an *aretalogus* (at the emperor Augustus' dinner parties, for instance), a man who told amusing—and preferably edifying—stories, fables to illustrate the vagaries of human nature.[175] And *comoedi*, whose profession was highly esteemed, recited passages from drama.[176] The reader, the musician and the *comoedus* were sometimes different men, artists each in his own field; but sometimes a household was fortunate enough to possess a slave or freedman of such versatile talent that he could play all the three parts.[177]

These at a polite party were the entertainments of the meal itself. When after dinner the guests relaxed, reclining over their wine, they turned to conversation—'conversation which should be decorous and

* This was a Roman aphorism, meaning that good fortune was rarely lasting (cf. Livy 45, 8, 6). Varro evidently adapted it for his own purpose.

gracious'.[178] Often it was literary talk, which took its start in a discussion of some passage which had been read aloud earlier. Aulus
Gellius records an evening when, the name of the wind Iapyx having
occurred in a poem which was read, Favorinus was invited to talk
about the names of the winds. He delivered a lecture on the subject,
suddenly cutting himself short with the remark, 'I have had more than
enough to drink, and I might go on babbling about the meaning of all
these names—but I have been talking and keeping you listening too
long already. It is a bad and a bad-mannered man who monopolizes
the talk in a large party.'[179]

The danger of one guest (or the host) monopolizing the talk was well
understood. Varro had much to say, evidently, on the subject: 'guests
should neither be chatterboxes nor mutes'; conversation should range
over the common affairs of life, subjects which there was no time to
discuss in the Forum.[180] Cicero in the De Officiis gave advice on
this as on most other branches of social life—sensible advice: that it
was a mistake to talk too much about yourself; that backbiting gossip
was to be deplored; and that conversation should be about domestic
matters, politics, or about the arts and sciences.[181]

There is in ancient literature a memorable picture of someone who
could kill conversation stone dead, correcting other people's mistakes
at one moment, making arrogant pronouncements the next. Juvenal
painted the picture. It was of a woman, married and a bluestocking.[182]

The Quaestiones Conviviales of Plutarch contain an interesting collection of light-hearted subjects (scarcely serious enough to satisfy
Cicero's requirements) which he had discussed after dinner with his
friends both in Rome and in Greece. Here is a sample: Why in old age
do you read things better at a distance? Why is fresh water better than
salt water for washing clothes? Which came first, the hen or the egg?
Is wrestling the oldest sport? Why do Jews not eat pork? On the supposed possession of the evil eye.[183]

Plutarch also suggested that if any of the guests was an experienced
diplomat or politician or an expert in any particular branch of knowledge or a man who had enjoyed unusual experiences or visited out-
of-the-way places, he should be invited to talk, for the information and
advantage of the rest of the company, about his subject. Such men
enjoyed answering questions about things which they knew, and were
generally reluctant to talk unless invited.[184]

When a coterie of the Emperor's friends was invited to stay at one
of his country houses for the purpose of sitting with him by day as his

advisers in administrative and judicial council, the occasion must have had similarities to a week-end party at Chequers. Pliny describes such a visit to Trajan at Civitavecchia (Centum Cellae). After the hard work of the day, the visitors relaxed at dinner in the Emperor's company. The dinner itself was a simple one 'by imperial standards'. At intervals there were delightful readings (*acroamata*); and there was 'entrancing conversation, which lasted well into the night'. Nero had entertained in Rome in a manner more cultural still, when after dinner he and his gifted young friends turned themselves into an amateur poetry society.[185]

At less cultured parties the place of conversation was often taken by quizzes and riddles (such as are contained nowadays in Christmas crackers). Tiberius was fond of asking people questions based on whatever books he happened to have been reading during the day—and inflicted sharp punishment on the *grammaticus* who tried to prepare himself for dinner by discovering what the Emperor's reading had been on that day.[186]

In the Roman world as well as the Greek 'μισῶ μνάμονα συμπόταν' was a familiar saying: 'I hate a drinking companion who remembers in the morning what happened the night before'.[187] It is embarrassing, as others beside Martial have found, to be confronted by a guest for dinner, responding to an invitation which you have forgotten that you ever issued.[188] Many *bêtises* and indiscretions of the drinking party are best forgotten. And in a spy-ridden society like Rome of the Caesars and certain states in the modern world the consequences of an indiscretion can be catastrophic. Many men died in the early Roman Empire because of some criticism of the régime coaxed out of them by the adroit questioning of a spy at a time when they had drunk too much. Not every man who was indiscreet in his cups was as fortunate as Rufus in the time of Augustus:

Under Augustus a man could get into trouble, yet not into positive danger, from words which he had spoken. At dinner a senator called Rufus said, 'I hope Caesar does not return alive from the journey which he is just starting and,' he added, 'all the sacrificial beasts, bulls and calves, are at one with me in this.' Ears were strained to catch his words. Next morning, as soon as it was light, the slave who had been standing at his feet during dinner reported his drunken remarks to him and urged him to lose no time, but to be the first to report the matter to Caesar. Rufus took the advice, went up to Caesar as he came down in the morning, swore on oath that he had not been himself the day before, asked that, if there were to be punishment, it might fall on him and his sons, and begged Caesar to forgive him and restore him to favour. When Caesar consented, he said, 'Nobody will believe this, unless you give me a present,' and he asked—and asked successfully— for what was a tidy sum to ask from anyone whose favour he enjoyed. Caesar said, 'For my own sake I will take care never to be angry with you.' It was good of him to forgive the man, and to show generosity into the bargain. You will not need to be told that the slave was given his freedom, its price being the sum which Caesar had paid.[189]

Singers were generally brought in from outside and had to be paid for; though there were rich people who kept a choir of slaves for their own pleasure, just as in the younger Pliny's time Ummidia Quadratilla shocked the strait-laced (including her prig of a grandson) by keeping her own troupe of pantomime actors, slaves and freedmen, who gave performances in her house as well as in the theatre. Trimalchio produced a troupe of acrobats to perform after dinner. At extravagant parties actors and ballet dancers sometimes came and gave a performance; Pylades the famous dancer played the mad Hercules at a dinner party of Augustus.[190]

The appearance of a fool or jester—scurra, coprea—was warmly welcomed even at respectable dinner parties. He was often malformed and clownish in his appearance, and he exercised his wit at the expense of the guests. It was a creditable convention that a man should show good humour in face of even outrageous abuse.[191] At the terrible dinner of the philosophers, which Lucian described with such brilliance in his Convivium, the scurra Satyrion, a man of grotesque appearance, first danced and gesticulated, and then pilloried the guests, who behaved well and laughed—until he called the Cynic Alcidamas 'a Maltese lapdog', at which Alcidamas made the bad mistake of engaging him in a bout of all-in wrestling.[192]

Maecenas had in his household two extremely talented performers, Sarmentus and Gabba, whom in due course Augustus was happy to inherit, Gabba's lively wit being good enough to be remembered and quoted by Quintilian a century after his death. Two scurrae might be matched against one another in a battle of wit and slapstick, as Sarmentus was matched against Messius Cicirrus at dinner in Cocceius' villa near Caudium when Maecenas was travelling with Horace and other friends to Brundisium. This performance was not unsimilar to the buffoonery and wit of an English pantomime.[193]

It stands to reason that a good *scurra* was a very well informed man, and in the imperial household such men were not denied the opportunity of power. Iulius Paelignus (who had some physical deformity or other), a close associate of Claudius before Claudius' elevation, found himself governing the province of Cappadocia, however ineptly, ten years after Claudius became emperor; and the *scurra* Vatinius, like Cyrano disfigured by his nose, was a rich, powerful and sinister freedman in Nero's household.[194]

Sombre parties relaxed with dice and gambling—indeed, even at the dinner table itself there was no relaxation which the emperor Augustus liked better[195]; lively and dissolute parties with performances by buffoons (the coarsest of *scurrae* and *moriones*), effeminate men, dancing girls from Syria or, best of all, from Cadiz. Sometimes there was—even at an imperial dinner party with L. Verus or Elagabalus for host—the spectacle of gladiatorial fighting. This indeed was a longstanding tradition of Campanian extravagance according to Strabo; there you were invited to 'dinner and gladiators', the number of pairs varying to match the number of guests.[196]

With or without such entertainment, this after-dinner period (when crowns of flowers were produced for people to place on their heads) was the time of the *comissatio*, the toasting and drinking. Sometimes men moved elsewhere, to another house, for the drinking session, casting lots or throwing the dice for the selection of the master of ceremonies (the *magister* or *arbiter bibendi*), who called the toasts and the measures to be drunk. More often, where they dined, there they drank. At the same time, people who had not been asked to dinner could be asked in for drinks afterwards. In this way Habinnas arrived at Trimalchio's house 'wearing several wreaths and with unguent running down his forehead into his eyes', having evidently dined all too well elsewhere, and called for wine and hot water.[197]

A census would no doubt have shown that on any day, both in Rome and in the country, in the great majority of households there was conversation after dinner and a little drinking; after which the party broke up because its members had occupations or amusements or studies to which they were anxious to turn before they went to bed. But quiet conversation was often a prolonged affair. Nothing can have been more sober than a dinner of the elder Pliny; yet he did not rise from the table in winter until after dark.[198]

Other parties went on until dark and into the night, not always an unqualified source of enjoyment to all the guests. Sober and serious men

4

were sometimes shocked at the dissipation by which they were surrounded; gay sparks, on the other hand, bored by the tediously learned
talk of a party in which they found themselves, when their patience
reached breaking point, called for their shoes and left. Always a com-
plaisant man, the younger Pliny sagely advised that you should take
every company as you found it and do your best to appear at ease.[199]

In some houses, whether occasionally or regularly, the evening
passed through a crescendo of drinking to an orgy of shouting,
quarrelling and brawling. The civilized old bachelor Periplectomenus
in Plautus' *Braggart Soldier* preferred always to leave and go home if he
felt tempted to quarrel with a fellow guest. A *graffito* in a dining-room
at Pompeii urged guests who could not stop quarrelling to leave and go
home. There was an accentuation of confusion (and of danger) when
the lamps were knocked over.[200] Severe sermons against the horrors of
drunkenness are to be read in the pages of Seneca and of the elder Pliny.
And there are the men who have left a name behind them for their
drunkenness: Cicero's son, who could drink a gallon and a half at a
draught and who once threw a drinking cup at M. Agrippa, when he was
drunk; M. Antonius, who wrote a book, 'Am I a drunkard?' (*De ebrietate
sua*); Torquatus Novellius Atticus, who sank a two-and-a-quarter-
gallon sconce at a single draught without taking breath and without
leaving a drop of wine in the sconce pot (and who died at the age of
forty-four in the early Empire, proconsul of Narbonese Gaul); L. Piso,
whom Tiberius is said to have appointed to the office of *praefectus urbi*
at the end of a drinking bout which lasted two days and two nights (a
man who stayed in bed until midday, but who otherwise performed
his duties admirably); his successor Cossus Cornelius Lentulus, a less
happy appointment, who fell into such a deep sleep at a meeting of the
Senate (because he had been drinking) that he could not be woken and
had to be carried home; Pacuvius, legate of Syria under Tiberius, who
at the end of each night's revel had himself carried to bed with all the
ceremonial of a mock funeral (just as, with less ceremony, the emperor
L. Verus in the second century A.D. had often to be carried off to bed);
the emperor Tiberius when he was young (some wit turned his name
Tiberius Claudius Nero into Biberius Caldius Mero, 'Boozy Hot-and-
Strong') and his son Drusus, who out-drank everybody except his
doctor, for his doctor had discovered a specific against intoxication
and started the evening by eating almonds.

They belong in the main, these great drinkers, to a very short period
of history. But there was always the possibility that a drinking bout

would end in wild disorder—like the dinner of the philosophers which was the subject of Lucian's brilliant pastiche. The guests were already very drunk indeed when the *apophoreta*, the gifts (in this case food) for taking away, were produced. Each of the guests was determined at whatever cost to secure the best for himself. So fighting started. Happily there was a doctor among the guests, and he was sober. There was a lot of work for him to do.[201]

The women of the house (including the young bride) were frightened spectators of the fighting at this dinner, and the experience was one which in real life no doubt women were sometimes forced to suffer. Since from the late Republic women reclined like men and no longer sat, they no longer raised but, in a certain social *milieu*, voluntarily or involuntarily, lowered the tone of dinners which they attended. The *graffito* on a dining room wall in Pompeii invited men to keep their eyes off other men's wives; and the provocation of the dinner table to adultery was something by which Horace and the elder Pliny alike professed themselves shocked. In Horace's poem the husband connived at his wife's misconduct; at the emperor Gaius' dinner table the husband, if he wished to remain alive, reflected that he was the subject of the Emperor and of his imperial whims.[202]

Early or late, the time came for the guests to make a move. Their shoes were produced. They said goodbye. Augustus once, after being given, the most commonplace of meals, said to his host as he left, 'I had not realized that I was such a close friend of yours'. Affluent people were carried home in a litter or a chair, or had a slave or slaves to escort them home. L. Cornificius, consul in 35 B.C., an eccentric, returned home on an elephant. In winter, and often in summer, parties broke up long after dark, those of Nero and Titus sometimes after midnight; and, if there was no moon and the lantern blew out, the guest's journey home, if he returned on foot, was not without its painful hazards. There were diners who did not reel home until after dawn—even, if the word of Caesar is to be trusted, the younger Cato, still an august figure even when he was wildly drunk.[203]

The slaves of the household were on their toes from the beginning of dinner until the party ended. The chef was the most important, one of the family's most valuable possessions. From being a chore, something that the cheapest slave could do, cooking in the second century B.C. turned into an art, Livy declares. So a cook cost as much as a horse; by the elder Pliny's time he cost as much as three horses, though only a third as much as a really expensive fish. 'No one is rated at so

high a value as a man who applies the whole of his great skill to bank-
rupting his master.' Sallust the historian is said to have paid a hundred
thousand sesterces to hire the cook of L. Cassius Nomentanus, who
himself squandered seven million sesterces on the gratification of his
gross appetite, 'gulae ac libidini'. With a fussy, ill-tempered or dys-
peptic master, the cook's life was not an easy one; but all masters were
not unreasonable. Ausonius went into the kitchen about an hour before
a lunch party, to make sure that all was well, encouraging his cook to
put his finger in the gravy and lick it, to check the taste.[204]

Trimalchio's household naturally contained not one cook but a
number of them, and in a carefully prepared frolic, a cook was brought
in to do the carving. But the carver—structor—was a specialist in his
own right. Trimalchio's was given the name Carver (Carpus), again
for the sake of a practical joke.* 'Another carves the priceless birds,
passing his skilled hand with regular motions over the breast and rump,
in order to carve nice helpings. Miserable man, with one object only in
life, to carve fat capons decently'; thus the bilious Seneca. There was a
wine-steward, often made up so as to give a false impression of youth.

In the course of a debauch the slaves had disgusting duties to perform
and Seneca, had he been a slave, would have hated it all. Those who
had the misfortune to serve a master as cruel as Augustus' abominable
friend Vedius Pollio lived in terror; let a precious glass be broken and—
if Augustus was not there to interfere—the unfortunate who dropped
it was thrown into the fish pond to feed the lampreys. But this was not a
typical household.

In all societies in which there has been extravagant entertainment,
however gross, the servants have enjoyed themselves as much as the
guests. There is plenty of good food and drink to be consumed outside
the dining-room; there are tips, and there is the immense pleasure of
watching the indecorous conduct of your betters. Trimalchio's slaves
obviously enjoyed every one of the carefully prepared practical jokes
in which the guests were fooled into thinking that they were to be
punished. The slave in Lucian's Symposium found it all very amusing.
Rufus' slave proved himself a better friend to his master than did certain
of his master's guests.†[205]

The slaves, indeed, reflected more often than not the master's
character and the manner in which he entertained. Here, whether true

---

* The summons 'Carpe' indicating, in W. D. Lowe's translation of the pun, 'Carver,
carve 'er.'

† See above, pp. 47f.

or not, is Cicero's description of the household of L. Calpurnius Piso, consul in 58 B.C.:

His house contains nothing of taste, charm or refinement, nothing expensive, in fact, his own appetites excepted. There is not a piece of chased or embossed silver; there are just vast beakers, marked (in case any one should think him ashamed of his origins) *Manufactured in Placentia*. There are no oysters or fish at his dinners, only an abundance of not very fresh meat. The servants who wait are filthy and some of them are decrepit; one man doubles the parts of cook and steward. He does not keep a baker or a properly stocked larder, and sends out for his bread and his wine (from the barrel). He entertains Greeks, packed five or more to a couch, while he has a couch to himself. Drinking continues until the drink runs out.[206]

After even the most orderly dinner there was plenty of cleaning-up for the slaves to do. The floor needed sweeping, for one thing; because guests customarily threw the objects of food which they discarded on to the ground—legs of lobsters, shells of snails, egg-shells, cherry stones, cores of apples. This habit, for which there was a long history (just as in European countries there was to be a long future for it) had extraordinary repercussions in art. A floor littered by such fragments appealed to a Pergamene artist called Sosus as a fascinating object of still life, and he started a fashion of designing mosaics in this *genre* (embellished with representations of doves drinking from a bowl), the name for which was 'asarôtos oikos' (the unswept pavement). Numerous specimens survive, a very remarkable one in the Lateran museum.[207]

Ancient literature admits us as spectators to the dining rooms of the affluent; it passes contemptuously by the homes of the great majority of Romans who were not rich at all. The basis of their meals was a thick soup of meal (often millet) and water or bread (very different from white bread, since it was ground husks and all), supplemented, in the main, by turnips, olives, beans, figs and cheese. Their meat (eaten rarely) was pork. Only those who lived near the sea or on rivers will have tasted fish. How well constituted their diet was, and whether a number of illnesses (especially skin diseases, which were prevalent) were the result of under-nourishment, just as many of the diseases of the rich were the result of over-eating, research has still to discover.[208]

4. The Workers' Afternoon

Not everybody's daily life, particularly in the short days of winter, followed this leisurely course. After lunch (and in summer a siesta) many people, perhaps the majority, returned to work. Farm labourers, whether they were slaves or free, will have worked on until dusk—in the gospel parable work was still going on in the vineyard at the eleventh hour of day—and then have returned home for an evening meal; and so will the majority of industrial workers. Apprenticeship contracts in Egypt were for work from sunrise to sundown, and there is no reason why the hours of work should have been different else-where, except in the case of men engaged on particularly arduous manual labour, like the miners in Portugal, who evidently started to come into the baths in the afternoon at the eighth hour; the baths were busy from then until the second hour of night. The miners were presumably working shifts.[209]

How regularly pupils returned to school after lunch, whether only in the shorter days of winter, we do not know. St. Augustine's duties as a teacher were apparently limited to the morning hours, but the scholarly M. Valerius Probus in the first century A.D., who took a small number of private pupils, taught them during the afternoon. And here is part of a schoolboy's account of his day in the early third century A.D.:

I finish my lesson and ask the master if I can go home to lunch. I say goodbye and he replies. I return home and change. I lunch off white bread, olives, cheese, dry figs and nuts, and have water to drink. After that I return to school, to find the master engaged in reading. He says, 'Get to work.'

After which, without (it seems) taking any physical exercise, the child goes off to the baths:

Time for the baths. I run to join the others who are going to the baths, saying to one and all, 'Have a good bath. Have a good supper.'[210]

Shops opened again in the afternoon, late in summer (as in Italy today) and doubtless very early in winter, for they closed, presumably, when it grew dark. It was growing dark when, evidently with buyers about, Encolpius and Ascyltus tried to dispose of their stolen cloak in Petronius' *Satyricon*. St. Augustine refers clearly to the opening of shops in the afternoon, and Martial mocks a man who spends the whole day in an expensive antique shop, and then leaves with a couple of cheap cups at the eleventh hour.[211]

Workers and shopkeepers must have fed when their working day ended. After which, with the coming of darkness, most people went to bed. For lamps did not give a bright light, and their smoke was no encouragement to lucubration.[212]

II

THE YEAR

++

DOWN TO 153 B.C. the year had two beginnings. The natural year started on January 1st after the winter solstice, the all-important civil year on March 1st (earlier, the 15th), from which the names of Quinctilis (fifth month, later renamed July in honour of Julius Caesar), Sextilis (sixth month, later August in honour of Augustus), September and October (seventh and eighth months, which we might well be calling Germanic and Domitian respectively today, if Domitian, who gave the months these names in his own honour, had not been the disaster that he was), November (ninth month) and December (tenth month) marked a numerical sequence.

Before 45 B.C., when Julius Caesar introduced the calendar which, with very small changes, we still enjoy, March, May, July and October had thirty-one days each, February twenty-eight and the remaining months twenty-nine each. The first day of every month was the Kalends. The fifth in the short months, the seventh in the long months, was the Nones, so called as being the ninth day before the Ides. The Ides, which in origin was the full moon of the lunar month, was on the 13th in the short months and the 15th in the long ones.

The days of the month were not numbered serially, but were reckoned by their distance from the following Nones, Ides or Kalends, as the case might be. March 16th, for instance, was the seventeenth day before the Kalends of April, 'a.d. xvii Kalendas Apriles', and that is how dates were given, past or future. Cicero wrote to Atticus in October 54 B.C., 'Pomptinus wants to hold his triumph four days before the Nones of November. Nine days before the Kalends of November I had letters from Britain from my brother and from Caesar, dated six days before the Kalends of October. The last letter I had from you was from Ephesus, dated five days before the Ides of Sextilis (August).' Describing his future movements in 59, he wrote, 'I want to get to my house at Formiae on the Parilia' (April 21st, ten days before the Kalends of May.) 'I shall leave on the Kalends of May, so as to be in Antium five days before the Nones of May. The games there are to last from four days before the Nones of May to the day before the Nones. I plan to get to Rome on about the Kalends of June.'[1]

The normal year was 355 days long, a day more than the lunar year of 354 days; and, as the Greeks discovered, in the course of eight lunar years, the year slips 90 days ahead of the sun. The Greeks made the correction very simply by inserting an extra month of thirty days three times in each eight-year period. The Roman solution was a great deal more complicated. An extra-intercalary-month was due for insertion into the calendar every other year, so as to make the length of the years over a four-year period 355, 377, 355 and 378 days successively, giving an average of $366\frac{1}{4}$ days (one day too many). The extra month was inserted on alternate years into February, which instead of ending in the normal way on the 28th was brought to an end on the 23rd (Terminalia) or the 24th (which, instead of being, as it should have been, the feast of Regifugium, was called 'the day after the Terminalia', 'Postridie Terminalia'). Then the intercalary month of twenty-seven days started (i.e. twenty-two intercalated days plus the five which were left over from the shortened February). The 23rd of the intercalary month was the date of the festival of the Regifugium— 'six days before the Kalends of March'—just as it was in a year in which there was no intercalation.[2]

The sequence of irregular years did not take place automatically, and there was no intercalation unless specific notice was given by the College of Pontiffs, in whose field of responsibility the calendar lay. It should, of course, have been their duty also to make periodical correction of the error which resulted from the calendar being one day too long; and there could be little excuse for their behaviour in periods when the calendar was allowed to get completely out of step with the sun. Carelessness and irresponsibility were sometimes to blame, sometimes intrigue. There were occasions when a politician or some important pressure-group like a big company of tax-collectors preferred a long year, others (as in the case of Cicero, a man who hated absence from Rome, yet was constrained to govern Cilicia for a calendar year) when they preferred a short one.

There had been bad patches in the earlier Republic, especially after the Second Punic War, during which intercalation had been suspended, and also at the end of the Republic, through the misbehaviour of the pontiffs, Caesar himself being their chairman, during the Fifties. At the beginning of 46 B.C. the inaccuracy was as large as two and a half months; the day celebrated as New Year's Day should in fact have been the 14th of October of the old year. The Roman equivalents of Harvest Thanksgiving were being celebrated in the case of corn and wine long before the harvest and the vintage started.³ With this kind of recurrent irregularity on top of the normal inequality in the length of the years, the civil calendar was useless to the farmer and the sailor; they had, both of them, to make their own calculations by the stars.

Minor, but still very considerable, inconvenience was suffered before the introduction of the Julian calendar from the fact that the public announcement of a forthcoming intercalation was sometimes made at the very last moment. When Cicero set out for Cilicia in the summer of 51 B.C., he was in a panic that 50 would be made an intercalary year. Four days before the date at which the intercalary month of 50 would have started, he still did not know, in Cilicia, whether there was to be intercalation or not. So, acknowledging a letter from Atticus received on February 19th, he did not refer to that date as 'a.d. xi Kal. Mart.' (which, if there was intercalation, would not be February 19th at all, but the 18th of the intercalary month); he called it 'a.d.v Terminalia', a safe date in either event.⁴

All these irregularities were brought to an end in the dictatorship of Julius Caesar. The year 46, 'the last year of confusion', was extended not by one but by three intercalary months, to last for 445 days.⁵ The Julian calendar was introduced on January 1st 45. After this in leap years February remained formally a twenty-eight day month, and there was no February 29th. Instead, a day was inserted between the 23rd and 24th, as a 'second twenty-fourth', '*bis sextum Kalendas Martias*', preceding the normal twenty-fourth, the Regifugium. So a leap year was later called *annus bisextilis*.⁶

To the Roman farmer of the Republic, as has been seen, astronomy was of more practical value than the calendar and even after the introduction of the Julian calendar farmers, always conservative people, may have continued to rely on the stars, just as a farmer today may prefer the evidence of his senses to an official weather forecast. In fourth-century Gaul a bad farm bailiff could be described as a man who blamed heaven for his poor crops, their poorness being in fact the result of his own ignorance; unable to understand the stars, he sowed grain too early or too late.⁷

Still, the Julian calendar was in fact reliable, and farmers' calendars of a simple kind, *menologia*, made their appearance in stone or in mosaic, rather for ornament than to remind the farmer of what he should know well enough already. Two have survived from Rome, one almost certainly as early as the first century A.D.

There are twelve columns, one for each month. At the head of each the zodiacal sign for the month is depicted. What for a farmer were the important features of the month are inscribed below it. For instance[8]:

MAY	SEPTEMBER
31 DAYS	30 DAYS
NONES ON SEVENTH	NONES ON 5TH
DAYLIGHT: 14½ HOURS*	DAYLIGHT: 12 HOURS*
DARKNESS 9½ HOURS*	DARKNESS: 12 HOURS*
SUN IN TAURUS	EQUINOX: 24TH
PROTECTOR: APOLLO	SUN IN VIRGO
WEED CORN	PROTECTOR: VULCAN
SHEAR SHEEP	PITCH-PAINT WINE JARS
WASH WOOL	PICK APPLES
BREAK IN YOUNG BULLOCKS	LOOSEN EARTH ROUND
CUT VETCH	ROOTS OF TREES
BLESS THE CORNFIELDS	FEAST IN HONOUR OF
SACRIFICE TO MERCURY,	MINERVA
FLORA	

In art the figure of the farmer at work in each of the twelve months was to have a long history. In the vast twelfth-century mosaic on the floor of the Cathedral of Otranto for each of the twelve months there is a medallion in which, under the appropriate zodiacal sign, the farmer is depicted. In September, for instance, he is treading the grapes; in October he is ploughing; in November he is cutting wood; in December he is killing a boar; in January he is crouched indoors over the fire. This was a favourite subject in medieval art.

Market days must be nearly as old as agriculture itself. On them the farmer exchanges his products for the goods which he needs. The townsman buys poultry and vegetables, and sells the farmer his tools and his wife her pots and pans.

From early times in Rome and in much of the Italian countryside, particularly in Campania, every eighth day was a market day,[9] called Nundinae, ninth-day affairs, because the Romans when they counted

* *I.e.* 60-minute hours, as calculated by astrologers and astronomers.

included both terminal figures. The period from one Nundinae to the next was *nundinum*. As soon as calendars existed, the letters A, B, C, D, E, F, G, H were placed against the successive days, starting with A on January 1st.[10] As the number of days in the year was never divisible by eight, and as the series of letters started afresh on January 1st each year, it is clear that in the calendars of any single place the market day must have been indicated by a different letter on each successive year.[11] Moreover, with increased population and prosperity, neighbouring towns necessarily had different market days. We known, for instance, that in Campania in the early Empire, Pompeii, Nuceria, Atella, Nola, Cumae, Puteoli had markets on different days, followed after a day's interval by Capua.[12]

The market day was the important occasion that in country life it has always been all the world over. It was, in early days, the day for cutting your nails and shaving and washing not merely your arms and legs but the whole of your body. People spruced themselves up, after seven days of hard work on the farm, before they went to market. It was also a regular school holiday, eagerly anticipated by children in the elementary and grammar schools.[13] As Varro wrote, 'The ancients devoted seven days to work and the eighth to business in town.'[14] Business could involve lawyers, who were to be found in towns. So the day was a *dies fastus*,* on which legal transactions could be effected. On the other hand, no public meetings could be held, since they would have interfered with the proper business of the day.[15]

Naturally there were often townspeople who wished to invite their friends from the country to a meal; so the stern Lex Fannia of 161 B.C.†

---

* Unless it happened to fall on a regular festival day (marked N or NP in the calendar for the year; see p. 77) or on Feriae Conceptivae or Imperativae (see pp. 70f).

† See p. 38.

allowed the entertainment of five guests, instead of the normal maximum of three, from outside the household on market days.[16]

The *nundinum* had many of the qualities of the later seven-day week, in that each of its eight days was identifiable in writing and conversation. The days were thought of and spoken of as 'the Nundinae', 'the day before the Nundinae', 'two days before the Nundinae', and so on.[17]

The interval between the first and the third of three successive Nundinae (counting both terminal dates, a period of seventeen days) was a *trinundinum* and, just as in England banns of marriage must be published in church on three successive Sundays, a number of public functions in Rome had necessarily to be performed on three successive Nundinae: the announcement of the text of a bill which was to be brought before a public assembly, the publication of the names of candidates for public election (and, once, in early Rome, the names of debtors after their arrest and imprisonment, in case anybody might be willing to come and bail them out). This had once been the best way of securing wide publicity, just as the calling of banns in church once was; it survived, like the calling of banns, when it had lost some of its appropriateness, since the Nundinae were no longer days when a majority of the voting population was likely to be in the city.[18]

The immense convenience of the seven-day week, as we use it, was still to come. In the East this was already a thing of long antiquity, the seventh day having been marked in Babylon by strong tabus: no baked bread or cooked meat might be eaten; the doctor might not lay hands on the sick; the King might not mount his chariot.[19] For the Jew it was a complete day of rest.

In the Hellenistic world, we do not know when, the seven days of the week received their planetary attributions and names and became, in succession, the days of Saturn, the Sun, the Moon, Mars, Mercury, Jupiter, Venus—attributions which, except in the case of Sunday,* survive in the Romance languages today.

The true order of the planets was different (Saturn, Jupiter, Mars, the Sun, Venus, Mercury, the Moon), and the weekly order of names was reached by starting with Saturn and then, in succession, leap-frogging the next two. In one of his after-dinner discussions which has not survived Plutarch investigated the origin of this changed order, and Dio Cassius was no doubt right in tracing it to the fact that each of the

* Northern Europe perpetuates this pagan name; in the Romance languages it is the Lord's Day, *dimanche, domenica, domingo.*

twenty-four hours of the day had its own planet (in the normal order), the planet of the first hour giving its general colour to the day. The planetary order of the first hours of successive days, calculated in this way, is the planetary order of the week.[20]

The Jewish Sabbath, the day of Saturn, will in some cases have been the Roman's first introduction to the seven-day week. Not only magistrates but everybody who had commercial dealings with Jews in the provinces and, from the second century B.C., in Rome, will have known that even in a crisis of the utmost urgency a Jew was inaccessible, and most people will have known that he fasted, every seventh day. By the time of the early Empire there were Romans who were proselytes and themselves observed the Sabbath.[21]

The rapidly spreading infection of astrology in the late Republic did most to familiarize Romans with the seven-day week. If every day felt the influence of a particular planet, the superstitious needed to know what that planet was; for there were lucky days and unlucky ones. Literature of the time of Augustus has references to Saturn's day (Saturday) as an unlucky day, particularly for starting a journey, but in nearly every case the day is referred to as being the Jewish Sabbath. The scholarly Diogenes lectured publicly in Rhodes on Saturdays in the years after 6 B.C. and was not prepared, even for Tiberius, the Emperor's step-son, to vary his practice.[22]

The first public record in Rome of the seven-day week, though the days are not given their names, is constituted by a calendar of between 19 B.C. and A.D. 14 from the Sabine country, with the days from September 14th, for example, marked in the following way:

E	A	F (astus)★
F	B	N (efastus)★
G	C	C (omitialis)★
A	D	C
B	E	C
C	F	C
D	G	C
E	H	C
F	A	C

The first column marks the days of the seven-day week, the second the eight days of the *nundinum*. There are two other very fragmentary

★ See pp. 75-7 below for the significance of this word.

calendars, one of the time of Augustus, the other from the early Empire, on which also the seven-day week is marked.[23] There was no regular correspondence between any particular letter and any particular named week-day, as the first of January was marked, just as it was in the case of the *nundinum*, with the letter A.

Pictorial and epigraphic evidence from Campania shows widespread familiarity before 79 A.D. with the seven-day week and with the names of the days. At Pompeii a wall-painting was found depicting, in their correct weekly order, the personifications of the divine powers which controlled each of the seven days. It was just such a picture as this that Trimalchio had on the door leading to his dining-room, marked to show which days were lucky and which unlucky.[24]

There are at least five inscriptions and one *graffito* from Latium and Campania designed to show the different market days in different towns.*[25] The inscriptions have the names of the towns and the names of the seven days of the week, and on some there are holes against each town and against each day; so by the insertion of a similar or a similarly coloured marker against the name of the town and against the day of the week indication was given of the particular week-day on which the next market day would be held in that town; for, with a planetary week of seven days and a market week of eight, where the market was held on a Tuesday, for instance, one week, it was held on a Wednesday on the week following.[26] There are *graffiti* at Pompeii, and therefore earlier than A.D. 79, 'Nine days before the Kalends of June, Sunday (*die Solis*)', 'Ten days before the Kalends of February, Ursa's child was born on Thursday.'[27]

A *graffito* at Pompeii gives a date in A.D. 60 in the fullest detail possible: 'In the consulship of Nero Caesar Augustus and Cossus Lentulus, eight days before the Ides of February, on Sunday, on the sixteenth day of the moon, market day at Cumae, five days before the market day at Pompeii.'[28]

This all confirms Josephus' statement, in the second half of the first century A.D., that the whole world, Greek and barbarian, was by that time familiar with the seven-day week and made use of it. Cassius Dio, writing early in the third century, said the same: that it was universally observed in his time by the Romans and by other peoples. And there is other evidence. A passage in Juvenal suggests that in the early second century A.D., schools followed a seven-day time table; for it was on a certain day of the week—*sexta quaque die*—that certain public

* See illustration on p. 60.

recitals took place, like the lectures of Diogenes in Rhodes a century earlier. And when Avidius Cassius was governor of Syria in the later part of the second century, he gave his troops a full military exercise 'every seventh day'—that is to say, once a week.[29]

From the third century even Christians dated by the days of the week, despite their pagan significance, the week still starting with Saturday on account of Saturn's planetary prestige. Mithraism and other forms of sun-worship displaced Saturn in the fourth century, when Sunday became the first day of the week, as we find it in Ausonius' poem on the names of the seven days.[30] At the end of that century, under Theodosius, the seven-day week was adopted for public and official purposes.

The idea of a regularly recurrent day on which all work was suspended had no appeal for the pagan Roman, and Roman writers generally stigmatized the Jewish observance of the Sabbath as a decadent glorification of sheer idleness.[31] The Roman Nundinae had never been such a day of rest; it was a day when traders and lawyers were at their busiest, and there was no ban at all on work.

The earliest evidence of Christian observance of Sunday (which from apostolic times was called the Lord's Day, *dies dominica*) as a weekly day of rest comes from Tertullian in A.D. 202.[32] Constantine, whose pagan, sun-worshipping father Constantius would have been pleased to hear him referring to it still as Sunday,* ordered its observance as a day of religious worship at the official acceptance of Christianity in two edicts in A.D. 321. By the first there was to be a general suspension of litigation and of work in cities, but there was no prohibition of agricultural work, since it might well happen that the ground and the weather were exactly right on a Sunday for sowing corn or transplanting vines; in the second an exception was made in the case of certain legal business— the emancipation of a son or the manumission of a slave, for which happy events the day seemed singularly appropriate. Theodosius barred the transaction of business and litigation and, in particular, the holding of public games on a Sunday, with one exception: an imperial birthday. This was between 386 and 395; in A.D. 409 even this exception was removed.[33]

A time came when, despite their natural conservatism, country people agreed to abandon the old eight-day cycle of Nundinae and to make one particular day of the seven-day week the market day.

---

* In A.D. 386 Valentinian and Theodosius referred to the day as 'the Day of the Sun, which our ancestors rightly called the Lord's Day', CT 2, 8, 18.

Alternatively markets might be held regularly on certain days of the month. An inscription shows that, when senatorial leave was given to a man in A.D. 138 to hold a market on his estate in the province of Africa, it was stipulated that the market should take place twice a month, four days before the Nones and twelve days before the Kalends. The markets would be held roughly once a fortnight, and successive market days always on different days of the seven-day week.[34]

In Italy outside Rome traditional non-Roman methods of dating had not died easily. An inscription from Ferentis in Etruria of 67 B.C., for instance, dated a death as happening 'Five days before the Ides of October in the month Chospher, on the third day of the moon.' In Etruria the days following the Ides, instead of being back-dated from the following Kalends, were most sensibly dated from the Ides and named accordingly, Triatrus, Sexatrus, Septimatrus, for instance. There was a reflection of this in the ancient Roman feast of Quinquatrus, so called as being the fifth day after the Ides of March and not because its festivities lasted for five days, as in fact they did.[35]

In pagan Rome, festivals apart, certain aspects and activities of life marked out certain days as having particular importance: debt chiefly and native Roman superstition.

Beside the Puteal in the Forum in Rome and beside the arch of Janus Medius by the Basilica Aemilia and at other places elsewhere the money-lenders were much in evidence on the Kalends, the Nones and the Ides, for it was on one or other of those days that interest on borrowed money had to be paid. The Kalends of July and of January were the days on which rent was due; and on the Ides schoolboys brought their monthly fees with them when they came to school.[36]

In all societies there are days which for known or unknown reasons are thought unlucky. The thirteenth of a month is commonly apprehended by the superstitious. In Greece there is still a reluctance to allow official ceremonies to take place on a Tuesday, the day on which Byzantium fell in the fifteenth century to the Turks.

Tradition and history supplied the Romans with a number of such days, 'black days', as they were called. Such days were *religiosi* and, though they were not marked in any particular way in the calendars, the year was uncomfortably full of them. There were the days following the Kalends, Nones and Ides for a start (and for highly superstitious people, the fourth day before the Kalends, Nones and Ides, whether or not because the disaster of Cannae happened four days before the Nones of August). There were the anniversaries of great military disasters: after 217 B.C. of Trasimene (June 21st or 23rd); after 105 B.C. of Arausio (October 6th) and, most grimly observed of all, July 18th, which was doubly inauspicious since it was the anniversary of the near-extinction of the Gens Fabia at Cremera in 477 B.C. and of the disaster of the Allia, which opened the way to Rome to the Gauls in 390 B.C. Nothing could have been more inauspicious than Vitellius' choice of this day for his inauguration as Pontifex Maximus in A.D. 69. With the anniversary of the Allia the people of Pisa equated the day on which Augustus' adopted son C. Caesar died; there were to be no public dinners on that day, no betrothal parties, no public entertainment, no races, no games.[37]

There were the days when the entrance to the underworld, the *mundus*, was open (August 24th, October 5th, November 8th), the days when families remembered their dead (the Parentalia, from February 13th to 21st), the days of the Lemuria (May 9th, 11th and 13th), when the ghosts of the dead were out and about.

More than eighty days of the year had some taint or other. And, just as there is a common reluctance to marry during Lent today, it was thought unlucky in ancient Rome to marry in May, the month of the Lemuria, or in the first half of June, until the temple of Vesta had been scoured on the 15th. Nor should a marriage take place on the Kalends, Nones or Ides, for in such an event it would be on the following day, which was always inauspicious, that the bride would be initiated into her religious duties as matron of the household. Roman armies should not engage when the underworld was open or, though for utterly different reasons, during the Latin Festival or during the Saturnalia; nor, of course, on the anniversary of one of the great Roman military disasters.[38]

We are told by Dio and by Macrobius that it was thought inauspicious for the public life of the State if the Kalends of the first month of the year (originally March, later January) or the Nones of any month should coincide with the Nundinae. The public disasters of the years 78 and 52 B.C. were attributed to such unfortunate coincidence on January 1st, and in 40 B.C. a day was specially inserted in the calendar, to be compensated by the withdrawal of a day later, to avoid a similar mishap. Nobody was certain of the reason for the superstition. It was said that the Nones—of what month, nobody knew—had been the birthday of King Servius Tullius, and so there was a risk that, with market crowds assembled on his birthday, there might be unhealthy talk in favour of a restoration of the monarchy.

There is no evidence of the superstition about the Kalends of January earlier than 78 B.C., and it is most unlikely that a single inter-calary day was ever inserted in the calendar because of such a super-stition. The extra day in 40 B.C. may well have been on account of a misplaced leap year in the new Julian calendar. It is certain that, how-ever unlucky the coincidence may have been felt to be, nothing could possibly have been done to avoid frequent coincidences of Nundinae with the Nones.[39]

It is impossible to know how deeply superstitious how many people were. Few can have known everything that was to be read on the sub-ject in Ovid's *Fasti*, and in the works of Varro, Festus and later Plutarch and others. It is remarkable that even Cicero, rationalist and sceptic as the *De Divinatione* shows him to have been, hesitated to negotiate his daughter's engagement in 56 B.C. during the two inauspicious days which followed the Latin Festival.[40]

The introduction of the Julian calendar brought a new unlucky day —the extra day, the 'second twenty-fourth' of February in leap years. In A.D. 364 Valentinian would not consent to be proclaimed emperor on that day.[41]

The Roman religious year, like the Christian later, embraced both fixed and movable feasts. In the Republic there were forty-five* regular festivals, *Feriae Publicae*, occurring each year on the same fixed day, *dies festus* or *feriatus*, and indicated by name in the public calendars. These were festivals whose expenses, mainly for sacrificial offerings, were met by the public treasury of the state, and the day was in most cases the anniversary of the dedication of the altar or temple of the divinity whose festival it was. Juppiter was the god most greatly honoured and, after Juppiter, Mars.[42]

The Kalends of March and the Poplifugia (July 5th) apart, no festi-vals were earlier than the Nones of any month, the day on which, by the survival of a practice dating from the time when there were no public inscribed calendars, public notice was given of the dates of forthcoming festivals. It was the opinion of antiquity—which modern scholarship, though it may not accept, cannot disprove—that the origin of every one of these festivals lay in the remote days of the eighth and seventh centuries B.C., the time of the monarchy. An extra-ordinary feature of the festival days, which has never been satisfactorily

---

* Fifty-eight, if you include the Ides of each month, sacred to Juppiter, and the Kalends of March, sacred to Mars.

explained, is that, apart from the Regifugium and the March Equirria, they never fell on even days of the month.[43]

A great many other days were devoted to public games (*ludi*), which were separate from the *dies feriati* of the calendars. There were no less than eighteen days of games in April, eight in July, fifteen (after Caesar's death, sixteen) in September and fourteen in November. To these were added towards the end of the Republic seven new days of games in honour of Sulla's Victory and, later, eleven days in honour of Caesar's.*

Here is a full calendar of festivals and games soon after Julius Caesar's death.[44]

January 9, Agonalia (to Janus)
           11, 15, Carmentalia (to Carmentis)
           13, Ides (to Juppiter)

February 13, Ides (to Juppiter)
           15, Lupercalia (to Lupercus or Faunus)
           17, Quirinalia (to Quirinus)
           21, Feralia (to the nether gods)
           23, Terminalia (to Terminus)
           24, Regifugium (to Juppiter?)
           27, Equirria (to Mars); chariot race in Campus Martius.

March 1, Kalends (to Mars)
           14, Equirria (to Mars); chariot race in Campus Martius
           15, Ides (to Juppiter and Anna Perenna)
           17, Liberalia (to Liber and Libera); Agonalia (to Mars)
           19, Quinquatrus (to Mars and Minerva)
           23, Tubilustrium (to Mars)

April 4–10, *Ludi Megalenses*
           12–19, *Ludi Ceriales*
           13, Ides (to Juppiter)
           15, Fordicidia (to Tellus)
           19, Cerialia (to Ceres, Liber, Libera)
           21, Parilia (to Pales?); birthday of Rome
           23, Vinalia (to Juppiter and Venus)
           25, Robigalia (to Robigus)
           28—May 3, *Ludi Florales*

* For full details of the Games, see pp. 245–48.

May 9, 11, 13, Lemuria (to Lemures)
     15, Ides (to Juppiter)
     21, Agonalia (to Vediovis?)
     23, Tubilustrium (to Vulcan)

June 9, Vestalia (to Vesta)
      11, Matralia (to Mater Matuta)
      13, Ides (to Juppiter)

July 5, Poplifugia (to Juppiter)
      6–13, *Ludi Apollinares*
      15, Ides (to Juppiter); from 304 B.C. for a period and regu-
          larly after Augustus, the mounted procession of
          Equites Equo Publico through the Forum to the
          Capitol, the *Transvectio Equitum*
      19, 21, Lucaria
      20–30, *Ludi Victoriae Caesaris*
      23, Neptunalia (to Neptune)
      25, Furrinalia (to Furrina)

August 13, Ides (to Juppiter)
        17, Portunalia (to Portunus)
        19, Vinalia (to Juppiter and Venus)
        21, Consualia (to Consus)
        23, Volcanalia (to Vulcan)
        25, Opiconsivia (to Ops Consiva)
        27, Volturnalia (to Volturnus)

September 4–19, *Ludi Romani*
           13, Ides (to Juppiter)

October 11, Meditrinalia (to Juppiter)
         13, Fontinalia (to Fons)
         15, Ides (to Juppiter); chariot race in Campus Martius and
             slaughter of the October Horse
         19, Armilustrium (to Mars)
         26—November 1, *Ludi Victoriae Sullae* (?)

November 4–17, *Ludi Plebei*
          13, Ides (to Juppiter)

December 11, Agonalia (to Sol Indiges)
          13, Ides (to Juppiter)
          15, Consualia (to Consus)

17, Saturnalia (to Saturn)
19, Opalia (to Ops)
21, Divalia (to Angerona)
23, Larentalia (to Larenta or Larunda and Juppiter)

This calendar of festivals is evidently, in its origin, largely a countryman's, a farmer's, calendar. In April the corn was in full growth and the vines were sprouting; so there was an accumulation of festivals to encourage fertility and to avert disease. There were few festivals in months when farmers were hard at work, in June, September or November; there were plenty in December and February and in the sweltering heat of August, when they had time on their hands.

Though its intensity varied from season to season, there was work for the farmer to do in all twelve months of the year. Fighting, vital for Rome's early survival and the extension of her power through Italy, had its own fixed season. The levies were held and conscripts were called up in March. So it was in March, when the *ancilia*, the sacred shields of Mars, were taken down by his priests, the Salii, and they executed their ritual dance, that Mars was honoured in a whole series of festivals; just as he was honoured again in October, which conventionally marked the end of the fighting season.[45]

Three times a year, on February 27th,* March 14th and October 15th, you could witness a two-horse chariot race, the Equirria, held in honour of Mars in the Campus Martius or, if there were floods, on the Caelian. On October 15th the outer horse of the winning pair was killed, its tail cut off and carried to one place (the Regia, to drip blood on to the hearth), its head to another; and had you watched this gruesome butchery as a Roman in the late Republic, you would probably have had as little idea of the reason as has the modern anthropologist who speculates about its origin in a time when Mars was a predominantly agricultural deity.[46]

But this was not the end. In addition, there were the movable feasts, the dates of whose celebration were fixed and announced each year by the competent authority, the consul, the praetor, one of the priestly colleges or minor religious or secular dignitaries. These festivals were called Feriae Conceptivae. The most important were the three- or four-day Latin Festival, which took place early in the year (because, in the days when consuls commanded armies in war, this festival had to be celebrated before they left Rome), and the Compitalia at the end of

* A.D. iii Kal. Mart. In the Republic this fell on the 26th of the intercalated month, when there was intercalation.

December or beginning of January. Other Feriae Conceptivae, as their names indicate, were mainly of primitive agricultural significance, and their number was not large.[47]

There were still other festival days, Feriae Imperativae, days of Supplicationes, which the Senate voted and for which the consuls fixed a day for offerings to be made to the gods. These were either intercession days on the occasion of public calamity, or thanksgiving days when some public crisis had been surmounted or a sensational victory won; or else they were days when triumphs were celebrated by victorious generals on their return to Rome. Supplicationes had rarely lasted for more than a day; three were enough when, after the victory of the Metaurus in 207 B.C., the issue of the Second Punic War was no longer in any serious doubt. But at the end of the Republic sycophancy inflated their number to bursting point. Fifteen days were voted in honour of Caesar's successes in Gaul at the end of 57 B.C. and twenty days were voted in his honour two years later. Cicero's last preserved utterance was a proposal, which the Senate accepted, that there should be Supplicationes of fifty days after the battle of Mutina in 43 B.C. Supplicationes were voted fifty-five times in honour of Augustus—a total of 890 days, an average of sixteen days each time.[48]

No comparable inflation occurred in the case of triumphs. Standards were maintained. Rarely were more than two celebrated in any year, often none at all.[49]

This in Rome. The major festivals of the Roman calendar were celebrated by Roman communities everywhere, and by the armies the whole Empire over.[50] Individual cities in addition celebrated their own traditional festivals, Praeneste (Palestrina), for example, in honour of Fortuna Praenestina on April 10th.[51]

The Empire brought a spate of new celebrations, official and unofficial. Achievements of Caesar and of Augustus, new temple dedications and imperial birthdays added, with imperial consecrations, thirty-two new festival days to the calendar between 45 B.C. and A.D. 37. The process continued under each successive emperor. Among these new celebrations, many of them shortlived, the birthday and anniversary of the accession day of the ruling emperor must always have been memorable occasions the whole empire over, days of great embarrassment to Jews and Christians, who could not share in such pagan jollification; so at Rome, after they became annual under Tiberius, were the Ludi Augustales which, once fully established, lasted ten days, from October 3rd to the 12th.[52]

In the absence of surviving calendars for the three hundred years after A.D. 37, apart from the third-century Feriale Duranum, we cannot know in detail what new festival days were added and how quickly the majority of them disappeared. In 225/7, as the Feriale Duranum shows, the army still honoured the birthdays of the consecrated emperors of the first and second centuries and of the consecrated women of the second; and, in addition, the birthdays of Julius Caesar and of Germanicus, whose memory evidently did not die easily.[53] By 354 the Calendar of Philocalus shows that Augustus, Vespasian, Titus, Nerva and Trajan were still remembered from the first century and Hadrian, Antoninus Pius, Marcus Aurelius, L. Verus and Pertinax from the second.[54]

At the same time with the growing infiltration of oriental cults there were new religious festival days. Once Gaius Caligula sanctioned the public worship of Isis, there was a seven-day festival starting on October 28th, which culminated in the three days of ecstasy (November 1st to the 3rd) which greeted the reincarnation, the Heuresis, of Osiris-Serapis; and at the harbours in spring there was the feast of the Navigium Isidis, the launching of the bark of Isis, which opened the sailing season on March 5th. The cult of the Great Mother, introduced to Rome at the end of the Second Punic War, which at the time of Augustus still had only one day of celebration on March 27th, when the statue was washed, expanded the number of its days of celebration, perhaps with the introduction of the *taurobolium*, in the second century A.D.[55] December 25th, the birth of the new sun, celebrated in Mithraism, became a great public festival with chariot-racing in the Circus as a result of Aurelian's monotheistic devotion to the sun-god and the erection of his great temple of Sol Invictus in A.D. 274.[56] Where such new cults obtained official recognition, their main festivals became *dies feriati*; where they did not, they were observed by their devotees none the less.

Not every day in a calendar of Saints' Days today receives attention even from the devout; and so it is to be assumed that, apart from Feriae Imperativae, which marked contemporary events of national importance, a large number of festival days had little significance except for the particular priests who had sacrifices to perform. Most of the old Roman festival days, being rooted in the life of a purely agricultural community, came to have no more significance for the city-dweller than have Rogation days for his modern counterpart. The

Robigalia, Floralia and Vinalia meant much to the wine-grower, especially the last, in August, since a single September hailstorm can destroy a vintage; they are unlikely to have meant anything to the townsman who bought his wine from shops. It is no surprise that in the fourth-century calendar of Philocalus only twelve of the original festivals survive to receive a mention. Macrobius suggested at the end of the fourth century that only the Agonalia, the Carmentalia and the Compitalia were still of any considerable significance.[57]

After paganism, Christianity. Now there were new public festivals, in particular Easter, and the old pagan festivals should have vanished. Indeed, with one or two unobjectionable exceptions like April 21st and May 11th, the birthdays of Rome and of Constantinople respectively, their celebration was forbidden by imperial ordinance in A.D. 389.[58] But superstition does not obey instructions, and the ordinary man is reluctant to turn his back on enjoyment. The Fasti of Polemius Silvius, of A.D. 449, among a haphazard recollection of imperial birthdays, circus days, birthdays of martyrs and the major festivals of the Christian Church, include nine of the old Roman festivals to whose pagan attribution a blind eye might be turned, including the Lupercalia and the Saturnalia, described inoffensively as 'the Feast of Slaves'. In some cases pagan practices transferred themselves to Christian worship. With the politic consent, if not with the approval, of the authorities the Memorials for the Christian martyrs were sometimes marked by the heavy drinking of the Roman Parentalia. December 25th remained, but changed its character. Sometimes pagan deities enjoyed an easy transformation and, retaining the jubilation of their festivals, became Christian. The Amburbium of February 2nd became the Feast of the Purification of the Virgin; at Syracuse Demeter turned into Santa Lucia.[59]

As evidence of how much attention was paid to religious festivals by educated men even in the Republic, Cicero's correspondence has a certain significance. None of his surviving letters, of which there are between nine hundred and a thousand, suggests that he ever observed any religious festival at all. On several occasions he dated a letter or an event by the name of a festival day instead of by the normal method. There are references of this kind to the Quirinalia, Terminalia, Liberalia, Cerialia, Saturnalia and Compitalia; also to three games, the Ludi Megalenses, the Ludi Ceriales and the Ludi Romani.[60]

His references to festivals for purposes other than dating are few. In Cilicia he proposed to confer the *toga virilis* on his nephew Q. Cicero on the Liberalia, that in the Republic (though not always later) being the day normally selected for the purpose; he refers to the high-spirited celebration of the Saturnalia by his army in Cilicia at the end of 51 B.C.; and once, with great consideration, he tells Atticus that he will not arrive at his Alban villa on the Compitalia (January 2nd, 49) because that would not be fair on his slaves, for whom the Compitalia was a holiday.[61]

Cicero's statement that festival days gave free men relief from quarrelsome litigation and slaves respite from toil and labour sounds well, but the only festivals on which the elder Cato would give extra wine to slaves were the Saturnalia and the Compitalia; and, while Columella explained that on a *dies feriatus* corn fields must not be fenced, sheep must not be dipped 'except as a curative measure', hay must not be cut or trees planted or thinned, he admitted that the prohibition on the use of yoked animals was disputed by good authority and made it clear that you could do most other things on a farm with a clear conscience. You could shear sheep, gather the vintage and even, if you took the precaution of sacrificing a puppy, sow corn.[62]

According to their nature, prominent men enjoyed the games and outstanding festivals by attending or by avoiding them. For Cicero and his like they gave the opportunity of a restful country holiday. So—in his fictional *De Republica*—Scipio Aemilianus spent the Latin Festival in January or early February 129 B.C. with a number of friends in the country. If we believe the *De Oratore*, most of the top lawyers and politicians spent the hot days of the Ludi Romani in September 91 B.C. at Tusculum, just as in 54 B.C. Cicero gave himself a holiday at Arpinum at the time of the Ludi Romani, so as to get away from the heat of Rome. Literary men, indeed, always liked to proclaim their avoidance of the games and of public festivities: the time could be spent better in writing or in leisurely relaxation.[63]

It is absurd to exaggerate the impact of festival days on the working life of Romans and to imagine that on all these days shops were shut and work ceased. This may have been true of the Games. Otherwise, workers had simply to down tools and stand about if a sacred procession was passing, since holy days were polluted if priests caught sight of men at work. Workers were given warning by a crier who went ahead of the procession.

A small number of festivals brought whole holidays, however, to certain classes of people.

March 15th (once New Year's Day), the festival of Anna Perenna, was a general holiday for the populace of Rome. On the river bank just north of the city, near the present Porta del Popolo, they lay about promiscuously in the open or in tents, drank heavily (one glass for every further year of life that was desired) and, in the evening, reeled back to the city in tipsy procession. Four days later, on March 19th, the Quinquatrus was a real holiday for those who owed particular dedication to Minerva as a goddess: to schoolchildren and their teachers, to doctors and artisans, in particular to drycleaners (*fullones*) and dyers.

On May 15th the merchants of Rome did honour to Mercury, their patron god, on the foundation-day of his temple, sprinkling holy water to secure forgiveness of past perjuries, and praying that the door might be open to fresh perjuries in the future and to the enjoyment of cheating the simple customer.

Tiber fishermen held their own games, the Ludi Piscatorii, in Trastevere on June 7th. June 9th, which was also the day when women celebrated the Vestalia, was a holiday for bakers. Flute-players had a holiday on June 13th. They feasted in the temple of Juppiter on the Capitol, after which, heavily intoxicated, they roamed the city, wearing masks. Gardeners took a holiday on August 19th. On July 23rd and August 17th the bargees and dock-hands of the Tiber celebrated the Neptunalia and the Portunalia respectively. Slaves had their own festivities and holidays, particularly on the Saturnalia in late December and the Compitalia at the end of December or beginning of January.[64]

As for the total number of days which workmen took off in the year as whole holidays, the only evidence available to us comes from Egypt, where apprentices were allowed a fixed number of holidays in each year, never to our knowledge more than thirty-six.*

When M. Aurelius curtailed the number of festival days and ensured that 230 days were left free for business and litigation, it is not to be imagined that on the remaining 135 days no shops were open and nobody was at work.†

The public business of the state was transacted on *dies fasti*, marked F in the calendars, and on *dies comitiales*, which were marked C. The public assemblies could meet on any *dies comitialis*, unless it happened to coincide with the Nundinae or with the celebration of one of the

* See further, p. 193.

† As we must hope that in the distant future no scholar, happening on an Italian calendar, in which every day of the year is a Saint's day of one sort or other, will suggest that Italians never did any work.

movable feasts or with Feriae Imperativae. Public meetings, however, could not be held on *dies fasti*, for these days were reserved exclusively for the judiciary, since on them by immemorial tradition there was no tabu on the use of 'the three words'—'*do*', '*dico*', '*addico*'—by the law officers, the praetors. Legal transactions could take place also on *dies comitiales* on which no public meeting was in fact being held, as long as it was not a day of Feriae Conceptivae or Imperativae. There were probably 193 or 195 *dies comitiales* before Julius Caesar, 191 after him.

The marked *dies fasti* of the Republican calendar were few, perhaps no more than thirty-nine, to which a number of Nundinae must be added.* There were, however, in addition fourteen 'split days', *dies intercisi or fissi*, on part of which legal business could legitimately be transacted.†

The fact that praetors were accessible for legal purposes only on *dies fasti*, *dies comitiales* on which public meetings were not being held and on parts of a few other days did not mean that all jurisdiction was subject to these limits. In the case of trials, for instance, the praetor's official action was completed when he had accepted a charge and delivered the *formula* for the trial and named a *iudex* or *iudices*. This was the proceeding *in iure*. The trial itself, the proceedings *in iudicio*, followed. Different factors, which will be considered later, determined whether or not the court sat on any particular day.

The number of *dies fasti* was evidently uncomfortably small, and the ten days added to the calendar by Julius Caesar when he revised it were all made *dies fasti* because he thought the number needed enlarging. By this and by certain changes he brought the number up to fifty-two. Augustus is said by Suetonius to have altered the designation of thirty days so as to make the number larger still.[66]

The number of *dies fasti*, once increased, was immediately decreased again, through encroachment from the new festivals established in honour of the imperial house.

In the second century Marcus Aurelius added *dies iudiciarii* to the *dies fasti*, so as to make the number of days available for legal and other

---

* See above, p. 60.

† Eight of these days were marked in the Julian calendar with the letters EN (short for *endotercisus*, i.e. *intercisus*, *endo* being an old form if *in*), three by F.P., which perhaps stood for *fasti principio*, two by Q.R.C.F. (*Quando rex comitiavit fas*, i.e. after the Rex Sacrorum had completed his duties for the day) and one, June 15th, by Q.ST.D.F. (*Quando stercus delatum, fas*, i.e. for the rest of the day after the Vestal Virgins had completed the spring-cleaning of the temple of Vesta and the rubbish had been removed).[65]

public business 230 in the year.[67] At the time of Julius Caesar the number had been 243.

106 or 107 days of the Republican year (108 of the Julian) were *nefasti*, days which were not available for public business of any kind. Of these, forty-five were the named festival days to which reference has already been made, and the rest also had religious significance of one sort or another. In the calendar of Caesar probably fifty-eight of them were marked 'N' (for *nefasti*) and 50 'NP', written or cut as a ligature of N and an archaic P, a symbol whose significance Festus explained in a passage which is unintelligible in its surviving state.[68] Mommsen thought the 'N' days were days of religious gloom (*nefasti tristes*) and that the 'NP' days were the joyful festivals (*nefasti hilares*), but his theory is one which the evidence does not fully support.[69]

Confusion can, and even in antiquity could, arise from the ambiguity of the word *nefastus*. In its technical sense it marked a day—not necessarily inauspicious—on which public business could not be transacted; in everyday language it came to be used instead of *ater* or *religiosus*, to mean a black or inauspicious day. When, after Agrippina was killed by her son Nero in A.D. 59, a sycophantic senator proposed that her birthday should be observed as a *dies nefastus*, he was not suggesting that the mark in the calendars should be altered to N or NP.[70]

Before the passing of a Lex Pupia of uncertain date in the Republic, there was no day in the year on which the Senate might not be summoned to meet; meetings could be held even on festival and on 'black' days.[71] The Lex Pupia, it seems, forbade meetings on any *dies comitialis*, or perhaps only on a *dies comitialis* on which the meeting of a public assembly was actually held. Senators were not prevented from meeting on a comitial day, however, once the meeting of the assembly had broken up,[72] and dispensation from the law could in any case be granted to the Senate by its own resolution, provided, of course, that no tribune interposed his veto.[73]

From 153 B.C. onwards, when January 1st was the beginning of the civil year, January, February and March were normally the months with the heaviest load of senatorial business. The new magistrates and officers—particularly the tribunes, who had entered office on December 10th, and the consuls, who took office on January 1st—had legislation to introduce; in February foreign embassies and provincial delegations were given a hearing; in March provincial governors were appointed.

After this there was a recess—the *discessus senatus* or *res prolatae**—from early April to mid-May, when senators were free to leave Rome whether for their estates or for their villas in Campania.[74]

Senators returned to Rome for the excitement of the period which preceded the elections of magistrates which, from Sulla's time to the end of the Republic, were held in July, the month in which the election of tribunes had always taken place.† When the elections were over, the main political life of the year was over too. By this time the magistrates of the year had usually shot their legislative bolt, and were thinking of the provincial administration ahead of them once the year was over. Eyes were on the consuls-designate, who were now called on to speak first at debates at which they were present, and on the tribunes-designate. If they had promised reforms when they were candidates, their proposals had to wait until the current year was over.

Without constituencies or organized parties or whips, senators were under even less binding an obligation to attend the Senate than are British Members of Parliament to attend the House of Commons. Except on public or administrative duty or on military service, senators could not leave Italy in the Republic, or travel further than Sicily or Narbonese Gaul, both highly Romanized provinces, in the Empire, without leave from the Senate or from the Emperor later.[75] But they could spend as much of the year as they wished in their country villas, even in their 'suburban' villas, which might be only a few miles outside the city. Once upon a time in practice, and still in the late Republic in theory, they might be compelled by force to attend the Senate if they were resident in Rome at the time, on the order of the presiding magistrate. When Antony threatened to have Cicero brought to the Senate by force on September 1st, 44 B.C., however, there was no precedent that was at all recent to justify his bluster.[76]

If a senator was empanelled as a juror in a trial which took place on a day when the Senate was meeting, he would naturally attend the court, for otherwise the whole hearing on that day might have to be suspended. But the Senate, if it wished, could by its ordinance force him to give priority to his duty as a senator.[77]

Senators' attendance at the House was determined by their health,

---

* This phrase was also used in the Empire for the Vacations of the Law Courts, *BGU* 611, col. 2, l. 4.

† The holding of elections at a time when farmers were busy over harvest and thrashing (and, in the case of tribunes before the time of Marius, when citizens on military service were not available) gave disproportionate weight to the city-dwellers' vote, anyhow in the Comitia Tributa and Concilium Plebis.

their sense of duty, their interest in the business on the agenda and also by their feelings of personal obligation (*gratia*). Younger members would attend at the request of their seniors, men from whom they might expect assistance in their own advancement, older members would come to oblige friends, from whom they might themselves expect a similar courtesy on another occasion.

In December attendance at the Senate was generally poor.[78]

The reduction of the business and importance of senatorial meetings under the Empire greatly simplified a senator's official life. While Augustus fixed a necessary quorum for all meetings, whatever the business, he reduced the stated general meetings of the Senate to two a month, on or near the Kalends and the Ides; so that the dutiful senator could plan his movements, with meetings of the Senate in mind, some time ahead. This did not debar the holding of supernumerary meetings in an emergency. Moreover Augustus took account of the fact that in September and October large numbers of members might wish to be out of Rome on their estates; so lots were cast and only those selected were required to attend in those two months.[79]

The only days on which in the Republic the courts were debarred from sitting were those on which a meeting of a public assembly was actually being held, and trials for the disturbance of the peace (*de vi*) could not be suspended on any other day. In other cases, however, the courts did not in fact sit on days of major festivals or when games were being held, because there was little chance of securing the attendance of a full jury on such days.[80]

April, as has been seen, was a month more than half of which was earmarked for games. This, no doubt, is the reason why the Senate was in recess in this month which, because of the games, was also something of a vacation for the law courts.

In general, however, the business of the courts, like the business of the Senate, was transacted as far as possible in the first eight months of the year, even through the stifling heat of July and August. There were slack times in the Republic and actual vacations in the Empire.[81] The younger Pliny speaks of July as a month when the courts were idle, yet only to emphasize the tiresomeness of having a case on his hands in that month. It was the last third of the year which, from all the evidence, was the slack time in the Republic. By the extortion law, the *lex Acilia* of 123 B.C., praetors were debarred from accepting cases for trial if the application was brought on September 1st or later. In 65 B.C. Cicero thought of going to Cisalpine Gaul 'for the period when the business of the courts cools off', from September to the end of December. Augustus, who divided the year into two 'terms' (*actus rerum*), summer and winter, ruled that the courts should be closed in November and December, September and October being the two months in which he had allowed the senators a considerable relaxation of their duties.[82]

The prosecution of Verres opened on August 5th, 70 B.C. and, if Cicero is to be believed, there was a fair chance that, if the case was allowed to run its normal course, the defence, by taking the fullest advantage of games and public holidays, would succeed in spinning it out to the end of the year.* After that, it would be necessary to empanel new jurors in place of these who as holders of magistracies in the following year would not be available; and also, of course, a different praetor would be president of the court. This startling statement explains the situation of the courts in the last four months of the year under the Republic. Cases which had started before the end of August would proceed to their conclusion, but no new prosecutions could be launched. In 65, therefore, Cicero can only have been free for the last four months of the year because he had no brief on his hands. Relief would not come automatically to counsel or to jurors on September 1st, but only when cases in which they were involved had come to an end. One must assume, therefore, that, if they had country estates to which they were anxious to go, nobody was more pleased than the jurors at Cicero's device for getting Verres' case over so quickly—unless, of course, there were other cases filed and waiting to come to a public court as soon as one was free to receive them.[83]

When Augustus established the fixed terms, there was always the equivalent of a 'vacation judge', and urgent actions could be brought before the praetor at any time at all. In origin, as quotations from Ulpian in the *Digest* make clear, the general suspension of litigation at certain times of year was designed to suit the convenience of the countryman, to prevent his being summoned to court when he had pressing duties on his farm, at harvest time in particular and during the vintage. That should have meant in June and July and in September and October.[84]

At the final conversion of the Empire to Christianity, Valentinian II, Theodosius and Arcadius sought in A.D. 389 to put an end once and for all to pagan practices, in an instruction starting with the brave words,

---

* Excluding the days of games and all the public festivals of the calendar, there would have been sixty-six days, less the number of days on which there were meetings of the Comitia, that would have to be spun out.

'We order all days to be court days'; but this generalization was immediately qualified by the elimination of the seasons of harvest (June 24th to August 1st) and vintage (August 23rd to October 15th); January 1st 'as a customary rest day'; the birthdays of Rome and of Constantinople; the seven days before and after Easter; all Sundays and imperial birthdays. Two more days were excluded in A.D. 400, Christmas Day and the Epiphany; and twelve years later, in an unexpected concession to the Jews, the courts might not sit on Saturdays. In time history repeated itself and the list of excluded days swelled still further; from Septuagesima to the Octave of Easter; from Ascension Day to Whitsun; from Advent to Epiphany; to which Ember Days, Rogation Days, Vigils of Our Lady and Saints' Days were added.[85]

III

FAMILY LIFE

✦✦✦

1. The Birth Rate and the Survival of Children

To ENJOY family life, it is necessary to have a family; and we are confronted at the start by the fact that in the last century of the Republic and in the early centuries of the Empire upper-class families, for which alone good evidence exists, were regularly dying out.

Was the absence of children the result of reluctance to marry? Metellus Macedonicus, censor in 131 B.C., made a powerful speech which was preserved and read aloud in the Senate on Augustus' instruction more than a century later. Given the nature of women, he said, married life was hardly endurable; but bachelor life was less endurable still.[1] It is true that the consuls saddled with the responsibility of introducing the second batch of Augustus' moral reforms in A.D. 9, whose object was in large part to penalize the unmarried, were bachelors, and reasonably enough people joked about the fact.[2] Yet in prominent families strong pressure was exerted on boys and girls to marry, both being in the *potestas* of their father, and there is as little mention of bachelors in such families as there is of spinsters. The old and lonely who were the prey of legacy-hunters, at whose expense the satirists amused themselves, were generally childless widowers or widows.

The misfortune of families which died out, despite marriage, was one which, through their own folly, the upper classes in Greece had experienced in the second century B.C. From anxiety that their children should inherit sufficient wealth to cut a figure in society, parents had deliberately limited their number by abortion or by exposure to one or two. Disease and war took their inevitable toll, and the parents found themselves left with no children at all. Whose fault was that but their own?[3]

In Rome the explanation is less easy. Physiological reasons have been suggested: that a daughter who was an only child was a particularly desirable wife because of the dowry that she would certainly bring with her and because of her reasonable anticipation of greater wealth to come. But genetically she carried a warning, which was not heeded; she inherited, and herself realized, a family curse of infecundity. The fate of the families of judges raised to the peerage and who married heiresses, or whose fathers or sons married heiresses, between 1660 and 1830 in England has been used to lend plausibility to such an explanation.[4]

Or is the failure of the Romans to have large families to be attributed to the fact—if, indeed, it is a fact—that they were victims of chronic lead poisoning? The water that they drank was piped through lead pipes. The food they ate was cooked in lead vessels. There was lead in the unguents with which they smeared themselves. It is even suggested, though without any evidence at all, that they used, as some other peoples have used, lead oxide (litharge) to sweeten sour wine. No wonder that some at least of their skeletons have shown an abnormally high lead content.[5]

How would this affect breeding? The male victim of lead poisoning, it is suggested, inclines to infertility; the female victim cannot hold her child, but suffers miscarriage after miscarriage.

If this is true, there must have been remarkable differences between individuals in resistance to the disease. The community's water came through the same lead pipes; within any class of society, food was cooked in the same kind of pots. Yet in eight years of marriage Agrippa and Julia produced five children; their daughter Agrippina and Germanicus produced six who survived to maturity, apart from others who died in infancy. Marcus Aurelius and Faustina had at least thirteen children, though only three of them grew up and married. Martial records a woman who was survived by five sons and five daughters. And when in A.D. 363 Julian gave honourable release from civic duties to the fathers of thirteen children, he presumably expected that there would be beneficiaries of his generosity.[6]

Legislation, however, first of Julius Caesar and then of Augustus, gave substantial advantages in public and in private life to the parents of three (in the case of freedmen, four) children[7]; and, as there is no point in dangling a carrot before a donkey which is incapable of eating carrots, one is bound to ask whether, as in Greece earlier, it was not by deliberate choice that so many parents had few children or none at all.

Was it the case that in the upper classes those who married did not want children and took the necessary steps to avoid them? Abortion, we know, was a common practice and one which the law did not condemn until, at the end of the second century, Septimius Severus made it a crime.[8] And there was no law to prevent the abandonment and exposure of babies.

Was contraception widely practised by the educated—that is to say, by the upper social—classes? This is a problem to which acute and imaginative scholarship has recently devoted energetic research. Ancient medical writers in profusion, the elder Pliny himself, knew of prescriptions for contraception. But most of these were superstitious, magical or, if neither, were, it appears, for the most part unlikely to be effectual. The subject is a difficult one for there is a great confusion in medical writings between abortifacients and contraceptives.[9] Medical writers apart, our sources are silent on the subject—even Juvenal and Martial, for both of whom it should have had a great appeal.

In extra-marital relationships (and the law closed its eyes, except in extreme cases, to the unfaithfulness of husbands) sound knowledge of contraceptives, if available, was to be prized, and it is true that in upper-class life (except for the occasional baseless scandal, such as that Brutus was Caesar's son or Drusus the son of Octavian) there is little mention of bastards. Yet Augustine refers to irregular unions as liable to produce unwanted children.[10]

In the free association of men with prominent ladies of pleasure knowledge of contraceptives, if it existed, was of obvious importance. Lucretius, indeed, describing a means of avoiding conception, but not by the use of contraceptives, states that it is common knowledge among prostitutes but no necessity in the case of married women.[11] The latest research on the subject reaches the conclusion that 'it would be rash to claim that the effect of contraception on Roman family limitation was negligible'.[12] In the present state of our knowledge it would be rash to claim that it supplies the key to the existence in ancient Rome of childlessness or of small families. After all, the use of contraceptives does not only prevent child-birth; it enables parents who are capable of having children and who want children to have the number of children that they wish and to have them at the time which they choose.

Old people, men and women alike, who have no children, are an inviting prey to the legacy hunter, in the modern world particularly to the charitable institution, in ancient Rome, men and women alike, to the *captator*, the shameless gigolo. This is a commonplace of Roman satire; it was the basis of social life in Croton, in the pastiche of

Petronius' *Satyricon*, a society whose members were fully occupied in displacing those ahead of them in the queue for the inheritance of the childless rich, a society in which the possession of children, natural heirs to a man's possessions, meant social ostracism. This was not an altogether groundless charge against imperial society; or that monument of ingenuous rectitude, the younger Pliny, would not have written of Asinius Rufus, 'In an age when for most people the prizes of childlessness make even a single son a cause of embarrassment, he has been willing to exploit the fertility of his wife and to have a large family.'

But how had Rufus achieved his purpose? By refusing to practise birth-control? Or by refusing to expose his infant children? Given Pliny's language, the first explanation is the easier. Yet in the *Satyricon* it is not said that prudent people did not *have* children, but that they did not bring them up: '*nemo liberos tollit*'.[13]

Yet, except in Petronius' satire, the notion that people at large did not have or bring up children because children would rob them of the rewards which old age had in store for the childless is too ridiculous to be entertained for one moment. For one thing, few people could feel any assurance in the prospect of old age ahead. And the whole of our surviving literature bears witness to the longing which married couples had for children and of their sorrow when they had no children or when their children died.

Suetonius tells an amusing and quite fantastic story, that in 63 B.C., the year of Augustus' birth, a hideous prodigy indicated that Nature had conceived a future king for Rome. So the Senate passed a decree ordering a wholesale Massacre of the Innocents. The decree was never registered at the Treasury, because all the men whose wives were pregnant combined to prevent this happening—not, it may be hoped, for Suetonius' reason, that every one of them hoped to be the father of a future king.[14]

The key to explain small Roman upper-class families is to be sought with some probability in medical ignorance and incompetence, and in the absence of any skilled knowledge of antiseptic.

So one passes to the high incidence of infecundity, miscarriage and infant and child mortality, about which our ancient evidence leaves no doubt at all.

The marriage of Scipio Aemilianus and Sempronia, the sister of the Gracchi, ended in disaster: 'she lost her looks and there were no children; so he hated her and she hated him.' Julius Caesar wanted a son and so did Augustus; so, without success, did most other emperors.

Pliny's letters introduce us to the grandson of Ummidia Quadratilla,* 'married at twenty-four and, but for misfortune—*si deus adnuisset*—a father.'

The nobler the family, the greater the distress at the absence of a male heir. at the extinction of the family's *genius*. A wife might resort to charms and spells, even—if she lived in Rome—go out into the streets at the Lupercalia so as to be struck by the leather strap of a Lupercus, which was supposed to engender fertility. The husband, confident in his own fertile virility, might divorce his wife and hope for greater success with another. This was believed to be the ground of the first recorded divorce in Roman history, that of Spurius Carvilius. That noble and childless woman whom we know as Turia at the time of the civil wars even advanced the suggestion to the distraction of her deeply affectionate husband. The same suggestion was made, but not by his wife, to Trimalchio and rejected by him.[15]

The adoption of unwanted, but not always illegitimate, infants by married couples who cannot have children, a not uncommon event in the modern world, was not a practice among the upper social classes in Rome and the Empire.† In such families girls were adopted very rarely,‡ and boys not below the age of puberty. When they were, as the two elder sons of Aemilius Paullus were adopted into the Cornelii Scipiones and the Fabii Maximi respectively in the second century B.C. or as when Galba adopted Calpurnius Piso in A.D. 69, it was generally to save a family from extinction, and at a respectable age when, as Hadrian said in adopting Aurelius Antoninus, there were none of the hazards and uncertainties which must exist in the case of a man's own children. When you adopted, you knew what you were getting.[16]

However, there was a use and a future for great numbers of exposed infants. They were often rescued, as Romulus and Remus had been rescued, and brought up in humble homes by people who wanted children or by those who had a simple eye to business. For the infant could by law be brought up either as a free child or as a slave, in which latter case he or she could be sold or exploited when adult, showing a handsome profit over and above the expense of upbringing. Freeborn children must have been tagged sometimes when they were exposed,§

---

* On whom, see p.48.

† Augustus' adoption of his two infant grandsons in 17 B.C. for dynastic reasons was exceptional.

‡ See p. 128 below, for an instance.

§ In the *Heauton Timorumenos* of Terence the girl is identified by a ring which her mother had attached to her when, as an infant, she was exposed.

and it was open to their parents to reclaim them later in life, on condition of paying the foster parents the expense of *alimenta*.

The happy dénouement of a comedy (Greek, of course, in its origins) was often the discovery that a girl, who had been brought up in such a way and, to pay for her upbringing, had been made a professional prostitute and then won the honest love of a free-born youth, was in fact herself free-born; so that she could be married and made an honest woman. And in Suetonius' catalogue of outstanding teachers, two in their origins were abandoned children, one indeed, C. Melissus of Spoletium, a man so talented and personable that he became a protégé of Maecenas. After he achieved this social prominence, his mother sought belatedly to recover him as her own free-born son, only to discover that the tables were turned, and that her grown and important son had no interest at all in acquiring freedom and a mother in one.

Inscriptional evidence, particularly from North Africa, suggests that there was often a very happy future for such exposed children. There are a great number of funerary dedications, both by foundlings of either sex to their *educator*, *nutritor* or *patronus* (or *patrona*) recording gratitude for kindness received ('*patrono benignissimo*', '*patronae benignissimae*') and also by patrons to their foster-children, in language of warm affection.[17]

Marriage was legal for a girl at twelve, for a boy at fourteen, and in the higher social classes, where the union of families through marriage had a political or social purpose, girls and boys were certainly married sometimes—we cannot say how often—as soon as this was legally possible, and the girl might be taken to live under the roof of her fiancé even before she was twelve and they could marry. Whatever the average age at which a girl achieved puberty in the Roman world, it is clear that in some cases this had not happened at the time of her marriage, and if the marriage was immediately consummated, she may have suffered harm and have been unable later to have children. But to exaggerate this occasional possibility into a general condition and to consider it an important reason for the decline in childbirth is a highly implausible fantasy.[18]

Miscarriage was common. Caesar's daughter Julia, married to Pompey, first suffered a miscarriage and after that died in childbirth. The empress Poppaea died of the same cause in A.D. 65. The case of the younger Pliny's third wife is startling: 'Silly girl, she failed to realize that she was pregnant . . . She has learnt her lesson. She might well have died.' She recovered, but never had children.[19]

Infant and child mortality, too, were extremely common. Of the twelve children of the elder Tiberius Gracchus and of Cornelia, only three (the two tribunes and their sister) survived. The child at whose birth Caesar's daughter Julia died did not survive her. The only child of Tiberius' marriage to Julia, daughter of Augustus, died in infancy-so did the only boy of the emperor Domitian. In the second century A.D. Fronto lost five children in succession: 'I never had a child born to me except when bereaved of another.' At Aquincum on the Danube a gravestone records a woman married at eleven and dead at twenty seven who was survived by only one of her six children. Quintilian's two sons died, one at the age of five, the other, already betrothed in marriage, at the age of nine.[20]

In the Empire, in regulations at law for tenure of municipal magistracy and for the inheritance of property from a husband or a wife, where the parenthood of children gave an advantage, a melancholy equation was made, itself the best possible evidence of the frequent deaths of young children. As the equal of one surviving child, you could count for municipal office at Malaca in Spain one child who had died after puberty or two who had died earlier, but 'after the naming ceremony'. For inheritance you could count as the equal of a surviving child, a child who had died after puberty, two who had died above the age of three, three who had died under three but after the ceremony of naming.[21]

If the death of infants and of young children was so common among the rich, malnutrition and the absence of medical attention would together ensure that it was commoner still among the poorer classes. The evidence of inscriptions must be used with care, for a child's death, causing greater emotional upset, is more likely to be recorded on a tombstone than that of an elderly person, unless he is very old indeed, and something of a prodigy; but even when allowance is made for this fact, the inscriptional evidence is incontrovertible. Of 164 surviving epitaphs of Jews in Rome, for instance, 65 are of children below the age of ten.[22]

Among the poor the exposure of infants had a very simple cause, like the surrender of children at birth to adoption sometimes in the modern world: the parents could not afford to bring them up. In A.D. 315 Constantine ordered immediate poor relief where parents were in danger of destroying a child which they could not afford to bring up. Fourteen years later, reversing a recent prohibition of Diocletian, Constantine allowed parents to sell their children, chiefly, no doubt, to slave nurseries, if they could not afford the expense of their upbringing, with the proviso that, if their economic condition improved, the parents had the right to buy them back.[23]

It is this same spectre of poor parents unable to afford to bring up children at all, or at least to clothe and feed them adequately, that induces the governments of civilized states in the modern world to make children's allowances to parents.

For this there is Roman precedent, in a stable and flourishing period of the Roman economy, in the late first and second centuries A.D., indeed until Diocletian put an end to it. The enterprise did credit both to a number of private benefactors, one of them being the younger Pliny, and to Nerva and his imperial successors.

The scheme started in Italy and spread to the provinces. So as to secure a regular annual income for the purpose, capital grants were made to municipalities and the money distributed among local landowners, on whose land a perpetual charge was laid, to be paid annually to the municipality. From this assured annual income the municipality made children's allowances for clothes and upbringing in respect of a fixed number of children—at Veleia in North Italy, by an imperial benefaction of Trajan, for 245 boys and 34 girls born in wedlock and for two illegitimate children, at the time from which the record survives. Boys were supported to an age not greater than eighteen, girls to an age not greater than fourteen. Something like five thousand children were so supported at the time of Trajan.

Here, known from an inscription, is a grant made by an African, who had had a distinguished career in the imperial service, to his native town of Sicca in the second half of the second century A.D.:

To my dearly beloved fellow-townsmen of Sicca I wish to give 1,300,000 sesterces. I trust you, my very dear fellow-townsmen, to ensure that from the interest of five per cent on that capital 300 boys shall receive subsistence grants and 200 girls, the boys to receive ten sesterces a month from the age of three* to fifteen, the girls eight sesterces a month from the age of three* to thirteen. The selection is to be made from citizens or from inhabitants of the city, provided these latter are staying within its boundaries. It will be best, if you agree, that the selection should be made by the annual magistrates, a replacement being found immediately in the case of a child who reaches the

---

* The starting age of three can only have been chosen because it was hazardous to select any one younger, and is another indication of the high death rate among very young children (see p. 88 above).

upper age limit or who dies, so that the number of beneficiaries may never fall short.

The institution, known as the Alimenta, is recorded in literature and on coins; it is portrayed—mothers bringing their small children to the Emperor—on the arch of Trajan at Beneventum; and evidence of government (apart from private) grants comes from forty-six Italian towns. Its clear intention was to increase the birth rate and to ensure that poor children, who might otherwise have been exposed at birth or have grown up with stunted instead of with healthy bodies, should be preserved and brought up to be 'soldiers in the making.'[24]

2. Birth of a Child

If a child was not exposed, three ceremonies followed its birth. There was first the moment when the father took it in his arms in open acknowledgement of the fact that he was its father. The child was 'raised', 'sublatus'.

The eighth day, if the child was a girl, the ninth, if it was a boy, was 'the day of purification', 'dies lustricus'; on this day the child was named.[25] The emperor C. Caligula, attending the ceremony in the case of his nephew (the later emperor Nero) and asked to give the boy his name, chose to play the fool and suggest that he should be given the name of his great-uncle Claudius, at that time the most despised member of the imperial court.*

Thirdly, after the legislation of Augustus (the lex Aelia Sentia and the lex Papia Poppaea), it was necessary in the case of Roman citizens to register a child's birth within thirty days. This act—the professio—could be performed by its father, its paternal grandfather or by its mother, directly or through an agent, in Rome at the Treasury (Aerarium Saturni), in a province at the provincial record office (tabularium publicum). Records of births were posted, and officially preserved in codices or on papyri, probably by imperial years. A birth certificate was obtained (a copy of the official entry, a diptych, with the signatures of seven witnesses), and it was probably such a birth certificate that St. Paul produced in evidence of his Roman citizenship. After M. Aurelius the births of illegitimate children had also to be

---

* The boy's name could not be anything but L. Domitius Ahenobarbus (his paternal grandfather's praenomen having been Lucius), and it was presumably out of courtesy that the Emperor, rather than the boy's father, was invited to announce the name.

registered.[26] A child's birth was evidently recorded not only by the day
but by the hour, this being necessary for any astrological calculation
concerning its nativity. A vast number of surviving tombstones record
the length of a life by years, days and, finally, hours.

3. Children's Games

The diversions and amusements of small children differ little from age
to age or from country to country. Roman children had terra-cotta
dolls, *sigillaria*.[27] They kept pets, mice which pulled little carriages,[28]
caged birds of all sorts, blackbirds, nightingales, parrots; and, if they
were lucky, they had parents less brutal than the old clothes-dealer in
Petronius' *Satyricon* 'My younger boy—there's something unhealthy
about his love of birds. I killed three of his goldfinches the other day,
and told him the cat had eaten them.' Children played with dogs; the
Satyricon contains, appropriately enough, a revolting child with a
revoltingly fat black puppy called Pearl (Margarita). The younger
Pliny tells us that, when the abominable M. Regulus lost his son, he
made a holocaust of the boy's pets around the funeral pyre: ponies,
dogs, nightingales, parrots and blackbirds.[29]

Children had hobby horses.[30] They played with tops and hoops.[31]
They built houses with bricks.[32] They played games with nuts and,
using nuts for stakes, they played simple games with knucklebones and
dice, games like Odds and Evens (*Par Impar*).[33] They also tossed coins,
shouting 'Heads' or 'Ships', though in doing this few of them are
likely to have known that they were preserving the memory of Rome's
earliest coinage, when one face of a coin was regularly stamped with a
ship's prow.[34] And they played the game of *mora*, which persists in
Italy still, a game in which each of the two opponents simultaneously
exposed and immediately withdrew his hand with a certain number of
fingers outstretched, and guessed the number of fingers exposed in his
competitor's hands.*

Children enjoyed playing at being grown-ups, and often no doubt
dressed up for their parts. When the younger Cato and his friends were
playing at Law Courts, with judge, prosecuting counsel and prisoner,
he took the game so seriously that, when another boy to whom he was
closely attached, playing the part of prisoner, was condemned and

---

* There was no higher testimony to a man's integrity than to say that he was some one
with whom you would be prepared to play the game (*micare*) in the dark, Cic., *De Offic.*
3, 77; Petron., *Sat.* 44.

hauled off to gaol, Cato rushed to deliver him from his warders, and then left the party in a fury. Children played at being judges, at being kings, at being gladiators. After the invasion of Italy by Julius Caesar in 49 B.C. they played at being Caesarians against Pompeians.[35] Masks were sometimes worn by which, understandably enough, small children were often terrified.[36]

Apart from innocent party games, children were capable of pranks which, in extreme form, were acts of theft and destruction; the classical instance is the theft of the neighbour's pears by Augustine when, at fifteen, he was old enough to know better.[37]

4. Schooling

From the Republic into the Empire there were two important developments in the upbringing and education of children. The first, of importance for their early years, lay in the fact that their mothers abandoned more and more of their natural duties to slave-women and to men-slaves, from breast-feeding at the start to the children's early education; so that history recorded as something remarkable the fact that the wife of the elder Cato, so far from having her own children suckled by slaves, herself suckled slave children of the household; and stress was laid, as on something remarkable, on the cases of men who owed the rudiments of their education to their mothers: the Gracchi, Sertorius, Julius Caesar and Octavian.[38]

The second change followed from the creation of a Roman literature of which Romans could feel proud—Cicero in particular, and Virgil. Before that the classics, on which education was based, were Greek classics, and so the child of an educated family was inevitably brought up to be bilingual, with Greek as his first language—because, in his schooling, Greek was the language which he would chiefly need. The results, in the governing class, were seen in the grown man. The great Roman statesmen of the second century B.C. were fluent 'in both languages'. The father of the Gracchi, when in Greece, made public speeches in Greek; and P. Licinius Crassus, consul of 131 B.C., when governor of Asia, was able to conduct cases in court in five different Greek dialects.[39] In the following century Cicero's culture was impregnated by Greek.

By the end of the first century A.D. things were changing. The younger Pliny's Greek has a certain superficiality. Later, though Marcus Aurelius wrote his *Meditations* in Greek, it was in horrible Greek that he wrote them. At the same time in the schools which were springing up in the provinces of the western half of the Empire, in many of which children were learning Latin as a foreign language, Latin was often taught, no doubt, without Greek. But by no means universally. In the fourth century A.D. Ausonius was learning Greek in Gaul and Augustine as a boy was learning it in North Africa, both finding it horribly difficult.[40]

A boy received his education at home until he was six or seven, once from his mother, later from slaves, a nurse at first and then a kind of governess. He learnt to talk Latin, and it was important that he should learn to talk with a good accent, not a *vitiosus sermo*; and he learnt to talk Greek.[41]

At six or seven he passed out of his mother's into his father's hands and in a conservative household like the elder Cato's in the second century B.C. his father then became his tutor, both in learning and in physical exercise. When a father relinquished this direct responsibility, it was first in favour of a slave or freedman of the household who was both skilled and trustworthy, or he might purchase a suitable slave, whether for the private use of his own household or to set him up as a teacher of other people's children as well as his own, to be a money-making proposition. So the *grammaticus* who, after manumission by Q. Catulus, consul of 102 B.C., was called Lutatius Daphnis, had passed hands twice, on each occasion for the fantastic price of 700,000 sesterces.[42]

Livius Andronicus, whose translation of the Odyssey into Latin in the late third century B.C. was a startling enterprise, the very foundation of Latin literature, may have been Rome's first schoolmaster, having earlier been a private tutor to the young Livius Salinator and being given his freedom in the year 240 B.C. in which Livius adopted the toga of manhood.*[43] But at first professional teachers were viewed with suspicion. Rhetorical teachers and philosophers were forced to leave Rome by a decree of the Senate in 161 B.C. Teachers of Latin rhetoric (*praeceptores*, who probably taught grammar too) were expelled by the censors of 92 B.C., on the ground that they taught their pupils to be idle and preternaturally clever, but the measure was ineffective and they were soon back again; Vultacilius Plotius, a Latin rhetorician, opened a school in Rome in 81 B.C., and after this teachers of grammar and

---

* The plebian family of Salinator had evident Greek interests. It was perhaps no accident that the year 219, when the first Greek doctor set up in practice in Rome (Plin., *NH* 29, 12), was the year of Salinator's first consulship.

rhetoric, constituting with medicine 'the liberal arts', were tolerated and even encouraged, in particular by grants of citizenship from Julius Caesar in 46 B.C. and by Augustus, who in the famine of A.D. 6 allowed them to remain in Rome when other foreigners were asked to leave the city.[44]

Doctors and teachers were professionals, who were paid. Jurists were different, because they should not dirty their hands with money; philosophers, too, were different, ostensibly because their profession also should be too noble to be mercenary, but really because from the moment when Cato, who also suspected doctors, persuaded the Senate to dismiss the embassy of three distinguished Greek philosophers in 155 B.C., teachers of philosophy were suspected of being the enemies of simple civic obedience. The history of the early Empire confirmed this fear, until in the end Trajan and Hadrian came to terms with philosophy and teachers of philosophy at last acquired respectability in the eyes of the ordinary Roman. The earlier view is admirably expressed by Tacitus: 'I remember Agricola's saying often that as a boy he became passionately absorbed in philosophy, beyond what was permissible for a Roman and a senator; but his sensible mother succeeded in putting an end to this intemperate enthusiasm.'[45]

From the time of the civil wars down to Domitian philosophy was, from the new Establishment's point of view, a chief weapon in the rebel's armoury—in the armoury of the younger Cato, of Brutus and Cassius, of Cicero, of the Stoic and Cynic opposition to the Flavian emperors; it brought contempt of death and a readiness at need to face death with courage. Its disciples like Seneca would have said that it taught a man how to live as well as how to die. And Quintilian, thinking of philosophy in less loaded terms, knew that it also taught how to think and so was a necessary part of humane education. Indeed an issue frequently debated was this: which had the greater usefulness—medicine, oratory or philosophy? Medicine, Quintilian thought. Tacitus thought Oratory. Seneca would have said Philosophy.[46]

There were three stages in schooling—primary education, education in literature (or, as it was called, grammar), and training in rhetoric. This last constituted 'higher education'.

For the affluent parent living in Rome or some other large city in which good educational facilities were available the first problem was whether to have his child educated at home by a private tutor or whether to send him to school. As between these two extremes, a middle course was possible—to have children taught at home at the first and perhaps the second stage, and then to send them to school for the latter stage or stages. Quintilian regarded this as a decision of importance, and strongly advised that children should be sent to school, because competition was a healthy stimulus and teachers gave a better account of themselves before a class than when they taught pupils singly.[47]

At all times practice varied. In the second century B.C., as has been pointed out, Cato kept his son at home and supervised the whole of his education himself on the ground that a teacher must sometimes punish his pupil, and that it was embarrassing for the son of a Roman and a gentleman to be punished by a slave. (At the same time he was glad to hire out the services of his talented slave Chilo for the education of other people's children.) In 56 B.C. Cicero's ten-year-old nephew was receiving private tuition in Cicero's house from the immensely distinguished Tyrannio. At the end of the first century A.D., as Quintilian's discussion indicates, there were still Romans who preferred to employ private tutors for their sons; indeed Marcus Aurelius congratulated himself on the fact that, instead of being sent to school, he had been educated by private tutors,[48] but by this time the general practice was to send boys to school rather than to have them taught by a private tutor. With girls, the case may have been different.

The decision having been taken, at whatever stage, to send a child to school, the question arose as to the particular school to which he should be sent. The younger Pliny, asked once to advise on this problem, himself inspected the establishments of a number of teachers before making a recommendation. A good school was one which, together with a high standard of teaching, had discipline (*severitas*), a good tone (*pudor*) and, in a homosexual society, exemplary morals (*castitas*); for the formation of a boy's character was regarded by sensible people as having comparable importance with the training of his mind.[49]

Apart from private schools, in Rome and a few other great cities of the Empire there were, from Vespasian's time onwards, 'public schools', the schools of public professors. Quintilian, as the first of Vespasian's professors of Latin rhetoric in Rome, presided over such a school, enjoying naturally a greater *cachet* than a private teacher, for he was 'a teacher by imperial appointment'; he received a public stipend of 100,000 sesterces a year and in addition he received fees, like a private teacher, from his pupils.[50] The scheme was extended into the provinces by Trajan, Hadrian and Antoninus Pius. In the late fourth century Augustine was appointed, on the recommendation of

Symmachus, Prefect of the City, to the chair of Latin Rhetoric at Milan. In inaugurating this reform Vespasian may have had a genuine interest in education; he may have wished to create 'plums' for gifted members of the teaching profession. But his motives may have been less enlightened. Who pays the fiddler calls the tune; and he may have hoped that objectionable rhetorical exercises with philosophical overtones on the subject of 'tyranny' and 'liberty' would be eliminated or at least soft-pedalled by his own nominees.[51] As has been seen, teachers of philosophy, a subject which naturally won no favour from the Flavian emperors, had to wait a little before they secured favoured recognition from Trajan and Hadrian.[52]

Cicero had stated in the De Republica that Rome had rejected the idea of introducing any regular system of state education[53]; but the Empire saw an improving change, the growing recognition of public responsibility for the provision of good educational facilities. Italian towns (with, after Vespasian, imperial example to follow) and provincial towns and communities, encouraged—often, no doubt, prodded—by the Roman administration, accepted the responsibility of creating public schools in grammar and rhetoric. That is to say, a teacher (which meant, in effect, a school) was officially established, or a number of teachers were officially appointed, by the local town council and provided with a basic stipend and premises. We hear of such a public teacher, a grammaticus, at Brindisi in the second century A.D. a stupid, opinionated man who thought that sheep, unlike other animals, had only two teeth, a man who was a poor advertisement for his profession. Strabo speaks of the official appointment of teachers by cities in Gaul at the time of Augustus. A school for the sons of chiefs, no doubt established by Augustus, was already in existence at Augustodunum (Autun) in Gaul in A.D. 21, and was still there at the end of the third century A.D. In Britain Agricola encouraged schools for the sons of prominent Britons, whose native wit he ranked above the cleverness of the educated young Gaul, with such great success that, while previously the young British had refused to learn Latin, they were now on fire to speak it well. We know of Annaeus Florus starting a successful school at Tarraco in Spain at the end of the first century A.D., and a little after A.D. 160 Fronto was writing to his son-in-law, the Governor of Upper Germany, asking him to find a post as public instructor in his province for a certain Antoninus Aquila.[54]

When Vespasian gave great privileges (for example, permission to form corporations) to doctors and extended certain of these, for instance, tax-exemption, to teachers,* the attractions of the teaching profession were immediately greater and receipts from taxation smaller. So the regulation ran into a certain amount of trouble. It was unpopular from the start with local authorities, who had the responsibility for tax-collection. And Domitian found that teachers were neglecting free-born pupils in favour of slaves, whose masters were prepared to pay large sums for their education.† So that a halt had to be called and a limit imposed on the number of public teachers that each city could officially approve—three, four or five, according to its status.[55]

In the end imperial concern with, and supervision of, education, like any other State control, killed individuality and private initiative among teachers and encouraged a sycophancy that was anything but healthy and a lowering of standards all round. It was the embrace of death.[56]

A letter of the younger Pliny introduces us to an interesting betwixt-and-between stage. At the end of the first century there was no good school, public or private, at Comum, and boys of Comum had to go for their education to Milan, burdening their parents with the expense of their board and lodging, dangerously removed from their parents' control. Pliny's solution of the problem was the creation of a 'parents' council' at Comum, who should club together and create their own school, appointing, evidently, a number of teachers. They would themselves be responsible for the appointment of the teachers, whose salaries they would guarantee. This was one of the most practical and sensible of all the younger Pliny's benefactions. Instead of subsidizing it himself, as he could easily have done, and allowing the parents to sit back and the scheme, ultimately, to run on to the rocks, he insisted that it should be the parents' responsible enterprise; his own contribution would be a third of whatever the parents, who were to govern the new foundation, were themselves prepared to contribute.[57]

The problem which confronted the parents at Comum before Pliny interfered, the problem of ambitious parents with clever children who lived at a distance from good educational facilities, will obviously have occurred at one place or another all over the Roman Empire. In North Africa Apuleius in the second century A.D. and Augustine in the fourth had to be sent away to school, Apuleius from Madauros to Carthage, Augustine from Thagaste to Madauros at a short distance of about twenty

* See p. 133.
† See pp. 132f.
7

miles for the second stage of his education and to Carthage for the third.[58]

In an affluent family a boy had, and retained, a personal tutor, a kind of 'moral tutor,' his *paedagogus*. This man, a slave of the household, escorted him to and from school, and was not always qualified to make a great contribution to his mental education. Ideally, Quintilian thought, he should be an educated man; if not, he should know his own limitations. If, lacking education himself, he had the ambition to acquire it, he could, given the necessary intelligence, improve himself by sitting in on the lessons which his pupil was attending at school—like Q. Remmius Palaemon of Vicetia (Vicenza) in the early Empire, who put his opportunities as *paedagogus* to such good use that he was freed and set up as a *grammaticus* himself in Rome. Nobody, in the opinion of Tiberius and of Claudius, was less qualified to be entrusted with the education of the young; still, whatever his morals, conceit and a prodigious memory gave him a great reputation and brought him a handsome fortune.

Martial introduces us to a different kind of *paedagogus*, a man who lived on in the household, 'a freedman Cato', who, though his former charge had grown up and was proud in the possession of a mistress, treated him still as if he were a child, rebuking his extravagance with the monotonous remark, 'Your father never behaved like that when he was your age.'

The rich boy was accompanied to school not only by his *paedagogus* but also by a humbler menial, a *capsarius*, who carried his books. Horace—the elder Cato would have approved of this—was taken to school in Rome and fetched home by his father. Poorer boys—and boys generally, perhaps, in country towns, even 'the sons of great centurions'—went unaccompanied to school, carrying their own satchels.[59]

The boy—or girl—who was taught outside the household went first at the age of six or seven to a primary school for four or five years. This 'school', in fact, was normally an establishment with one master, *primus magister*, or *magister ludi* or *magister ludi litterarii*, though sometimes he was assisted by an usher. The pupils were taught reading, writing (both in Greek and Latin) and elementary arithmetic: '*ubi legere et scribere et numerare discitur.*'[60] Augustine as a grown man still had nightmares of this period of his education, of being thrashed for idleness and an overfondness for ball games and Ausonius urged his grandson even at a later stage in his education to steel himself against fright at the sight and sound of the cane: 'Your father and mother faced this in their time and survived.' A fresco from Pompeii depicts such a thrashing before a pillared forum. For elementary and grammar school teaching, it seems, was generally given in rooms on the edge of Fora, or under the colonnades or in the *exedrae* of Fora, separated by a mere curtain from the bustling world outside and around. The screeches of the boys' unbroken voices and the ranting of their teachers were audible to the passer-by[61]; but on market days the noise outside would have drowned the teacher's voice. That was why children in primary and grammar schools had holidays every eighth day, on the *Nundinae.**

Work started very early in the morning, soon after dawn, was broken off for lunch at midday and, anyhow in winter, probably resumed in the afternoon.[62]

Secondary, which followed primary, education was education in grammar, syntax and literature.[63] The same *grammaticus* might teach both Greek and Latin, or a child might be sent to a different teacher for each of the two languages. Procedure was that of the 'construe'. The master read a passage aloud, explaining the main difficulties. Then a pupil, or a number of pupils in turn, read the same passage aloud, an operation the more difficult because of the fact that he read from a text (a roll) in which there were no intervals between words. After this the detailed construe started. It was an approach which stressed every aspect of literature but the aesthetic, and it must often have been oppressively tedious. In Greek, Homer, the tragedians and Menander were read to the exclusion of most other authors; in Latin, in the Empire, Terence, Virgil and Horace, though until the end of the first century A.D., when attention was riveted on them as the established Latin classics, other poets, even Lucan, were read. History and rhetoric —which meant Sallust (not Livy) and Cicero—belonged properly to the sphere of higher education, to the *rhetor*, but sometimes they too received cursory attention in secondary schools. The elements of the medieval quadrivium, arithmetic (and geometry), music and astronomy, were 'fringe subjects', cursorily studied to relieve tedium in spare hours.[64]

A child was thirteen or fourteen when the first two stages of his education were surmounted, and he advanced to higher education, at the hands of the *rhetor*.[65] This school, somewhat grander than the premises of the primary or secondary school teacher, was also in the

* See p. 60.

vicinity of the Fora—in imperial Rome, in the *exedrae* of the Forum of Augustus, in rooms attached to the libraries in the Forum of Trajan (the *Schola Traiani*) and in the mysterious Athenaeum of Hadrian.

This, like the other branches of Roman education, was based directly on Greek educational practice. It was education for the advocate, not for the lawyer. Two things were taught: fluency of speech and ingenuity in argument. Exercises, 'declamations', were worked out and then performed by pupils before an audience—their teacher and their fellow-students and sometimes before invited friends. They consisted either of *suasoriae*, speeches on a set theme (for instance, 'Hannibal after Cannae debates the pros and cons of marching on Rome') or of *controversiae*, in which the (fictitious) law on a particular issue was stated, a dilemma was posed, and the pupil was called on to argue on one side or the other. For instance[66]: 'The law states that, if a woman has been raped, her assailant shall be executed or forced to marry her without dowry, according to her choice. On one and the same night a man raped two women. One demanded his execution, the other that he should marry her. So what?' All this against a background of formal oratorical rules and conventions which were painstakingly imparted to the pupils. At the end the gifted pupil knew how to convince a jury that black was white; but as yet he knew little of Roman law.

There was an artificiality about the themes. In the *suasoriae* the subjects were chosen from Greek and Roman history, but from a Greek history which ended (as it did also for the rhetorical schools in Greece) with the death of Alexander the Great, and from a Roman history which ended on the battlefield of Philippi—for the reason, presumably, that few people knew any Greek history later than 323 B.C. and, in the case of Roman history, because the treatment of a subject later than the end of the Republic might be held to involve criticism of the imperial régime. Not, of course, that in *suasoriae* about Cicero or Brutus and Cassius there was not great room for subtle innuendo on the subjects of 'liberty' and 'tyranny'. Again, the subjects of *controversiae* belonged to a world of fantasy, far removed from any issue which was likely to arise in the contemporary courts.

To some extent this education in rhetoric was better, and indeed more Roman in character, under the Republic. The elder Cato had claimed that an orator should be 'a morally good man, skilled in speaking', and in Cicero's day philosophy (natural philosophy, logic and particularly ethics), Roman civil law and Roman history were fundamental constituents of oratorical training.[67] By the end of the first century A.D., to the regret both of Quintilian and of Tacitus, this was no longer the case.[68] Philosophy, as has been seen, was suspect; 'history' was restricted to a collection of *exempla* (like that of Valerius Maximus) to which an orator might appeal at need, and law had its own schools.

In the Republic, among the upper classes in Rome, a young man's introduction to the theory and practice of law came after he left school and was accepted as a pupil by a jurisconsult or by a barrister in practice, as Cicero studied under Scaevola the augur and then under Scaevola the pontiff. He learnt the intricacies of the law by seeing the law in action, by listening to the discussion of a case, and of the issues which it raised, by lawyers among themselves or with their clients. In the Empire there were public law teachers, who instructed in the vicinity of the great libraries (like that created by Augustus in the temple of Apollo on the Palatine in Rome). Legal texts, the earliest of which we know being the Digest of P. Alfenus Varus, consul in 39 B.C., were the subject of the same sort of detailed study as the *grammaticus* devoted to literary texts. Great law schools grew up, not only in Rome but also in the provinces, the greatest of them in the East, at Berytus (Beirut).[69]

Women were presumably excluded from these schools, since in the Empire they were forbidden to plead in court.[70] Students came in the late Empire from a great distance to the schools at Rome and Berytus, and their education and deportment were strictly supervised by the authorities, as we know from regulations of Justinian forbidding them to play practical jokes on their teachers or fellow-students. Earlier, in 370 A.D., students were only admitted at Rome after an official scrutiny of their documents; their 'residence permit' expired when they were twenty; and in the meanwhile 'the office of tax assessment shall carefully investigate the life of the students at their lodging houses, to see that they actually do bestow their time on the studies which they assert that they are pursuing . . . Nor shall the students attend shows too frequently nor commonly take part in unseasonable carousals.'[71]

There is no evidence to suggest that in any Roman school of whatever grade there were either examinations or reports or certificates of proficiency.

Contemporary education is never immune from criticism, and criticism from informed sources deserves attention. Seneca was not alone in thinking that, in the hands of the *grammaticus*, close analysis of literary texts degenerated into tedious pedantry. Quintilian detected a growing inclination to scrap the hard groundwork which should be the basis of a literary education in favour of superficiality which, requiring neither knowledge nor thought, was more immediately attractive to the young. The *grammaticus* sometimes brought his pupils on too fast and encroached on what was the proper preserve of the *rhetor*; 'the High School was undertaking to do University work.' Tacitus' criticism was severer still: discipline was dangerously relaxed and children left school ignorant of history and literature with which they should have been familiar. In this the poor schoolmaster was not wholly to blame. His income depended on his filling his classes; and pupils, encouraged often by their parents, came to shape their own curriculum. 'A teacher', Agamemnon the rhetoric-master said in Petronius' *Satyricon*, 'is like a fisherman; unless he baits his hook with what attracts the fish, he will sit the day out on his rock without a bite.' As other countries too have found, education is in danger of floundering with youth at the helm.[72]

From a modern point of view a striking weakness of Roman education was its extreme narrowness and conservatism. Apart from the medical schools in Greece, there was no scientific education, and higher education generally was restricted to rhetoric, declamations which, though they may have sharpened the wits and the imagination, were monotonously confined through the centuries to the same threadbare topics—pirates, changelings, Xerxes debating whether to cross the Hellespont, Cicero debating whether to burn his books and save his life.[73] Youth was being trained to argue in court and to debate in politics at a time when forensic opportunities hardly survived except in the centumviral courts and politics did not survive at all. There was only prize oratory, dreadful stuff like Pliny's *Panegyricus* and all the other panegyrics or, in Greek, the endless tedium of Dio Chrysostom's and Aelius Aristides' public orations. There remained the study of law, which had always been the finest and most Roman part of Roman education, a basic training not only for the lawyer, the *jurisprudens* or *jurisperitus*, but also for the administrator; and this function it continued to the end to discharge.[74]

There were good and bad teachers; and there were, as there always have been and always will be, good and bad parents.

The easiest butt for the satirist and the moralist, educated men themselves, was the parent who was culpably indifferent to his children's education, the parent who professed that he had succeeded in life himself without any education or, alternatively, the parent who took his

own education for granted and thought that the education of his
children was an item on which money could be saved. He would
squander sesterces by the hundred thousand on luxurious building or on
domestic amenities and grudge two thousand on a tutor for his child.
So Juvenal. Or, if Plutarch[75] is to be believed (and what was true of
contemporary Greece was true of Rome), such men would select the
best of their slaves for posts in the household which promoted their
own material well-being, but when it came to selecting a tutor for their
children (in Philemon Holland's splendid translation), 'If they meet
with one slave among the rest that useth to be cupshotten, given to
gluttony and belly cheere or otherwise is untoward in any good service,
him they set over their children to bring them up.'*

Most parents, however, were concerned over their children's education; in the wealthiest class generally at Rome, because education was
accepted, and therefore good; among those who were not so fortunate
as to have a good education themselves, because a good education was
a passport to material success. This was the motive which, no doubt,
filled the schools in the western provinces, in which the promotion of
education—primarily for the sons of prominent men[76]—was one of the
very best features of Romanization. And as, from the end of the first
century A.D., Greeks were increasingly admitted to the imperial
administrative service, parents in Greek-speaking provinces will have
seen the value for their children of a knowledge of Latin, however much
the cultured Greek professed to despise Latin as a barbarous language
and its literature, by comparison with his own, as a barbarous literature.

In Italy, too, among the lower middle class, the desire to see children
educated as a means of getting on in the world is admirably represented
by Echion the rag-seller in Petronius' *Satyricon*, addressing Agamemnon, the teacher of rhetoric:

You remember that little shaver of mine? Well, he'll be your pupil
one of these days. He's already doing division up to four and, if he
comes through all right, he'll sit at your feet some day. Every spare
minute he has, he buries himself in his books. He's smart all right, and
there's good stuff in him. His real trouble is his passion for birds . . .
And, you know, he's mad about painting. And he's already started
wading into Greek, and he's keen on his Latin. But the tutor's a little
stuck on himself and won't keep him in line.

* Compare Roger Ascham: 'And it is a pitie that commonlie more care is had, yea and
that among verrie wise men, to find out rather a cunnynge man for their horse than a
cunnynge man for their children.'

The older boy, now, he's a bit slow. But he's a hard worker and teaches the others more than he knows. Every holiday he spends at home and, whatever you give him, he's content. So I bought him some of those big red law books. A smattering of law, you know, is a useful thing around the house. There's money in it too. He's had enough literature, I think. But if he doesn't stick it out in school, I'm going to have him taught a trade. Barbering or auctioneering,* or at least a little law. The only thing that can take a man's trade away is death. But every day I keep pounding the same thing into his head: 'Son, get all the learning you can. Anything you learn is money in the bank. Look at Lawyer Phileros. If he hadn't learnt his law, he'd be going hungry and chewing on air. Not so long ago he was peddling his wares on his back; now he's running neck and neck with old Norbanus. Take my word for it, son, there's a mint of money in books, and learning's a trade never killed a man yet.'†

The value of a good home background was appreciated as keenly by Roman as by modern educationalists. Livy deplored the loss of parental authority in the emancipated world of the early Empire. Quintilian stressed the advantages which came to a child from having not only an educated father but also an educated mother; and pointed out that uneducated parents carried an even heavier responsibility.[77]

Over-fond and over-proud parents could be, as they always have been, an embarrassment to their children. 'I remember,' Persius wrote, 'as a small boy, I used to give my eyes a touch with oil if I did not want to learn Cato's grand dying speech, sure to be vehemently applauded by my wrong-headed master, that my father might hear me recite in a glow of perspiring ecstasy with a party of friends for the occasion. Reason good, for the summit of my scientific ambition was to know what that lucky treble-six would bring me, how much that ruinous ace would sweep off—never to be balked by the narrow neck of the jar (when throwing tali‡) or to let any one be cleverer at whipping the top.'§

Children could be harmed by being spoiled, worse still they could be harmed by the bad example of their parents. Juvenal, Quintilian and

---

* Cf. Martial 5, 56: If your boy is a dullard and wants to make money, make him an architect or an auctioneer.

† Petronius, *Satyricon* 46. I quote W. Arrowsmith's spirited translation (University of Michigan Press, 1959).

‡ On these games, see pp. 155f.

§ Persius, *Sat.* 3, 44–51, tr. J. Conington, Oxford, 1871.

Tacitus all labour the point. As Quintilian wrote, 'We have no right to be surprised if our children say something over-free and use words which we should not tolerate from the lips even of an Alexandrian page. It was we who taught them . . . We have no right to be surprised. The poor children learn these things before they know them to be wrong.' Parents infected their children with degrading appetites—for the stage, gladiators, horses. So Tacitus. In his fourteenth satire Juvenal exploited the theme. Do not be surprised if your son turns out a criminal, your daughter a libertine. By whom were they first taught to despise moral standards? The boy by his father, the girl by her mother.[78]

Happily there is the younger Pliny to remind us of what, dazzled by the satirist, we might overlook: the existence of normal, happy families, with parents who took no responsibility more seriously than the responsibility for the upbringing of their children.

There is evidence, too, of a less happy kind in funerary reliefs (often with inscriptions) erected by devoted parents all over the Empire for their sons and daughters who died, as large numbers of children evidently did, during the period of their schooling. These frequently depict children at school reading aloud from a book (*volumen*, a roll) before their masters. The inscriptions refer in terms of fulsome praise to genius sadly cut short—for instance, to a mathematical prodigy, a boy of thirteen, to gifted little girls of seven, to a boy of six who, sent to school to learn Greek, succeeded in teaching himself Latin.[79]

All education had to be paid for. Teachers in receipt of imperial or municipal stipends still collected fees from their pupils* or at least expected gifts from their parents. The question arises: what proportion of Roman children received any education at all? What proportion of the Roman Empire was literate? The children of household slaves may, as will be seen, have enjoyed particular advantages; the children of other slaves and the children of the free-born poor, particularly in country districts, however, can have had little education beyond what was acquired by native wit—anyhow an ability to handle coinage. A great number must have been unable to read or write, and a great many others had nothing better than the elementary teaching of a primary school.

Armies in the modern world are a good testing ground of literacy and even in an enlightened socialist state there are soldiers whom the

---

* In fourth-century Rome students of rhetoric frequently defaulted on their debts by abandoning a school at the moment when fees were due to be paid and transferring to a different teacher (Aug., *Conf.* 5, 12, 22).

army schoolmaster is called on to teach to read and to write. In the case of the Roman army we can unfortunately appeal to no evidence earlier than the fourth century A.D., when Vegetius in his admirable manual of military instruction points out that, in the selection of recruits, while physical size and strength are essential, there are certain posts which call for educated men—*litterati milites*—to keep duty rolls and pay-sheets, no very arduous intellectual exercise. The clear implication is that such proficiency was beyond the reach of many recruited men; and it would be a bold assumption that this was not the case at all periods of Roman history.[80]

The part played by physical training in education is discussed elsewhere (pp. 159-63).

Pupils at elementary and grammar schools had the equivalent of a weekly holiday—every eighth day on the Nundinae.* In the Christian Empire, Sundays became holidays. There were also certain pagan festival days and, after the conversion of the Empire to Christianity, Easter and Christmas, when schools were closed.

The general distribution of longer holidays was what it is in Europe today—a short break in winter and in the spring, and a very long holiday indeed in the summer.

The winter holiday was the Saturnalia.† The spring break was for the Quinquatrus, the festival of Minerva, from March 19th to 23rd, a period which, Symmachus said, you remembered all your life as having been a holiday when you were a schoolboy. The summer holiday started at the beginning of July and lasted until October 15th.‡

In an epigram on this subject Martial observed that, if children could only manage to avoid illness in that unhealthy season, they had achieved what was worth more than anything that they might have learnt in the time at school.[81]

5. Slaves

The family consisted not only of husband, wife and children; there were also, technically known as the *familia*, the family slaves, subject to the *dominica potestas* of the master of the house, acquired, like any other real property, by inheritance, gift, sequestration or purchase, or else bred in the house from slaves of the household. These last, who as

---

* See p. 60 above.
† On which see pp. 124f.
‡ See, further, p. 210.

children played freely with the master's children, were *vernae*, particularly profitable, like calves and colts (so Varro encouraged his slaves to breed), particularly loyal as a rule and particularly favoured. They started with the great advantage of speaking Latin as their native language; while mature slaves, brought from the market and freshly imported (*novicii*) found Latin, as all Greeks found it, a very difficult language to learn. Cicero's friend Atticus would have no other kind of slave.[82]

As inscriptions show, slaves were often, in their occupations and crafts, specialists in quite minute fields, and it is tempting to think of the ordinary Roman household as a place in which there were bevies of slaves at every turn. That collector of records, the elder Pliny, knew of an owner of vast estates who died in 8 B.C. leaving a household of 4,116 slaves, stating that, but for losses in the civil wars, the number would have been higher. Pedanius Secundus, Prefect of the City, murdered in A.D. 61, had four hundred slaves and that, in fact or in boastful pretence, was the size of Trimalchio's slave establishment, divided into forty decuries, one in ten slaves being known by sight to his master. The younger Pliny made provision at his death for the support of a hundred of his freedmen, not all of whom were necessarily freed by his will, and this clearly implies a large family of slaves.[83]

In the case of such startling figures, the majority of slaves were farm workers or employed in industry, and the number of house slaves was far smaller. Augustus fixed twenty as a maximum number of slaves and freedmen that a man might take with him into exile, and this was probably a generous figure. The inscriptions of slaves and freedmen in the tomb of the Statilii at Rome, a family of great prominence, from 40 B.C. to A.D. 65, suggest that T. Statilius Taurus Corvinus, consul in A.D. 45, had eight slaves. So it is probable that most people of moderate means in Rome had only one or two, and that many households had no slaves at all.[84]

This might, indeed, have been deduced from the extremely limited living accommodation, one or two rooms at the most, of those who lived in blocks of flats at Rome or Ostia. The wealthier, in houses, had more room, but even so slaves probably slept in the attics or were boarded out. Indeed sleeping quarters for slaves are known only in rare cases, from archaeology, for instance at the Casa del Menandro at Pompeii (on the second floor of a back yard, with kitchens and latrines, and in rooms off the *triclinium* wing) and at the *villa rustica* of Agrippa Postumus near Pompeii (diminutive single rooms) and, from literature, in the case of the younger Pliny's extensive Laurentine villa, where the slave quarters were at a distance from the rooms of the family but good enough in themselves to be used as spare rooms for guests; when occupied by slaves they were seemingly dormitories.[85]

Slaves, who were chattels and with no rights at law, were in the absolute power of their master. Except when the charge was incest or conspiracy, they could not be called as witnesses in court against him— until in the early Empire it was ingeniously discovered that, if they were acquired by compulsory purchase by the State, the ban was automatically removed; there was nothing to prevent them from testifying against their former master. Their evidence, whenever taken, was taken under torture.[86]

They were bound to promote their master's welfare at every turn, because there was no limit to the punishment which he could inflict on them if he was dissatisfied; and they were encouraged to preserve his life by the strongest of all imaginable deterrents; if he was murdered, the whole of his slave-household were put to death without even the formality of a trial, on the ground that, since they had not prevented the murder as they should have done, they were all accessories after the crime. This, which was Republican law, was reinforced in the early Empire and extended to cover the murder of the master's wife.[87]

In A.D. 61, stung by a personal grievance, a slave of the City Prefect Pedanius Secundus killed his master; the whole vast slave household of four hundred slaves was executed. A proposal was even made in the Senate, but not carried, that all the freedmen resident in the household should be deported.[88]

In about 100 A.D. an ex-praetor Larcius Macedo, an unpleasant man, himself of slave ancestry, was assaulted in his baths by all the slaves in attendance on him and left for dead. However, he revived, to live for a few days longer, in which time he saw the slaves, who naturally had run away, recaptured and executed; so he enjoyed the sadistic pleasure of living to see his murderers punished.[89]

Death, however, was not always murder and, in the political distemper of the times, the first century A.D. saw an epidemic of suicides among people in the highest position in Roman society. They were, for the most part, considerate men, and remembered, even in the last emotional crisis, to send their slaves away or to leave evidence that they were not implicated in their death. Even so, the slaves could be held responsible on the ground that, as long as it was within their power, it was their duty to frustrate their master's intention.

In A.D. 105 the consul Afranius Dexter was found dead and, as we know from a letter of the younger Pliny, there was no evidence to show whether he had been murdered or had called on a slave to assist him in suicide. His slaves (of whom Pliny says nothing) were presumably executed; the Senate then discussed the fate of his freedmen. They were to be examined under torture. After that, there were three different proposals: that they should be executed, that they should be banished or that—presumably if they did not incriminate themselves under torture—they should be spared. Pliny's letter, which does not show him at his clear-headed best, relates everything except the decision which the Senate reached.[90]

It is clear that from the first century A.D. onwards there was increasingly strong public disapproval both of the ruthlessness of the law and of the arbitrary power of masters. In A.D. 61 the Roman populace, a body which was predominantly of slave descent itself, rioted in protest against the execution of Pedanius Secundus' four hundred slaves and, despite C. Cassius' eloquent protest that society would collapse if the slaves were not killed, a number of senators had doubts and troops had to be fetched in before the execution could take place.[91]

However, in the course of the Empire a greater humanitarianism invaded the law. If a sick slave was abandoned by his master and then recovered his health, he was to be free, by an edict of Claudius. Slave-prisons (ergastula) were abandoned by Hadrian, who also restricted the punishment of slaves in the event of a master's murder to those who were near him when he was killed. Under Antoninus Pius a master's right to kill any of his slaves was greatly restricted: 'In these times it is not permissible . . . to exercise severity against slaves beyond measure and without cause.' Also if in the provinces a slave fled from his master and took refuge at a statue of the Emperor, the provincial governor was to hold an enquiry and, if he was convinced of the master's brutality, the master was to be forced to sell the whole of his slave-household.[92]

Economics explain the change of policy; slaves were scarcer and therefore not so easily expendable. Stoic teaching had always urged kindness to slaves, and had stressed that a master was as completely in slavery to Fortune as his slaves were in slavery to himself. Stoics preached, however; they did not act. The rule of that great Stoic M. Aurelius was marked by no considerate legislation whatever, where slaves were concerned. Christianity too. It accepted slaves into the Church; individual Christians often, particularly at the moment of their conversion, gave freedom to their slaves; but officially Christianity saw nothing wrong with the institution of slavery itself.[93]

Given the uncontrolled power of the master and the existence in Roman as in all other societies of vicious men, slaves were sometimes treated with hideous cruelty. Galen tells the story of a sadist and masochist in one (a Greek, in fact, from Crete) with whom he travelled, a man who, irritated over a trifle, struck two of his slaves on the head with the sharp edge of his sword-sheath, wounding them seriously— and then came to Galen with a strap and asked for a thrashing. The slaves who evoked Seneca's pity, waiters at a large and intemperate dinner party, however, would have been surprised by the idea that they deserved sympathy; like all other servants, they doubtless enjoyed their master's parties, just as Trimalchio's servants entered heart and soul into the tricks, often at their own expense, which were played on his guests.[94]

However, whether considerate by nature or not, most Romans appreciated that, except with the incorrigibly idle and vicious (who were best taken to the market and sold), kindness to slaves paid rich dividends. In the hideous proscriptions of 43 B.C., when nothing but dangerous subterfuge could save the lives of the proscribed, 'the utmost loyalty was displayed by their wives, considerable loyalty by their freedmen, a little by their slaves, and none at all by their sons.' So Velleius Paterculus. Appian, on the other hand, records case after case in which slaves saved their masters' lives, often at the sacrifice of their own. A fugitive Restio, hiding in the marshes, was startled by the appearance of a *verna*, a slave whom he had branded for ill-conduct. 'I have forgotten the branding,' the slave said. 'I only remember the kindness I had from you before,' and saved his master's life.[95]

Among the Pisonian conspirators of A.D. 65, none after arrest showed heroism comparable with that of the freedwoman Epicharis, who was submitted to hideous torture; 'under terrible constraint she, a freedwoman, refused to divulge the names of men unconnected with her and whom she hardly knew at all, and so gave a finer example than all the free men, knights and senators who, though they suffered no torture, were only too anxious to give away the names of their closest kin.'[96]

We need not therefore think that Cicero and the younger Pliny, about both of whom we happen to know so much, were unique in their friendly relations with their slaves and freedmen, in particular in their concern over their health. Tiro, who had been freed three years earlier, had to be left behind at Patras when Cicero and his staff were returning from Cilicia in 50 B.C., because he was seriously ill. A whole series of letters testifies to Cicero's and his family's deep concern on this account. When Zosimus, a highly accomplished slave of the younger Pliny, a nice reader and a musician, contracted tuberculosis, Pliny sent him on a cruise to Egypt, from which he returned, seemingly cured, and threw himself ardently into his work. Soon he sickened again. This time Pliny sent him to a friend's villa at Fréjus (Forum Iuli), whose climate and milk were recommended for victims of the disease.[97]

A nice satire of Horace describes the amusing and confident raillery of a cheeky slave contrasting the untroubled nature of his own amorous peccadilloes with the perilous consequences of his master's. And there could be no better evidence of the real affection of a whole family for a favourite slave than the letter written to his brother by Q. Cicero when he was serving on Caesar's staff in Gaul, on the news of Tiro's manumission, at about the age of fifty, in 53 B.C.:

I have just heard about Tiro. He ought never to have been a slave, and now you have decided that he should be our friend instead. My delight at the news is matched only by the longing I have to see you all, you, your children and my own boy. After reading your letter and Tiro's, I jumped with joy. Thank you for what you have done. And many congratulations. The loyalty which I receive from Statius is a sheer delight to me*; so how much you will gain, in the same way, from Tiro—and more, because Tiro is a scholar, a conversationalist, a humane man, and these are qualities which count for more than material values. I have innumerable reasons for loving you, but this tops them all, especially because, as was right, you wrote to send me the news. I read your letter, and it was *you* all over.[98]

We think of Roman slavery, perhaps, in too heavily loaded and emotional terms, and forget two things: first, that there was a greater potential of varied genius among slaves (a great many of whom came from the Greek-speaking East) than in any other section of the Roman community and, secondly, that in a large, and particularly, in the Empire, in the imperial, household a quick and bright young slave had the possibility of a really exciting future. The world was crying out for men of educated talent in fields in which the freeborn Roman

---

* A clever dig, this; for M. Cicero had disapproved strongly of Quintus' act in manumitting his slave Statius.

would not (for social reasons) or could not (because he lacked the skill) engage. The slave's interest and his master's were in this matter the same; at the crudest assessment, there was money in it for them both. The elder Cato was shrewd enough to realize this in the second century B.C. 'He was willing to lend money to any of his slaves who asked, and they bought slave-boys whom, at Cato's expense, they educated and trained. At the end of a year, they sold them—in a number of cases to Cato himself, who paid the highest price that the market offered.' A century later another astute financier, Crassus, 'with all his extensive real estate, seemed to have more money still tied up in slaves, of whom he had great numbers of all sorts; readers, secretaries, connoisseurs of silver, accountants, waiters. He himself supervised their education and training, thinking that nothing had a greater claim on a master's attention than his slaves, human factors of his prosperity.' Atticus' staff of librarians and copyists were slaves born in the house and trained in the house. An even better advertisement for this kind of training (because it can hardly have been undertaken as a financial investment) is the case of Epictetus, who as a slave of the imperial freedman Epaphroditus was allowed to attend Musonius Rufus' lectures in Rome; he was given his freedom by Epaphroditus and became an important philosophical teacher (with Arrian as one of his pupils), first in Rome and then, after the expulsion of philosophers by Domitian in A.D. 89, in Nicopolis.[99]

Apart from technical specialists of all kinds, there was always an extensive need in public service, in the imperial household and in commercial life for linguists, anyhow men who 'spoke both languages', for shorthand-writers (*notarii*), for clerks and accountants and, in private life, for slaves of good literary education.* Inscriptions perpetuate the memory of slave children, infant geniuses, who died young, of a *calculator* of thirteen, 'whose ample knowledge would fill volumes', of a shorthand-writer who could take dictation at lightning speed.

With the need of such specialists in view, two great imperial training schools (*paedagogia*) for slave-boys were set up in Rome, one on the Palatine and the other, *Ad Caput Africae*, on the Caelian. Similar schools for the training of young slaves were established by wealthy individuals

---

* But Calvisius Sabinus, a rich freedman vulgarian in the early Empire, was presumably unusual in possessing, instead of a library of books, a library of literate slaves worth over a million sesterces, since he had paid 100,000 sesterces for each of them, one to know Homer by heart, one Hesiod, and nine the nine Greek lyric poets; so that they might be at hand at any moment to supply him with an appropriate quotation—which, because he was such a fool, he rarely managed to repeat correctly (Sen., *Ep.* 27, 5–8).

with large slave households, and it has been conjectured that the younger Pliny had such an establishment at his Laurentine villa. To judge from inscriptions, the education continued at least to the age of eighteen and, during the period of their training, the boys were often employed in their spare time both in the imperial and in private households as pages and waiters at table*—uniformed so as to enhance their good looks (which shocked Ammianus Marcellinus)—or, in the country, as hunt servants. The instructor, who appears often in inscriptions, was *paedagogus puerorum*: a dedication by twenty of them *Ad Caput Africae* shows the size of that establishment.[100]

An easier alternative for the normal master of a promising young slave was to apprentice him or to send him as a trainee, just as boys who were not slaves were trained, to a suitable instructor, with differing financial arrangement according as he would or would not begin to earn money for his instructor during the period of his training. We have evidence from Egyptian papyri of such apprenticeship, training in shorthand-writing, for instance, and in weaving. As evidence in such a matter could hardly survive except on papyri, and papyri have generally survived only in Egypt, it can safely be assumed that such arrangements were made throughout the empire.[101]

Seneca pointed out that it was a master's duty to clothe and feed his slaves. If he gave them an education, that was charity. It was a charity, however, which paid handsome dividends to the slave himself, to his master and to the Roman world at large.[102]

Though there were many who lived and died as slaves, the intelligent and enterprising slave lived in the hope of eventual manumission. This was something that he might buy with part or the whole of his *peculium*, capital which he acquired if he was set up in business of any sort, which by law was the master's property but in practice was treated as belonging to the slave, or he might receive freedom without payment, by gift of his master, whether in his master's lifetime or by his will when he died. Certain restrictions were placed on the freeing of slaves by legislation passed under Augustus, the *lex Fufia Caninia* of 2 B.C. and the *lex Aelia Sentia* of A.D. 4. By the former a limit was placed, no doubt in the interest of the heir, on the number of slaves who might be freed by testament—half in a household of three to ten; a third if there were more than ten and not more than thirty; a quarter

---

* Some, of course, may have been receiving training in waiting, cooking, etc., such as is admirably given today in the Hotel School of the Westminster Technical College in London.

if there were more than thirty but not more than a hundred; after that, not more than a fifth, with an absolute maximum of one hundred. By the *lex Aelia Sentia* except in circumstances of the utmost formality no slave could be freed under the age of thirty and, no doubt to protect the young against intemperate generosity, no master might confer freedom if he was under the age of twenty. However the law allowed for exceptional cases.[103]

Full manumission brought freedom and Roman citizenship in one. Benighted reactionaries like Juvenal deplored the conversion of Rome into a nation of mongrels. A far wiser man, Philip V of Macedon at the end of the third century B.C., at a time when he was at war with Rome, had urged a Greek city, Larissa, to copy the Roman example.[104]

The intimate association of the new freedman's family with the source of its freedom was marked, as long as the family survived, by its gentile name, what in England we should call its surname. This was the name of the Roman family from which, in the person of its liberated slave ancestor, its citizenship derived.

The first act of the freedman, if he had lived in intimate association with a slave woman, was to free and marry her as soon as he could afford it. He might continue to live in his former master's household, as has been seen (and many, lacking any means of their own, had no alternative), or he might move to live outside it. If he had been a close friend of his master and of his master's friends, he felt at once the cold draught of prejudice in the free society into which he moved. Not only were there strict rules (for instance that his children could not marry into families descended even three generations back from a senator) but in general, as is clear from the whole of ancient literature, Romans who were not conscious of having slave blood in their own veins were supremely contemptuous of these who had. Still there were those who overcame this prejudice. Larcius Macedo, killed by his slaves, was of slave origin, yet rose to be praetor. A happier instance is supplied by a man whose name we do not know, whose talent earned him a spectacular career. A slave from Smyrna, he was acquired by the imperial household, in which he served under ten emperors, from Tiberius to Domitian, rising to the highest post in the imperial service, that of Financial Secretary (*a rationibus*). In the course of his career he acquired freedom and after that equestrian rank, and he married a woman, Etrusca, whose brother was a consular.[105]

Slaves might, of course, powerfully influence or destroy happiness and good order within a family. Some were young, handsome, highly sexed, a contrast often in all respects to the master, but not always to the mistress, of the house. Sex, indeed, to Petronius' amusement, often ran counter to the social order, slave-women admitting none but the gentry, their mistresses only slaves and the coarsest exemplars of male virility, to their beds. So scandals occurred. The unfortunate *dispensator* (who could have been a freedman) who was the object of public sympathy in Petronius' *Satyricon* because his master, having discovered him in an intrigue with his wife, had condemned him to death in the arena, was, according to table-talk in Trimalchio's dining room, the helpless victim of a disagreeable sex-starved mistress. Juvenal, in a hateful satire, lampoons an impotent sexual pervert who used a slave to father children who, passing under his name, would give him the political and economic advantages of the father of a family.

And there were free women and widows who lost their heads to attractive slaves. If they were independent and there were children from the union, the children were free and Roman citizens since, by Roman law, the mother determined the child's status. This was perfectly safe as long as the slave belonged to the woman's household. Trouble started when he was somebody else's slave, and this was the impropriety which the freedman Pallas encouraged Claudius, in the form of a *Senatusconsultum Claudianum*, to repair in A.D. 52. After this, if a women contracted such a liaison with the knowledge and approval of the slave's master, she sank to the status of a freedwoman, but the children were still free. If the master was not consulted, or disapproved, then she became a slave, and her children too. Accommodations were possible. Masters were always pleased to increase the size of their slave-household. And so the master and the other two parties might come to an agreement by which the liaison was overlooked and the woman's status unaffected, as long as the offspring became members of his slave household: an arrangement which suited all parties, until Hadrian forbade it.[106]

6. Life in the Family

There was, of course, every variety of family. There were husbands and wives without children but still happy, as the younger Pliny and his wife Calpurnia seem always to have been or, like Scipio Aemilianus and Sempronia, acutely unhappy. By Augustus' moral legislation a childless woman between the ages of twenty and fifty, once married, could hardly avoid the married state; she was given two years if her husband died, eighteen months if she had been divorced, in which to marry again.

There was, in Lucretius' vivid description, 'your happy home, your splendid wife, your adorable children running to meet you to claim a kiss and a hug'; there was Juvenal's unideal home: an unprincipled father, a profligate mother, with children modelling themselves on the unimproving examples of both their parents. There was nothing uniquely Roman about families in which there was a conflict of parents, the mother mollycoddling the children, while the father reduced them to tears, bullying them to work harder at their lessons, even on holidays.[107]

There is a nice letter of Pliny on the subject of the over-stern father:

Some one I know was pitching into his son for having too expensive tastes in horses and dogs. I waited for the young man to leave, and then said, 'Now, look here, have you never done anything which was open to criticism by your father?' 'Have done,' do I say? 'Do you not sometimes do things today which, if you suddenly changed places, your son could rebuke just as ponderously? Haven't we all got our weaknesses? One man indulges himself in one way, another in another.'

Stung by this instance of excessive severity, I write to you, as one friend to another, in case you should ever be too hard on your son, Remember he is only a boy, and you were a boy once yourself and. in playing the heavy father, don't forget that you are a man and the father of a man.[108]

There were homes in which children had fathers, but whose mothers were dead or divorced, like the home in which the later Emperor Tiberius spent his first boyhood, after his mother Livia had abandoned her husband in favour of the man who was to be Augustus Caesar. If widowed or divorced, the father might marry again, and the children in that case had a stepmother. Or he might take a concubine to live with him, as Marcus Aurelius did, for the very reason that he did not want his children to suffer from a stepmother.[109]

There were other homes in which there were mothers and no fathers. The sister of Augustus was such a dutiful, if in the end tragic, widow, his niece Antonia such a dutiful and attractive one, conscious, each of them, that her children's future, and therefore their moulding, were of importance not only to herself and to her family, but possibly to the government of the Empire itself.

The outstanding feature of the Roman family was the absolute power of its male head, the *paterfamilias*.[110] He could kill his wife only if he discovered her in bed with another man; he could not only sell but could also kill any of his children, though in the latter case he was expected to summon and consult a family council first. This, according to one account, was how Spurius Cassius, on resigning his third consulship, was executed in 485 B.C. The passage of time did not weaken this absolute power of the father. Seneca remembered the case of a Roman knight who condemned his son to death, and was nearly lynched by the angry public; also the case of a son who attempted to kill his father. The father, a forgiving man, summoned a council, which Augustus himself attended, but so far from killing his son, as he was entitled to do, he allowed him to live in relegation at Massilia and even made him an allowance.[111]

In the late Republic and early Empire a father could probably no longer compel his son or daughter to marry against their wills; but girls were very young when the arrangements for their marriage were made, and sons could not easily forget that, after marriage as before it, they would be in financial dependence on their fathers. If, as by this time was the general rule, his daughter was not married by *confarreatio*, so as to pass into the arbitrary power (*manus*) of her husband, but remained in the power of her father, she had no alternative but to divorce her husband, if those were her father's instructions.

A son was as much in the *potestas* of his father after marriage as he had been before it. He could not hold property in his own right, and either lived on an allowance from his father, or else he received a settlement (*peculium*), to which he could add by investment and earning, but which, even so, his father could control at will. And even his own children were not under his authority; they were under that of their grandfather.

In A.D. 4 Tiberius was forty-five years old; he had been married twice and he had a son about sixteen years old. He then, on Augustus' instruction, adopted his nephew Germanicus, who was eighteen years old. After which, Augustus adopted Tiberius, who ceased in that moment to be the head of a family. Thenceforth he was no longer entitled to make gifts, to manumit or to receive an inheritance or legacy unless he booked it to the credit of his *peculium*.[112] Yet in public life he was in effect now joint ruler with Augustus of the whole Roman world. His sons Drusus and Germanicus will have lived in the same dependent state until their deaths.

It was, of course, possible for a father to emancipate his son when he grew up and married. Emancipation was a complicated process. The father sold his son as a slave to a friend, who at once manumitted him, so that the son returned automatically to the *potestas* of his father. The process was repeated not once only but twice. At the end of it all the son was free of his father, independent, *sui iuris*. And we do not, until the very late Empire, hear of any simpler way of securing emancipation. By gaining his freedom the son at first penalized himself, for if his father, not having explicitly disinherited him, died intestate, he would not have a claim to a proper share in his father's estate (as, in similar circumstances, he would have done, had he not been emancipated). This applied under the *ius civile*, until it was modified by praetorian rulings in the late Republic which validated such a claim on his part, despite his emancipation.[113]

Here is one of the dark spots of Roman history, where we simply do not know the facts. We do not hear of grown sons who in their fathers' lifetimes expressed frustration on account of the lack of financial independence. We do not hear of grandsons appealing to their grandfathers over the heads of their fathers or of men whose fathers were still alive complaining that they had no authority over their children. The *peculium* may have been treated as being in fact, what it was not in law, the son's absolute property, and a father may have been allowed conventionally to exercise full *patria potestas* over his children. Or emancipation may have been commoner than the evidence suggests. It is true that there are references to it as a means by which a father rid himself of an undesirable son, cheated the law to his own and the family's material advantage or enabled his son to acquire an inheritance which could not otherwise have come to him. Yet there is Constantine's sanctioning of emancipation, with manumission, as a legal act which could be performed, despite the general ban, on a Sunday, on the ground that these were happy acts; 'the better the day, the better the deed'.[114]

A father must never appear naked in the presence of his son, once his son reached puberty, or of his son-in-law; so they did not go to the baths in one another's company.[115]

In the young married household the first and most momentous event was the birth of a child. A table was laid out in the *atrium* to Lucina, the goddess of childbirth, and it remained for a *nundinum*, until the day of purification, the *dies lustricus*. Then, as has been seen already, the child was named.[116]

The children who survived infancy were brought up and, in families which could afford the expense, given a schooling. For a girl, childhood might be a very brief affair, since the law allowed her to marry at the age of twelve. Though such early marriages were probably uncommon, her engagement might well be arranged and announced before that—not before she was ten, Augustus ruled; not before she was seven, the law stated later. Still, Claudius' daughter Octavia was betrothed at the age of one—and a party held to celebrate the event, the *sponsalia*. When Augustine at the age of thirty-one aspired to correct profligacy by marriage, a child of ten was selected as his *fiancée*; there were two years to wait, in the course of which he decided not to marry.[117]

The legal requirement that a daughter should consent not only to her marriage but also to her engagement can have meant little; anyhow she was unlikely at that age to know much about moral turpitude, which was the only ground on which she could refuse her father's choice of a husband. The *sponsio* was not made by the girl herself, but on her behalf, normally by her father; and from the second century B.C. it was not legally binding. There could not be an action for breach of promise.[118]

While others might deal with the forming of the young girl's mind, her mother attended to equally important things; in particular she taught her daughter to hold herself well and to move with elegance. A girl was under the strict surveillance of her mother until the moment of her marriage.

Boys, however, as they grew up, took or were given greater licence. So the elder Cato, when he saw a youth of his acquaintance emerging from a brothel, said, 'Good'; when, a short time later he saw him in similar circumstances, he said, 'By "Good" I did not mean to suggest that you should make this place your home.' In fourth-century Africa, when Augustine was sixteen, his mother lectured him on the evils of fornication and, in particular, adultery; but after that his parents did not concern themselves over his promiscuous and licentious habits.[119]

The girl said goodbye to her childhood on the eve of her marriage, when she devoted her *toga praetexta* and her toys to the Lares of the family; the boy on his coming of age, when he too laid his *tunica recta* and his *bulla* (the golden locket which he wore as something of a charm*) before the household Lares.[120]

---

* Freedmen's children wore a leather collar with an amulet instead; later on poor children might wear this, or a leaden *bulla*. Graves of children show that the *bulla* was buried with them.

The age at which a boy came of age differed at different periods and, between families, at the same period. In individual cases it was often determined, no doubt, by the strength of mind of the boy's parent or guardian in face of strong pressure from the boy himself. It could not happen before he achieved puberty at about fourteen, but it need not happen as early as that—unless, of course, he was required to marry at fourteen and marriage clearly required that he should be a man. In the top social families in early Rome the public aspect of his coming of age overshadowed the private. He was now ready to enter on his public service, his apprenticeship to public life (the *tirocinium fori*) under the tutelage of his father or some other eminent figure who would teach him the rules and introduce him to the practices of public administration for a year or so; after which, he would enter on his *tirocinium militiae*, and start his military service. This was a tradition which Augustus tried to revive; he wanted senators' sons to adopt the broad stripe, the *latus clavus*, immediately on assuming the *toga virilis*, to attend meetings of the senate as spectators, to engage quickly in military service. This at the age originally of eighteen, later of sixteen or seventeen. Cicero's nephew came of age at sixteen, Gaius Caligula at what was an abnormally late age, eighteen.[121]

The occasion, one of great ceremony, took place regularly in the Republic and after that generally, if not universally, on March 17th, the festival of Liber and Libera. Ovid suggests a number of fanciful reasons for the selection of this date though not, with modern scholars, that, as Liber and Libera were sponsors of fertility, they were particularly qualified to ensure that, when he married, the young man should have children.[122]

The young man on this day assumed his grown-up clothes, the white *toga pura* instead of the striped *toga praetexta*, which he had worn as a boy. He was escorted by the family and friends—this was the *deductio in forum*—to the *tabularium* under the Capitol, where he was registered as a full citizen and his name was placed on the roll of his tribe. Augustus wished the temple of Mars Ultor in his new Forum to be visited as part of the ceremony.[123]

There was, on the part of the rich, public entertainment of their clients and a great dinner and reception in the family itself.

Materially this was a landmark of the first importance in the young man's life. If his father and grandfather were dead and he had before been in the charge of a guardian (*tutor*), he shed his guardian at this moment and assumed full control of his property. But in one's teens one is not always fully grown-up, and there are vultures everywhere; so a *lex Laetoria* of the second century B.C., reinforced by a subsequent praetorian edict, took account of this fact and fixed a second 'coming of age' at twenty-five, giving great protection to those who at twenty-five might otherwise have realized that, in the interval, they had been victimized or cheated in the conduct of their private affairs. So at his first 'manhood' the wise 'man', persuaded doubtless by his elder relatives (who had, all of them, a great interest in his property, in case he should die unmarried) applied, on taking the *toga virilis*, for a *curator*, an older man to authorize transactions which he performed in his first years as a man.[124]

It is hard to know at what age a girl normally married. A patient count of 145 inscriptions, recording women of probably moderately well-off families, shows that eight per cent married below the age of twelve,* ten per cent at twelve, eleven per cent at thirteen. The majority, therefore, married when they were fourteen or older. They married boys or men older than themselves. In the poorer classes it has been inferred from the alimentary schemes, under which boys were supported to a higher age than girls, that girls married generally at thirteen or fourteen, boys between fifteen and eighteen.[125]

Marriage, as far as the family was concerned, was a more spectacular event in the case of a daughter, who was symbolically 'snatched' forcibly from her mother's arms, to be taken to her new home.† The son would normally have been provided by his father with a new home to which to bring his bride. Only very rarely did he bring his bride to live in his father's house; the ménage of the Licinii Crassi in the early first century B.C. was clearly a most unusual one, with two married sons and their wives living and feeding with their father, P. Crassus, consul of 97 B.C., and with their younger brother, the future triumvir.[126]

7. Family Festivities

The birthday of a member of the family, an excuse for festivity, had greater religious significance in Rome than it is apt to have in the modern world. In the house a turf altar was erected, gaily decked with flowers, and on it offerings of food and wine were made, to the Genius

---

* That is to say, set up house with the boys or men whom they would marry formally when they were twelve.

† For the details of the marriage ceremony, see my *Roman Women*, 179–89.

in the case of a male member of the family, to the Juno in the case of a female member; candles were lit and incense was burnt—until in A.D. 392 Theodosius forbade such pagan practices.

Everybody wore white. There was a birthday party, a dinner to which guests, relatives and friends, were invited and brought presents —or, if they could not come, sent them. Martial, who had great interest in the presents which he received, suggested that a successful barrister might expect on his birthday to be the recipient of handsome gifts from grateful clients.

Seneca has a splendid discussion of the appropriate choice of presents. Do not be so gauche as to send hunting kit to the senile or to a woman, books to the illiterate, nets for game to a dedicated scholar. Do not pander to weakness by sending wine to a toper or patent medicines to a valetudinarian. Send something unusual, something that will not wear out, something conspicuous, an inescapable reminder of its donor.

Sad poems of Ovid in Tomi reflect his loneliness on his own birthday in exile, his feeling of doleful relegation on his wife's: 'Look how the wind blows the smoke from the incense towards the happy places, towards Italy.'[127]

In the Republic anybody born in an intercalary month celebrated his birthday on the last day of February. What happened in the case of all the people born in 46 B.C., the last year of the old calendar, with its three intercalary months, two of them at the end of the year, we do not know. After that under the Julian calendar there was no problem at all. If born on the extra day of a Leap Year, you were born 'six days before the Kalends of March', and every year the calendar contained such a day; its peculiarity in a Leap Year was that it repeated itself, and occurred twice over. Not that this entitled you in a Leap Year to claim two birthdays.[128]

From February 13th until the 21st, on the *Dies Parentales* the family remembered its dead, and on the 21st made offerings at their tombs. After which, on the 22nd, it turned its attention to itself. This was on the Caristia, the day of the *Cara Cognatio*. Relatives dined together, and everybody brought a contribution to the meal, preferably—if Martial is to be trusted—birds, fieldfares for instance. The meal, marking the unity of the family, had a particular purpose; family quarrels were ironed out, and family disputes settled. Offerings were made to the Lares and, Ovid suggested, this was an appropriate moment for the family to drink the Emperor's health.[129]

March 1st, which was once New Year's Day in the Roman calendar, was a day of honour to Lucina, the goddess of childbirth; and in the household it was a day on which the women could look forward to receiving presents from their relatives and friends. In particular for the mistress of a household it was a kind of Mother's Day, *Matronalia*. It was no day for the bachelor, Horace sighed, inviting Maecenas to feed with him; he might send gifts to the ladies, but dinner in the household was evidently a close family occasion. Indeed the household slaves were entertained, just as they were at the Saturnalia, this time by the mistress of the house, at the Saturnalia by the master. It was, therefore, presumably a less rowdy occasion.[130]

The five days from March 19th to 23rd, the Quinquatrus, the Festival of Minerva, were notable days in the family, if there were children, since they constituted a five-day school holiday.[131]

April 4th and April 12th were the only two days in the year on which, in society, it can have been of any great account in the late Republic and Empire whether you were a patrician or a plebeian. On these two days, however, the distinction determined your social life. On the 4th patricians entertained other patricians to dinner; *mutitationes*, which also meant 'changing horses', was the technical word for such exchange of hospitality. By the severe sumptuary law of 161 B.C. a host had to make a declaration before the courts that he had not exceeded a certain expense on the dinner.

Eight days later, on the 12th, members of plebeian families exchanged hospitality in a similar manner.

What was the origin of the convention? This was one of the conundrums which was put forward for solution when a number of young Roman students celebrated the Saturnalia in Athens in the second century A.D. by dining together. It was answered evidently, Aulus Gellius does not tell us how. Presumably the patrician dinners originated in patrician snobbery quite early in the Republic; and the plebeians, when their social position was assured, retorted in kind. This would be on the analogy of the altar of Plebeian Chastity (*Pudicitia Plebeia*), which was erected in pique by a Verginia, herself a patrician, when she was debarred from the temple of Patrician Chastity for having married into a plebeian family.[132]

August 13th was a holiday for slaves. Why, nobody knew. Festus' suggestion was that this was the day on which King Servius Tullius, a slave by birth, had dedicated the temple of Diana on the Aventine. For Plutarch the antiquarian, the problem was greater still: why did slave-women wash their hair on this day in particular? He answered the question by another: was this how the washing of women's hair started? Did slave-women start to wash their hair on this holiday because they could think of nothing else to do? Was their example then copied by free women?

For an answer to the conundrum, one goes to the scholar, and stays for an answer. Professor H. J. Rose has written, 'Neither question can yet be answered. We know that the date named is the foundation date of the ancient temple of Diana on the Aventine, and there seems to be some connexion between that goddess and slaves. As to the hair-washing, this is, as is well known, a ceremonious business among underdeveloped peoples, but why August 13th should be specially chosen, we do not know; perhaps because Diana, like Artemis, was closely connected with the life of women and might be expected to protect them in this critical operation. In Christian times babies' hair was washed on Palm Sunday.'[133]

The greatest of all the annual holidays and celebrations was the Saturnalia on December 17th, lasting officially in the Republic for a single day, though in the late Republic it extended over two or three. In the Empire the festival lasted three days under Augustus and over four from the reign of Gaius. By the end of the first century A.D., though it was a five-day holiday in theory, it lasted in fact for seven days, from the 17th until the 23rd. Schools were closed. Beforehand there was the pleasure and excitement of buying presents (followed, if you were as greedy as Martial, by the disappointment of receiving them), in particular the gifts of the season, which came to be more extravagant than the original symbolic candles and clay dolls (*sigillaria*),* for whose sale there was a special market, also called Sigillaria, first in the Colonnade of the Argonauts, then in a Colonnade of Trajan's Baths, like the market which is held today in Rome before Christmas in the Piazza Navona. Presents were *Saturnalia et sigillaricia* and included tips, the equivalent of the 'Christmas box'.[134]

For the whole of the festival legal restrictions were relaxed, so that everyone, children and slaves included, could dice and gamble, the children with nuts for stakes, without fear of punishment.† On the

---

* The modern equivalent of which is the Christmas card, in contrast to the Christmas present.

† In the sixteenth-century statutes of my own Oxford College students were allowed to play cards in Hall for moderate stakes on three occasions in the year: All Saints' Day, Christmas Day and the Purification of the Virgin.

17th itself (and we do not know for how many other days of the pro-tracted festival) the toga was discarded in favour of the more comfort-able *synthesis*, the dinner suit, and on their heads men wore the felt cap, *pilleum*, the mark of freedom; and slaves, whose particular festival this was, were exempt from punishment. More than this, in the household the rôles of slave and master were reversed. Either the master and his family dined with the slaves, or, as happened at Macrobius' Saturnalia, the slaves ate in style in the dining-room and not until their meal was over did the butler (who on such occasions was not always perhaps at his sober best) announce that the dining-room was at the disposal of his master and his master's guests.[135]

After dinner each night there was drinking, clowning and merri-ment, degenerating sometimes into wild horse play. The dice were thrown to select a member of the party (he might be a slave) as Saturnalian King to hold office for the whole length of the festival. Every member of the party had to obey his instructions. He could command people to dance, to sing, to commit any absurdity—even to having their faces blacked as a preliminary to being thrown into a tub of cold water. Nero, when the dice selected him for this office in the imperial Saturnalia party in December A.D. 54, chose the opportunity to humiliate Britannicus by making him sing.[136]

On the 24th life returned to normal. Children went back to school. There was no more licence for the drunken gambler, now dragged from his pothouse by the police.[137]

The Compitalia at the end of the Republic followed the Saturnalia, in late December or early January, and some time in the early Empire it was fixed to the three days from January 3rd to 5th. This, like the Saturnalia, was particularly Roman in its origin, a festival to mark the end of the corn-sowing, and, as celebrated on country estates, had features in common with the Saturnalia. The slaves were given extra rations, wine included, and the bailiff (*vilicus*) and his wife dined with them. It may be the case that the Saturnalia, as celebrated in the late Republic and Empire, grew up at a time when the rich property-owner spent the winter at his town house; that earlier, when he lived at his farm in the country, he and his family made merry with his slaves at the Compitalia and that, in dining with the slaves, as in so much else, the bailiff came to represent his master.[138]

The Saturnalia, a target for the abuse of Christian writers from the second century onwards, certainly survived into the fifth century. From the late fourth century onwards, however, it was chiefly the

Kalends of January that Christian writers attacked. This had evidently developed into a five-day festival, from the 1st until the 5th of January, including the three days of Ludi Compitales, and had become something more boisterously pagan even than the Saturnalia. It started riotously on New Year's Eve, when the streets were thronged with revellers who knocked on people's doors and there was little chance of sleep. On New Year's Day laurels decorated front doors, as they did on other days of family rejoicing, and there were presents, lamps (like the candles of the Saturnalia) and money-boxes in particular. As at the Saturnalia, slaves dined with their master and his family. Astrology may explain the change. The New Year had its horoscope, prediction of what the coming twelve months had in store.[139]

8. Death in the Family

Roman families lived in the presence and expectation of death, as in the eighteenth and early nineteenth centuries European families lived still. Not only was the rate of mortality in infants and children very high indeed, as has been seen; but, though some men and women lived to prodigious ages, life-expectancy of grown people was, by modern standards, short. So that parents did not live in the expectation, as parents in affluent societies live today, of seeing their children grow up and marry and, probably, their grandchildren grow up too. This means a family psychology which is difficult for us to understand. In Christian countries where the death rate has been high, the Christian Church encouraged a patient resignation: 'The Lord gave, and the Lord has taken away.' In pagan Rome these facts help to explain the cult of the family Genius which survived as a form of real devotion when other parts of pagan Roman religion had lost their appeal. By prayer and cult alone could a family hope to survive from one generation to the next.

After death, there was the funeral. This, in the case of outstanding men of state, was in the Republic a startling sight, the corpse being followed by the family and by a procession in chariots of men wearing the death masks of all the dead man's distinguished ancestors (borrowed from the *tablinum* of the house), and clothed in their robes of office or triumphal insignia. To the Greek Polybius this was one of the most startling and impressive ceremonies of Roman public life. It could happen in the case of distinguished ladies too; Tacitus describes the funeral in A.D. 23 of a very old lady indeed, the widow of one of the tyrannicides, C. Cassius, the half-sister of another, M. Brutus. 'There were twenty masks of her distinguished ancestors, Manlii, Quinctii and the rest—with Brutus and Cassius outshining them all, from the fact that their masks were not included.' The funeral procession made its way to the Rostra in the Forum, the representatives of all the ancestors sat on thrones and a funeral address, in praise of the dead man and of each of his ancestors, was delivered by his son or by some distinguished relative.[140]

But with the advent of Empire the day of the great families was soon at an end. Such funerals were reserved for Emperors and their favoured kin.

After the funeral, there was a period of family purification—the *feriae denicales*—which, with the funeral itself, excused members of the bereaved family from the most urgent public functions: a magistrate from appearing in court, a recruit from obeying his calling-up instructions. On the ninth day after the funeral, this period of strict mourning ended, and in normal circumstances there was a funeral feast, *novendialis cena*; in desperate circumstances the dead man's possessions could now be auctioned.[141]

Finally, the will, which, in the way of wills, might, or might not, be a surprise. Trimalchio's wife and slaves and a whole succession of his guests will have heard his will at some stage or other at one of his drunken parties: 'I am setting all my slaves free in my will'—which, in fact, the law forbade*—'and I am making Fortunata my heiress.' Valerius Maximus, on the other hand, has stories of more than one man who handed over his rings and said farewell on his deathbed to his friends, with an indication that, when his will was read, they would find that they had not been forgotten. The will was subsequently read, and there was no mention of their names.[142]

In his will a Roman named his heirs, and he also made personal legacies. From the time of the Twelve Tables onwards there was trouble from the fact that the legacies might exhaust the estate, and the heir be left with nothing—or worse, only a collection of unpaid bills. A number of unsuccessful attempts were made to amend the law, until finally by the *lex Falcidia* of 41 B.C. the total of legacies might not exceed three-quarters of the whole estate, leaving the heir or heirs at least a quarter, and this law held good during the Empire.[143]

By the *Lex Voconia* of 169 B.C. women might not be named as heirs to an estate of greater value than 100,000 *asses*, the lower limit of the

* On the freeing of slaves by will, see pp. 113f.

top property class in the census, a limit which was probably raised later to 100,000 sesterces.[144] There were various ways of circumventing the law. Women could, of course, receive legacies—after 41 B.C., up to three-quarters of the estate. Or the father of an only daughter might make over the whole of his property as a trust to a male friend, a *fideicommissum hereditatis*, on the understanding that he, the *heres fiduciarius*, would proceed to transfer the whole estate as a gift to the daughter. This was all right as long as the friend was honest, for such trusts were not actionable. Cicero records a shameless case in which the dead man's wishes were deliberately flouted, but this would have been difficult in the Empire, when the procedure was recognized as legally proper, on the part of any trustee who valued his own reputation and standing, his *dignitas*.[145]

Or a woman might be granted exemption from the terms of the law. Livia received such exemption, and was named as Augustus' heir in his will in respect of a third of his estate. With the Empire, however, the law was evidently greatly relaxed in practice, and a daughter could certainly inherit her father's estate.[146]

The Romans knew no law of primogeniture. So, on a father's death, his sons, unless explicitly disinherited, might expect to be named as heirs in equal parts; and if he died intestate, they could claim an equal division of his estate among themselves.

Pliny records a remarkable case in which a testator's intentions were frustrated by a pair of brothers, rich, respectable ex-consuls. Curtilius Mancia, who had a strong dislike of his son-in-law Domitius Lucanus, left his money to Lucanus' daughter Lucilla, his granddaughter, on condition that she should pass out of the control of her father. So she was emancipated by her father—but then adopted by her father's brother, Domitius Tullus. The two brothers administered their affairs as partners in a *consortium*; so when the daughter had received her legacy and was then adopted by her uncle, she passed, with her new wealth, into that very control by her father which her grandfather had been determined to end. However, all worked out happily. Lucanus left his entire fortune to his brother and Tullus made a model will, treating his wife very handsomely, also his grandchildren and grandson and, for the rest, leaving Lucilla heiress to his vast estate (and hers).[147]

A will might always be invalidated by the praetor or by a decision of the centumviral court on the ground either of the unfitness of the testator or of the unsuitability of a legatee (a eunuch, for instance, or a pimp).

An ingenious device of one profligate who felt apprehensive on this account was to give his mistress an I.O.U. for a large sum of money, which she was to present to his heirs as a debt due from his estate when he died. In the event the testator was unexpectedly slow in dying, and the lady too impatient. She presented the I.O.U. while he was still alive, and her claim failed.

Under the rule of bad emperors, the will of any one of wealth and prominence might be overturned for more serious reasons still, namely that the Emperor's name did not appear among the legatees. So a nice calculation had to be made. What was the minimum sum likely to satisfy the avaricious ruler, so that something at least might descend to a man's own family?[148]

A will could be overturned for better reasons. A close relative who had been disinherited, or whose name had been omitted, could bring a suit against 'an undutiful will', a *querela inofficiosi testamenti*.[149]

If a woman who died was dependent on her father (*in manu*), her possessions reverted to him automatically. Only if she was a Vestal Virgin had she the full ownership of her property in her father's lifetime.

If her father was dead, a woman was—under her guardian—independent, and could bequeath what she possessed, but she could not leave her property to her sons and daughters if they were in the *potestas* of their father. If the sum was large and the father as unscrupulous as M. Regulus at the time of the younger Pliny, he at once emancipated his son when he was placed in this predicament, and all was well.[150]

Unmarried people and women without children were free to dispose of their property as they wished; hence the *captatores*, the pestering fawners and flatterers, who had at least ensured that the sufferings of wealthy old age should not include loneliness.

Others beside relatives and friends had a deep interest in the will: the household slaves, for whom there was the hope of manumission (see pp.113f). The slave manumitted by testament, unlike the slave freed in his master's lifetime, normally lost his *peculium*.

IV

WORK AND LEISURE

1. Work; Life in the Sun

THE TRADITION of public service, *negotia publica*,[1] was an inheritance of the aristocracy in Rome's best days and was quickly absorbed by the *parvenu* as soon as he entered the Roman governing class.

Public service embraced a variety of skills such as no single career in any modern state includes. In the course of his career the active and successful senator was called on to practise as a young barrister in Rome, to do military service as a junior officer, to discharge, in various magistracies, a number of complicated administrative functions in the capital, to sit as a judge in court, to understand public finance, to govern provinces, sometimes to command large armies in war—and all through his life, when he was in Rome, to share in the Roman government, a politician and, at the best, a statesman. Rome demanded a large professional versatility from its essentially amateur governing class.

In the Empire a junior branch of the public service developed for men of certain means (400,000 sesterces, as against the senator's compulsory 1,000,000), the Equites. This too embraced a variety of talents, sometimes in combination: a skilful understanding, again, of public finance, military ability (the Equites commanded the auxiliary units of the Roman army, the praetorian guard in Rome and the legions in Egypt) and administrative talent of a high order (the Equites provided the governors of Egypt and also of a large number of minor provinces).

By the exalted notions of the republican aristocracy paid employment was servile and money-making was sordid. A gentleman's landed property produced an income to satisfy his needs and until the second century B.C. those needs were not large. His public service was unremunerated. The law—the *lex Claudia* of 218 B.C.—forbade him, if he was a senator, to trade.[2]

130

Other men, less fortunate, needed or wished to increase their means and devoted a lifetime to the purpose. At the start of his book on agriculture (always a respectable occupation) in the second century B.C. Cato wrote, 'There is more money to be made in commerce—but at a risk.* There is more to be made in money-lending, but no gentleman would be a money-lender' ('*si tam honestum sit*'). Cato would have approved of Bacon's 'The ways to enrich are many, and most of them foul.' In Plautus' *Trinummus* Lysicles, in enquiring how a fortune has been lost, lists the different fields of the businessman: contracting for the State, commerce, slave-dealing.[3]

When in the second century B.C. Rome adopted the more luxurious standards of living which prevailed among the rich in the Hellenistic world, prominent Romans needed, and acquired a greater appetite for, wealth. For the senatorial proconsul provincial administration and big wars were a new means to supply a private fortune, however corruptly. For the contractor, tax-farming in the provinces offered the chance of disproportionate profits, and quickly developed ancillary avenues to wealth, banking and money-lending. And for the speculator of whatever class huge money was to be made at home in ranching, which developed in Italy in the second century and put to shame the smaller gains to be made from arable farming. Asked the best way to make money in land, Cato said, 'Own a good ranch'. What second? 'Own a fair ranch.' What third? 'Own a ranch.' What fourth? 'Own a poor ranch.'[4] And with such fortunes to be made by any Roman or Italian who had money—it need not be his own—to start with and with bad debts, however unjustly incurred, to be honoured by the provincial subject, there were queues at the doors of the money-lenders. Indeed persons of the highest standing in the late Republic—Cicero, Caesar, Brutus—lent and borrowed money, though they would have eschewed comparison of themselves with professional money-lenders. With their capital tied up (as, for safety, all capital in antiquity was tied up) in real estate, land or house property, and with no such economic system as the modern world enjoys with banks that lend money against security and pay interest on deposit, the money-lender provided a vital service.†

Obsessed though Cicero was by the superiority of public service, he

* Trimalchio could have agreed, who lived to be worth thirty million sesterces, but at his first adventure in trading bankrupted himself by the loss of ships and cargo worth as much (Petron., *Sat.* 71; 76).

† Just as in the early nineteenth century a man in financial difficulty often requested a friend to sign a bill against some future date.

admitted that there were other professions and occupations (*negotia privata*) in which men worked hard to earn a living. He divided them into two categories, according to their respectability.[5]

The higher sort called for more than average intelligence, '*prudentia maior*', and had the great merit of contributing usefully to the welfare of society: the professions of the doctor, the architect and the teacher. These were respectable, but only for people of a certain social class, '*iis quorum ordini conveniunt*'. It was not from delicacy that Cicero did not write, 'but only for slaves and freedmen'; his readers will have understood what he meant.

Architects, in fact, whose profession was a profitable one, were generally Greeks, and so were doctors, the medical profession being one for which the Roman was too heavy-handed; he had too much *gravitas*.

Not everybody shared Cicero's respect for doctors. In a long and choleric passage the elder Pliny abused them as roundly in the first century A.D. as the elder Cato, who dosed his own family, had abused them more than two centuries earlier: they were always changing their modes of treatment; they made far too large fortunes; 'they learnt at the expense of their patients, experimented at the cost of their patients' lives and, unlike the ordinary man, could get away with murder.' The emperor Tiberius lived to a great age and enjoyed excellent health; the fact that he never consulted a doctor did not go unnoticed.[6]

In Greece the profession had been reserved for free men, and in republican and imperial Rome there were such doctors. If the profession was commonly held in poor esteem, that was because the majority of doctors in Rome, men like Antonius Musa, who cured Augustus and almost immediately killed Augustus' son-in-law Marcellus by his cold water cure, were freedmen or slaves, most of them poorly qualified quacks. They had picked up the elements of medicine by acting as assistants to qualified doctors—Martial's statement that his doctor Symmachus was accompanied by a hundred pupils on his private rounds may have been an exaggeration—or they had attended short courses of instruction given by doctors. It is a good commentary on their training that, while the length of an apprenticeship in weaving in Egypt, as we know from papyri, was never less than twelve months, the notorious Thessalus of Tralles at the time of Nero professed himself able to turn a young slave into a trained doctor in six months. It may well have been this kind of crash-course to which Domitian was objecting when he cancelled the fiscal privileges given by his father to doctors and teachers, if their pupils were found to be slaves and not free. And this act of Domitian may help to explain the fact that in the second century A.D. we hear more in literature of fully qualified doctors like Galen, who studied for eleven years before he practised, and less of the imperfectly trained slave—or freedman—practitioner. The doctors known to us from inscriptions, however, were mostly freedmen. They include specialists—oculists, for instance—and they also include women doctors.[7]

Teachers were graded: at the bottom the elementary school master, at the top the teacher of rhetoric and, a little below him, the grammar school master (*grammaticus**). The middle and lower ranks of the profession, the *grammatici* and the elementary school masters, were largely recruited from Greeks, slaves or freedmen; though some teachers came from the Italian country towns and from Spain and Gaul. From the time of Augustus teachers of rhetoric were generally free-born Romans.

With a few notable exceptions, teachers were badly paid,† and ended their often extremely long lives—for then, as now, the profession encouraged longevity—in abject poverty. In the Empire they received some alleviation from Vespasian in that, with doctors, they received certain tax rebates—to the considerable annoyance of municipal authorities, who were responsible for much of the tax-collection and, as the Empire floundered to its collapse, had to make good any deficit from their own pockets. This was the concession which Domitian cancelled in the case of those whose pupils were slaves.

The elementary schoolmaster was universally despised. *Grammatici* and teachers of rhetoric had greater pretensions to scholarship and their writings were often published, commentaries—often very arid commentaries—on classical texts or on philology in the first case, *suasoriae and controversiae*‡ in the second. In Rome itself many, particularly in the last century of the Republic, were remembered and became the subjects of anecdote because of the subsequent public distinction of those who had been their pupils. In the Empire a *grammaticus* might rise to hold the important post of librarian in one of the

---

* On schools, see pp. 94–7.

† Notable exceptions were Verrius Flaccus, who taught Augustus' grandsons and earned 100,000 sesterces a year and Q. Remmius Palaemon in the early Empire, who earned 400,000 (Suet., *Gram.* 17; 23). Under Vespasian, Quintilian received 2,000 sesterces a year per pupil (Juv. 7, 186f.). Under Diocletian's wage freeze of A.D. 301, when the sesterce was worth far less (Edict vii), an elementary teacher received 200 sesterces per pupil per month, a *grammaticus* 800, a *rhetor* 1,000. The preferential scale for the *rhetor* as against the *grammaticus* was preserved, even enhanced, in the fourth century A.D. (*CT* 13, 3, 11).

‡ On which, see p. 100 above.

great public libraries, the Palatine library or that in the portico of Octavia. And when two professional chairs of rhetoric were established at Rome by Vespasian, and one of rhetoric and four of philosophy in Athens by M. Aurelius, their holders were prominent and distinguished scholars. Quintilian was the first to hold the chair of Latin Rhetoric in Rome.

For anyone who had tutored a prince, from Nero's tutor Seneca in the first century, through Fronto, who failed to make an orator out of M. Aurelius in the second, to Ausonius, the tutor of Gratian in the fourth, there was the prospect of the highest distinction in public life. Consulships were in store for such favoured ex-tutors.[8]

Cicero's list of the types of employment which were utterly discreditable embraced the activity of the tax-collector and of the professional money-lender (in whose favour nobody ever spoke), the manual worker, the middle-man in business, the mechanic (*opifex*) and, towards the bottom of the list, people to whom he and his friends owed the delicious food that they ate—the butcher, the cook, the poulterer, the fishmonger and even the man who caught the fish. Below this came those who dealt in scent and who danced on the stage.

The discredited tax-collector was the man whose hands were dirtied by the sordid collection of people's taxes. The higher executive of the great tax-farming companies, who were Equites, could not be so sweepingly condemned; after all, a relative of Cicero by marriage was highly placed in the tax collection of Bithynia.[9] And, as for the servitude of employment, by the end of the first and the beginning of the second centuries A.D. Equites were prepared to accept employment as heads of the great departments of the imperial household (*a rationibus*, *ab epistulis* etc.) which, involving subservience to the Emperor as employer, had previously been thought suitable only for freedmen.

Even in the most rigidly conservative societies, wealth and success can cover a multitude of sins; and Cicero exempted from his general condemnation the business man who operated on a big enough scale and amassed large profits—such men, no doubt, as those whose interests he commended unblushingly in letters to his friends who governed provinces; for their profits were likely to be invested in land, and the successful trader might retire to set up as a country squire. Agriculture (farming your own land) was always a creditable occupation. This, in Petronius' *Satyricon*, was the achievement of Trimalchio, who had started life as a slave.[10]

Not that the working class, the shopkeepers and the others on whom

society depended for its very existence, would have been greatly dis-
tressed by Cicero's strictures, had they been literate and leisured
enough to read them. Their monuments and epitaphs which survive
in large numbers, often with reliefs in which the carver has portrayed
them at work, indicate a robust pride and satisfaction in the work by
which they earned their livings, such as scarcely survives in epitaphs
from eighteenth and nineteenth century Europe. One would be surprised indeed to find in a churchyard the gravestone of a man of whom
it was recorded that he had been a good pork-butcher in the High
Street.

Among Romans you will not find an epitaph of a gladiatorial
trainer (*lanista*), though you will find plenty of epitaphs of gladiators.
Nor will you find the epitaph of a slave-dealer, *mango* (though there
was one who did not blush to mention his trade in erecting a dedication
on the Great St. Bernard in thanksgiving for a safe crossing of the Alps,
perhaps with a contingent of his human merchandise); and obviously
you will not find a pimp (*leno*). He, like the gladiatorial trainer, was
disqualified from holding municipal office by Caesar's law. Auctioneers
and undertakers suffered the same disqualification, but only as long as
they were in practice (just as publicans may not be Justices of the
Peace in England). An auctioneer may not have enjoyed great esteem,
but he generally made a lot of money.

For the rest, there are few occupations which are not proudly recorded in surviving epitaphs: bathmen, barbers, dry-cleaners, veterinary surgeons, shopkeepers of every kind, bootmakers, jewellers,
workers in linen, wool and silk, carpenters, painters, candlestick-
makers, stone-cutters, shorthand-writers, organ-builders and a variety
of others.* Often the address of their premises is recorded, their rise
from slavery or poverty (the champion reaper, for instance, from
North Africa, who became a town-councillor and a rich man), the
happiness of their married life and the exemplary standard of their
business integrity.[11]

Trimalchio positively flaunted his slave origin. As soon as you
entered the hall of his villa, you were confronted by a fresco on which
his education in book-keeping was depicted.[12]

---

* Compare the occupations listed in Diocletian's prices—and wage—freeze of A.D. 301
(*Edict* vii, xx, xxif., xxx, xxxi): farm-workers and veterinary surgeons, brickmakers,
builders and decorators, blacksmiths, bakers, shipwrights, drivers, barbers, metal-
workers, water-carriers, polishers, scribes, tailors, teachers, barristers, bath-attendants,
gold- and silver-smiths, dry-cleaners, textile-workers of all kinds.

2. Leisure; Life in the Shade

Public life was hard, competitive, often dangerous; and it gave little opportunity for relaxation. Cicero declared that in the time of his active public life he never took a siesta. 'Even in my spare time I never relaxed. At the games and festivals I was busy writing speeches,' just as, even at the public games, Julius Caesar and M. Aurelius later spent time poring over official papers. This was in the tradition. Had not the elder Cato said that a great man was accountable for every moment of his spare time as much as for every moment of his working day?[13]

Public life was 'life in the sun', and in Mediterranean countries the sun in summer is merciless and beats hard on those who are exposed to it. It is an enemy, not a friend.

The Mediterranean shade, on the other hand, is a kind refuge; 'life in the shade' is an easier, less exposed life. But by the severest Roman standards there was, for men of any social standing, a certain weakness in preferring the shade, in shrinking from exposure to the sun.

The active politician, the soldier and the administrator lived in the sun and the dust. The soldier's scorn for the civilian was contempt for the man who lived in the shade. In Plautus' *Curculio* the soldier who has been let down by his banker says, 'What is the good of my making kings my servants if I am to be mocked by this shady character, this *umbraticus*?'[14]

The orator, too, lived in the sun; his active life was contrasted favourably with the lives of those who, possessing his talents, chose or were forced to exercise them less pugnaciously, whether by teaching rhetoric to the young or becoming jurisconsults, men who sat in chambers and gave counsel's opinion. 'If you can't play the cithera you learn the flute; if you can't make an orator, you become a jurisconsult.' Teachers of rhetoric and consultant legal specialists lived in the shade—like athletes who trained, but never entered for championships.[15]

'Life in the shade'—the *vita umbratilis*,[16] the cloistered life, which was a form of *otium*—was always a second-best life. The choice of such a life, the pursuit of *tranquillitas*[17] or *quies*, might in certain circumstances be excusable: if your health did not enable you to face the rigour and strain of a political, administrative or military career, or if you had the misfortune to live at a time when 'liberty and the state failed'. Under a despotism or a tyranny, for instance, it might be better to live in retirement than to cooperate as a servant in a corrupt régime.[18]

So much would be agreed generally. For the rest, Stoicism laid it down as a man's duty to engage himself publicly in the service of his community unless he was debarred by some impediment; Epicureanism, on the other hand, recommended against a public career, unless there was some singular and compelling reason why a man should take it up.

Virtue was the Stoic's aim, Pleasure the Epicurean's—true pleasure, which the virtuous life alone embodied. But by opponents of Epicureanism the concept was travestied. Virtue was 'tall, royal, invincible, tireless; you could find her in temples, in the forum, in the senate house, guarding the walls, dusty, sunburnt and with hands calloused.' Pleasure, on the other hand, was 'humble, servile, weak, decrepit; her stand and habitation the arches'—where prostitutes hung about—'and cook shops.' Pleasure was to be seen, more often than not, 'slinking away, hiding in the dark, round the baths and sweat-chambers and places which lived in fear of the police—soft, nerveless, saturated with drink and perfumes, pallid or rouged.'[19]

The Epicurean retorted that the life which he advocated was not spineless or inactive; that man was the citizen of two societies, of the Universe and of his particular community (whose service was a matter of rushing about and getting into a sweat, *discursus et sudor*).[20] The philosopher in his retired (shady) life lived as a citizen of the Universe.

Still, in the general opinion, Stoicism belonged to the sun; about Epicureanism there was something not a little shady.

Cicero wrote, 'We may perhaps excuse men for not going into politics if they are exceptionally clever and have devoted themselves to scholarship, or if bad health or some more serious reason still has led them to withdraw from public life . . . but so far from regarding it as praiseworthy, we should, I think consider it discreditable if, without any such excuse, they simply profess to despise a career in the army and politics, which most people admire. In that they despise and think little of public distinction, it is hard not to commend their judgement, but it looks as if, in fact, they are frightened of the work and the trouble and of making enemies and of being defeated at the polls, as if this involved something discreditable.'[21]

As the Empire advanced, an increasing number of men, alerted by the examples of those commoners for whom distinction in public life was the prelude to catastrophe, refrained from the risks of a senatorial career, and instead chose the safety (*quies*) of non-administrative equestrian life, largely as country landowners.[22] When in the third century Gallienus debarred senators from holding commissions in the army and later when they were all but excluded from provincial administration, the senator's career was less exposed to danger and the Senate itself lapsed into a body little different from a town council, unconcerned with such problems of empire as the formidable self-assertion of the soldiery as a sovereign power. 'Revelling in their relegation (*otium*), terrified for their riches, the enjoyment of whose abundance they rate higher than eternal life, they opened up a broad highway for the army (which was practically barbarian) to power over themselves and their successors.'[23] The sun had gone in, and even the senator's life had turned shady.

Nobody's life could be more shady than a writer's, above all a poet's. Curiatius Maternus came under attack in Tacitus' *Dialogus*: a man with the virile gifts of an orator and an administrator, who turned his back on public life and preferred to write poetry.[24]

Writing seriously about serious subjects—history, oratory, philosophy even—was more creditable, and this was how Cicero consoled himself for his relegation from public life. He wrote three important books, including the *De Republica*, between 52 and 50 B.C., and eighteen between 46 and 44, on political theory, general philosophy, oratory and religion. He was certainly not unconscious of the literary heritage that he would bequeath to posterity, and from the point of view of the late Roman, the medieval and the modern world it is a piece of priceless good fortune that he should have been edged out of politics and forced to employ his pen.

But Cicero did not think so.[25] He has made it very clear indeed that he viewed writing (other than polishing up his political and forensic speeches for publication) as a poor substitute for playing an active part in public affairs.[26]

Sallust despised farming[27] as much as Cicero in his heart of hearts may well have despised it (for Cicero wrote no dialogue on the subject of agriculture and much of the sentimental panegyric of farming which the elder Cato was made to deliver in Cicero's *De Senectute* would, if he had heard it, have made that sturdy and practical old farmer wince).[28] Sallust devoted his retirement to writing history. He defended his change of life, but there is a certain hollowness in the bravado with which he did so: 'Now that I have decided to abandon public life, I have no doubt that, in respect of the important and useful work to which I have turned, I shall be dubbed work-shy (*iners*), certainly by those whose idea of hard work is toadying to the proletariat and canvassing by means of dinner parties.' This has not a little of the taste of sour grapes.

Historians, of course, had their critics. For Juvenal they were 'spineless people who enjoyed lying on their backs out of the sun'— '*genus ignavum quod lecto gaudet et umbra*'. Polybius had criticized Timaeus on this very ground, that he spent all his time in libraries. It was the 'bookish' historian who was condemned and it was to avoid this criticism that so many historians, like Polybius, went out of their way to emphasize the fact that their research had not been bookish at all, but conducted in the harsh glare of the sun, in travelling to see places (always a dangerous and expensive process), and that they had acquired their qualifications as historians the hard way, by lives spent in politics, even on the battlefield.[29]

If you did not possess the original talent of an author, you could none the less give a good account of yourself in the shade—'*humaniter vivere*'—by devoting your time to study, as long as it was the right kind of study. Of this type of life Seneca wrote much, advocating the study of philosophy. In studying philosophy a man brought the great philosophers of the past into his own home. He adopted them into his family and, whereas in ordinary life he might disapprove of the parents whom, by no choice of his own, Nature had given him, in his studies he could give himself new and distinguished parents, parents of his own choosing. If he called on them, as at the daily *salutatio*, they were not asleep but awake, glad to receive him. If he conversed with them, there were no eavesdropping spies listening in.[30]

Philosophy, as Seneca envisaged it, embraced metaphysics and, indeed, the physical study of the Universe—geography and a great deal of what we should call natural science.[31]

Pure academic scholarship, on the other hand, he despised as having no useful purpose.[32] Indeed, if Seneca were alive today and called on to formulate a curriculum to be followed in a new university, he would certainly exclude literature and history and propose a course which was a combination of philosophy and natural science.

The practical value of moral philosophy was that it taught a man to live (in the sense of making the best possible use of every second of his life) and how to die (in the sense of accepting the fact of death, not fearing, but perhaps looking forward to, the moment of its coming). Philosophy taught him to be self-dependent for the whole richness of existence, to escape servitude to Fortune, which was the concomitant of worldly ambition and worldly wealth and greatness. For the rich man, the man of importance in public affairs, stood on a treacherous platform which might be snatched away at any moment from under his feet. The philosopher was not beguiled by the worldliness of human ambition.

This noble doctrine had, of course, to be accommodated to the facts of real life—and there were critics, men like Quintilian, who said openly that philosophy could be counterfeited. Seneca himself was, by the standards of the times, a millionaire. So, if you were rich, he explained, you accepted the fact, but you did not base your happiness on it. You would survive as a contented philosopher even if the basis of your riches was swept away.[33] And if some critic charged you with living a useless life, you pointed to the great philosophers of the past and retorted, 'Have their lives and writings, a constant inspiration to posterity, been useless?' On the contrary, they might seem to have devoted the fruits of their 'retirement' to the service of those engaged in public life.

Some education in philosophy was indispensable to the orator, who was by the elder Cato's definition 'a good man, skilled in speaking' ('*vir bonus dicendi peritus*'), for moral goodness is not an inborn quality; it has to be taught. So the budding orator had to go to the philosopher for this part of his education, and Cicero and Quintilian alike deplored the fact that, from Socrates onwards, philosophy had parted company from public affairs; it had left the sun and chosen the umbrageous part. Quintilian, indeed, hoped for a time when philosophy would once again come out into the sun, when the same man would combine the qualities of a distinguished philosopher and a distinguished orator, and so the student of rhetoric would go to one master, not two.[34]

There were two charges which a man in prominent society must be careful to avoid. The first was *luxus*, self-indulgence. The second was *inertia*, idleness—*iners otium*. This was the criticism which Sallust anticipated, and tried to parry, when he left politics to become a historian. It was a charge which had evidently been made against Atticus. *Inertia*, fatally seductive, habit-forming to its devotees, was the opposite of *industria*; and it was a bad thing that a man should not be working at something. Sallust claimed that writing history, so far from being a form of idleness, was substantial and useful work (*tantus tamque utilis labor*).[35] When Tiberius poured cold water on Claudius' aspirations to a career in public life (*dignitas*), and Claudius turned for companionship to the dregs of society, this was *iners otium*.[36] The loathsome P. Suillius insulted Seneca's reputable studies in public, calling them '*studia inertia*'.[37] Indeed, the lesson of Agricola's career, heavily underlined by Tacitus, was that even under bad emperors a man could do valuable public service, if he combined self-effacing loyalty with a strong will to work (*industria ac vigor*).[38]

When chaffed or charged with *inertia*, a man put a bold face on his chosen way of living; he called it the pursuit of *quies* or *tranquillitas*. And Romans were not complete prigs. It was impossible to withhold admiration, however grudging, from men in responsible positions who made exhibitions of themselves as idle wasters, effeminate men like Maecenas under Augustus, devotees of *somnus et inertia* like Sallustius Crispus, the great-nephew and adopted son of the historian, under Tiberius. Both had declined senatorial careers; yet when the need arose, both proved alert, intelligent, capable of hard thinking and of resolute action.[39] And there was L. Calpurnius Piso, the Pontifex, Prefect of the City under Tiberius for eighteen years, 'who often spent the whole night at a party and stayed in bed until midday—yet discharged his onerous duties admirably', as even Seneca admitted, just as he admitted that a successor of Piso as Prefect of the City, Cossus Cornelius Lentulus, a responsible man, whose discretion Tiberius trusted more than he trusted the discretion of any of his ministers, once arrived in the Senate so drunk that he had to be carried home.[40]

Life in the shade could, of course, be a very discreditable existence indeed if it was devoted to nothing better than self-indulgence, in particular lust and the satisfaction of the belly.[41] Cicero was loud in his disparagement of libertines. Their exemplar was that protégé of Sulla, L. Lucullus for, after his eastern campaigns, Lucullus as good as retired from public life to the shocking enjoyment of his villa,[42] whose very existence was an offence against nature: he built out on to the sea, and channelled sluices through the rock to bring the sea into the land. Nothing so titillates the virtuous as the viciousness of others; and there is a pleasing story of Cicero's inquisitiveness (and Pompey's) as to the style in which Lucullus lived when he was by himself at home, not entertaining others. They met him, and invited themselves to dinner. Lucullus prepared to send for a slave, but they stopped him, saying that they simply wanted to take 'pot luck', and to discover how he dined when he was alone. 'But,' he answered, 'you must at least allow me to tell the servants that I have guests?' They agreed. So he summoned a slave and said, 'I have two guests, and we will dine in the Apollo room.' It was an understood thing in his house, though strangers did not know it, that when Lucullus dined in the Apollo room the most extravagant imaginable dinner was to be served, a meal costing not less than 200,000 sesterces.[43]

The progress of the moneyed Roman rake was no different from any other rake's progress and his vices, sententiously underlined by our self-righteous sources, were monotonously uniform. He ate too much, he drank too much, he whored too much.[44] He spent too much time asleep; in an observation of the elder Cato, which did not stale with repetition, he never saw the sun rise and he never saw it set.[45]

This was the life of the libertine, of T. Petronius under Nero, of Elagabalus—also, in the early Empire, of a man called Buta, who gave plenty of exercise to the wit of the eques Varus who, when a tedious poet recited his stilted description of sunrise, exclaimed, 'Ah, Buta's bedtime'. It was the life of Sextus Papinius, who practised singing at midnight, ordered his carriage at two in the morning, shouted loudly for his servants to bring dinner just before dawn and for anybody but the good-tempered was an insufferable neighbour. We hear about these men. There were probably not many of them.[46]

Men who were no philosophers made no secret of their venial weaknesses. Man was weak, prone to enjoyment, as a favourite scribbling in the Roman baths admitted:

> *Balnea vina Venus corrumpunt corpora nostra,*
> *At vitam faciunt balnea, vina, Venus.*

Baths, drink and mating are disintegrating;
Yet what is living but baths, drink and mating?

There is a comparable inscription from Timgad, done by someone who could not manage his aspirates* (like many other people in North Africa, to judge from Augustine's bitterness on the subject):

> *Venari lavari ludere ridere occest vivere*

Hunt, bathe, gamble, laugh—ave a good life.[47]

For self-indulgence was not a failing of the upper classes alone. Trimalchio could take on any aristocrat at his own game and beat him.[48]

Seneca tells us what he regards as a shocking story of a certain Vatia, the last descendant of a distinguished family of the late Republic.[49]

---

* But cf. p. 158 for this *genre* of inscription.

This man inherited a luxurious villa in Campania, from which he never emerged, his life—as people believed—wholly devoted to gluttony, sleep and lust. The ordinary man—not Seneca himself—as he passed, would sigh with envy and say, 'Vatia is the only man alive who knows how to live.'

But dissolute worldliness for Seneca was wider than the simple catalogue of natural appetites; its victims embraced collectors of expensive *objets d'art* (Corinthian plate, an alloy of gold, silver and copper, of which Trimalchio boasted in the *Satyricon* that he had a prize collection), coin collectors, men interested in athletes, dandies (particularly dandies who spent long hours at the barber's), musical enthusiasts, people who played games and sunbathed and even people (like the emperor Tiberius) who enjoyed literary or historical quizzes.[50]

The trouble about philosophy has always been that at some stage or other it parts company with common sense. And Seneca's thunderings against even the simplest and most innocent kinds of pleasure have not unreasonably prompted the suggestion that he railed jealously at certain pleasures for no other reason than that they were pleasures which he was constitutionally debarred from sharing with other people.

Dinner parties are not what I should call periods of relaxation, considering the anxiety which attends the laying out of the silver, the fuss made over ensuring that the pansy waiters have got their dress exactly right, the concern over the state in which the cook serves up the boar, the frenzy with which at a given sign the young waiters scuttle about their various duties, the skill with which the birds are carved into small slices, the way in which the unfortunate page boys keep their eyes skinned to clear up the mess where any of the drunken guests has been sick.[51]

To judge from Seneca, there was never a dinner party at which people were not sick. Not without reason has it been conjectured that he was a gastric neurasthenic, that he hated good food (which other people so much enjoyed) because he had a queasy stomach.[52]

The best possible contrast between the creditable and discreditable forms of 'shady life' is that between the manner in which Tiberius in fact spent his time when he was living on Capri in the last ten years of his principate and the stories which circulated about the depravities in which he indulged. Tiberius' constant companion on Capri was the astrologer Thrasyllus, whom he had known intimately for over thirty years, a man who, so far from being a charlatan, was both a scholar and a philosopher[53]; he also took with him the most distinguished legal consultant of the age, M. Cocceius Nerva, ex-consul, water-controller in Rome, grandfather of the future emperor. And there were a number of literary men, chiefly Greeks, chosen as being good conversationalists.[54] Meanwhile vulgar persons, Neapolitans in chief perhaps, imagining how with all the wealth and opportunity of an emperor they would be amusing themselves in the solitude of Capri, pictured an orgy of depraved lust and declared this to be the Emperor's daily life. Their stories might even have had a ring of possibility if the Emperor had been as young and virile as they were, instead of being a tired old man in his seventies.[55]

3. Relaxation

No society has ever existed in which there were not people, particularly young people, who did not know what to do with their spare time. The earliest expression of this dilemma in Roman literature was by the chorus of Q. Ennius' *Iphigenia* in the early second century B.C.: 'A man who does not know how to use his spare time has more trouble than when it is his troublesome work that he is troubled by . . . Look at us now. We're neither at home nor at the war. We go here, and we go there, and once we get there, we want to turn back. We drift about aimlessly. It's being half-alive, not alive at all.'[56]

Oscar Wilde in his plays made capital of the fact that boredom is a congenital disease of the upper class in a society which has little else to pursue but its own amusement; and critical observers of the upper range of Roman society, satirists and moralists alike, flayed this quality which in the late Republic and early Empire made havoc of the lives of many men (and women too) who enjoyed easy circumstances in Rome. When at the end of his life Seneca was in a mood to urge men to turn their backs on public life, he emphasized its hollowness. Politicians fought for power and, having achieved it, discovered that power too was hollow. They rose to hold the consulship even; then, bored with its duties, longed only for the day when they would relinquish office. Other great men have had the same experience in other societies.[57]

But the boredom against which the moralists chiefly railed was the boredom of men who not only had nothing to do, but were bored with themselves and with everything around them. So we have lively pictures of those who believed pathetically that a change of scene would provide them with a stimulus and a cure, not realizing that their disease was a part of themselves, something that they carried with them wherever they went.[58]

He does not know what he wants and is always seeking a change of scene, as if by this means he could rid himself of some burden. Bored at home, he opens the door of his great *palazzo* and goes out—then is back again, because he feels no better outside than at home. He drives like a madman to his house in the country, with not a moment to spare, as if it was on fire and he was coming to help. He arrives—yawns or falls sound asleep, seeking oblivion that way; or else, in a fever, he rushes back to Rome.

If only he would study philosophy, he would be cured; so Lucretius.[59]

Seneca likewise:

People set out on journeys with no particular objective in view. They wander down the coast. In a purposeless way they go by sea, they go by land, always wishing that they were doing something else. 'Let us go to Campania.' 'No, smart resorts are a bore; rough country is the thing to see. Let us go to Bruttium and see the ranches in Lucania.' Once in the bush, they must find a nice resort; after the extensive tedium of these uncultivated districts, something civilized is needed for their cultured gaze to feed on. 'Let us go to Taranto. People are always talking about its harbour and its splendid winter climate' . . . 'No, let us go back to Rome.' It seems a lifetime since they last heard the applause and din of the games. 'It might be rather nice, too, to see somebody killed.'[60]

For Seneca too, philosophy is the cure.

There was yet another disease from which society suffered, an unexpected form of *inertia—strenua inertia*. This was the disease of men whose escape from the boredom of their own company (for only a philosopher was capable of relishing and profiting from *solitudo*) was to steal a leaf from the good man whose life was absorbed in *negotia* (preferably the *negotia* of public life), and always to be busy, never to have a moment to spare. This was *occupatio*, but *desidiosa occupatio*. Its exponents were '*occupati*'; and this was not a flattering term. They turned futility into a full-time occupation:

If you meet one of these men coming out of a house, and ask, 'Hullo, what are you up to?', he will answer, 'I'm hanged if I know.

10

But I shall be seeing some people, I shall have something to do.' . . . .
Their progress is purposeless and futile as that of an ant which climbs
to the top of a tree and then climbs down again empty. You will see
people rushing as if there was a fire, and you will feel sorry for them
for on the way they push other people aside, knock them over and even
fall flat themselves. In fact they are simply in a hurry to say good-
morning to somebody who will not say good-morning back. Or
they are on their way to join the funeral procession of a man whom
they have never met; or to the courts to the case of a man who is
perpetually litigating; or to attend the wedding party of a man who
gets married every other day. They will walk beside a litter and even
carry it some part of the way. Then they return home, worn out by
this futile exhaustion and swear that they cannot think why they ever
went out at all, or where they have been. And yet tomorrow they will
follow exactly the same course.[61]

These frenzied attempts to kill boredom were indications of a neu-
rosis to which the educated man falls victim more easily than the uneducated. Associated with it was an anxiety-complex (in Greek,
athumia) to which a number of people of the upper classes in the
hazardous political life of the late Roman Republic and early Empire
were understandably subject; and the affliction evidently assailed a wider
class still. Lucretius' poem is alone in suggesting that fear of an after-
life, of punishment after death, was in pagan Rome a vital constituent
of this alarm. In Seneca and in Plutarch, both of whom wrote essays
on the subject, it is defined in no such clear terms, but is a general
malaise, fear of what may happen in life itself, disillusion with a man's
achievement and surroundings, inability to appreciate to the full the
good things which exist already, in every man's possession. 'Do not
overlook the blessings that are common to all; we should rejoice that
we are alive, that we are well, that there is peace and freedom to till
our land and sail the seas, to speak and not to speak, to work or to be
idle. Imagine the opposite of these, and you will see what blessings
they are.' This was the achievement of *tranquillitas*, of *euthumia*.[62]

There were many people, of course, whose psychological disturbance
was not to be adjusted so easily by the smooth reasonableness of the
philosopher; and these were the people who sought comfort and ad-
justment, indeed excitement, in the oriental and mystery cults, whose
success indicated a growing spiritual anxiety which the orthodox
religion of Rome neither recognized nor catered for. Christianity, with

the very promise of an after-life—and this might have surprised Lucretius—brought the greatest comfort and assurance of all, spreading fast in the late second and third centuries A.D. at a time when the blessings of ordinary everyday life which, on Plutarch's prescription, a man only needed to appreciate in order to be happy, had either disappeared or were in close prospect of disappearance.[63]

It would be a mistake, however, to think of the streets, the *fora* and the baths of Rome and of cities in the Roman world in the late Republic and early Empire as filled by men and women who were either yawning from boredom or frenzied automatons in unrewarding pursuit of a change of air. Such people were known only within their small society. Members of that society and the hangers-on who wrote for its edification or amusement mocked or abused abnormality according to their natures, whether they were satirists or moralists.

Most people had serious business on hand, whether it was in public life or, at a lower level, in coping with the economics of survival; and hard-working men need relaxation, though some, like Marcus Aurelius, are so foolish as to think that they have not the time for it. 'Nature herself does not allow a man to work continuously without a break,' Valerius Maximus wrote; and in Cicero's *De Oratore* L. Crassus, who at first playfully shied from the idea of participation in a serious dialogue in highly gifted and critical company as being too strenuous a form of relaxation, said, 'A man does not seem to me to be free unless every now and then he is completely idle.' What more splendidly active men ever lived than Scipio Africanus and Laelius? And what did they do in their spare time? They walked on the seashore and picked up shells.[64]

Festivals were invented, Seneca wrote, for the sake of relaxation. Sensible men, he declared, were aware of the necessity for relaxation. There were those who took a day off every month. Others made it a habit never to work (not even to open letters) after a certain hour of the day, Asinius Pollio never after four o'clock in the afternoon.[65]

Few people's working life can have been the unremitting servitude which Seneca describes as the fate of Polybius, the legal secretary (*a cognitionibus*) of the emperor Claudius: 'You can never stay in bed of a morning. You can never escape from the rush of business and take a peaceful holiday in the country; worn out by the uninterrupted discharge of your laborious duties, you cannot relax by taking a pleasure-tour or forget everything in enjoying the varied entertainment of the games. Your life is not your own.' Yet, some time or other, this over-worked man found the leisure to translate Homer into Latin and Virgil into Greek.[66]

Escape from the town to the country offered the most satisfactory relaxation to those who had the time and the means. In the country a man could relax, if rest was what he needed. Or he could ride or fish or hunt.*

For educated men, whether they lived in Rome or resided in the country or were abroad on public service, great relaxation was to be found in reading.

A persistent curiosity is the mark of an educated mind. In the culti-vated society of the late Republic the dialogues and letters of Cicero reflect this curiosity—about history, the law, ethics, religion, literature; and curiosity, now something more pedantic, marks the educated world of the Empire, from Varro and Verrius Flaccus, a freedman who taught Augustus' grandsons, through Aulus Gellius in the second century to Macrobius at the end of the fourth.

Educated men had their own private libraries.[67] They bought books from the book-shops and they borrowed books from one another; and their interests acquired a fillip from the excellent public libraries which came into existence during the Empire in Rome and in all considerable towns.

In Rome in the fourth century A.D. there were twenty-nine libraries. Eight are well known to us. Five of these were the great foundations of the early principate: Pollio's in the Atrium Libertatis, Augustus' two, in the temple of Apollo on the Palatine and in the Porticus of Octavia by the theatre of Marcellus, the library of the temple of Divine Augustus below the Palatine and that in the Domus Tiberiana on it. Later came Vespasian's library in the Forum Pacis and the great Bibliotheca Ulpia flanking the court of Trajan's Forum; and, later still, the library on the Capitol. They suffered heavily from fires, particu-larly the two great fires of 80 and 191 A.D.[68]

Literature, inscriptions and the spade attest the existence of libraries in seven country towns of Italy, the best known being that established by the younger Pliny at Comum; at six cities in Greece; at five in Asia Minor, the one at Pergamon going back to Hellenistic times. We know of one in Cyprus, of a number in Alexandria (also Hellenistic) and of two in North Africa, at Carthage and Timgad. They were either given as

* On these diversions see pp. 219–22.

benefactions to their cities by rich individuals or else built at municipal expense, involving a capital outlay at the start and a trust fund for their upkeep—for salaries, repairs and the purchase of new books.* The libraries seem generally to have been in the vicinity of temples, to have been approached through handsome porticoes and, apart from the liberal ornament of busts of famous writers and thinkers, to have contained book-stacks (*armaria*), closed cupboards whose contents were indicated by subject-catalogues, and reading rooms. The very fine library about which, thanks to the archaeologist, we have the best knowledge of all is that built at the time of Trajan at Ephesus by the consular Ti. Iulius Aquila in memory of his consular father, Ti. Iulius Celsus.[69]

You could take books out, as we know from a letter written from the country to Fronto by Marcus Aurelius: 'I have been reading two of the elder Cato's speeches, one "On the property of Pulchra", the other his impeachment of a tribune. "Here, boy," you are shouting, "go as fast as you can to the Library of Apollo, and bring me these two speeches." That's no good, I'm afraid. I have taken the books out, and have them with me here. So you will have to try the librarian of Tiberius' library, and see what a tip will do.' We hear from Aulus Gellius of taking a book out of the library at Tibur (Tivoli). You could even, with permission, take out manuscripts.[70]

You went to a library to browse, or to see if it had a particular book that you wanted to read. If you were a well-known reader, the librarian might bring you a book to show you, as when Aulus Gellius and a friend were in the library of Tiberius and 'a book was brought to us, written by M. Cato Nepos'. Or you might come on an unexpected book as you browsed. So Aulus Gellius, looking for something in Trajan's library, happened on a book containing the edicts of early praetors.

It is improbable that libraries were such havens of silence as the modern reader seeks. The ancients, when they read to themselves, read aloud (Augustine was startled by the fact that Ambrose read to himself in silence). When Gellius went to a library with a friend, they evidently engaged in lively conversation about the books that they read.[71]

Cultured men not only read for relaxation; they also wrote, even translated for amusement from Greek into Latin or from Latin into

---

* At Comum the capital outlay was probably a million sesterces, at Dyrrachium 170,000. At Ephesus the annual allowance for upkeep was 8,000 sesterces, interest at 8% on 100,000; at Comum the interest, probably smaller, on the same sum.

Greek. While serving on Caesar's staff in Gaul, Q. Cicero astonished his brother, no slow writer himself, with the news that he had written four tragedies in sixteen days,[72] and his commander Caesar sought distraction in writing even when on campaign, with extraordinary fertility and success. Apart from the books on his own fighting, he wrote a book on grammatical analogy (*De Analogia*) while crossing the Alps one spring, on his way back from the winter assizes in Cisalpine Gaul to a summer of arduous campaigning—a book which Aulus Gellius could quote two centuries later as an authority on the proper use of Latin words. (You must never say '*inimicitia*', for instance, but always '*inimicitiae*'.[73]) Caesar's retort to other people's eulogies of M. Cato, the 'Anticato', was written when he was fighting the sons of Pompeius Magnus in Spain in 45 B.C. Another book, 'The Journey', was written in twenty-four days, in the course of travelling out to Spain.[74] Most remarkable, as illustration of the literary relaxation of great men, is the story that on the afternoon before the battle of Pharsalus in 48 B.C., while the rest of the republican troops were sound asleep in the sweltering heat, M. Brutus was awake, busily engaged in making an epitome of the voluminous history of Polybius.[75] And, despite his protesting about having no time to relax, M. Aurelius must have derived great satisfaction from turning his back on the corroding anxieties of public life and communing with his own tortured soul as he wrote his *Meditations*.

For the mordant wit entertainment was to be found in the composition of sharply satirical lampoons against leading personalities of the day (and, of course, in publishing them among a close circle of friends). We have specimens in the three outrageously abusive lampoons of Catullus at the expense of Julius Caesar.[76] At the end of his life Augustus objected so strongly to the lampoons of Cassius Severus against a number of leading men and women in Roman society that he made such writing a criminal offence.[77] However, emperors in the Julio-Claudian house were better game, and better material even, than prominent commoners. The lampoonist took risks, enjoyed himself, amused his friends and often, no doubt, got away with it. Sometimes he was denounced by an informer, and exile or death was the penalty.[78] Few men can have had the satisfaction of lampooning an emperor who was already dead and consecrated with the approval of his successor and for the open amusement of the Court. This was Seneca's pleasure when in the *Apokolokyntosis* he described Claudius' rejection from heaven and his subsequent trial and condemnation in Hades.

The younger Pliny was not the man to venture into such dangerous waters (not, of course, that in the virtuous Nerva or Trajan there was anything to criticize); on safer ground he was the prince of scribblers, writing poems of all sorts (in his carriage, in his bath and even at the dinner table).[79] And, if there was no sense in courting danger, there was fun in being naughty, in writing erotic poems. Strait-laced people might accuse him of *lascivia*, but he could point to an army of great men—Cicero and Augustus among them—who had indulged in this form of relaxation in the past. He had a number of friends who amused themselves by writing too, and they exchanged their products for mutual criticism, even gave recitations to invited audiences—not, as Pliny made clear, from vanity, but in order to improve what they had written in the light of comments and criticism, to be detected even in the moving of a muscle on a listener's face. There was much pleasure in this. It did no harm. But invitations to such parties no doubt drove others beside Juvenal to fury. '*Semper ego auditor tantum?*' There was no literary task which such enthusiasts were not prepared to tackle themselves or to encourage their friends to tackle. Pliny even played with the idea of being a historian.[80]

There were countless other forms of relaxation. Nero had his music; though, entering the lists in competition with the professionals both as vocalist and as instrumentalist, he would not himself have called it relaxation: '*Qualis artifex pereo.*' Titus also sang. Hadrian and Valentinian, both highly talented men, were painters and sculptors in their spare time. Marcus Aurelius, too, took lessons in painting.[81]

People kept birds and animals. Women and children in particular kept dogs (with a preference, it seems, for bitches), giving them names like Missy (Issa), Fly (Myia), or Lydia; and then, as now, pet dogs were often far too fat. Cats, however, do not seem to have been common before the first century A.D. Juvenal mentions a woman who kept a lion (guaranteed tame), which proved expensive to feed. Some people had pet monkeys. Tiberius kept a pet snake.[82]

As for birds, Catullus' Lesbia had her favourite '*passer*', probably a bull-finch. And there were talking birds, not only parrots but also starlings, magpies (when you arrived to dine with Trimalchio, one greeted you), crows and ravens—like the raven hatched from a nest in the roof of the temple of Castor at Rome which made its home with a cobbler, greeted the great, members of the imperial family even, by name on the Rostra, was killed by another cobbler, whose shoes it befouled, and then, on March 28th, A.D. 35, after rough justice had been executed on its murderer, given a public funeral, escorted by two Aethiopians and burnt on a pyre on the Appian way.[83]

Rich men who were bird-fanciers possessed aviaries, walled round and netted over, the first known to us belonging to a knight who lived at Brindisi in the early first century B.C. These included a rich variety of birds—even, from the first century A.D., pheasants. There was pigeon-breeding, largely for eating, for pigeons were thought a great delicacy; some people kept carrier-pigeons.[84]

Cock-fighting and quail-fighting were amusements of the raffish, as once among the 'cocks' and the 'bucks' in English society, and were extremely popular among the lower classes. They gave the opportunity often for heavy betting. They are represented in Pompeian art. When their relations were good, Antony and Octavian contended against one another at this sport, Octavian always winning; so, in their youth, did Caracalla and his brother Geta. Marcus Aurelius, on the other hand, expressed thanks in his *Meditations* for the fact that he was taught when young 'not to cock-fight or to be excited about such sports.'[85]

There was little respectability about dancing or drinking; of the two, dancing was the more discreditable. From being a simple manly exercise—'*virilem in modum tripudiare*'—as it once had been in the time of the elder Scipio (the equivalent of Scottish reels and jigs, perhaps), dancing had rapidly changed to being a soft, unmanly, discreditable diversion. When the younger Scipio was taken to see a young people's dancing class—a *ludus saltatorius*—attended even by children of upper-class families, he could not believe his eyes. And, if you wished to vilify L. Afranius, the consul of 60 B.C., you said that he was better at dancing than at public business.[86] In the case of drinking, on the other hand, as has been seen above, more than one highly respectable public figure (including, indeed, the emperor Tiberius—'Biberius Caldius Mero') was notoriously a heavy drinker; and, however loudly you trumpeted the long list of the younger Cato's inimitable virtues, you could not deny—and in his *Anticato* Caesar made much of the fact—that he was often drunk[87].

But, by the canon of august respectability, you should drink in the privacy of your own or a friend's house.

In every town, the whole Empire over, in addition to inns (*cauponae, deversoria, hospitia, stabula, tabernae*) there was an abundance of cook-shops, restaurants and bars (*popinae, ganeae, tabernae*) which are identified and reconstructed (even to their inn-signs) by archaeologists in

such excavated cities as Ostia and Pompeii*,[88] and which are the object
of a barrage of disparaging abuse in all our ancient literary sources.
Ausonius describes the stench of pike being fried in oil in a cook-shop.
Despite the epitaph of a woman (*popinaria*), 'whose cooking attracted
numbers of people to Tibur (Tivoli)', it may be doubted whether the
best of them even began to approach the standard of what today we
should call a respectable restaurant. The worst of them—in great cities
like Rome and the ports—were very discreditable indeed, often
hardly disguised brothels which lived in constant fear of the police.[89]
Their clientèle consisted largely of working men and of slaves, for
whose relaxation they catered—at Ostia for 'bargees, thieves, runaway
slaves, executioners, undertakers', which is Juvenal's scornful and not
necessarily accurate description of a whole social class, the class to
which his patrons did not belong.

To their clients they were one of the great attractions of town as
contrasted with country life.[90] Some, no doubt, performed a useful
service during the day, providing cooked food and snacks, in particular food which could be carried away (like fish and chips today);
for it must be remembered that there were no fireplaces in the tene-
ments at Ostia or, presumably, elsewhere, and that for poor people
there was nothing but a brazier or portable oven to cook on in their
homes.

Some bars were open all night—*pervigiles popinae*—and were rowdy
houses where singing, dancing and gambling often degenerated into a
series of free fights.

That these establishments did big business, whatever their clientèle, is
beyond all doubt. At Pompeii there were twenty inns and a hundred
and eighteen bars; and if at Ostia there were, for certain, only two inns
and fourteen bars, that is plausibly explained on the hypothesis that at
Ostia drinking habits were different, and that men who wanted to drink
resorted to their clubs (guild-houses) instead.[91]

In Rome itself authority waged constant and ineffective war against
such establishments. Claudius ordered the closure of all drinking houses;
an urban prefect of the fourth century tried to stop early-morning
drinking by the introduction of opening hours (from ten a.m. onwards);
and in the early Empire there were prohibitions on the sale of hot water
(for mixing with wine) and of foodstuffs more appetizing than cooked
vegetables. Brave measures, none of which had the smallest effect.[92]

---

* One at Antibes (*CIL* xii, 5732) had a notice outside, 'Listen, traveller, come inside if
you please. There is a list of prices that tells you everything.'

We cannot tell how many people idled and drank in bars the whole day through. Bohemian characters patronized them, like the poet Florus, whom Hadrian mocked wittily.[93] We need not pay too much attention to statements in the courts and in politics in the late Republic, for it was clearly a convention that, in your abuse of a man, the catalogue of his vicious practices should include familiarity with these low haunts. His breath knocked you over as he emerged from one at eleven in the morning; or he was seen to slink into one at four o'clock in the afternoon, and drank there until dark.[94]

In Rome, however, some of these establishments offered a regrettable temptation to the young sparks of society who found enjoyment not only in discovering how the other half of society lived, but in competing with it at its own game. Wearing coarse clothes, even disguised as slaves, they set out in bands sufficiently strong to assure themselves of survival in any rough house; they patronized the *popinae* and the *tabernae* and assaulted people whom they met in the streets. Nero enjoyed such pranks, even when he was emperor, often returning home with several cuts on his face; and the young L. Verus, in similar escapades, broke a lot of glass and ended up sometimes with a black eye.[95]

In all classes of Roman society gambling and gaming (*alea*) were favourite relaxations, borrowed in every one of their many forms from the Greeks. You could not be prosecuted for gambling during the Saturnalia or, at any time of the year, for betting on athletic events[96]; with these exceptions the law frowned on the practice, with penalties as severe as exile and, at the lightest, a fine four times the value of the wager.[97] It offered no protection against loss or damage to the keeper of a gaming house.[98] However, it is doubtful if the law was ever enforced seriously, and from the early Empire onwards it does not seem to have been enforced at all. Labourers played with dice and knucklebones when the weather drove them indoors from their work. Men at the table absorbed by the dice made a good subject for a mosaic. Books about dicing and games-playing were on sale, one written by Suetonius, one in his supposedly degenerate youth by the later emperor Claudius.[99] Among the well-to-do stakes might run high, and as much as 100,000 sesterces be lost in a single night. Raffish men might stake articles of their own expensive wardrobe; on the other hand, some grown-ups, like children, only played for nuts.[100]

Women of all ages enjoyed themselves with the counters; and a smart young woman with her questionable way to make could not hope to attract an enviable clientèle unless she was able to play the various games and to keep her head at the table.[101] It was the last pleasure left to old men[102]; schoolchildren played surreptitiously and were caned if detected.[103]

Most emperors were enthusiasts. Augustus not only made a present of a thousand sesterces to each of his guests for their stakes, but also refrained from taking advantage of his own skill; he was capable of saying at the end of an evening, when he had lost twenty thousand sesterces, that if he had driven home all his advantages he might well have finished the evening fifty thousand to the good.[104] Gaius Caligula not only shocked people by playing when the Court was in mourning for his sister Drusilla, but—as might be expected—was known to cheat.[105] In the satire on Claudius' consecration, the Emperor, a gambling enthusiast, was first condemned in Hades to dice with a bottomless box cutting a more undignified figure even than usual, down on his knees, trying to find the dice.[106]

Simple dicing called for a dice-box (*fritillus*), a board (*abacus, alveus* or *alveolus*) and knucklebones (*tali*) or dice (*tesserae*[107]).

Knucklebones, large numbers of which have been unearthed, whether natural or artificially made, were oblong with four sides, two wider and two narrower, and rounded at the two ends. When thrown, the *talus* should fall with one of the flat surfaces upwards, though it might alight on one of the rounded ends and then fall over, this not being accounted a true throw.[108] The surface of each of the four flat sides differed recognizably (plain, convex, concave and twisted) and each had a name and a number (1, 3, 4, 6 respectively), though these were not marked or inscribed. The player threw his four *tali*. If each showed a different surface, this was the top throw, Venus, a Royal (*basilicus*[109]). Scoring, therefore, was not on a simple numerical basis. The lowest throw was four aces; this was the Dogs, *Canes*, or the Four Vultures. A six in some combination or other, *senio*, was also a bad throw.[110]

We know how Augustus and his friends played the game. Each of them threw in turn. A player who threw the Dogs or a Six (which was normally a good throw), put sixteen sesterces into the pool. Whoever first threw Venus, scooped the pool.[111] But from the fact that in Greece every different combination of numbers appears to have had a different name, it is evident that a number of other games were played with *tali*.[112]

The *tali* could be used, like dice, in the service of any game which was played with counters. And there was a game in which the players competed in throwing the *tali* into the narrow neck of a jar, an achievement which evidently called for great skill. This was called *tropa*.[113]

The die, of which numerous specimens have been excavated, was like a modern die, with the numbers one to six on its six sides. The player seems never to have thrown more than three dice, and when three dice were thrown, the highest throw (Venus, again) was of three sixes. Dicing with the *tessera* was for higher stakes than dicing with *tali*.[114]

Dice were thrown to determine moves in certain games played with counters of bone, glass or crystal on boards which were marked out in squares. The two most popular—which it is a mistake to try to reconstruct as if they bore analogies to draughts, backgammon or chess—were *Duodecim Scripta* (Twelve Lines) and *Latrunculi*.

Duodecim Scripta was played on a board marked out in twenty-four squares, marked successively one to twelve in the first row and then backwards from thirteen to twenty-four in the second, square 24 being directly above square 1. Some or all of the squares had names, 23 being '*Divus*', 19 '*Summus*' (the square which you could reach by throwing three sixes from the starting point), 14 '*Antigonus*'. Each player had fifteen pieces, and moves were determined by the throwing of three dice. At the start of the game the white pieces were on square 1 and moved forward, the black on square 24, moving backwards. The winner was the player who first succeeded in moving all his pieces from square 1 to square 24, or from square 24 to square 1, or was perhaps the player with the highest score on points. If one enemy piece was on the square to which your throw took you, it was driven back to base; if two or more enemy pieces held the square, then you yourself could not occupy it. This, at least, is the most plausible reconstruction yet made of the game, which evidently had something in common with tric-trac.

There were players who took the game as seriously as people today take chess and bridge; for we have the story of Scaevola who, setting out for the country after losing a game, went over every move in his head. He was so delighted when he discovered the mistake which had cost him the game, that he returned to confirm with his opponent that he was right. A professor of Rhetoric at Bordeaux in the fourth century A.D. had the same prodigious memory. He could recall a game when it finished, throw by throw and move by move.[115]

Latrunculi (Robbers or Soldiers)—a Roman war game—was far more complicated, and its reconstruction is possible only in a very general way, thanks largely to Isidore of Seville, who wrote in the first half of the seventh century A.D. and to the fact that an enthusiastic games-player of Perugia was buried with the whole of his gaming tackle. This included eight hundred and sixteen pieces in glass and sixteen of bone, and has since been dug up—as at the Roman villa of Lullingstone in Kent has a coffin with thirty gaming counters. The label-shaped bone counters from Perugia and others found elsewhere are inscribed each with a word and number, for instance *MORARIS* ('Check') XIIII; *ARGUTE* ('Smart') XV: *MALEST* ('Bad luck') XXIIIA.[116]

The board was divided into a number of squares, we do not know how many. Opponents, playing with pieces in different colours, protected their own and attacked the enemy's 'sheepcote' (*mandra*), the robbers' lair or perhaps a military encampment, for in early Latin '*latro*' meant a mercenary soldier.[117] The pieces were called 'robbers' or 'soldiers' (*latrones, latrunculi, milites, bellatores*) and were of three kinds: the pawns (*ordinarii*) who could only advance or retire a square at a time, forward or backward; *vagi*, the rangers, who could move freely in any direction; and the *inciti*, who could not move at all. These last were, presumably, the 'home guard' defending the *mandra*. They were not functionless, because a piece which found itself between two enemy pieces was taken[118]; so that, if a piece broke into the enemy *mandra*, its advance might prove purposeless. Victory belonged to the player who succeeded in capturing or immobilizing all the enemy's pieces, for which purpose he would evidently need to break into his *mandra*. His opponent was then 'penned down in his *mandra* by the glass *latro*'.[119] The victor was hailed as *Imperator*.[120]

There were other popular games[121]: *Terni Lapilli*, played with three counters on a marked board, perhaps on the principle of our noughts and crosses, and another which has left much evidence, but which we have little hope of reconstructing. The evidence comes from all over the Empire but particularly from Rome, and in Rome largely from the catacombs, and is none of it earlier than the middle of the second century A.D. It consists of rare specimens of the tops of gaming tables with a peculiar type of inscription, and of large numbers of other inscriptions of this particular type.

The inscription is generally of six words, each of six letters. On the table they were inscribed in three lines in pairs with a gap in the middle; so that there were eighteen letters on either side of the table. On the eighteen letters on his side of the table each player evidently moved his pieces—but how, we cannot tell.

Read consecutively, the words made interesting reading. For the most part they constituted useful advice to the games-player, warning him of the fickleness of fortune, the danger of gambling and the folly of losing one's temper. For instance:

SPERNE   LUCRUM
VERSAT   MENTES
INSANA   CUPIDO

In the same *genre* are the hexameter 'lines of the twelve philosophers', all concerned with gambling; for instance, LUDITE SECURI QVIBVS AES EST SEMPER IN ARCA, 'Play without concern when your purse is full.' Some inscriptions of this type express simple euphoria; for instance, PARTHI OCCISI BRITTO VICTUS LUDITE RO-MANI, 'The Parthians are killed, the British defeated; sport, Romans;' or from a tomb near the Porta Portese in Rome, CIRCUS PLENUS CLAMOR INGENS IANUAE TE[NSAE], 'The Circus is full, there is a roar of shouting, the gates are bulging.' One evidently reproduces the inscription on a table in a tavern: ABEMUS IN CENA PULLUM PISCEM PERNAM PAONEM, 'For dinner: chicken, fish, ham, peacock.'[122]

The keen player, or a man as ostentatiously rich as Trimalchio, provided himself with his own handsome set of pieces, perhaps of ivory or precious stone.[123] Also, since rich Romans took pride in the possession of expensive tables, he might have the kind of gaming table which Martial describes, one panel of which was engraved for the game of *Duodecim Scripta*, the other for *Latrunculi*.[124]

Evidence abounds of the widespread passion for gaming in Rome.*
Lines were cut out on the steps of public buildings (the Basilica Julia in the Forum at Rome, for instance), on which games could be played. Ammianus Marcellinus was shocked in the fourth century A.D. by what seemed to him to be a positive mania for gambling among all classes in Rome; he was interested in the fact that some well-to-do Romans objected to being called '*Aleatores*' (gamblers), but did not object to the name '*Tesserarii*' (dicers).[125] People would stop to watch a champion at play and would look over players' shoulders to mark the progress of a game. *Latrunculi* was played by prisoners. When in the principate of Gaius the centurion came to fetch the philosopher Julius Canus to the execution-chamber, he was playing *Latrunculi* with a

* An epitaph survives from Aquitania of 'an elementary schoolmaster, a keen player of *Latrunculi*', ILS 7752.

fellow-prisoner; he insisted that the centurion should first check the state of the game, in which he was a point ahead, in case his opponent should claim later to have won it.[126].

4. Exercise and Sport

The majority of those who took exercise took it in the afternoon during the eighth and ninth hours—that is, between 1.15 and 3.45 p.m. at midsummer and between 12.45 and 2.15 at midwinter.[127] Young men of the upper social classes in Rome and in the youth organizations (*Iuventus*) were not so restricted in time and must have spent much of their mornings too in arduous physical exercise. These youth organizations for free-born boys of the upper social class, started by Augustus and encouraged by succeeding emperors, spread quickly through the country towns of Italy and, in the first and second centuries A.D., into the western provinces and into Greece. They developed in due course into '*collegia*' with magistrates, and were eventually to perform something of the function of a local militia. They are a part of Roman life which has been brought to light in the main by inscriptions and in particular by the excavations at Pompeii.[128]

An aristocracy like the Roman is in its origins an aristocracy of country-dwellers; its sons are brought up to ride and to hunt. Hunting was internationally the sport of aristocrats and of kings. There were Ptolemies who were great hunters. It was on the estates of the vanquished Macedonian monarchy that the youthful Scipio Aemilianus acquired in 167 B.C. that passion for hunting which Polybius shared and afterwards encouraged. Polybius' enthusiasm also infected Demetrius of Syria, who, as a hostage in Rome, used to hunt in southern Latium; so, when in 162 Demetrius sent his hounds and his servants to Anagni in preparation for a hunt at Circeii, there was no reason for anybody to suspect that, instead of following them, he was slipping on board a ship at Ostia, fooling the Roman government and on his way to Syria to take possession of his kingdom.[129]

The young aristocrat hunted and, since he must be ready for war if war came, he was trained in the art of fighting. As in medieval times there was jousting; so the young Roman (like the elder Cato's son) trained with shield and javelin. When the Equites hailed Gaius Caesar and Lucius Caesar as 'Principes Iuventutis', their symbolic gift consisted of silver shields and silver spears.[130]

When Ovid pictured Romulus and Remus exercising themselves in boxing, throwing the javelin and putting the weight, his imagination got the better of his historical sense, for these, like running and wrestling, were sports which reached Rome later, through contact with the Etruscans and the Greek cities in the south. They then became a part of Roman education,[131] starting in boyhood and continuing after the age of fourteen (in *adulescentia*) until the age of seventeen, when military service started. This, Cicero says, was a period of life devoted to exercise and sport in the Campus.[132]

The Campus in Republican Rome was the Campus Martius, described by Strabo[133] as 'a vast area with unlimited space for driving chariots and riding and at the same time for all the people playing ball, trundling hoops and wrestling.' Those exercising were mainly youths, but older men were to be seen—prodigious sights sometimes, like Marius when he was nearly seventy, 'practising weapon drill and riding every day among the young people', and the younger Cato,' oiling himself and playing ball' after his failure to secure election to the consulship in 52 B.C.[134] The runners were oiled, the wrestlers oiled and dusted. At the end of their exercise they plunged into the neighbouring Tiber. 'So the Romans of old, who from successive wars and incessant danger acquired mastery of the art of war, selected the Campus Martius as being near the Tiber so that, after their fighting exercises were finished, the young people might wash off the sweat and dust and by hard swimming recover from the exhaustion of the races.'[135] They still swam in the Tiber after their sports in Cicero's time and later.*

Though Sallust does not make the point explicitly, relaxation of this hard military training was no doubt considered by some to be a part of the decadence which attacked the wealthy aristocracy especially in the years after Sulla's dictatorship. Horace once complained bitterly that contemporary Roman boys had not been taught to ride and were frightened of hunting; they would rather indulge in Greek sport[136]— just as English traditionalists complained in the late nineteenth century when hunting and rowing, both manly sports, were challenged by the new organized games which appealed so strongly to the public schools and the middle classes. Hunting the hare and breaking in a horse were for Horace '*Romana militia*', in contrast to other exercises, whose devotees were 'playing the Greek'.[137] Cicero, however, considered

---

* Indeed the *genius loci* is not dead today. Up-river on both sides of the Tiber above and below the Ponte Risorgimento in Rome are the Dopolavoro clubs, with their tennis and net-ball courts, and their barges.

exercise and sport in the Campus on a par with hunting as unexceptionable relaxation.[138]

By the late Republic and early Empire there were three sorts of exercise or sport. In the oldest and best tradition of the Roman aristocracy were hunting, riding and competition in arms. (No mention is made of horse jumping.[139]) Second came the sports which ranked highest in Greek esteem: boxing, wrestling, running, throwing the discus and the javelin. There were also swimming and jumping, both part of the recruit's training in the army. Lastly there were weight-lifting, trundling a hoop and a great variety of ball games. Rowing was never a serious Roman sport.

Boxing and wrestling were sports of emperors. Augustus was an enthusiastic spectator of boxing. Marcus Aurelius enjoyed boxing and wrestling; a man should face life, he thought, as a wrestler, prepared for any contingency. He also hunted and played ball. The young Gratian in the fourth century, lauded as a gifted all-rounder by Ausonius, ran fast, wrestled skilfully, high-jumped well, threw the javelin and cast darts with great skill and was also an excellent horseman.[140]

Julius Caesar had been an excellent rider and was skilled in weapon-fighting, and Octavian, though he did not match his great-uncle's skill, kept up his riding and his arms-drill until the civil wars were over.[141] He then decided that the training of boys and youths in military exercises and sport was to be an important feature of Roman life, and inaugurated the Youth Movement, the *Iuventus*. In Rome he revived the *Lusus Troiae*, an immensely complicated military tattoo, not unlike a medieval tournament, in which the young sons of the aristocracy, after ceremonial riding and counter-riding, engaged in mock battle, and then re-formed.[142] There were other cavalry exercises in Rome, and his two grandsons received their titles '*Principes Iuventutis*'.[143]

The *tirones* of the new youth organizations were boys at school, taking—in the manner of English public school boys—a great deal of exercise; and it is no accident that on the stucco reliefs of the ceiling of the central nave of the underground basilica of the Porta Maggiore at Rome,[144] the scene in which a seated schoolmaster is watching a pupil in some part of his schooling is directly above another in which three boys are playing ball and two others, exercising with shields and short swords or staves, are being supervised by a coach (see pl. 8b). On the opposite side of the same ceiling two boys with shields and light swords are attacking wooden posts, *pali* (as recruits did both in the army and in gladiatorial schools),[145] again under the supervision of instructors, just

II

as the runners in a portico painted on a wall of Trimalchio's house were training under a coach.[146]

Older were the boys who had left school and who had not yet started their military service or their careers. Older men still, particularly in the country towns, no doubt came and played or practised later in the day when their day's work was at an end. And there were evidently numbers of keen alumni. There were honorary members (financial benefactors in particular) and older men, officials responsible for the organization.[147]

Seneca naturally took a jaundiced view of it all.[148] 'It is unbecoming folly for an educated man to devote time to developing his muscles, broadening his shoulders and strengthening his lungs. However good the results of your training-meals may be and however strong your sinews, you will never be as strong or as heavy as a respectable bull. Moreover, the more weight you put on, the more constricted and sluggish your mind becomes. You ought, therefore, to reduce your body and to give more play to your mind. There are numerous disadvantages about being an athlete. There is first of all the laborious training, which exhausts a man's vitality and disqualifies him for concentration and serious study. Then there is the sheer size of the training meal, enough to deprive a mind of its agility. There are the slave-coaches, dreadful men who behave like tyrants. Oiling and drinking make up their lives and a perfect day for them is one in which they have had a really good sweat and, to make good the loss, take a good swig of liquor, which will sink the deeper if they have had nothing to eat. Drinking and sweating—it is the life to which people are condemned who suffer from chronic indigestion.'

There were evidently good trainers, and bad. Quintilian recognized the existence of such trainers as Seneca abused, 'men who spend part of their time in rubbing themselves with oil and part in drinking* and who stultify the mind by over-attention to the body'. But he appreciated that physical training under good instructors was an important part of education.

There seem always to have been conservative opponents of those athletic exercises which had come to Rome from Greece, on the general ground that the highly-trained athlete was brittle, while the well-trained soldier, on the other hand, was tough. It is, of course, true

---

* The masseurs in the baths drank heavily in Petronius' *Satyricon* (c. 28). The person massaged also contracted a great thirst—the disgusting woman, for instance, in Juvenal 6, 425–33.

that a trained athlete, with specially developed muscles, is often not as robust as a well-trained soldier, a point which Quintilian made when he said that the good orator required not the 'swelling thews' (*tori*) of athletes, but the 'wiry muscles' (*lacerti*) of soldiers. The athlete was even accused of a certain softness, sometimes for surprising reasons; by Quintilian, for instance, on the ground that tough, energetic figures in real life, soldiers or orators, men 'who lived in the sun', had to en dure the extreme discomfort of being hot under thick clothing, while the athlete, who ran naked, endured no discomfort at all.

Celsus wrote with good sense of over-specialization in athletics: 'Special athletic training and training diet are a mistake because, once public duties interfere with regular training, the body suffers, and men who have followed such a diet age prematurely and are always getting ill.'[149]

Members of the *Iuventus* not only paraded ceremonially in public[150]; they also played games and competed in sport before spectators.[151] If they fought sometimes in the manner of gladiators, as Vespasian's son Titus once did in his home town, it was with this difference, that they were amateurs, while gladiators were professionals, and they fought with dummy weapons, not to kill.[152] Medieval tournaments were described by Roger de Hoveden as 'military exercises carried out not in the spirit of hostility but solely for practice and display of prowess', and young Romans trained and demonstrated the results of their training in similar displays. *Graffiti* from the great Palaestra in Pompeii show that, just as 'jousters travelled from land to land like modern cricketers on their tours, offering and accepting challenges',[153] teams of *iuvenes* from one town engaged in competitions with teams from another.[154]

For most grown men, particularly in the baths, exercise took the form of one or other of different games of ball.[155] Manuals of instruction were published, which do not survive; but we have Galen's interesting little essay 'On Exercise with the Small Ball,' in which he discussed exercise in general, stressing its psychological side—the greater the enjoyment derived from it, the better—and insisting that, at its best, it should bring every muscle of the body into play.[156] Hunting, the best exercise of all, was expensive and time-consuming; it was therefore barred to men in public life and to those who had their living to earn. The 'small ball game', better than wrestling or running because it exercised every part of the body, took up little time and cost nothing. It was a profitable training in strategy; serious accidents

were rare and, as it could be played with varying degrees of strenuous-
ness, it was a good game for men of all ages.[157]

The 'small ball game' *par excellence* was *harpastum*, and was the game
which the Greek world had once called *phaininda*. Pollux,[158] who gave
an intelligible account of a game called *episkyros*,* unfortunately took
refuge in wild etymological speculation to account for the game
phaininda, and evidently had little more idea of the game than that
feinting played an important part in it. It was certainly played with a
hard ball, and 'dusty' was the epithet which Martial used of it.[159] It
was perhaps a little more dangerous than Galen suggested, for we
know of a spectator who became involved and had his leg broken.[160]
Athenaeus wrote of the game as follows[161]:

> The game called *harpastum* was formerly called *phaininda*, which is
> the kind I like best of all.

> Great are the exertion and fatigue attendant upon contests of ball
> playing, and violent twisting and turning of the neck. Hence Anti-
> phanes, 'Damn me, what a pain I've got in my neck.' He describes the
> game of *phaininda* thus: 'He seized the ball and passed it with a laugh
> to one, while the other player he dodged; from one he pushed it out
> of the way, while he raised another player to his feet amid resounding
> shouts of 'Out of bounds', 'Too far', 'Right beside him', 'Over his
> head', 'On the ground', 'Up in the air', 'Too short', 'Pass it back in
> the scrum'.

Scholarship has done its best to reconstruct the rules of the game,[162]
but in the absence of any surviving representation of it, whether in
painting or in stone relief, little is to be gained by such speculation. We
can only be certain that, like the Greek *episkyros*, it was a team game.

Other ball games were individual games, played only by two or
three players.

Two men might throw and catch a small hand ball.[163] Lending
money, Seneca said, borrowing an image from Chrysippus, was like
this kind of game. You suited the size and nature of your loan to the
character of the borrower, just as you threw one way to a tall opponent,
another way to a short one; you sent a difficult ball to a skilled player,
and practically handed the ball to your opponent if he was an un-

---

* 'It is played between teams of equal numbers who face each other. They scratch a
half-way line with a stone, and call the line *skyros*. On this they place the ball. The side
which gets hold of the ball throws it over the heads of its opponents, whose business it is
to seize the ball and to throw it back, until one side drives the other over its own dead-ball
line.'

skilled beginner. A player who exhibited *malignitas* spoiled the game.[164]

If there were three players, they stood as if at the three points of a triangle[165] and the game, called *trigon* (as was the hard ball with which it was played), was a serious matter, each player having his own— often very raucous—scorer (*pilicrepus*) and his own ball-boy.[166] This was the game that Trimalchio, in his red shirt, was playing in the baths, with scorers; his ball-boys, saved the indignity of stooping to recover the dropped balls, handed Trimalchio new ones whenever he needed them, from a bag.[167] More balls than one might be in play, and each player feinted, trying to mislead his opponents as to the direction in which he was about to throw the ball. It must have been something like a three-man cricket fielding-practice. A good player was a man of quick reactions and great agility, some one born under Lepidus in Gemini, if Manilius was to be believed.[168] Either hand could evidently be used; for when Gaius Caligula gave a hundred thousand sesterces to those who played with him, but only half that sum to a certain L. Caecilius, Caecilius said, 'Does this mean that I only use one hand when I play?'[169] A skilful left-handed catch was greatly admired.[170]

The scorer evidently counted missed catches which dropped to the ground; so that the winner was the player with the smallest score.[171] Only if this was the case, can sense be made of Martial's sycophant in the baths who, evidently standing behind the player whom he wanted to flatter, caught in either hand the balls which this player missed. It is surprising that the other two players did not protest—unless they too had similar supporters behind them. For when *trigon* was played at the baths, it was evidently common for others who were exercising—an '*uncta corona*'—to stand round and watch.[172]

When a lackadaisical player muffed his catches, Galba said sarcastically, 'Don't strain yourself; you might be Caesar's candidate at the elections', Caesar's candidates being certain of election without any effort on their own part.[173]

To play these last two games was '*datatim ludere*'.[174] There was a third game—'*expulsim ludere*'—in which the ball was thrown against a wall. You might see slaves or children doing this in the street.[175] Played more seriously, it was evidently like Fives. The player took the ball off the wall full-toss or else at the first bounce. This, it seems, was the game at which Calpurnius Piso, whose eulogy survives, excelled; he repeatedly hit the ball full-toss (*volantem geminare pilam*); he 'brought it back into play when it fell'—i.e. took it on the first bounce—'and he surprised his opponents by reaching a ball which seemed to have beaten him' (*non sperato fugientem reddere gestu*).[176]

This game, unlike the others, was evidently played in a special court. Such courts (*sphaeristeria*) existed, no doubt, in a great many baths, as they existed in those of Claudius Etruscus, and also in a number of private villas.[177] There was one in the younger Pliny's Laurentine villa and another in his villa in Tuscany.[178] An inscription records the building of one by the magistrates of Centuripae in Sicily. A court was evidently partly open, and was sited so as to receive the afternoon sun, that being the time when exercise was normally taken.[179] The room, or 'court', could evidently be used for more than one purpose; but it is hard to know why it was in a court of this kind that Vespasian took the only pains that he is ever known to have taken to encourage his admirable good health, 'rubbing his throat and other parts of his body a fixed number of times.'[180]

However the ball game which most middle-aged and elderly men played before their bath was less vigorous than any of these. Whether or not in any very strongly competitive spirit, they threw and caught a larger and lighter ball, either a *paganica*, which was stuffed with feathers, or a *follis*, which was inflated with air—a medicine ball, in fact. The *follis* is said to have been invented for Pompeius Magnus by his trainer Atticus of Naples, perhaps when Pompey was recovering from his serious illness in Campania in early summer 50 B.C. Martial describes this as a ball for small boys and for old men. Augustus played it when he abandoned serious exercise after the civil wars; Pliny's elderly friend Spurinna played it at the age of seventy-seven; and if in Cicero's *De Senectute*, the elder Cato did not recognize any form of ball game as suitable for old men, that may be for the very good reason that Cicero knew that the *follis* was only introduced a century after Cato was dead.[181]

As today some men stop playing tennis at thirty, while a few still play vigorously in their seventies, it is impossible from the bare mention of '*palla*' to know whether it was a lazy game with the *follis* or a strenuous game with the small hand ball that a man was playing— Maecenas, for instance. When Maecenas was dead, Seneca for one could not abuse him too soundly for being sloppy and soft; yet Horace, his contemporary, reveals that he was a passionately enthusiastic ball-player. So later was Marcus Aurelius.[182]

Inevitably there were enthusiasts who continued to play when they would have been wise to abandon the game. Martial has an amusing and untranslatable epigram at the expense of a man who was a champion when young, but who went on playing when he was long past the game.[183]

There was one more ball game, once recorded. Loudly applauded by large audiences in all the four great *thermae* in Rome, a certain Ursus did what no Roman citizen had done before; he played a game with a glass ball, at which only one person in Rome could beat him, his patron, the distinguished Annius Verus, prefect of the city and consul for the third time in 126 A.D. Ursus, who wrote poetry, composed his own epitaph, because he wanted posterity to know of his achievement. His wish has been granted.[184]

The ball, the discus and the hoop were 'campestria arma'. Exercising in the Campus Martius with one or other of them, a man attracted spectators. So, if he did not play well, he was wise not to play at all, if he did not want to be laughed at.[185]

Ball-players, strenuous or lethargic, apart, there were young men who fenced with staves (*clavae*) or tilted at posts; there were the weight-lifters and men exercising with dumb-bells; and there were others who indulged in one or other of the exercises in which the *Iuventus* was trained—who ran, rode, drove chariots and wrestled. There were men, according to Seneca, who spent the entire day in taking exercise.[186]

And what of women?

There are occasional representations in art of young women throwing balls, either alone, to one another, or against a wall; but there is nothing anywhere comparable with the early fourth-century mosaic from Piazza Armerina in Sicily, where a number of agile young women, stripped for exercise, are seen, two running (one of them perhaps a trainer), two playing with a light ball, one throwing the discus and one running with dumb-bells in both hands.[187]

It is to be assumed, therefore, that some women took exercise, in particular that they played the gentler ball games—but to a far smaller extent than men; for women's baths, where they have survived, seem not to have had access, like men's, to *palaestrae*.

Juvenal and Martial were interested only in the abnormalities of the female sex—in the woman who stripped and played *harpastum*, lifted heavy weights, wrestled and submitted to the severe training of the gladiator. 'Think of a poor husband present at the sale of his wife's property, seeing her gladiatorial kit, whether as Thracian or as Samnite, coming under the hammer.' And there were rare occasions, under

Nero and the Flavians, when women fought wild beasts or took part in gladiatorial engagements at public spectacles. Indeed the practice survived spasmodically, until Septimius Severus forbade it. These were exceptional women—as, one hopes, was Juvenal's hostess, who after heavy exercise and massage, took a sweat bath and a heavy drink to follow, just as if she was a man, and, just like a man, was flushed and violently sick afterwards when welcoming her dinner guests, again to the horror of the poor husband.[188]

Except for chariot driving and riding, for which, as a general rule, greater space must have been needed, exercise took place in the *palaestrae*, which from late Republican times onwards were attached to the baths, in the open when the weather allowed, under the surrounding porticoes or in covered *xysti* when the sun was too fierce or the weather too cold for exercise in the open air.[189] Vitruvius' remark that the building of *palaestrae* was unusual in Italy[190] is at first sight surprising. The Republican Stabian baths of Pompeii, after all, had their *palaestra*. But Vitruvius wrote before 27 B.C., before the inauguration of the new Youth Movement by Augustus. This movement is seen by the archaeologists as the background to the construction of two new and magnificent *palaestrae*, one by the amphitheatre at Pompeii, a vast enclosure surrounded by porticoes, planted with beautiful trees and provided with a swimming bath (*piscina*) and the other, one third smaller, at Herculaneum, not all of which has yet been exposed, which also had a swimming bath. After this, towns of the western Empire increasingly copied what had long been an important amenity in Greek towns of importance in the East.[191]

V

RETIREMENT

━━

AT FORTY-SIX a man ceased to be a 'junior' when voting in the centuries at elections and became a 'senior', and this normally signified the end of his liability for military service, though in a crisis he might still be called on to serve up to the age of fifty. At sixty he was exempt from jury-service. This was the age at which, from Augustus' principate onwards, a senator was excused attendance at the Senate.[1] Peregrinus in Lucian's satire strangled his father at that age on the ground that, at sixty, he had lived long enough. Indeed there was an old saying, '*Sexagenarios de ponte*', 'Sexagenarians from the bridge,' interpreted generally as meaning that, once they reached the age of sixty, old men should be thrown into the Tiber and drowned. Legends arose in illustration of this as a primitive Roman custom, including one of the tender-hearted son who concealed his old father. The origin of the expression was in fact less picturesque. The 'bridge' was not a river-bridge at all, but the 'bridge' which the voters crossed on the way to vote. The meaning, therefore, was that men over sixty should be debarred from voting.[2]

Retirement (*otium*) was for those who lived in the sun, whether they lived the creditable life of a politician, a public servant or a barrister, or the—by Roman aristocratic standards—less creditable life of a business man or, if they survived so long, the highly discreditable life of an actor, a charioteer or a gladiator.* It was '*usurpare otium post labores*'.[3] For those who spent their lives in the shade retirement was hardly meaningful; they lived in retirement already. Not that they might not make a certain re-adjustment of their lives in old age. The poet Statius, for instance, wanted—if only he could secure the agreement of his wife—to leave Rome and go back to Naples, to which a number of Greek teachers in Rome retired, because Naples was so much more a Greek than a Roman city.[4]

* On the retirement of gladiators see p. 302.

For even the greatest of professional barristers a moment came when his powers began to fail, when, as he spoke in court, cruel men tittered and even friends blushed. This was the time to move out of the sun into the shade, to abandon practice at the Bar, to retire to the less exacting life of a law-teacher or a jurisconsult. If this in its turn proved too exacting, a man could write. It was in such retirement that Quintilian wrote his great book on education. 'We should see this, perhaps, as the happiest time of an orator's life,' Quintilian wrote. 'Revered in his retirement, unassailed by envy, he will enjoy that regard which comes to most men only after death, and he will know in what respect posterity is going to hold him.'[5]

What was to be sought in retirement was *quies* and *tranquillitas*.[6] This meant escape from the strain and bustle of public life or business, but did not imply the existence of an anchorite; and, as will be seen, it certainly did not imply idleness. For at all periods the graver among the Romans believed that, if a man was not making a serious and useful contribution to the life of his community, he should, at all stages of his life, in some sense or other be improving himself.

The quiet pleasures of retirement were, as they still often are, a distant mirage in the hard-working man's outlook; but the further he advanced, the further the mirage receded. Men said, 'I will retire at fifty,' 'I will retire at sixty.'[7]

The satirist enjoyed himself at the expense of the man who pursued riches, yet was never satisfied with his wealth. Horace's money-lender Alfius spoke lyrically of the countryman's life, yet never abandoned money-lending in order to sample it. Like Juvenal, Horace mocked the idiocy of men who lived the lives of paupers in order to die as millionaires, men who did not enjoy their wealth but lived in rags, starving themselves. Such men were psychological cases; why did they not go to doctors, as they would do if they found that the more they drank the thirstier they became? Ask a ploughman, an innkeeper, a soldier or a sailor why he endured the hardships of existence, and he answered that it was to be able to retire safely when he was old, '*senes ut in otia tuta recedant*'. Yet for most of them the moment of retirement never came.[8]

Roman emperors enjoyed this pipe-dream of retirement as much as other men. Seneca tells us that, in all the crises, dangers and disappointments of his long principate, Augustus buoyed himself up with the hope (which he knew to be a false hope) of ultimate retirement. 'He satisfied other people's prayers, but he could not satisfy this, which was his own'.[9] Tiberius, addressing senators at his accession, made dark hints of ultimate retirement, 'when I reach the time at which you may think to give me some respite in my old age'. He had already shocked Augustus by his five years of self-banishment to Rhodes in 6 B.C., and in the end he managed in an extraordinary and irresponsible fashion to combine the last ten years of his rule as emperor with partial and singularly unhappy retirement in Capri.[10]

Claudius, indeed, in the second year of his rule received an invitation to retire, 'an impertinent, threatening and arrogant letter telling him to abandon the government and to retire quietly into private life'. The letter came from the governor of Dalmatia, who aspired to replace him, and Claudius is said to have called a council meeting to ask whether he should do as he was told.[11]

At the end of the first century A.D. Nerva was so complacently satisfied with his own rule as to say, 'There is nothing to prevent me from resigning and living in safety as a private individual.' Had he lived longer, he could have shown whether this was a serious thought.[12]

History, it seems, got Nerva a little wrong. His adoption of Trajan was construed as an act of resignation and quoted perhaps—certainly, if Lactantius is to be believed—in 305 A.D., when after twenty years of rule Diocletian, an exceedingly sick man, performed his startling act of resignation, a resignation which was imposed also on his fellow-Augustus, Maximian. Diocletian, whether or not he resumed his simple private name of Diocles, retired to an anything but modest dwelling, his palace at Spalato, Maximian to Lucania (or, perhaps, to the villa of Piazza Armerina in Sicily, with its splendid mosaics). This was on May 1st, 305, when Diocletian was a very old man; he died after some ten years of retirement. Hostile authors declared that he retired not of his own will but under pressure from his Caesar, Galerius, who was impatient for the succession. Friendlier sources remark that 'with singular excellence he did what no earlier Roman emperor had done, and of his own will stepped down from the summit of power to the status of a private individual.' In retirement he grew cabbages, and their cultivation brought him a new happiness; so, though not on the best of authority, we are assured.[13] Later on Lactantius, loathing Galerius as the author of the great persecution, smugly imagined him planning a future for himself at the moment of Diocletian's resignation. He too would celebrate the twentieth anniversary of his rule (his *Vicennalia*); then, having assured himself that the men in whose favour he resigned were creatures of his own, he would retire to the enjoyment of a quiet and peaceful old age. In fact six stormy years of active life were all that were in store for him.[14]

In Rome, as in other countries, political careers were successful careers or they were unsuccessful careers.

The end of a successful political career under the Republic was a calm Indian summer of revered, distinguished eminence, what Cicero called 'cum dignitate otium'.[15] The treacherous ladder of the cursus honorum had been successfully climbed. With the consulship behind him, a man was consularis and his family (if it had not that distinction already) was noble.[16] The arduous 'toil in the sun'—provincial administration, hard pleading in the courts—was concluded. The old statesman was a reservoir of wisdom and experience which the State, the wiser element in the younger generation of politicians in particular, was anxious to tap, both informally outside the Senate and in the Senate, when he chose to attend its meetings; there, as a senior consular, he was always invited to speak at a very early stage in every debate. He had resources (opes); he had standing (dignitas); his advice (consilium) commanded assent.[17] The blind Appius Claudius was such a man; when he was brought to the Senate in 280 B.C. in extreme old age, his voice was strong enough to persuade the Senate not to negotiate a settlement with Pyrrhus.[18] And the elder Cato, portrayed in the contented assurance of his successful old age in Cicero's De Senectute, was the very exemplar of the type. This was retirement at its happiest.

There were senators of smaller stature too who were content to relax in their old age, men who had not reached the top of the ladder, who had not got beyond the praetorship, if they had risen as high as that. Their disappointments lay behind them, and they accepted old age with philosophic content.

Of all the men who were cheated of the influence and prestige to which they had looked forward, we know Cicero's disappointment best. Instead of living to be the Grand Old Man of republican politics, he endured the humiliation of exile in 58 and after his return in 57, so far from initiating policy, his first concern was not to give offence. Finally under Caesar's dictatorship government by senatorial debate was at an end. At sixty Cicero the consular had no auctoritas; no Senate waited on his consilium.[19] For a moment, when Caesar was killed, the clouds lifted—only to descend again.

Others were disappointed, but with less good cause. There were always those who were conscious that they had not succeeded, but were not so conscious of their own shortcomings. They blamed the system, not themselves, and even became rebels.

Worse than disappointment, disgrace.

There was the bitter tragedy of Coriolanus. There was the example of M. Livius Salinator who triumphed for his victory over the Illyrians as consul in 219 B.C., and then was accused by a junior officer of having made an unfair distribution of booty to his troops and spent the first eight years of the Second Punic War in disgrace—until the consuls of 210 extracted him from his retirement and told him to cut his hair, discard his rags, dress properly and attend the Senate; after which he was elected to a second consulship and in 207 won the battle of the Metaurus, which destroyed Hannibal's last hope of winning the war. Salinator was restored to public prominence, but with a chip on his shoulder which never disappeared. And in the years after the defeat of Antiochus the Great in 189, P. Scipio Africanus, whom many would have pronounced the greatest man in Roman history, an ex-censor, twice consul, was forced at the very end of his career to retire from public life in Rome to his farm at Liternum under a heavy cloud; for both he and his brother had been suspected, though they had not been proved guilty, of being light-fingered in their handling of public money.[20]

Then there were the senators who, when—normally at five-year intervals under the Republic—the Censors published the list of members, found that, for reasons which they did not need to be told, they were senators no longer. This was the fate of the brother of the great T. Flamininus, when the elder Cato was censor in 184 B.C. He was an ex-consul and had marred an excellent career of public service by a bestial act of cruelty as a military commander. The censors of 70 B.C. removed as many as sixty-four men from the Senate, one of them the ex-consul Lentulus Sura, who was to conspire with Catiline seven years later.*[21] It calls for little imagination to picture the embarrassment of such men and indeed of others who had made a mess of their careers. Sallust, who in his writings was to sermonize so pontifically on the subject of public corruption, was saved by Caesar's personal intervention from the charge of pilfering when he governed Africa after Thapsus, and after Caesar's death there was no more place for him in public life.[23] M. Lepidus, who had been Master of the Horse to Caesar and colleague with Antony and Octavian in the triumvirate, a member

---

* Similarly members of town councils were unseated if, after investigation, charges against them were confirmed.[22]

of one of the most distinguished of Roman families and High Priest of the State, endured greater humiliation still after he had opposed Octavian in the fight against Sextus Pompeius in Sicily in 36 B.C.[24] He lived on to 12 B.C., stripped of the exercise but not of the title of his priesthood, compelled to endure a kind of open arrest at Circeii. At the end, some time after his son had been executed as a conspirator against Octavian, Octavian—now Augustus—amused himself in no very pleasing way by rubbing salt into the old man's wounds. He brought him to Rome and forced him to attend meetings of the Senate. As senior ex-consul, he should have been asked to speak first in debate; Augustus waited and called on him to speak last.[25]

Worse than humiliation in Rome was, in the late Republic and later, the penalty of exile.

Exile (*exilium*) was not in origin a penalty at all. If a man changed his residence from Rome to a city in the Latin League, or a Latin came to live in Rome, he automatically acquired the citizenship of his new place of residence and, as he could not be a citizen of two different communities, he shed the citizenship of the city which he left. As far as migration to Rome was concerned, the practice was brought to an end in the the early second century B.C., but for the migrant Roman it survived and indeed had been extended to cover Latin colonies and certain other cities in Italy—for instance, Naples, Tarquinii, Nuceria and Ravenna. Of the old Latin cities, Tibur (Tivoli) and Praeneste (Palestrina) were at Rome's very doorstep.

People thus moved their residence and their citizenship at first for business or other personal reasons. In due course such migration was the means of evading the penalties of the law in Rome. A Roman who was threatened with prosecution or who, after proceedings had started, foresaw inevitable condemnation, flitted to Tibur, Praeneste, Naples or some other convenient haven. He ceased to be a Roman, and the law could not touch him. All that it could do was to ban him from re-entering Rome or living on Roman territory by 'interdicting him from fire and water'—forbidding him access to these fundamental constituents of life.

After the Social War in 90 B.C. the whole of the Italian peninsula south of the Po acquired Roman citizenship; so this easy subterfuge was at an end, and the fearful defendant who sought to escape capital punishment had to go further afield. If he was denied fire and water whether by the people in one of its assemblies or by the courts, he was conventionally allowed to pass unmolested through Italy on his way to his chosen place of exile outside it; so profound was the Roman dislike of capital punishment.[26]

Unless the exile had been very clever or was very fortunate, he was likely to have a considerably smaller income than before. Sometimes, if the offence for which he escaped condemnation in Rome was corrupt practice as a provincial administrator, he had taken the earlier precaution of salting money away somewhere outside Italy, perhaps the very sum that he had pilfered. After all, Pompey before his return to Rome in 62 B.C. had invested large sums in the East, and Cicero, an honest governor if one ever was, left over two million sesterces banked in Asia when he returned from governing Cilicia.[27]

Exile brought great humiliation for a man who had enjoyed prominence in public life at Rome. He was separated not only from his friends and sometimes even from his wife and children, but from the magnetic life of Rome itself. This was a separation which Cicero hardly found tolerable even when he was governing a province,[28] and we have evidence enough in the letters which he wrote in exile of the desperation of a man who felt at home in Rome and nowhere else. He was like a ship which has broken from its anchor. On some other men exile weighed less heavily. P. Sittius (not a senator, admittedly), who could not return to Rome in safety because of his supposed involvement in Catiline's plotting in the Sixties, set up as a *condottiere* in North Africa and opened up a big business for the supply of animals—panthers and lions—for the games in Rome.[29] And P. Rutilius Rufus, who returned to Asia after his scandalous condemnation in the courts in 92 B.C., could sustain himself with the comforting assurance of his own rectitude, the knowledge that in the opinion of every honest man alive he had been condemned for his integrity and for no other reason.[30]

On the other hand, the exile was free—outside Italy—to choose his new home. He naturally chose to live in the most congenial surroundings possible—if he had any culture, it would be in Greece (preferably in Athens) or in Asia Minor, in Smyrna perhaps, or on the island of Rhodes, where the lectures of distinguished philosophers gave opportunity of self-improvement, however belated. Of such men, L. Memmius, praetor in 58 B.C., who was banished by the findings of one of Pompey's courts in 52 for extensive bribery when he sought the consulship in 54, is a most interesting enigma—the man to whom Lucretius dedicated his great poem as to a Roman patron of Epicureanism, who retired to Athens, acquired what had once been Epicurus' house, and then infuriated local feeling in Athens and feeling among Epicureans everywhere by proposing to pull it down and build on the site.[31]

There were cultured and agreeable cities in the West too, particularly Marseilles, to which Catiline lyingly said that he was retiring when he left Rome on the night of November 8th, 63 B.C. and to which the gangster Milo retired when driven from Rome in 52. Milo blamed his exile less on his own long and established record of crime than on his counsel's failure in court. Cicero had muffed his defence. When Cicero later composed at leisure and sent him that masterpiece of polished oratory, the *Pro Milone* which survives, he replied that if this speech had been made at his trial, he would never have been exiled and so would never have had the enjoyment of eating red mullet (*triglia*) as it was cooked in Marseilles. But as Dio, who tells the story, is careful to emphasize, this did not mean that he was happy in his exile; his only object was to score a point off Cicero.[32]

For a senator in the Empire a successful career was to be made in imperial administration, no longer in politics. Indeed there were no more politics worth the name, no more critical issues to be resolved. Increasingly the senatorial agenda consisted of trivialities. The Emperor alone made policy, even if he sometimes flattered the Senate by first announcing it to that body.

As a result, senators, who had little to lose (since they had no anticipation of further promotion in their careers) spent more and more time in the country[33] or, if they were in Rome, did not bother to attend the Senate's meetings. Paetus Thrasea—admittedly registering a strong moral protest against Nero's practices—had not been to the Senate for three years before he came under attack in A.D. 66.[34] At the end of the first century the elderly consular Silius Italicus retired to his favourite villas—mark the plural—in Campania and was not even impelled by courtesy to travel to Rome to greet Trajan on his return from Pannonia in A.D. 99.[35] And there is an interesting letter in which Pliny chides Bruttius Praesens after his praetorship (in about 104). He was a southerner and so was his wife, and he was idling his time away in Lucania, laying the foundation of his retirement (*otium*). Had he forgotten his *dignitas*, his duties as a senator? Why had he abandoned Rome? It is a fair conjecture that he thought that his career was at an end and had no more ambition for himself. If so, he was wrong. Ten years or so after his praetorship—we should like to know how and why—he was serving under Trajan in the Parthian war. In the twenty-five years after that he was to govern five different provinces and to hold two consulships. A modest man? Or a man to whom for some reason or other Trajan had once taken exception?[36]

A whole succession of emperors rebuked the members of the Senate for the spirit (*segnitia*) in which so cavalierly they disregarded their public duty (*publica munia*): Augustus, Claudius, Nero, Caracalla. Augustus and Claudius tried to enforce attendance by the imposition of sanctions.[37] Claudius even told the senators to their faces that, instead of muttering 'Agreed' to any proposal put before them, they should interest themselves in their business to the extent of getting up and making speeches[38]; but to no effect. At a rare moment when Vespasian's armies had taken Rome but Vespasian himself had not arrived, Helvidius Priscus urged his colleagues to be strong, to show what they could do on their own; but he had no following.[39] What prudent man would put his neck into a noose? So attendance continued to fall off. The quorum which had been 400 at the time of Julius Caesar fell in the third century to seventy, to fifty a century later.[40]

A senator might want to sever himself completely from public life, or he might not want to retire at all. In the first case he consulted his conscience and if his conscience told him that, in Johnson's words, 'he had done very well, he need say no more' (that is to say, he could not reasonably be charged with *inertia*, *desidia*, *segnitia*), then he could retire with a good conscience, and turn a bold face to his critics. 'The first two stages of a man's life should be devoted to his country, the third and last to himself.'[41]

The smoothness, ease and completeness of a man's retirement from public life depended increasingly on his personal relationship with the Emperor.

It was not hard for a man who was not one of the Emperor's personal *amici* ('a friend of Caesar') to draw the correct inference from the fact of being passed over for an appointment which he could reasonably have expected. C. Sulpicius Galba, brother of the later emperor, consul in A.D. 22, retired from public life because of shortage of money, but still anticipated that in due course his would be one of the two names put forward for the proconsulship of Asia and Africa (offices normally awarded about fifteen years after the tenure of the consulship). Instead in A.D. 36 he received a letter from Tiberius telling him that his name would not go forward; so he committed suicide.[42] The same disappointment was shared by a far greater man than Galba. When Agricola, who was never an *amicus* of the Emperor, returned in A.D. 84 from seven years of distinguished administration in Britain, it was a

12

reasonable expectation that his experience would be called on for Domitian's wars on the Danube; but no such call was made. His appointment to the proconsulship of Asia or Africa, however, in about 91 should have been automatic; instead it was represented to him by others, closely in touch with the Emperor, that he would be wise to ask if he might be excused. We have only Tacitus' tendentious account of the transaction. It is possible that Agricola's health was already failing (he died in 93); just as it is possible that Salvius Liberalis who, after actual appointment to Asia, 'excused himself' under Trajan, was not being discriminated against but was thought to be too old for the job.[43]

There was no future for an *amicus* of the Emperor from the moment when his conduct gave offence. Antonius Primus, a legionary commander in Pannonia in A.D. 69 and a chief architect of Vespasian's victory, was, despite his earlier criminal record, a 'friend' of Vespasian. When he joined Vespasian's staff, his conceit and arrogance sufficiently ensured that he should have no further advancement; but still Vespasian did not renounce his personal 'friendship'.[44]

The formal renunciation of ' *amicitia* ' had always been a feature of the political life of the Roman upper class,[45] a most famous instance being the severing of the close friendship of M. Livius Drusus (tribune in 91 B.C.) and the younger Servilius Caepio.[46] Renunciation of 'friendship' by the Emperor, however, was of a far greater seriousness. At its lightest it might indicate only personal disfavour (*privatae inimicitiae*[47]). Still, the rejected 'friend' could not be certain of that. So when D. Silanus, implicated in the exposure of the younger Julia in A.D. 8, was debarred from Augustus' friendship, he interpreted this as an instruction to retire into voluntary exile. This was wise of him; had he stayed, he might have been prosecuted. Instead Augustus died and after a few years Tiberius allowed Silanus to return. His 'exile' had been voluntary. There had been no trial or sentence. Tiberius could say that it was nice to see him back after the long time that he had chosen to spend away.[48]

The renunciation of imperial friendship might be the prelude to sinister mischance, disgrace, prosecution. When in Syria Germanicus renounced the friendship of Cn. Piso the governor, and ordered him out of the province, Piso was (and would have been even if Germanicus himself had not died) a doomed man. And when Pomponius Labeo, faced by prosecution for maladministration of Moesia on his return to Rome in A.D. 34, received formal renunciation of Tiberius' friendship, he knew what to do; he cut his veins.[49]

The prudent politician who foresaw trouble might seek to avert it by taking the initiative in requesting the Emperor's permission to seek retirement. Augustus' close relationship with his equestrian adviser Maecenas was damaged in 23 B.C. when Maecenas' brother-in-law was detected in a conspiracy against the Emperor's life. A few years later Maecenas retired altogether from public life—perhaps at his own request—and for the remaining eight years of his life enjoyed in his house on the Esquiline 'a retirement so remote that he might have been abroad'.[50] At the time of Burrus' death in A.D. 62 Seneca would have been insensitive indeed not to appreciate the formidable strength of the opposition which was building up against him inside and outside the Court. So he solicited an audience and begged the Emperor's leave to retire. Tacitus depicts a splendid exchange of flowery insincerity in the prepared speech of the tutor and the extempore reply of his gifted old pupil, Nero. 'Your elderly "friends", like myself, are entitled to ask for retirement (*quies*) as our due'. So that honour might be satisfied, the request was formally refused; but by an arrangement which suited all parties Seneca withdrew from the Court. He spent more and more time in the country and survived for three years, finding consolation in writing as in similar circumstances Cicero had once done. These were the years in which he wrote his surviving letters.[51]

All governors of imperial provinces and men in such outstanding positions as the Prefect of the City (a senator), the two Prefects of the Praetorian Guard and the Prefect of the Corn Supply (equestrians), together with the whole of the imperial bureaucracy in Rome, with the *a rationibus, a cognitionibus, a libellis, ab epistulis* as heads of the most important departments (freedmen at first, equestrians from the early second century A.D.) held office at the emperor's pleasure.

There was no such thing as a retiring age, no anticipation of a pension. A man's tenure of a post ended with the intimation of the appointment of a successor. He might be succeeded on promotion: a Prefect of the Praetorian Guard, who was advanced to the Prefecture of Egypt (like Sejanus' father in the early empire) or the Prefect of the Vigiles at Rome who was promoted to be Prefect of the Praetorian Guard. And, unless he had been conspicuously unsuccessful, or was explicitly recalled to stand trial, like the procurator under Tiberius who, in such a case, swallowed a lethal dose of leek-juice[52] a provincial governor need not anticipate on his recall that he would not shortly be appointed to another provincial command or to some further office in Rome. In other cases the replacement of a man was in fact the end of his career, as when C. Septicius Clarus, Prefect of the Praetorian Guard and his close associate C. Suetonius Tranquillus, Hadrian's *ab epistulis*, both the emperor's 'friends', were discharged from their offices because of their bad influence on the empress Sabina.[53] And at the end of Hadrian's principate the Prefect of the City, L. Catilius Severus, a very distinguished man with two consulships behind him, who even anticipated adoption by Hadrian whose 'friend' he was, made so little concealment of his disapproval of Hadrian's adoption of Antoninus Pius that he had to go: '*successore accepto, dignitate privatus est.*'[54]

When at the end of Tiberius' principate efforts were made to incriminate the commander of the Upper German army, Cn. Lentulus Gaetulicus, as having been involved in Sejanus' plotting, because his daughter had been engaged to Sejanus' son, Gaetulicus wrote with great effrontery to the Emperor stating that he would regard the appointment of a successor as a death sentence; and so succeeded in holding his command for another five years until he was in fact involved in a conspiracy and executed by Gaius.[55] And there is a comic story about C. Turranius, who was discharged by Gaius at the advanced age of eighty —or perhaps even ninety—from the Prefecture of the Corn Supply. Heartbroken, he had himself laid out for burial in his house, and his household stood round him and sang funeral dirges. At the news of this extraordinary behaviour, the Emperor restored him to his post— which he held for at least another eight years. We know of a similar case, the father of Claudius Etruscus who, starting life as a slave and ending it as an *eques*, held high bureaucratic office under ten successive emperors (from Tiberius to Domitian). Domitian dismissed him, but later restored him to his office.[56]

In most cases, of course, the appointment of a successor meant honourable discharge (*citra indignationem principis*) and carried no connotation of disgrace. A man was allowed to go, because he had earned his retirement. In such cases the blameless emperor Severus Alexander formally thanked the displaced man in the name of the State for his services—'*Gratias tibi agit res publica*'—and made generous provision for setting him up in private life.[57]

A man might ensure his own retirement, like Pliny's friend Terentius Iunior of Perugia who, after a successful equestrian career, was offered promotion to the Senate and to a further career of a different sort, but declined the offer.[58] Or he might petition the emperor for leave to resign, '*successorem petere*', '*reverti ad otium*'. Seneca urged Lucilius Iunior, to whom his letters were addressed, to resign his equestrian post in Sicily: 'Get out of the rat-race; it grows worse all the time, the higher you advance in the Service.'[59] And there is a quite remarkable story of a Prefect of the Praetorian Guard in the early years of Trajan, one of his '*amici*' (it is extraordinary that we should not know his name). Trajan was dismayed by his request for retirement, but granted it and, to mark his respect for the man, went down to Ostia with his other friends to say goodbye to him when he set sail for the place which he had chosen for his retirement. But, as Pliny told Trajan in the *Panegyricus*, Trajan was that kind of man. However great his own reluctance, he never stood in the way of a man's retirement (*vacatio*).[60]

Indeed, when there had been no flagrant inefficiency or scandal, it suited both the convenience of an emperor and the personal reputation of the man whose career was being brought to an end that he should appear to have resigned of his own free will. Hadrian was not a little embarrassed at the start of his principate when he wanted to get rid of P. Acilius Attianus, one of the two Prefects of the Guard and the man who, to Hadrian's convenience, had carried the odium of the murder of the four consulars at his accession—a dangerous man who knew too much. When Hadrian could not appoint a successor to him, because Attianus made no application to be succeeded, he took steps to enforce such an application. But Attianus stated his terms clearly, and the Emperor had no alternative but to accept them: that he should be raised to the rank of senator and given *consularia ornamenta*. Though Nero is said to have discharged the all-powerful Pallas soon after his accession, it is evident that Pallas laid down the conditions on which he was prepared to accept discharge.[61]

The ingenious suggestion has been made that all the elaboration of Seneca's published *De Brevitate Vitae*, in which he urged his father-in-law Pompeius Paulinus to resign from the office of Prefect of the Corn Supply and to seek retirement, was in fact an elaborate cover for the fact that resignation was being forced on Paulinus for political reasons. How much better for Paulinus' *dignitas* that the public should think that he had accepted Seneca's published view that his great talents were being wasted as long as he continued to hold an office whose function was merely to ensure that people had enough to eat.[62]

The extremes of success and disaster at the end of a public career were not greatly different under Republic and Empire, the status of an elder statesman at one extreme, exile at the other.

Under the Republic, as has been seen, the reward of a successful public career was 'cum dignitate otium', the unchallenged primacy of an elder statesman. In the Empire again the knowledge and experience of such a man were not wasted; he was a consiliarius of the Emperor, invited from time to time to the Emperor's Council where, in periods of responsible government, his opinions carried weight.[63] The tragedy of the last years of Agricola's life was that, for whatever reason, he did not enjoy this esteem.

Under the Empire exile became a recognized form of punishment for members of the upper social class (the honestiores) not only in Rome but throughout the Empire. There were two forms of exile, relegatio, which might have extenuating circumstances, and deportatio, which was merciless and irrevocable. Sentences of either kind could be passed by the Emperor or the Senate at Rome, and in due course by the Prefect of the City and the Prefect of the Praetorian Guard. Provincial governors could, within certain limits, pass sentence of relegation, but for deportation they had to secure the consent of the Emperor.[64]

Relegation was for a limited period of time, or alternatively, without any time limit, it was a life sentence. It could either, as 'liberum exilium', take the form of prohibition against living in certain named places (as when, for pointing a finger at an ill-behaved member of the audience, the actor Pylades was excluded by Augustus from Rome and Italy[65]) or it could state the place of exile, whether on the mainland or an island (relegatio in insulam). The Emperor Claudius' perverse sense of humour led him sometimes to sentence a man to residence in Rome, forbidding him to travel more than three miles from the city.[66] Deportation was always to some explicit spot, unhealthy, remote, disagreeable: the bare, rocky island of Gyaros, Sardinia, which was brigand-ridden and notoriously unhealthy,[67] or an oasis in the Libyan desert.

The relegatus retained his Roman citizenship with full civic rights; the deportee, on the other hand, lost his citizenship and his property, and retained only his freedom. He reached his place of sentence with little more than the clothes on his back.

As a punishment deportation, which involved loss of citizenship, was considered equivalent in severity to condemnation to the mines or to fighting in the arena (sentences which were passed on members of the lower orders, the humiliores, for comparable crimes); relegation was the equivalent of hard labour or imprisonment.[68]

A man who violated the conditions of his exile and was caught was automatically transferred to the next most severe grade of penalty. If he had been relegated to an island, he was deported; if he had been deported, he was executed. It was possible also by misbehaviour in exile to suffer an aggravation of sentence. Cassius Severus was relegated to Crete by Augustus in A.D. 12 because of the outrageous libels which he had published against leading members of society in Rome. In exile he continued his offensive practices; and so in A.D. 24 his property was impounded and he was deported to the island of Seriphos.[69]

There was great disparity between the places to which exiles were relegated. The small islands around the Italian coast (which Mussolini was to use later for a similar purpose) were unpopular; they were under easy supervision and some, like Pandateria (Ventotene), to which Agrippina, the widow of Germanicus was sent, are exiguous, sea-girt prisons. It was less reasonable to complain of Capri or Sorrento (or perhaps even of Reggio, to which Augustus' daughter Julia was moved by Tiberius). Sardinia and Corsica (in which Seneca spent the years from A.D. 41 to 49) were unpopular. For the rest, scattered round the Mediterranean, many places of Roman exile are today the most envied of holiday resorts: Majorca and Minorca, Crete, Cyprus, Sicily, Rhodes. Other places were Massilia, Lugdunum and Vienna in Gaul, Tarentum in Italy and large numbers of the islands in the Aegean.[70]

Once a man had been condemned by the Senate, it was not unusual for the first speaker to propose relegation to some barely inhabited rock like Gyaros. This made a good impression; it was a patent recognition of the heinousness of the crime. But the quality of mercy is not strained. So a later speaker, perhaps the Emperor himself, might propose some more congenial place of exile—Cythnos, for instance, or Amorgos. So honour was doubly satisfied.[71]

The *relegatus* might have been stripped of a portion of his property, but he normally retained most of it, and he might be accompanied into exile by his wife (whose dowry he still held) and even by friends and relations. When Augustus' daughter Julia was sent into exile in 2 B.C., her mother Scribonia went with her—the woman whom Augustus had divorced years earlier because her moral standards were considerably higher than his own. Martial in an epigram praised the loyalty of the adventurous Q. Ovidius, who joined his consular friend Caesennius Maximus in Sicily when he was exiled in A.D. 65, Caesennius himself having gone to Corsica in similar friendliness to join the exiled Seneca some twenty years earlier.[72] When Glitius Gallus and Novius Priscus were sent into exile after the exposure of the Pisonian conspiracy in A.D. 65, their wives went with them. Gallus' wife was an exceedingly rich woman, and surviving inscriptions show that the island of Andros gave a new home not simply to an exile and his wife but also to a pair of most generous benefactors—unwisely generous indeed, for, we do not know how, the Roman government proceeded to mulct the wife of much of her fortune.[73]

The exile might choose to occupy himself profitably; indeed, if he was deported and had lost all his property, unless friends were willing and able to send money to him, he had no alternative if he wished to survive. Valerius Licinianus, a barrister and ex-praetor, who was culpably involved in the scandal of the Vestal Virgin Cornelia in A.D. 90, gave public instruction in the art of rhetoric in Sicily.[74] In a fictional dialogue, recorded as history by Cassius Dio, a certain Philiscus, meeting Cicero in his exile, had advised him to accept misfortune in a philosophical spirit and, following the example of Thucydides and Xenophon, to buy a farm and settle down and do a little writing.[75] And the unhappy A. Avillius Flaccus, deported to Andros by Gaius Caligula after his prefecture of Egypt, managed to buy a little land and farm it.[76]

It was all too easy for those who were not in exile themselves to overlook its hardships and to paint an almost idyllic picture of the exile's life. Cicero had remonstrated with Philiscus on this score[77]; yet this was the type of consolation which he sought to convey to his friends in exile when he wrote to them from Rome during Caesar's dictatorship: they were well out of Rome at such a time.[78] And under the Empire an exile could be congratulated on his freedom from the worrying boredom of life in Rome—from political anxiety, from the necessity of courting the great with flattering insincerity, from the tedious formality of the daily *salutatio*. Plutarch's *De Exilio* reflects the supposedly brighter side of an exile's life: he could be certain of a roof over his head, of a bath and of fish and hares, if he troubled to catch them; nobody would try to borrow money from him; he could relax in *otium* and *quies* (ἡσυχία).[79]

Fiction, indeed, masquerading as history, has ascribed a view something like this to Gaius Caligula. His act in sending executioners to dispatch Avillius Flaccus, who already had been deported, has been generalized into an imperial decision to execute all exiles everywhere. Different motives were ascribed. According to one account Gaius, meeting a man who had been recalled, asked him how he had spent his time in exile. 'In prayer,' the man answered, with what seemed expedient sycophancy. 'I never ceased to pray for Tiberius' death and your own accession to the principate.' So, struck by the thought that all the people whom he had sent into exile might be praying for his own death, Gaius at once ordered them all to be executed. But there was another account, according to which, reflecting as he lay in bed on the nature of exile, Gaius exclaimed suddenly that it was not punishment at all but one long holiday; and so acted as he did.[80]

In the life of some exiles there was room for hope. Those exiled for a fixed period could anticipate an end to their relegation. And a profound change in the régime, as when Gaius succeeded Tiberius, after Nero's death, and when Nerva succeeded Domitian, brought amnesties. This, when Augustus died, was one of Ovid's vain hopes.[81] The career of the abominable P. Suillius (half-brother of the great general Corbulo) was marked by such interesting vicissitudes. Once quaestor of Germanicus, he was banished for corrupt practices by Tiberius and recalled by Gaius Caligula, Germanicus' son. Back in Rome, he entered on a career of sinister success as a prosecuting counsel, held the consulship under Claudius, whose 'friend' he was; then, with another change in régime, he was brought to book under Nero and, utterly unrepentant, banished once more, this time to the Balearic islands.[82]

Still, not every exile slept soundly. A criminal exiled for malpractices might reflect that there were still other crimes in his past which might yet be exposed. There is an ugly story of Vibius Serenus, recalled from exile in Amorgos in A.D. 24 to face further accusation, this time of encouraging insurrection in Gaul. The slick young prosecutor was his own son. He was condemned and, after a suggestion that he might be sent to Gyaros or Donusa, he was in fact allowed to return to Amorgos.[83] Or the executioner might come, as he came for Flaccus under Gaius, for Helvidius Priscus under Vespasian.

For outspoken advocates of philosophical views opposed to the notion of hereditary monarchy in the late first century A.D. relegation was—as it has been for 'politically objectionable persons' in the modern authoritarian state—something of an occupational hazard. The victims were Stoics and Cynics in the main. Under Nero Musonius Rufus accompanied Rubellius Plautus into exile in Asia Minor out of friendship. When Rubellius Plautus was driven to suicide, he returned and was himself exiled after the Pisonian conspiracy—to Gyaros, whose benefactor he then became by discovering a spring in what had previously been thought a waterless island. People came to Gyaros in great numbers to enjoy his teaching. Recalled by Galba (probably), he was exiled once more by Vespasian, but brought back to Rome by Titus.[84]

Helvidius Priscus and his wife Fannia were banished by Nero, recalled by Galba, and banished once more (and Helvidius then executed) under Vespasian. Fannia came back to Rome, and, with her mother, the younger Arria, widow of Paetus Thrasea, was banished again in A.D. 93 and had her property confiscated. She returned to Rome after Domitian's death—the most exiled woman in Roman history.[85] It would have shocked the younger Pliny, who held both her and her mother in the highest esteem, to hear them rancorously described by a modern historian as 'a tedious pair'.[86]

Epictetus, a Phrygian slave protégé of Domitian's a libellis Epaphroditus (who gave him his freedom), a man greatly influenced by Musonius, left Rome when the philosophers were banished in A.D. 93 and went to Nicopolis in Epirus, where he stayed and taught to the end of his life, having, happily, among his pupils one who made copious notes at his lectures, Arrian. Unlike other philosophers, he was not tempted to return to Rome when Domitian died and times were happier.[87]

Apart from men of high position in the governing class at Rome, there were among the 'martyred' philosophers men of inferior status, not Roman citizens, who shared their fate. For them society cared little, as it cared little for the fate of astrologers (Chaldaei, mathematici), who were expelled from Rome and Italy with monotonous regularity.[88] Their temporary disappearance mattered no more than the sudden disappearance of an exotic psychiatrist or a racing tipster would matter today. You had only to wait. They were always back again.

We know something of the feelings of two highly sensitive and cultured men in exile, both of them punished for their allegedly amorous indiscretions with princesses of the imperial house. Seneca, banished by Claudius under the influence of Messalina and the powerful imperial freedmen in A.D. 41 on the charge of adultery with the emperor's niece Iulia Livilla[89]—who was herself exiled and later put to death—spent eight years in 'terrible Corsica' until, after Messalina's death Agrippina, Iulia Livilla's sister, married Claudius and secured Seneca's recall in order that he might act as the young Nero's tutor.

The barbarous language of the natives of Corsica was in some danger, Seneca feared, of corrupting the purity of his own Latin style; but, for the rest, he sought in a highly artificial consolatio to his mother to persuade her (and so himself) that his predicament was not to be deplored. So far from missing rich food and clothing, he had achieved, in poverty and the simple life, what every Stoic should aim at achieving.

Unattractive as Corsica was, many people lived in the island from deliberate choice:

Where will you find a place which is just bare precipitous rock, like
Corsica—a place so lacking in natural resources, with a lower standard
of civilization among its natives, more unattractively situated and with
such a bad climate? Yet the native-born Corsicans are in a minority.
So, if even a place like this has tempted people to move from their own
home-towns, there cannot be anything so awful in changing your
place of residence.

As for occupation, he was as free in Corsica as in Rome to con-
template the operations of nature and of the physical universe, and to
speculate on their causes. This has a brave, if slightly hollow, sound.[90]

Ovid, on the other hand, relegated at the age of fifty to Tomi on the
coast of the Black Sea, was unable to find one single consolation. His
condemnation followed and arose (we do not know exactly how)
from the public disgrace of the younger Julia, Augustus' granddaughter, in A.D. 8. He survived nine years of exile, without his wife,
who remained in Rome. The selection of Tomi was a piece of brutal
vindictiveness on Augustus' part. Had Britain been conquered already,
it might well have been to Britain that Ovid was sent (for men were
banished to Britain later), as being equally far from Rome and even
more barbaric.

The climate of Tomi was insufferable. In winter the gates were
closed and people lived in a beleaguered citadel, under attack from
marauders who crossed the frozen Danube and shot poisoned arrows
into the town. There were no books. Hardly anybody spoke Latin and
those who spoke Greek spoke it with a vile Getic accent. Even his own
Muse, he felt, had deserted him. In the end he was driven to learn the
hateful language of the place and, in an exhibition of virtuosity, wrote
and recited a poem in Getic in Augustus' honour. In the *Tristia* and
the *Epistulae ex Ponto* we have the record of his inconsolable nostalgia
for Italy and Rome.[91]

For the fortunate who had not incurred disgrace happy retirement was
the reward of a life well led. People said, 'He has worked hard to earn
this respite,' '*Multo labore hoc otium meruit.*'[92] And, moving out of the
the sun into the shade, a man was expected to spend his time creditably;
his should be '*laudabile otium*'.[93] It should not be the life of the rich
bachelor or widower surrounded by sycophantic legacy-hunters,

captatores. It should not be Lucullus' life or Vatia's, a last spree of wanton self-indulgence.

There was no better relaxation than in farming your own land. This had been the retirement of the heroes of the history books, from Cincinnatus to Scipio Africanus and the elder Cato. 'Nothing,' Cicero had written, 'is better, nothing more profitable, nothing more becoming to a gentleman.'

Ovid had always looked forward to retiring when he reached a certain age and farming the land which he had inherited from his father. '*Non ita dis visum est*'; for when his white hairs indicated that the moment had come, he had no chance of retiring to Sulmona, frozen as he was in exile on the Black Sea. When Remigius, marshal of the Court, was under a cloud after his scandalous doings in North Africa in A.D. 373, he retired to his estate near Mainz: '*a muneribus rei publicae quiescens negotiis se ruralibus dedit prope Moguntiacum in genitalibus locis.*' But vengeance pursued him. His earlier public actions were being investigated; and so he hanged himself.[94]

Retiring to the country life, a man farmed, even interested himself in experimental agriculture—in grafting or in methods of transplanting grown trees.[95] Reading and writing and philosophical reflection were, all of them, creditable exercises.

There is an agreeably ingenuous letter of the younger Pliny, written after he had been invited to dine in the country with Terentius Iunior who, after a successful career in the equestrian service, had turned his back on further promotion and had retired to farm. Regarding him as a specimen of the squirearchy, Pliny primed himself with dull questions on farming and prepared for a thoroughly tedious evening. His host, however, determined the conversation, and Pliny was amazed to find himself challenged in literary talk by a man whose Greek was as fluent as his Latin. 'You might have thought we were in Athens.'[96]

Much, of course, depended on the state of your health. Vestricius Spurinna was for the younger Pliny the supreme example of happy old age. At seventy-seven, with a distinguished public career behind him, he retained all his faculties. Living in his country villa, he called for his shoes in the morning at the second hour and walked three miles. Then, after a rest, he went for a seven-mile drive, accompanied by his wife or by a friend, and after that walked another mile. Then, after a quiet period of writing, at the ninth hour in the afternoon in winter (a little earlier in summer) he went to the baths, undressed and walked naked in the sun on a fine day and after that played ball strenuously. He took his bath and, after a short interval, lay down to dinner—a nice, cultured meal which might be prolonged even in summer until after dark.[97]

As in all societies there were men whose retirement took a form which, perhaps not unexpected by themselves, was unexpected by other people, like the boxing champion Horus who retired from the ring and took up philosophy.[98]

The nicest testimony to retirement which has come down to us is that of Ser. Sulpicius Similis, who was Prefect of the Guard with Attianus* and on whom Hadrian evidently found it easier to force retirement than he did on his colleague. Similis was an attractive man. Once, when Trajan summoned him to his presence as a centurion before he summoned the tribunes, Similis said, 'Sir, this is contrary to discipline.' So, when Hadrian retired him—'*successorem dedit*'—he withdrew to his farm and enjoyed seven happy years as a farmer. He composed his own epitaph: 'Similis died, so many years old; he lived for seven.'[99]

From the time of Augustus a man who signed on for service in any branch of the Roman armed forces knew that, if he was not killed, discharged sick (with *causaria missio*) or cashiered (*ignominiae causa missus*),[100] and if he was not promoted to officer-rank, he would be due for retirement at a certain date, so many years ahead. Return to civilian life was '*ad Lares redire*', '*ad Lares suos redire*' or '*discedere in otium*'.[101]

After the establishment of the *aerarium militare* in A.D. 6 (a treasury exclusively devoted to the payment of military gratuities), the Guardsman's honourable discharge (*honesta missio*) would normally come after sixteen years, the legionary's discharge from full service after twenty years (with a further five years on active reserve—*sub vexillis*—after that) and the auxiliary soldier's after twenty-five.[102]

Until Septimius Severus it was a condition of legionary (but not of auxiliary) service that a man should not marry[103]—a condition which is reflected in the fact that nearly all the surviving gravestones and monuments of legionaries in the early Empire were erected by parents, brothers or fellow-soldiers. In the absence, therefore, of any system of widow's or dependents' allowances, the legionary had no official family to worry about. If he kept a woman in the civilian settlement attached to the camp (the *canabae*), and if he was killed, his savings in

* On Attianus, see p. 181 above.

his unit's bank could be transferred to her, if he had made a will to that effect, and his contribution to the unit's funeral fund would cover the expenses of his burial.[104] His woman would probably find some other soldier to replace him, and would have to support any children who might have been born to them (who would not, of course, have Roman citizenship). Once a son of his was eighteen, though illegitimate, as long as he was fit and active, the army would be delighted to recruit him into an auxiliary unit or even, giving him citizenship, into the legions.[105] For the existence of sons born out of wedlock to legionaries there is ample evidence.[106]

The sum that the legionary received on discharge was at first 12,000 sesterces (just over thirteen times his annual pay of 900 sesterces). This was raised by a third when Domitian was emperor, and then spiralled rapidly in the general monetary inflation which started at the end of the second century. The pay of a Guardsman was considerably higher, indeed more than three times as high by the time of Augustus' death, partly perhaps because of the greater prestige of the Praetorian Guard, partly perhaps because of the greater cost of living in and around Rome —though the Guardsman's corn allowance, at least from the time of Nero, was additional to and not, like the legionary's, a stoppage from his pay.[107]

Although we have numerous discharge certificates (*diplomata*) of auxiliaries, showing that they received Roman citizenship for themselves and their sons,[108] we do not know what gratuity they received, just as we do not know their pay on service.

In his early forties, then, an ex-legionary, a 'veteran', faced civilian life unmarried, with his gratuity and whatever he may have saved from his pay, from the donatives distributed at each emperor's accession and on other red-letter days or from any booty shared out after a victory in which he had taken part.

If his unit was under strength, as was often the case, he might be pressed to soldier on, with what financial inducements we do not know; and we have evidence of legionaries who had done thirty, even forty, years' service in the ranks. Alternatively he might have been commissioned during his service and so extend his period of service or, after accepting his discharge, he might sign on again, this time with the commissioned rank of a centurion. There are numerous inscriptions which show the careers of such men. Juvenal's 'centurion at sixty' was no fantasy.[109]

Before the discharge system was regularized by Augustus in A.D. 6, it had been normal practice in the late Republic, one followed by Julius Caesar and by Augustus himself in the extensive discharges after the end of the civil wars, to settle veterans in new colonies in which whole units turned civilian (we should like to know how they acquired their wives), and in which each man received his own grant of land.

An attempt was made under Nero in A.D. 60 to revive this practice, in order to repopulate cities in the south of Italy (Antium and Tarentum) which—perhaps because of the spread of malaria—were becoming seriously under-populated. But the scheme failed: 'The men slipped back to the provinces where they done their service. They left no children, because marriage and bringing up children was something outside their experience.' The experiment might have had a greater chance of success if the new settlers had known one another already. Instead they seem to have been picked haphazardly from a variety of different units. For Antium (Anzio), indeed, confirmation of Tacitus' account of the failure of the experiment has been found in the dedication of the funeral monument of an ex-centurion who settled down and became a municipal magistrate. When he died, he seems to have had no family to make his heirs; instead he left his property to four other ex-centurions—though it must be admitted that two of the four were ex-centurions of the Vigiles and of the Praetorian Guard in Rome, and do not fit easily into Tacitus' description.[110]

However, the old system was not abandoned, and it continued profitably on the frontiers of the Empire. Veterans were settled at Cologne (Colonia Agrippinensis) when it was made a colony in A.D. 50 and at Camulodunum (Colchester) in Britain in the same year— 'a strong post against rebels, and to communicate to the natives the notion of obeying the law'. In eleven years (before the Britons sacked the place in A.D. 61) the veterans earned nothing but hatred for their behaviour. In Cologne, on the other hand, a successful integration of veterans and natives occurred; they intermarried, got on well together and within twenty years were conscious of themselves as a single society—as they explained to the Tencteri from across the river in the Rhine revolt of 70, when it was suggested that they might care to slaughter all the Romans in the town.[111]

The great city of Timgad in North Africa was established as a colony in A.D. 100 on Trajan's instruction, as a settlement for veterans of the Third Legion, stationed in Numidia. Its position was attractive, and it grew rapidly; at the same time it was a strategic outpost against marauders from the South.[112]

After the settlement of A.D. 6 individual gratuities were sometimes given in land, not in cash—generally in land near the frontiers, in the districts where the men had served. Inevitably there were complaints about the quality of these land grants.[113] If a discharged soldier did not want to take this land and farm it, presumably he sold it. With the proceeds and his savings, or with his gratuity in cash, he might return to his home town, if he had one,[114] marry and settle down to a job in civilian life. Soldiers from the Rhine in particular returned to their homes in Spain or Provence, in search of a kinder climate. In particular men of commissioned rank (ex-centurions and ex-tribunes) often returned home. They tended to belong to a higher social class and so might have property to return to; and they often proceeded to take a full part in local municipal life, holding magistracies and belonging to the local senate.[115]

On the other hand, a veteran might remain in the district in which he had served—a large number of the discontented veterans whom Nero had tried to settle at Antium and Tarentum slipped back to the frontier country which they knew well—and there he might either farm or set up in civilian life in a trade which he had learnt on service, for the army trained great numbers of specialists—in the building trade, farriers, blacksmiths, cooks, men with extensive veterinary knowledge. We know of a soldier who, on discharge, opened a shop at Mainz and sold swords.[116]

VI

HOLIDAYS

✦✦✦

ALL OVER the Roman world some festivals were holidays for some people and some, like the Saturnalia, were holidays for everybody; and the public games clearly constituted holiday-breaks for a number of people. But we do not know at all to how many days of holiday in the year, paid or unpaid, working men were entitled. Our only evidence concerns a small number of apprentices (to weavers, for instance, or jewellers) in Egypt, whose apprenticeship-contracts or work-sheets have survived on papyrus. In one case eighteen days a year were allowed, in another twenty, provided these were festival days. In a third case thirty-six days a year were allowed, and there was no stipulation about their being festival days. Lucian's Parasite says that every craftsman had one or two days holiday a month. It can, therefore, be assumed that every working man was entitled to a certain number of days off in the year.[1]

1. Country Houses and Estates

Protracted holidays were a different matter, and such holidays were an experience only of the rich, who could afford them, and of school-children (and, therefore, of teachers) and, in the form of leave, of members of the fighting services. So restricted are our sources that even in the case of the rich our knowledge mainly concerns those whose life centred on Rome.

Luxurious country and seaside hotels not having been devised, the rich Roman went to stay at his own or at a friend's country house. To this the only occasional exception was the spa, sought for its particular cure. More than a hundred spas have left their records in Italy and the provinces, particularly in the West, places where invalids sought alleviation from such common complaints as rheumatism, gout and intestinal disorders—and even, in some cases, persons hoped to be cured of alcoholism or lechery.[2] Their names proclaimed—and often still proclaim—their use: Aquae in Roman times, Bains, Baden or Bagni today. Aix-en-Provence (Aquae Sextiae) was a Roman settlement from the first conquest of Gaul in the late second century B.C. 'because of its abundant supply of water from warm and from cold springs.'[3] People went to a spa sometimes for the sake of its baths, sometimes in order to drink its waters.[4]

In Italy the sulphur baths of Albulae* were in easy reach both of Rome and of Tibur[5]; there were a number of watering-places in Etruria[6]; and a large number of cure-places were in the bay of Naples in the vicinity of Cumae and Baiae, the most famous being the Aquae Cumanae, the vast complex of whose baths delights the tourist today. Here a Roman of the late Republic or early Empire, if he did not possess a villa of his own, was unfortunate if he could not invite himself to stay with a friend.[7] Otherwise he took lodgings, perhaps in the accommodation which was attached to the baths themselves. Here were the enclosed sweat-baths 'in the myrtle-groves above Cumae', where the hot sulphurous steam which rose out of the ground was found to alleviate rheumatism in particular.[8] These baths were tried in a final and unsuccessful attempt to arrest the last illness of Hadrian.[9] Sinuessa, further north on the coast, had baths which were claimed to cure, among other complaints, sterility in women, madness in men. The freedman Narcissus, whose presence might have ruined her plans, was persuaded by Agrippina to go down here to take a cure for his gout, so as to have him out of the way while she murdered her husband, the emperor Claudius.[10]

Spas took a natural pride in their reputation. Popularity and patronage brought big profits, and a change in medical fashion could cause disaster—to the establishments at Cumae, for instance, when the doctor Antonius Musa recommended cold baths instead of hot as a universal panacea, curing the emperor Augustus with sensational success in B.C. 23 and killing his nephew by the same treatment a few months later. The fad was revived by a Massiliot doctor under Nero.[11]

Apart from actual spas, there were particular environments which were recommended for invalids—for instance, pine woods for the tubercular; also Fréjus (Forum Iulii) because of its climate and its milk.[12]

An exceedingly rich man might possess a house with a park (horti) in Rome, a country house within easy reach of the city (villa suburbana),

---

* For a story about which, see p. 32 above.

an expensive house at the sea, probably in Campania (*villa maritima sumptuosa*) and even other country houses which might or might not have farms or estates attached to them. It was a mark of unostentatious thrift in Atticus that, while he could have afforded all of these luxuries he was content merely to possess two country estates, one at Arretium (Arezzo), the other at Nomentum (Mentana), just over twenty kilometres out of Rome.[13]

The fashion among a limited number of the very rich of building villas in Rome surrounded by gardens which were often as large as parks (comparable with the modern grounds of the Villa Torlonia and the Villa Doria Pamfili) started, under Hellenistic influence, in the last century of the Republic and continued into the Empire.[14] We know the names of about seventy owners of such properties. They lay chiefly on the right bank of the Tiber, starting at the river and running back into the hills of Monte Mario and of the Gianicolo, and, on the left bank, on the Pincio. It was not until Maecenas buried the stinking graveyards of the Esquiline under tons of earth that this district too became a part of Rome's Green Belt.[15]

With the establishment of the Empire some of these great gardens— in particular Julius Caesar's in Trastevere, where Cleopatra and her consort had been lodged when they were in Rome in 45/4 B.C., and Agrippa's, on the left bank of the Tiber, between the Corso (Via Lata) and the river—were bequeathed to the populace of Rome and became public parks. In Trastevere an artificial lake fifty acres large was constructed by Augustus amid the parkland for naval displays, the *stagnum navale*.[16] Many other gardens which emperors or empresses coveted passed on their owners' often accelerated deaths into imperial possession. This was the case with most of the Esquiline parks. Likewise the great gardens of Sallust and Lucullus, which covered the greater part of the Quirinal and of the Pincio, had become imperial by the mid-first century A.D., Lucullus' gardens having been greatly improved by their owner Valerius Asiaticus—at the cost of his life, for Messalina wanted them. After having his pyre moved to a position where its heat could do no damage to the trees, Valerius took his life there in A.D. 47. Messalina's enjoyment was short, for only a year later she was herself driven to the merciless extremity of suicide in those same gardens. Much stress was given to the magnificence of the gardens which Seneca had laid out by those who set out to poison Nero's mind against him.[17]

The finest of all the imperial gardens in Rome was also the most short-lived, the parkland of the Golden House which with intemperate and tasteful extravagance Nero laid out after the great fire of A.D. 64, over an area extending from the Palatine to the Esquiline, 125 acres on one calculation, 370 on another.* The chief feature of the gardens was a great lake 'like the sea' on the site later occupied by the Colosseum. 'There was country, the variation of tilled fields, vineyards, grazing land and woods, with domestic and wild animals.' The life of these gardens which, to the public anger, encroached heavily on the city's highways and amenities, was a short one. After fifteen years the lake had disappeared and the Colosseum had taken its place. After fifty years the great house itself was underground, a foundation for Trajan's Baths.[18]

Even so, a considerable number of *horti* still survived in private hands at the end of the second century A.D. Central Rome was, in fact, surrounded by a Green Belt, a thing highly pleasing from aesthetic considerations, but a barrier to any convenient extension of the heavily overbuilt residential quarters of the city.

Such *horti* afforded to their exclusive owners something of the quiet, coolness and relaxation for whose sake most rich Romans possessed a house in the country within easy reach of the city. The empress Livia's villa at Prima Porta was only eight miles from Rome. The suburban villas of two of the richest men known to us in the first century A.D. were no more than four miles out, those of Seneca[19] and of Martial's patron, the sinister and successful informer, M. Aquilius Regulus,[20] who also possessed *horti* in Rome.[21]

In general, however, the suburban villas of the rich were at a greater distance, down on the sea, like Pliny's Laurentine villa just south of Ostia, or up in the hills, chiefly at Tibur, which was twenty miles from Rome, or at Tusculum (Tusculo), which was nearer. Access to Rome was easy (Pliny could get out to his villa at the end of a day's work in the capital[22]) so that there were practical advantages by comparison with relegation to the more distant Campanian coast. The fortunate owners of such villas, if they were not detained in Rome by official business, were able to avoid the scorching summer heat of Rome; they went out to them regularly in early July, and did not return to Rome until September was over, September being regarded as the most treacherous of all the hot months, the time when fevers spread in Rome and the undertakers did a flourishing business.[23] Shade and the scent of laurels

* See *TDAR* 167f. The Vatican grounds cover 75 acres, Hyde Park in London 390.

were thought to give immunity from plague. Suburban villas, more-over, were convenient resorts for convalescence—Tusculum, as we know, to Cicero, when his stomach was out of order, Tibur to Catullus after a bout of bronchitis.[24] And they offered quick and convenient refuge to their owners when there was disorder in Rome itself. In the chaos which followed the murder of Pertinax in A.D. 193 it was to his suburban villa that every prominent man in Rome most prudently scuttled.[25]

It was on Tibur, behind which Horace had his little farm at Licenza, that the poets chiefly spilled their epithets: Tibur was cool (*gelidum*) in summer; it had an equable climate in winter ('*mite solum Tiburis*'); it sprawled down the hillside (*supinum*), and the river Anio ran through it, cascading down to the plain below, then as it does now.[26] Metellus Numidicus, consul of 109 B.C., had a villa here, which passed in due course to his grandson Metellus Scipio (consul of 52 B.C., and father-in-law of Pompey), on whose death it was annexed by Antony and so no doubt passed in due course to Augustus, for Tibur and Praeneste were the hill-towns to which he chiefly resorted, travelling slowly by litter and only by night.[27] Another prominent man who in the age of Trajan owned a villa at Tibur with grounds on both banks of the river Anio was the poet P. Manilius Vopiscus, son and father of Roman consuls; Statius has left a description of its luxurious appointments and of its natural charm.[28]

On the plain close under Tibur Hadrian built the most remarkable of all Roman villas, whose pillage in stone has built much of modern Tivoli and whose pillage in works of art has helped to fill the museums in Rome. It was the inspiration of the most travelled and in some ways the most cultured of all Rome's emperors, and was probably designed by himself. Its buildings, each to suit a different mood, a different purpose, its pleasances, gardens, pools, fountains and watercourses cover an area of over seven hundred acres. Hadrian himself can have spent little time here, respites in his extensive travels. How much or how little it was used after his death, we cannot say, for ancient historians hardly thought it worth a mention. Its vast and extensive remains, often skilfully restored, with water once again filling Canopus, the marine theatre and the great *piscina* of the Pecile, are a provocative challenge even to the least imaginative.[29]

For all Tibur's attractions, Tusculum—on the hill above Frascati—was evidently by far the most popular place for a suburban villa, at least in the last fifty years of the Republic. The sites of a hundred and thirty-one Roman villas have been identified by the archaeologists, and from literary sources we know the names of thirty-four distinguished men who owned villas there, from the elder Cato in the second century B.C. to the younger Pliny at the time of Trajan. Sulla, Hortensius, Lucullus, Catulus, Cicero and Pompey all possessed villas there.[30] It was Cicero's Tusculan villa (which had once been Sulla's) that Clodius' louts ravaged at the time of his exile, doing damage to the tune of half a million sesterces, so that, depressed and out of pocket on his return, Cicero looked for a purchaser and even thought of dispensing with a suburban villa altogether; and it was the Tusculan villa of the spendthrift M. Scaurus, aedile in 58 B.C., that was burnt down by his infuriated slaves.[31]

Other popular sites for villas up in the hills were 'tall', 'chill' Praeneste (Palestrina), Lanuvium, which Augustus liked and, further north, Nomentum, where Atticus had one of his only two Italian country properties, Seneca had a villa, and Martial had a small property.[32] This was a district where, with attention, vines could be made to flourish and big money was to be made by enterprising vine-growers.[33]

There was also Alba, where Pompey and later Domitian had great villas above the lake, and where Statius had a little property which Domitian improved by giving it running water.[34]

The suburban villa might be a luxurious country house, finely furnished with works of art, having well-watered gardens, which were laid out in cool splendour, the prototype of such magnificent villas as the Villa d'Este at Tivoli or the Villa Aldobrandini at Frascati. On the other hand, it might have a farm attached and be a *villa rustica*. Horace at Licenza behind Tivoli, with his eight slaves and his foreman, and Martial at Nomentum, farmed land and made money by so doing.[35] Indeed Columella, writing at the time of Nero, made the point that, with the greater and greater calls of public life in Rome, there was much to be said for the possession of farm property at no great distance from the city, so that an owner could slip out to it every day after his business in Rome was finished. There was an old Roman saying that nothing fertilized land as well as its master's eye.[36]

Most Romans of consequence in the last century of the Republic and in the early Empire possessed a villa, either on high ground overlooking the sea or on the sea shore itself.[37]

Of coastal resorts north of Rome we hear far less than we do of those to the south. Traversed by the Via Aurelia, the Etruscan coastland was perfectly accessible, but, while it produced wines* and, especially off Cosa and Monte Argentario, good fish, the land was swampy and for large stretches the climate was unhealthy; with whatever etymological impropriety, the elder Cato derived the name Graviscae from 'gravis aer.'[38] Cosa, which stands on high ground, and where there are numerous holiday villas today, was an important town; Monte Argentario, just north of it, also the site of many enviable modern villas, may have been the property of the Domitii Ahenobarbi in the late Republic, but there is no evidence that it was greatly frequented†.[39]

But between Civitavecchia (Centum Cellae) and Rome the climate was healthy enough, and on this stretch of the coast there were numerous villas. Civitavecchia itself was a clever discovery of Trajan; there he built a villa for himself, of which the younger Pliny, an official visitor to an imperial Council, has left us a description; its site, and the sites of a number of neighbouring villas, have been identified but not yet excavated.[40] Trajan's genius, moreover, made Centum Cellae what it is today, a splendid harbour. South of Centum Cellae lay Pyrgi, site of startling recent excavations concerning its earlier history, where Nero's 'utterly detestable' father, Domitius Ahenobarbus, evidently had a villa, for it was here that he died of dropsy.[41] Further south, a little way off the Via Aurelia, was Alsium, where there were plenty of villas in the late Republic. It was here that M. Aemilius Porcina built higher than the regulations allowed, and was fined by the censors of 125 B.C. for doing so; and in 45 B.C. Cicero could think of four different friends to whose villas in Alsium he might invite himself to stay. In the second half of the first century A.D. that noble character Verginius Rufus possessed a villa at Alsium which passed into the hands of the mother-in-law of the younger Pliny. The Antonine emperors, too, had a villa here, where, as we know from Fronto, Marcus Aurelius, who was so bad at relaxing, allowed himself short holidays.[42] Inland between Alsium and Rome there was Lorium, where in the second century A.D. Antoninus Pius was brought up and where he built himself 'a palace', which was truly 'suburban', being within a day's distance of Rome—a villa which Marcus Aurelius inherited and used.[43]

Most seaside villas were south of Rome on the coast below Anzio

---

* Present-day Maccarese, a heavy red wine much drunk in Rome, comes from the ancient Graviscae.

† There is a persistent local tradition that the name comes from Domitii who were bankers (argentarii).

(Antium), in particular round the bay of Naples, from the Capo di Miseno in the north to the extreme tip of the Sorrentine peninsula (Athenaeum, Punta Campanella) in the south.[44]

Possession of such villas went back to the second century B.C., when Scipio Africanus had a country villa at 'swampy' Liternum, a squalid enough establishment if judged by later standards, though it continued to be inhabited and its land to be farmed. Indeed it received something of the respect due to an historic monument, and in the elder Pliny's time people were still shown a giant olive tree and a myrtle, both planted, it was said, by Africanus himself two and a half centuries earlier.[45] And towards the end of the second century B.C. Cornelia, mother of the Gracchi, retired after the death of her sons to a villa at Misenum and lived there, a gracious and generous hostess. M. Antonius the orator, consul in 99 B.C., possessed a villa at Misenum which was inherited in succession by his son and by his grandson, the triumvir.[46]

On the coastline of the bay of Naples from Misenum in the north to the Sorrentine peninsula in the south there were two important cities and a number of small towns. The two important cities were Greek, Puteoli and Naples.

Puteoli was the most important harbour-town in Italy until the time of Trajan. Its sea-front is known to us from engravings on glasses which were sold to tourists. It was handsome but predominantly a commercial city.

Naples, on the other hand, was an isolated portion of Greece, a wholly Greek city, talking Greek, enjoying Greek games from Augustus' time onwards, Virgil's city, relaxed and cultured.[47]

There were rich men, often of Campanian origin, who lived all the year round in or near the towns, many of them engaged in business or commerce, and there were rich Romans who built, inherited or bought holiday villas at one place or other round the bay. We know the names of over forty prominent Romans who were the owners of such villas at the time of the late Republic.[48]

An occasional very rich man like L. Lucullus possessed two maritime villas, one at Misenum, one at Naples; Pompey had estates at Cumae, Alba, Formiae and in the ager Falernus which sold for seventy million sesterces[49]; but we know of nobody in the late Republic or early Empire who possessed as many villas as Cicero, who was not rich at all.[50] Apart from his inland villas at Tusculum and at Arpinum, he possessed at one time or other villas on the coast at Antium, Astura and Formiae, and three in Campania—at Cumae (on the eastern slope of the Lucrine Lake), at Puteoli and at Pompeii. His Pompeian villa he possessed before 60 B.C., and always retained. He seems to have purchased his 'Cumanum', something far smarter, some time after his return from exile in 57 B.C., and the villa at Puteoli, like that at Astura, was acquired towards the end of his life, probably as a legacy from his banker-friend, M. Cluvius.*

The history of the ownership of many of these villas in the Republic was a melancholy reflection of the politics and economics of revolution. C. Marius owned two villas, one at Misenum, another at Baiae, no distance away. In the Sullan proscriptions they both came on the market. The villa at Misenum was acquired by Sulla's daughter Cornelia for the equivalent of a song, three hundred thousand sesterces; she subsequently disposed of it to Lucullus for ten millions, over thirty times the price she paid for it. The villa at Baiae passed into the hands of an erratic Sullan henchman, the elder Curio, and in due course was inherited by his son.[51]

Business might always be combined with pleasure, and there were those who were prepared to invest money in commercial property in the big Campanian towns. The family of Q. Hortensius, the distinguished orator of the late Republic, owned so much property in Puteoli that a district of the city, the regio Hortensiana, was named after them; and Cicero's inheritance from M. Cluvius in 45 B.C. included dilapidated shops in Puteoli which, once repaired, brought him profit.[52]

Emperors naturally shared the tastes of their rich subjects and were able to outshine the richest, for as a legacy of the civil wars Augustus acquired in a comparatively small area Julius Caesar's villa at Baiae, Pompey's at Cumae and Antony's at Misenum. Augustus also inherited the villa and fishponds of the vile son of a freedman P. Vedius Pollio at Pausilypon, owned yet another villa at Surrentum and possessed, in addition, the islands of Pontiae (Ponza) and Pandateria (Ventotene), with villas which proved their value when one of his relatives required banishment—his daughter, for instance, to Pandateria, where the remains of the imperial villa are to be seen today. For himself, there was Capri, which he acquired by exchange from the city of Naples, and where there were twelve villas in three great complexes, one in the north-east, the Villa Iovis, one under Monte Solaro, the third west of Marina Grande.[53]

* At the same time Cicero sold his villa at Antium to M. Lepidus.

These villas were inherited by Tiberius, who possessed in addition a villa at Circeii on the mainland and Lucullus' (once Marius') villa at Misenum, in which he died. Other famous republican villas passed into the hands of members of the imperial family, that of Hortensius at Bauli to Antonia Maior and so, probably, to Agrippina, the mother of Nero; this was where she was staying in the spring of 59 when her son Nero decided that the time had come for her to die.[54]

But still under the Empire there were rich private owners of villas. At Baiae there was the sumptuous villa of Servilius Vatia, whose elegant splendour, together with the dissipation of its owner, provoked Seneca to write Lucilius a letter as tedious as a sermon in praise of the simple life.[55] Nero's aunt Domitia had a villa here which Nero coveted, and so she lost her life; and the conspirator C. Piso had a villa where Nero was frequently entertained and where in A.D. 65, if Piso's notions of hospitality had been as crude as those of his associates, Nero might well have been murdered at the dinner table.[56]

Three events in early imperial times affected the character of the Bay.

The first was Agrippa's act in 37 B.C. in the war against Sextus Pompeius. He blocked the Lucrine Lake* from the sea, widened the canal connecting it to Lake Avernus and connected the whole complex by a tunnel to Cumae. The two lakes constituted the Portus Iulius, a vast dockyard and training area for the fleet. However, the Lucrine Lake was far too shallow for the purpose and, once the crisis was over, the enterprise was abandoned and the fish and oysters came into their own once more.

The dockyards then moved a very short distance to Misenum, whose splendid harbour was improved by a pair of parallel arched moles and connected to a vast inner harbour, the present Mare Morto. Here for four centuries was Rome's 'Pompey', the headquarters of the western Mediterranean fleet with barracks for some ten thousand sailors, whose families required accommodation both in Misenum, now Colonia Iulia, itself and in the surrounding neighbourhood as far as Puteoli. A number of villas must have disappeared in the process and for the rich on holiday the attraction of the northern part of the bay must have been greatly lessened.[57]

The third event was the eruption of Vesuvius in A.D. 79. Herculaneum and Pompeii were buried and, though the Government took prompt

* Which was considerably larger then than now. See the article of R. F. Paget in JRS 1968, 152–69.

measures to recompense the stricken survivors, a number of property-owners must have sustained serious financial loss. Statius wrote, 'When crops grow again and the stricken land is green once more, will future generations believe that underground lie cities and people whose ancestral estates perished with them? And still the mountain-top issues its lethal threat.' Stabiae, on the fringe of the stricken area, recovered ('*Stabiaeque renatae*') and neither on the Sorrentine peninsula nor on the northern stretch of the bay does there seem to have been any fear of another such disastrous eruption. Statius tried to persuade his wife to leave Rome and settle in Naples. And from A.D. 95 the amenities of the area were greatly improved when, after the construction of the Via Domitiana, the journey to the bay from Sinuessa, where you left the Via Appia, coming from the north, was made on a strong stone highway instead of on a treacherous boggy track; though Statius exaggerated when he said that after this you could leave Rome in the early morning and be sailing on the Lucrine Lake that same evening.[58]

The habit of possessing villas on the coast, if men could afford them, continued into the following centuries, and at the end of the fourth century Symmachus, a prodigiously rich man, had villas in Campania at Bauli, Cumae, Puteoli, Naples and on the Lucrine Lake.[59] In A.D. 476 Lucullus' villa, which had had such a fantastic and long history, was chosen by Odoacer as a place of pensioned retirement for Rome's last emperor, Romulus Augustulus.

Between 100 B.C. and A.D. 100 the appearance of the Bay of Naples was transformed. Outside existing commercial cities—Puteoli, Naples, Pompeii—the wild and barren coast acquired the charming, if artificial, elegance which marks the French Riviera today. Instead of scrub there were handsome stone-built villas, set in what seemed a woodland of green trees. On the hill of the Sorrentine peninsula villa rose above villa. Bare rock was transformed. 'What was that site, that land, before it had the fortune to fall into your hands? You set a path over the bare rocks. Once there was only a track; now you have a tall colonnaded portico, so that there may be no dust on the road. On the curved shore you have set hot baths under their twin domes.' 'Here, in a spot which Nature favoured, Nature has met her master and given way to the planner; she herself has been mastered and tamed. A hill has been levelled. Where there was scrub, there are now roofs to live under. Where no soil existed, there are now tall trees. The owner has established his dominion. He has shaped and conquered the rocks and the land has submitted gladly.' Statius' language is extravagant, but his meaning is clear.[60]

Baiae in particular was a positive nest of rich villas and even by Augustus' time was almost the size of Puteoli. Though Romans tended to possess villas round the bay and not in Naples itself (the hot baths of Naples, though every bit as good as those of Baiae, were much less frequented), Naples, retaining so much of the character of a foreign city, was always a resort for those who were staying or living in the neighbourhood.* Its general atmosphere—and this sounds odd today—was one of profound relaxation. It was 'otiosa Neapolis', 'in otium nata,' a place where it did not matter what you wore, where even high-born senators were to be seen in the tunica pulla, which normally they wore only in the privacy of their own gardens. And, after a working life in Rome, Greeks who had never shed their nationality, teachers in particular, retired to live here.[61]

Roman grandees had not the whole of Campania to themselves. Eleven farms (villae rusticae) outside Pompeii on the lower slopes, then green and flourishing, of Vesuvius have been excavated and their owners identified. One belonged to Agrippa Postumus, the grandson of Augustus, and perhaps to his father before him, while the other ten belonged to local citizens of Pompeii.[62] And many villas, no doubt, just as tastelessly furnished, belonged to freedmen as opulent and vulgar as the fictitious Trimalchio, with his large house at Puteoli, land at Pompeii and estate at Cumae.[63] The loose women out boating, the parties singing and brawling late at night, by which Seneca was shocked, could well have been Trimalchio's friends.[64]

We think of the country homes of rich Romans as being chiefly on the Alban and Sabine hills near Rome or on the sea-coast, particularly in Campania, because so much of our evidence derives from the poets and concerns their patrons in the last years of the Republic and the early years of the Empire; and Campania is an area in which archaeological excavation has been particularly fruitful. But in a world in which there were no government bonds, no safe equities, a very considerable part of every rich man's capital was invested in land which, whether he farmed it directly through a bailiff or let it out to tenants, had to be made to pay. Pompey's family, whose influence was so strong in Picenum—from which Pompey raised a private army and brought it to Sulla's aid in 83 B.C.—certainly had large holdings of land there.[65] The younger Cato had property in Lucania, which he visited.[66]

* See p. 324 for its Greek-type games.

Thanks to Caesar's account of the Civil War we know that L. Domitius Ahenobarbus, Cato's brother-in-law, had estates at Corfinium just north of Sulmona so large that he could promise the soldiers whom he levied twenty-five acres a man, to say nothing of his other property on the Etrurian coast round Cosa, from which he secured slaves, freedmen and tenants to crew his ships in the war.[67]

From Julius Caesar's time onwards the complexion of the Senate changed. The distinguished families, whose names featured on every page of republican history, died out fast and a steadily increasing number of senators were men of new families from the country towns of Italy, just as Cicero's family in the late Republic had come from Arpinum; they even came from such romanized provinces as Sicily and Narbonese Gaul. By Vespasian's time it was an exceptional senator who had not such a background.[68] So, just as Cicero and his brother inherited family estates in the vicinity of Arpinum, these men had country houses and property in their home districts; what was new for them was the acquisition of a town house in Rome. When they could get out of Rome it was their family property which had first call on their time. They retained a strong civic loyalty and local attachment, which is admirably illustrated by the act of T. Labienus, Caesar's second-in-command in the Gallic wars, who devoted the bulk of the fortune won in that campaign to the embellishment of his home town Cingulum in Picenum.[69] Also they had financial reasons for wanting to keep an eye on their own property. Senators from Sicily and Narbonese Gaul were even dispensed from the necessity of procuring the Emperor's leave to travel outside the boundaries of Italy to visit their estates.[70]

In the younger Pliny at the turn of the first century A.D. we have an admirable example of a man with remote Italian origins. His family came from near Comum (Como) and he possessed extensive landed property both on Lake Como and in Tuscany (now in Umbria) at Tifernum Tiberinum (Città di Castello) about half way between Arezzo and Gubbio. He had villas at Como[71] and it is hard to think of any amenity which his Tifernum villa lacked; we have Pliny's very detailed description of it.[72] However welcome the relaxation that he found there, it was the business of an extensive landlord which made a first call on his time. Large sums of money were involved, rents of four hundred thousand sesterces in the case of his Tuscan estates.[73]

From the end of the first century A.D. Italian senators began to lose ground to men of provincial extraction. To ensure that senators showed proper concern for the economic welfare of Italy, Trajan enforced a regulation by which every candidate for office was bound to have a third of his capital invested in Italian land.[74] So the provincial senator's Italian country house will have been on the estate which he bought; he formed new local associations in Italy. In the third century Cassius Dio, whose home was in Bithynia, found Capua a congenial place of retreat: 'I stay there when I am in Italy. I chose Capua because of its peace and quiet as a place for writing when free from business in Rome.'[75]

Once established as a social necessity for people of means, the villa acquired more and more luxurious features, many of them borrowed from Greece, and these soon became standard.[76] The ideal situation was thought to be on high ground facing south-east, so as to catch the winter sun, and great importance attached to a good view.[77] But as owners resided chiefly in the spring, summer and early autumn, coolness and shade were the chief requisites, as they are in Italian gardens still— the movement, splash and sparkle of water in fountain, nymphaeum and artificial channel[78] and shade from stone porticoes, which were serviceable also for exercise when it rained,* or from avenues of trees (*xysti*), in whose shadow you could walk and talk.[79] Particularly favourite trees were the cyprus and plane, whose roots connoisseurs watered with wine. The plane tree, indeed, was symbolic of uncreative leisure; it was 'the tree that gave shade to drinkers', 'widowed', 'barren', 'unmarried', in sharp contrast with the 'serviceable' elm; for the moralizing Roman expected even trees to behave like good Romans and be useful. The elm served as a prop for the climbing vine, as it does in Campania today.[80]

Favourite shrubs were the myrtle, box, oleander, laurel and bay, and there were fruit trees like the peach and the cherry (which Lucullus introduced to Italy from Asia Minor in the late Republic). Ivy was very popular.[81] Trees and shrubs were treated in a manner which has since, from the Renaissance onwards, been a feature of the distinctively Italian garden. They were closely clipped, *nemora tonsilia*. This was a novelty thought to originate with C. Matius in the time of Augustus, and there was topiary, the earliest mention of which occurs in a letter written by Cicero about a villa of his brother in 54 B.C.[82]

There were also flowers, to be enjoyed as they blossomed and to be plucked to make the wreaths which men wore when they drank, once

---

* There might even be a completely underground passage or a covered passage with windows for walking, a *cryptoporticus*, such as is to be seen on the Palatine today and also in Hadrian's villa.

dinner was over.* Roses were best of all, the roses of Paestum enjoying particular renown. Moralizing again, Quintilian contrasted ground used to produce a rich corn harvest with that employed to grow lilies, violets and anemones.[83]

If the owner's pride bordered on megalomania and a poor neighbour's tree overhanging his boundary offended him, he might decide to burn it down; if the neighbour's cottage burnt down too, that was an unfortunate accident—if we may believe a specimen lawsuit of the elder Seneca. And there were Roman parallels to the story of Naboth's vineyard; just as, on a larger scale, if you wished to extend your estate at the expense of your neighbour and he was unwilling to sell, you might turn starving beasts on to his fields by night to consume his crops until he was persuaded to change his mind.[84]

Nature was improved by art. There were statues, copies of Greek originals, bought or pilfered in Greece, Asia Minor or Sicily—where Verres could scarcely see or even hear of a respectable statue without deciding to make it his own. These stood about the grounds or broke the bare austerity of the porticoes. And, dotted about the ground, there might be little temples. There was not only the marble villa; there were also the marbled gardens, *horti marmorei*.[85]

Other luxuries included enclosed courts for ball games, open—even heated—swimming pools, *piscinae*.[86] There were, of course, always luxurious hot baths in the villa itself.

The villa should have its kitchen garden (*hortus*) and, if the situation warranted it, its vineyard—for, as long as it was drinkable, there was great pride in offering a guest a home-grown wine. Martial mocked a certain Bassus who was seen driving out of Rome to his villa, his carriage crammed with vegetables of all kinds, a cage of small birds, a hare and a sucking pig—packed, in fact, with the produce which a man should be bringing back with him when he returned from his country house.[87]

Certain villas, from the late Republic onwards, while not surrounded by large property, had extensive fishponds which served for use and for spectacle, for Romans, like other people, enjoyed watching fish and, if they were rich, they were prepared to pay handsomely for the pleasure. Such were the *piscinarii*, whom Cicero despised. Some fish were eaten in the household, others presumably disposed of in the market—except from the villas of such fish-lovers as the orator Hortensius, who wept over the death of a favourite fish in the ponds of his

* See p. 49.

villa at Bauli and refused ever to eat his own fish, buying fish instead
from the market in Puteoli. Better this than the example of the notorious
P. Vedius Pollio, in Augustus' time, who, when he decided to rid
himself of an unsatisfactory slave, threw him into the pond to feed his
lampreys.[88]

In the matter of fish, Campania was particularly favoured. First of
all there were the oyster-beds in the Lucrine Lake, started early in the
first century B.C. and developed successfully by a prominent speculator,
C. Sergius Orata, the inventor of shower-baths.[89] Secondly, refined
taste increasingly disparaged freshwater fish and appreciated sea-fish.
Marcius Philippus, consul of 56 B.C., is said once at dinner to have spat
out the fish (which was freshwater) with the remark, 'Damme, if I
didn't think this was fish.' Hence the engineering and tunnelling by
which seawater was admitted through sluices at regular intervals to
fishponds of villas near the sea, the showpieces of such extravagance
being Lucullus' villas at Naples and Misenum; 'a Roman Xerxes'
was what Pompey called him.[90]

Today you have only to descend a short distance to the shore from
the National Archaeological Museum at Sperlonga (just south of
Terracina) to see such fishponds, still stocked with fish, at the so-called
Grotto of Tiberius. 'Here we can check word for word the truth of the
things the classical writers described; the knowledge and capital outlay
involved in selection, excavation and construction, filling and func-
tioning of such highly complicated pools, some with rock bottoms and
others with sand. They were provided with mazes of passages and locks
for regulating the flow and dosage of the waters which were provided
as sweet or as brackish as their precious charges required.'[91]

As has been observed, Lucullus' fishponds were a byword. After his
death his fish were sold and, according to the elder Pliny, fetched four
million sesterces.[92] C. Lucilius Hirrus' comparatively small estate sold
soon after Julius Caesar's death for the same sum, because of the value
of its fish-ponds.[93]

Not only fishponds (*piscinae**). There were preserves of wild animals
(*leporaria* and *vivaria*†) of hares and boars, for instance, and of poultry
and birds of all sorts, from thrushes, which the Romans considered a
great delicacy and netted in the bushes, to peacocks (*pavones*), with
special dining-rooms, so that you could eat in full sight of, almost

* The word *piscina* means either a fish-pond or a swimming bath.
† *Vivaria*, enclosures for live things, could be used of fishponds as well as of enclosures
for birds and animals.

among, the animals and birds. Birds kept for profit were geese (for *foie gras*), hens, doves, storks, pigeons, peacocks. Dormice were profitably bred too.[94] And some men had apiaries on a large scale.[95]

In the general economy of Italy villas differed. The majority of those in the Bay of Naples were, to judge by the literary evidence, no more than extremely luxurious seaside houses, and archaeology has established that the same was the case with some of the villas at Circeii.[96] Yet from his villa at Puteoli the fictitious Trimalchio farmed vast estates. Martial describes the villa of Faustinus at Cumae who, disparaging planes, myrtles and clipped box, went in for general farming (vines, poultry, cattle), evidently with great success.[97] And it should not be forgotten that one of the most luxurious villas of which we have a detailed record, Pliny's in Tuscany, was the villa of a man who had estates there which were leased to tenants and, as we can judge from the rents, four hundred thousand sesterces a year, were very large.[98]

A 'villa' was a country house. If, as all country houses had once been, even to the time when the great Scipio Africanus came home at night sweating from his work in the fields,[99] it was a working farm house, it was a *villa rustica*[100]—like the well-appointed Villa Item and others excavated near Pompeii, or like the republican villas recently excavated at Francolise near Capua. If it was on the sea, it was a *villa maritima*. It might, or might not, have property, a *praedium*, or even an estate, a *fundus*.

Standards of luxury among the rich were rising all the time, culminating in vast imperial country mansions, Hadrian's below Tivoli, Diocletian's palace at Spalato and (if it really was imperial[101]) Piazza Armerina in Sicily.

Extravagance in villa-building on the part of private individuals in the late Republic and early Empire, an extravagance which sometimes led to bankruptcy, was mocked, gently or savagely, by satirists and roundly abused by philosophers like Seneca. They objected to the great expenditure on the import of precious marbles from overseas, especially from Greece and Asia Minor. This practice dated from the early first century B.C.[102] They deplored the turning of good agricultural land to such uneconomic use, particularly in the crowded villa-area of Campania.[103] And they never tired of abusing the 'unnatural' craze for tunnelling through rocks to bring the sea into the land and at the same time building out over the sea on piers, so as to bring the land into the sea. Paintings survive to show the existence in Campania of such piers (see pl. 5), but one may suspect that in a great many of the literary

14

passages the target was one and the same—the republican Lucullus.[104]

2. Holidays out of Rome

It is not easy to ascertain the times at which holidays were taken by the general mass of those who could afford them, because the surviving literary evidence comes from extremely limited sources, ch˙ ⌐ ᶜrom poets and from men heavily committed in public affairs like Cicero and the younger Pliny. The evidence comes from men, and in nearly every case from men who had no young children. So we do not know whether wives and children (who, if they were at school, had a long summer holiday from July 1st to October 15th*[105]) were packed off to the country or to the sea for long periods, particularly in summer, when the father of a family had himself to remain in, or within easy reach of, Rome; it is to be assumed that they were.

Students generally enjoy longer holidays than their elders; and Aulus Gellius, writing in the second century A.D., more than once recollects with pleasure summer holidays when with other students (and perhaps with a tutor, a *rhetor*, a *grammaticus* or a philosopher; so that it was something like a Reading Party) he went up to Tivoli or down to the sea at Naples or Puteoli, to escape the heat of Rome.[106]

In so far as they were not oppressed by the financial necessity of dancing regular attendance on their patrons, poets seem to have been enviably free to take what holidays they liked when they liked. Horace, persuaded by Maecenas to leave Rome in August on account of bad health, informed him that he proposed to spend September too in the hills, and that after that he would go to the sea for the winter months. Campania was good; in deep winter the far south was even better. Horace loved Tarentum and the country round it; so did Virgil.[107]

When Horace became a patient of Antonius Musa, who recommended against the hot baths of Cumae, he wondered whether to spend the winter at Salernum or further south down the coast at Velia, and wrote to a friend for information. Which had the better water, which the better wine? And, for food, how did the two places compare as concerned game and fish?[108]

The highly individual list of Martial's basic needs, whose satisfaction would bring him complete happiness even in a dismal town in Calabria,

---

* In the late fourth century school holidays may have been made to conform with the law vacations, and have lasted from June 24th to August 1st and from August 23rd to October 15th, with a short resumption of work from August 1st to 22nd. Cf. *CT* 2, 8, 19 (A.D. 389) with Aug., *Conf.* 9, 2, 2 and 4 (school in session in early August).

was as follows: an inn-keeper, a butcher and a bath; a barber and a gaming table and pieces; a small selection of his favourite books; one companion with whom he could have intelligent conversation and a young man accompanied by his girl friend.[109]

The smartest season of the year in Campania was evidently the spring, for, when times were sufficiently settled in the Republic, the Senate was regularly in recess—*discessus* or *res prolatae*[110]—for a period of a little over a month (in 56 B.C. from just after April 5th to just before May 15th), and the smart world seems to have moved down to the sea. This was the lively gossiping crowd which for a moment reduced Cicero to humility in 74 B.C. They none of them realized that he was on his way home from the tenure of his first public office, a year's quaestorship in western Sicily; they had not even noticed that he had been out of Rome. Cicero's letters of 60, 59, 55 and 54 B.C. show that he was down at one or other of his maritime villas in April and in early May.[111]

It does not seem that prominent people went down to the sea so much during the summer, and the villa at Formiae belonging to Domitius Apollinaris, suffect consul in A.D. 97, may not have been untypical, a villa which its owner adored but which he was rarely able to visit, so that its amenities were chiefly enjoyed by his resident staff of slaves.[112] In view of the fact that Rome today is deserted, except by tourists, in August and in view of the ancient fear of September as an unhealthy month,[113] this is surprising at first sight. There were many reasons. Except at night, when it might be dangerous, travelling must have been extremely uncomfortable in hot weather. The cool breezes of the hills were more refreshing than those from the sea, and snow (preserved all the year round for cooling drinks) was no doubt more easily kept in the cool ice-chambers of villas on the hills. And there were advantages, even in the dog days, in not being too far away from Rome.

The keen politician was reluctant to be at any great distance from the city, and for anybody with a big practice at the Bar absence might be impossible. So at the best he slipped away to his suburban villa, from which he could always return at short notice. In the late Republic elections were normally held in July; candidates must be on the spot, with their supporters. And the Senate might be convened on important business, as it was in 51 B.C. on August 13th and on September 1st.[114]

At the end of August 54 B.C. Cicero wrote to his brother, who was on Caesar's staff in Gaul, 'I have never been so busy in court, and this at the worst time of year, in stifling heat', and a little later, 'I escaped from the heat (I do not remember it ever being hotter) to Arpinum'— during the Ludi Romani, which then lasted from September 5th to 19th. 'I left my freedman Philotimus in Rome, to get seats for the games for members of my tribe, and I revelled in the delight of my stream.'[115] The aediles, who were responsible for the organization of the games in Rome, were less lucky.[116] In the Empire, too, July and August could be a busy time in the courts. Claudius is said to have sat in judgement from morning to night during these stifling months.[117]

The courts affected more people than learned counsel. There were also the jurors. These, according to the law prevailing at the time, were senators or equites or partly one and partly the other. Since C. Gracchus' time qualified jurors were selected from those with a Roman domicile, and the jury for any particular trial was chosen from those who were within reach of Rome at the time. No prosecution was admitted later than September 1st[118] but, even so, litigation which had started earlier might continue fitfully for the remainder of the year, the number of days on which the courts were in session being limited by the fact that they did not sit on days of major festivals or games, of which the later months of the year, particularly September and November, were full.*

The autumn games, then, were safe holiday periods for men in public life and for lawyers who would rather be in their villas or on their estates than at the games themselves in Rome. Cicero took advantage of the September Roman games in 54 B.C.; so, in his fictional dialogue, the De Oratore, did most of the outstanding public figures in 91 B.C., to meet in L. Crassus' villa at Tusculum, to sit under his great plane tree and talk.[119] In October landowners had a further reason to get away: they wished to attend their estates at vintage time. Also, if they had outgoing tenants, this was the time of year, directly after the vintage, when tenancies changed hands, so that the incoming tenant could do his own pruning of the vines against the following year's vintage.[120]

The lives of senators, barristers and jurors were greatly eased by considerate regulations which Augustus made. Each year a number of senators sufficient to constitute a bare quorum was chosen by lot and, while they had to be available for senatorial meetings (only two a month now, in the ordinary way) in September and October, other senators were free to spend those months with a clear conscience as far away from Rome as they liked. As for lawyers and jurors, who were now given

* See above, pp. 79–81.

one year's full leave in four, the courts were no longer to sit during November or December, a vacation which Claudius perhaps extended into January.[121]

Still, however, there were official duties to keep a number of prominent men in or round Rome during the hot weather. Pliny's spell of active duty as Prefect of the Treasury of Saturn concluded at the end of August A.D. 98 or 99, and with special imperial permission he then absented himself for a bare month to visit his estates in Tuscany. And September 1st was the day on which, from the late first century A.D., one set of suffect consuls went out of office and another came in. Politeness demanded that the friends of the new consuls should be in attendance, if they could possibly manage to be there.[122]

There were various modes of travel from Rome to the country and, in the country, from place to place. You could ride on horseback or, if you were not grand enough to possess a horse, on a mule. You could be driven either in a spacious four-wheeled carriage with more than two horses, a *carruca*, *rheda* (*raeda*) or *petorritum*, or in a light, fast, two-wheeled, two-horse gig, a *cisium*, with a driver and, at the most, one other passenger. Or you could be carried in a litter, *lectica*.

All three ways of travelling are illustrated in the story of the fatal *rencontre* on the Via Appia near Bovillae just over ten miles south of Rome in the afternoon of January 18th, 52 B.C. Clodius, returning to Rome with three companions from Aricia, where he had been making a speech to the local senate, was on horseback, their safety guaranteed, it would have seemed, by their escort of thirty slaves. Milo, on his way south to Lanuvium for the installation of a priest on the following day, was driving with his wife Fausta in a *raeda*, also with a heavy escort of thugs. Clodius' dead body, abandoned on the highroad after the engagement, was found by a senator who was on his way back to Rome in a litter.[123] He got out, and the corpse was put in.

The *carruca* and *raeda*—both Gallic in origin, as probably was the *petorritum*—were not fast conveyances; when employed at a stage in Horace's journey from Rome to Brundisium, a *raeda* covered twenty-four (Roman) miles in a day.[124] In nature something like a *char-à-banc*, it might be very smartly ornamented in metal and could be adapted for sleeping.[125] This was the carriage which carried or accompanied the family into the country, bearing its household plate and other such necessary accompaniments of gracious living, attended by an escort of household slaves in case of highwaymen. When Seneca, travelling with one friend and a few slaves in his mule-drawn farm-cart, envied a party of the rich which drove past him in a cloud of dust, he moralized later in a letter to Lucilius on his own weakness. A good Stoic should not be humiliated by the vanity of worldly splendour.[126]

The sight of a man travelling in such a conveyance to Tivoli with five slaves, a wine chest and a commode, was amusing to Horace, presumably because, if you travelled in so stylish a manner, you should have more stylish luggage.[127]

When the journey back to Rome was made, the carriage would be packed high with farm delicacies, if its owner had a garden at his villa or came from his estate.[128]

Anyone who was unencumbered by luggage and who wished to travel fast drove in a *cisium*, which had something of the glamour of the nineteenth-century phaeton, either his own or one hired with its driver from a stand. There were stands outside most cities, and by changing carriages and horses at regular intervals it was possible to cover long distances at considerable speed. Cicero records a night journey of fifty-six (Roman) miles—eighty-two kilometres—between Rome and Ameria which was made in ten hours. 'There are some things,' Seneca states, 'that you can write even in a *cisium*', which implies that nobody would choose to travel by *cisium* if he had serious writing to do on the journey.[129]

Roman carriages cannot have been very comfortable even on firm highways. Once you left the highway, your journey might be perilous. Pliny gave warning that the final sandy approach to his Laurentine villa, though admirable for anybody arriving on horseback, was not good for wheeled vehicles; and on the track which did duty for a road from Sinuessa to the Bay of Naples before the Via Domitiana was built, carriages might sink up to their axles in the boggy ground.[130]

The most comfortable way of travelling was also the slowest—by litter. The most luxurious litter was covered and curtained, and some even had windows.[131] Carried by up to eight bearers, it was slung on straps which passed over their shoulders and were easily detachable, if you wanted to give a man a thrashing.[132] The smartest bearers were Bithynian, the litter being supposed to have come originally from Bithynia.[133]

With good bearers you doubtless travelled very comfortably indeed. Reading and writing were easy; when you were tired, you could sleep. Augustus regularly travelled by litter when he went up to the hills from Rome, covering the distance in a couple of nights and lying up by day. Cicero made the journey from Astura to Tusculum, to Rome or to

Atticus' Nomentine estate in two days, resting for the night at Lanuvium. In December of A.D. 303, when Diocletian's health was beginning
to fail, he travelled by litter most of the way from Rome to Ravenna.[134]

It was possible, of course, to reach the Campanian coast by sea from
Ostia. Augustus preferred to travel by sea when he could; and the
reason why, on the famous journey to Brundisium, Maecenas and
Cocceius only joined Horace at Terracina may be that they had made
the first part of the journey by sea. When Claudius set out for Britain
in A.D. 43, he sailed from Ostia as far as Marseilles.[135]

Though it was always possible, with change of horses, particularly
if the journey was being made by hired carriage, to travel by night
as well as by day, this was exhausting and dangerous not only on
account of the possibility of a brush with highwaymen. So on a journey
of any length the traveller had to seek lodging for the night.

There were hotels on all main roads and in the cities,[136] the better
ones having a restaurant, a lavatory, bedrooms with keys or bolts—
Encolpius locked his bedroom door at the inn in Petronius' *Satyricon*—
and also a yard and stabling. An inn at Pompeii had six bedrooms,
round two sides of an inner court yard, with a kitchen on the third
side. Its large bar and its restaurant were a little way away, on the main
street.[137]

Sometimes, no doubt, travellers dossed down in dormitory-like
conditions,* but *graffiti* from Pompei record numbers between one and
four in a room. In one case there is a record of the sorrow of solitude:
'Vibius Restitutus slept here by himself and wished he had his Urbana
with him.'[138]

Horace spent the first night of his journey to Brundisium in a
'*modicum hospitium*' at Aricia. Forum Appii, where he spent the next
night, was distinguished, among other disagreeable features, by
'*caupones maligni.*'[139] Hotel-keepers, indeed, as a class, were not kindly
spoken of. They probably made good money, for Varro suggests that
a farmer whose property bordered on a main road could increase his
income substantially by building a hotel and restaurant, *taberna deversoria*, on the road.[140]

An inscription from Aesernia in Samnium gives the specimen of an
itemized bill: 'Pint of wine, bread, one as; other food, two asses; girl
for the night, eight asses; hay for mule, two asses.'[141] On the other
hand, in Cisalpine Gaul in the second century B.C., where food was
extremely plentiful and cheap, the traveller stayed *en pension*, agreeing

* As in remote places in Italy one still does.

terms with the innkeeper on arrival. You could stay for half an as a day, everything included, Polybius records.[142]

Inns in general were no doubt as uncomfortable and primitive as those in southern Italy half a century ago. Also they lacked respectability, and the gentry did not patronize them. Instead they stayed the night in a friend's villa or bought and kept a shack, a *deversorium*, at a convenient resting place on the roads between villas on which they frequently travelled.

A friend might lend the use of his villa even when he was not himself in residence, and in such cases travellers often bought their own food, even their own tents.[143] The baths would not be heated if the villa was unoccupied, and the traveller who wanted a bath would visit the nearest public baths.[144] On the fourth night of Horace's journey to Brundisium the travellers stayed the night at the villa of Maecenas' brother-in-law, the man who was to conspire against Augustus and to meet his death in 23 B.C.[145]

Cicero, who quite often stayed with friends for the night[146], bought and used a number of his own *deversoria* on the Via Appia (at Lanuvium, Sinuessa, Minturnae and Terracina) and on or just off the Via Latina (at Frosino, Anagnia and Cales), those being the two roads on which he would normally travel to and fro from his villas. This purchase has been counted against him by an ill-tempered modern critic as a senseless extravagance[147]; but we have no means of knowing if Cicero's practice was exceptional. One reason which Cicero gave for buying such a rest-house was anything but discreditable: he did not wish, by frequently soliciting hospitality, to be a nuisance to his friends.[148] Their cost was from thirty thousand to fifty thousand sesterces,[149] and it is clear that they were little more than shacks, for Cicero once wrote that it would be impossible to stay for an entire day in any of them.[150] It may be suspected that, in addition to giving the owner a roof over his head for the night or shade during a prolonged rest in the middle of the day, the *deversorium* discharged the function of a *poste restante*. If a slave was left in charge, he would be kept abreast of the owner's movements and plans, and would be able to direct letter-carriers to the villa at which his master was staying, or to hold letters if his master's arrival was anticipated.[151]

When a man went into the country, he did not necessarily spend all his time in his own villa or villas; he also paid visits to his friends. The surviving record of Cicero, the younger Pliny and, centuries later, of Symmachus, gives evidence of such exchange of hospitality. Pliny accepted an invitation to stay with Junius Mauricus at Formiae, 'but only on condition that you will not put yourself out. It is not the sea or the coast that I want; I want to see *you*, to relax and feel completely free.' When Vesuvius erupted in A.D. 79, the elder Pliny had a friend from Spain staying with him at Misenum.[152]

Visitors can give considerable extra work to servants, and there is an amusing passage in Plautus' *Miles Gloriosus* illustrating this. When the old gentleman Periplectomenus says to his young guest Pleusicles that he must buy something in the market for their dinner, Pleusicles replies, 'I am ashamed to think how much I am costing you. Any guest who has stayed with a friend for three days has outstayed his welcome, but after three days he is a thorough nuisance. The master of the house may not mind, but the slaves start complaining.' Their complaints, no doubt, often preceded the guest's arrival. Juvenal describes (as Plautus had described earlier) the turmoil in a household when a guest was expected, the cleaning of the silver, the attempts to remove the traces of spiders and of dogs.[153]

Out of Rome the tired man laid aside his cares and worries. Yet for the kind of middle-aged and elderly men who have left their records this was anything but light-hearted relaxation. The Roman destined for public life was born, one is tempted to think, with a pen in his hand and a platform under his feet. In the country he wanted to write as well as to read, often to polish up his own speeches for publication.

Still, even with writing to do, retirement to the country contrasted with the crowded programme of daily life in Rome (*occupatio*) was relaxation (*otium*). The younger Pliny nicely describes such relaxation in his Laurentine villa:

I read or write or exercise my body, on whose well-being mental life depends. I hear nothing said, I say nothing myself, which I might subsequently regret. I never have to listen while somebody is being criticized or abused. I criticize nobody—except, occasionally, myself when I am writing badly. I am not hoping for anything to happen or frightened of anything that could happen. There are no rumours to disturb me. I have myself and my books to talk to. This is my idea of the simple, honest life—enviable, unimpeachable relaxation; there is nothing in one's business life to match it.[154]

Educated men in the country liked to walk up and down their porticoes or their shady avenues of trees or even to take more extended walks, and to think; or, if they had guests, to walk up and down and to talk about the very serious matters which occupied their minds: literature, philosophy, history, politics. When a number of friends assembled, they would sit down and enjoy the kind of serious discussion which Cicero has made the basis of his elaborate dialogues. They recreate the atmosphere of the great Greek philosophical schools, of the Academy, of the Garden. Exercise was an interruption, taken to the extent to which it was thought necessary for good health.

If Marcus Aurelius had taken Fronto's advice and given himself a really good holiday each day when he was spending four days at Alsium, he would have read in the morning, taken a siesta in the sun at midday, then have walked or been rowed out to sea. A good sweat in the baths would have followed, as the prelude to a delicious dinner.[155]

Here is the younger Pliny's account of a day in summer at his estate in Tuscany:

I wake as I please, usually at seven, often earlier, not often later. I keep the shutters closed. In the quiet and the dark, with no distractions, free and left to myself, instead of thinking about what I see, I direct my gaze towards whatever I am thinking about, which eyes can do when they have nothing else to look at. I concentrate on whatever I have in hand, just as if I was writing or correcting word by word a long passage or a short one, according to the ease or difficulty of composing and remembering what I have composed. Then I call in a writer, let in the daylight and dictate the result. He goes away, and then I keep calling him back and sending him away again.

At roughly ten or eleven—because we do not observe exact time—I move either to the walk (*xystus*) or to the covered portico according to the weather, and think out and dictate the rest.

Then I get into a carriage and go on with what I had been thinking about in bed and when I was walking; my concentration is freshened and strengthened by the change of motion.

After that I take a short siesta before I go for a walk, and then I read aloud a speech either in Greek or Latin, distinctly and with emphasis, not so much for the sake of my voice as for the sake of my digestion; though, of course, my voice benefits at the same time. Then I have another stroll, oil and exercise myself, and have a bath.

At dinner, if my wife is there or if there are a few guests, a book is read aloud and afterwards there is light recitation or music. Then I go for a walk with my companions, many of them scholars. So, with talk about this and that, the evening is spun out, and the longest of days is over in a flash.

The programme is not always exactly the same. If I have been in bed or on my feet for a long time, then sometimes after my siesta and reading I mount a horse and ride instead of being driven in a carriage. Riding is faster and takes up less time.

Friends drop in from neighbouring towns and take up part of the day. When I am tired, I welcome the interruption and am revived by it.

If I hunt, as I sometimes do, I always take a writing tablet with me, so as to bring something home, even if it is not game.

My querulous tenants get too little of my time; so they would tell you.[156]

The composition on which so much of the day had been concentrated would, after it had received its final polish, be sent for criticism to a friend, whose flattering comment might crown the work—as when a friend read his 'Avenging of Helvidius' and told him that it reminded him of Demosthenes' speech against Meidias (which, as Pliny admits, he had in front of him when he was writing).[157]

As a professional financier, Pliny was shrewdly interested in the profitability of his own estates. This is evident from more than one of his letters. It is true, too, that when he wrote from the country to his literary friends and disparaged rusticity, this was largely an affectation. None the less, for a man with such extensive property and the considerable income derived from it, Pliny's attitude to his tenants is strange. He would have liked the income, one feels, without the tenants. They were always complaining, perhaps because they had good reasons for complaint. 'I sometimes get on a horse and play the landlord to the extent of riding round a part of my estate, but my real object is the exercise.'[158]

The letters of Symmachus are markedly different. He enjoyed the country for its own sake and not simply as a place of refuge from town, and writes vividly about what is going on around him—the vintage, the pressing of the olives, hunting.[159]

For the fit and healthy there was riding and, in the autumn and winter particularly, hunting (of which Hadrian was criticized for being too ardent a devotee).[160] Hunting was a matter of driving game (especially hares) into nets and of detecting, pursuing and spearing deer, boars or bears.[161] Hounds, of course, were a prime element of the hunting, together with skilful slave-huntsmen. Trajan was praised by Pliny in the *Panegyricus* for being a real hunter who ranged over the mountains —not the man to chase after broken-down beasts which had been transported in cages and liberated, to make an easy quarry.[162]

Visible records of outstanding success in the hunt were antlers and the fangs of boars fastened to the walls of shrines. Different and more embarrassing records were the hunter's scars which he might insist on revealing, stripping, if need be, for the purpose. Sallust, in his under-bred way, had declared hunting a slavish pastime and, centuries later, Ammianus Marcellinus mocked the type of hunting-party in which all the serious work was done by the slaves. Once when the emperor Valentinian was hunting, a page, bitten by the hound which he was holding, slipped its leash too quickly. The page was killed for this.[163]

We have from the end of the fourth century a most interesting letter of Symmachus which reflects harshly on Sallust and clearly echoes what Horace had once written:

You are hunting—which shows that you are vigorous and healthy; and nothing pleases me more than that you keep yourselves fit by country sport. After that, I am delighted that your hunting has been so successful, that you can honour the gods and gratify your friends—the gods by nailing up antlers of stags and fangs of wild boars on the walls of their temples, your friends by sending them presents of game. I have no sympathy with the opinion that hunting is a slavish pursuit. Ad-mirable as the literary style of the exponent of this view may have been, his own moral obliquity hardly qualified him to respect as an authority on the good life. I would rather see you being countrymen with Atilius and pursuing tough sport than being seduced by literary precepts to the cult of soft living. This is the right occupation for men of your age. Young men should relax from their studies not in dicing, playing ball or trundling a hoop, but in exhausting spirited activity and in the enjoyment of exercising courage in a way that can do no harm. I shall encourage my boy to hunt as soon as he is old enough, even though he is my only son.

The time will come when old age weighs heavily on you and you will have to give up hunting. When that time comes, you can rightly talk of hunting in terms of slavery, for a man *is* a slave if, when his bodily strength goes, he refuses to avail himself of the respite from such strenuous exercise which old age affords.[164]

When holidaying, you were in the hills or at the sea. Symmachus wrote to Decius, 'You tempt me by your description of the Campanian coast. Still, I find that there is just as much pleasure to be had in staying in the country at Praeneste. Though most people would rather be at the sea than in the hills, I prefer woody country to the open shore when it is a matter of evading intense heat.'[165]

Propertius' epithet for Baiae was 'corrupt', and he had fears for Cynthia's morals when she went there without him; and it was not the heat but the morals of the Campanian Riviera which persuaded Seneca to leave Baiae—that resort of vice, *deversorium vitiorum*—after staying there for a single night. Drunkards staggered about the shore. There were noisy and intemperate boating-parties, *comessationes navigantium*. There were performances of music on the lakes, '*symphoniarum cantibus strepentes lacus*.'

More than three centuries later Symmachus wrote, 'Indulgence begins at Formiae', and further south he contrasted his own decorum with the manners of those round him. 'When *we* are boating, we do not sing. We feed without eating ourselves sick. We keep away from the baths. We do not watch wanton exhibitions of swimming by the young.'[166]

We hear much of rowing and sailing on the Lucrine Lake, in the Bay of Naples and in the sea off Formiae, as also on the inland lakes.[167] Poorer people hired boats, rich people possessed one,[168] which at one extreme might be a small rowing-boat, at the other an *aerata triremis* or such a splendid barge as those (recovered from below the water of Lake Nemi before the 1939 war, in the course of which they were wantonly destroyed) in which Gaius Caligula floated in comfort. Domitian, we are told, was towed in a dinghy on the Alban Lake and on the sea some distance in the wake of a rowing boat, because his shattered nerves could not stand the noisy splash of the oars. When Trajan took to the sea, on the other hand, in a rowing boat, he was at the sculls, in a sailing boat his hand was at the tiller.[169] At the end of the fourth century Ammianus Marcellinus laughed at the kind of sailing that was done in the south: 'People sail in painted boats from the Lucrine Lake to Puteoli and think themselves the equals of the Argonauts.'[170]

There was also swimming in the sea during the summer and, if you had such luxury as the younger Pliny enjoyed in his Laurentine villa, there were even heated bathing pools, where you could swim and look at the sea (presumably on days when the sea itself was chilly).[171] It is evident that most Romans were able to swim, for it was thought remarkable that Gaius Caligula could not.[172]

Fishing, too, was popular, and Martial described the acme of luxurious fishing when he wrote of a villa at Formiae where you could fish not merely from your bedroom window but even, if you wished, from your bed, and one of Pliny's villas on Lake Como enjoyed this same amenity.[173] Cicero has a nice story of a Roman knight, C. Canius, who was attracted by property on the shore near Syracuse, which he tried to buy from its owner, a wily Syracusan banker called Pythius. Pythius invited him to dinner in the grounds. The sea was thickly crowded with fishing boats from which fishermen landed and pre-sented Pythius with their heavy catch. So, with thoughts of the fishing, Canius bought the property for a fancy price. He took possession the next day and, surprised to see no fishermen, asked a neighbour the reason. The neighbour told him that no fisherman was so foolish as to waste time fishing that particular stretch of water. 'In fact,' he said, 'I could not imagine what all those fishing boats were doing here yesterday.'[174]

3. Soldiers on Leave

In the late Republic and in the Empire soldiers had holidays in the sense that they were entitled, presumably in the winter when there was no campaigning, to a stated period of leave. A military tribune in the late Republic was entitled to two months, and the younger Cato used his leave when serving in Macedonia in 67 B.C. to travel to Pergamon in Asia to visit the philosopher Athenodorus Cordylion, knowing that Athenodorus was very old and would not live for ever and trusting in his own transparent integrity to open a door on which even kings knocked in vain. He did more than succeed; he triumphed, persuaded the old man to come back with him, and even produced him, like a prize trophy, in his own officers' mess.[175]

The majority of officers are unlikely to have devoted their periods of leave to such high-minded self-improvement, though many of them travelled to see famous sights, just as Germanicus went off from Syria to Egypt in the winter of A.D. 18/19 'cognoscendae antiquitatis', on an archaeological tour.*[176]

The common soldier seems often to have turned huckster during his periods of leave, going from town to town to make what money he could.[177] In the Empire a legionary, who was not allowed to marry before the time of Septimius Severus, if he kept a woman in the local town no doubt spent his leave with her, and married auxiliary troops passed the time with their families. Some soldiers took the opportunity to slip away and desert. It appears that in 169 B.C. a number of soldiers

* See further pp. 231f below.

had returned home to Italy from Macedonia, and the censors took special measures to identify them and to return them to their units.[178]

In the Empire the soldier who overstayed his leave stood to face a charge of desertion. But the law was sensible. If the soldier could establish that he had started back in good time, but had been delayed by circumstances beyond his control—illness, for instance, or highwaymen or floods—he was excused. It is unlikely that soldiers were often the victims of pathological generals such as Cn. Piso, the governor of Syria who quarrelled with Germanicus in A.D. 19, of whom Seneca has recounted this horrible story. Two men serving under him went on leave together and when only one returned Piso ordered his execution on the suspicion that he had killed his companion. At the moment when the execution was to take place, the missing soldier returned to camp, to the relief of his companion and of the humane centurion in charge of the execution. The execution was suspended. The centurion presented the two men to Piso who, intemperately angry because his order had not been carried out, ordered the execution of both soldiers and of the centurion as well.[179]

In the Empire a soldier secured his leave from or through his centurion, and for this service the centurion exacted a fee (*vacatio*). The practice was bitterly resented by the troops, particularly as the centurion turned this exaction of money into a refined art.

The common soldier was burdened by this payment, which was like a tax, falling due each year. A quarter of the troops were either away on leave[180] or loafing about in the camp itself, provided they had paid the centurion his fee. No one considered what a heavy burden this was, or cared how the soldier raised the cash (for they robbed on the roads, thieved and sank to doing the work of slaves in order to purchase their leave). If a soldier was rich, he was worn down by hard fatigues and by cruel treatment until he paid up. When his pockets had been emptied and he was further demoralized by idleness, he returned to his unit no longer rich but penniless, no longer fit but in miserable shape.[181]

Every general in the Roman army must have deplored the existence of such a system, of which the troops complained over and over again[182]; but the entrenched privilege of the centurions was hard to break. The abuse was brought to an end in the year of civil war, A.D. 69, by Otho and Vitellius—but only by an addition to centurions' pay equivalent to the sum which they would otherwise have lost, payable by the Emperor from the imperial treasury.[183]

VII

TRAVEL

◆◆◆

SOME MEN travelled long distances because their profession or calling left them with no alternative: senators, knights, freedmen and slaves in the imperial administration; soldiers recruited in one area of the Empire for service in another (in Asia Minor, for instance, for posting to the legions in Egypt[1]); young Romans, more often than not from the upper class, who left home to complete their education in Massilia (Marseilles), Athens, Rhodes, Alexandria or one of the other great university cities; business-men and traders. Innumerable people, few of them of any considerable substance, travelled in search of a new life with better economic prospects, as immigrants travel to North America or to Australia today. The traffic of these last was increasingly a traffic from east to west because the new world, the world of economic opportunity, was in the main the world of the fast-developing western provinces of the Empire, North Africa included; and Italy, in particular Rome itself, was a magnet. There were explorers, men who travelled from curiosity, Greeks in particular, like Polybius, who was given a ship by Scipio Aemilianus after the sack of Carthage in 146 B.C. to sail west, out into the Atlantic, and who earlier had been to Spain with Scipio in 151, returning overland and crossing the Alps with eyes and ears wide open in the hope of discovering a clue to the route by which Hannibal had brought his army into Italy some seventy years earlier.[2] But of 'holiday travel', of travel for the sake of going abroad and seeing interesting places, of the kind of travel which is one of the greatest enjoyments of modern civilized life, there was—on the part of Romans living in Italy—very little indeed.

Opportunities for wide travel existed such as had never existed before. In the second century B.C. Polybius, who took advantage of those opportunities, emphasized that this was by no means the smallest of Rome's gifts, through conquest, to the Mediterranean world.[3] Admittedly the gift became less effective in the century after Polybius

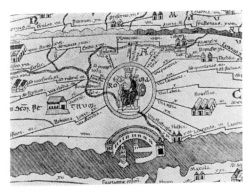

1(a) Air photograph of the Piazza Navona (the Stadium of Domitian) in Rome (*Fototeca Unione*)

1(b) Rome as the centre of the world in the Peutinger Table

1(c) The Theatre of Pompey in Rome with the Temple of Venus Genetrix on the *Forma Urbis* (*Fototeca Unione*)

(a)

(b)

(c)

2 Pompeian *graffiti*

3 Portrait of L. Vibius, Vecilia Hilara and their son (*Alinari*)

(a) Hall (*atrium*) with *impluvium* (*Anderson*)

(b) Peristyle and garden (*Anderson*)

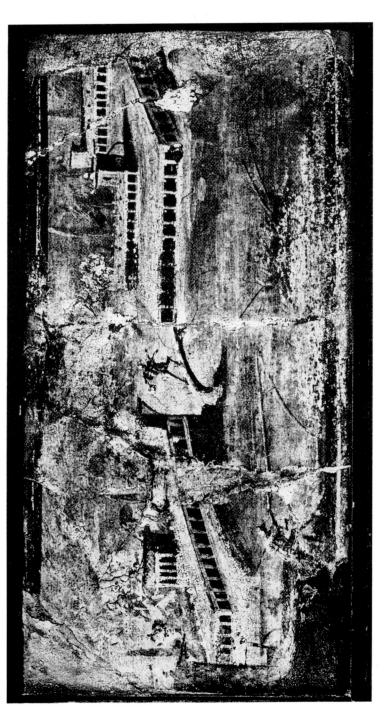

5 Villas on the sea in Campania: fresco from Pompeii, Museo Nazionale, Naples (*Anderson*)

6(a) Dinner in the household, with the slaves baking and cooking in the kitchen, 3rd century A.D., from Trier (*Anderson*)

6(b) Scene in a tavern, Vatican Museum (*Anderson*)

7(a) Childbirth: relief from Ostia (*Fototeca Unione*)

7(b) The upbringing of a boy. He is first being suckled, then held by his father, then driving a goat-cart and finally confronting his teacher (*Musée du Louvre, Paris*)

(a) Two boys reading to a schoolmaster: relief from Trier (*Fototeca Unione*)

(b) Boys at school and exercising: stucco relief from ceiling of the underground basilica near the Porta Maggiore, Rome (*Fototeca Unione*)

(a) Butcher's shop: relief from Ostia (*Fototeca Unione*)

(b) Sale of cloth, Uffizi Museum, Florence (*Alinari*)

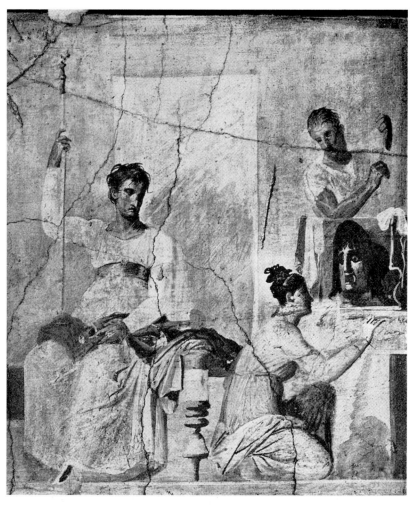

12 Green-room scene of actors and actress before a masque: fresco from
Pompeii, Museo Nazionale, Naples (*Anderson*)

(a) Musical accompaniment with, in the background, the bier (*sandapila*) for carrying out corpses

(b) Fighting in progress

(c) An appeal. The defeated man has dropped his shield. The *lanista* (in white) holds the victor off until the audience has given its verdict

(a) Coursing: mosaic from Oudna, Tunisia (*Professor J. C. M. Toynbee and the British School at Rome*)

(b) Taking animals on board for transport to Rome for the games: mosaic from Piazza Armerina, Sicily (*Sopraintendenza alle antichità, Sicilia Orientale, Syracuse*)

(c) Wall painting of animal-fighting in the arena, from extra-mural baths, Lepcis Magna (*Superintendency of Antiquities, Tripolitania*)

15(a) 'Silence; don't wake the bulls': mosaic from El-Djem (*Direction des Musées Nationaux, le Bardo, Tunisia*)

15(b) Boys racing hoops, Mosaic Museum, Istanbul (*Haluk Doganbev*)

(a) Racing in the Circus: mosaic from Lyons (*M. le Conservateur, Musée de la Civilisation Gallo-romaine, Lyon*)

(b) The famous charioteer Scorpus driving a *quadriga* (*Superintendency of Galleries, Urbino, Professor J. C. M. Toynbee and the British School at Rome*)

wrote because of Roman failure to suppress the piracy which their own foreign policy and the interests of their own slave-dealers so greatly encouraged; but for the first two centuries of the Roman Empire conditions for travel were better over a wider area than they were to be again until nineteenth-century Europe. The sea was generally free of pirates.[4] Through Italy and all the provinces of the Empire there were firm main roads, well built and well repaired.

So that a large element of that danger which travellers, particularly travellers who wrote history, boasted of having confronted so manfully, disappeared—but not all. Ships were sometimes wrecked. Terence was believed to have died on his way back from Greece to Italy in 159 B.C.; there was one story that he was drowned, another that he perished from grief at the loss of a ship which contained his baggage, including new translations of a hundred and eight of Menander's plays. Octavian's doctor, M. Artorius Asclepiades, author of works on Longevity and Hydrophobia, perished in a shipwreck after Actium. The ship in which Josephus travelled to Rome in A.D. 61 sank in the Adriatic and its six hundred passengers had to swim all night. Eighty, including Josephus, were picked up in the morning by another boat.[5]

On land, too, travel retained its discomforts. The first quality of a journey to be stressed was its length: 'the way was exceeding long'.[6] By land, if you rode or drove your own horses, a sharp limit was imposed on your travelling time each day by your horses' endurance rather than by your own.

Travellers on official government business under the Empire were given special facilities for fast travel. At regular intervals on the great roads of Italy and the provinces there were posting-stations (*stationes*) with fresh horses. The privileged traveller was armed with an official warrant (*diploma*), which authorized officials at the station to provide fresh horses and to do everything to expedite his journey, *diplomata* being issued in the Emperor's name in Rome and by governors in the provinces. Like modern motor licences they were valid only to a certain date[7] and in any case they were automatically cancelled by the death of the emperor in whose name they were issued. One can easily imagine the scrutiny of such documents by minor officials at the posting station; in the east Pertinax, then a private individual, is said to have been found travelling with false papers and to have been forced to continue his journey on foot.[8]

With all the facilities of the *cursus publicus* at your disposal, you were unlikely in a carriage to average more than five miles an hour* over a long journey—that is to say, forty to fifty miles a day.[9] In an emergency if necessary by dint of travelling by night as well as by day, greater distances could be covered—as, under the Republic, Julius Caesar once covered a hundred miles in twenty-four hours.[10]

On horseback, of course, you travelled faster. Tiberius, racing from Italy to his brother's death-bed in Germany in 9 B.C. and changing mounts as each horse was exhausted, covered two hundred miles in twenty-four hours.[11]

Private travellers, like officials, could hire fresh horses at the stations on the roads, if horses were available and they could afford the price.

Not every traveller was mounted or driving in a carriage or a cart. Letter-carriers, for instance, of whom there must always have been many on the roads, were slaves travelling on foot. In urgent circumstances dispatch-carriers were, or should have been, on the run. The ordinary man walked and might hope to average up to twenty-five miles a day.[12]

The sailing season, marked by the festive launching of the bark of Isis (the *navigium Isidis*) on March 5th, opened on March 10th and lasted until November 11th. Even within this period a traveller might be held up for some days on account of unfavourable winds, as Cicero was held up at Corcyra on his way home to Brindisi in the second half of November (early October by the Julian calendar) 50 B.C.; less cautious travellers ahead of him braved the storms and were wrecked. When the 11th of November came, the cautious traveller accepted his misfortune and might have to settle down to spend the winter months in the harbour-town from which he had planned to sail. Yet even in winter there were passages to be had for those who would face the risk because, apart from cargo-boats whose owners ranked profit above safety, there were ships carrying imperial officials, prisoners and the like.[13]

Given good winds, a ship in normal conditions might make a hundred and twenty sea-miles in a day and, if conditions were good, travel by sea was generally far faster than by land. You might reach Ostia from Cadiz in seven days, from Marseilles in three. Two days was a record for a voyage from North Africa to Ostia. In good weather a traveller might reach Puteoli from Corinth in five days. Aristides

---

* Where distances and speeds are given in terms of miles in this chapter, the mile is a Roman mile, 1·5 kilometres.

in A.D. 145 took fourteen days to get from Miletus to Rome by sea, but he was held up on the way by bad conditions.[14]

Travellers to the east mostly sailed to Corinth and, since the project of a canal through the isthmus (which Julius Caesar envisaged and Nero actually started) was never achieved, they landed at Lechaeum and their boats were conveyed over-land on rollers or, more commonly, they embarked on different boats at Cenchreae to continue their voyage.[15]

The voyage round the south coast of the Peloponnese meant braving Cape Malea and was a dangerous project: 'Round Malea, and forget your family.' But between July and September you might find a north-west wind if you travelled by this route, while the wind was likely to be in the north-east in the Corinthian and Saronic gulfs. So the younger Pliny, a man of no spectacular daring, sailed round Malea on his way out to Bithynia in A.D. 111. Still, this was evidently an achievement of which to boast. A business man in Asia Minor erected a memorial to record the fact that he had rounded Cape Malea in journeys to Italy seventy-two times.[16]

The largest ships were the corn ships on the Puteoli-Alexandria run, a voyage which in the most favourable summer conditions (in the forty days after July 20th, when the Etesian winds blew) might be expected to take about twelve days, though it had been done in nine. These ships might have a capacity as large as 1575 tons. They could carry several hundreds of passengers. Six hundred people were aboard the ship in which Josephus was wrecked. Aelius Aristides even speaks of a helmsman holding the responsibility for a thousand lives.[17]

The voyage to Egypt was recommended by doctors for victims of tuberculosis, for those whose eyes troubled them and for sufferers from headaches. Sea-sickness in itself was considered salutary.[18]

Arrangements for sailing were simple. You went down to the harbour and looked for a ship which was bound for the right port. You asked the price of a passage and, no doubt after a little haggling, you reached an agreement, paid your money and, armed with food, drink and wrappings for the voyage, went on board.[19]

In the provinces as in Italy itself* inns and lodging-houses were not the least discomforts of travel. Whenever possible, you enjoyed the hospitality of friends and acquaintances; and if you were a person of any consequence, distinguished provincials were happy to put you up, just as in Rome itself, Cicero thought, a man of standing should give hospitality to distinguished foreigners, not always for completely

* See above, pp. 215f.

altruistic reasons. Residents in a province might, however, find themselves put to intolerable expense in this way, like the inhabitants of Hippo Diarrhytus in Africa in the elder Pliny's time; so many Roman officials from the province came to see their tame dolphin (which played in the sea with children), expecting to be given hospitality, that the townsfolk were driven to kill the dolphin. In A.D. 238 the Scaptopareni in Thrace complained to the Emperor of the intolerable expense to which they were put in providing hospitality for provincial officials, soldiers and others who arrived—and stayed—to enjoy their natural hot baths. When P. Vedius—probably the young Vedius Pollio—was in Cilicia in 50 B.C., he stayed in Laodicea with a freedman of Pompey, Pompeius Vindullus.[20]

If the traveller put up in inns, he was liable to fare worse in the provinces even than in Italy. Aelius Aristides describes a journey from Smyrna to Pergamon in the second century A.D. when he was forced to travel the whole night through, since the first two inns that he came to were too repulsive to stay in; the third was locked up for the night and it was impossible to attract attention. So he went at dawn to a private house in which there was no comfort, not even a fire.[21]

There were further discomforts: extreme cold (from which, in the night, Aristides suffered), lack of safe drinking water, as Sidonius Apollinaris found in the fifth century at Ravenna, in which water had always cost more than wine. If the traveller did not enjoy robust good health, there was the further risk of sickness, indeed of being stranded in a foreign city, seriously ill. Such was the fate of Cicero's freedman Tiro, who was stricken by a fever which turned into malaria at Patras in November 50 B.C. and forced to remain there for several months. Virgil died at Brindisi in September 19 B.C. from an illness which he contracted in Greece, at Megara.[22]

At times of crisis in the Republic the Senate imposed severe restrictions on the movements of its members and in ordinary times, as late as the early Empire, a senator required the Senate's permission to travel outside Italy. He requested a *libera* or a *votiva legatio*, his reason usually being a mercenary one in connexion with his private affairs, entering on a legacy, for example. Armed with his official permit, he enjoyed all the privileges—the right to claim free travel and free hospitality—which would have been at his disposal had he been travelling on public business, on an official diplomatic mission. The thing was a scandal, bitterly resented, naturally, by the provincials, who were called upon to pay his bills. Cicero tried, but with only partial success, to restrict the abuse when he was consul. Where Cicero failed, Caesar succeeded.[23]

From the earliest days of the Empire senators were forbidden to leave Italy, unless on official duty, without the Emperor's permission. An exception was made in the case of visits to Sicily and, after Claudius, Narbonese Gaul because so many senators owned property in these two provinces.[24]

The western provinces offered few attractions to the Roman tourist; what he wanted to see were the famous sights of the old-world: mainland Greece, the Greek islands and the Greek cities of Asia Minor. In Greece itself Athens had to be visited; it was 'the star of Greece', with buildings, sculptures and pictures to be seen and admired. When Nero avoided it in his Greek tour in A.D. 67, an explanation was called for. People said that the Areopagus would have recalled memories of Orestes and the Furies, and Nero on holiday did not wish to be reminded of his mother's death. More curious is the possibility that Strabo, who claimed to have travelled from the Euxine to Ethopia and from Armenia to Etruria, crossed the isthmus of Corinth yet never went to Athens.[25]

After Athens, the traveller should see Epidaurus and, naturally, Olympia and Delphi, Delphi being visited for its buildings and works of art rather than for the oracle itself which by the end of the first century A.D. was in decline. At Delphi—and, naturally, at Olympia—the traveller hired a guide, a *periegetes*, and suffered. Inscription followed inscription; what exhausted tourist wanted to hear every one of them read out and explained?[26]

Of the islands, Chios and Lesbos and Samos were visited. Rhodes was thought the most attractive island of all—a well-ordered, handsome city, with interesting surviving vestiges of its earlier naval power and with a population whose decorum and avoidance of flamboyance made a good impression on visitors. The Colossus was a remarkable sight, even in ruins on the ground. And, among paintings, the visitor was shown the Satyr of Protogenes and told how the artist had painted out the partridge at the top of the column because it had been too lifelike, mistaken even by partridges for a real bird.[27]

After the islands Ionia offered every attraction—a delightful climate, remarkable temples (of which the surviving temple of Apollo at Didyma gives some conception), a great number of spas. Cities to visit were Sardis, Smyrna, Ephesus and Colophon.[28]

No country had more to show the tourist than had Egypt. With its perfect climate, Alexandria, 'the crown of all cities', 'placed at the cross-roads of the whole world', was, until challenged for the title in the third century by Antioch and Carthage, second city of the Empire, after Rome. Chief object of attraction was the Serapeum with its pillared halls and its library. This and the library at Bruchion, also in Alexandria, were two of the greatest libraries in the world until their destruction in A.D. 391 and 272 respectively.[29] And there was the Museion, the foundation of Ptolemy Soter, which was not a museum at all, but a great university with dining-hall and lecture-theatres. Its life must have interested the puzzled tourist of antiquity as much as the life of a great Oxford or Cambridge College puzzles the foreign tourist today. An emperor, of course, like Hadrian, or a distinguished academic from the outer world, would be admitted to the lectures and take part in discussions himself.[30]

The visitor travelled up-river to Memphis, just above the Delta, near the site of modern Cairo, and there he would be incurious indeed if he did not visit the sanctuary of the bull Apis at the hour when it was brought out to frisk round an open court adjacent to the sanctuary of its mother 'particularly for the sake of tourists', and was fed.[31]

Finally Thebes, which covered the area between the two great sanctuaries of Amon, Karnak to the north, Luxor to the south. Here were the pyramids and, greatest of all fascinations, the vast statue of Amenophis III of the eighteenth dynasty, only the lower part of which remained intact after the earthquake of 27 B.C. The visitor must be up before sunrise so that, if he was lucky (like Strabo, when he visited it in the entourage of the governor of Egypt, Aelius Gallus), he might, at the moment when it was struck by the rays of the rising sun, hear it emit a melodious twang, like the snapping of a chord of a cythera or lyre.[32] In the first half of the first century A.D., it seems, Greeks spread the belief that the statue was of Memnon, son of the Dawn, whom Achilles slew at Troy. Romantic imagination went further, holding that it had been deliberately destroyed by Cambyses and that, when intact, it had spoken at dawn with a human voice.

All over the image's vast legs and feet tourists left the record of their experience of the miracle, and the inscriptions have survived, the earliest from A.D. 20, the latest from A.D. 196 or even 205, forty-five in Latin, sixty-three in Greek and one bilingual. The simple tourist left his name and the date, reckoned sometimes in consular sometimes in imperial years; sometimes he recorded a wish that his mother or some other relative had been there to share his experience. The sophisticated went further; heedless of their lack of versifying talent, they translated the marvel into a few lines of Greek verse. There are four different compositions, evenly tedious, done in Aeolic Greek by the learned Balbilla, who attended the empress Sabina as a lady-in-waiting when Hadrian came in A.D. 130.[33] The prize should go to an imperial official:

Here under the Libyan dunes of Egypt, where swift Nile cleaves Thebes of the fair gates, know, Thetis of the surge, that at the warm touch of his mother's torch Memnon lives on and speaks loud—while Achilles, who spoiled always for a fresh fight, is silent in the fields of Troy and in Thessaly is silent too.

Done by Asclepiodotus, poet and imperial procurator.[34]

Septimius Severus visited Memnon in A.D. 200.[35] The latest inscription may date from 196. So it has been suggested that the Emperor had the constructive idea of repairing the statue—with disastrous consequences. Memnon henceforth was as silent as Achilles.

Members of the imperial family and their entourage apart, there are no records in the Empire of Roman senators at Thebes or indeed elsewhere in Egypt. They would have needed special dispensation from the Emperor; for Augustus had forbidden them, as he had forbidden high-ranking Equites (other than those in charge of the administration of the country) entry to Egypt. The Alexandrians were an excitable people, as Germanicus found when, without bothering to ask Tiberius' leave, he arrived there in the winter of A.D. 18. At least a third of Rome's corn was shipped from Alexandria. A disaffected senator was a potential rebel and, with Alexandrian support and the opportunity of starving Rome, he would constitute a formidable threat. The lesson taught by Antony was not to be forgotten.[36]

Nobody, not even an emperor, set out to make the ancient equivalent of the 'grand tour'. In the early Empire it was dangerous for an emperor to leave Rome for too long a time and, when so much of public administration called for his personal assent or decision, great delay and even disaster might follow from his not being quickly accessible in the capital. Capri is not a great distance from Rome; yet it is clear that the efficiency of imperial administration suffered greatly from Tiberius' irresponsible withdrawal there for the last ten years of his rule. Who is to say how different history might have been if Nero had not been in Greece collecting the last of his 1,808 victory crowns when Vindex prepared to revolt at the beginning of A.D. 68?

Apart from Gaius' visit to Sicily after the death of his sister Drusilla (where he mocked the famous sites and, it was said, left Messina in a panic when Etna erupted)[37] and Nero's Greek tour,* no emperor journeyed abroad except for official reasons. Even Hadrian, the only emperor who from choice and under no compulsion spent half his rule in travel, visiting all but the Danube provinces and acquainting himself with the problems of the Empire's frontiers, was never on holiday. Seeing the sights was, naturally, a great joy to a man so cultured and so curious, and many of the features of his villa below Tivoli —the Canopus waterway, for instance—were to remind him of what he had seen. He travelled on business, even if he missed no opportunity for pleasure, however strenuous. He climbed Etna to see the sunrise from the summit; also, for the same purpose, Mount Casius in Syria.[38]

Other emperors who were summoned to the provinces on account of urgent crises and princes who were out of Italy on state business took the opportunity of seeing interesting sights whenever the opportunity offered. When Germanicus was sent out to the East at the end of A.D. 17, his journey to Syria was something of a pleasure-tour, embracing Nicopolis and the site of the battle of Actium (where his grandfathers had fought one another), Athens, a number of Greek islands and the Bosphorus. Turning back, he visited the site of Troy and landed at Colophon in order to visit and question its oracle; so at last he reached Syria. He was evidently in no great hurry.[39]

In the following winter Germanicus went down to Egypt from Syria, to see its ancient monuments, 'cognoscendae antiquitatis', though he announced his visit publicly as 'for official purposes'. He saw Alexandria. He went up the Nile. At Memphis the bull Apis, released in the courtyard, refused the food which he offered it; he saw the Pyramids; he listened at sunrise to Memnon; and after that he proceeded up-river to the first cataract.[40]

In A.D. 69 Titus, who was sent home from Syria to convey the loyal greeting of his father Vespasian to Galba, heard of Galba's murder when he reached Corinth and decided to return. On the return voyage he put in at Rhodes and Cyprus and in Cyprus visited the temple of Paphian Venus, but not only as a sight-seer. He consulted the priest about the voyage and received an answer suggesting that for him and for his family the future had good things in store. Later, in the winter of 70, after the conclusion of the Jewish war, he travelled extensively

---

* Earlier Nero had planned to visit Egypt, but abandoned the plan at the last moment, frightened by a portent.

and in Memphis took part in the ritual consecration of a new-born bull Apis.[41]

After his Parthian war Septimius Severus visited Egypt, partly for reasons of state, partly for holiday—a holiday from which he derived great enjoyment 'because of the cult of Serapis, the antiquities that he saw and also the novelty of the wild animals and of the countryside'. Outside Alexandria he visited the stock sights—Memphis, Thebes, the Pyramids, Memnon. Illness prevented him from travelling further up the Nile.[42]

In taking the fullest advantage of opportunities of foreign sight-seeing which their official duties offered, emperors and princes acted as proconsuls and generals had always acted. Athens and Rhodes were on the direct route for those who took up postings in the eastern Mediterranean; Cicero wrote of Athens (where he had previously lived as a student) on his way out to govern Cilicia, 'I was delighted with the place and its buildings.'[43] And proconsuls and other administrators took time off in order to see interesting places. In 167 B.C., after his victory in the third Macedonian war, Aemilius Paullus did an extensive round tour of Greece, visiting Delphi, Lebadia, Chalcis (to see the Euripus and the bridge), Aulis, Corinth, Sicyon, Argos, Epidaurus, Sparta and Olympia, making the appropriate sacrifices at the various shrines. Whether his experience justified Livy's sour comment that, seen by the naked eye, the famous places in Greece generally fell below their reputation, we cannot tell.[44]

The inscriptions at Memnon are the best possible illustration of this practice. Nine record visits from governors of Egypt, and a great number of the other visitors were Roman or Greek officials serving in Egypt, or else officers or rankers of the legions stationed in the province. A centurion, whose home was at Vienne in Gaul, evidently enjoyed frequent leave and spent it in Thebes (unless, perhaps, he was on duty in the vicinity), for he heard the voice of Memnon on twelve different occasions between November A.D. 80 and June 81.[45]

In the upper social classes travel was indeed regarded as a part of a young man's education, to be enjoyed in one or both of two different ways.

There was first the completion of his education. For this purpose if, under the Empire, he lived in the west, he probably went, like Agricola, to the university at Marseilles (Massilia). If he lived in Italy, he naturally went to Athens and perhaps also to Rhodes, from which centres he was able to visit other show places in Greece and Asia Minor;

though the reputation of Marseilles was so high that some Romans sent their sons there rather than to Athens.[46] Other distinguished 'university cities' in the eastern Mediterranean were Tarsus, which had an excellent reputation and produced a number of distinguished philosophers and rhetoricians, but was little visited by foreigners, Berytus (Beirut), which had an eminent law school in the late Empire, and Alexandria, whose distinguished medical school won a reputation which survived through the centuries. 'As evidence of his mastery in his profession, the mere statement by a doctor that he has been trained in Alexandria is better than any testimonial.' Anatomy was studied more thoroughly at Alexandria than anywhere else and Galen thought it essential for a medical student to go to Alexandria in order that he might have experience in the dissection of the human cadaver. Medical students were, in the main, Greeks, not Romans.[47]

Romans went for their higher education to Greece mostly in their early twenties. Caesar at twenty-five and Cicero at twenty-seven were a little old; Cicero's son went at the age of twenty. They were likely to gain most from their studies in Quintilian's view if they had already made their début as pleaders in court, academic work having greater value if it was based on practical experience.

Young men who were friends went to pursue their studies together, Cicero with his brother, his cousin L. Cicero, Atticus and M. Pupius Piso, whom Cicero would have been shocked to envisage as a political enemy of the future. They consorted with other Romans according to their personal likes and dislikes. In 45/4 B.C. students at Athens included Horace and young Cicero, both aged twenty, Cato's grandson (the one surviving son of Bibulus), a young Manlius Acidinus, perhaps a young Manlius Torquatus and, a young man with a distinguished future ahead, Valerius Messalla Corvinus. Their studies ended abruptly when the world disintegrated at Caesar's death and soon, as good republicans, they joined M. Brutus and were swept into the civil war.[48]

Ovid was a student at Athens in the middle-twenties B.C. when he was in his late teens and it may well have been after this that he travelled with his friend Pompeius Macer in Asia Minor (where Macer, as the son of Pompey's freedman Theophanes, a native of Lesbos, should have been a very good guide) and then stayed for some time in Sicily. In Asia Minor he visited the ruins of Troy.[49]

As we know from Cicero's letters, the higher education of these young men might cost their fathers a lot of money. If they were to live in style, they must have their own houses. They entertained and received entertainment, young Cicero entertaining his tutor, the disinguished philosopher Cratippus, to dinner and even receiving calls from him unannounced. In the second century A.D. Aulus Gellius and other Roman students in Athens dined together on the Saturnalia, as American students in a European university may dine together today on Thanksgiving Day.[50]

University education edifies. Also, in its long history, it has often corrupted. Cicero was doubtless not the only father whose son's letters were a catalogue of mounting debts, and who heard rumours that his son was too fond of the bottle. A letter survives, written by young Cicero to his father's freedman Tiro, which is a splendid profession of zeal and repentance.[51]

Residence in Athens gave an opportunity of wider travel in Greek lands. From Athens Cicero visited the Peloponnese, where he winced at the first sight of the ruins of Corinth but not, apparently, at seeing boys kicking and biting one another, collapsing rather than admit defeat, in their sports at Sparta or at being told of their still being beaten to death at the altar, in the continuing enforcement of improving Lycurgean discipline. His son, when at Athens, formed plans—and with greater stability, would have carried them out—to visit Greek cities in Asia Minor.[52]

In the latter part of the first century A.D. the pursuit of particular philosophers sometimes led to less conventional seats of instruction than Athens and Rhodes—to Nicopolis, even to Gyaros.*

There was a two-way traffic in students. Young men went from Rome to Greece. But other students, as the great law schools in Rome developed, came from the provinces to study there.†

The second means by which young Romans of the upper class could broaden their horizons as boys and as young men was by going out with their fathers or by securing posts as cadets (*comites*) on the staffs of their parents' friends and relatives who held administrative posts in the provinces. Young Cicero, having announced his wish to visit Asia Minor, was invited by the governor, C. Trebonius, to join him, and Trebonius wrote to assure the young man's father that he would ensure that Cratippus came with him, so that it would not be simply one long holiday. In fact young Cicero had already been taken out to Cilicia on his father's staff in 51 when he was only fourteen, together with his cousin Quintus who was still younger. They saw Athens for

* See above, p. 185.
† See above, p. 101.

the first time, and Cicero was anxious that the boys should see Rhodes on the way home. At the same time Bibulus, as governor of Syria, took his two elder boys out with him, with tragic consequences; they were sent from Syria to Egypt to be out of harm's way when a Parthian invasion threatened, and there they were both killed by rioting Roman soldiers.[53]

In this way Catullus spent some unprofitable months in Bithynia in 57/6 B.C. on the staff of C. Memmius, a man who impressed the rest of the world less favourably than he impressed Lucretius, and he looked forward to seeing the great cities of Asia on the way home; but in fact he enjoyed no part of his toil abroad—his *peregrinus labor*'—as much as he enjoyed being back at home at the end of it all, at Sirmio on Lake Garda.

Propertius received an invitation, which he declined, to join his friend Volcatius Tullus when Tullus was on an official mission to Asia. Tibullus, who had previously seen heavy fighting under Valerius Messalla Corvinus in Gaul, fell ill and had to be left at Corfu when he was on his way out to Syria later with a place on Messalla's staff; he had been excited by the thought of visiting Egypt when he was in the East. Persius sometimes travelled abroad with Paetus Thrasea. Seneca went to Egypt as a young man to visit his uncle C. Galerius, who was governor for sixteen years; but as his writings reflect nothing of his experience of Egypt, he was perhaps simply sent out as a sickly young man for the benefit of the voyage to and fro—not a happy experience, for his uncle died on the journey home.[54]

In the Republic young men of good family were sometimes attached to the staffs of provincial governors as *comites* or *contubernales* for more practical reasons than merely to give them experience of foreign parts. When Q. Pompeius, governor of Africa in 62/1 B.C., was pressed to take out M. Caelius Rufus, the fact that Caelius' father had estates in Africa was certainly not irrelevant. Under a generous and successful governor these young men might hope not to lose money on the venture; indeed M. Brutus' interest in the corrupt and illegal floating of a loan in Rome to the city of Salamis in Cyprus may well have originated in the year 58 B.C. when he accompanied his blameless uncle Cato on Cato's sinister public mission to the island to eliminate its king and to transfer his exchequer to Rome.[55]

For a keen young man with aspirations to a distinguished career there could be no better introduction to the administrator's life than attachment as a junior to a good governor or a good general; and a magistrate or ex-magistrate who was about to govern a province was often embarrassed by requests for places on his staff from relatives and political friends on behalf of their sons or themselves. A strong man like Scipio Aemilianus was ready to meet such applications with a blunt refusal; he invited people to join him and did not accept those who invited themselves. Those who were less resolute paid the price of their generosity. P. Clodius was an acute embarrassment to his brother-in-law L. Lucullus in the third Mithridatic war; given a commission in the army, he encouraged the troops to mutiny. Julius Caesar was the worst sufferer of all. At Vesontio before the engagement with Ariovistus in 58 B.C. his army panicked, 'starting with the junior officers and cadets who had joined Caesar's staff on personal grounds ("*amicitiae causa*") and had little experience of fighting. Finding a variety of different reasons which made their urgent departure necessary, they asked leave to go. Some stayed because they were ashamed of being thought cowards, but they could not control their expression, sometimes even their tears. They retired to their tents, lamenting their own sorry plight or, with their friends, deplored the danger that faced them all. In every part of the camp men were occupied in making their wills.'[56]

In the Republic few women of the senatorial class travelled beyond the borders of Italy, for the law forced senators to leave their womenfolk at home when they were out of Italy on service, whether engaged in fighting or in provincial administration. Indeed a husband often said goodbye to his wife 'at the gate' on the occasion of his ceremonial departure from Rome—which did not mean that in her absence he denied himself the pleasure of intimate female companionship.[57] In times and places of danger the regulation was sensible, but in the case of the peaceful provinces by the end of the Republic it might well have been relaxed. Sons were sometimes taken out by their fathers, but were not the better for the experience. Wives left at home consoled themselves, in the absence of their husbands, in what ways they could. Often the husband returned, like Pompey in 62 B.C., and a divorce followed.

After the civil wars in whose turmoil husbands, wives and families fled overseas together, it would have been difficult to reimpose the old restriction; anyhow, when Augustus was in the provinces, he liked to have his wife with him.[58]

There were a few hard-suffering wives of austere upholders of the old régime, like the patient wife of A. Caecina in the early Empire,

who bore her husband six children but was never allowed to accompany
him in any of the forty years in which he was on active service.[59]
But most husbands were accompanied by their wives, and when emperors travelled, their womenfolk always went with them—Gaius'
sisters to Gaul in A.D. 39, Statilia Messalina to Greece with Nero in
67, Plotina to the east with Trajan, Sabina to Egypt with Hadrian.

Administrators too. Husband, wife and family travelled about the
Empire together and family life was no longer interrupted by the
demands of a husband's career. Claudius, later to be emperor, was born
somewhat unexpectedly at Lyons in 10 B.C. at the anniversary of the
dedication of the great altar of Rome and Augustus by his father
Drusus. When Germanicus was in command of the Rhine armies, his
little boy Gaius was dressed in uniform with military boots and so
acquired his name Caligula, and Germanicus' wife had a baby at Ara
Ubiorum on the Rhine, Agrippina, who later became empress and
gave her birthplace its new name, Colonia Agrippinensis (Cologne).
When Germanicus was touring the Greek world on his way out to
Syria, his wife had another daughter, her last child, born at Lesbos.
Agricola's wife bore a daughter in Asia when her husband was quaestor
and later a son in Britain during Agricola's governorship of the island.[60]

A strong and assertive governor's wife could be an embarrassment to
others beside her husband, and it was an unfortunate chance which
brought two such women, who were not likely to consort well together, into close association when Germanicus was in the East in
A.D. 19. Munatia Plancina, the wife of Cn. Piso, governor of Syria,
was said even to take part in military parades and manœuvres; the
elder Agrippina, Germanicus' wife, had herself assumed no small
military prominence when Germanicus commanded the Rhine
armies.[61] The clash of these two women's personalities was not a small
factor in the subsequent tragedy, Germanicus' death and Piso's recall,
trial and suicide. The women survived—for a time.

The notoriety of these two women's behaviour, however, together
with his own recollection of the fact that in the mutiny of the lower
German legions in A.D. 14 Agrippina and her small boy Gaius had been
in considerable danger of their lives,[62] encouraged the austere A.
Caecina to propose in the Senate in A.D. 21 that Republican practice
should be restored and women should be left at home when their
husbands were on service in the provinces. The proposal was resisted
vigorously (by the Emperor's son Drusus among others) and was killed
for lack of support.[63]

The perfect wife of an administrator should no doubt leave administration to her husband; but one may wonder if Seneca's aunt, the wife
of C. Galerius, the governor of Egypt, did not perhaps overdo things
a little. According to her nephew's panegyric, 'in all the sixteen years
in which her husband governed Egypt, she was never once seen in
public, and she never admitted a resident of the province to her house.
She allowed no requests to be addressed to her and she addressed no
requests to her husband.'[64]

It is true that no commercial ambition lay behind the acquisition of
Rome's earliest provinces or of Rome's first penetration into the Greek
world east of the Adriatic; yet as soon as imperial expansion started,
Romans and Italians saw the opportunities for trading enterprise
and grasped them. Traders were to be found outside the imperial
frontiers, ahead of Roman conquest, and in this they ran serious risks.
They took part in the defence of Cirta against Jugurtha in 112 B.C.
and, when Jugurtha took the town, they were put to death; as were
the Roman traders at Cenabum and at the Aeduan city of Noviodunum
in Gaul in 52. Even in the settled provinces they were not always
altogether safe. Asia had been a province for over thirty years in 88 B.C.;
then Mithridates invaded it and eighty thousand Romans and Italians,
most of them traders and business men, were put to the sword. Great
numbers, too, must have been slaughtered when Mithridates' forces
sacked Delos.[65]

The delegation of a large amount of tax collection to private enterprise (to *publicani*) brought a large number of Romans to the provinces
as employees of the tax-farming companies; they added to their wealth,
but not to their popularity, by indulging in various not particularly
scrupulous forms of money-lending.

Occasionally—not often—Romans abroad are spotlighted in our
literary sources. The seventy-nine letters of the thirteenth book of
Cicero's correspondence with his friends are mostly written to provincial governors and commend the interests (business interests, not
necessarily uncorrupt) and the persons of his friends and connexions.
Romans are ubiquitous in the Sicily which his Verrine orations
describe—also in Narbonese Gaul as portrayed in the *Pro Fonteio*,
Narbonese Gaul being hardly a province at all, but almost a part of
Italy. Plutarch's account of Cato's brave end in Africa in 46 B.C.
reveals the fact that in the town of Utica there were three hundred
Romans, 'business men in Africa, trading and lending money'. They
were evidently rich for, when Caesar spared them, he did this at the

price of an enormous indemnity—200 million sesterces (an average of over 650,000 sesterces a man).[66]

Inscriptions, however, supply most of our evidence. They show active trading with Egypt, both from South Italy and from Delos in the second century B.C. They attest the presence of large numbers of Romans and Italians—free and freedmen, with their slaves—on Delos in the eighty years of its vast prosperity, a slave-market handling thousands of slaves a day, the most important link in the east–west commercial chain. This prosperity followed the punitive measures taken by Rome against Rhodes in 166; it was increased by the punitive measures taken by Rome against Corinth in 146; it ended with the pillage of the island by Mithridates' forces, and there was never any considerable revival.[67] An inscription reveals that at the time of Augustus there were 250 Romans resident in Cyrene who possessed capital worth 10,000 sesterces, which is a very small sum. Inscriptions give us tantalizing evidence of individuals—like the two Romans who left a record of their presence in Egypt on the Coptos–Berenice road under Augustus; one was coming home from India.[68]

There were men who went abroad for business reasons, like many of the employees of the great tax-farming companies, but later returned to Rome. And there were also settlers, Romans who moved out to the provinces and made their homes there. We have a strange glimpse of an extraordinary settlement at Carteia in Spain as early as 171 B.C., of 4,000 men whose fathers, Roman soldiers, had remained in Spain after the second Punic war and had married—though Roman law did not recognize such marriages—Spanish women. They were established as a Latin colony, the first outside Italy. When he returned to Rome from Spain in 206, Scipio had left a number of soldiers behind, wounded men chiefly, to form the settlement of Italica, which later was Trajan's and Hadrian's home town.[69]

The civilian settlers, like the Roman soldiers, are elusive people, though a little less elusive than they once were; for it is in connexion with such people that the recent cult of prosopography has achieved some of its greatest successes. The appearance in Spain, for example, of a family name which is common in Campania may indicate the descendants of a Campanian immigrant. Immigration is also indicated in the case of Romans by membership of a tribe different from that to which a man's neighbours belonged.[70]

Sometimes, generations later, the descendant of a settler travelled in the opposite direction from that taken by his pioneer ancestors. He came to Rome, entered politics, became a senator perhaps, or even an emperor. This, perhaps, was Trajan's background, and Hadrian's.

Even larger was the number of Greeks and of eastern Mediterranean people who travelled west, bringing their gods with them. Isis, for instance, was brought to the western Mediterranean ports by sailors and travellers from Egypt. Casually preserved tombstones record the deaths in Rome of men, women and children who had been born in Greece, Asia, Cilicia, Syria, Crete, Egypt. Juvenal's intemperate abuse would suggest that Rome was full of Syrians.[71] Fellow-nationals would meet over the celebrations of their native cults; and they formed their own business and social communities, *stationes*. The traders from Tyre, as we know, had one such *statio* in Puteoli and another in Rome; at Puteoli, indeed, and at Ostia there were corporations of a whole variety of eastern Mediterranean and of north African traders.[72]

Greeks in general were more addicted to travel than were Romans, and there were professional travellers among Greeks who had no Roman counterparts. There were, first of all, the orators, men like Aelius Aristides in the second century A.D., who moved from city to city for the sake of delivering, whether or not in response to invitations, the tedious and flatulent public speeches which Greek audiences so greatly relished. There was hardly a great city from Alexandria to Rome in which Aelius Aristides did not deliver some speech or other. Philosophers travelled too, men like Artemidorus and Euphrates of Tyre whom Pliny first met on his military service in Syria, both of whom came to Rome. The journeying of philosophers, like that of astrologers, was not always spontaneous, for there were periods when they settled down in Rome only to be evicted from it—by Tiberius, by Nero, by Vespasian and by Domitian. An aggressive religion, too, prompted extensive travel; witness the journeyings of St. Paul and other missionaries of the early Christian church.

The outspoken Timagenes of Alexandria, who was to write history and make an enemy of Augustus, when he first arrived in Rome, after capture by Gabinius in the late Republic, opened a school of rhetoric there. An inscription records a man from Nicaea in Bithynia who came to Rome, set up as a mathematics teacher and, as his epitaph states complacently, found this a paying occupation.[73]

Greek professional athletes, too, in the short period of five years or so in which they were at their peak, travelled from one race meeting to another, together with poets and musicians, for whom also there were competitive events. The *periodonikes* had won victories at each of the four great games in Greece, at the Nemea, the Isthmia, the Pythia and Olympia. An inscription records the stupendous achievement of the pancratiast M. Aurelius Asclepiades in six years racing between 177 and 182 A.D. He was 'aleiptos' (always in the van) and 'anekkletos' (too good to be challenged). In none of the events in which he competed in Asia, Greece and Italy was he ever beaten. He won at Alexandria, at every available race meeting in the Greek towns of Asia Minor, in Greece itself and in Italy at Naples, Puteoli and in the Capitolia at Rome.* At the age of twenty-five he retired. Relentless competition was dangerous, and his successes provoked jealousy, which he resented.[74]

There were also, Greek rather than Roman, men with a bent for exploration. We meet two interesting men of this sort in dialogues of Plutarch (himself a considerable traveller). The Spartan Cleombrotus travelled not for business but because he liked seeing and finding out things; he had travelled a lot in Egypt, had visited the Troglodyte country and had sailed out into the Red Sea. The other was Demetrius of Tarsus (whose record survives in York) who 'under imperial escort' had sailed out to the western isles off Scotland—probably when Agricola was governor of Britain, and probably as a preliminary to the voyage made round the north of Scotland which established for the first time that Britain was an island. 'This,' Sir Ian Richmond wrote, 'gives us a rare glimpse into the methods of Imperial exploration, using educated and inquisitive Greeks for its intelligence officers.' There are earlier examples: Polybius with Scipio Aemilianus in Spain and Africa in the second century B.C.; Strabo in Egypt in attendance on the governor Aelius Gallus more than a century later.[75]

Apart from foreigners who settled in the city, Rome was probably visited by more tourists than any other city in the world, numbers of them Romans from the provinces. We have a glimpse of some who came from Baetica to Rome to witness Domitian's Capitoline Games† and who after a subsequent visit were forced by bad weather on their way home to land at Tarraco. Here they encountered Annaeus Florus. This highly sensitive man was deeply offended by his failure to secure an award at previous Capitoline games; the men from Baetica assured him that they had shouted for him and that they too had been disappointed when the prize-winner was announced. So he left Rome and travelled to Sicily, Crete, Rhodes and Alexandria. Then he returned and went west, crossing the Pyrenees into Spain (Tarraconensis), where he

* On which, see p. 326.
† On these games, see p. 326.

settled down—to be a schoolmaster. This, he assured his hearers, was his métier; he could ask for no greater happiness. However, as a friend of Hadrian, he later returned to live in Rome.[76]

So there *were* Romans who travelled. There was a Q. Ovidius of Nomentum who, under Nero, moved to Sicily of his own free will, so as to live with the consular Caesennius Maximus, who had been banished to Sicily. Later in A.D. 98, when he was an old man, he decided to go to Britain to see a friend, a Roman, presumably, who had settled or was stationed in the province. A poem of Martial suggests that, for a man of his age, this was a courageous undertaking.[77]

VIII

HOLIDAYS AT HOME:
PUBLIC ENTERTAINMENT

◆◆◆

1. Festivals, Games and Shows, their origins
and differences

THE HISTORY of holidays at home in ancient Rome is a history—
for the austere moralist, a depressing history—of progress in the entertainment business.

In the beginning there were established festivals (*feriae, dies feriati*),
each of them in honour of a particular divinity[1]; they were spread over
the twelve months, all on odd and none on even days of the month,
none but March 1st and July 5th (the Poplifugia) falling earlier than
the Nones, for it was on the Nones that the dates of the festivals in
each month were publicly announced. There were fifty-eight such
days (including, in every month, the Ides). The origin of the festivals
lay in the time of the kings, in the supposed religious calendar of King
Numa; and it was bad history which dated the institution of the Regifugium, which was thought to have something to do with the expulsion of the last king, Tarquinius Superbus, and the Poplifugia to a
date later than the monarchy. They were for the most part festivals
closely connected with the vicissitudes of the countryman's life, and
many of them had the object of placating the benign, and averting
the malignant, influences to which the farmer and his crops were
exposed.[2] Their sacrifices were in every case the business of the
appropriate priest, and in some cases the sacrifices were attended by
sports and frolics. By the end of the Republic few can have held any
significance at all for the ordinary city-dwelling Roman. The festival
day was still *nefastus* in the calendar; so it was a day on which he could
not consult his lawyer. But it would be absurd to imagine that shops
were not open, and that ordinary people did not go about their business as much on these as on other days of the year.

From the time of the kings to the end of the Republic the list of festival days was unchanged. Then came the Caesars, and the beginning of a novel era of sycophancy.[3] The Senate knew no better way of marking Julius Caesar's great victories (in Spain in 49 B.C., at Pharsalus, at Alexandria, at Thapsus and at Munda) than by decreeing that their anniversaries should be festivals. By the time of Tiberius' death in A.D. 37, the number of such imperial anniversaries had risen to thirty-two, and after that the process continued. In each principate it became customary to make an annual festival of an emperor's birthday, of his day of accession, of his notable victories, even of his alleged escapes from assassination. If after death he was consecrated, that was yet another day for celebration. If, on the other hand, he was judged to have ruled badly, then the anniversaries established in his honour during his lifetime were conveniently forgotten. Still, the additions were more numerous than the subtractions. In A.D. 70 the Senate appointed a committee 'to purge the calendar which had been befouled by the flattery of the times, and to reduce the strain on the exchequer'—for the State treasury (the *aerarium Saturni*) had to meet the expense of the sacrifices[4]; and a similar committee was set up with similar terms of reference by Nerva in 97.[5] In both cases the end of a discredited dynasty was an obvious moment for reform.

Inevitably, however, the nuisance continued, and Marcus Aurelius set a limit of one hundred and thirty-five to the number of days which were marked as festival days on the calendar, and on which legal business could not be transacted.[6]

The Games (*Ludi*) were something altogether different in their origin and in their nature.[7] At first generals vowed games to Juppiter which, if they won their battle and were accorded a triumph, they celebrated (*ludi magni, votivi*) at the conclusion of their triumph, going in procession (*pompa*) from the Capitol to the Circus.* These occasional triumphal games were dissociated from the triumph and became a regular annual event, the Ludi Romani, perhaps at the institution of the curule aedileship in 366 B.C.

At all times a Roman magistrate might seek in a crisis to win divine favour for the state by vowing *ludi magni* to Juppiter Optimus Maximus, the games to be held in five or ten years time if general prosperity was then such as to warrant their celebration; or he might vow games to other gods as the price of delivery from plague or famine. And from

---

* This was the origin of the *pompa* with which in later times the Games always opened, though they were no longer directly connected with a triumph.

the elder Scipio's time generals on the eve of battle might seek any god's aid by something more powerful than prayer—by the offer of a temple and public games to be held in Rome in the god's honour in the event of victory.[8] In 212 B.C., when Hannibal's fortunes still seemed alarmingly in the ascendant, the Sibylline books were consulted and advised that games should be held in honour of Apollo 'as a specific for the expulsion of the foreign plague'. Four years later the games, the Ludi Apollinares, were revived for the purpose of eliminating a different kind of plague, and it was resolved that they should be celebrated annually on July 13th each year. They were extended to three days in 190 and by the end of the Republic lasted for eight, from July 6th until the 13th. The regular Ludi Romani, as has been seen, were probably instituted in 366 B.C., the other five fixed Republican games in the half-century following 220 B.C.[9]

At the beginning of the first century B.C. the year contained fifty-seven days of games (one day less than the number of *feriae*). They spread over nearly the whole of April. First came the Ludi Megalenses, or Megalensia, in honour of the Great Mother, that stone from Pessinus in Asia Minor representing the goddess, whose transport to Rome in 204 in accordance with the instructions of the Delphic oracle had fulfilled the most sanguine of expectations by giving Rome the final victory over Hannibal. First celebrated on her arrival in 204, they were firmly fixed in the calendar with theatrical performances from 194, filling the seven days from the 4th to the 10th. After the mere break of a day the games of Ceres (Ludi Ceriales or Cerialia), which certainly existed in 202 B.C., were celebrated for eight days, from the 12th to the 19th. Another break of eight days—and then there were the licentious games of Flora (the Ludi Florales) from the 28th until May 3rd. They dated certainly from 173 B.C. With the winter over and the crops sown, April was a good month for festivity.

In July there were the eight days of the Ludi Apollinares from the 6th to the 13th.

In September and November the two greatest sets of games took place—the Ludi Romani from September 5th to the 19th[10] and the Plebeian Games from November 4th to the 17th. The Roman Games, in honour of Juppiter, were thought to go back to the time of the kings, though their regular annual celebration dated from 366. The Plebeian Games are first recorded in 216 B.C., and date perhaps from 220.

These six Games supplied a number of people living in Rome with their relaxation in the early years of the first century B.C. Then, as was to happen in the case of the festivals, men usurped the privileges of gods and the later divinity of emperors was foreshadowed. Sulla won the battle of the Colline Gate in 82 B.C. and so became master of Rome; in the following year new games were established in honour of his victory, the Ludi Victoriae Sullae, for seven days from October 26th to November 1st, finishing only three days before the Ludi Plebei started. People at large may have proclaimed their hatred for the name of Sulla from the moment when he was dead; but people loved games, and his games continued, we cannot say for how long.

After Sulla, the chief enemy of his name, Marius's nephew, Julius Caesar. Sulla was for him a bad precedent, but he—or his flatterers—built on it and in 46 B.C. games in honour of the Victory of Caesar (the goddess, or the word would have been in the plural) were established, to extend for eleven days, from the 20th to the 30th of July, following hot on the heels of the Ludi Apollinares. These were the games which Caesar had vowed to Venus* before the battle of Pharsalus and nothing could have been more appropriate than that the period of their celebration soon after his death in 44 B.C. should have been the moment for the unexpected appearance of the comet (*sidus Iulium*) which set everybody's mind at rest with its incontrovertible assurance that Caesar had already become a god.[11]

Further, as if to link these new-style Ludi with the old, the Ludi Romani were extended by a day in Caesar's honour on a proposal of Antony after Caesar's death.[12]

As the empire of the Caesars was consolidated, public games were subject to the same inflation as festivals. New festival days, marking births, accessions and consecrations of emperors, were, unlike the festival days of the Republic, made the occasion of regular games. Games even came to be held on certain of the ancient festival days on which in the Republic no games had been held at all—for instance, in the second century A.D., on the Parilia (April 21st), the birthday of Rome, to mark the dedication on this day of Hadrian's temple of Venus and Rome (between the Colosseum and the Forum), 'the temple of the City', perhaps the most magnificent temple ever built in Rome. And there were such new games as the Ludi Augustales, first celebrated in Augustus' honour in 11 B.C., which Tiberius turned into a ten-day

---

* His temple, vowed to Venus Victrix, was dedicated to Venus Genetrix, ancestress of his family. But Pompey, with his temple to Venus Victrix, surmounting his theatre (see pl. 1b) and already dedicated in 52 B.C., helped to necessitate this convenient change of plan.

affair, from the 3rd to the 12th of October. So powerful was the inflation that in the middle of the fourth century A.D., as the surviving
calendar of Philocalus (A.D. 354) shows, a hundred and seventy-seven
days of the year were the occasion of some regular games or other.[13]

The days of the Republican public games were explicitly devoted
either to theatrical performances (*ludi scaenici**) or to chariot-racing
(*ludi circenses*[15])—in all but three of the games to theatrical performances on every day except the last, when the chariot races took place,
normally in the Circus Maximus. In the Ludi Romani the chariot-
racing lasted for the final five days, in the Ludi Plebei for the final three
and in the games in honour of Caesar's Victory for the final four. Both
in the Ludi Romani and the Ludi Plebei one day was the Epulum Iovis
and one was devoted to the ceremonial parade of the mounted Equites,
the Transvectio Equitum.

Gladiatorial fighting was no part of the public games in the Republic
and only a trifling part under the Empire.† And with small exceptions
(the release at the Cerialia of foxes with lighted torches attached to their
tails,[16] a practice which in its unknown origin must have had the purpose of averting some disaster to the crops) and the hunting of roes
and hares in the Circus on the last day of the Floralia,[17] there was,
until 169 B.C., no considerable exhibition or hunting of wild beasts
(*venatio*) as part of the ordinary games.

So on fifty-six of the seventy-seven days of regular public games at
the time of Augustus, on 101 out of 177 days in the mid-third century
A.D., any Roman who could secure a seat sought his entertainment in the
theatre; on seventeen in Augustus' time, on sixty-six in the fourth
century, he sought it in the Circus. Chariot-racing was, of course, a
far more expensive entertainment to mount than was a performance in
the theatre. But this at least is clear, that the impression that every
citizen of Rome spent every day of the public games at the races or even
watching gladiators, is a very wrong impression indeed.

Exhibitions of gladiatorial fighting and of wild beast fighting which,
more often than not, accompanied it, were *munera* (shows), not *ludi*.[18]
The origin of *munera* was, like that of *ludi*, deeply religious. Gladiatorial fighting was an Etruscan practice; men fought to the death at
the tomb of a dead chief, whose spirit needed, for its strong survival,

---

* These might consist of coarse farces, pantomimes, comedies or tragedies. A feature
of the Floralia was a strip-tease performance by prostitutes, rather than witness which the
younger Cato once left the theatre.[14]

† See below, p. 250.

the sacrifice of blood. And when gladiatorial fighting was first introduced to Rome, whether directly from Etruria or by way of Campania[19] its purpose and spirit were the same; it was an exhibition of fighting and slaughter staged from time to time by high-ranking members of the Roman nobility in honour of their distinguished dead—at first as a part of the actual funeral celebrations, later often after the death and funeral, but always in explicit memory of a particular dead man. Among a number of implausible explanations of Celer ('Fast') as a third name in the family of the Metelli, one attributed its origin to a Metellus who was in a fever of haste to give gladiatorial games when his father died. Our earliest record comes from the year 264 B.C. when, with his brother, D. Iunius Pera, who was consul and triumphed in 266, put on men (prisoners, perhaps, from his campaigns) to fight as gladiators at funeral games in honour of his father in the Forum Boarium in Rome.[20] In 216 B.C. the three sons of M. Aemilius Lepidus put on twenty-two pairs in the Forum at funeral games in honour of their father.[21] When Scipio Africanus mounted such fights in Spain in 206 B.C. (mortal duels between noble Spanish gentlemen rather than contests of professional gladiatorial riff-raff, as Livy emphasized[22]), he honoured the memory of his father and uncle who had been killed five years earlier; when Julius Caesar showed 320 pairs of fighters (all in silvered armour) in Rome in 65, this was in memory of his father, who had been dead for twenty years.[23]

By Caesar's time gladiatorial games had become a vast public entertainment, to be enjoyed by as many of the public as could secure places to watch, a means of attracting popularity and of winning votes. What, in Tertullian's words, had once been, by the belief of its promoters, a *munus*, a dutiful service (*officium*) to the dead, had become an entertainment, something to enjoy.[24]

At first the gladiatorial games may have been an exclusive performance, given by the members of a noble family and witnessed by their peers. It was—by one of two conflicting accounts—a *nobile scortum*, a pleasure-boy from a noble house, who tempted the proconsul L. Flamininus to an act of singular bestiality, the execution of a prisoner at the dinner table, in the early second century B.C.; he told Flamininus that he had missed the chance of witnessing death at gladiatorial games in Rome when he consented to join his staff in Gaul.[25] As tribune in 122 B.C. Gaius Gracchus tore down the boxes of the nobles which had been built around a temporary arena for gladiatorial fights in the Forum, preventing the proletariat from witnessing the spectacle.[26]

Gladiatorial fighting was not the sole constituent of the funeral games of the Roman nobility in the Republic. At least in the early second century there seem in nearly every case also to have been theatrical performances (*ludi scaenici*). Indeed the first performance of the *Adelphi* of Terence and the second performance of his *Hecyra* took place at the funeral games given in 160 in honour of the great L. Aemilius Paullus by his two sons.[27]

The very late statement (in a panegyric to Theoderic) that under the consuls of 105 B.C.—one of them Rutilius Rufus, who drafted gladiatorial trainers into the army to teach the troops commando warfare—there was a display of gladiatorial fighting at the public games is certainly untrue[28]; and there is no reason to think that gladiatorial fighting was ever displayed to the Roman public under the Republic except when privately given at his own expense by some individual Roman, always on the pretext of honouring a dead relative. The first recognition of gladiatorial encounters as a part of public games comes from the months just before Julius Caesar's murder in 44 when, in an orgy of sycophantic voting, the Senate decreed that at all gladiatorial games inside and outside Rome in Italy one day should be devoted to Caesar's honour; and in the celebration of the Cerialia in 42 B.C. the plebeian aediles substituted gladiatorial fighting for chariot-racing and by their act perhaps made history.[29]

Even so the *munus* and the *ludi* retained their distinction, and gladiatorial fighting (together with wild beast hunting and fighting) was hardly to be witnessed in Rome except in particular celebrations, given usually by the Emperor, and not at the regular games. The eight occasions, for instance, on which Augustus gave gladiatorial shows (three times in his own name, five times in the names of his adopted sons and grandsons), shows in which some ten thousand gladiators fought, all marked particularly significant events or achievements. One was given in honour of his friend and son-in-law M. Agrippa after his death, another was in honour of his dead stepson Drusus, in A.D. 6, fourteen years after he was dead. This last was given in the name of Drusus' sons Germanicus and Claudius.[30]

So in A.D. 80 the emperor Titus marked the opening of the Colosseum (presumably in memory of his father Vespasian, who had built it and who had died in the previous year) by a hundred days of gladiatorial fighting, wild beast hunts and other such spectacular entertainments[31]; and Trajan, who had a mania for gladiatorial fighting as for other public entertainment, marked the conquest of Dacia by 117 days of celebration in 108 and 109 in which eleven thousand beasts were killed and ten thousand gladiators fought. This was his 'second show'; we know no details of his first. Even Hadrian put on 1835 pairs of fighters at six days of games which he gave in A.D. 126.[32]

As will be seen, it was to the Emperor's interest to take the exclusive control of the gladiatorial schools in Rome into his own hands. In 22 B.C. there was legislation to ensure that, imperial displays apart, gladiatorial shows should be given at public games only with the Senate's permission and then not more than twice a year or with more than sixty pairs of combatants—which, by the standards which Augustus and some of his successors set for themselves, was very small beer indeed.[33]

That even in the fourth century A.D. gladiatorial fighting was no large element in the regular public games is shown by the calendar of Philocalus, according to which there was gladiatorial fighting on only ten days (all in December) out of the hundred and seventy-seven days of annual Ludi.[34]

Christianity protested vigorously against the licence of festivals, games and shows. In 389 Theodosius abolished all pagan festivals and substituted the severer relaxation of the weekly 'Lord's Day', and of certain seasonal holidays and Christian festivals.[35] Yet the games continued, though no longer under their pagan titles. There were games still on April 4th and 10th (no longer called the Megalensia), on five or six days between April 12th and 19th (a considerable survival of the Ludi Ceriales), and on four days between July 6th and 12th, the period of the Ludi Apollinares.[36]

Christians protested against gladiatorial fighting as being cruel in itself and an encouragement to cruelty in the spectators (a point which Seneca had stressed far earlier), as being wasteful of money and as being staged in the amphitheatre, which was a 'temple of demons', whom the blood attracted. So in A.D. 325 it was forbidden, though ineffectively, by Constantine who, perhaps persuaded by the Council of Nicaea, had already forbidden the exposure of criminals to death in the arena and for heinous offences had substituted condemnation to the mines.[37] Christian preachers preached against it, as against all other *spectacula*, but in vain; in their enjoyment of watching gladiators, people forgot about the demons.

The story that gladiatorial fighting came to an end in Rome in A.D. 392 when a monk, St. Almachius, rushed into the arena to stop the fighters and was killed himself is not acceptable. Gladiatorial exhibitions did not in fact stop in 392.

Such fighting disappeared in Gaul early, in the East late, in the fourth century. At the end of the century gladiatorial schools were closed in Rome but still gladiatorial fighting continued, perhaps as late as A.D. 439/40.[38]

Wild beast fighting and hunting persisted longer. In the eastern empire it seems that Anastasius in 498 forbade contests of men against wild beasts, but allowed the fighting of beasts against one another. Theoderic may have done the same in Rome, for the last we hear of *venationes* in the Colosseum at Rome is a highly coloured denunciation of them by Theoderic, written by Cassiodorus, in A.D. 523.[39] Why spend money on mounting an exhibition of death, the struggle of the hunter pitted against a beast more powerful than himself, his only chance of survival lying in trickery and deception? How much better to spend it to the benefit of the living.

Chariot-racing continued to flourish in Constantinople; at Rome the last recorded races in the Circus Maximus took place under Totila in A.D. 549.

As for the stage, the severer spirits among the Christian clergy and Christian writers would have liked to see an end to all play-acting, for plays perpetuated pagan myth and were more often than not indecent; but their congregations had not lost the pleasure-loving instincts of the pagan past. Legislation against the performance of the mime, particularly the *maiuma*, a licentious aquatic spectacle, was ineffective, and ecclesiastical sanctions (refusal of baptism) against performers as against charioteers did not succeed. Pompey's theatre was restored in the sixth century under Theoderic, and in Cassiodorus' letters there are frequent references to pantomimes, just as there are to charioteers.[40]

2. Places of Entertainment

At the time of Julius Caesar's first consulship (59 B.C.) Rome, unlike Capua and the Greek cities to the south, had no permanent stone theatre and at the time of his death in 44 B.C. it had no permanent amphitheatre. For the primary purpose of chariot-racing, however, there were two circuses, the Circus Flaminius in the Campus Martius, constructed in 221 B.C., where the Ludi Plebei were held, and the Circus Maximus between the Palatine and the Aventine, whose open track, stripped of all ornament, is familiar today to anybody who has ever been in Rome. In the centre was an underground shrine of Consus, in whose honour, if legend was to be believed, Romulus held the races which tempted the

Sabine maidens to their doom. The Circus, then, was thought to be very old. Its historical existence seems established in 329 B.C., and we know of alterations and improvements made in 174 B.C., but it was not until the time of Augustus that it achieved great magnificence. At the west end of the ellipse were the twelve starting boxes, the richly painted *carceres*, sometimes called 'the fortress', the *oppidum*.⁴¹ Through the centre ran an axial rib, the long *spina*, on which Augustus placed one obelisk (the one which now stands in the centre of the Piazza del Popolo) and in A.D. 357 Constantius placed another (the obelisk which is now in the Piazza del Laterano). From 174 B.C. the *spina* held seven large wooden eggs (*ova*) and, by the gift of M. Agrippa in 33 B.C., seven bronze dolphins from whose mouths water poured into basins (*Euripus*). At either end were three *metae*, turning posts, which after Claudius were of gilded bronze.⁴²

The box of the presiding magistrate, who was starter, was above the *carceres* in which the chariots awaited the race, held back by a rope across the front.

The length of the *spina* was 344 metres, and the length of the arena just under 600; its width, at its greatest, was 87 metres.

The surrounding seats were in three stories, the lowest of stone with marble facing, the two highest of wood. Outside, the building was arcaded with shops where you could get food and where, if such was your need, you had no difficulty in finding a prostitute or an astrologer.⁴³

A third Circus was built by Gaius across the river in the gardens of Agrippina, called the Circus of Gaius and Nero or the Circus Vaticanus, whose north side was destroyed in the fourth century A.D. to create space for the first basilica of St. Peter.

The Piazza Navona (see pl. 1a) in Rome still perfectly reproduces the shape and size of a small-scale circus, for it is the stadium which Domitian built in the Campus Martius for athletic contests, some of the original stone still being visible; it was used, too, for a time, after the Colosseum was burnt in A.D. 217, for gladiatorial exhibitions. Its arcades served the same sordid purposes as those of the Circus Maximus, and it was in one of their brothels that S. Agnese was martyred; which explains why her church stands in the Piazza Navona where it does.⁴⁴

That the Romans should have lagged so far behind the rest of the civilized world and have had to wait for Pompey to give them their first permanent stone theatre may at first occasion surprise. In fact, almost exactly a century before the building of Pompey's theatre a contract for the building of a permanent stone theatre at Rome was

given out by the censors of 154 B.C. and the work had made some progress when that scourge of moral disintegration, P. Scipio Nasica
Corculum, persuaded the Senate to order its destruction and to pro-
hibit any such building for the future.[45] This was probably not, as the
sources suggest, because he disapproved of Romans sitting down while
they watched plays because, though they may have stood up to watch
plays a century or more earlier, they watched seated from the early
second century, as the prologues to Plautus' comedies show clearly.[46]
The reason for which he thought the existence of a permanent stone
theatre would be harmful to public morals was that in Greek cities,
where public political life had disintegrated seriously enough, theatres
were used for deliberative public assemblies, people sitting down to
listen to the speeches. Give the Romans a theatre, and they would
transfer their public meetings (*comitia* and *contiones*) to the theatre and
sit down. It was a firm Roman tradition that in public assemblies and
elections people stood on their feet.[47]

Even at the end of the Republic prejudice against the notion of a
permanent stone theatre survived, and Pompey faced criticism over
his great theatre in the Campus Martius, remains of which still survive;
indeed it was perhaps partly with an eye to such criticism that he built
a temple of Venus Victrix above the auditorium (see pl. 1c), in just
such a position as was occupied by the temple (now the site of the
museum) above the top row of seats of the theatre at Praeneste (Palestrina). In inviting the people to the dedication of his theatre in 52 B.C.
Pompey invited them not to the theatre but to 'the temple of Venus,
under which we have set stone seats (*spectacula*)'.[48]

This was no sharp practice on Pompey's part; he was observing
tradition. For in the beginning and we cannot say for how long performances at the games were given in front of the temple of the divinity
in whose honour the games were held. That was what Cicero meant
when he said that at the Ludi Megalenses (at which Plautus' *Pseudolus*
and Terence's *Andria* were first performed) the plays were acted 'before
the temple of the Great Mother and under her very eyes'.

Later on when the permanent theatre was a familiar feature of Rome
Quintilian revealed an interesting side of Roman public character
when he suggested that a proposal to build a theatre for enjoyment's
sake would shock; the orator should stress not only the practical value
of his proposal (relaxation for the worker, orderliness if the spectators
were seated and not jostling one another to get the best view) but also
its religious significance, the last being the point which he would make

if he was advocating the institution of new games: 'he will describe the theatre as a kind of temple for sacred purposes.'

Jostling for a view, at least, was avoided even before there were permanent theatres; plays were performed on temporary wooden stages before an audience on wooden seating erected for the performance and afterwards taken down.[49]

In the Empire (when there were no more deliberative assemblies that mattered and public business was no longer liable to disintegration if people sat down as in the Senate, of course, even in the days of its greatest deliberations, senators had done), there were three stone theatres, Pompey's (which was modelled on the theatre at Mytilene, a building which had specially delighted him, and which does not survive)[50] and the two which were built under Augustus. One of these was the theatre of the younger Balbus, that Spaniard who, enfranchised as a boy through Pompey in 72 B.C. together with his father and his uncle (who was Julius Caesar's trusted agent), had, as we know from a highly critical letter to Cicero from Asinius Pollio, under whom he was serving in 43 B.C. in Spain, a strong interest in the stage.* His theatre at Rome, started in 19 and dedicated in 13 B.C., when Augustus returned from Gaul, was near the Tiber, just north of the island, occupying part of the site of the present Palazzo Cenci.[51]

The third theatre was 'the theatre of Marcellus', whose shell is still one of the most striking sights in Rome, built on a site 'under the Tarpeian rock', and perhaps to a design which Julius Caesar had planned. This is 'the theatre near the temple of Apollo', the god connected with the theatre by early Roman ideas, built by Augustus as a memorial, after his death, to his nephew and son-in-law C. Marcellus. It was started in 23 and was publicly dedicated in 11 B.C.[52]

These were, and continued under the Empire to be, Rome's 'three theatres'.

The fact that Rome had no permanent stone amphitheatre before the time of Augustus need surprise nobody, for amphitheatres did not exist in Greece and, as far as we know, the first amphitheatre ever built was the one which survives in its full splendour at Pompeii today. It was built between 70 and 65 B.C. by two prominent magistrates and benefactors of Pompeii, before the word 'amphitheatre' itself had been invented; for in its dedicatory inscription, which survives, it is called *spectacula*, the word which Pompey was to use for his theatre at Rome.[53]

* See pp. 272f below.

Before the building of a permanent amphitheatre in Rome, exhibitions of gladiatorial and of wild beast fighting took place in temporary enclosures, no doubt elliptical in shape, in the Forum or elsewhere, or else in the Circus Maximus. These involved the expensive structure of temporary seating and expensive precautions for the safety of spectators. When the elephants which Pompey exhibited at his games in 55 B.C. stampeded and made for the iron railings with which the centre of the Circus Maximus had been surrounded, there was a panic in the audience. Profiting by this experience, Julius Caesar, when he showed wild beasts in the Circus Maximus in his great games in 46 B.C., had a canal dug round the arena, ten feet wide and ten feet deep, and filled with water, and this evidently guaranteed the safety of spectators. This canal (*euripus*) remained until the time of Nero.*[54]

Pliny has a remarkable account of 'a great lunacy', a permanent wooden contrivance erected by the younger Curio in memory of his father in 53 B.C., with the object of outclassing a fantastically expensive wooden theatre erected by Scaurus five years earlier. It consisted of two theatres back to back, which were used for separate theatrical performances in the mornings and then were swivelled through an angle of a hundred and eighty degrees, a number of spectators remaining in their seats during the operation, so that in combination they formed an amphitheatre for gladiatorial encounters in the afternoon. Pliny's circumstantial account of this contrivance is buried in a long jeremiad on the subject of Roman decadence. Since it is hard to believe that, with all the resources of modern engineering, such a contraption could be designed and made to work today, Pliny's story (a fantasy, perhaps, of some etymologist, trying to explain *amphitheatrum* as in fact being two *theatra*) has never been taken seriously, and is a warning against uncritical readiness on other occasions to accept all Pliny's 'facts'.[55]

The first basically stone amphitheatre in Rome was built by T. Statilius Taurus, one of Octavian's generals, probably in the southern part of the Campus Martius, and was dedicated in 29 B.C., and this was in effect the only permanent stone amphitheatre in Rome until Vespasian constructed the Colosseum.† It burnt down in the great fire of A.D. 64.[56] Seven years earlier Nero had built a wooden amphitheatre, a building

---

* See p. 311 below, for precautions taken later. The situation is reversed when the suggestion is made, as it has recently been made in England (*Times* 26.1.68), that football grounds should be surrounded by dykes of water, to keep the spectators from breaking on to the ground.

† Called the Amphitheatrum Flavium. It did not receive the name Colosseum until five hundred years or so after the fall of Rome.

which Tacitus thought below the dignity of history to describe, something which should be left to the newspapers, the *acta diurna*. It evoked rhapsodies, however, from Calpurnius Siculus' rustic on his first visit to the capital: 'It rose into the sky, and looked down on the Tarpeian rock.' It was opened with a remarkable exhibition of gladiatorial fighting, at which nobody at all was killed.[57]

The site of Vespasian's stupendous amphitheatre was made available by his crude destruction of Nero's Golden House. Vespasian lived to dedicate it in 79; Titus completed the building and opened it with a hundred days of magnificent games in the following year[58]; and from then onwards, except for periods when it was under reconstruction after damage by fire, lightning or earthquake, it was the scene of all the greatest exhibitions in Rome both of gladiatorial encounters and of wild beast fighting until such entertainments were brought to an end.

To an audience seated in the open air in a Mediterranean climate for long hours in summer and even in spring and autumn, the chief cause of discomfort is likely to be the sun and the heat; and to the mind of the Roman moralist it was yet another mark of disintegration that even before the end of the Republic the Romans had taken a tip from the Greeks who lived south of them in Italy, and started to shield themselves in public from the sun. This was 'Campanian luxury', and Q. Catulus was responsible for its introduction when at the dedication of the restored temple of Juppiter on the Capitol in 69 B.C. he had an awning (*velarium*) erected to protect spectators from the sun.[59] This excellent amenity was almost at once introduced for theatrical performances, and in 23 B.C., to mark the aedileship of Marcellus, Augustus erected, as Julius Caesar had earlier erected, a great awning over the Forum for the whole summer.[60] Involving tall central poles and a cumbersome tackle operated by sailors, the *velarium* came to be a regular fitting of the permanent theatres and of the amphitheatres, including the Colosseum.[61] It was quoted as an instance of the disagreeable caprice of the emperor Gaius that at gladiatorial games on days when the sun was scorchingly hot he would have the awnings drawn back and refuse to allow any spectator to leave. Martial mocked a notorious napkin-thief by suggesting that, as soon as he entered the theatre, the awnings were drawn back for safety.[62]

These awnings were difficult to manipulate in a high wind and on windy days their flapping was a distraction: 'as at times the canvas awning stretched over a great theatre cracks flapping between poles and beams, sometimes tears and flies wild under the boisterous winds.'[63]

17

Lucretius, who has given us this vivid picture, has also shown how the illusion of the theatre was increased by the artificial lighting which resulted from the colours of the awnings themselves. 'This is often done by yellow and red and purple awnings, when outspread in the public view over a great theatre upon posts and beams they tremble and flutter; for then they dye, and force to flutter in their own colour, the assembly in the great hollow below and all the display of the stage... All within laughs in the flood of beauty, when the light of day is thus confined.'[64]

When the Parthian Tiridates came to Rome in A.D. 66 to confess himself Nero's slave and to receive from Nero the throne of Armenia (the most spectacular reception of a foreign potentate ever given in the Empire), special purple awnings were stretched over the theatre of Pompey, which was specially gilded for the occasion, and on them was painted a picture of Nero driving his chariot among the stars.[65]

With the awnings Ovid coupled, as the second luxury of the civilized theatre, the diffusion of saffron water. It was sprinkled on the stage, giving a strong and pleasing scent[66]; to the performers it created an additional hazard, for, if it was sprinkled too liberally, they were liable to slip.[67]

Public entertainment was free in Rome, and men, women and children, free and slaves, might attend—as long as they could get places.[68] In the Republic it was part of a great man's patronage to secure tickets[69] for members of his tribe and for his clients (including people from the provinces staying in Rome); when Cicero escaped to the country during the Ludi Romani in 54 B.C., he left a freedman to perform this duty for him. It was only after 63 B.C. that, when a man was standing as a candidate for public office, the bribery laws reasonably enough forbade him to exercise this patronage directly, though nothing stopped his friends from exercising it on his behalf.[70]

Women had always been allowed—and in the Empire were always allowed—to sit with men in the Circus, but at the theatre they were segregated.[71] At first they could sit where they liked at the gladiatorial shows because, under the Republic, these were *munera*, given under private auspices, and not official *ludi*, given under the authority of the State, for which the State naturally made and enforced its own regulations.[72] Indeed it was thanks to this freedom that at a gladiatorial show the coquette Valeria was able to attract the attention of Sulla, a recent widower, who soon after married her.[73]

It was an indication that the *munera* had lost their private character when Augustus enacted that the rules of the theatre should in this respect apply to the amphitheatre also. He placed other limitations on the freedom of women when he forbade them to witness athletics, presumably because he thought they should not see men naked. (Was this when his wife Livia observed that, in the eyes of a sensible woman, men without clothes were just so many statues?[74]) Augustus once had a boxing match postponed to the following morning, issuing an edict that no woman was to come to the games on the next day before eleven o'clock.

His prohibition against women seeing athletics may have held good, since Nero fell back on Greek precedent when he issued a special invitation to the Vestal Virgins to attend athletic sports.[75] His segregation of women to the highest row of seats at gladiatorial and wild beast fighting certainly remained.

Though there were not separate tiers, there were three ranges of seats in theatres and amphitheatres and at the Circus. They were known in the theatre as the *cavea ima*, *cavea media* and *cavea summa*; in the Colosseum as the *maenianum primum* (with twenty rows of seats, *gradus*) and the *maenianum secundum* (with about sixteen), while above them, behind a Corinthian colonnade, there were wooden seats under a roof (*maenianum summum in ligneis*), where the women sat.

Below each *maenianum* there was a sharp drop (a perpendicular wall, *balteus* or *praecinctio*, sometimes gaily decorated) on to a wide passage-way which encircled the whole auditorium (also called *balteus*, *praecinctio* or *praecinctionis iter*). Having climbed the steps from outside, the ticket-holders walked along the appropriate passage, and then climbed by stone steps into the block (*cuneus*) where they were to sit. People who had no seats could stand and watch the spectacle from the passage-way.

On the roof over the women's seats, which itself may or may not have been covered, there was standing room for the poorer classes, *pullati*, people of little means, who would not be wearing the toga. At the theatre it was to the *cavea summa*, where the most uncultured part of the audience sat, that the actor directed his crudest and coarsest shafts.[76]

The 'best people' naturally occupied the best seats, and in the Empire the Emperor with his attendants occupied the best seats of all. He was conspicuous especially in the amphitheatre, since it was he who was the patron who gave the *munera*. In the Colosseum the imperial box[77] (*pulvinar*—literally a couch on which statues of the gods were exposed) was on the *podium* (the raised platform surrounding the arena, like the platform which surrounded the Circus, from which the spectators' seats rose). It was on the north side, approached by a wide passage; it faced, across the arena, the box of the Prefect of the City.

From 194 B.C. it was the senators' privilege at the theatre to occupy seats directly under the stage, and when there were permanent theatres, the senators sat in the orchestra. This privilege of front seats was extended to the Circus by Augustus and after Claudius' expensive refurbishing of it, they had a specially reserved block of front seats.[78] Later they enjoyed the same favour in the Colosseum. There was enough room for them to be joined by representatives of allied states and distinguished foreign delegates who were present on official business in Rome.[79] In a moment of pique Augustus cancelled this concession for the theatre, when he discovered that descendants of freedmen had been sent to Rome as delegates,[80] but evidently it was soon restored. Tacitus tells a pleasing story of two chiefs of the German Frisii who, repulsed from Roman territory which they had annexed, were sent to Rome to make their peace with Nero in A.D. 58. While awaiting an audience, they were taken to the theatre of Pompey in the hope that its magnificence would impress them. Since they could not understand a word of the play that was being acted, they asked loud questions: why, for instance, were people in non-Roman dress sitting among the senators? They were envoys from Rome's valiant and loyal allies, they were told. At which, announcing that in loyalty and valour nobody was better than a German, they marched down to sit among the senators. 'The audience was delighted by such an exhibition of old-fashioned impetuosity and noble pride.' The Emperor conferred citizenship on the pair of them.[81]

The reservation of fourteen rows of seats in the theatre for the Equites, the second social order in the State, by the Lex Roscia of 67 B.C. caused great popular resentment, which Cicero's honeyed tongue assuaged,[82] and the privilege, which was greatly prized by the Equites, was not withdrawn. They also had special seats of some kind at the Circus, though here their privilege, like the senators', did not receive its final expression until the principate of Claudius. Then Nero filled in the canal which had surrounded the Circus since the time of Julius Caesar and, if Pliny is to be trusted, made this the place where the Equites had their reserved seats. In that case they must have sat at ground level, below the *podium*, and therefore in front of the senators— unless the *podium* itself was built forward and reconstructed.[83]

A proposal in the Senate in A.D. 32 that men who had served in the Praetorian Guard should be allowed to sit in the equestrian seats at entertainments—that is, that they should, like most centurions, acquire equestrian standing on discharge—whipped the emperor Tiberius into a fury and brought disgrace to its misguided author.[84]

From inscriptions on the surviving seats of the Colosseum and from the records of the Arval Brothers in the year when the building was opened (A.D. 80), we know that in the Colosseum a large number of special bodies—priestly and secular colleges, corporations etc.—had permanently reserved seats, which were not numbered individually, but were marked off by lengths in feet; it was therefore left to the body itself to distribute as few or to squeeze as many of its members as it chose into the space.[85] This explains Clodius' statement in 60 B.C. in respect of some public games that though his sister, wife of the consul Metellus Celer, had 'all the space allowed a consul at her disposal', she would only give him a single foot.*[86] Augustus had segregated various classes of spectators in special blocks of seats—children under age, tutors, married men from the commons, soldiers—and, sparse as they are, the surviving marks of reserved seats in the Colosseum suggest that this segregation continued.[87]

The Vestal Virgins occupied specially reserved seats in a prominent position at the theatre and at the gladiatorial games in the Empire, where they might be joined by ladies of the imperial family.[88]

Those who sat, like other women, at the very top seats of the amphi-theatre must, even with the best of sight, have appreciated very little of the skill of gladiatorial combat or of the men who fought the wild beasts. Nero, even in his privileged box, used a cut emerald to improve his vision of the gladiatorial games. He was, of course, short sighted.[89]

3. Cost and Presidency

Particular victory games were the responsibility of the general who had vowed them. The regular public games were the responsibility of the aediles (of the two plebeian aediles for the Ludi Plebei and of the two curule aediles for the others) except for the Ludi Apollinares and, after 81 B.C., the Ludi Victoriae Sullae, which were the responsibility of the urban praetor. The aediles made all the arrangements and presided over the celebration itself.[90]

A most prominent feature of the games at all times was their expense.

* Modern calculations of seating generally allow a foot and a half for each individual.

When a general held games after his triumph, the cost was met from the booty which he had captured; he might even, like M. Fulvius Nobilior after his successes in Greece between 189 and 187, raise a special levy for the purpose from the people whom he had defeated. Latins and other allied communities in Italy were similarly distrained on by the aediles for the expense of the regular games.

In the early second century B.C. the senate was reasonably concerned by the rapidly increasing monetary extravagance of games of all kinds and by the hardships of such enforced contributions. So they restricted the amount which Fulvius Nobilior was allowed to spend on his victory games in 187 and tried to make this reduced figure the norm; and ten years later, because of distraints made on the Latins and Italian allies by Tiberius Gracchus as aedile, they imposed a limit on the sum which might be spent on the regular public games also.[91]

These measures may have succeeded in cutting down requisitions, but they did not effectively reduce the sums spent on the regular public games. The aediles in charge were usually men in their middle thirties with a career to make and, as most of the spectators were also voters, there was every temptation to give games of unusual splendour,[92] costing far more than the allowance which the Treasury made. This was a vote-catching preparation for later candidature for the praetorship and the consulship, magistracies which led to provincial governorships and military commands in which, however corruptly, there were big fortunes to be made. This was a consideration for the poor man like Caesar when he was aedile in 65 B.C. To find the money the impecunious aedile went to a rich friend or to a money-lender, and it was in the hope of deterring the money-lender from making such advances that, in the general economic instability of the declining Republic, a law was passed in 52 B.C. to delay a provincial appointment until five years after the tenure of the praetorship and consulship; if money-lenders had to wait some ten years for the repayment of their loans, perhaps they would be more reluctant to lend large sums of money to the impoverished. For by the end of the Republic, as Livy observed, expenditure on the games had reached a pitch of insanity which even the wealth of kings could hardly have supported.[93]

The responsibility for the games was jointly shared by the two aediles (whether curule or plebeian), and it is easy to imagine the embarrassment of a pair of colleagues, one of whom was rich, while the other was not rich at all. This, indeed, was the case in 65 B.C. Bibulus, who could afford the expense, put down most of the money;

Caesar made a smaller contribution from his borrowings; yet, to Bibulus' chagrin, it was Caesar, not Bibulus, who received the cheers of the crowds.[94] So in 58 B.C., when fantastic sums were spent on the games, it was the wild spendthrift M. Aemilius Scaurus who, to judge by the records, attracted people's attention, though his colleague P. Plautius Hypsaeus, as the coins confirm, was equally involved.[95]

In 22 B.C. Augustus transferred the responsibility for the games to the praetors, a College by this time of twelve magistrates or more, with the excellent proviso that, where colleagues gave games jointly, neither was to spend more of his own money than the other.[96] By what means, whether or not by casting lots, the various public games were distributed between the praetors, we do not know, except in a few cases. The Ludi Augustales, for instance, were from the start of Tiberius' principate the charge of the Praetor Peregrinus.[97] We know that Agricola gave games in his praetorship, and also the younger Pliny.[98]

In the new government of the Caesars heavy expenditure was unlikely any longer to pay rich practical dividends. Still, it was expected of a man. The public Treasury (*aerarium Saturni*) still put down a very considerable amount of money in some cases (just over three quarters of a million sesterces for the Ludi Romani; 600,000 sesterces for the Ludi Plebei; 380,000 sesterces for the Games of Apollo) but only a laughable sum—10,000 sesterces—for the new Ludi Augustales.[99] If he was to give spectacular games, the praetor still had to dig heavily into his own pocket. Augustus sanctioned the expenditure by praetors of three times their public allowance. At the end of the first century A.D. the Megalensia cost a minimum of 100,000 sesterces; if given spectacularly, four times that sum.[100]

If the praetor could not afford the expense, he might, if he was lucky, get help. Trajan, when emperor, gave Hadrian two million sesterces for his praetorian games; and we know that Antoninus Pius gave the impoverished Gavius Clarus a large sum from his private exchequer to help him over his games—a sum which, once he could afford it, Clarus insisted on repaying.[101] Even when the praetorship had ceased to be a magistracy of any great public significance in the fourth century, it was still heavily encumbered by this traditional expenditure which the Roman proletariat considered its right. When men tried to avoid the office under Constantine, they rarely succeeded. The games given by Symmachus on behalf of his son, the urban praetor, in the fourth century, were said to have cost 2,000 pounds' weight in gold.[102]

Gladiatorial games under the Republic were given by individuals of their own free will and without constraint, and naturally they had to meet the expense themselves. This was considerable from the start; in the middle of the second century B.C. it might be nearly three-quarters of a million sesterces.[103] Milo in 53 B.C. ran through three fortunes on shows which he expected to attract votes when he stood for the consulship.[104]

In the Empire gladiatorial games were rarely given by private individuals in Rome, and then only with special permission,[105] and, as has been seen,* they might be given twice a year, on stated conditions, by the praetors at the public games.

The giving of special and regular gladiatorial games (*munera*) was, from Claudius' principate onwards, an obligation laid on the quaestors, to be discharged at their own expense before their entry on office (replacing a previous obligation to undertake road-paving) and, though Claudius' measure was rescinded by Nero, it was re-introduced by Domitian. These official gladiatorial games were massed together in December and by the fourth century lasted for ten days—the 2nd, 4th, 5th (the day on which the quaestors entered office), the 6th, 8th, 19th, 20th, 21st, 23rd and 24th. Severus Alexander had ruled that only those candidates who enjoyed the Emperor's personal nomination need dip into their own pockets, and that the others should have their expenses paid from the imperial treasury (*arca fisci*); and this distinction was marked in the titles of the shows. They were called *candida* or *arca*, unsubsidized or subsidized.[106]

The scale of these shows, of course, was nothing by comparison with the holocausts which were mounted from time to time at their own expense and to their own glory by individual emperors. It is hard to imagine what Titus' hundred days of games must have cost, or Trajan's orgy of public shows.

There were more features of the games and of the shows than their simple entertainment.

Cicero said in 56 B.C., 'There are three places where popular feelings find expression, at public meetings, at public assemblies and at the games and fights'.[107] With the establishment of the Empire, the public meetings and the public assemblies soon disappeared; the games and the gladiatorial fights survived.

The theatre—which was never subject to any official censorship, for Pompey's appointment of Sp. Maecius Tarpa to select plays for per-

* See above, p. 251.

formance at the opening of his theatre was an isolated happening, greeted with disapproval[108]—was a sounding board for contemporary political feeling, whose importance in the Republic Cicero perhaps exaggerated. The volume of applause which greeted prominent persons as they entered the theatre was carefully noted. At the Ludi Apollinares in Caesar's first consulship in July 59, when his popularity was very low, there was hardly a cheer when he arrived in the theatre, while the entry of young Curio, by whom he was being severely baited in politics, was acclaimed with roars of applause; and when in the tragedy which was being acted the actor spoke the words, 'Miseria nostra magnus es' ('At the cost of our misfortune you are Great'), which could be a hit at Caesar's association with Pompey the Great (who was not present), he was encored over and over again.[109]

After this, under the Caesars, criticisms of the régime and scurrilous lampoons on the rulers were loudly greeted.* These are the kinds of insults which persons of prominence may expect to receive from the cartoonist today.[110]

Moreover, there was no other place better suited for effective public protests than the public performances at the games and the shows. These protests might reflect genuine hardship (during a food shortage, for instance), or they might be deliberately inspired and organized for political purposes.[111] In the late Republic gangs had been coached by men like Clodius to cause disturbances and to shout well-rehearsed answers to questions at public meetings. The man Percennius, who had been trained to lead a body of shouters (not always claqueurs) in the theatre and who found himself drafted into the army, made full use of his professional expertise in helping to instigate the mutiny of the Danube legions in A.D. 14. To ward against one common source of such trouble it was recommended that youths arrested for hooliganism should be whipped and forbidden entry to public spectacles.[112]

Although, as represented pictorially in mosaics, the spectators exhibit decorum appropriate to a stained-glass window, in fact the fanatical enthusiasm of the supporters of the different colours in the Circus sometimes led to wild disorder, and that was a reason why in the fourth century a succession of racing days (such as had occurred, for instance, on the last five days of the Ludi Romani) was avoided.[113] Rome, however, never experienced anything comparable to the terrible Nica insurrection which occurred at Byzantium in 532, in which thirty

* Examples are given below, pp. 279 and 284.

thousand people perished and Justinian came near to being deposed. Its origin lay in an ordinary riot of the Circus factions.*

The downfall of the hated praetorian prefect Cleander in A.D. 190 was achieved by what was evidently a very carefully rehearsed incident in the Circus at Rome. After the seventh race a body of children led by a tall, conspicuous girl, ran on to the course protesting against the current corn shortage and reviling Cleander. A large part of the spectators followed them, and then moved off in a body towards the Emperor's residence outside Rome. They overcame the troops sent against them, and Commodus in terror ordered Cleander's execution.[114]

In the early sixth century instructions reached the City Prefect: 'A check must be placed on the habit of insulting persons in the Circus. If a senator is insulted, the offence is to be punished with the full severity of the law. If a senator so far forgets good manners as to kill a free-born person, he is to be fined'.[115]

In the Republic the maintenance of order at public gatherings was one of the aediles' duties. In the Empire responsibility rested with the Prefect of the City, once that office had been permanently established under Tiberius, and the Prefect stationed troops from the urban cohorts, which he commanded, to keep order in the theatre, the amphitheatre and at the Circus during public entertainments. The praetor in charge of the games, like the aedile before him, could inflict summary punishment on actors and performers.†[116]

In A.D. 15 a centurion and some soldiers were killed and an officer was wounded in trying to restore order in the theatre at Rome. In the mood of quixotic idealism with which his principate opened, Nero tried in A.D. 55 to do without pickets of soldiers at the games, so as to give the people a taste of liberty and to remove the soldiers from the temptations of the entertainment world. So far from making things better, the removal of the soldiers made them worse. In the following year the soldiers resumed their duties.[117]

For the Emperor attendance at, and the display of lively interest in, the *munera* which he gave were politically prudent, whatever his personal feelings about wild beast and gladiatorial fighting. Tiberius' popularity suffered through his not giving shows and not concealing his dislike for them. Julius Caesar even caused offence by studying official

---

* The antagonism of football supporters has produced startling disasters in modern times—300 killed and 1,000 injured at Lima in May 1964, 42 killed and 600 hurt at Kayseri in Turkey in September 1967.

† See p. 280.

papers at the games which he attended, instead of devoting his whole attention to the proceedings, and Augustus was careful not to make the same mistake.[118] Though an emperor like Commodus might degrade his office by the exuberance of his interest in the contests, the occasion was one when the emperor was among his people, sharing their amusements.[119] He was also extremely accessible, and it was not difficult for a commoner to approach him and to thrust a petition into his hand. Even in the changed conditions of the modern world, while royalty may or may not have won popularity from its visits to the opera, it has never lost popularity from its interest in the horses.

4. The 'Demoralization' of the Games

If a modern satirist observed that the English, who had once been a great imperial people, were now obsessed with two things only, free state medicine and the football pools, he would make a valid point, but he could hardly be thought to have provided a key to the interpretation of modern English history. A whole chapter of Roman history, however, is commonly based on Fronto's statement in the second century A.D. that Trajan knew that the Roman people was held fast by two things, the free corn distribution (*annona*) and the shows (*spectacula*) and on Juvenal's cutting observation a little earlier (a *cliché*, first made perhaps about the inhabitants of Alexandria), that the Roman people, once the repository of sovereign imperial power, worried about and looked forward to two things only, bread and the games, '*panem et circenses*'.[120]

So a frightening picture is painted. In Rome, a city of around a million inhabitants, 150,000 people were completely idle, another 150,000 did no work after midday—all three hundred thousand of them, nearly a third of the whole population of the city, kept alive by corn doles and the frenzied excitement of public spectacles.[121]

As for the '150,000 unemployed', however, there is the best of authority for the fact that man cannot live by bread alone. He requires clothes, at least, and a roof over his head. Even if a portion, and it could only be a small portion, of the 150,000 were helped out by the miserable *sportula*,* which they received as clients attending the daily *salutatio* of the rich, this would not keep them alive. There was no state aid to the unemployed; in the first two centuries A.D. there were no such charitable gifts as the Church dispensed in poverty-stricken

* On which see above, p. 22.

areas in nineteenth- and early twentieth-century Italy. Had such unfortunates existed, Rome must have been full of beggars; and one of the
most striking features of our extensive literary evidence about life in
ancient Rome is that it hardly ever mentions a beggar. Begging,
Martial suggested contemptuously, was something which Jewish
children were taught by their mothers to do.[122]

As for the second figment of the modern historian's imagination,
the 150,000 who only worked till midday, a man working the first
six hours of the day (and it is clear that in Rome work started very early
in the morning) would be working on an average, the whole year
round, what we should call a forty-two hour week.

This army of unemployed idlers did not exist. And had it existed, it
could not have spent, as is alleged, more than half the year at the games.
As has been seen, the great majority of days of the public games were
devoted to the theatre, to *ludi scaenici*. There is no reason to think that
on such days performances were given concurrently at more than one
theatre. The *Eunuchus* of Terence was performed twice in a single day,
presumably to two different audiences, but we do not know how common an event that was. The theatre of Marcellus held between ten and
eleven thousand spectators, the theatre of Pompey between nine
and ten, the theatre of Balbus between six and seven. The Colosseum
held a maximum of 50,000 people, but for the *pullati* there was standing
room on the roof for a mere five thousand.[123]

The life, therefore, of practically the whole of the million or so
inhabitants of Rome must have been unaffected on days of *ludi scaenici*
by what was going on in the theatre. One person in every twenty could
squeeze into the Colosseum—if he had a ticket. The only occasion on
which there was room for as much as a quarter of the inhabitants of the
city to be at the games was when there was chariot racing in the Circus,
which could probably accommodate a quarter of a million spectators.
This explains the fact, which has often received comment, that the
populace at large took far more interest in chariot racing than it did
in gladiators. They saw chariot racing; they did not often see gladiators.
And chariot racing occurred, as has been noted, on seventeen days of the
year at the time of Augustus, on sixty-six in the fourth century.

We ourselves see nothing wrong with the idea of a man who, with
two non-working days a week, gives himself the enjoyment on one of
those days of watching racing, football or cricket. We should be wise
to observe the same sense of proportion before we pass scathing judgement on the Roman who, at the start of the Empire, can only have spent

a few more days than seventeen a year in such indulgence or even perhaps on the man who in the last days of the Empire spent something over
sixty-six.

The games, particularly the chariot races, were a major interest, a
subject of constant discussion, among the commons in Rome. Maecenas
discussed leading gladiators by name when Horace drove with him in
his carriage. Messalla in Tacitus' *Dialogus* said, 'The peculiar vices of
the Romans seem to me almost to be conceived in the womb—interest
in the stage and enthusiasm for gladiators and horses.'[124]

Men of culture despised or affected to despise the games, though they
might concede, as Dio Chrysostom conceded, that, human nature
being what it is, some relaxation was inevitable. Cicero has left a very
carefully composed account of his distress in watching Pompey's
games in 55 B.C.; yawning over hackneyed mimes in the morning,
shocked by the vulgarity of a production of *Clytemnestra* in which the
stage was like a ranch, packed with mules, disgusted by the wild beast
fighting. Marcus Aurelius' complaint was the same, of the repetitive
monotony and boredom of contests in the arena. Seneca too: the spectacles encouraged an infectious blood-lust in those who watched them;
a man returned home at night from the amphitheatre less of a man and
more of an animal than when he set out in the morning.[125] For Tertullian, the games were deplorable in themselves and the worse for
being held in honour of heathen gods.

Yet the good life was a fight against great odds, a resolute struggle
against worldliness, against Fortune. For a lively image of the good fight
Seneca might have gone to the army, to the Roman legionary on the
field of battle. But soldiers on battle fields were remote from his
experience and from the experience of many of his readers. So, however
grudgingly, he found himself compelled to go time and time again
to the arena for his images—to the resolute wild beast fighter, '*adulescens
constantis animi*', in his way another Cato, and to the unflinching courage
of the gladiator, who showed that it was possible to face death with
resolution.[126] And, besides courage, they had cool skill. A good gladiator did not go berserk; he fought with his head.[127]

The fatal temptation of the spectacles is well illustrated in the case of
St. Augustine's pupil Alypius. Cured by St. Augustine in Carthage of
his intemperate enthusiasm for horse-racing, he came to Rome and
succumbed to worse temptation still. For when his friends dragged him
against his will to the amphitheatre, he determined to spite them by
keeping his eyes tightly closed. But he could not plug his ears; and when

there was a crescendo of shouting from the spectators, he opened his eyes—with fatal results. From that moment he was an impassioned enthusiast for gladiatorial fighting.[128]

5. The Theatre

The writing of plays for private reading continued for long to be a relaxation of the cultured; Quintus Cicero, a fast composer, wrote four tragedies in sixteen days of soldiering in Gaul,[129] and nine tragedies of the young Seneca survive. On the other hand, the period in which a great number of new plays were written for stage performance was, in Rome, a short one. It began when the first Punic war ended, in 240 B.C., and it was virtually at an end by the time of Sulla.[130] Plays were adaptations of Greek models, tragedies based sometimes on Euripides but more often on contemporary Hellenistic works, comedies based on Greek New Comedy, particularly Menander. The name given to this type of drama expressed its Greek origin: *palliata*, from *pallium*, the Greek word for a cloak. None of the notable playwrights was Roman. They were men who had emerged from slavery or who came from the country towns of Italy. Outside the twenty-one comedies of Plautus and the six comedies of Terence, nothing survives but the titles of plays and scattered, usually very short, quotations from them; yet it is clear that their authors were writers of bold and versatile genius.

L. Livius Andronicus, author and actor-producer, brought to Rome as a prisoner of war from Tarentum, a home of Greek cultural life, was the pioneer, with the production of tragedy and comedy in Latin in 240 B.C. He also did the *Odyssey* into Latin, in Saturnian verses. Cn. Naevius, who came from Campania and who had fought in the first Punic war, apart from composing an epic on that war, wrote both tragedies and comedies. Both Livius and Naevius produced a *Trojan Horse*—the Romans took a particular interest in their own supposed Trojan origins—and a *Danae*. Q. Ennius, a Messapian, served in Sardinia in the second Punic war and was brought to Rome by the elder Cato; he was a *protégé* of the Scipios and of Fulvius Nobilior, whom he accompanied on his Aetolian campaign. He received citizenship from Fulvius' son. We know the titles of twenty of his plays, including a *Thyestes*. He also wrote an epic poem on the history of Rome. His nephew, M. Pacuvius, who was born at Brindisi, wrote some twelve tragedies, one of them, the *Teucer*, very highly spoken of. Tragedy reached its peak in the hands of L. Accius from Pisaurum in Umbria, a man of slave origin, born in 170 B.C. He competed with Pacuvius in 140, when he was thirty years old and Pacuvius eighty. Quintilian, like Horace, considered Pacuvius and Accius the finest Roman tragedians, Accius the more powerful of the two, Pacuvius the more erudite.[131]

Greek-type comedy (also *palliata*) triumphed in the hands of T. Maccius Plautus, an Umbrian from Sarsina, who survived an up-bringing in circumstances of great poverty—his plays were written between 204 and 184, when he died—and of P. Terentius Afer (Terence), who was of North African, but not Punic, extraction; he was born in Carthage. He took his name from the senator Terentius Lucanus who freed him. His plays were produced in the years between 166 and his death in 159.

Plautus' plots were the plots of Greek New Comedy, set in a bourgeois world of pimps and prostitutes, of swaggering soldiers, of gay, raffish, irresponsible young men (who often had hearts of gold) and of stern, sometimes doddering, sometimes lecherous, sometimes miserly fathers (who often had hearts of gold themselves). The prostitute, if it was with her that the young hero had fallen in love, turned out to be no prosti-tute at all, but a free-born girl who had been captured as a child or exposed and sold into slavery. The vicissitudes of the plot, which always ended happily, were more often than not the contrivance of an amiable and utterly amoral slave of the household.

Plautus evidently took great liberties with the Greek originals of his plays (which unfortunately do not survive), cutting some passages, expanding others, so as to give them a Roman complexion. And he made great fun of the Latin language itself. To read, every one of his plots is extremely funny,[132] and the plots of more than one of them have a universality of appeal which has given them a permanence in litera-ture. There have been countless versions of *Amphitryon* between Plautus and Giraudoux; and the plot of the *Menaechmi* (the confusion caused by identical twins) is the plot of Shakespeare's *Comedy of Errors*.

To latinize New Comedy in the manner of Plautus was to vulgarize it. So Terence thought, and he wrote comedies which were throughout closer to the Greek originals. As a consequence his plays appealed to sophisticated taste, but had none of the popular glamour of Plautus. Even so, though he became a standard 'classic' in Roman education,* he was condemned by Roman literary critics of a later age, if not as

* And in English some of the most familiar Latin tags come from Terence: *Fortuna fortes adiuvat; Quot homines, tot sententiae; Verbum sapienti.*

sharply as Plautus; these critics searched for the graceful wit of New Comedy, and did not find it.[133]

As for the rowdier sections of the audiences to which Terence's plays were performed, his prologues describe conditions frightening enough to deter the most resolute of playwrights. In the prologue to the *Phormio* the audience is requested to listen in silence, 'that we may be more fortunate than when an uproar drove our company from the stage'. At its first performance the *Hecyra* was not able to finish because of the rumour of a boxing-match, which set the spectators talking to one another about the rival skill of the boxers, at its second performance because the theatre was stormed by a crowd of people who had been wrongly informed that a gladiatorial show was about to take place there.[134]

An interesting theatrical innovation—though there were remote precedents, of course, in early Greek tragedy, in Aeschylus' *Persae*, for instance—was the historical play on a Roman subject, the *fabula praetexta*, this being the tragic form of what was called generically the *togata*, a play in Roman instead of in Greek dress.[135] Naevius was its originator. These were historical plays either about great Roman heroes of the past, such as Romulus or Brutus, or about great contemporary heroes, written for performance at their triumphal games or else at the funeral of the man whom they commemorated. Ennius wrote an *Ambracia*, probably for performance at the triumphal games of M. Fulvius Nobilior, who defeated the Aetolians and captured Ambracia in Greece in 189/8; and Pacuvius' *Paullus* was performed either at the triumphal games of L. Aemilius Paullus, who won the third Macedonian war or at the funeral games celebrated by his sons in 160. Accius produced a *Brutus*—on the subject of Rome's first consul, the founder of the Republic—in honour of his patron, D. Iunius Brutus Callaicus, consul of 138.[136]

Historical plays continued to be written for the stage by men of the highest social standing even into the early Empire, for instance by P. Pomponius Secundus, consul in A.D. 44, who at an earlier stage in his career wrote an *Aeneas*. Quintilian, indeed, thought him better than any other tragedian whose plays he had seen. The genre must have touched its nadir in Spain in 43 B.C., when the young Cornelius Balbus put on the performance of a play by himself about himself—a description of his attempt as a Caesarian in the civil war of 49/8 to break through the enemy lines in order to discover his one-time benefactor, Lentulus Crus, the Pompeian consul of 49, and to persuade him to desert Pompey and come over to Caesar. Balbus alone wept copiously during the performance, moved by the pathos of his own composition.[137]

In the theatre Roman audiences were always restive, liable when bored, according to Horace, to shout, 'We want bears', 'We want boxers'. Indeed Horace suggested that if Democritus, the laughing philosopher, was raised from the dead and taken to the theatre in Rome, he would be entranced not by the performance but by the extraordinary behaviour of the audience. In tragedy, as time went on, it was more and more spectacle that the audience demanded—*Clytemnestra* with six hundred mules, something like a prodigious production of *Aïda* today in the Baths of Caracalla.[138] And tragedy had smaller appeal than comedy, as long as it was not Terence's sort of comedy. When Plautus, in the person of Mercury, mentioned the word 'tragedy' in the prologue of his *Amphitryon* ('You shall hear the argument of our tragedy'), he quickly proceeded, 'What? Frowning at the notion of this being a tragedy? Right. I am a god. I will change it and turn it from a tragedy into a comedy without altering a single line.'[139]

An attempt was made, but not a very successful one, to create a specifically Roman genre of comedy, the *tabernaria*, a comic form of the *togata*. Naevius was its inventor and L. Afranius, who wrote some forty comedies in the middle period of the second century B.C., was its master. With only a few fragments and the titles of plays to go on, it is hard to estimate its quality. Its scenes were set in Italian not in Greek cities. It dispensed with those characters in Greek New Comedy which were strangers to Roman life and concerned itself with the lower stratum of Roman society—the baker, the tailor, the barber, the freedman and the prostitute and, for good or bad, Romen women made their strong influence felt on events around them. In this last respect the difference between Greek and Roman comedy was the difference between Greek and Roman life. Yet, paradoxically, Afranius, so admirable in all other respects, made much play with homosexuality, which the Romans considered to be a Greek, not a Roman, weakness.[140]

If the writing of such comedies ceased, it was no doubt because their place was taken by the mime. Still, classical comedies were revived from time to time—Afranius' *Simulans* (*The Pretender*), as we know, in 57 B.C. and, appropriately enough, his *Fire* (*Incendium*) with Nero among the spectators.[141]

The writing of tragedies for performance stopped in the late Republic perhaps because the classical Greek themes had been exploited to the

full and no genius was capable of developing the *praetexta*. Yet tragedy
was not dead. From casual references, chiefly by Cicero, we know of
numerous revivals of plays by Ennius, Pacuvius (the actor Rupilius
never missed a chance of playing in Pacuvius' *Antiope*, because the part
suited him so well) and by Accius, whose *Tereus* was performed at
M. Brutus' games in July 44 B.C., when Brutus himself could not be
present. In happier times, of course, his *praetexta*, the *Brutus*, would have
been chosen.[142]

Moreover Greek tragedy was still presented to the public in different
forms—either, as will be seen, in ballet by *pantomimi* or in 'musicals'
in which, masked and costumed, a performer sang a tragic part. Nero,
as we know, sang the part of Canace in birth-pangs, Orestes the matri-
cide, the blind Oedipus and the mad Hercules.[143]

6. Pantomime and Mime

As Lucian pointed out in his brilliant essay on Dancing,* one of our
most important sources for the Roman pantomime,[144] mimetic
dancing was in the earliest tradition of most Greek and foreign peoples.
It is recorded that in 364 B.C. in a time of plague dancers were brought
to Rome from Etruria who performed, presumably to a musical
accompaniment and, according to Livy, this was the start of acting
at Rome.[145]

On the public stage at Rome ballet-dancing (*pantomimus* was the
word both for the dancer and the dance), in a form whose origin was
Greek, achieved under Augustus a startling popularity which it never
lost; and the vogue spread through the provinces, particularly in the
East.[146] Attractive masks were worn, unlike the forbidding masks of
tragedy: the mask of the father, for instance, indicated a mixture of
irritability and complaisance with one eyebrow raised and the other
not. The actors were nearly always men, but sometimes there were
women.[147] As a general rule it was a solo performance, one dancer
playing many different parts, each indicated by a change of mask[148];
very occasionally there were more dancers than one. For success, like
all ballet-dancers, they needed to be not only supremely clever and
imaginative but also strong, supple, well-built and in perfect training.[149]
Their gesticulation was elegant and so meaningful that the cynic
Demetrius under Nero, converted by a dancer's performance, said—

* Written probably between A.D. 162 and 165 when that enthusiastic patron of the
pantomime, the emperor L. Verus, was in Antioch.

as people often said of good pantomimists and actors—that 'he talked with his hands'; and in the same period a barbarian prince from Pontus who ruled a polyglot kingdom begged Nero to give him a *pantomimus* whom he had seen on the stage in Rome, in the hope that, with such a man at his side, he might dispense with interpreters.[150]

The performance was accompanied by music, either by a single flute, a flute and cithera or a full orchestra, and also by singing, either by a soloist or a choir. A bad dancer was one out of time with the music.[151]

We know the titles of nearly two hundred of these ballets, which were mainly on Greek—not Roman—mythological subjects or on the subjects of Greek tragedy. Sometimes the theme was historical; there were ballets on Plato's dialogues and on Ovid's poems.[152] A good dancer's repertoire was enormous, from 'Chaos' at one extreme to 'Cleopatra' at the other.[153] He should know the whole of Homer, Hesiod and the Greek tragedies.[154] The ballets were evidently to a degree conventional, for it was a bad mark against a performer who was dancing Chronos in the act of eating his children that he slipped into the part of Thyestes engaged in the same grim operation.[155] The dancer who captivated Demetrius stopped the music and danced the capture of Ares and Aphrodite in bed by Hephaestus, representing each of the characters in turn and even the gods as they stood round and chuckled.

It is a bad actor who submerges himself too deeply in his part. There was the story of a *pantomimus* dancing the mad Ajax (after his defeat by Odysseus) who achieved such a frenzy of madness that he nearly killed the player who was Odysseus. And his example was infectious. The audience went mad too.[156]

Severe men found much to criticize in the pantomimes, in particular the private morals of the dancers. Dio Chrysostom fulminated against them in his speech to the Alexandrians.[157] However in works which survive two enthusiasts wrote in their defence. Lucian in the second century A.D. claimed that not only did the pantomime give pleasure but that it had a serious and useful purpose: 'It sharpens the wits, it exercises the body, it delights the spectator, it instructs him in the history of bygone days, while eye and ear are held beneath the spell of flute and cymbal and of graceful dance. . . . I say nothing of the excellent moral influence of public opinion as exercised in the theatres, where you will find the evil-doer greeted with execration and his victim with sympathetic tears',[158] this last a defence which might have been offered later for Victorian melodrama. Two centuries after Lucian, Libanius protested that, if pantomime-dancers were long haired and immoral, that did not mean that pantomime itself was immoral. And, like Lucian before him, he claimed, that, at the worst, it was less degraded than other forms of popular entertainment: 'One wrestler breaks another's bones; a pancratiast loses an eye; a charioteer knocks another over and kills him. The death of a horse sets the whole population of a city at one another's throats; there is stoning, arson, murder. Dancing, on the other hand, does no harm and never will'.[159]

There are plenty of anecdotes to illustrate the lively give-and-take between performers and audience in pantomime: of an audience in Antioch in Syria shouting, 'Hullo, Astyanax, where's your father?', when a very small man started to dance the part of Hector and, 'Step over it; you don't need a ladder', when a remarkably tall man danced Capaneus scaling the walls of Thebes.[160] In Rome there are two anecdotes of Pylades and his pupil Hylas under Augustus. Dancing the part of 'the great Agamemnon', Hylas sought to give the impression of tallness. Pylades from the audience shouted, 'Tallness is one thing, greatness is another' and then, challenged to give his own interpretation of the part, he played Agamemnon deep in thought, like Lord Burleigh in Sheridan's Critic. When Pylades thought that Hylas was dancing the blind Oedipus too firmly and confidently, he shouted out, 'You are using your eyes.' When the audience indicated that Pylades was over-acting the part of the mad Hercules, he took off his mask and said, 'Idiots. It is a mad part that I am acting.'*[161]

There were flourishing training schools in pantomime-dancing in which the traditions of the great dancers, in particular of Pylades, who wrote a book on the pantomime, and of Bathyllus were perpetuated and their names appropriated, generation after generation in the Roman Empire.[162]

While the sophisticated enjoyed pantomime, the ordinary man and woman found greater pleasure in the obscene frivolities of the mime.[163]

The mime had a long history in Sicily and in the Hellenistic world. It embraced the poems of Theocritus and of Herodas on the one hand and, on the other, a wide range of public performances, acrobatic, spoken and musical. What all these writings and performances had in common was a primary concern with the everyday life of the common man and, as far as the Romans were concerned, the coarser that life, the better.

* As Nero might have done on the occasion when, dancing the same part, he was put in chains and a simple recruit on guard duty rushed to his defence (Suet., Nero 21, 3).

Subjects of popular mimes were often such as win headlines in the newspapers today—sudden changes of material fortune, for instance: 'Wealthy Overnight' (*Modo egens, repente dives*) or, by contrast, 'Millionaire Goes Bankrupt' (*Dives fugitivus*). Some were melodramatic like 'Laureolus, the Highwayman Crucified' (appropriately performed before the murder of the emperor Gaius), a fascination of which lay in the flooding of the stage with imitation blood.[164] Another popular mime called *Faba* ('Beans') depicted a parvenu god, Romulus, for instance, who, so far from taking to ambrosia as food, clamoured still for beans, the common man's staple food.[165] Most popular of all was what we should call bedroom farce: 'Love Locked Out' (*Exclusus Amator*), the break-up of marriages, 'the smooth adulterer, the artful wife, who successfully fools her husband'.[166] Indeed it was the pre-occupation of the mime with adultery which persuaded that model city Marseilles (Massilia) to ban the performance of mimes altogether.[167] As Minucius Felix was to write, 'Mime either exposes adultery or it displays it.'

There were mimes which mocked the lascivious antics of the Olympian gods and in the late Empire, when the times were appropriate, there was blasphemous mockery of the Christian religion, this being one of the reasons why mimes were so vehemently attacked by the writers and dignitaries of the Church: 'they were inventions of devils, not of God.' Their seduction was infinite. Had they not delighted St. Augustine himself in his young, unregenerate days?[168]

The texts of the mimes were at the mercy of considerable improvisation, particularly in the way of sharp criticism of contemporary politics and politicians. In this way they might be a sounding-box of current political opinion; and so politicians like Cicero kept their eyes on them in the late Republic, as did Emperors later.[169]

At the same time the pithy aphorism received warm applause.[170] 'A good companion on the road is as good as a lift'; 'Tears of a legatee are laughter under a mask'; 'If you have been wrecked once, don't blame the sea if you are wrecked a second time'; 'Refuse a request smartly, and you confer a benefit'. Such aphorisms, all ascribed to the successful *mimus* Publilius Syrus, whom Julius Caesar rewarded,* together with other such sayings gained currency, were collected together to make school-books and were quoted with approval by sedate philosophers like Seneca.[171]

Mimes were usually in prose, but might be in verse. They might be

* See p. 284 below.

accompanied by music and songs. Occasionally, as in the pantomime, there was one actor but generally there were a number, with an *archimimus* as their leader. Parts were graded, the 'second part' being that of the parasite or buffoon (*stupidus*), whose head was shaved, who wore a phallus and carried a stick, for thrashing.[172] The actors were barefooted; they wore patchwork coats (*centunculi*) if men, the *recinium*, a veil thrown over the head, if they were women (*mimae*). Unlike the *pantomimi*, they did not wear masks, and facial distortion, like exaggerated gesticulation, was one of the means by which they diverted their audiences*[173]

The Atellan farce,[174] named after the town of Atella, north of Naples, was an indigenous Italian form of entertainment, called also the *ludicrum Oscum*. It was brought to Rome early and still performed sometimes in the original Oscan language as late as the time of Augustus, if Strabo is not mistaken.[175] It achieved great popularity with the groundlings (though it was disparaged by the sophisticated) particularly in the period between the Gracchi and Sulla. The Atellan play was then performed, like the satyr-play in Greece, for light relief after a tragedy, and so acquired a new name, the *exodium*, and its actors the title *exodiarii*.[176] In the late Republic it was superseded for a time in popularity by the mime.[177] Appearance in an Atellan play brought no social stigma on the actors, who in the Republic were men with full citizenship.[178] It was to preserve the *dignitas* of the Roman citizen that (by a practice which pre-dated the general wearing of masks in theatrical performances other than mimes†) the actors wore masks from the very start.[179] As against professional actors, they had amateur status.

They gesticulated extravagantly; their language, so far from being polished, was the common language of the countryside or of the streets; and their talk abounded in witticisms, *doubles entendres* and political double-talk.[180] The parts were as traditional as in a Punch and Judy show: two different buffoons, Maccus, the glutton,[181] and Bucco, whose mask had inflated cheeks; Pappus, the old gaffer, in whose person all the follies and comic afflictions of old age were mocked; and Dossenus, the hunch-back, butt for the many gibes which could be levelled at such oddities as schoolmasters, philosophers and other tricksters. The titles of the performances were derived largely from the countryman's life and the farmyard ('The Gelded Boar', *Maialis*, for instance); some from the *Palliata* ('The young Companions', *Synephebi*), some

---

* See p. 305 below for a mime in which a dog played a leading part.
† See p. 283 below.

from private and commercial life ('The Pregnant Virgin', 'The Baker'). After the Social War there were Italian subjects, like 'The Women of Brindisi', 'Soldiers of Campania'.[182]

The genre was revived under Augustus, and achieved great popularity in the early Empire; Trimalchio kept a troupe of *comoedi* to give private performances.[183] It may be doubted, however, whether during the Empire the actors long retained their privileged status or were treated in any way differently from actors in the ordinary mime.

For playwrights and actors alike the temptation to satirize imperial shortcomings was hard to resist—a reference to Tiberius as 'the old goat'; under Nero, the line 'Goodbye, father; goodbye, mother', accompanied by the gestures of eating—was Claudius not thought to have died from a surfeit of poisoned mushrooms?—and of swimming —for Nero's first attempt to rid himself of his mother was a crude attempt to drown her. If they were lucky, actor and author got away with it; if not, they were banished, perhaps executed.[184]

In the second century A.D. there was a revival of the Atellan farce in its original form, this time for the pleasure of the sophisticated, when archaism was the literary fashion.

7. Actors

A difference most frequently emphasized when Greek and Roman social habits were contrasted in antiquity was the fact that acting, a respectable profession in Greece, was not considered respectable at all in Rome, on two grounds: that the actor 'showed himself off to the people' and that he was paid for doing so.[185] Also the performers were to a large extent foreigners: Greeks, Egyptians, Syrians. The status of the profession was lower under the Empire than it had been under the Republic, for straight plays had practically disappeared and pantomime and mime held the stage. Yet it is hard to accept the extreme view that 'ars ludicra' as a term of disparagement dates from the late Republic and applies only to *pantomimi* and *mimi*, and that in earlier Rome actors had never been slaves and the profession had not been disreputable at all.[186]

Most actors and actresses were slaves or freedmen and freedwomen. Under the Republic there had certainly been some free-born men who acted and under the Empire there may well have been stage-struck citizens who were professional actors just as there were Roman citizens who became gladiators. Except, originally, in the case of the Atellan farce,[187] any Roman who acted on the public stage was stigmatized formally (*infamis*), in that his name could not appear on the official list of property-owning citizens and he could not be called up for military service, a hardship which he may not have considered a hardship at all.* If we can judge from Julius Caesar's draft regulations, he was disqualified from taking part in local government.[188]

By the terms of Augustus' moral legislation men and women who had senatorial blood even three generations back were forbidden to marry actors or the children of actors, just as they were forbidden to marry the children of freedmen. An actress was classed with prostitutes; she was '*humilis abiectaque persona*'.[189]

Actors were expelled from Rome for the first time, we do not know for how long, in 115 B.C. They were liable to summary punishment by magistrates, until Augustus limited this liability to the theatre itself.[190] For gross misbehaviour during a performance, presumably of a sort to encourage disorder in the audience, they could be whipped on the spot by the presiding magistrate. In A.D. 17, after serious rioting, the Senate decreed that no senator might enter the house of a *pantomimus* and no one of equestrian rank might be seen with one in public.[191] Six years later a number of actors were expelled from Italy—to be recalled by Gaius in 37.[192] A number were banished under Nero in 56 A.D., but they were soon recalled.[193] Pantomimes were forbidden by Domitian, restored by Nerva and forbidden again by Trajan; and in the oily sycophancy of his *Panegyricus* the younger Pliny declared that, for their conflicting behaviour, Nerva and Trajan deserved equal praise, 'for it was right to restore what a bad emperor had abolished and, once restored, abolition was the right thing.'[194]

The official prohibitions of A.D. 17 indicate clearly enough that there were senators who were anxious to visit *pantomimi* in their homes and equestrians who liked to consort with them in public. That was the trouble. Scipio Aemilianus in the second century B.C. had been shocked when he was taken to a large dancing class and found even the son of a man who was standing for public office among the pupils.[195] The wife of the consul of 77 B.C., a highly educated woman, played music, sang and danced, in Sallust's words, 'more elegantly than is necessary for a respectable woman.' Strong prohibitions were issued by Augustus against the appearance of society women and of men of senatorial or equestrian families on the stage, but even in his own presence these regulations were flouted and in the end he turned a blind eye. If Mar-

---

* In the case of good actors, it was certainly no hardship to the theatre-going public. Was this a consideration?

cellus, his son-in-law, exhibited a Roman knight and a woman of high birth as dancers on the stage in his public games, and if Nero caused men and women not only of equestrian but even of senatorial standing to dance and play music in public, these performers were obviously no blundering amateurs who had been taught their tricks overnight.[196] Indeed husbands and wives competed, Seneca says, each anxious to be the more voluptuous dancer.[197]

Acting has at all times been a profession in which both materially and socially the rewards of success were very high. In the Roman world actors were paid, it seems, by the performance, *diurna merces*, five *aurei* (five hundred sesterces) in the Empire.[198] One of the punitive measures taken in A.D. 17 was to restrict the size of actors' fees.[199]

Eminent actors and actresses, however, were little affected by such regulations. We hear of a *mima* who earned 200,000 sesterces a year in the late Republic,[200] and in the early Empire Seneca suggests the possibility of *pantomimae* making respectable marriages, bringing with them a dowry of a million sesterces.[201] In the late Republic Roscius earned over half a million sesterces a year.[202] His contemporary Aesopus was worth twenty millions when he died.[203] Good actors, in fact, made more money than playwrights, who normally sold their copyright to a producer outright. Terence sold the *Eunuchus* in the second century B.C. for a mere 8,000 sesterces.[204] We hear, however, of one tragedy—*palliata*—which made very big money for its author. This was the *Thyestes* of L. Varius Rufus, a friend of Maecenas, Virgil and Horace, a play so good as to be a match for any Greek tragedy in Quintilian's view. This was performed in 29 B.C. at the great games with which Octavian celebrated his victory at Actium; he paid Varius a million sesterces.[205]

Clever actors are made as well as born. So actors of distinction took pupils, and to have been trained by an actor as eminent as Roscius in the late Republic was in itself a passport to success. A gifted well-trained slave could be a valuable investment for his or her owner. The case in which Roscius was defended by Cicero turned on the value of a slave who had been murdered, a man whose owner had contracted with Roscius for his training on condition that the pair of them should share equally in his earnings.[206] The slave himself, presumably, received a share too; how otherwise could he have built up any savings in the hope of buying his freedom? For slaves on the stage, like other slaves in domestic, commercial and cultured employment, could buy their freedom, subject to their master's consent. In the case of actors this consent was sometimes extorted, when an audience was delighted by their performance and cried out for them to be freed. Under the Empire such appeals were often made to the Emperor, if he was present in the theatre and he responded by a popular, if not inexpensive, gesture; for he had to compensate the owner of the slave. One of the reasons for which Tiberius is said to have avoided the theatre was to prevent the repetition of an occasion when, confronted by a popular outcry, he was left with no alternative but to give freedom to a *comoedus*. Such occurrences were frequent, until Marcus Aurelius strictly forbade the granting of liberty to actors in response to outcries in the theatre by members of the audience.[207]

For the member of a theatrical troupe freedom must have been harder to secure. Such troupes were possessed by individuals—for instance by Trimalchio; by that tough old lady Ummidia Quadratilla, whose puritanical grandson's commendable disapproval of the practice was shared by his friend, the younger Pliny; and by some emperors. They gave performances in the household as well as in the public theatre and, as a troupe, might be put onto the market and sold or bequeathed by will to a legatee.[208]

In England, before acting became a respectable profession late in the nineteenth century, there were distinguished players like David Garrick and Mrs. Siddons, who were accepted in the best society, though they could not be hosts at such a social level themselves. In France, too, in the eighteenth century, actors were disparaged and could not receive Christian burial; yet actors of distinction were received in the best society.

The social position of actors was similar in Rome. The great majority led obscure, sordid lives. For people more fortunate than themselves they were a despised necessity. Actresses in the mimes, even those who were past their prime, were kept in Rome in the fourth century at times when food was short and respectable people, scholars, were driven from the city. What could be more paradoxical, Tertullian asked, than so to glorify an art and to disgrace the artist.[209]

In the middle range there were actors who attracted honours in the Italian country towns. As freedmen in the Empire, they were sometimes elected members of the Augustales (the very prominent and honourable priesthood of the imperial cult) and even given the honorary status (*ornamenta*) of municipal magistrates and councillors. Sometimes statues were set up in their honour.[210]

There was also a corporation of actors, with patrons and priest, of

which there is slight literary mention, but which has left its record in a
number of inscriptions from southern Latium and Campania, the
corporation of the 'Parasites of Apollo'. They were, perhaps, in their
republican origin, a guild of minor actors (hence their title, taken
from the character of the parasite), modelled in some degree on the
famous Greek travelling companies of actors, 'the artists of Dionysus'
(one of which was fetched to perform in Rome in 167 B.C. at the games
of L. Anicius, and given a reception which must have made the actors
wonder whether the Romans were a civilized people at all). In the
Empire the Parasites of Apollo evidently gained greater prestige and
numbered even outstanding actors among their members.[211]

In Rome itself the social prizes were naturally higher than elsewhere.
In most periods of the Empire, Society, even the Court, opened its
arms to the successful actor, particularly if his skill was enhanced by
natural good looks. There were always smart women, often women of
the Court, who were stage-struck and who lost their hearts to actors—
and, in a free-loving society, also men. Thanks to Galen we know of a
society woman who consulted her doctor in Rome in the late second
century A.D. because she could not sleep. She denied having anything
on her mind. Her perceptive doctor put his finger on her pulse and
mentioned various names. At the mention of the famous *pantomimus*
Pylades, her pulse raced, and her complaint was diagnosed.[212]

The chief patrons of actors were raffish characters—Sulla and Antony
in the Republic, Maecenas under Augustus, Gaius, Messalina, Nero.
Yet later Hadrian and the Antonine emperors, who were not raffish at
all, encouraged and befriended prominent actors.

That is why we know the names of a number of great actors and
dancers—respectable men in the late Republic; slenderer characters in
the Empire who knew that they played for high stakes and who, more
often than not, came to a violent end.

The two men (both free Roman citizens) who made fortunes by their
acting in the late Republic, Q. Roscius Gallus and Clodius Aesopus,
were close personal friends of Cicero, of Catulus and, before that, of
Sulla. Roscius, 'a man fit to be a senator', was, despite a slight squint
(which was the reason for his introducing the wearing of masks in
about 110 B.C. to the straight Roman stage), one of the handsomest men
in Rome. He was a superb actor, and excelled in comedy. After Sulla
honoured him with the gold ring, he was an equestrian, and it was a
mark of his new social standing that henceforth he declined to accept
a fee when he acted. He died, an old man, just before 62 B.C.[213] Clodius

Aesopus was a full-blooded and highly emotional tragic actor, and we have a vivid account from Cicero of his performance in Accius' *Eurysaces* directly after the Senate passed the decreee which preceded Cicero's recall from exile in 57 B.C. He made the most of every line in the play which could be construed as referring to the glory of Cicero and to his undeserved misfortunes, and he even gagged to the same effect: an ecstatic performance ecstatically received—if we may trust the word of Cicero who was, naturally, a long way from Rome at the time.[214]

A notorious episode in Caesar's games of 46 B.C. introduces us to two figures of eminence in the contemporary theatrical world, the writer of mimes, D. Laberius, who was an *eques*, then sixty years old, and the up-and-coming young freedman mime-actor Publilius, a Syrian slave in origin; both of them were the source of frequently quoted aphorisms.* On this occasion Publilius challenged Laberius to appear on the stage in a mime in competition with himself, and Laberius, notoriously an outspoken man, was told by Caesar to accept the challenge—which forced him, by appearing on the stage as a mime-actor, to divest himself of equestrian status. His prologue, deploring this misfortune, survives. With great wit he decided to appear in the part of the freedman Publilius himself, recoiling, as he made his first entry, from the effects of a thrashing and crying, 'Citizens, we are free no longer.' The eyes of the audience turned to Caesar, 'Still,' he continued, 'when many people are afraid of anybody, he must be afraid of them too?' Again all eyes turned to Caesar. Caesar's behaviour was typical. Far from being angry, he awarded Publilius the prize, and then gave Laberius the gold ring, restoring him to the equestrian rank from which he had been temporarily degraded.[215]

The distinguished actors of Augustus' age were acquaintances of the Emperor. They were all *pantomimi*—Pylades, the Cilician, his own freedman, spoken of as 'the creator of the pantomime', who excelled in tragic parts (for instance in playing 'Semele's death and the Birth of Dionysus'), Bathyllus, the freedman of Maecenas, who played comic parts, and Pylades' pupil, Hylas. Indeed they were on familiar terms with the Emperor, if the story is true that Pylades, when reproved with Bathyllus (or Hylas) for causing a disturbance in the theatre, told Augustus he should be grateful to them for diverting the interest of the people from politics. However, these men's enjoyment of imperial favour was precarious. Pylades was banished for a period because he had pointed

* See p. 277 above.

his finger in an obscene fashion at a member of the audience who had
hissed him, and Hylas was once thrashed in the hall of Augustus' own
house before spectators.[216]

The emperor Gaius was infatuated by Mnester, a pantomime-actor;
so, after him, was the empress Messalina. Gifted, handsome and
popular, Mnester was withdrawn from the stage on Claudius' com-
plaisant instruction to serve, however unwillingly, Messalina's lascivious
caprices, which from time to time he escaped to enjoy an intrigue with
a distinguished and very beautiful woman, Poppaea, the mother of
the later empress. Messalina secured Poppaea's death in A.D. 47, and
the death of two knights who had lent their house for the intrigue of
the lovers. In the following year Messalina met her end, and Mnester
was executed in the holocaust that followed.[217]

For that 'pearl of the stage', L. Domitius Paris, freedman of Nero's
aunt Domitia, death too was the ultimate price of social prominence.
Having easy access to the imperial dining-room as an after-dinner
dancer, he was employed in A.D. 55 by his patroness to frighten Nero
by revealing a fictitious plot of his mother Agrippina to depose him.
The stratagem did not succeed. Paris then sued his patroness and, by a
decision of the Emperor which was widely questioned, recovered
ten thousand sesterces, the price of his emancipation, on the ground that
he was free-born and therefore had never been a slave or in need of
emancipation. But at the end, in A.D. 67, he fell from imperial favour
and was executed—some said because Nero was jealous of his talent,
others because Nero was angry on account of the fact that, however
hard he tried, Paris was unable to teach him how to dance—a failure
all the more humiliating in view of Nero's hope of dancing Virgil's
'Turnus'.[218]

Success and imperial favour were attended by no such precariousness
in quieter times. The slave Pylades, a favourite of Trajan, received his
freedom from Hadrian. He trained and gave his name to another slave,
whom M. Aurelius and L. Verus freed—L. Aurelius Pylades, 'first
pantomime-actor of his time', a popular benefactor of Puteoli. He was
the actor whose name set the rich society-lady's pulses racing.[219]

And so it continued, success sometimes proving fatal and sometimes
not, up to the moment when in Byzantium (where the old Roman
rules against marriage with actors and actresses prevailed) in A.D. 523,
in defiance of all convention, the notorious strip-tease mimist Theodora
became the wife of the emperor Justinian.[220]

From the surviving writers of antiquity actors receive little but abuse and contempt, and it is easy to forget that, wherever there has been acting, there have been men and women wholeheartedly devoted to their art, artists of a very high order.

Quintilian has high praise for two outstanding contemporary actors whose strong personalities determined the parts that they played. One, Demetrius, was tall, handsome and graceful; so he was cast always for reputable rôles, gods, young men and respectable old ladies. The other, Stratocles, had only to laugh in order to captivate his audience; he was cast always for lively parts, ill-tempered old men, cunning slaves, parasites and pimps.[221]

Two attractive stories of gifted actors survive. The first is of a Latin called Saunio, a favourite on the Roman stage, 'a buffoon with a wonderful gift for gaiety. Not only could he stir up laughter by what he said, but even without a word his slightest motions would bring smiles to all who watched him, so winning was his natural appeal.' In the grim days preceding the outbreak of the Social War in 90 B.C. Romans who were present in Picenum, perhaps at Asculum, killed an actor for his outspoken anti-Roman utterances, and the Picentines, wildly angry, decided to retort by killing Saunio, because he was such a favourite with the Romans.

'Foreseeing what was about to happen, he came on the stage soon after the comedian had been killed, and said, "Members of the audience, the omens are favourable. May the evil that has been done bring good fortune. Know that I am no Roman but subject to the *fasces*, as you yourselves are; I traipse around Italy, peddling my graces in quest of merriment and laughter. Spare then the swallow that belongs to all men alike, to whom God has given the privilege of building her nest without risk in any man's house. It would be unfair for you to bring bitter tears upon yourselves." Continuing at length in a conciliatory and humorous vein, by the persuasive charm of his discourse he wheedled them out of their bitter and vengeful mood and thereby escaped the danger that threatened.'[222]

The second story, of a veteran comedian, is told by the elder Pliny. An old actor finished a performance amid great applause. It being his birthday, he gave a dinner party and, at the end, called for a warm drink, set his mask on a table opposite and transferred to it the diner's crown of flowers from his own head. He lay back and relaxed. A neighbour at the table called out to him that his drink was getting cold. But the words failed to rouse him—for he was dead.[223]

As well as acting and actors, there were music and musicians There were instrumentalists: flautists, cithara-players, trumpeters, horn-players, who accompanied or supplied background to the singers; there were vocalists, both soloists and chorus-singers; and there were *citharoedi*, who accompanied themselves on the cithara as they sang. We know the names of many such performers[224] and also of teachers of music and singing[225] from their epitaphs, but it is only rarely that one was sufficiently prominent to be mentioned by name in our literary sources—like Terpnus, a singer who accompanied himself on the cithara, whom Nero invited to his Court and made his music-master.[226]

The emperor Nero himself, indeed, is the only outstanding Roman musician whom history knows by name. He first performed privately to the Court, where failure to conceal the fact that music—or Nero's music—bored him, nearly brought Vespasian's career to a sudden end[227]; then to invited audiences in his gardens in Trastevere. At Naples, undeterred by an earthquake, he made his début on the public stage in A.D. 64, a performance which he repeated in Rome at the second cele-bration of his quinquennial games in A.D. 65 and then in a musical tour of Greece at all the major festivals in A.D. 67.[228] He sang to his own accompaniment on the cithara. He sang major tragic parts, in mask and costume. It was rumoured that, while Rome was burning in A.D. 64, he was so deeply moved by the spectacle that he sang a passage, 'The Capture of Troy', from his own epic on the Trojan war. He took his singing, perhaps, more seriously than he took his imperial responsi-bilities; he trained arduously, lying on his back and lifting weights on his chest, so as to strengthen his singing muscles; he followed the musician's diet; in public he observed rigorously all the rules of pro-fessional decorum.[229] Naturally in every public contest he won the victor's crown. He was an artist, perhaps an artist of distinction, in love with his art. '*Qualis artifex pereo*', indeed, are said to have been almost his last words.[230] Even without the professional claqueurs whom he employed,[231] his performances could not have failed to entrance the general public. The faithful Burrus watched and applauded (he had to), but was close to tears.[232] Respectability shuddered. When Nero was dead, historians and satirists[233] were to heap contumely on him. Rightly, no doubt. For an emperor of Rome, it was all shockingly undignified.

Apart from actors, singers and dancers, there were many others who performed publicly, often in the theatre, before large audiences. In-deed, few of the acts which are to be seen in a modern circus or music hall would be altogether unfamiliar to an ancient Roman, if he was re-born today.

There were circus-performers, like acrobats (*petauristarii*) who, together with Atellan farces, gave Trimalchio such great pleasure. They walked and danced on tightropes or at the top of tall ladders which their fellow-performers supported. There were conjurers (*praestigiatores*), whose deception Seneca so much enjoyed. There were jugglers, 'so skilful that the objects which they throw into the air seem to fly back into their hands of their own accord', men like the brilliant Agathinus whose skill, Martial observed elegantly, had only a single flaw: he was incapable of dropping the shield with which he juggled. There were puppet-shows; and there were exhibitions of human prodigies, like the Lycian boy at the time of Augustus, who was less than two feet tall, weighed seventeen pounds and had a stentorian voice.[234]

For cultured audiences there were public readings; Aulus Gellius describes readings of Ennius in the theatre at Puteoli.[235] And there were exhibitions of wrestling and of boxing, a sport which Augustus loved to watch and so, according to Horace, did the populace at large.[236]

8. Gladiatorial Games

Had you surveyed the contestants before many gladiatorial games, you could have divided them into two classes: those who might hope to survive and those for whom there was no hope at all.

The doomed men were criminals of the lower orders (*humiliores*) who had been condemned to death[237]—'*damnati ad mortem*' or '*damnati ad gladium*', condemned to death by the sword; just as there were other unfortunates '*damnati ad bestias*', condemned to killing by wild beasts. Such were the men who engaged in the mock sea-battle on the Fucine lake for the entertainment of the emperor Claudius and the Court in A.D. 52 and who cried, '*Morituri te salutant*'; for they were not to guess that on this occasion Nemesis* would be a kind goddess, and that some of them would be spared.[238]

At first this had been a convenient means of disposing of prisoners of war and of deserters,[239] and this may well be the origin of the names of certain types of gladiator, Thraeces, Galli, Samnites; later it was a form of punishment for men found guilty of capital crimes in the courts—*noxii*. A patron of gladiatorial games applied to the authorities for such condemned men, and advertised them, if they were obtainable, as one of the attractions of his show. Money was paid to secure them—in Gaul in M. Aurelius' time, six *aurei* a man—and the purchaser was

* See p. 296 below.

required to give an undertaking on oath that they would be disposed of within a specified period of time, normally a year.[240] They were put into the arena with no defensive weapons, to kill one another or to be butchered by other gladiators who were properly armed.[241]

For gladiators proper—the criminals condemned to death hardly deserve the title—there was hope, however slender.

Of these some also were criminals of the lower orders (*humiliores*) but, their crimes being less heinous, they had been sentenced not to death, but to the arena, to a gladiatorial school; '*in ludum damnati*'. This was an alternative sentence to condemnation to the mines or to deportation, and was considered a lighter punishment than consignment to the mines, for if the man survived his engagements in the arena, he might be discharged (*rude donatus*) at the end of three years and set free at the end of five.[242]

Secondly, there were slaves who had been sold to a gladiatorial trainer. These might be prisoners of war or the captives of highwaymen or pirates, who were immediately disposed of in this way. Or they might have displeased their master in private service and have been sold by him. The Thracian Spartacus and his associates, whatever their immediate background, seem to have been sold in some corrupt manner to a gladiatorial school. As an instance of the instability and servitude to his inferiors of the future emperor Vitellius, the story was told that when one of his favourite slaves tired of his advances and ran away and was subsequently discovered selling drinks at Puteoli, Vitellius put him in irons, then made a favourite of him again; after which, finding him excessively easy-fingered, he sold him to an itinerant gladiatorial trainer. Later, discovering that the youth was billed to appear late in a gladiatorial show, he stole him away and freed him. Under Hadrian the sale of slaves to gladiatorial schools was forbidden, except with the slave's consent, unless he had committed some offence. If a runaway slave sold himself to a gladiatorial establishment and his identity was subsequently discovered, he had, by a ruling of Antoninus Pius, to be returned to his master.[243]

The third class of gladiators were free Roman citizens who 'signed on'—*auctorati*—voluntarily, or under some kind of compulsion.[244] The compulsion was rarely as forcible as when, among other acts of brutality in Spain in 43 B.C., the younger Cornelius Balbus* forced a soldier who had fought for Pompey to enter a gladiatorial school and, when the man refused to take the oath, had him burnt to death, or

* The playwright; see pp. 272 f.

19

as when Gaius Caligula insisted on the fulfilment of his oath by a man who had sworn that, if Gaius recovered from illness, he would become a gladiator.[245] Generally the compulsion was an economic one; Livy, indeed, recognized two categories of gladiator, 'slaves and free men, who sell their blood'. The wanton spendthrift—so the moralists and satirists of the early Empire never tire of telling us—was confronted by the spectre of bankruptcy and grasped this as his only means of escape.[246] He was paid money down on joining (a sum which, in an effort to stop the practice, Marcus Aurelius reduced to two thousand sesterces); he lived free as a member of a gladiatorial school. There was prize money. If he survived and won his discharge, he could sign on again as a trained fighter, at a higher fee.[247] Though he was stigmatized socially—*infamis*—he never surrendered his status as a free Roman citizen. And his decision, when he first signed on, was not utterly irrevocable; a relative or a friend could always buy him out.[248]

There were also genuine volunteers, for in any society there are men to whom danger appeals. They liked fighting—like the gladiator whom Seneca heard complaining that so few games were held when Tiberius was emperor: 'All my lovely youth is going to seed'.[249] There were men of the highest social background, of senatorial and equestrian families, who fought in the arena, encouraged by such emperors as Nero and Commodus, who is said himself to have fought in a thousand engagements against opponents with dummy weapons, 365 in the lifetime of his father; in other cases they fought in disregard of imperial prohibition (by Augustus, for instance, or Vitellius), a prohibition which could never be enforced for any long period of time. Of Vitellius' regulation Tacitus wrote, 'A severe warning was issued against Roman knights degrading themselves by gladiatorial fighting. Earlier emperors had bribed and, more often, forcibly compelled knights to fight, and numbers of country towns in Italy competed by the offer of high sums to entice really degraded young men to do the same.'[250]

In Tiberius' principate, at Drusus' games in A.D. 15, two knights fought, and one was killed; Tiberius then forbade the killer ever to fight again.[251] This, perhaps, implies that it was not expected to be a mortal engagement; and it may be supposed that in many cases these sprigs of society were not *auctorati* or strictly members of gladiatorial schools, that they gave exhibition bouts and fought with dummy weapons, or at least did not fight to kill. And this must have been the case when women engaged publicly as gladiators. The literary sources refer to women fighting in this way from the time of Nero onwards, until Septimius Severus forbade the practice, and there is in the British Museum a relief from the eastern part of the Mediterranean on which two women—the sculptor has left their sex in no doubt—are shown bare-headed but otherwise armed, hotly engaged in a gladiatorial bout.[252]

It can be assumed that candidates were not accepted without a test of physical fitness and aptitude. Recruits—*novi auctorati, tirones*—were certainly accepted at the age of seventeen,[253] and were perhaps accepted younger still. When they signed on, they took a formidable oath: 'I undertake to be burnt by fire, to be bound in chains, to be beaten, to die by the sword.'[254] Now, or at a later stage, the gladiator often adopted a name different from his own, under which to fight: Narcissus, for instance, or Nicanor or Pugnax or Swan (Cycnus) or Dove (Palumbus), just as *pantomimi* often assumed such famous names as Pylades or Paris; there was, no doubt, an element of superstition in this.[255] The proportion of criminals, slaves and free volunteers differed no doubt from time to time and from place to place. The incomplete inscriptions of two *familiae* at Venusia show eighteen slaves and ten free men, *auctorati*.[256]

A troop of gladiators was a *familia*[257]; its place of residence and training, its 'school' or barracks, was a *ludus*.

The possession of troops of gladiators by Romans and Italians who could afford the expense was already common in the last century of the Republic, particularly in Campania, which was always the home of gladiatorial fighting. Once, Strabo tells us, Campanians used to exhibit gladiatorial fighting to their guests at the end of dinner parties, the number of bouts varying in accordance with the number of their guests.[258]

In Rome itself such *familiae* played a significant and sinister part in the corruption of political life and in the breakdown of law and order in the late Republic. Gladiatorial games being popular, vote-winning events, candidates for office acquired bands of gladiators (borrowing money heavily for the purpose, if they could not afford the expense), in order to give games—which, as has been seen,* were no part of official *ludi*—on the pretext of commemorating some death or other in the family. The games over, the survivors were sold to another politician who had similar ambitions, or they might be employed as a formidable bodyguard for their employer as he moved about the streets, ideal

* See pp. 248 f. above.

instruments of hooliganism and intimidation.[259] Once Spartacus' revolt in 73 B.C. had demonstrated the danger to public safety of a large band of gladiatorial malcontents, precautions were taken in moments of crisis (Catiline's revolt in 63 and the outbreak of civil war in 49) to disband the *familiae* and lodge them in a number of smaller units, whether in different towns or in a variety of different households. Already in 65 B.C., in apprehension perhaps of the extravagant gladiatorial games which Caesar planned to hold in his aedileship, the Senate had placed a restriction on the number of gladiators that any private individual might possess in Rome itself. In 63 Cicero introduced a law forbidding the giving of gladiatorial games by any politician in the two years preceding his candidature for public office.[260]

There were gladiatorial schools (the property of private individuals) in Rome, like that of C. Aurelius Scaurus, whose trainers the consul of 105 B.C. borrowed to be army instructors in commando tactics.* There were numerous private establishments in Campania, particularly at Capua. It was from a school at Capua that Spartacus with seventy-seven other gladiators made their fateful escape in 73 B.C. Julius Caesar owned a school at Capua which had armour for five thousand fighters; this was the school which, with reasonable apprehension, the Government broke up when Caesar invaded Italy in 49.[261]

Gladiatorial schools are recorded in the Empire at a number of Campanian towns, particularly at Pompeii, where remains of a barracks survive, and in large cities in the provinces, both in the western and in the eastern Empire.[262]

A gladiatorial school was a source of profit as well as of interest to its owner, who hired his gladiators out to patrons who wished to give games (*munerarii*), charging a certain sum for the service of those who survived and a capital payment for all those who were killed. Atticus, who did not invest money foolishly, sank capital in gladiators and Cicero, whatever his feelings about gladiatorial fighting, showed interest in his venture: 'I hear your gladiators are marvellous fighters; if you had wanted to hire them out, you would have covered your expenses in a couple of games'.[263] Julius Caesar, too. In describing his conduct on the day before he crossed the Rubicon in 49, both his biographers think he gave the impression of having nothing on his mind but gladiators. Plutarch says that he spent the day watching gladiators in training, Suetonius that at dinner he was entirely absorbed by plans for the building of a new gladiatorial school.[264]

* See p. 250.

In Rome itself privately owned gladiatorial establishments survived into the early Empire, but not beyond the Julio-Claudian period.[265] Such ownership was hardly compatible with the régime of the Caesars. Given the wish and the means to keep and train gladiators, a private individual was tempting providence; at any moment he might be summoned for treason, faced by the allegation that he was planning a Putsch. And indeed, from the Emperor's point of view, this could have been a real danger. Also the giving of gladiatorial shows in Rome was to be the prerogative of the Emperor and of members of the imperial family and of certain magistrates* just as, outside Rome, however formally, games were only given by private individuals with his consent. So the enlistment of gladiators called for the creation of a special department of civil servants, the *procuratores familiae gladiatoriae*, who often covered vast districts of the Empire. And in Rome itself it seems that, from Domitian's time onwards, no more private *ludi* survived.[266] Instead there were the four imperial training schools, each under an imperial procurator, a *ducenarius*[267]—the Ludus Matutinus on the Caelian, used probably for the training of wild beast fighters (*bestiarii*), which came into existence in the Julio-Claudian period,[268] and the three schools created later than the Colosseum, to which they were connected. These were the Ludus Magnus, which is marked on a surviving portion of Septimius Severus' *Forma Urbis*, and which has recently been excavated, between the Via Labicana and the Via di S. Giovanne in Laterano and, smaller in size and importance, the Ludus Dacicus and the Ludus Gallicus. In Trajan's time, *bestiarii* apart, these schools must have been able to accommodate ten thousand gladiators.[269] There were also training schools belonging to the Emperor outside Rome in Italy at Praeneste and at Capua and in the provinces, at Pergamum and Alexandria.[270]

The director of training in a gladiatorial school was the *lanista*. Presumably because he made money (and he might make a lot) in trafficking with human lives, he was some one whom the world at large contemned—'*contemptissimus quisque ac turpissimus*', in Seneca's judgement. He ranked with the dregs, pimps and procurers, and like them was debarred—even after his retirement, when he might be a rich man—by Julius Caesar's regulation, from holding municipal office. Caesar, whose interest in gladiatorial fighting is manifest, did not even think him good at his job, for he insisted that his own gladiatorial recruits (*tirones*) should have private training. And,

* See p. 251 above.

it seems, the *lanista* and his relatives shared the world's low opinion of himself; for, in the abundance of surviving inscriptions in which the profession of the living or the dead is described, there is not one inscription in which a *lanista* as such has left his record. He may have passed himself off, with some grandiloquence as 'Business Manager', *Negotiator familiae gladiatoriae*.[271]

Other functionaries of the gladiatorial schools, to judge from the inscriptions, felt no such embarrassment about their calling. There were doctors (*medici*), experienced especially in staunching wounds and in repairing muscular sutures; Galen took pride here in a certain technique of his own invention. There were masseurs. There were makers of the complicated arm-bands (*manicae*) which gladiators wore, tailors (for the gladiator was very smartly turned out) and armourers, the keeper of the armoury shouldering a large responsibility, for arms were kept under lock and key when training or fighting was not in progress. Spartacus and his associates only secured arms by a piece of unexpected good fortune. They were unarmed when they escaped from barracks, but they captured a cart on the main road which was loaded with armour and on its way to a gladiatorial school.[272]

Most important of all were the trainers.

The *tiro* in a gladiatorial school started, as a recruit started in the army, with a very general course of training. He was given a wooden sword (*lusoria arma*) and practised against a wooden dummy (*palus*); it was in this kind of elementary training that Juvenal's monster of a woman-athlete engaged. He learnt the vulnerable points at which to strike, and he learnt quickness in recovery from the thrust to the on-guard. This he did under skilled supervision, for the object of this introduction to his training was to discover for which of the numerous types of gladiatorial fighting he was best suited. So, when we find frequent mentions of a *primus palus* and a *secundus palus*, these may well have been his instructors (highly skilled gladiators or ex-gladiators themselves) in the initial stage of his training.[273]

At the second stage of his training he was turned into a professional; and such different qualities in temperament, physique, talent and resilience were demanded by the different forms of fighting (of which there were at least sixteen), that the selection at the first stage must have been a matter of the utmost skill and importance. No one who was not a good horseman could qualify as an Eques (who generally fought an opponent mounted like himself). Chariot-fighters, Essedarii (British in their origin), who fought other Essedarii (and, occasionally, it seems,

Retiarii), had to be able to fight from a chariot and to work in harmony with their drivers. For fighting on foot—and this is how most of the engagements were fought—the phlegmatic, tough men capable of standing up to a long fight, made the best heavy-armed fighters— Galli, Myrmillones, Hoplomachi, Samnites, Secutores. Others were better suited to be light-armed fighters, Thraeces, who carried a light shield and were armed with a reversed sickle. The agile, quick-footed daredevil was cut out to be the most interesting gladiator of all, the Retiarius, who fought bare-headed, wore a tunic and was armed with a net, in which he hoped to encompass his opponent, a three-pronged trident and a dagger. He was a dead man, once he was cornered; his object was to provoke, irritate and exhaust the heavily-armoured opponent against whom he fought, baiting him to lumber after him across the arena, shouting at the Myrmillo (whose ensign was a fish on his helmet), 'It's not you I'm after, it's your fish; why are you avoiding me, you Gaul?'—'Non te peto, piscem peto; cur me fugis, Galle?'[274] Society, which disapproved naturally when any of its members debased himself by fighting as a gladiator, disapproved particularly of anyone who fought as a Retiarius because, fighting bare-headed, he could be recognized. The kind of gladiator that a man dreamed he was fighting indicated, curiously, the type of woman that he would marry; dreaming of a Retiarius meant that your wife would be penniless, erotic and a light-o'-love.[275]

In the second stage of training there were special instructors (doctores) for each several sort of fighter—a doctor Murmillonum, a doctor Thraecum, and so on.[276] The summa rudis and the secunda rudis, ex-gladiators, often mentioned in inscriptions, may have been general overseers of training.[277] At a certain point the trainees started to fight with bare steel (decretoria arma). Whether or not by invitation, spectators were admitted to watch gladiators in training (the excavated Ludus Magnus at Rome has an elliptical practice-ring, with seats around it); but it was not thought a sign of good character in a young man if he was constantly hanging round a gladiatorial school.[278]

Gladiators were divided, in the schools, into two classes, tirones, those who had not yet fought their first fight, on the one hand, and veterani on the other.[279]

Living conditions were bad, and Spartacus and his associates were not the only gladiators who broke out and deserted. There were complaints about the cells; in the excavated barracks at Pompeii the bedrooms, though single, were tiny, each about twelve feet square. There was a prison at Pompeii with stocks—though it was not from being in stocks that eighteen persons (one a woman) perished there in A.D. 79.[280] They were given plenty to eat, but their food was simple and coarse, largely 'barley and beans.'[281]

The society was demoralizing. Many of the trainees had a criminal record. They were all of them murderers in the making. Yet there was a certain *esprit de corps* and there were friendships. We have, for instance, a dedication in memory of a young Thraex, who died or was killed as a *tiro* at the age of twenty, erected by all his fellow-Thraeces, '*armatura Thraecum universa*', and another raised by a whole *familia* to a veteran of 99. And there are others, erected by one friend in memory of another, by an Eques 'to his good fellow-slave, a Thraex', for instance.[282]

Advancing the cynical view that in social life every man is every man's enemy, Seneca instanced gladiators, 'who drink with a man, and then fight him', and Quintilian pointed out that trainees of the same gladiatorial instructor were often matched against one another in the arena.[283] Why, it may well be asked, were combatants not regularly selected from different schools?

Mars was the god, naturally, whom gladiators chiefly honoured; also Victory. Mars and Venus are depicted on the walls of the gladiatorial barracks at Pompeii. Inevitably, like all athletic competitors at all times, gladiators were extremely superstitious; they paid cult to Fortune and, catching an infection which was widespread in the East and which spread to the West, chiefly to the Danube provinces, they did all they could to placate the frightening goddess Nemesis, evidence of whose cult has been found in amphitheatres in the western Empire as well as in the East. There is an inscription from Verona, in the name of a vanquished Retiarius, a married man who at the age of twenty-three had been killed in his eighth engagement: 'Observe, every man, his own planet. That is my advice. Have no trust in Nemesis. She deceived me'.[284]

In the Empire (unless, presumably, they were bad and dangerous characters) gladiators were evidently not confined rigidly to their barracks except, perhaps, at the first stage of their training and in the days immediately before their fights. At Pompeii there is a house— 30 Nola Street—from whose decoration and *graffiti*, which are entirely concerned with gladiatorial fighting, it appears that a number of gladiators lived there. Inscriptions show that gladiators often married (one at the early age of fifteen) and that some had children. Indeed, there is the story that, by a popular gesture, Claudius gave an honourable discharge to a gladiator at the intercession of the gladiator's four sons.

Gladiators visited brothels; a *ludia* was a gladiator's Moll. The *graffiti* in the house at Pompeii show that some of them had, or believed themselves to have, an irresistible attraction for women. A Thraex called Celadus was 'the man the girls sighed for' ('*suspirium puellarum*'); the Retiarius Crescens was 'Lord of the Dolls' ('*puparum dominus*'). They had a fatal attraction for some high-ranking women in society. Juvenal's Eppia, who abandoned her husband and children and eloped with a gladiator, may have had her counterpart in real life. And one of Juvenal's cynical warnings against marriage—'Do you want to marry and find yourself father to a gladiator's offspring?'—suggests that gladiators were not always to be found in barracks. In an age when slander was of little consequence, it was commonly said both of Curtius Rufus, a consul under Claudius, and of Nymphidius Sabinus, Nero's Prefect of the Praetorian Guard, that they had gladiators for their fathers.[285]

The patron of the *munus* was the *munerarius*, a word introduced to the Latin tongue by Augustus. He entered into a number of contracts, the most important being that with a *lanista* for the number and quality of gladiators that he required. A passage from Gaius' *Institutes* suggests a contract by which the *munerarius* undertook to pay eighty sesterces for each gladiator who survived the engagement and 4,000 for every man killed or wounded. The senatorial decree of 177/80 A.D., which envisaged buying gladiators outright (for re-sale, no doubt, if they survived), laid down that half the gladiators engaged were to be 'common gladiators', whose price was not to exceed two thousand sesterces. For the rest, the maximum sums payable varied according to the total outlay on the show, which might be as low as 30,000 sesterces or as high as 200,000. If this was between 150,000 and 200,000 sesterces, the highest permitted price for a gladiator was 15,000 sesterces, 'for a man of top class and high reputation'.[286] Famous retired gladiators commanded quite fancy prices—100,000 sesterces, even 240,000.[287]

Advertisements for the games were, no doubt, painted everywhere on the walls, as we know them to have been at Pompeii: the date, the promise of shade (*vela*), the number of fighters—sometimes their names —and the number of *noxii*, if there were to be executions.[288]

On the night before the engagement, the combatants dined together. It must have been a macabre occasion, and Plutarch can be believed who says that the gladiators were little interested in the food, but were absorbed in making their last dispositions (as, of course, were Roman soldiers on the eve of a great battle), arranging for the care of their womenfolk, some—the *auctorati*—for the freeing of their slaves; contingent arrangements, operative only if they were killed. There were some whose nerves broke, like the twenty-nine Germans, brought to Rome for the *munus* of Symmachus' son in the fourth century who, rather than face the morrow, strangled one another to death.[289]

In the morning they were occupied in sharpening and testing their weapons, and the whips were got out.[290]

Our liveliest account of the horror of it all comes from one of the declamations falsely attributed to Quintilian. In this masterpiece of sensational fiction, the poor son of a poor, ancient and ailing father was the intimate friend of the son of a very rich man. Their fathers were not on speaking terms. The rich son travelled, was captured by pirates and, when his father refused to pay the ransom, sold to a gladiatorial school. The poor son, more concerned than his friend's own father, set out to find him, and discovered him in all the distress of the night before his first fight. He prevailed on him and on the patron of the show to agree to their changing places, on condition that, if he was killed, his friend would support his own poor old father. He fought and was killed. His rich friend was forbidden by his rich father to carry out his undertaking. He defied his father and was disinherited. Whether legitimately or not, was a question for the lawyers.[291]

The show started with a procession through the arena, the *pompa*. The *munerarius* presided, in *toga praetexta*, with lictors, like a magistrate.

The morning was devoted to wild-beast fighting. From 61 B.C. there was a break at midday, and spectators had the option of going off for lunch or staying for the *meridianum spectaculum*, the execution of the *noxii*. This was the 'gloomy sight of punishments whose justice could not be questioned', '*iustissimorum suppliciorum tristis aspectus*'. Were the victims not highwaymen, murderers—later, Christians, enemies of society? Many of the audience stayed to watch. The emperor Claudius revelled in the spectacle. Seneca protests vocally against it. He had gone to the arena at midday, expecting light relief, comic bouts, he declares.[292] This suggests—for he was old enough at sixty to know what happened at the midday break—that, in the absence of criminals condemned to death, midday was the period for an utterly different kind of display, a time for relaxation and amusement. For there certainly were bouts which should not in any circumstances have been fatal—when beast-fighters past their prime contended with mangy and toothless lions, and when *paegniarii*, old gladiators (the old man who died at ninety-nine and was honoured by his *familia* was a *paegniarius**) fought one another with dummy weapons. Indeed, M. Aurelius refused to watch except when the fighting was with foils, and nobody was killed. These were *prolusiones*. There was no limit of bad taste to which the joke might not be carried. Under Domitian women and dwarfs fought; 'Father Mars and Bloodstained Valour smile'. And Gaius Caligula, for whose perverse sense of humour this kind of event had a great appeal, amused himself still further at the general expense. He forbade anybody to leave the theatre (when at the midday interval the audience normally dispersed) and, the sun then being at its hottest, had the awnings drawn back.[293]

The same word *prolusio* was used for the beginning of each bout of serious fighting when, after the formal procession of combatants (the *pompa*), the real encounters started in the afternoon. For, to a musical accompaniment, they started with feinting and shadow-fighting, even with spears, which were later discarded. The combatants whipped themselves up into a fury by shouting abuse at one another. Then the shrill blast of the trumpet ended the preliminaries. The music grew more raucous—trumpets, horns, flutes, even a water-organ—and the real fight started.[294]

Charioteers and horsemen excepted, the majority of bouts seem to have been between a Thraex with his small shield and reversed scimitar, less often a *retiarius*, on the one hand and a heavy-armed fighter (a *murmillo*, *hoplomachus*, Samnite or *secutor*) on the other. Evidence is afforded by detailed records of bouts from Pompeii and from the series of fights shown on the remarkable mosaics from a villa at Zliten in N. Africa (see pl. 13).[295]

A poor fighter received little sympathy. His opponent felt insulted in fighting such a man, and the crowd showed no mercy. But, as a general rule, the fighting must have been very skilful indeed.

Though without the enthusiasm with which they backed one colour or another in the chariot races in the circus, members of the watching public generally favoured one type of fighter; they were either *parmularii* or *scutarii*—'small-shield men' or 'big-shield men'; '*Ego parmularius sum*', as the cretin answered when asked which school of rhetoric he favoured. Imperial enthusiasm here as elsewhere could border on the intemperate—Gaius' and Titus' on the side of the Thraeces, Domitian's in hostility to them. Claudius disliked Retiarii.[296]

---

* See p. 296 above.

There were no referees, no rules; though, to judge from the Zliten mosaics, the *lanista* or some other unarmed person was in the arena. If the combatants fought to a standstill, the bout was called off, and the fighter recorded, after his victories, the number of such occasions, when he was '*stans missus*'. Martial describes such a contest, which had the happiest of issues: 'While Priscus and Verus each drew out the fight and the prowess of each was long equal, there were loud shouts for an end to be called to the bout, but Caesar* obeyed his own regulation that, with a prize of victory at stake, the fight should go on until one appealed ('*ad digitum*'). Still, a way was found of ending the equal contest. There was nothing to choose between them in the fight—and nothing when they *both* appealed. Caesar awarded each the prize— and discharge (*rudis*) too, the reward of splendid courage.'[297]

When a wound was inflicted, the audience cried, 'A hit, a hit'— '*Habet*', '*Hoc habet*.' A wound could be fatal. Or a wounded fighter could disdain the notion of appealing, and fight on to the death.[298] Otherwise, when he was at his opponent's mercy, he could drop his shield and raise a finger of his left hand in appeal—if his victor gave him the chance. The victor might be berserk, intent on killing, if the *lanista* could not stop him. For, to judge by the Zliten mosaics, the *lanista* (if that is who he was) rushed at this moment to grip his hand and stop him from dispatching his victim until the result of the appeal was known. But often the victor was merciful, even to his own cost, as one inscription suggests, recording the death of a gladiator at the hand of a man whom in a previous fight he himself had spared.[299]

In the case of an appeal, the decision rested with the *munerarius*, who generally followed the declared wishes of the audience, which waved handkerchiefs or made a downward movement of the thumb (*pollicem premere*), a sign to drop the sword, if it wanted a fighter spared. Anyone who was against mercy pointed his thumb to his own chest ('*pollicem vertere*'), indicating the *coup de grâce*. At the same time there were shouts, '*Missos*,' 'Let them be spared'—or '*Iugula*'—'Cut his throat.' Few *munerarii* were as ready to disregard the public's wishes as Julius Caesar; when they called for a fighter's death, he often spared him.[300]

If the appeal failed, the victim 'received the sword'. The brave man only wanted assurance from his master (presumably the *lanista* in the arena) that he had fought manfully. Credit was given to him if he then died with courage. Such men's examples supplied a text to the philosophers when they preached sermons on the inconsequence of death.[301]

* Domitian.

Once the fight was over and the victim dispatched, an attendant in the mask of Mercury came out with a hot iron to make sure he was really dead and not bluffing, and boys ran out with clean sand to cover the pools of blood. The body of the victim was taken out on a bier (*sandapila*) to the mortuary (*spoliarium*), where his armour and kit were removed and, if it was found that he was not dead at all, his throat was cut. The victor meanwhile preened himself, parading his palm of victory. He would receive a crown, and also prize money.[302]

At the end of bouts in which the victim was spared and no killing was done, the wounded were rushed to hospital. A man who was judged by his trainer not to have fought hard enough might be thrashed. Otherwise the *missus*, with a fresh infusion of valour, now that he was out of danger, was soon spoiling for another fight. 'The wounded gladiator swears never to enter the lists again. Then, the wound forgotten, he picks up his arms once more.'[303]

Sometimes—perhaps when it was thought that he had not been seriously tested—the victor was required to fight a second time. For this purpose there were reserves—*suppositicii*—kept in waiting in case of need.[304]

After the show was over, gladiators, if they were slaves and had been bought outright, not hired, by the *munerarius*, were sometimes put up for auction and sold, like animals. Such sales are said to have been a favourite caprice of the emperor Gaius, and there was a story that a man who had slept, nodding his head, during the auction, woke to find that thirteen gladiators had been knocked down to him at a price of nine million sesterces.[305]

The most important and interesting questions about gladiators can none of them be answered. What, when he signed on, was the average gladiator's chance of survival? While we have the record of a *tiro* who in the games after Trajan's death fought in two separate bouts, and Caracalla forced a man to fight three engagements in a day, the last of them fatal, a number of surviving inscriptions suggest that few men fought more often than once a year.[306]

Some gladiatorial shows were evidently sheer carnage: 'cold steel for the crowd, no quarter and the amphitheatre looking like a slaughterhouse.' An inscription from Minturnae records eleven bouts with eleven men killed. Other inscriptions record fighting when the percentage of deaths was not nearly so high. We have the record of a gladiator who won eighty-eight victories, but this figure is exceptional. However, a number of men are recorded to have fought and even to have won crowns of victory more than thirty times.[307]

Few great gladiators are known to us by name. An exception is Pacideianus, described by Lucilius as 'far and away the best gladiator in history', who fought in the mid-second century B.C. and whose name, thanks to Lucilius, was still famous in Rome a hundred years later. And Martial honours an invincible gladiator Hermes, 'who always wins and never kills', who fought with equal skill as a Retiarius and as an Andabata (on horseback).[308]

It would seem probable that, after a very good fight, a slave would be given his freedom, and a number of inscriptions have been interpreted as showing this happening. '*Lib. viii*', for instance, has been taken as indicating that a slave gladiator was given his freedom— *liberatus*—after his eighth fight. But this interpretation is wrong. '*Lib*' stands for '*liber*', and shows that the man was an *auctoratus* and not a slave, and the following figure gives the number of engagements in which he fought.[309]

However, it was often the reward of a good fighter to be given his discharge—'*rude donari*'. He was then a *rudiarius*. In the case of a slave, it may be assumed that such honourable discharge carried freedom with it. In many cases the retired gladiator became an instructor in a gladiatorial school. He might, if he wished, fight again in the arena—at his own price.[310]

9. Wild Animals[311]

The Roman's interest in wild animals was intense and catholic; he liked looking at them, he liked seeing them perform tricks and he liked watching them being hunted and killed. Wolves (the caged wolves under the Tarpeian rock today are a reminder, like the bronze *lupa* on the Campidoglio, of the miracle of Rome's foundation), bears, boars as well as deer, hares and wild goats were indigenous. More exotic animals brought the succession of Rome's imperial conquests to Rome's doorstep, visible evidence of the expansion of Roman power to the furthest corners of the inhabited world. Elephants were the first to be seen, four in 275 B.C. in M. Curius Dentatus' triumph after fighting Pyrrhus, from whom he had taken them at Beneventum. Then, after the second Punic war, came ostriches, leopards, dangerous animals whose general importation was forbidden by the Senate until perhaps 170 B.C., and lions, both first seen when M. Fulvius Nobilior triumphed for his victories in Greece in 186 B.C. The Romans, who had their own Cockney-type wit, called the elephants, which had been captured in Lucania, 'Lucanian cows'; ostriches were 'sea sparrows' and leopards 'African mice'.

The first hippopotamus and crocodiles were on show at Aemilius Scaurus' games in 58 B.C.; the first rhinoceros, an animal in whose existence there had been common interest a century earlier, and the first Gallic lynx, sent no doubt by Caesar from Gaul, at Pompey's games in 55. A giraffe (camelopard) was shown for the first time, a present perhaps from Cleopatra, in Caesar's great games of 46 B.C. Tigers were sent from India to Augustus, and the first tiger, tamed and caged, was exhibited in Rome in 11 B.C., at the dedication of the theatre of Marcellus; Claudius later exhibited four. There was no end to the novelties. By the time of Nero Romans had seen polar-bears in pools chasing seals.[312]

Animals exhibited at the shows increased all the time in number and variety. The menagerie collected at Rome by the emperor Gordian III for his Persian triumph and taken over by Philip and exhibited at his secular games in A.D. 248, the thousandth anniversary of the foundation of Rome, consisted—if the report is to be believed—of 32 elephants, 10 elks, 10 tigers, 60 tame lions, 30 tame leopards, 10 hyenas, 6 hippopotami, 1 rhinoceros, 10 wild lions, 10 giraffes, 20 wild asses and 40 wild horses.[313]

In view of the great interest that Romans showed in animals (they popularized the keeping of cats in western Europe), it is surprising that there was never a great zoo in imperial Rome. There was the example of Alexandria, where Ptolemy II had established one, and already by the end of the Republic, as has been seen,* a number of wealthy Romans had created exotic animal and bird preserves (*vivaria, leporaria, aviaria*) on their estates. At his Laurentine villa in the late Republic Q. Hortensius had an enclosed animal preserve fifty (Roman) acres large and in it there are was a raised spot on which he would dine with his guests. 'Orpheus was summoned, and arrived in costume, with cithara and horn. The sound of his horn attracted herds of deers, boars and other animals from the woods. It was every bit as good as a wild-beast show without leopards at the aediles' games.'†[314]

L. Cornificius, consul in 35 B.C., kept an elephant on which he rode out to dinner in Rome, and on which he rode home afterwards. An imperial herd of elephants, supervised by a *procurator ad elephantos*,

---

* See pp. 208 f. above.
† Almost as good in fact as Longleat with its lions in modern England.

was kept near Ardea, south of Rome, probably from the time of Julius Caesar (who mounted the Capitol in his triumph in 46 B.C. and rode home at night between lines of elephants holding torches in their trunks) or from the time of Augustus. Nero kept various wild and tame animals in the gardens of his Golden House, but they must have disappeared when Vespasian destroyed the Golden House itself. It was left to Byzantium to follow the example of the Ptolemies and to establish a great zoological garden.³¹⁵

In the Republic animals were exhibited and animal-fighting took place, at victory games given by successful generals and also (though not on the scale on which they were shown under the Empire) in the official *ludi* given by the aediles, for whom the expense of exotic entertainment might be expected to bring, as its dividend, a heavy vote when they stood as candidates for higher political office. So, to judge from the manner in which Cicero as governor of Cilicia in 51/50 B.C. was pestered by his young friend M. Caelius Rufus to secure and dispatch leopards to him in Rome ('The moment you receive news that I have been elected, get straight down to this business of leopards'),³¹⁶ it is likely that aediles took advantage of every influential connexion in the provinces that they possessed. Under the Empire the giving of such shows was increasingly the prerogative of the Emperor though, as the letters of Symmachus at the end of the fourth century show, in the late Empire rich men might give animal shows if they received permission.³¹⁷ Outside Rome Nero forbade the giving of such shows under their own patronage by imperial officials, allowing them to be given only under imperial patronage, whether by his procurators or by private individuals. They were, in the Empire, a part of *munera* not of the *ludi*, and on days when there were both animal fights and gladiatorial encounters, the animal fighting took place in the first part of the day—the *matutinum spectaculum*—before the midday break.

Animals were frequently exhibited in the theatre, the arena or the circus or in some other public place, for interest and entertainment alone, and with no thought of killing. The simplest exhibitions were of animals in cages—Augustus showed a tamed and caged lion in 11 B.C. and Martial writes of a caged bison whose flanks were worn bare by rubbing against the bars—or in other conditions in which the public was protected against the possibility of harm. Augustus showed a rhinoceros in the Saepta, a tiger on the stage and a vast snake in the Comitium. You might even see tamed wild animals without going to the theatre; Androcles, after his miraculous salvation, is said to have walked about the streets and to have looked into taverns with a collecting box in one hand and his lion on a lead in the other. If you dined with the emperor Elagabalus, you might be startled to find a lion or a leopard as your close neighbour at the dinner table, particularly as you had not been told that the animal was in fact perfectly house-trained.[318]

Great interest was taken in the tricks of performing animals. In Rome Plutarch witnessed a remarkable performance by a dog in the theatre of Marcellus on an occasion when the emperor Vespasian was a member of the audience. The dog appeared in a mime in which he was given food on to which had been poured what the audience believed to be poison. He ate it, exhibited hideous convulsions and fell down, to all appearance dead. He was picked up by the actors, carried about and laid down again, an evident corpse. Then, at the correct cue, he roused himself very slowly, rose to his feet, then frisked about, clearly in perfect trim. And so the illusion was created that what had been thought to be poison was in fact a sleeping draught.[319]

There were performing monkeys, which were dressed as soldiers and rode on goats or drove teams of goats harnessed to a chariot. Strabo describes a fascinating exhibition of crocodiles in a large pool, beside which a platform had been built, where they could sun themselves and be seen by the spectators. Skilled Egyptians from Tentyra, whose inhabitants paid cult to the crocodile and were never harmed by it, dived into the water, swam among the crocodiles and drew them up by nets on to the platform, to exhibit themselves.[320]

The elephant was probably the most popular show-animal of all. There were stories of its intelligence and of the seriousness with which it applied itself to its training (in particular of one elephant which was so humiliated by its own backwardness that it would go out alone at night and practise the tricks which it learnt much more slowly than its companions). A party of diners was set out in the arena, and trained elephants moved among them with such delicacy that they did not disturb the dinner. Aelian, in a fascinating panegyric of the elephant, describes a scene at Germanicus' games which was even more remarkable. Places were laid for dinner in the arena. Six male and six female elephants, costumed for their parts, entered, reclined in their places and ate and drank—all with ostentatious politeness, so as to give no impression of ill-manners or of greed. And elephants were miraculously skilled tight-rope-walkers, moving forward, moving backwards and even walking down a tight-rope from the extreme summit of the theatre to the ground.[321]

20

Lions were trained to play with hares, like cats with mice, picking them up in their jaws, dropping them and then catching them again, without ever doing them the slightest harm.

There were performing bears, which climbed poles and performed other tricks, popular favourites many of them and known by name to the public as, thanks to mosaic and other artists, some of them are known to us: Eirene (Peace), Simplicius (Frank). There were even tame seals which had been trained to answer when called by name.[322]

In the building of the amphitheatre at Pompeii between 70 and 65 B.C. there was little thought, evidently, of extensive wild-beast fighting, for there are no substructures (like those in the Colosseum at Rome) for the holding and release of wild animals. At Rome, however (always in improvised conditions, whether in the Circus or elsewhere), vast animal shows already had a century of history behind them.

There was a show of animals at the otherwise predominantly Greek Games of Fulvius Nobilior in 186 B.C. In 169 B.C. in the Circus Maximus there was a display of sixty-three leopards (the ban on whose importation had perhaps been lifted in the previous year), forty bears and also elephants, given by the aediles, one of whom was Scipio Nasica who later was to prevent the building of a stone theatre in Rome.*[323]

The end of the Jugurthine war facilitated extensive importation of lions from North Africa. A greater number than ever before were seen at the games of the aediles L. Licinius Crassus and Q. Mucius Scaevola in or just before 100 B.C., and a hundred lions (a gift, with hunters, from his friend King Bocchus of Mauretania) were hunted with javelins at the games given by Sulla in his praetorship a few years later. These were both famous games, which found their way into the history books. In his wildly extravagant games in 58 B.C. M. Aemilius Scaurus exhibited a hundred and fifty leopards (variae).[324]

Elephant-fighting was seen for the first time in the aediles' games of 99 B.C. and twenty years later elephants fought bulls.[325] At Pompey's games in the Circus in 55 B.C. which were planned naturally to be the games of all time with six hundred lions (Sulla had only showed a hundred) and over four hundred leopards (more than twice the number shown by Scaurus), the eighteen elephants came near to wrecking the whole show. They were hunted by men with javelins, fetched from Africa with the elephants for the purpose. One was killed by a direct shot beneath the eye. Another, forced to the ground, snatched the shields of its attackers and threw them into the air, like a juggler

* See above, p. 254.

throwing plates, to the delight of the audience, as if this was a rehearsed trick. But then the rest stampeded and made for the iron railing between the arena and the audience; they raised their trunks and cried, as if imploring mercy. Among the spectators terror for their own safety combined with a rush of pity to the heart, and they shook their fists angrily at Pompey. Was there not some affinity between man and this noble, clever beast? Had the elephants not been promised before they left Africa—and, in their intelligent way, understood the promise—that their lives would be spared and that they would return home in safety? Later, when Pompey was murdered on African soil, people were to say that his death was, in a sense, the elephants' revenge.[326]

For the Romans were always sentimental about elephants (of which they never made any considerable use in war). As Cassiodorus was to write some six centuries later in a profusion of artificiality, 'There is a sort of kingly dignity in the elephant's appearance and, while it recognizes with pleasure all that is honourable, it seems to despise scurrilous jests.'[327] It objected even more to being killed. The scene in 55 B.C. is no flourish of later historians' imagination; we have an account of it from Cicero, who was a spectator.

Pompey's—indeed all previous—games had to be eclipsed by those which Caesar gave in the Circus in 46 B.C. He might have thought it wise to dispense with elephants, just as he dispensed with leopards, about which there was no longer any novelty.[328] Instead, he showed elephant-fighting of a 'different kind, elephants carrying 'castles', from which armed fighters did battle with one another; also there was a tournament, in which two armies, each accompanied by elephants, fought in a mock battle. Forty elephants altogether were engaged.[329]

Thessalian bull-fighting was a novel feature of these games of Caesar. The Thessalians on horseback rode the bulls down; then grasped their horns and, by a quick twist, broke their necks. When the emperor Claudius showed bull-fighting later, the horsemen are described as jumping on to the backs of the exhausted bulls and bringing them to the ground by their horns.[330]

The last great show of animals given by a private individual was that of P. Servilius in 25 B.C.; he exhibited three hundred bears and three hundred leopards.[331] Such shows henceforth were given by the emperors, and the main interest of our sources lay in recounting the fantastic number of animals that were killed, as records were made and broken—3,500 in twenty-six *venationes* of Augustus; 9,000 killed in a hundred days at Titus' great games at the dedication of the Colosseum in A.D. 80; 11,000 animals killed at Trajan's Dacian triumph in A.D. 107, which lasted 123 days.[332]

Apart from the exhibition of animals, there were three different kinds of spectacle: armed men fighting animals, animals pitted against other animals, unarmed men and women exposed to starving vicious beasts.

The last was the killing by animals of men condemned for the most serious criminal offences—*noxii*.

No one can fail to be repelled by this aspect of callous, deep-seated sadism which pervaded Romans of all classes. In 167 B.C. L. Aemilius Paullus, victor in the third Macedonian war, had non-Roman deserters trampled to death by elephants and his son, the younger Scipio, who destroyed Carthage, had deserters and runaway slaves thrown to the beasts—'excellent measures for discipline, both of them', in Valerius Maximus' view. Four and a half centuries later a panegyrist claimed that Constantine, the first Christian emperor, achieved 'something lovelier even than his victory' when, 'for the pleasure of all of us' ('*ad nostrum omnium voluptatem*'), he had his German prisoners thrown to the beasts. Human bestiality was even made a fine art when a Sicilian brigand Selurus, 'the son of Etna', was caught and in the games at Rome placed on a model of Etna, which disintegrated, plunging him into a cage of wild beasts below. Strabo saw it.[333]

Normally the victim was tied to a stake—'*ad palum deligatus*'—on a small platform, wheeled out into the arena and there exposed to a starved beast. The owner of the villa at Zliten in North Africa was happy to have such an episode represented on one of his mosaics. This was the punishment which young Balbus inflicted in Spain on Roman citizens who offended him; the fate, in Petronius' *Satyricon*, of a steward who was detected in an intrigue with his mistress.[334]

The occasional romantic story does nothing to lighten the black horror—neither the sparing of Androcles by his friendly lion (with the crowd shouting for both to be given their lives) nor the report that Caracalla as a boy endeared himself to the audience by bursting into tears and averting his eyes rather than witness such killing.[335]

Animals shown at the games were of two kinds, wild or domesticated, *ferae* or *pecudes* (or *mansuetae*). They were 'toothed' (*dentatae*), like lions, leopards, bears or else they were grass-eating (*herbariae, herbaticae, herbanae*), like cattle, deer, pigs.[336]

There were two kinds of fight. In the first beasts contended against each other—elephants against bulls, for instance, a tigress against a lion, a rhinoceros against a variety of beasts; in the second men— *bestiarii* or *venatores*—contended with animals. Both are represented on the Zliten mosaics; there a bull is shown fighting a bear, while men fight bulls and hunt deer, wild asses and ostriches.[337]

The *bestiarius*, armed with knife or hunting spear (*venabulum*), fought one or more wild beasts. The issue was a simple one: his survival or theirs.

The picture of a contest of leopards against hunters armed with spears (from the late second or third century A.D.) has been preserved on a frieze of the Hunting Baths at Lepcis Magna in Tripolitania. Here is the archaeologists' vivid description of it:

Ten hunters, four of whom have their names inscribed beside them— Nuber, (V?)incinus, (L?)ibentius and Victor are engaging six leopards, the names of three of which, Rapidus, Fulgentius and Gabatius(?), are likewise extant. On the whole the hunters have the situation well in hand. But two are down, and Victor is about to collapse; his auspicious name, written twice beside him, has not saved him from disaster. All the men are dark-haired and swarthy. Most of them wear short, long-sleeved tunics of pink and mauve or blue, green and red, or red, or green, while Victor is naked, save for a white loin-cloth. The hunter who is dispatching Rapidus is wreathed with flowers.[338]

Fighting with beasts in this manner lacked the glamour of gladiatorial fighting; so we do not hear of free men who signed on voluntarily, like the *auctorati* among gladiators. This class apart, *bestiarii* were on all fours with gladiators, condemned to their dangerous life after criminal sentence in the courts or, if they were slaves, sold or consigned to trainers—though after the *lex Petronia* of A.D. 19 it was criminal for a master to consign a slave or for a trainer to accept him without the explicit consent of a court. In imperial Rome their training school was the *ludus bestiariorum*, the *ludus matutinus* established on the Caelian in the early Empire. For some the training held nothing but terror, and Seneca tells a revolting story of a German killing himself rather than face the arena. On the other hand, there were highly skilled fighters like Carpophorus at the time of Domitian, whose success inspired Martial to write a succession of epigrams; he speared a boar, a bear and a lion, and he killed a leopard with a far shot; he once killed twenty beasts in a single bout. Such men might be honoured and manumitted as a reward for their courage and success at the insistence of the admiring audience.[339]

There is a romantic story of a *bestiarius* who had once been an animal-keeper, and evidently a considerate one. Pitted against a lion and other beasts in the arena, he owed his life to the fact that the lion, recognizing him as an old friend, took his part and joined him in fighting the other beasts.[340]

The *venator*, the hunter, ranked higher than the *bestiarius*. Often men were brought over from Africa to stage the kind of animal-hunting which was their livelihood, shooting the animals from a distance with javelins, or hunting them down with the aid of hounds. It was in this way (and no doubt from a very safe position) that amateurs shot animals in public, not only men of social distinction and even women, but emperors themselves. Tiberius at the end of his life shot at a boar in 'camp games' at Circeii. Commodus, as a marksman, can have had few rivals in history:

Everybody was amazed by the accuracy of his shooting. Using arrows with curved tips, he shot at Moroccan ostriches, running as fast as their legs and flapping wings would carry them and, the tops of their necks severed by the force of the blow, they went on running, though decapitated, as if nothing had happened. A leopard charged and got its teeth into the hunter who challenged it, and was on the point of mauling him when Commodus at the vital moment struck it with his spear, killing it and saving its victim. A hundred lions were released from below ground. With a hundred shots he killed them all and there they lay, all over the arena, and people had plenty of time to count them and see that not one single shot had failed to gain its mark.[341]

An elaborate material setting was often given to the hunts, by trees and shrubs (temporarily planted), rocks and cascading water in the arena. The bucolic Corydon, a spectator of the games in Nero's amphitheatre, was startled (in Calpurnius Siculus' poem) when the ground opened to release not only wild beasts 'but also golden arbutes amid a sudden spray of saffron'. This, no doubt, was a Neronian touch.[342]

Though we hear once of a spectator being killed accidentally by a *retiarius* at gladiatorial games, we have no record of such mishaps during *venationes*. The greatest precautions against accidents must have been necessary in the improvised conditions in which such shows were given in the Republic. We have already seen what panic was caused at Pompey's games in 55 B.C. when the audience feared a break-out by the elephants. When Caesar gave his great hunting games in the Circus Maximus in 46 B.C., a canal ten feet wide and ten feet deep was constructed, separating the audience from the arena.[343] Calpurnius Siculus describes the measures taken in Nero's amphitheatre and these, it seems, were copied later in the Colosseum. The platform (*podium*) which surrounded the arena of the Colosseum, and above which the spectators' seats rose, was thirteen feet above ground level. At ground level between it and the arena itself was a wooden barricade from which at regular intervals rose the tall masts for the awning. On these masts at a certain height were fixed elephant tusks, from which strong netting hung. As an additional precaution in Nero's amphitheatre there was an ivory cylinder, which rotated easily on its axis, at the foot of the *podium*, so that an animal which broke through would be frustrated if it tried to climb over it to reach the *podium*. Similar devices must have been employed when the games took place in the Circus after Nero had filled in Caesar's canal or indeed, as happened often outside Rome, when they were held in a theatre.[344]

However, there were also the shots of the hunters, the javelins and the arrows; and there is no means of knowing why these seem never, when fighting was at the edge of the arena, to have endangered the spectators.

There can be no doubt of the immense popularity of the *venationes*, though they did not outshine chariot-racing in popularity in Rome, as they evidently did in Syria, of which Libanius wrote: 'People like racing, as you know, and they enjoy stage shows, but nothing attracts them as much as men fighting animals; escape from the beasts seems beyond the bounds of possibility, yet through sheer intelligence the men succeed in mastering them. The crowds go off to the other games early in the morning, but for the wild-beast shows they queue up all night.'

There were protests from the sensitive—from gentle Plutarch, who hated the idea of killing animals; from Cicero, who wrote, 'How can there be any pleasure for a civilized being in the mangling of a weak man by a powerful beast, or in the transfixing of a splendid beast by a hunting-spear?' There were other Romans whose macabre sense of humour has left its record—in a *graffito* at Pompeii of a *bestiarius* prodding a reluctant lion—if that is what the animal is meant to be—with a long spear, to induce it to interest itself in the proceedings (pl. 2b); in a mosaic from El-Djem (Thysdrus) in Tunisia (pl. 15a) depicting the lunch-time interval on the arena or perhaps the stables on the night before a show. In the spectators' seats a hilarious drinking party is in progress; in the arena there are bulls, enjoying a siesta, with a slave entreating the topers to make less noise: '*SILENTIUM, DORMIANT TAVRI*', 'Less noise: don't wake the bulls.'[345]

Just as in modern battle great numbers of men are required in the rear in order to support those in the fighting line, a vast organization lay behind the showing and hunting of animals in the Roman games. Few provinces of the empire were unaffected. First of all the animals had to be caught; then they had to be transported; finally they had to be in good trim when they were let loose before the spectators.

Elephants came from India or, more commonly, from Abyssinia and northern and central Africa (the African elephant being larger than the Indian, not smaller, as Pliny mistakenly thought).[346] Lions and leopards (to which last the Romans gave a variety of different names: *Libycae ferae, Africanae bestiae, variae, pantherae* and *pardi*) were brought from North Africa, whose inhabitants were encouraged to believe that their capture was a benefit to farmers, and also, more expensively, from Syria. Bears came from North Africa and also from central and northern Europe, the Balkans and Italy itself. Tigers were brought the long way from N. Persia, India or the Caucasus. When Symmachus was collecting animals for his son's games in A.D. 393 and 401, he got horses from Spain, hounds (including Irish wolfhounds, *Scottici canes*, which were very popular) from Britain, lions and leopards from North Africa and crocodiles from Egypt.[347]

Animals were trapped, caught in pits (elephants, lions and leopards) or driven by numbers of heavily-armed hunters into nets or cages.[348] This might, no doubt, sometimes be an army exercise on the frontiers; but in the main it was a work of private enterprise on the part of hunters, who sold the animals to animal-dealers. These dealers in turn handed the beasts over to transporters. Some, like elephants, ostriches, antelopes and bison could travel loose, roped or chained and under close supervision of keepers; others, like lions, leopards, crocodiles, were boxed or in cages. In the mosaics of Piazza Armerina in Sicily (pl. 14b) we have splendid representations of the animals being taken aboard in Africa for shipping across the Mediterranean.[349]

At every stage of the journey precautions had to be taken to prevent any of the animals from escaping. There is the story of a sculptor who was making a model of a caged lion which had been landed at the docks in Rome, when he was attacked and nearly killed by a leopard which had escaped from a neighbouring cage. On the other hand, the simple Megarians in Greece could hardly blame anyone but themselves for their disaster in 48 B.C. In their city, which was then under attack by troops in Caesar's interest, were a number of caged lions, which must have started their journey to Rome from Syria for C. Cassius' prospective aedilician games before the civil war broke out. When the Caesarian troops were on the point of breaking into the city, the Megarians let the lions out of their cages, expecting them to attack the invading troops. Instead they made for easier victims, the Megarians themselves.[350]

A duty was payable on the import of animals like lions and leopards to Italy.[351]

After this the animals had to be held, properly fed and kept in good trim for the show. Symmachus' crocodiles had to be exhibited a second time and killed in something of a hurry; they had refused to eat for fifty days, and had little fight left in them. Worse still was the fate of the man from Plataea in Greece in Apuleius' *Metamorphoses*. The bears which he had secured at great expense died in the hot weather before the games started.[352]

In Rome the emperors had a *vivarium*, a holding place, for the animals between their arrival and the show. It was outside the Porta Praenestina. Here the animals were in the hands of *magistri*, who prepared them for the shows.[353] The last stage on their long journey to extinction was when they were taken in their cages to the Colosseum. There they required more expert attention; they had to be smoked out of their cages and driven along the passages into the arena itself, to face the crowds and the noise, by which at first they were terrified. If they were employed to kill criminals, starvation was their goad and, after the carnage was over, men had the difficult business of rounding them up and driving them back to their cages, largely by the temptation of water, for they were by that time tortured by thirst.

If they were being released for a fight, their tempers had to be roused, perhaps by the whip. Straw dummies were thrown before the bulls, which tossed them in growing anger.[354] Then at last they faced other beasts which had already suffered like themselves, or else the *bestiarii* and *venatores*, the last in the long chain of men who had dealt with them from the moment when the trappers and the hunters had caught them in their native habitats. From capture to death they entailed a vast extravagance both in highly skilled manpower and in money.

Of the men who made their living from handling beasts for the shows, the most skilful and interesting were those who trained performing animals. The best animal-trainers came from Egypt, particularly from Alexandria. Seneca writes of small Ethiopian boys who could make an elephant kneel and walk the tight-rope.[355]

10. The Races

With the horses, we return from *munera* to *ludi*.*

The empire-wide Roman passion for chariot-racing, nowhere more exuberant than in Rome itself, has none of the grim overtones of gladiatorial and wild-beast fighting, even if it was stigmatized just as sententiously by pagan and Christian writers and, indeed, is stigmatized by modern historians of ancient Rome. It was a living interest and excitement which bound together men and women of all classes. Together with the stage and gladiators, horses were the only subject, according to Tacitus, about which young men conversed freely with their tutors. But not the young Marcus Aurelius who, in giving thanks that he was not as other men were, praised his tutor for the fact that he was not a partisan of the Greens or of the Blues any more than he was a *parmularius* or a *scutarius*.[356] As a general rule, however, emperors enjoyed racing as much as did the meanest of their subjects.

In the Republic drivers of chariots (*aurigae*, *agitatores*) competed under either of two colours, as white (*albus*, *albatus*) or as red (*russatus*) and rivalry between the colours was already fierce soon after 77 B.C. when at the cremation of Felix, a driver of the Reds, a supporter threw himself on the funeral pyre. The supporters of the Whites declared that he was out of his mind at the time, overcome by the smell of the spices burnt at the cremation.[357]

Since no republican writer mentions 'factions' (official organizations of the colours), the provision of horses, as well as of chariots and drivers, was seemingly left under the Republic to the initiative of the magistrates responsible for the races, and Augustus allowed even senators to contract for supplying horses.[358] In the Empire very rich men—like Symmachus at the end of the fourth century—may have sought *réclame* by providing their own horses; but the great organizations, the *factiones*, of the four colours—green (*prasinus*), blue (*venetus*), red and white—came into existence in the early Empire no doubt because they suited the convenience of magistrates responsible for the races as well, probably, as improving the standard of racing itself.

Domitian added two new factions, the purple and gold, which were short-lived. At the end of the third century the Reds and Whites, while racing under their own colours, seem to have amalgamated organizationally with the Blues and the Greens respectively.[359]

* See above, p. 248.

The faction, once organized, embraced all aspects of racing–owner, stable, trainer and driver. It was housed in a great building, probably below the Capitol, near the Circus Flaminius,[360] and presumably it also had stables outside the city. It was a large organization, under the control of a *dominus* or of *domini* in partnership. These were evidently business managers of great talent; they might be of equestrian rank, they might be men who had once been drivers.[361] The staff of a faction included numbers of highly skilled specialists, for the organization bought and owned its own race horses; it must constantly have commissioned new chariots and have seen that its chariots and their equipment were in first-class order; and it was in the market the whole time for the best drivers, who were either brought to Rome from the provinces or else were slaves or freedmen. Some must have started as stable-boys and have been trained because they showed promise; we know of a famous driver who started his racing at the age of thirteen. Others, already trained, will have been bought, often from rival factions.[362]

A vast staff was employed by each of the factions—buyers, trainers, doctors, horse-doctors, harness-men, grooms—mostly slaves and freedmen. There were also clerks and club-servants, for the building had its social amenities. The emperor Gaius dined more than once in the stables of the Greens. So we are not surprised to find a *cellarius*, a club-steward, among a faction's employees.[363]

The extent to which these factions were under imperial supervision and depended on imperial financial subvention is uncertain.

Horses were not raced below the age of five, according to the elder Pliny; but Columella says that three-year-olds raced.[364] The best horses came from the provinces of the Empire, in particular from Spain and from North Africa. In a surviving list of victorious horses, out of seventy-one whose provenance is given, fifty-two were African, together with three Moorish and two from Cyrene; three of the seventy-one were Greek.[365] They were brought to Italy by sea. A mosaic from Tunisia shows three horses, Ferox, Icarus and Cupido, on a horse-transport whose technical name, *hippago*, appears twice on the mosaic, in Latin and in Greek.[366]

Good horses were also bred in Italy itself, in Lucania and Apulia in the south. The only stud-owner we know by name in this part of the world was not an attractive character. The handsome son of a banished father, banished himself by Gaius as a suspected paramour of the emperor's married sisters, he earned a living for a time as a fisherman in

Greece. Allowed by Claudius to return on condition that Claudius never set eyes on him, he started business as a horse-breeder in Apulia. Here Nero met him, caught his enthusiasm for horses and, disastrously, appointed him Prefect of the Praetorian Guard in Rome. He was Ofonius Tigellinus.[367]

The magistrate in charge of the races approached the managers of the factions and entered into a contract for the supply of horses, chariots and drivers for the Games. In the year of Nero's accession the prices asked were so outrageous that the responsible magistrate staged a sensational protest. He prepared to put on chariots drawn by trained dogs. The Reds and the Whites were prepared to accept these extraordinary conditions, but the Blues and the Greens refused. At which point Nero intervened. Horses made their appearance and he paid the bill himself.[368]

There were races of two-horse chariots (bigae), in which the novices among the charioteers competed[369]; of four-horse chariots (quadrigae), which were the most common; also, less often, of chariots drawn by three horses (trigae) or by six (seiuges) or even eight or ten, octoiuges, decemiuges.[370]

The first race of the day, following the opening procession of religious images and magisterial dignitaries (the pompa) was called the 'a pompa', and was one in which only experienced drivers competed because the horses were apt to be nervous after the procession. There were races for horses which had never raced before (equorum anagonum) and occasionally a race pedibus ad quadrigam, in which the chariot raced with two men up and, as soon as the driver crossed the finishing line, his companion had to sprint once round the course. Victory went to the chariot whose runner came in first.[371]

There were twelve starting boxes (carceres), six on either side of the gate above which the starter sat, set in a curve so that no box had an unfair advantage over any other, though, even so, a middle stall was thought better than an outside one. When there were four colours, the race was for one, two or three chariots from each faction. In the first case the starting boxes on the right were used, in the third case all twelve. The drivers cast lots for boxes at the start. The chariots were held back by a rope stretched across the front of all of them.[372]

The charioteer stood erect, a striking figure in his distinctively coloured tunic, with whip and knife (in case of a crash, when he could only save himself by cutting the traces.) Once the race started, he would be extended almost horizontally over the horses. The heads of the nervous and excited horses were held by grooms 'who talked to them to calm and encourage them.' The starter, a consul or praetor in Rome, held up, then dropped, a napkin. A trumpet sounded. The horses were off.[373]

> *Ut cum carceribus sese effudere quadrigae,*
> *addunt in spatio, et frustra retinacula tendens*
> *fertur equis auriga neque audit currus habenas.**

The chariots raced down one side of the *spina*, keeping it on the left, turned at the *metae* and raced back on the other side. An egg was lowered and later also a dolphin, to mark each lap as it was accomplished.[374] There were seven laps, a distance of roughly five miles (8·4 kilometres); a race lasted about quarter of an hour.

The trickiest moments were at the turn; that was why the best horse ran on the inside, on the left of the team. It was here that the driver's skill was demonstrated; he must not take the turn too wide[375] and allow the chariot behind him to come up and occupy the inside place, with its advantages, if the driver was skilful, at the following turn.

There were a variety of other skills: to crowd opposing chariots into one another in the hope of causing a collision; and, the problem of every jockey, to know when to hold his horses in and when to extend them, for victory was won more often than not *septimo spatio*, on the home stretch in the last lap, 'the driver's happiest hour.'[376]

From Sidonius Apollinaris in the fifth century we have a splendidly vivid account of a race of four *quadrigae* each of a different colour, running as two competing teams.† Consentius (our hero) was in fourth place on the outside, his partner in the lead in the inside station. But the leader drove his horses too hard and at the fifth turn they were exhausted; so he pulled out. This left the two opponents in the lead. The foremost one of the two, however, took the turn at the end of the sixth round too wide, which gave Consentius the chance of slipping in to the gap and snatching the lead. One of his adversaries then tried to foul him by forcing a collision, but he was not skilful enough and only succeeded in crashing his own chariot, which left Consentius an easy winner.[377]

---

* Virgil, *Georg.* 1, 512–4: 'As when the chariots burst from the stalls and meet on the course, the driver, vainly seeking to hold back his team, is carried away by them and the chariot heeds not the reins.' Cf. Horace, *Sat.* 1, 114–6.

† See above, p. 314, on the ultimate amalgamation of the colours.

Mosaics show men on foot on the course (pl. 16a). They were, presumably, the *hortatores* of each Faction, shouting encouragement to the chariots of their several stables, using the Greek word, *Nica*[378] ('Win').

Each race was for an advertised sum of prize money, up to sixty thousand sesterces, and there were second, third and fourth prizes according, presumably, to the number of chariots racing in any event.[379] When two or three chariots competed from each stable, they evidently raced, as in the race which Sidonius Apollinaris described, as a team and not as individuals. There were a number of technical terms, understood by all Romans, of whose meaning we cannot be certain, for different kinds of victory: '*occupavit et vicit*' (perhaps meaning that he led from the start), '*successit et vicit*', '*praemisit et vicit*', '*eripuit et vicit*' (perhaps, he won on the post[380]).

The race was *a carceribus ad calcem*, from the starting boxes to a finishing line at the same end of the circus as the start. The result could be a dead-heat, indicated by the victor as '*ad album*', '*ad venetum*' or whatever the colour was with which he dead-heated.[381] Few more remarkable races can ever have been seen than one in which the driver was thrown before the chariot was out of the starting-box, but the horses none the less brought the chariot in, to win.[382]

There may have been stewards of the course (see pl. 16a). Charioteers evidently, as in the race described by Sidonius Apollinaris, sometimes endeavoured to crowd their adversaries and to force them into a collision. And it appears that there were cases when, in response to a general outcry by the spectators, a race was stopped and re-run; the drivers were *remissi* or *revocati*.[383] There were also cases such as are sometimes suspected in racing today, when a driver deliberately held back his horses so as not to win. He might be bribed to do this or he might, in his prudence, think it wise to allow a rival who had powerful, in particular, imperial, support, to win.[384]

A more intangible hazard for a charioteer, as the vogue of magical practices increased in the Roman Empire, was that a rival or a supporter of a rival colour might have 'poisoned'—that is to say, doped—his horses or might have taken the opportunity to cast a harmful spell on him by means of an inscribed tablet, of the sort of which many specimens survive. 'I adjure you, demon, whoever you are, and I demand of you this day, from this hour, from this moment, that you torture with pain and kill the horses of the Greens and the Whites, and that you kill and bring into collision the drivers Clarus, Felix, Primulus and

Romanus.' On the other hand, if he was himself consistently successful, his jealous rivals were likely to accuse him of practising magic arts. The use of magic against charioteers was forbidden by an ordinance of the year A.D. 389.[385]

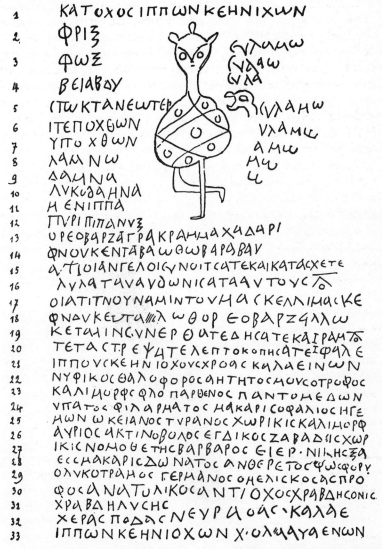

1   ΚΑΤΟΧΟϹΙΠΠΩΝΚΕΗΝΙΧΩΝ
2   ΦΡΙΖ
3   ΦΩΞ
4   ΒΕΙΑΒΟΥ
5   ϹΠΩΚΤΑΝΕΩΤΕ
6   ΙΤΕΠΟΧΘΩΝ
7   ΥΠΟΧΘΩΝ
8   ΛΑΜΝΩ
9   ΔΑΜΝΑ
10 ΛΥΚΩΔΑΗΝΑ
11 Η ΕΝΙΠΠΑ
12 ΠΥΡΙΠΙΠΑΝΥΖ
13 ΥΡΕΟΒΑΡΖΑΓΡΑΚΡΑΗΔΑΧΗΔΑΡΙ
14 ΘΝΟΥΚΕΝΤΑΒΑΩΘΩΒΑΡΩΒΑΥ
15 Α ΤΟΙΑΝΓΕΛΟΙϹΝΟΙΤϹΑΤΕΚΑΙΚΑΤΑϹΧΕΤΕ
16 ΛΥΛΑΤΑΝΑΥΩΝΙϹΑΤΑΑΝΤΟΥϹΤΩ
17 ΟΙΑΤΙΤΝΟΥΝΑΜΙΝΤΟΥΗΑϹΚΕΛΛΙΜΑϹΚΕ
18 ΦΝΑΥΚΕΝΤΑΜΛΩΘΟΡ ΕΟΒΑΡΖΩΛΛΩ
19 ΚΕΤΑΛΙΝϹΥΝΕΡΘΥΑΤΕΔΗϹΑΤΕΚΑΙΡΑΜΤΩ
20 ΤΕΤΑϹΤΡΕΨΩΤΕΛΕΠΤΟΚΟΠΗϹΑΤΕΙΦΑΛΕ
21 ΙΠΠΟΥϹΚΕΗΝΙΟΧΟΥϹΧΡΟΑϹΚΑΛΛΕΙΝΩΝ
22 ΝΥΦΙΚΟϹΘΑΛΟΦΟΡΟϹΑΗΤΗΤΟϹΜΟΥϹΟΤΡΟΦΟϹ
23 ΚΑΛΙΜΟΡΦϹΦΛΟΠΑΡΘΕΝΟϹ ΠΑΝΤΟΗΕΔΩΝ
24 ΥΠΑΤΟϹ ΦΙΛΑΡΗΑΤΟϹ ΗΑΚΑΡΙϹΟΦΑΛΙΟϹΗΓΕ
25 ΗΩΝ ΩΚΕΙΑΝΟϹΤΥΡΑΝΟϹΧΩΡΙΚΙϹΚΑΛΙΜΟΡΦ
26 ΑΥΡΙΟϹΑΚΤΙΝΟΒΟΛΟϹΕΓΔΙΚΟϹΖΑΒΑΔΙϹΧΩΡ
27 ΙΚΙϹΝΟΜΟΘΕΤΗϹΒΑΡΒΑΡΟϹ ΕΙΕΡ · ΝΙΚΗϹΖΑ
28 ΕϹϹΗΑΚΑΡΙϹΔΩΝΑΤΟϹΑΝΘΕΡΕΤΟϹΨΩΦΟΡΥ
29 ΟΛΥΚΟΤΡΑΗΟϹ ΓΕΡΗΑΝΟϹΟΗΕΛΙϹΚΟϹΑϹΠΡΟ
30 ΦΟϹΑΝΑΤΟΛΙΚΟϹΑΝΤΙΟΧΟϹΧΡΑΒΔΗϹΟΝΙϹ
31 ΧΡΑΒΔΗΛΑΥϹΗϹ
32 ΧΕΡΑϹΠΟΔΑϹΝΕΥΡΑΟΑϹ · ΚΑΛΛΕ
33 ΙΠΠΩΝΚΕΗΝΙΟΧΩΝ Χ · ΟΛΩΜΑΥΑΕΝΩΝ

At the end of the race the prizes were awarded, a palm for the victor and substantial sums of money. When Nero's father, a man without grace or integrity, presided as praetor at the games, he made a point of holding back a part of the money for himself and the scandal was such that the *domini* of the four factions combined in making a public protest.[386]

Probably from the time of Gaius, there were regularly twenty-four races (*missus*) on each day. Previously the number had been smaller. Allowing quarter of an hour for each race, an interval between races and a lunch-time break, the programme would occupy a whole day. Later in the Empire, when two festival days coincided, forty-eight races were run, but it is clear that the races on these occasions must have been over a shorter distance than the normal seven laps.[387]

What of the spectators, the quarter of a million people in the circus, and of the public at large? They were the subject of one of the younger Pliny's stuffiest letters[388]:

The races are on, a spectacle which has not the slightest attraction for me. It lacks novelty and variety. If you have seen it once, then there is nothing left for you to see. So it amazes me that thousands and thousands of grown men should be like children, wanting to look at horses running and men standing on chariots over and over again. If it was the speed of the horses or the skill of the drivers that attracted them, there would be some sense in it—but in fact it is simply the colour. That is what they back and that is what fascinates them. Suppose half way through the race the drivers were to change their colours, then the supporters' backing will change too and in a second they will abandon the horses on which a moment earlier their eyes were fixed and whose names they were shouting. Such is the overpowering influence of a single worthless shirt, not only over the crowd, which is worth less than a shirt anyhow, but over a number of serious men.

When I think of their wasting their time so insatiably over such tedious, repetitive inanity, I derive not a little enjoyment from the fact that such enjoyment is not one to which I am a slave. These are days which other people squander on utterly idle activity (*otiosissimis occupationibus**), but days when I am at my happiest, occupying my leisure (*otium meum*) with a pen.

Just as in England there are numbers of people who, without having any personal interest in either Oxford or Cambridge, habitually favour either the Dark Blues or the Light Blues in the Oxford–Cambridge Boat Race, so most of the people in Rome and Italy and in districts of

* See p. 145 above on the significance of these words.

the Empire where circus-racing was popular, were confirmed supporters of one particular colour, though Rome never went to the extreme which was reached in Byzantium later where the Blues and the Greens were, in effect, rival political parties, fanatically opposed to one another. In Rome the two most popular colours and the chief rivals were the Blues (whom Vitellius and Caracalla backed, and whom Domitian particularly disliked) and the Greens, who evidently enjoyed the greatest popularity.[389] The supporters of the Greens ranged from a whole gallery of emperors at one extreme (Gaius, Nero, L. Verus, Commodus and Elagabalus) to Trimalchio's cook at the other[390]; and Juvenal states that, in the prevalence of ensuing depression, a defeat of the Greens was like a second Cannae.[391]

It would be a mistake, however, to think that the general public was not greatly interested both in the horses themselves and in its favourite charioteers. This interest both among the wealthy and the poor was one of the features of Roman life in the fourth century which struck Ammianus Marcellinus most forcibly—and not particularly favourably —when he visited the city.[392] And there are abundant references in ancient literature to the wide knowledge which people possessed of the pedigrees of outstanding horses.[393]

Bets (*sponsiones*) were laid, and this was an evident attraction of the races. People betted both off the course—Trimalchio's cook wanted to lay a bet with his master in favour of the Greens—and, whether or not there were bookmakers, on it. Ovid's young ladies and their bucks both had their flutter.[394]

For such young people were among the keenest of the racegoers. The young man liked to be seen in the company of a pretty girl, well dressed; and at the races men and women were allowed—as at the theatre and the amphitheatre they were not—to sit together. Ovid has given us a delightful account of a day at the races spent by a young man who had no interest in racing at all, with his *inamorata*, who was an enthusiastic race-goer. He had eyes only for her, she only for the horses. But he did his best, giving her aggressively male protection by rebuking the man behind for sticking his knees into her back, her neighbour on the other side for giving her too little room.[395]

People at a distance from Rome were evidently anxious to have the earliest news of the winners. Pliny tells the story of a *dominus* who sent the results of the races to Volaterrae, his home town, by carrier-swallows, whose legs were marked with the victorious colour.[396]

At the start of their racing careers many charioteers were slaves, to whom success commonly brought freedom, whether or not as a result of popular acclamation by the spectators. (Hadrian once refused to respond to such an appeal and published his reasons; it was not for him to coerce the master to whom the driver, as a slave, belonged). Others came, or were brought, from the provinces of the Empire. They were, like gladiators and actors, *inhonestae personae*, and Tertullian emphasized the paradox of their social position, popular heroes, yet at the same time men whom the law held in the lowest esteem. Some traded on their popularity to behave arrogantly and offensively in public. Some were spoilt—and often subsequently ruined—by the dangerous friendship of emperors like Gaius who, after a party, once gave two million sesterces as a going-away present to a charioteer called Eutychus. Others were universally popular, without popularity going to their heads, like Scorpus (pl. 16b), whose death Martial lamented in a couple of poems.[397]

The successful driver made a fortune—ten bags of gold in an hour, by contrast with the poor client's dole of a hundred farthings, according to Martial; a hundred times what a lawyer could hope to earn, according so Juvenal.[398] And inscriptions survive in confirmation, records of outstanding drivers, giving not only the names of their most successful horses, the number of times that they represented the various colours and the number of their victories, but also the prize money which they won for their stables, of which they naturally received a considerable share themselves.

P. Aelius Gutta Calpurnianus,[399] who erected his own monument on the Via Flaminia, won 102 victories (*palmae*) for the Whites, 78 for the Reds, 583 for the Blues, 364 for the Greens—1,127 in all. These included, for the Blues and Greens alone, one prize of 50,000 sesterces, twelve of 40,000 and twenty of 30,000. His leading horses when he raced for the Blues were all African; with one of them he won a hundred and five times.

Crescens, a Moor,[400] who started racing at the age of thirteen in A.D. 115 and died in A.D. 124 at the age of twenty-two, won a total of 1,558,346 sesterces in prize money.

In a monument which he erected at the age of forty-two near the Circus of Gaius and Nero in Trastevere, C. Appuleius Diocles, who also raced in the first half of the second century A.D. and probably started his *quadriga* racing at the age of eighteen, recorded a quite remarkable series of achievements. He raced over 170 times a year and in one year won a hundred victories. The total of his victories, first prizes alone, was 1,462—81 for the Whites, 216 for the Greens, 205 for the Blues and 960 for the Reds, the faction to which he finally became attached. He won prizes which totalled close on four million sesterces. He then retired to live at Praeneste (Palestrina), where a record of him survives in a dedication in his name to Fortuna Primigenia, erected by his son and daughter.[401]

There were always young men of the upper social class at Rome who protested against the fact that chariot-racing was a professional occupation, not a sport for amateurs. Sometimes, to the horror of respectable society, they managed to compete. It was more reprehensible still when an emperor like Nero appeared in public as a chariot-driver.[402]

In Caesar's games of 46 B.C., however, men of the highest social grading took part in races of *equi desultorii*, riding bareback (and without stirrups, for stirrups did not reach Europe until about 700 A.D.). This type of racing went back at least to the year 169 B.C. and may well have been respectable, for it is represented on certain moneyers' coins in the late Republic, presumably to record ancestral victories in such contests. It was not straight riding, as we know it, for the jockey had a pair of horses which were reined together and he vaulted from one to the other—in the circus, perhaps at the end of each round. The records of the Secular Games held by Augustus in 17 B.C. and the records of the Arval Brothers suggest joint programmes of chariot-racing and of this kind of bareback riding. Cicero says that a *desultor* ranked lower in esteem than the driver of a four-horse chariot, and Varro states that the horse which made a good mount for a *desultor* differed in points and training from a good chariot-horse. Otherwise literary references are few and there is nothing to suggest that such events were a significant feature in the Circus games. We have no inscriptions of *desultores*, such as we have of chariot-drivers. Why the Romans never raced horses in Circus games as horses were raced in Greek games and are raced today is an unanswerable question.[403]

There were other sporting events.

There were exhibitions of trick-riding, based in particular on the performance of the *desultores*, but by men who displayed even greater virtuosity. They stood erect on the back of one horse and then stepped lightly onto a second horse's back in full course, or they sank back and lay on the horse's back, a performance which is familiar to anybody who has ever visited a modern circus. A mosaic discovered in a cellar of the Palazzo Farnese shows eight horses, each ridden by a man standing on its back.[404]

There were occasional races on foot, held in the Circus and else-where. We have accounts of them under Augustus, in Claudius' cele-brations for the invasion of Britain in A.D. 44 and under Nero. The elder Pliny records the outstanding performance of a runner who covered 160 Roman miles in a day and of a boy of eight who in A.D. 59 ran seventy-five miles between midday and dusk. And, as has been seen, there were boxing matches and wrestling bouts.[405]

11. Greek Games

Augustus established quinquennial games in honour of Apollo at his new foundation Nicopolis, to commemorate the victory of Actium, games which ranked equal in importance with the traditional games at Delphi, Olympia, Nemea and the Isthmus.[406] Such regularly recurrent games had already been established from time to time in the Greek-speaking countries of the eastern Mediterranean in honour of Roman proconsuls, as they had been established earlier in honour of Hellenistic kings; and others were to be established later in the Empire in honour of other Roman emperors. Augustus instituted similar games at Naples in A.D. 2. These were to be quinquennial in the Greek sense (celebrated every four years); they consisted at first of athletic and equestrian contests only, but after Augustus' death—perhaps in A.D. 18—musical competitions were added. These 'Italian' games—the *Italika Rhomaia Sebasta Isolympia*—enjoyed great repute from the start, attracting professional competitors from the Greek world, and they ranked in importance directly after the four great Greek games and the *Actia* at Nicopolis. They were patronized by Augustus himself and, indeed, attended by him very shortly before his death in A.D. 14. They were attended by later emperors also.

It was a novelty, however, when Augustus introduced such Greek games to Rome, in honour of Apollo—games which were repeated in his lifetime, but which seem not to have survived his death.[407]

Greek games were utterly different from Roman. In Greece the games (*agones*), held, each of them, every fourth year at one or other of the great religious centres, respected the tradition of centuries. Candidates competed in a variety of events for the prize, a laurel or a parsley crown, and the honoured title of *hieronica*, 'victor in the sacred games'.

Though, as has been seen, athletic events took place from time to time in Rome and were popular, and chariot racing was a familiar enjoyment, Nero broke with tradition in A.D. 60 in the wide variety of events which constituted his new games, the *Neronia*, at Rome. These games were *sacra*, like the great games in Greece, and their expense was a charge on the public treasury. They were to be celebrated in the summer every five—not, as in Greece, every four—years; and they were to consist, in the Greek manner, of competitions in singing, in instrumental music, in the recitation of original poems (Lucan was victorious with his '*In praise of Nero*', *Laudes Neronis*) and in original declamation. These events took place in Nero's freshly built amphitheatre. There were also athletic events, held in the Saepta in the Campus Martius, and chariot-racing in the Circus of Gaius and Nero, whose site was near that of the present Basilica of St. Peter. Certain of the events took place at night, in brilliant artificial light. Participation as a competitor, so far from involving 'infamy', was to be honourable, as in Greece it always had been, and open to the highest rank in society. Indeed the son of a consular is reported as competing in a wrestling bout against a Spartan girl.[408] The *Neronia* were given a status higher than that of the ordinary games, for the president, instead of being a praetor, was an ex-consul, chosen by lot. It was evidently considered smart for members of the audience to wear Greek dress.[409]

A great part of the programme of these games represented a cultural innovation out of keeping with Roman tradition and offensive to a great many Romans' taste. So there was plenty of criticism, which Tacitus has represented and embellished: competitions of this sort were degenerate, certain to corrupt the young—as if the young were not corrupt enough already. Liberal sentiment, however, approved: at least nobody would be out of pocket, for the public treasury was to meet the whole expense. The populace had mixed feelings. Why, they asked, were there no pantomimes? The fortuitous appearance of a comet was fastened on as inauspicious by the critics.[410]

Five years later in A.D. 65, soon after the dire punishment of the Pisonian conspirators, the games were held for the second and last time —for by 70 Nero was dead and Rome was ruled by a very different kind of man, Vespasian, who did not like music.

In 65 the Senate thought it prudent to offer Nero the prizes of victory in advance, before the competitions started, but that was no proper way in which to treat an artist. Nero competed, both as singer and as instrumentalist, his cithara being carried in formal procession by the two Prefects of the Praetorian Guard. He sang *Niobe*. This time, in his description, Tacitus concentrated not on the feelings of high society, but on the dilemma of those members of the audience who had come from the simple milieu of the Italian country towns. What they witnessed was something altogether outside their experience. Prodded by the soldiery who were stationed in the auditorium, they applauded nervously, often at the wrong times.*[411]

In A.D. 86 Domitian launched a similar project, to mark the rebuilding of the temple of Juppiter on the Capitol.[412] This was the *Agon Capitolinus*, or the *Capitolia*, games in the same Greek tradition, in honour of the Capitoline Juppiter, contests in literary creation and music, in athletics and horse-racing. The musical events took place in Domitian's new Odeum, the athletic events in his new stadium, on the site of which the present Piazza Navona is built (pl. 1a). The prizes were wreaths of oak. The programme was more extensive than Nero's. The poetical and oratorical contests were both in Greek and in Latin; the instrumental events covered a wide range and included musical accompaniment of singers. We have preserved on his funeral monument, for he died soon afterwards, the forty-three hexameter lines in Greek delivered extempore by a child of eleven, a freedman's son, at the third celebration of the *Capitolia* in A.D. 94 on a stock rhetorical theme, Zeus rebuking Helios for lending Phaethon his chariot. There were fifty-two candidates in the event, and the judges gave the boy a special commendation because he was so young. It was on this occasion that Statius competed without success in the Latin verse competition, to his great humiliation.[413]

Domitian's *Capitolia* survived his death. The rhetorical events and the races for girls were abandoned early, but the prizes for Greek and Latin poetry continued to bring the highest *réclame* to their winners. In 106 the competition in Latin verse was won 'by the unanimous verdict of the judges' by a boy of thirteen.[414]

The *Capitolia*, indeed, were still being held in the third century, for it was at their conclusion that the Praetorians killed the emperors Maximus and Balbinus in A.D. 238. Two years later, in 240, Gordian revived Nero's Greek Games, in honour of Minerva. The year was correctly chosen. On quinquennial reckoning from the foundation, it was the year for the thirty-seventh celebration.[415]

12. Tournaments and Displays

Apart from the ordinary spectacles and exhibitions so far described,

* A similar story is told of a recent performance of Beethoven's ninth symphony in the great Roman theatre of Aspendus, packed for the occasion largely by local peasants.

extraordinary displays were mounted on occasions of particular celebration. Under the Republic and from time to time under the Empire
after some outstanding military success the citizens lined the streets
to watch a triumphal procession. First came the cars carrying booty and
pictorial representations of the fighting—Pharnaces in hot flight and the
caption *Veni, vidi, vici* at Caesar's triple triumph in 46 B.C. Select
prisoners followed. Finally there was the triumphator himself, erect
on his chariot, his cheeks painted red, until he descended to climb
the Capitol on his knees. Under the Republic this was a general, under
the Empire the emperor himself—Claudius, for instance, in A.D. 44
after the invasion of Britain.*

On other occasions in the late Republic and in the Empire military
displays were given by young boys of good family who were fetched
from Greece or Asia Minor to dance the Pyrrhic dance, an exercise of
which even Plato had approved. This was one of the features of Julius
Caesar's triumph in 46 B.C.; it was repeated frequently under the Julio-
Claudian emperors, and later.[416]

More startling, while it lasted, was the military tournament given
by Roman boys of the highest social extraction, the *Lusus Troiae*.
In its remote, probably Etruscan, origins it has no connexion at all
with Troy. The word was properly *truia*, and meant a labyrinth.[417]
By Sulla's time it was the *Lusus Troiae*, which will have accorded with
his notion of Venus, mother of Aeneas, as his own special protectress
and Rome's.[418] Two squadrons (*turmae*), each perhaps of twelve
members, one of boys between the ages of twelve and sixteen, the
maiores, the other of boys under twelve, the *minores*, paraded in armour,
with helmets and lances, on horseback. They performed complicated—
labyrinthine—drill movements, and then fought a mimic battle.

This was a tough disciplining of the scions of the upper class which
had an immediate appeal for Octavian and for Agrippa. Performances
were given in 40, in 33 and in 29 B.C.[419] At some stage before 19 B.C.,
when Virgil was still alive, Augustus evidently decided to reconstitute
the exercise, so that it should be performed by three *turmae* instead of
by two, and Virgil warmed to his task, describing the—quite fictitious
—origin of it all with young Priamus, Atys and 'handsome Iulus' as
the three youth-leaders in the fifth book of the *Aeneid*.[420] 'The folk of
Alba taught it to their sons; from Alba great Rome took it and preserved the fine tradition.'

* See Bibliography, p. 341, for a splendidly imaginative sixteenth-century picture of a
Roman triumph.

It was celebrated in 13 B.C. and again in 2 B.C., with the three grand-sons of Augustus leading each of the three *turmae*. However, fighting on horseback was a dangerous exercise for such young boys and when one was dangerously injured and Asinius Pollio's grandson broke his leg, Pollio protested in the Senate and his protest was evidently effective. If such exercises persisted, they were no longer performed in public and presumably they were performed on a gentler scale.[421]

There were other public tournaments given by the six *turmae* of Equites Equo Publico, the *Ludi Sevirales*. The participants were older men, capable of surmounting the hazards of their exercises, whatever those hazards were.[422]

Other displays were given before the public by a very different class of performer, on a very large scale, to mark significant occasions, such as military victories or the dedication of public buildings of importance.

In his great games in 46 B.C. Julius Caesar gave displays of troops in action, a thousand infantry against an infantry contingent as large, two hundred horsemen against another two hundred, and a mixed engagement of horsemen and cavalry. And in his celebration of the suc-cessful invasion of Britain, Claudius mounted in the Campus Martius a realistic re-enactment of the siege and capture of a British stronghold and the surrender of the British kings.[423]

More exciting still were the representations of naval battles, *nau-machiae*, whose participants were gladiators or prisoners condemned to death. Caesar had a great lake dug for the purpose in the Campus Martius for his games in 46 B.C.; it was filled in, because of plague, three years later. Augustus, to mark the dedication of the temple of Mars Ultor in 2 B.C., constructed a vast lake on the other side of the Tiber under the Gianicolo, between the Lungara and the Villa Lante, 536 metres long and 357 metres wide, with an island. Landscape gar-deners were employed to create a garden with trees round it, which survived long after the lake itself had evaporated.[424] Another lake, perhaps on the right bank of the Tiber, was constructed for Domitian, who watched a naval engagement on it in pouring rain.[425] On the false assumption that Narcissus and his contractors had been successful and that the Fucine Lake would be drained dry once the sluices were opened, Claudius decided to mark its last hours in A.D. 52 by a great naval fight, witnessed by Nero and himself in full military uniform and by Agrippina in a golden cloak.

Always in that age of extravagance there had to be novelty. So Nero's engineers designed his new amphitheatre in such a way that the arena could be flooded. Here was the very latest thing in applied science. The arena was cleared. The water poured in and formed a lake. There was a sea-battle. The water was drained away and, on firm ground, the gladiators resumed their fighting. The same devices were employed in the construction of the Colosseum and at its opening in A.D. 80 Nero's programme was repeated on Titus' instruction. Titus also held a second sea-fight in Augustus' lake across the Tiber.

The sea-fights were pages from the history books, with the victims in appropriate costume: in 46 B.C., Tyrians against Egyptians; in 2 B.C., Athenians against Persians (it was the battle of Salamis, and the Athenians won); on the Fucine Lake, Rhodians fought Sicilians. In Nero's amphitheatre the fight was between Athenians and Persians once more; in A.D. 80 between Corcyreans and Corinthians in the Colosseum and on Augustus' lake between Athenians and Syracusans.

Roman history was not without its own naval encounters. There were the battles of the first Punic war. There was Actium which, according to Horace, was once reproduced as a private enterprise by two brothers, one acting Octavian, the other Antony. Yet these were never represented on public occasions. Perhaps the wrong side might have won.[426]

An interesting problem arises, which is not easily answered. How were such great numbers of prisoners and condemned criminals available for slaughter in these mock battles when the occasion arose? There were three thousand in 2 B.C.; for Claudius' spectacle on the Fucine lake, nineteen thousand.[427]

13. Outside Rome

The citizens of Rome were not alone in their addiction to the theatre, the amphitheatre and the Circus. Their tastes were shared by the inhabitants of every city in Italy and in the provinces of the Empire.

Roman colonies in particular celebrated official *ludi* comparable, though on a far smaller scale, with the Roman *ludi*, on fixed days of the year, which it was the duty of the magistrates to arrange, with an official grant from the city treasury which they were expected to supplement from their own resources. At the games given by the *duumviri* of Caesar's colony Urso in Spain, for instance, the local treasury advanced 4,000 sesterces and each of the *duumviri* was expected to contribute at least another 2,000. The aediles for their games received 2,000 from the local treasury and were expected to contribute not less than 4,000 sesterces themselves.[428]

The duumviral games at Urso, which extended over four days, were given in honour of Juppiter, Juno and Minerva, and were either gladiatorial (*munus*) or theatrical (*ludi scaenici*); so were three of the four days of the aediles' games; the fourth, which was to be held in the Circus or Forum, and was presumably to consist of chariot-racing, was devoted to Venus. We know of similar regular games in honour of Apollo (Ludi Apollinares) at Pompeii, starting on July 5th, at which a certain A. Clodius Flaccus in his first duumvirate exhibited a procession (*pompa*), bull-fighting, *succursores*, three pairs of *pontarii*, amateur and professional boxers (*catervarii et pyctai*), games complete with entertainers, pantomime actors and the great Pylades—all at an expense of 10,000 sesterces; and in his second duumvirate he celebrated the Apollinares more lavishly still, in the Forum on the first day with a procession, bull-fighting, *succursores* and amateur boxers, on the second with sixty athletes and, jointly with his colleague, thirty-five pairs of gladiators, wild beast hunting, bull-fighting, boars, bears and other animals.[429]

We know of official games at Capua as early as 108 B.C., given by district-officers, because from 211 until 59 B.C. Capua was not a civic community with magistrates. There were three days of games at Antium (Anzio) from May 4th to the 6th, which Cicero's daughter Tullia insisted on seeing in 59 B.C. Inscriptions record such official games (*munus publicum*) at Fundi, Naples (four days of gladiatorial fighting), Grumentum and Caieta.[430]

With the Empire the number of official celebrations increased, to mark the Emperor's birthday and other notable days in the imperial calendar, just as they did in Rome. Iguvium (Gubbio) in Umbria created games in honour of the Victory of Caesar Augustus.[431] At Urso and, no doubt, elsewhere there were also official priestly *ludi*, like the most ancient celebrations at Rome. At Urso these were chariot races, *ludi circenses*.[432]

There was a restriction on the size of gladiatorial fighting in the municipalities, imposed no doubt by Augustus when he limited the number of times when gladiatorial shows might be given as part of the public games at Rome. When a municipality wished to exceed the prescribed limit, it had evidently to apply formally to the Senate in Rome. Paetus Thrasea chose to oppose such an application from Syracuse in A.D. 58, and was criticized for not moving motions of opposition on more important subjects. Pliny suggests in the *Panegy-ricus* that, before Trajan's benign rule, the Senate was flooded by such applications.[433]

The most important games of all were those given by the provincial high priests of the imperial cult, for instance by the Asiarch in the province of Asia. It seems that when he entered on office, he took over a whole troupe of gladiators for use in his official spectacles, keeping experts to deal with them (Galen, for instance, was medical officer to the establishment at Pergamum under five successive Asiarchs); he re-plenished it as necessary and in turn sold it off to his successor.[434] And we know of the obligations which fell on the priests of the imperial cult in Gaul, who likewise kept their own bodies of gladiators.[435]

Apart from obligatory *ludi* written into the charters of cities, like that of Urso, which it was the magistrate's duty to give, there were a far larger number of shows (*munera*) which a municipal magistrate or priest gave at his own expense because such generosity was expected of him. We have numerous inscriptional records, in the form of appre-ciatory dedications, of men who gave games in honour of their election to a municipal magistracy or priesthood, or to a municipal senate. There was, indeed, strong public pressure on men who achieved such local distinction to celebrate it by giving games. The priest at Theveste in North Africa 'who was the first man since the foundation of the city to give a show—six pairs of gladiators—in honour of his priesthood' no doubt set a precedent which his successors were con-strained to follow. In Apuleius' *Metamorphoses*, written in the second century A.D., there is the story of the man who celebrated his election to the chief magistracy in Corinth by giving superlative games, and who went up to Thessaly to procure outstanding wild beasts and gladia-tors for his show.[436]

As the Empire wore on, the financial strain of such official and semi-official games weighed more and more heavily on local magistrates, priests and town councillors (*decuriones*) and was one of the reasons for the increasing reluctance of men to accept public office. When the Senate at Rome passed a resolution on the proposal of Marcus Aurelius and Commodus in or soon after A.D. 177 to reduce the financial outlay on games in the provinces, the prosy senator, whose speech is recorded, said, 'At the news of this proposal the priests of your most loyal pro-vinces of Gaul met, rejoiced and talked. There was one who on his election to the priesthood had deplored the effect on his finances. He had turned over in his mind the possibility of an appeal to the Emperors.

Now he was the first to speak, in agreement with his friends: "Why think now of appealing? Our most reverend Emperors have removed the whole of the burden weighing on my estate. Now I *want* to be priest. Once I cursed the obligation to give games; now I grasp at the opportunity."'437

Games and shows were given spontaneously and under no legal obligation by a number of rich men, including Augustales, freedmen who constituted the colleges in charge of the imperial cult in cities of Italy and western provinces, and even, in vanity, by men who were not rich at all and who bankrupted themselves in the effort. They had at first to obtain the permission of the local town council (*decurionum decretum*) and, when this requirement was dropped, they required formal imperial approval, '*ex indulgentia*'. The decree inspired by M. Aurelius and Commodus required a strict scrutiny of the expenses of the games, to be conducted by officials of the imperial administration.438

A benefactor, whether in his lifetime or by his will, could either put down money for a single celebration of games or he could give or bequeath a capital sum to his municipality whose income after investment was to be devoted to the holding of regular games.439 Auximum received a legacy to enable it to buy six pairs of gladiators on alternate years and to put them to fight some time in May.440 In the north of Italy a man took every precaution in the second century A.D. in drafting his will when he left money for annual games 'to be held in due accordance with all laws, plebiscites and decrees of the Senate'.441 As governor of Bithynia Pliny wrote to Trajan about the legacy to the cities of Heraclea and Tium, to be spent at Pliny's discretion, either on public buildings or on the institution of quinquennial games in Trajan's honour.442

Local populations might show an indecent interest in such legacies— in that, for instance, of Horace's miser whose heirs, if they failed to record the size of his fortune on his tomb, were condemned to give a gladiatorial show with a hundred pairs of fighters and a vast feast to his townsfolk. It is recorded, indeed, that when a centurion, evidently a rich centurion, died at Pollentia, the populace held up the funeral until his heirs promised to put down money for gladiatorial games; news of which so incensed the emperor Tiberius that he sent troops to arrest the local senate among others for allowing such a scandalous thing to happen.443

Towards the end of the first century A.D. the younger Pliny, a most generous benefactor to his native Comum, when opening the public library that he had given to the city, took the opportunity of explaining why, instead of giving money for games, he had made the city a considerable gift, five hundred thousand sesterces, whose income was to be devoted, in accordance with current imperial policy, to children's allowances (*alimenta*) for poor parents.[444]

Where—chiefly from inscriptions from Italy and the north African provinces—figures of gifts and legacies survive, enabling us to calculate the expense of games given outside Rome, they vary very greatly indeed, and none reaches as high as the 400,000 sesterces which in Petronius' *Satyricon* 'our good Titus, who has just come into thirty-two millions, could spend on games which would perpetuate his name to eternity, and never feel the pinch'.[445] At Concordia at the north of the Adriatic a public legacy of three hundred thousand sesterces was to be spent partly on games and at Pisaurum (Pesaro) and Aeclanum in Samnium we know of games which perhaps cost 150,000 sesterces, at Pisaurum games held under the terms of a legacy every five years, at Aeclanum games lasting three days and, therefore, costing 50,000 sesterces a day.[446] From north Africa we have records of gifts as high as 200,000 sesterces (for a four-day display of gladiators and wild animals), some of a few thousand (as at Iguvium in Italy the sum spent was 7,750 sesterces) and some even of a mere few hundreds.[447]

It seems possible that outside Rome, even when games were given by a benefactor, there may have been a charge for admission, at least to those who neither belonged to the plebs nor held a position which entitled them to official seats. An inscription from Cirta in north Africa, probably of the third century A.D., records the dedication of a statue by a benefactor 'from the takings for seats in the amphitheatre at the show which he gave.'[448]

There were certainly other shows and games given by entrepreneurs for their own profit, at which the public was charged for admission. When the charms of one of his favourites failed, the young Vitellius sold him to a gladiatorial trainer who went round the towns giving shows. Juvenal refers to such men with scorn and one, of freedman ancestry (the snob Tacitus underlines the fact), was responsible for a spectacular catastrophe in the early Empire when, on marshy ground and without adequate safety precautions, he built a temporary amphitheatre for a gladiatorial show at Fidenac in A.D. 27. At the height of the spectacle the crowded stands collapsed and thousands of spectators were killed or maimed. This was judged to be the result of building on the cheap by a man of inadequate means, and the Senate decreed that for the future nobody with capital of less than four hundred thousand sesterces should be allowed to engage in this kind of enterprise.[449] The *munera assiforana* mentioned in the senatorial resolution of A.D. 177/80 about the expenses of games seem to have been shows which charged for admission, an *as* for a seat, and to have been given for a cost of less than 30,000 sesterces.[450]

In small places which did not possess theatres or amphitheatres temporary stands were put up for games as in the disastrous case of Fidenae. Neither Cremona nor Bononia (Bologna) seems to have possessed an amphitheatre in A.D. 69; or the soldiers of the vanquished Thirteenth would not have been put on to building them for the victory games of Vitellius' generals. The amphitheatre of Placentia, which was burnt down in the fighting earlier in 69, an object of great local pride 'because it held more people than any other amphitheatre in Italy', was presumably mainly a wooden building. In southern Latium Casinum (Cassino) owed its amphitheatre as well as the construction or restoration of its theatre to that splendid doyen of entertainment, Ummidia Quadratilla.[451]

But most great cities in Italy and in the provinces had their own permanent stone theatres, which in the absence of an amphitheatre were used for gladiatorial fighting and for the display of wild animals on a small scale, and indeed the finest surviving Roman theatres are from outside Rome—at Ostia, probably the oldest Roman theatre to survive, and at Beneventum in Italy; at Arles, Orange and Vienne in the south of France; at Timgad, Dougga and Sabratha in north Africa; at Aspendus in Asia Minor. In Britain there were theatres at St. Albans and at Canterbury (Durovernum). There were also, but more rarely, small theatres especially designed for the hearing of music, the most famous of which, still happily used for the purpose for which it was built, was the Odeon of Herodes Atticus under the acropolis at Athens. There were two in Gaul, at Lyons and Vienne.[452]

It was as easy to develop an intemperate enthusiasm for the theatre in the provinces as in Rome. In Africa this was the young Augustine's experience.[453]

There are remains of more than seventy amphitheatres in the Roman empire, and there were many more of which nothing remains. Striking survivals are those at Pompeii, Capua and Verona; at Arles, Nîmes and Trier. In Britain the shell of the amphitheatre at Caerleon survives.[454]

There were amphitheatres, like the one at Lyons, and theatres which were built and used in antiquity but which have left no traces. And there were others, we do not know how many, whose construction started in a fever of municipal pride and vanity but which, because of the inefficiency or corruption of architects or contractors, were never completed. A letter written to Trajan by the younger Pliny when he was governing Bithynia in the second century A.D. gives a horrifying list of abortive public building enterprises. At Nicaea, for instance, a theatre was built of bad stone on marshy ground. Ten million sesterces were spent—and then the project, in collapse long before completion, was abandoned.[455]

Alexandria had both an amphitheatre and a hippodrome (circus) at the time of Augustus; and there were evidently circuses in a great number of cities, whose remains have not survived, for instance in the Rhineland[456]; and, where there was space, there is likely in some cities to have been racing (as, for instance, at Pompeii there were other games) in the Forum itself.[457] It is hard to believe that there were no precedents in the ancient world for the excitement of the Palio in Siena.

Lyons, the most important town in Gaul, had, in addition to its surviving theatre and Odeon, both an amphitheatre and a circus.

As for capacity, the Odeon in Lyons held 3,000 and the theatre 5,700 until it was enlarged to hold just over 10,000.[458] The amphitheatre at Verona held about 30,000 people. In country and provincial towns, therefore, a far larger proportion of the local population had the chance of getting into the games than was the case in Rome.

The games in Campania were held chiefly in the spring and early summer months; in north Africa the climate is such that they could be held comfortably in winter.

Though there are records of *ludi scaenici* and of athletic contests,[459] the municipal games of which records chiefly survive were *munera*, exhibitions of wild beast fighting and of gladiatorial games. These come from Campania and, in unexampled profusion, from north Africa, whose mosaics and paintings give us the most vivid and plentiful illustrations of wild beast hunting and fighting that we possess.

As for gladiators, private gladiatorial establishments evidently continued to flourish in Italy and the provinces after the time, at the end of the first century A.D., when they appear to have been superseded in Rome itself by the great imperial schools. We have archaeological evidence of a gladiatorial barracks at Pompeii earlier than this in the courtyard of the great theatre, which was evidently converted to such use after the earthquake of A.D. 62.[460]

The number of gladiatorial engagements that took place on a single day was considerably smaller in the municipalities than in Rome; there seem normally to have been between five and ten a day.

Enthusiasm for gladiatorial fighting, which Rome had caught like an infection from the Etruscans, spread from Rome to the East. In about 175 B.C. Antiochus Epiphanes, the Syrian monarch, 'gave a gladiatorial show in the Roman style before an audience which felt more terror than enjoyment in watching something the like of which they had never seen before. Fights were repeated—sometimes to the death and sometimes not—and so people acquired the habit of watching them with pleasure, and in the case of most young men a fillip was given to their fighting spirit. So while at first the King had generally secured his gladiators ready-trained from Rome at very high prices, he was soon able to provide them locally from his own subjects.'[461] Under the Empire there were gladiatorial fights in the theatre of Dionysus at Athens and in the great cities of Asia Minor and of Syria they were immensely popular. So was chariot-racing and wild beast fighting. In the fourth century Libanius railed against such obsession.[462]

Wild beast fighting was extremely popular in north Africa where animals, particularly lions, leopards (*Africanae*), elephants, bears and ostriches were easily obtainable. In southern Italian towns the number of beasts exhibited was considerably smaller than at Rome. Bulls and boars (*herbariae*) and bears were easily obtainable; more exotic animals such as leopards were difficult and expensive to procure. Tigers, perhaps, were never seen in Italy outside Rome, and elephants must have been uncommon.[463]

Two stories illustrate the practical difficulties of anyone who wished to exhibit wild beast fighting in country districts where supply and transport was not as highly organized as it was for the shows at Rome. A friend of the younger Pliny ordered a number of leopards for a show which he was giving at Verona but, because of bad weather conditions, the animals did not arrive in time. And there is Apuleius' story of the man at Plataea in Greece who had advertised an extravagant *munus* of gladiatorial and wild beast fighting. In this case the bears, which had been billed as a special feature, arrived too soon. The summer heat of Boeotia was too much for them, and they were almost all dead before the show began.[464]

In the Greek East there was traditionally a greater interest in athletics than there was in Italy. There, of the great athletic Games, some survived from the ancient days of Greek independence, others were later, having their origins in the Roman Republic or Empire. In some cases there were races for women as well as for men. Ancient traditions survived by which victors at the great games were honoured, even pensioned, by their home towns, to the point where this sometimes became a heavy burden on public funds. An interesting letter of the younger Pliny records games of this type, a *gymnicus agon*, established by bequest with the sanction of the local authority at Vienne in Gaul, which a local magistrate cancelled on his own responsibility because of their corrupting influence. Trajan was every inch the Roman when, on appeal, he supported the magistrate's act. However, there are records of such games at thirteen places in the West.[465]

In Alexandria, where enjoyment of public entertainment was more intemperate even than in Rome and which was castigated publicly by Dio Chysostom in a not unhumorous speech for the kind of exuberance which is anything but uncommon among football spectators today, chariot racing was one mania; the other, which ran it close, was devotion to pantomime dancing and the mime, which was popular in other Egyptian cities and in the East generally.[466] One papyrus from Oxyrhynchus, indeed, of the second century A.D., contains fragments of two mimes. The first—complete with stage and musical directions, is typical of the early Greek romance and concerns the rescue of a young Greek woman by a naval expedition led by her brother from an Indian king who, with his companions, jabbers in a foreign tongue and is made drunk by the agency of the coarse *stupidus*. The second fragment, reminiscent of the fifth mime of Herodas, is about a rich woman whose advances have been rejected by her slave; having made arrangements for the execution of the slave and his lover (which are not carried out), she proceeds to arrange the poisoning of her tiresome old husband.[467]

Notices of forthcoming shows were painted on the bare walls of streets and, as the ash from the eruption of Vesuvius in A.D. 79 preserved so much of the streets and buildings of Pompeii against the erosion of time, the archaeologists have discovered and recorded, even where their skill has not been able to preserve, the appearance of the walls with their paintings and *graffiti* just as they were when the disaster occurred. Most of the notices are of gladiatorial and wild beast fighting; most of them announce that there will be a canopy and protection from the sun: '*Vela erunt.*'[468] A famous fighter is starred by name[469]: 'Felix will fight bears.' One very interesting notice gives the names of the gladiators who are to contest each bout with the previous record of each, and later, after the games were over, somebody has marked up the results: 3 killed, 6 spared, 9 victorious.[470]

Theatrical entertainment in Greece was largely supplied by troupes of strolling players, 'the artists of Dionysus', a company of whom were summoned to Rome from Greece in 167 B.C. The Parasites of Apollo, who have left many records in cities south of Rome, may have been similar. Though we have no evidence of actors from Rome appearing in other cities in Italy, it is to be assumed that they did this, indeed that they had to, to make a living.[471]

Local dignitaries (magistrates, priests, *decuriones*) occupied the best seats and careful provision to this effect was made in local charters, if we may judge from that of Julius Caesar's colony of Urso in Spain. After Augustus heard with annoyance that a Roman senator had not managed to secure admission to games at Puteoli, the Senate passed a decree that seats in the front row at all games and shows outside Rome must be reserved for senators, in case any were present and wished to attend.[472]

Rioting and disorder were liable to occur at public gatherings outside Rome, just as they occurred in Rome itself. At a gladiatorial show given in Pompeii in A.D. 59 by a disgraced Roman senator spectators from the neighbouring city of Nuceria were first abused, then set on, by the Pompeian section of the audience. A number of people were killed and the Roman Senate, after investigating the facts, banned the holding of public games and shows at Pompeii for ten years. A vigorous painting of the scuffle survives, found on the wall of a Pompeian house near the theatre in 1869 (see p. 338).[473]

Troops on service required entertainment like other men, and by a happy chance two inscriptions have survived from a military unit to give us the only evidence of amateur theatricals that we have from the ancient Roman world. The unit seems to have been a composite one of the Fire Guard (*Vigiles*) from Rome and of sailors from the fleet at Misenum. It was stationed, probably, at Ostia. There was a Director (aedile) and service men took the traditional parts. There were *archimimi*, rogues and buffoons, *stupidi* and *scurrae*. They seem to have performed on the Emperor's birthday, under Septimius Severus and under Caracalla.[474]

Syrian legionaries were addicted to the theatre as to most other dissipations and, when they were campaigning in the East, both Trajan and L. Verus sent to Rome for actors to come out and perform to the troops.[475]

BIBLIOGRAPHY

Where references to a book are frequent in the following notes, they are to the name or short title added in brackets.

GENERAL

J. P. V. D. Balsdon, *Roman Women*, London, 1962 New York, 1963 (*Roman Women*).

R. H. Barrow, *Slavery in the Roman Empire*, London, 1928.

J. Carcopino, *La Vie quotidienne à Rome à l'apogée de l'empire*, Paris, 1939. English translation, ed. H. T. Rowell, tr. E. O. Lorimer, *Daily Life in ancient Rome*, London, 1941 (Carcopino).

F. R. Cowell, *Everyday Life in ancient Rome*, London, 1961.

J. A. Crook, *Law and Life of Rome*, London, 1967.

F. M. de Robertis, *Lavoro e lavatori nel mondo romano*, Bari, 1963.

S. Dill, *Roman Society from Nero to Marcus Aurelius*, 2nd edition, London, 1905.

A. M. Duff, *Freedmen in the early Roman Empire*, Oxford, 1928.

L. Friedlaender, *Darstellungen aus der Sittengeschichte Roms*, 9/10th editions, rev. G. Wissowa, Leipzig, 1919–21 (Friedlaender). English translation of 7th edition, tr. J. H. Freese, A. B. Gough, L. A. Magnus, *Roman Life and Manners under the early Empire*, London, 1908–13; reprinted 1965 (Friedlaender, E. T.).

J. Gagé, *Les Classes sociales dans l'empire romain*, Paris, 1964.

P. Grimal, *Les Jardins romains à la fin de la République et aux deux premiers siècles de l'Empire*, Paris, 1943.

T. Kleberg, *Hôtels, restaurants et cabarets dans l'antiquité romaine*, Uppsala, 1957.

Ramsay MacMullen, *Soldier and Civilian in the later Roman Empire*, Harvard Historical Monographs, 1963.

J. Marquardt–A. Mau, *Das Privatleben der Römer*, 2nd edition, Leipzig, 1886 (Marquardt).

J. Marquardt–G. Wissowa, *Roemische Staatsverwaltung* iii, 2nd edition, Leipzig, 1885 (pp. 482–589, on the games, is by L. Friedlaender) (Marquardt–Wissowa).

U. E. Paoli, *Vita Romana*, Florence, 1940; very well illustrated. English Translation by R. D. Macnaghten, *Rome, its People, Life and Customs*, London, 1963.

Tutto su Roma antica, Forence, 1963, with superb illustrations.

W. Warde Fowler, *Social Life at Rome in the Age of Cicero*, London, 1908 (reprinted 1965).

W. L. Westermann, *The Slave Systems of Greek and Roman Antiquity*, Philadelphia, 1955.

THE ROMAN CALENDAR
PARTICULARLY CONCERNING FESTIVALS AND GAMES

A. Degrassi, *Inscriptiones Italiae*, xiii, 2, Rome, 1963 (Degrassi or *Inscr. Ital.*).

A. K. Michels, *The Calendar of the Roman Republic*, Princeton, 1967.

Ovid, *Fasti*, edited by Sir James Frazer, London, 1929.

W. Warde Fowler, *The Roman Festivals*, London, 1899.

LIVING IN ROME

Axel Boethius, *The Golden House of Nero*, Ann Arbor, 1960.

D. R. Dudley, *Urbs Roma*, London, 1967.

A. P. Frutaz, *Le Piante di Roma*, Rome, 1962, three mammoth and wonderfully produced volumes, with plans of the city starting with the *Forma Urbis*, and including Stefano du Pérac's picturesque notion in the sixteenth century of an ancient Roman triumph, pianta xxii, 9–12, tav. 46–9.

H. Jordan–Ch. Huelsen, *Topographie der Stadt Rom in Altertum*, I, iii, Berlin, 1907 (Jordan–Huelsen). [Huelsen completed this volume after Jordan's death.]

G. Lugli, *Monumenti minori del Foro Romano*, Rome, 1947.
    Roma Antica, Il centro monumentale, Rome, 1946.

E. Nash, *Pictorial Dictionary of ancient Rome*, London, 1961/2 (*PDAR*).

S. B. Platner–T. Ashby, *A Topographical Dictionary of ancient Rome*, Oxford, 1929 (*TDAR*).

LIVING OUT OF ROME
Italy

J. Beloch, *Campanien*, Berlin, 1890.

P. Grimal, *Les Jardins romains*, Paris, 1943.

G. Hahn, *Der Villenbesitz der röm. Grossen in Italien zur Zeit der Republik*, Diss. Bonn, 1922.

Georgina Masson, *Italian Gardens*, London, 1961.

H. Nissen, *Italische Landeskunde*, Berlin, 1883–1902.

Hadrian's Villa

S. Aurigemma, *Villa Adriana*, Rome, 1962.

H. Kähler, *Hadrian und seine Villa bei Tivoli*, Berlin, 1950.

Herculaneum

A. Maiuri, *Ercolano, i nuovi scavi* 1, Rome, 1958.

Ostia

R. Meiggs, *Roman Ostia*, Oxford, 1960 (Meiggs, *Ostia*).

Pompeii

R. Étienne, *La Vie quotidienne à Pompéi*, Paris, 1966.

A. Maiuri, *Pompeii* (English translation), Rome, 1929.
  Pompei ed Ercolano fra case e abitanti, Padua, 1950.

A. Mau, *Pompeji in Leben und Kunst*, 2nd edition, Leipzig, 1908.
  English translation by F. W. Kelsey, *Pompeii, its Life and Art*,
  London–New York, 1899.

Sicily, Piazza Armerina

G. V. Gentili, *La Villa Erculia di Piazza Armerina, i mosaici figurati*,
  Rome, 1964, with splendid coloured illustrations of the mosaics.

Biagio Pace, *I Mosaici di Piazza Armerina*, Rome, 1955, very well illustrated.

North Africa

S. Aurigemma, *I Mosaici di Zliten*, Rome, 1926.

Britain

A. Birley, *Life in Roman Britain*, London, 1964.

ECONOMICS OF LIVING

R. Duncan-Jones, 'Costs, Outlays and *Summae Honorariae* from
  Roman Africa,' *PBSR* 1962, 47–115.
  'An Epigraphic Survey of Costs in Roman Italy,' *PBSR* 1965,
  189–306.

Tenney Frank, ed., *An Economic Survey of Ancient Rome*, Baltimore,
  1933–40 (*ESAR*).

M. Rostovtzeff, *Social and Economic History of the Roman Empire*, 2nd
  edition, rev. P. M. Fraser, Oxford, 1957 (*SEHRE*).

RELAXATION

J.-M. André, *Recherches sur l'Otium romain*, Paris, 1962.

L'Otium dans la vie morale et intellectuelle romaine, Paris, 1966.

L. Becq de Fouquières, *Les Jeux des anciens*, 2nd edition, Paris, 1873.

C. E. Boyd, *Public Libraries and Literary Culture in ancient Rome*, Chicago, 1916.

M. R. Cagnat, 'Les Bibliothèques municipales dans l'empire romain,' *Mém. Acad. Inscr.* xxxviii, 1, 1909, 1–26.

M. della Corte, *Iuventus*, Arpino, 1924.

FAMILY LIFE AND EDUCATION

A. Gwynn, *Roman Education from Cicero to Quintilian*, Oxford, 1926.

H. -I. Marrou, *Histoire de l'éducation dans l'antiquité*, sixth edition, Paris, 1965 (Marrou)
English Translation by G. Lamb, *A History of Education in Antiquity*, London, 1956 (Marrou, E. T.).

Roberto Paribeni, *La Famiglia romana*, Rome, 1947.

STUCCO RELIEFS IN UNDERGROUND BASILICA OUTSIDE PORTA MAGGIORE

G. Bendinelli, 'Il Monumento sottoterraneo di Porta Maggiore in Roma,' *Monumenti Antichi*, 1926, esp. 672–8, tav. xviif.

E. L. Wadsworth, 'Stucco Reliefs of the first and second centuries A.D. still extant in Rome,' *MAAR* 1924, 79–87, and plates xlif.

THE THEATRE

W. Beare, *The Roman Stage*, 2nd edition, London, 1955.

M. Bieber, *The History of the Greek and Roman Theater*, 2nd edition, Princeton, 1961.

J.-P. Cèbe, *La Caricature et la parodie dans le monde romain antique*, Paris, 1966.

J. A. Hanson, *Roman Theater-Temples*, Princeton, 1959.

H. Reich, *Der Mimus*, Berlin, 1903.

L. R. Taylor, 'The Opportunities for Dramatic Performance in the time of Plautus and Terence,' *TAPA*, 1937, 284–304.

GLADIATORS AND ATHLETES

M. Grant, *Gladiators*, London, 1967.

P. J. Meier, *De Gladiatura Romana*, Bonn, 1881.

Th. Mommsen, 'Senatus Consultum de Sumptibus Ludorum Gladiatorum minuendis factum a.p.C. 176/7', *Ges. Schr.* 8, 1913, 499–531 (*Eph. Epig.* 1890, 388–428).

L. Moretti, *Iscrizioni agonistiche greche*, Rome, 1953.

J. H. Oliver, R. E. A. Palmer, 'Minutes of an Act of the Roman Senate,' *Hesperia*, 1955, 320–49.

André Piganiol, *Recherches sur les jeux romains*, Strasburg, 1923.

L. Robert, *Les Gladiateurs dans l'Orient grec*, Paris, 1940.

HUNTING AND ANIMAL SHOWS

J. Aymard, *Essai sur les chasses romaines*, Paris, 1951.

J. Jennison, *Animals for Show and Pleasure in ancient Rome*, Manchester, 1937 (Jennison).

O. Keller, *Die antike Tierwelt*, Leipzig, 1909–20.

G. Loisel, *Histoire des ménageries de l'antiquité à nos jours*, Paris, 1912.

J. M. C. Toynbee, 'Beasts and their Names in the Roman Empire,' *PBSR*, 1948, 24–37, with excellent illustrations.

ADDITIONAL BIBLIOGRAPHY

John H. D'Arms, *Romans on the Bay of Naples*, Harvard U.P., 1970.

S. C. Gilfillan, 'Lead Poisoning and the Fall of Rome', *Journal of Occupational Medicine* 7, 1965, 53–60.

J. Kleberg, 'Römische Wirtshäuser und Weinstuben', *Das Altertum* 15, 1969, 146–61.

I. and P. Opie, *Childrens' Games in Street and Playground*, Oxford, 1969.

J. E. Packer, 'Housing and Population in Imperial Ostia and Rome', *JRS* 57, 1967, 80–95.

Stewart Perowne, *The Caesars' Wives*, London, 1974.

J. E. Skydsgaard, 'Nuove ricerche sulla villa rustica Romana fino al epoca di Traiano', *Analecta Romana Instituti Danici* 5, 1969, 25–40 (with excellent bibliography).

H. Solin, M. Itkonen-Kaila, '*Graffiti del Palatino I, Paedagogium*', Helsinki, 1966 (*Acta Instituti Romani Finlandiae* III).

Paul Vigneron, *Le cheval dans l'antiquité gréco-romaine*, Nancy, 1968.

J. B. Ward Perkins, 'Nero's Golden House', *Antiquity* 30, 1956, 209–19.

D. G. Weingartner, *Die Ägyptenreise des Germanicus*, Bonn, 1969.

LIST OF ABBREVIATIONS
USED IN NOTES

AE	*L'Année Épigraphique.*
AG	Aulus Gellius, *Noctes Atticae.*
AM	Ammianus Marcellinus.
AP	*Anthologia Palatina.*
App. *BC*	Appian, *Bella Civilia.*
Carcopino	*See* Bibliography.
CD	Cassius Dio.
CI	*Codex Iustinianus.*
CIG	*Corpus Inscriptionum Graecarum.*
CIL	*Corpus Inscriptionum Latinarum.*
CJ	*Classical Journal.*
CN	Cornelius Nepos, *Vitae.*
Col.	Columella, *De Re Rustica.*
CQ	*Classical Quarterly.*
CR	*Classical Review.*
CRAI	*Comptes Rendus, Académie des Inscriptions et Belles Lettres*
CT	*Codex Theodosianus*
Degrassi	A. Degrassi, *Inscriptiones Italiae xiii, 2 (Fasti),* Rome, 1963.
DH, *AR*	Dionysius of Halicarnassus, *Antiquitates Romanae*
Dig.	*Digest*
D–S	C. R. Daremberg–Edm. Saglio, *Dictionnaire des Antiquités grecques et romaines.*
EJ	V. Ehrenberg, A. H. M. Jones, *Documents illustrating the Reigns of Augustus and Tiberius,* 2nd editn., Oxford, 1955.
ESAR	*See* Bibliography.
FGH	F. Jacoby, *Die Fragmente der griechischen Historiker*
FIR	G. G. Bruns, *Fontes Iuris Romani Antiqui,* seventh editn., Tübingen, 1909.

FIRA	S. Riccobono, *Fontes Iuris Romani Anteiusti-niani*, 2nd editn., Florence, 1941.
Friedlaender	*See* Bibliography.
Herod.	Herodian.
Hor., *AP, Car., Ep., Sat*	Horace, *Ars Poetica, Odes, Epistles, Satires*
IGR	*Inscriptiones Graecae ad Res Romanas Pertinentes*
ILS	H. Dessau, *Inscriptiones Latinae Selectae.*
Inscriptiones Italiae	*See* Degrassi; all refs. are to xiii, 2 unless otherwise stated.
JC, *BC*, *BG*	Julius Caesar, *Bellum Civile, Bellum Gallicum.*
Jennison	*See* Bibliography.
JRS	*Journal of Roman Studies*
L.	Livy.
Luc., *De Salt.* etc.	Lucian, *De Saltatione* etc.
MAAR	*Memoirs of the American Academy in Rome.*
MAI	*Memoirs, Institut national de France, Académie des Inscriptions.*
Marquardt, Marquardt–Wissowa	*See* Bibliography.
Marrou	*See* Bibliography.
Mart.	Martial.
McCrum–Woodhead	M. McCrum, A. G. Woodhead, *Select Documents of the Principates of the Flavian Emperors*, Cambridge, 1961.
Meiggs, *Ostia*	R. Meiggs, *Roman Ostia*, Oxford, 1960.
Mommsen, *Staatsr.*	Th. Mommsen, *Roemisches Staatsrecht*, 3rd edition, 1887/8, reprint, Basle, 1952.
MRR	T. R. S. Broughton, *The Magistrates of the Roman Republic*, New York, 1951/2.
NSA	*Atti della Accademia nazionale dei Lincei, Notizie degli scavi di antichità.*
ORF	H. Malcovati, *Oratorum Romanorum Fragmenta*, 2nd editn., Turin 1955.
Ovid, *AA, Fast., Tr.* etc.	Ovid, *Ars Amatoria, Fasti, Tristia* etc.
P.	Polybius
PBSR	*Papers of the British School at Rome.*
PDAR	E. Nash, *Pictorial Dictionary of Ancient Rome.*
Petron., *Sat.*	Petronius, *Satyricon.*
PIR	*Prosopographia Imperii Romani*, 'A' to 'I', second editn., 1933–66; remainder, 1st editn., 1897.

Plin., *Ep.*	Pliny's *Letters*; S–W, edition of A. N. Sherwin-White, Oxford, 1966.
Plin., *NH*	Pliny, *Natural Histories.*
PLM	*Poetae Latini Minores.*
Plut., *Ant., Cato mi., JC* etc.	Plutarch's *Lives* of Antony, the younger Cato, Julius Caesar etc.
Plut., *Mor.*	Plutarch, *Moralia.*
Quint.	Quintilian, *Institutio Oratoria*
RE	Pauly–Wissowa, *Realencyclopaedie der classischen Altertumswissenschaft.*
Reinach, *RPGR*	S. Reinach, *Répertoire de peintures grecques et romaines*, Paris, 1922.
RG or *RGDA*	*Res Gestae Divi Augusti*
Roem. Mitt.	*Mitteilungen des deutschen archaeologischen Instituts, Roemische Abteilung.*
Roman Women	*See* Bibliography.
Sall., *Cat., BJ*	Sallust, *Catilina, Bellum Iugurthinum.*
Schanz–Hosius	M. Schanz, C. Hosius, *Geschichte der roemischen Literatur*, 4th editn., Munich, 1927–35, reprinted 1959.
SEHRE	M. Rostovtzeff, *Social and Economic History of the Roman Empire*, rev. P. M. Fraser, Oxford, 1957.
Sen., *Ep.*	The younger Seneca, *Letters.*
Sen., *Apok., De Clem., De Ben., De Brev. Vit.* etc.	The younger Seneca, *Apokolokyntosis, De Clementia, De Beneficiis, De Brevitate Vitae* etc.
Sen., *Controv., Suas.*	The elder Seneca, *Controversiae, Suasoriae.*
SHA, *Hadr., MA, AS* etc.	Scriptores Historiae Augustae, *Lives* of Hadrian, Marcus Aurelius, Alexander Severus etc.
Smallwood	E. M. Smallwood, *Documents illustrating the Principates of Gaius, Claudius and Nero*, Cambridge, 1967; *Documents illustrating the Principates of Nerva, Trajan and Hadrian*, Cambridge, 1966 (the context will show which volume is intended.)
Suet., *DJ, DA, Tib., C. Cal.* etc.	Suetonius' *Lives* of Divus Iulius, Divus Augustus, Tiberius, C. Caligula etc.
T*A*, T*H* etc.	Tacitus, *Annals, Histories* etc.

TDAR	S. B. Platner, T. Ashby, *A Topographical Dictionary of Ancient Rome*, Oxford, 1929.
VM	Valerius Maximus.
VP	Velleius Paterculus.
Wissowa, *RK*	G. Wissowa, *Religion und Kultus der Roemer*, 2nd editn., Munich, 1912.

NOTES ON THE ILLUSTRATIONS

Plate 1

(a) The present Piazza Navona in Rome preserves the form of Domitian's Stadium, remains of whose building are still to be seen on the site. The dome on the left is of Borromini's church of S. Agnese in Agonia, who was martyred here (see p. 253).

(b) The Peutinger Table was a road map of the Roman Empire dating, probably, from the late second century A.D. This section shows Rome at the centre of the world, all roads leading to it, and the neighbouring towns (Nomentum, Tibur, Praeneste, Alsium, Lorium, Laurentum, etc.) where the rich had their *villae suburbanae*. The Anio flows through Tibur, to join the Tiber above Rome. Ad Aquas Albulas on the road to Tibur is marked (see p. 32). In the foreground is Trajan's great harbour of Portus, near Ostia.

(c) The *Forma Urbis* was a vast plan of Rome cut in stone at the time of Septimius Severus, of which valuable fragments survive, for instance for the Ludus Magnus (p. 293), the Saepta Iulia and, here, the Theatre of Pompey. It shows clearly the site of the Temple of Venus Victrix which surmounted the seats of the audience, the *cavea* (see p. 254).

Plate 2

(a) A gladiatorial fight. *Severus l(ib.) (victoriarum) xiii (periit)*
    Albanus Sc(auri?) l(ib. victoriarum) xix vicit
'Severus, a free man, victor in 13 previous engagements, was killed; Albanus, freedman of Scaurus, victor in 19 previous engagements, was winner.'
Severus has dropped his shield and awaits the *coup de grâce*. This can hardly be the same man as the Severus of *CIL* iv, 4870, who fought in 55 engagements.
CIL iv, 8056.

(b) Comic drawing of a beast-fighter prodding an animal (apparently, from the caption, intended to be a lion) into activity. He is called Venustus, and the word before the last appears to be *lione* (i.e. *leone*).
CIL iv, 8017.

(c) Record of a tragic romance. The *graffito* is evidently composed by Severus, threatening his unsuccessful rival in love: *Dixi, scripsi. Amas Hiredem quae te non curat. Sev(erus) Successo* . . . 'I have spoken, I have written. You are in love with Iris, who does not care for you. Severus to Successus . . .' The epigram follows:

> *Successus textor amat Coponiaes ancilla(m)*
> *nomine Hiredem, quae quidem illum*
> *non curat; sed ille rogat, illa comiseretur.*
> *Scribit rivalis, Vale.*
> *Invidiose quia rumperes, sedare(?) noli formonsiorem*
> *et qui est homo pravessimus et bellus.*

'Successus the weaver is in love with Coponia's maid, Hiris [sic]. She does not care for him. He begs her to have pity on him. His rival writes: "Be off with you. Villain, do not, just because you are in torment, abuse a man handsomer than yourself, a man who is a very devil and a powerful lover".'

But not highly literate, writing *Hiridem* for *Iridem*, *rumperes* for *rumparis*, *sedare* for, presumably, *sectari*, to say nothing of *illa commiseretur*.

CIL iv, 8259. Cf. M. della Corte, *NSA* 1929, 459.

Plate 3
    CIL vi, 28774.

Plate 4
    House of the Silver Wedding, Pompeii. The name of the house derives from the fact that it was excavated in 1893, the year of the silver wedding of King Umberto I. In addition to the entry hall and peristyle here illustrated, the house had both a winter and a summer dining-room, baths (on one side of the peristyle), an open swimming pool (*piscina*), kitchen and bedrooms. The open sky-light (*impluvium*) of the *atrium* let smoke out and light (and rain) in. See A. Maiuri, *Pompeii*[10] (ET), 53; A. Mau, *Pompeji in Leben und Kunst*, Leipzig, 1908, 315-24.

Plate 8
(b) In the upper band a schoolmaster watches, rod in hand, while a boy holding a writing tablet addresses an unidentifiable object at the top of a post. Behind it a second naked boy stands facing the first; he also holds a writing tablet. A third boy, arms outstretched, steals up behind the master.

In the lower panel one boy has caught in his left hand the ball which a second boy has thrown with his left hand (on catching with the left hand see p. 165). To his left, not in the photograph, a third boy has both hands outstretched, waiting in turn to receive the ball.

The boy on the right of the lower panel stands holding a large round shield. To his right, not in the photograph, two naked boys are advancing, each with a small shield in the left hand and a short sword in the right, towards a trainer who, like the seated teacher, has a rod in his hand.

See E. L. Wadsworth, 'Stucco Reliefs of the first and second Centuries still extant in Rome', *MAAR* 1924, 9–102, esp. 83f. and plates xli f.

Plate 15

(a) This startling mosaic in which five reclining and animated figures, to whom wine is being handed, are requested not to wake the five sleeping bulls (*Silentium; dormiant tauri*) was discovered in 1954 at El-Djem (Thysdrus) in Tunisia and has provoked a succession of highly improbable speculations. First of all, the date. Fourth century A.D. (probably), or third? Is the drinking party (whose figures for convenience will be referred to, from left to right, as A, B, C, D, E) a male drinking party or are B and E women? And what is the significance of their attributes and of the captions above their heads? A waves an ivy-branch; his caption is seemingly (*N*)*os nudi* (*f*)*iemus*, which suits his near-nakedness: 'We will take off our clothes.' Is he Dionysus? B has a radiate crown with, in the centre, an anchor or perhaps a cross. His or her caption is *Bibere venimus*, 'We have come here to drink.' A marine goddess? Next C with his radiate crown, one ray spearing a fish, with the caption *Ia*(*m*) *multu*(*m*) *loquimini*, 'You are talking too much' The Sun? Then D, the rather bored master of ceremonies, with his caption *Avocemur*, 'Let us go away', or alternatively, 'Let us relax'. And finally E with a crescent at the end of his or her staff and the caption *Nos tres tenemus*, 'We have had our three (cups)', i.e. 'We have had quite enough to drink'. Luna, the Moon? (At first it was not appreciated that C, D and E had each his own caption, and the reconstruction made was *Iam udulo avocemur qui minimos tres tenemus*, 'Let us leave this drunkard [A]; we have had our regulation three drinks.') And what of the bulls? Something sexy, was the first suggestion. In due course common sense abandoned the

notion of religious ritual and thought the human party was enjoying an after-dinner drinking orgy, a *comissatio* (cf. p. 49),
perhaps of a drinking-club in which guests dressed up as gods, as
in the club to which Octavian once belonged (Suet., *DA* 70, 1;
VP 2, 83, 2). What, then, could be the occasion of this drinking?
The Saturnalia, it was suggested. The five drinkers were slaves,
one the Saturnalian King (see p. 125); the two waiters, one
saying, 'Less noise', were their masters, playing the slave, as
masters did at the Saturnalia (see p. 125). But drinking out of
doors in December, even in north Africa? Improbable. So at last
common sense was given a look-in. The bulls were going to fight
in the arena—is a *bestiarius* not marked on the haunches of one of
them?—and the five drinkers were not unconcerned. Tertullian,
Apol. 70, describes the dinner of *bestiarii* on the eve of the beast-
fighting at the Liberalia, on March 17th. Climatically possible.
But psychologically? Surely no keen bull-fighter whose life might
depend on the skill which he displayed on the following morning
would get drunk the night before. Miserable victims, then?
B a prospective Christian martyr, with the mockery of a cross on
his head? By now, once again, the nadir of absurdity had been
reached. What, then, of bull-masters and bull-trainers having an
orgy the night before their 'pupils' fought?
The history of this academic awakening of sound common sense
is to be traced through C. Gilbert-Picard, *CRAI* 1954, 418–24;
M. H. Seyrig, *CRAI* 1955, 521–6; J. Bousquet, *Karthago* 1954,
213f.; M. F. Squarciapino, *Archeologia Class.* 1957, 245–9 to
C. Gilbert-Picard, *La Civilisation de l'Afrique romaine*, 1959, 242–4;
348. See *AE* 1955, 84; 1956, 64 and 120; 1959, 18; 1961, 66;
1964, 238.

(b) Mosaic showing boys trundling Greek hoops (the *trochi Graeci* of
whose popularity with Roman boys Horace disapproved so
strongly, see p. 160), evidently in a Circus, whose *metae* they are
passing. It was found in Istanbul. Children can be seen in Turkey
today trundling two hoops in this way. I am grateful to my old
pupil Antony Sutch, English Director of the Ottoman Bank in
Istanbul, for his kindness in securing me this photograph.

Plate 16
(a) Mosaic of racing in the Circus. There are eight starting-boxes, not

the normal twelve, in the *Carceres*, above which sits the starter, flanked by two other persons. There are eight *quadrigae* in the race, with single men on horseback (stewards of the course?) and on foot (*hortatores?*).

(b) The funerary *stele* of T. Flavius Abascantus, a high imperial civil servant (*a cognitionibus*) in the Flavian period, at the top depicts Abascantus at dinner in the world to which after death he has been transported. Below is a relief of Scorpus, the famous and popular charioteer of the time of Domitian, with four horses, whose names are given: Ingenuus, Admetus, Passerinus and Atmetus (*ILS* 1679, *CIL* vi, 8628). On another relief (*ILS* 5289, *CIL* vi, 10052) his victory is recorded with four other horses, Pegasus, Elates, Andraemon (named by Martial 10, 9, 5 as a famous horse) and Cotynus (also mentioned in *ILS* 5287, 16, driven by Diocles (see p. 322)).

23

NOTES

(See page 345 for explanation of abbreviations)

Introduction

1. There were no government bonds or equities; so if you had wealth, inherited or acquired (in trade, for instance), it was invested, as until the eighteenth century all safe capital was invested, in real property. For emergencies you may have had a certain amount out at loan, sums which could be called in easily if you needed ready cash. Money was loaned in Rome itself on good security, whether by private individuals or by professional money-lenders, in the late Republic and early Empire at a lower rate of interest than can be obtained from banks today—sometimes as low as 4% (Cic., *Ad Att.* 4, 15, 7). In the provinces it was higher, normally 12%. As for capital, you required a hundred thousand sesterces to be a local town councillor (Plin., *Ep.* 1, 19, 2), four hundred thousand to be an Eques, a million in the early Empire to be a senator. Nine to fifteen millions represented comfortable wealth for a senator. The wealthiest men known to us possessed four hundred millions: Lentulus the augur under Augustus (Sen., *De Ben.* 2, 27, 1) and Narcissus, the freedman of Claudius (CD 60, 34, 4; no wonder such men were hated, as they were). Pallas, another Claudian freedman, and Seneca had fortunes of three hundred millions (TA 12, 53, 5; 13, 42, 6; CD 61, 10, 3). At the other extreme soldiers (legionaries), who never in history have been highly paid, received 900 sesterces a year in the early Empire (part of which went into savings, McCrum-Woodhead 405) and 12,000 sesterces when they were discharged (H. M. D. Parker, *The Roman Legions* 214–24; 246). A general labourer is thought on the evidence of St. Matt. 20, 2, to have earned 4 sesterces a day. Grain, the foundation of living, cost something over 3 sesterces a *modius* (a sixth part of a bushel), Cic., *In Verr.* 2, 3, 163; TA 15, 39, 2; Plin., *NH* 18, 90. Except in periods of temporary economic crisis, prices were reasonably stable in the late Republic and early Empire, as is shown by the fact that soldiers' pay was unchanged for a hundred years, from Augustus to Domitian, then raised by a third and stable again for another century until Septimius

Severus. After that a galloping inflation set in and figures of income and expenditure no longer have comparable significance. Cf. J. Szilágyi, 'Prices and Wages in the western provinces of the Roman Empire', *Acta Antiqua* 1963, 325–89.

2. Excellent illustration of umbrella and woman's handbag Paoli (see Bibliography), E.T. pl. 36. Money in belts, Plaut., *Truc.*, 954–6; L. 33, 29, 4. Purse (*loculi*), Hor., *Ep.* 1, 1, 56; Juv. 1, 89; 10, 46. Money-bag (*crumena*) round neck, Plaut., *Truc.* 652; 654f.; 956; Hor., *Ep.* 1, 4, 11; Juv. 11, 38.

3. The general fact is certain enough, though there can be no even roughly reliable actuarial calculations. All that can be done is to make a patient count of all surviving funerary inscriptions in which the length of life is recorded (see, e.g., J. Szilágyi, 'Die Sterblichkeit in den nordafrikanischen Provinzen', *Acta Arch. Hung.* 1965, 309–34; 1966, 235–77; 1967, 25–59). But this evidence is highly misleading for (a) in the case of people of any standing, many of whom supervised the inscription of their own epitaphs in their lifetime, age at death is generally not recorded and (b) in other cases the high incidence of round numbers suggests guess work: A. Mócsy, 'Die Unkenntnis des Lebensalters im röm. Reich', *Acta Antiqua* 1966, 387–421. Still, in general, people lived longer south of the Mediterranean than north of it and longer in the country than in the towns (on the unhealthiness of Rome, see Sen., *Ep.* 104, 6; Herod. 1, 12; AM 14, 6, 23). Their expectation of life if they survived to their midforties was perhaps higher than it is today, but the expectation at birth or even at ten of surviving the forties was slender. See A. R. Burn, 'Hic Breve Vivitur', *Past and Present* 1953, 1–31.

4. Cf. A. D. Nock, *Conversion*, Oxford, 1933; A. Alföldi, *The Conversion of Constantine and Pagan Rome* (tr. H. Mattingly), Oxford, 1948; *A Conflict of Ideas in the late Roman Empire* (tr. H. Mattingly) Oxford, 1952; *The Conflict of Paganism and Christianity*, ed. A. Momigliano, 1963.

5. On which something is said below at the start of chap. 3.

6. See books by Carcopino, Cowell and Paoli in the Bibliography, p. 340.

7. Suet., *C. Cal.* 38, 3.

8. See T. S. Jerome, *Aspects of the Study of Roman History*, New York-London, 1923, esp. 66–107.

9. *ILS* 5163.

10. Jack Lindsay, *Daily Life in Roman Egypt*, London, 1963. Also *Leisure and Pleasure in Roman Egypt*, London, 1965; *Men and Gods on the Roman Nile*, London, 1968.

Chapter I

1. See Marquardt, 250–340.

2. Plin., *NH* 7, 212–15. Their complicated construction is described by Vitruvius 9, 8. There is an illustration in the Loeb edition of Vitruvius, pl. N.

3. Clock in Trimalchio's dining-room, Petron., *Sat.* 26. In the baths, Lucian, *Hippias* 8.

4. AG 3, 3, 5; cf. Sen., *De Brev. Vit.* 12, 6, 'Some people would not know they were hungry without a clock to tell them so'.

5. AM 23, 6, 77; Cassiod., *Var.* 1, 46, tr. T. Hodgkin.

6. *ILS* 5392, 5617–25, Plin., *NH* 7, 182; Mart. 8, 67, 1. Varro, *LL* 6, 89 states that the *accensus*, later a private secretary to a pro-consul, was once employed by the praetor to shout the time 'at the 3rd, 6th and 9th hours'.

7. Juv. 10, 215f.

8. Sen., *Apok.* 2.

9. See for details Marquardt 257f.; see p. 16 above.

10. Varro, *LL* 6, 7; Macrob., *Sat.* 1, 3, 12–15; Fronto, *Ad M. Caes.* 2, 6, 3 (Loeb i, p. 142).

11. Mart. 12, 57, 5; cf. Cic., *Tusc.* 4, 44, '*opificum antelucana industria*', (a quotation from Demosthenes).

12. Fronto, *Ad M. Caes.* 4, 5 (Loeb i, 178f.); *De Fer. Als.* 3 (Loeb ii, 4–18).

13. Plin., *Ep.* 3, 5, 8f. (Pliny and Vespasian); Philostratus, *Vit. Apoll. Tyan.* 5, 31 (Vespasian); Fronto, *Ad M. Caes.* 4, 6 (i, 180 Loeb); CD 76, 17, 1 (Septimius Severus); AM 16, 5, 4 (Julian); Suet., *Galba* 22; Suet., *C. Cal.* 58.

14. Suet., *Galba* 4, 4.

15. AG 3, 4; 6, 12, 4f.; Plin., *NH* 7, 211. Shaving in the house, *Plut., Ant.* 1, 2f. On barbers, Carcopino 157–64.

16. Plaut., *Curc.* 72f.; Mart. 8, 67, 10; Plin., *Ep.* 3, 5, 10, of the elder Pliny, '*Post cibum, quem interdiu levem et facilem veterum more sumebat*'; see Marquardt 264f.

17. Mart. 14, 223.

18. *TH* 1, 62; Suet., *Vit.* 7, 3; 13, 1.

19. Galen, *De Venae Sect. adv. Erasist. Romae deg.* 9 (xi, 242 K); Cic., *In Pis.* 13; *Phil.* 2, 104; Plut. *Cato mi.* 44, 2. Galen vi, 332f. and 412 K do not seem to justify Marquardt's belief (p. 265) that the *ientaculum* was generally consumed by people at the third or fourth hour.

20. AG 20, 1, 2 and 55; *TA* 25, 23, 5.

21. E.g. *SIG*³ 656, the two citizens of Teos who represented the case of Abdera in Rome in about 166 B.C.

22. Sen., *De Ben.* 6, 34, 1f.

23. See, for references, M. Gelzer, *Kleine Schriften* 1, 1962, 105-7; *ILS* 1320, an Eques of the time of Augustus and Tiberius, '*ex prima admissione*'. As a general rule, the Emperor received Senators at the first admission, Equites at the second.

24. Cic., *Ad Att.* 1, 18, 1.

25. Praetors sent their lictors to pay a formal call on rich childless widows, Juv. 3, 126-30.

26. Mart. 10, 10; Juv. 1, 101 and 117f. pretends that the magistrate's call is on a par with that of the *clientes* and that he accepts the dole.

27. See Friedlaender, E.T. iv, 77-81 for the details and date of the change.

28. *TA* 16, 22, 1; *PLM* 1, 15, 109-137 (pp. 229ff.). Canvassing at Pompeii, *CIL* iv index, pp. 773-5.

29. Sen., *Ep.* 4, 10; Galen vi, 758 K; Juv. 3, 184-9.

30. Columella 1, pr. 9; Juv. 5, 59-66, '*Maxima quaeque domus servis est plena superbis*'.

31. *Laus Pisonis*, *PLM* 1, 15, 134-6; Mart. 12, 18, 4-6; Galen vi, 758 K. Baths at the tenth hour, Mart. 3, 36; 10, 70.

32. Juv. 5. However there were Roman hosts who refused to emulate such ill manners, Pl., *Ep.* 2, 6; see page 43.

33. *De Brev. Vit.* 14, 3f.

34. Sen., *Ep.* 19, 4.

35. *TA* 13, 19, 3; 14, 12, 6; 16, 32; *TH* 4, 40.

36. Ancient sources: Sen., *De Brev. Vit.* 14, 3f.; Epict., *Man.* 33, 13; Mart. 3, 4, 36, 46; 4, 8, 26; 9, 100; 10, 14, 18, 75, 82, 96; 12, 68; 14, 125; Juv. 1, 95-135; 3, 126-132 and 249f.; 5. See for more

detail, Friedlaender i, 88–97; 223–32 (E.T. i, 86–97; 195–212; iv, 77–81 (appendix 14)); Marquardt 259f.; *RE* iv, 23–55, esp. 53f., s.v. '*Clientes*'; iA, 2060–72, s.v. '*Salutatio*'.

37. Mart. 4, 8, 2, 'Exercet raucos tertia causidicos', on which, G. Bilfinger, *Die antiken Stundenangaben*, Stuttgart, 1888, 117–24; A. H. J. Greenidge, *The Legal Procedure of Cicero's Time*, Oxford, 1901, 139.

38. Asc., *In Milon.* 41C.

39. *FIR* 28, 102; *FIRA* i, 21, 102.

40. AG (Varro) 14, 7, 8; *RE* Supplb, vi, 702.

41. Livy 44, 20, 1; Senate in session at midday (3rd century A.D.), SHA, *Elag.* 15, 6.

42. *Comitia quaestoria* at the second hour, Cic., *Ad Fam.* 7, 30, 1.

43. Mart. 8, 44, 8.

44. Hor., *Car.* 1, 1, 20 (cf. 2, 7, 6); Sen., *Ep.* 83, 3; *AP* 10, 43–ZHΘI; Plut., *Mor.* 284D (QR 84); Sen., *De Tranq. An.* 17, 7.

45. School hours, Auson., *Ep.* 13, 10; Galen 11, 242 K.; Mart. 9, 68; 12, 57, 4f. Children home for lunch, Apul., *Met.* 10, 5. Libraries, Vitruv. 6, 4, 1, '*Usus enim matutinum postulat usum*'.

46. Asc., *In Milon.* 43C; Suet., *DA* 73; Balsdon, *Roman Women*, 268, 270; *ILS* 6891, 19–23.

47. See Marquardt 265–9 and, for England, Arnold Palmer, *Movable Feasts*, Oxford, 1952. On 'merenda', used once of the evening, then of the midday meal, see Marquardt 367f. For fanciful speculation on this subject, see Plut., *Mor.* 726D ff. (*Quaest. Conv.* 8, 6, 4).

48. CD 37, 46, 4; Suet., *D. Cl.* 34, 2.

49. Cic., *Ad Fam.* 7, 30, 1.

50. Sen., *Ep.* 83, 6; T. S. Jerome, *Aspects of the Study of Roman History*, New York-London, 1923, 102–7.

51. Plaut., *Men.* 208; *Curc.* 323; wine, Sen., *Ep.* 122, 6.

52. Sen., *Cons ad Marc.* 22, 6; guests might be invited, Macrob., *Sat.* 3, 17, 6; Suet., *Domit.* 21.

53. Plin., *NH* 6, 89; Cic., *De Div.* 2, 142; Varro, *RR* 1, 2, 5 ('aestivo die'); Mart. 4, 8, 4; Plin., *Ep.* 3, 5, 11; 7, 4, 4; 9, 40, 2; Celsus 1, 2, 5.

54. JC, *BG* 7, 46, 5; *BC* 2, 14, 1; 3, 9, 6.

55. Mart. 4, 8, 4, 'Sexta (sc. hora) quies lassis, septima finis erit'; SHA, *AS* 61, 3; *Max. duo* 23, 6; Procop., *De Bell. Vandal.* 1, 2, 17; JC, *BC* 2, 14, 1.

56. CD 76, 17, 2f.; SHA, *AS* 30, 4f.

57. Galen vi, 757f. K.

58. Mart. 3, 44, 12.

59. '*In thermis et circa balnea*', Mart. 12, 82, 1. For a discussion of the two words, and an account of the baths at Ostia, see Russell Meiggs, *Roman Ostia*, Oxford, 1960, 404–20.

60. *Pro Rosc. Am.* 18; *Pro Cluent.* 141; *Pro Cael.* 62f.; *De Orat.* 2, 223; cf. *CIL* x, 221; xiv, 3013.

61. Hor., *Sat.* 1, 3, 137; Mart. 3, 30, 4; Juv. 6, 447; *ILS* 6891, 22f.

62. *ILS* 5723 (on these considerable baths, now excavated at the end of the Via dell' Abbondanza, see M. della Corte, *NSA* 1958, 123f.). Cf. Juv. 7, 4; *ILS* 6891; *Dig.* 20, 4, 9.

63. CD 49, 43, 3; 54, 29, 4 (Agrippa's *Thermae* in Rome); *CIL* v, 376 (Istria), ix, 5074f. (Interamna); *Dig.* 32, 35, 3 (Tibur).

64. Plin., *NH* 36, 121; Severus Alexander (*Vita* 39, 4) added a large number; L. Preller, *Die Regionen der Stadt Rom*, Jena, 1846, 105–12.

65. Maecenas, CD 55, 7, 6. See inscriptions listed under *balneum* and *thermae* in the index of *ILS* (pp. 882, 903). Fifty of these inscriptions record gifts of baths, in 3 cases out of 5 of new baths to replace ones which had fallen out of use.

66. *ILS* 5686; Plin., *Ep.* 10, 23f., replacement of old *balineum* by a new at Prusa in Bithynia.

67. *Balnea muliebria*, *ILS* 5683f., *AE* 1961, 109; *balneae feminarum*, SHA, *AS* 23, 5; 24, 2; the *Lex metalli Vipascensis*, *ILS* 6891. See my *Roman Women*, 268–70. Prohibition of mixed bathing by Hadrian, *Vita* 18, 10; by Marcus Aurelius, *Vita* 23, 8; by Severus Alexander, *Vita*, 24, 2. Men's and women's baths adjacent, Vitruv. 5, 10, 1.

68. Mart. 3, 36, 6.

69. Lighting the great *thermae* must have been impossible. For short periods—after Severus Alexander and before the emperor Tacitus—baths in Rome were open after dark (SHA, *AS* 24, 6; *Tac.* 10, 2).

70. Plin., *Ep.* 2, 17, 26. Of the excavated baths at Ostia, two are shown as certainly and one as possibly pre-Trajanic in the plan on p. 418 of Meiggs, *Ostia*.

71. Mart. 3, 36, 5; cf. 10, 70, 13.

72. Lamps have been found in the baths at Pompeii; *lex metalli Vipascensis* in Portugal, baths open until second hour of night (*ILS* 6891).

73. Mart. 10, 48, 1–4; SHA, *Perc. Nig.* 3, 10.

74. Juv. 11, 204–6.

75. Suet., *DA* 76, 2; Petron., *Sat.* 72f.; Fronto, *De nep. amiss.* 1 (ii, 222 Loeb), '*vesperi loto*'. Death from undigested peacock, Juv. 1, 142f.; Pers., *Sat.* 3, 98–106; Celsus 2, 17 (a warning against such practice). Athaenaeus 11, 484b on a vomit and a bath after drinking. SHA, *Gord. iii*, 6. 6.

76. Plin., *Ep.* 9, 36, 3.

77. Mart. 4, 19; 14, 126; Juv. 6, 246.

78. Hor., *Car.* 3, 12, 7; Ovid, *Tr.* 3, 12, 19–22; Epict. 1, 1, 29.

79. For detail, see *RE* ii. 2756f., s.v. 'Bäder' (A. Mau); on the construction of baths, Vitruv. 5, 10.

80. Galen, *In Hippocr. de acut. morb. vict.* 47 (xv, 715 K).

81. In *tepidarium*, Celsus 1, 4, 2; sweat bath, Galen, *In Hippocr. de acut. morb. vict.* 47 (xv, 715 K); at the end, Galen, *De meth. med.* 8, 6 (x, 479, 481); 11, 10 (725 K); Cic., *Ad Att.* 13, 52; Petron., *Sat.* 28.

82. Plaut., *Stichus* 230; Mart. 12, 82, 7–10; 14, 51; Petron., *Sat.* 28; Apul., *Met.* 1, 23; Apul., *Flor.* 9, 34f.

83. Mart. 12, 70.

84. Plin., *Ep.* 3, 5, 14; AM 28, 4, 9; Sen., *De Brev. Vit.* 12, 7. Cf. Lucian, *Nigr.* 34, 76.

85. Philo, *Leg. ad Gai.* 27, 175.

86. Mart. 7, 32, 6.

87. SHA, *Hadr.* 17, 6f. Titus in the baths, Suet., *D. Tit.* 8, 2.

88. Sen., *Ep.* 56, 2.

89. Literally, 'Your offscouring.' See the Brescia mosaic, *ILS* 5725.

90. 28, 4, 19.

91. Mart. 12, 82, 6. Profit on such sales, as on theatre bars today, was perhaps a not unimportant part of the economy of the establishment.

92. Sen., *Ep.* 56, 2.

93. Mart. 12, 19.

94. Mart. 12, 70; Sen., *Ep.* 122, 6; Plin., *NH* 14, 139; Quint. 1, 6, 44.

95. Mart. 1, 23; 12, 82, 14; Petron., *Sat.* 27.

96. Petron., *Sat.* 42; Sen., *Ep.* 86, 12; Non. 155 L, s.v. *ephippium*; Suet., *DA* 82, 2; Celsus 1, 1f; Galen, *De sanit. tuend.* 5, 4 (vi, 333f. K).

97. SHA, *SS* 18, 3; Colum. 1, 6, 20.

98. T., *Agr.* 21, 3; Sen., *Ep.* 51, 6 and 86 passim.

100. *De meth. med.* 9, 2 (x, 536ff. K).

101. SHA. *SS* 4, 6, Septimius Severus dining *en famille* with his children; Hor., *Sat.* 2, 7, 29–37.

102. Plin., *Ep.* 5, 6, 19–23; 9, 36, 4.

103. Mart. 2, 11; 2, 14; 5, 78, 1; 12, 77, 5f.

104. Cic., *Ad Q.f.* 2, 6 (5), 3; Sen., *Ep.* 8, 1; Plin., *Ep.* 3, 5, 13; Quint. 10, 3, 26f.

105. 9th hour, Cic. *Ad. Fam.* 9, 26, 1; Hor., *Ep.* 1, 7, 71; Mart. 4, 8. Sometimes for the 10th hour, Nic. Damasc., *FGH* 90, F. 128, 28; Mart. 1, 108, 9; 7, 51, 11f. (cf. A. H. J. Greenidge, *O.c.* (n. 37), 139). Auson., *Ephem.* 5.

106. AM 28, 4, 17. Cf. Sen., *De Ben.* 4, 39, 3, '*Ad cenam, quia promisi, ibo etiam si frigus erit; non quidem, si nives cadent*'.

107. Plin., *Ep.* 1, 15, 1. On unpunctuality, cf. Plut., *Mor.* 725F–727A (*Quaest. Conv.* 8, 6).

108. Hor., *Sat.* 2, 7, 32–5; Lucian, *Gall.* 9 (cf. Juv. 5, 12–106).

109. Hor., *Sat.* 2, 8, 2; Mart. 7, 51, 11; 11, 52; 12, 48, 17; 12, 82, 14.

110. Hor., *Ep.* 1, 7, 46–61. Cf. *RE* xiv, 1567.

111. Mart. 10, 29, 4. Cf. Petron., *Sat.* 30, *vestimenta cubitoria*; SHA, *Maximini ii*, 30, 5, *vestis cenatoria*.

112. Petron., *Sat.* 56; Mart. 5, 79 (cf. 2, 46); 10, 87, 12; 14, 1, 1; 14, 141; Suet., *Nero* 51. The dress is clearly described by L. M. Wilson, *The Clothing of the ancient Romans*, Baltimore, 1938, 169–72, following W. B. McDaniel, *CP* 1925, 268–70. Under Hadrian and his successors togas were worn at the emperor's parties, *SHA SS* 1, 7.

113. Sigma for seven, Mart. 10, 48. *Hexaclinon*, Mart. 9, 59, 9; Auson., *Ephem.* 5. Sigma for eight, Mart. 14, 87; SHA, *Elag.* 29, 3. Prejudice against even number and other superstitions of the table, Plin., *NH* 28, 26f. On places at table, reclining to eat etc., Marquardt 302ff. Varro, *AG* 13, 11, 1.

114. Mart. 10, 48.

115. Cic., *Ad. Fam.* 9, 26. Carcopino is shocked: 'libertinism aggravated by hypocrisy.' *Cicero, the Secrets of his Correspondence*, 85–7.

116. Hor., *Sat.* 2, 8. On the practice of inviting guests to bring 'shadows', Plut., *Mor.* 707A–710A (*Quaest. Conv.* 7, 6).

117. Urso, see n. 145 below. Suet., *DJ* 48; Cic. *Ad. Att.* 13, 52. Rooms to hold more than one *triclinium*, Cic., *In Verr.*, 2, 4, 58 (reading *trigeminos* or *trinos*); Vitruv. 6, 4; Plut., *Mor.* 679B (*Quaest. Conv.* 5, 5); Athen. 2, 47f.; Petron., *Sat.* 77.

118. Juv. 11, 11 (cf. Hor., *Sat.* 2, 7, 104, 'obsequium ventris'; 111, 'gulae parens'); Sen., *De Benef.* 1, 10, 2, 'foedissimum patrimoniorum exitium, culina'.

119. Hor., *Sat.* 2, 2, 98f.; Juv. 11, 20.

120. Hor., *Sat.* 2, 4; 2, 8.

121. Petron., *Sat.* passim; AM 28, 4, 13.

122. Matius, Col. 12, 4, 2; 46, 1. Apicius, Plin., *NH* 19, 143; Sen., *Cons. ad Helv.* 10, 8f.; *PIR*² 'G' 91; E. Brandt, 'Untersuchungen zum röm. Kochbuche', *Philol.*, Supplb. xix, *Heft* 3, Leipzig, 1927; J. André, *Apicius, L'art culinaire, De re coquinaria*, Paris, 1965; B. Flower—E. Rosenbaum, *Apicius, the Roman Cookery Book* (English Translation), London, 1958. On Roman cooking, see *RE* xi, 957–82, s.v. 'Kochkunst' (Orth).

123. AM 28, 4, 34.

124. Hor., *Sat.* 2, 2; Juv. 11, 1–20; 35ff.; Sen., *Cons. ad Helv.* 10, 3ff.; *De Benef.* 1, 10, 2; *Ep.* 47, 1–8; 89, 22; 90, 7f. (greed for fish); Lucian, *Nigr.* 31, 72f.

125. Sen., *Ep.* 95, 41; *Cons. ad Helv.* 10, 4; SHA, *L. Ver.* 5, 1–5; *Elag.* 24, 3; Plut., *Lucull.* 41, 5; CN, *Att.* 13, 6. Cleopatra's ten million sesterces dinner hardly counts, Macrob., *Sat.* 3, 17, 15–17.

126. Macrob., *Sat.* 3, 13, 13; Petr., *Sat.* 49.

127. Macrob., *Sat.* 3, 16, 11–16; Lucil., 1176M.

128. Macrob., *Sat.* 3, 15, 13.

129. Hor., *Sat.* 2, 2, 120; Plut., *Cato mai.* 8, 2; Plin. *NH* 9, 67; Macrob., *Sat.* 3, 16, 9.

130. Macrob., *Sat.* 3, 13, 1.

131. Plin., *NH* 10, 52.

132. Juv. 1, 141; Plin., *NH* 8, 210; cf. Suet., *Tib.* 34, 1 (half-, not whole-, boars at Tiberius' dinners).

133. Macrob., *Sat.* 3, 16, 4; Hor., *Sat.* 2, 2, 47; Plin., *NH* 9, 60; Sen., *Ep.* 95, 25.

134. Sen., *De Tranq. An.* 1, 6; *Ep.* 123, 1 (cook and baker in the household); Cic., *In Pis.* 67 (Piso had not even a baker); AG 15, 19.

135. SHA, *Did. Julian.* 3, 8f.

136. AG 2, 24; Macrob., *Sat.* 3, 17.

137. *ORF²*, pp. 54–6; H. H. Scullard, *Roman Politics, 220–150 B.C.*, Oxford, 1951, 265f.

138. Scullard (n. 137), 221.

139. Lucil, 1172 M; AG 2, 24, 2–6; Macrob., *Sat.* 3, 17, 3–5; Plin., *NH* 10, 139; Athen. 6, 274 c–e. *Poussin*, Plin., *NH* 10, 140. Fattening hens in the dark, Sen., *Ep.* 122, 4.

140. Macrob., *Sat.* 3, 16, 15f. On the date of C. Titius, *RE* vi A, 1555–6, no. 7.

141. Macrob., *Sat.* 3, 17, 6; AG 2, 24, 12. Macrob., *Sat.* 3, 17, 13 mistakenly attributes the *lex Aemilia* to M. Aemilius Lepidus, consul in 78 B.C. Plin., *NH* 8, 223 and *De vir. ill.* 72, 5 are to be preferred as sources, it being most unlikely that there should have been two *leges Aemiliae*.

142. AG 2, 24, 7; Macrob., *Sat.* 3, 17, 7–10; Plin., *NH* 14, 95. On the date, *RE* xiii, 288.

143. AG 2, 24, 11; Macrob., *Sat.* 3, 17, 11f.

144. Most of the *spécialités* to which Varro objected in his satire 'On Foodstuffs' came from outside Italy, AG 6, 16. According to the author of the *Life* of Pertinax (SHA 8, 9–11) the reduction of extravagant banqueting under Pertinax led to a general lowering of the price of food.

145. AG 2, 24, 13; Macrob., *Sat.* 3, 17, 13. Cf. *Lex. Col. Gen. Iul Urs.* (*FIR*, 28) chap. 132, which allowed a candidate for the local magistracy to have nine men to dinner, but forbade him to give more extensive entertainment or to allow anyone else to entertain on his behalf.

146. CD 39, 37, 2; Macrob., *Sat.* 3, 17, 14.

147. Cic., *Ad fam.* 7, 26; 9, 15, 5; 9, 26, 3; Suet., *DJ* 43, 2; CD 43, 25, 2. The bigoted M. Favonius' speech against extravagant eating habits (AG 15, 8) may have been made in 55 or 46 B.C., *RE* vi, 2074.

148. CD 54, 2, 3; Suet., *DA* 34, 1; AG 2, 24, 15. Whether these limited expenditures were per meal or per person dining is never made clear in our sources. A.D. 22, TA 3, 52–5.

149. Mart. 11, 79; Hor., *Ep.* 1, 13, 15; *Sat.* 2, 8, 77; Mart. 3, 50, 3; 12, 87; Plin., *Ep.* 3, 1, 4; 9, 17, 3.

150. *NH* 14, 143; Petron., *Sat.* 31; Juv., *Sat.* 6, 424–433.

151. *Conv.* 1 (418f.) and 20 (433).

152. Plut., *Mor.* 619 (*Quaest. Conv.* 1, 3); Hor., *Sat.* 2, 8, 20–26; cf. TA 3, 14, 2. For a table plan, see Marquardt 304. The propriety of giving guests their places is discussed in Plut., *Quaest. Conv.* 1, 2 (*Mor.* 615D–619A). Four to a couch, Hor., *Sat.* 1, 4, 86.

153. Plut., *Cato mi.* 37, 7f.

154. Plut., *Brut.* 34, 4, 8.

155. See Friedlaender ii, 282–311 (E.T. ii, 131–164) for a sane assessment of the degree to which the Romans were grossly extravagant in their eating and drinking, and Marquardt, 297–331 for the history and detailed analysis of Roman practice. Augustus' dinners were normally of three courses, never of more than six, Suet., *DA* 74. For Elagabalus' fantastic dinners, SHA, *Elag.* 30 (22 courses); 32, 4 (variations on a single course); Severus Alexander's dinners, *Vita.* 37.

156. Mart. 11, 31, 4; 11, 52, 1–12. Constituents in full detail, Marquardt, 323–6. For examples, Mart. 10, 48, 7–13; Macrob., *Sat.* 3, 13, 12. *Polenta*, Sen., *Ep.* 110, 18.

157. Marquardt, 326–331; 414–474 for details. Hadrian was particularly fond of *tetrapharmacum* (pheasant, sow's udders, ham and pastry), *Vita* 21, 4.

158. On *garum* and fish sauces, see C. Jardin, 'Garum et sauces de poisson de l'antiquité', *Riv. di Stud. Liguri* 1961, 70–96.

159. Ter., *Phorm.* 342; Hor., *Sat.* 2, 2, 77.

160. For specimen menus and good cooking, see Hor., *Sat.* 2, 4; 2, 8; Mart. 5, 78; 10, 48; Plin., *Ep.* 1, 15; Juv. 11, 65ff. *Bellaria*, AG 13, 11, 6f. (Varro). Pears, Colum. 5, 10, 18.

161. Sen., *Cons. ad Helv.* 10, 3; Cic., *Ad Att.* 13, 52, 1 (cf. Suet., *DJ* 53); Suet., *D.Cl.* 33; *Vit.* 13; Fronto, *De Eloq.* 1, 4 (ii, 56 Loeb); Marquardt, 330; Friedlaender ii, 291–3 (E.T. ii, 153f.).

162. Cic., *Ad Att.* 13, 52; Juv., *Sat.* 5, 114–173 (details of the different foods served); Lucian, *Cronosolon* 17f (399f.); Mart. 1, 20; Plin., *Ep.* 2, 6; Hadrian, *Vita.* 17, 4.

163. Cic., *Ad fam.* 9, 26, 1; cf. *Ad Q.f.* 3, 1, 19, 'Hoc inter cenam Tironi dictavi'.

164. Plin., *NH* 14, 94–7; Petron., *Sat.* 34.

165. Varro, *RR* 1, 65; Athen. 1, 26c–27c. Vintages, Plin., *NH* 14, 94 (Opimian); Mart. 10, 48, 20; Juv., *Sat.* 1, 5, 32; Sen., *Ep.* 114, 26.

166. Hor., *Car.* 3, 19, 11–17; Auson., *Griphus ternarii numeri* 1–4.

167. Lucil. 1122f. M; AG 13, 11, 3 (Varro); Plut., Mor. 660B (*Quaest. Conv.* 4 pr.).

168. E.g. CN, *Att.* 14, 1, '*Nemo in conviviis eius aliud acroama audivit quam anagnosten*'. Plin., *Ep.* 6, 31, 13, *acroamata* when Trajan entertained his guests at Centumcellae. *Acroamata* discussed, Plut., *Quaest. Conv.* 7, 8 (*Mor.* 711B–713F).

169. Cic., *Ad Att*, 1, 12, 4, death of the 'gay and amusing' *anagnostes*, Sositheos; *Ad Fam.* 5, 9, 2, a runaway (*fugitivus*) *anagnostes*; Plin. *Ep.* 5, 19, 3; 8, 1, 2; cf. *ILS* 7770, '*Grammaticus lectorque fui*'. Women so employed, *ILS* 7771 (*lectrix*), *CIL* vi, 33830, 34270 (*anagnostria*).

170. Plin., *Ep.* 3, 5, 12; Juv. 11, 182; AG 18, 5. Cf. Petron., *Sat.* 68.

171. Mart. 3, 50; cf. 5, 78, 25.

172. Plin., *Ep.* 9, 34; Mart. 11, 52, 16–18.

173. AG 1, 22, 5 (Varro); 2, 22, 1; 3, 19, 1 (Gavius Bassus); Juv. 11, 180ff. SHA, *AS* 34, 6–8, Severus Alexander's highly cultured dinner parties.

174. *Lyristes*, Plin., *Ep.* 1, 15, 2; 9, 17, 3; 9, 36, 4. *Tibicen*, Quint. 1, 10, 20 (with chorus, Mart. 9, 77); *Citharoedus*, Mart. 5, 56, 8f.; Singers, AG 19, 9; Macrob. 2, 4, 28.

175. Suet., *DA* 74; Juv. 15, 16; Plut., *Mor.* 673B (*Quaest. Conv.* 5 pr.).

176. *Comoedus*: Plin., *Ep.* 1, 15, 2; 3, 1, 9; 9, 17, 3; 9, 36, 4; Plut., Mor. 673 B (*Quaest. Conv.* 5 pr.). Cf. SHA, *MA* 2, 2.

177. E.g. Plin., *Ep.* 5, 19, 3.

178. '*Sermones, ut castitate integros, ita adpetibiles venustate*', Macrob., *Sat.* 1, 1, 4.

179. AG 2, 22, 1–26.

180. AG 13, 11.

181. *De Offic.* 1, 132–7.

182. Juv. 6, 434–56.

183. *Quaest. Conv.* 1, 8f.; 2, 3f.; 4, 5; 5, 7 (*Mor.* 625D–627F; 635E–638F; 669E–671C; 680C–683B).

184. *Quaest. Conv.* 2, 1, 2 (*Mor.* 630).

185. Plin., *Ep.* 6, 31, 13f.; TA 14, 16, 1f.

186. Plut., *Quaest. Conv.* 5 pr. (*Mor.* 673A); Suet., *Tib.* 56.

187. Mart. 1, 27, 7; Plut., *Mor.* 612C; 645A (*Quaest. Conv.* 1 pr.; 3 pr.); Lucian, *Symp.* 3.

188. Mart. 1, 27.

189. *De Ben.* 3, 27; cf. Quint. 6, 3, 10, a similar lucky escape of some young men who maligned King Pyrrhus in their cups. Mart. 10, 48, 21–4, '*Nec faciunt quemquam pocula nostra reum*'.

190. Plin., *Ep.* 7, 24; Petron., *Sat.* 53; Macrob., *Sat.* 2, 7, 17; 3, 14, 4; Suet., *DA* 74. The 'Court Players' (at the time of Hadrian)—*histriones aulici*—SHA, *Hadr.* 19, 6; Entertainment at Hadrian's banquets, *Vita* 26, 4.

191. Plut., *Quaest. Conv.* 2, 1, 5–13 (*Mor.* 632A–634F).

192. Lucian, *Symp.* 17–19, 'Μελιταῖον κυνίδιον'; Athen. 10, 421a, b on the danger of this leading to brawls.

193. Juv., *Sat.* 5, 1–5; Quint. 6, 3, 27 (also 62 and 64); Hor. *Sat.* 1, 5, 51–70. See for further refs. *RE* vii, 418f. (Gabba); iiA, 25 (Sarmentus).

194. TA 12, 49, 1; 15, 34, 3; Mart. 14, 96.

195. Hor., *Sat.* 2, 7, 15–18; Petron., *Sat.* 33; Suet., *DA* 71, 2.

196. Plin., *Ep.* 9, 17; Hor., *Sat.* 1, 2, 1; Mart. 5, 78, 26–8; 6, 71; 14, 210; Juv. 11, 162–70; Macrob., *Sat.* 3, 14, 4 (*moriones* and dancing girls). *FGH* 90, F. 78 (Nic. Damasc.), cf. Strabo 5, 4, 13, 250C and SHA, *L. Verus* 4, 9; *Elagab.* 25, 7 (gladiators).

197. Hor., *Car.* 2, 7, 21–8; Mart. 1, 71; 9, 93f.; 11, 36; Petron., *Sat.* 65. T. Vinius takes his widowed daughter to drinks with Tigellinus after dinner, Plut., *Galba* 17. Invitation to drinks after dinner, SHA, *Elag.* 20, 2. On the whole subject, Marquardt, 331–40.

198. Plin., *Ep.* 3, 5, 13. Cf. SHA, *Pertinax* 12, 7, cultured talk after dinner when Pertinax dined *en famille*.

199. *Ep.* 9, 17.

200. Plaut., *Mil. Glor.* 652–5; Juv. 5, 25–9; Athen. 10, 421a and b; *CIL* iv, 7698c; Lucian, *Symp.* 46.

201. Drinking: Sen., *Ep.* 83; 12, 8 (Pacuvius, on whom see *RE* xviii, 2158f., no. 3); SHA, *Verus* 4, 9; Plin., *NH* 14, 137–148; *ILS* 950 (Novellius); Mart. 2, 72; Suet., *Tib.* 42, 1; Galen x, 3 K; *Apophoreta*, Petron., *Sat.* 40; Lucian, *Symp.* 38; SHA, *Elag.* 22.

202. *CIL* iv, 7698b, '*Lascivos vultus et blandos aufer ocellos/coniuge ab alterius, sit tibi in ore pudor*'; Plin., *NH* 14, 141; Hor., *Car.* 3, 6, 21–32; Suet., *C. Cal.* 25, 1.

203. Cic., *De Sen.* 46; Plin., *Ep.* 3, 1, 9; 3, 5, 13; Macrob., *Sat.* 2, 4, 13 (Augustus); Suet., *Nero* 27, 2; *D. Tit.* 7, 1; Mart. 1, 28; CD 49, 7, 6 (Cornificius); Apul., *Met.* 2, 32; Plin., *Ep.* 3, 12 (Younger Cato).

204. L. 39, 6, 9; Plin., *NH* 9, 67; Acr. on Hor., *Sat.* 1, 1, 101f. Auson., *Ephem.* 6.

205. Petron., *Sat.* 36–50; Sen., *Ep.* 47, 5–8; 95, 24; Vedius Pollio, Plin., *NH* 9, 77 and Sen., *De Ira* 3, 40; Trimalchio's slaves, Petron., *Sat.* 30; 41; 47–50; 54; 67 (well fed themselves after the dinner); Lucian, *Symp.* 15 (428). On cooks with difficult masters, Mart. 3, 13; 3, 94; 8, 23; 14, 220.

206. Cic., *In Pisonem* 67.

207. Plin., *NH* 36, 184; Stat., *Silv.* 1, 3, 55f.; W. Deonna—M. Renard, *Croyances et superstitions de table dans la Rome antique*, Brussels 1961, 107–39 and plates xv, xvii, xix–xxii.

208. J. André, *L'Alimentation et la cuisine à Rome*, Paris, 1961; M. Johnston, 'Vitamines', *Cl. Weekly* xxv, 1931/2, 31; 119.

209. Matthew 20, 1–16; *P. Oxy.* 4, 725, 12; 14, 1647, 18–21; *BGU* 1021.

210. Aug., *Conf.* 6, 11, 18; Suet., *Gram.* 24; *C. Gloss. Lat.* 3, 377f.; 646f.; Marrou, 394.

211. Aug., *Conf.* 3, 7, 13; Petron., *Sat.* 12; Mart. 9, 59.

212. Quintil. 11, 3, 23, '*Fuligo lucubrationum bibenda.*'

Chapter II

1. *Ad Att.* 4, 18, 4f.; 2, 8, 2.

2. See Th. Mommsen, *Röm. Chron. bis auf Caesar*, Berlin, 1859, esp. chap. 1, as revised by A. K. Michels, 'The Intercalary Month in

the Pre-Julian Calendar', *Hommages à Albert Grenier*, Latomus, Brussels, 1962, iii, 1174–8. See also A. Degrassi, *Inscr. Ital.* xiii, 2, 314f. and now A. K. Michels, *The Calendar of the Roman Republic*, Princeton, 1967, esp. 145–72. The chief source is Macrob., *Sat.* 1, 13.

3. Suet., *DJ* 40, 1.

4. Cic., *Ad Att.* 6, 1, 1.

5. Suet., *DJ* 40; CD 43, 26, 1; Censor., *De Die Nat.* 20, 8; Macrob., *Sat.* 1, 14, 3 (wrongly giving 443 days).

6. Isid., *Orig.* 6, 17, 25; *RE* iii, 503, s.v. '*Bissextum*'.

7. Auson., *Ep.* 26, 13–18.

8. *CIL* I², 280–2; *Inscr. Ital.* 284–98; *ILS* 8745; *SEHRE*, pl. xxxvi.

9. Macrob., *Sat.* 1, 16, 30–6, quoting Cassius Hemina, F. 14P, '*Servium Tullium fecisse nundinas ut in urbem ex agris convenirent urbanas rusticasque res ordinaturi*', and Rutilius, F. 1 P; Fest. 176 L.

10. *RE* xvii, 1467–72, s.v. '*Nundinae*' (W. Kroll). For the letters see *CIL* i², 210–53; *Inscr. Ital.* 325f.

11. Macrob., *Sat.* 1, 13, 17, '*Dies qui addictus est nundinis*', without doubt, the correct reading.

12. Inscriptions, *Inscr. Ital.* 301–6.

13. Fest. 177 L; Sen., *Ep.* 86, 12; Plin., *NH* 28, 28; Non. 316, 19ff. L., quoting Varro (F. 279), '*Utri magis sunt pueri? Hi pusilli nigri qui expectant nundinas, ut magister dimittat lussum?*' See L. Halkin, 'Le Congé des Nundines dans les écoles romaines', *Rev. belge de phil. et hist.* 1932, 121–30.

14. *RR* 2, praef. 1.

15. See Macrob., *Sat.* 1, 16, 28–36 for pronouncements on this subject; Th. Mommsen, *Staatsr.* iii, 1³, 373.

16. Athen. 6, 274 C. The *nundinalis*—better, *nundialis*—*cocus* of Plaut., *Aul.* 324 has nothing to do with Nundinae. He was the cook, hired for a funeral banquet (*novendialis cena*), as Plaut., *Pseudol.* 796 indicates; Fest. 176, 27 L.

17. This is established by the combined evidence of the Pompeian *graffito*, *CIL* iv, 4182 and a wall-scratching at Dura-Europos, *Preliminary Report of the Sixth Season at Dura-Europos*, New Haven, 1936, 40–4, no. 622. See W. F. Snyder, 'Quinto Nundinas Pompeiis,' *JRS* 1936, 12–18.

18. See A. W. Lintott, *CQ* 1965, 281–5 for a convincing demonstration that this was the meaning and purpose of the *trinundinum*. For a restatement of the traditional view that it was a 25-day period, see A. K. Michels, *O.c.* (n. 2) 191–206.

19. See *RE* vii, 2553.

20. Plut., *Quaest. Conv.* 4, 7; CD 37, 18f.

21. Cic., *Pro Flacc.* 66–9; VM 1, 3, 3; Suet., *DA* 76, 2; Juv. 14, 96–106.

22. Sabbath, Tibull. 1, 3, 18 (*Saturni dies*); Hor. *Sat.* 1, 9, 69f.; Ovid, *AA* 1, 76 and 414. Hor., *Sat.* 2, 3, 291 (Thursday, *Dies Iovis*, according to Porphyry.) Diogenes, Suet., *Tib.* 32, 2.

23. *CIL* i², 220; *Inscr. Ital.* 51–4 (Fasti Sabini), with A. Degrassi's notes; 156 (Fasti Foronovani); 229–31 (Fasti Nolani). Mommsen attributed the seven-day lettering of the Fasti Sabini to '*privata sine dubio superstitio*'. See A. Degrassi, *Inscr. Ital* 326, and now, 'Un nuovo frammento di calendario romano e la settimana planetaria di sette giorni,' *Scritti vari di Antichità*, Rome, 1962, 681–92.

24. W. Helbig, *Wandgemälde* . . . . . *Campaniens*, Leipzig, 1868, 200, n. 1005; Petron., *Sat.* 30.

25. *CIL* i², 218; *Inscr. Ital.* 300–6.

26. Parapegmata, *Inscr. Ital.* 299–301 and 304; 306f.

27. *CIL* iv, 6838; 8820 (Pompeii); 6779, a list of the days of the week.

28. *CIL* iv, 4182. For the correct interpretation, see W. F. Snyder, *JRS* 1936, 17f.

29. Jos., *C. Ap.* 2, 282; Aug., *Civ. Dei* 6, 11; CD 37, 18, 1f.; Juv. 7, 160f.; SHA, *Avid. Cass.* 6, 3.

30. Aus., *Ecl.* 8.

31. Seneca, quoted by Aug., *Civ. Dei* 6, 11; Juv. 14, 105f., *lux ignava*; TH 5, 4, *inertia, ignavia*.

32. *Rev.* 1, 10; Tertull., *De Orat.* 23.

33. On the whole subject, *RE* vii, 2547–78, s.v. '*Hebdomas*' (F. Boll) is excellent, but published before most of the Pompeian evidence was available. See also L. Halkin, *O.c.* (n. 13), 128–30. Constantine, *CI* 3, 12, 2 (3); *CT* 2, 8. Theodosius, *CT* 2, 8, 18, 20, 23 and 25; 15, 5, 2, etc.

34. *FIRA* i, 47, *S.C. de nundinis saltus Beguensis*.

24

35. Varro, *LL* 6, 14; Fest. 304–6 L.

36. Debts, Cic., *In Verr.* 2, 1, 149; Hor., *Epod.* 3, 69; *Sat.* 1, 3, 87; Ovid., *Rem. Am.* 561. Rent, Petron., *Sat.* 38; Mart. 12, 32. School fees, Hor., *Sat.* 1, 6, 75 (whatever reading is adopted).

37. Cannae, AG 5, 17, 3–5; Trasimene, Ovid., *Fast.* 763–8 (reading uncertain); Arausio, Plut., *Lucull.* 27, 8f.; July 18th, L. 6, 1, 11. Vitellius, Suet., *Vit.* 11, 2; TH 2, 91. Pisa, *ILS* 140, 25ff. Augustus would not travel on the day following *Nundinae*, and avoided serious business on the Nones, Suet., *DA* 92, 2.

38. Fest. 144–7 L, s.v. *Mundus*; Macrob., *Sat.* 1, 15, 21f.; 1, 16, 16–19; G. Wissowa, *RK* 443–5. On *dies atri* and *religiosi* generally, A. K. Michels, *O.c.* (n. 2) 62–7.

39. Macrob., *Sat.* 1, 13, 16–19; CD 40, 47, 1f.; 48, 33, 4. See A. K. Michels, *O.c.* (n. 2) 164–7, who thinks the superstition about January 1st to be late and astrological.

40. AG 4, 9, 5; Macrob., *Sat.* 1, 13, 16f.; 1, 15, 21f.; 1, 16, 13–18; Plut., *Mor.* 269 E ff. (*QR* 25); Ovid, *Fast.* 5, 490; 6, 225; Cic., *Ad Q.f.* 2, 4, 2; Petron., *Sat.* 30; 39.

41. AM 26, 1, 7.

42. Fest. 284 L, '*Publica sacra, quae publico sumptu pro populo fiunt*'; Macrob., *Sat.* 1, 14, 11; 1, 16, 3; G. Wissowa, *RK* 129–53; 432–49.

43. Varro, *LL* 6, 28; A. Degrassi, *Inscr. Ital.* 364–8.

44. On dates of Feriae and Ludi, see *CIL* i², 297–304; *Inscr. Ital.* 364–76. On the Feriae, see Varro, *LL* 6, 12–26; W. Warde Fowler, *The Roman Festivals*, London, 1899; E. O. James, *Seasonal Feasts and Festivals*, London, 1961, 159–198.

45. G. Wissowa, *RK* 143–6.

46. Varro, *LL* 6, 13; Fest. 71 L; 117 L; Ovid, *Fast.* 2, 857–60; 3, 517–22; G. Wissowa, *RK* 144f.

47. On Feriae Conceptivae and Imperativae, see Macrob., *Sat.* 1, 16, 6. The major Feriae Conceptivae were the Feriae Latinae (three or four days, fixed by the consuls on entering office); Compitalia (one day, in the Empire extended to three, selected by the praetor, in late December or early January); Sementivae (two days in January, separated by a seven-day interval, chosen by the Pontifices, Varro, *LL* 6, 26); Fornacalia, the Feast of Ovens (a day in February fixed by the Curio Maximus for each Curia,

on the understanding that people who missed it or who did not know what their Curia was, could celebrate the Quirinalia, the Feast of Fools, on February 17th instead, Ovid, *Fast.* 2, 527–32); Paganalia (the date fixed by Magistri Pagi); Ambarvalia (three days in May); Augurium Canarium (sacrifice of a red dog at a date fixed by the Augurs, when the corn was in ear before harvest, Plin., *NH* 18, 14); Amburbium (perhaps, though Feriae Conceptivae, celebrated on February 2nd); Florifertum (late April or early May). For details, see the separate articles in *RE*.

48. L. 27, 51, 8; JC *BG* 2, 35, 4; 7, 90, 8; Cic., *Phil.* 14, 29 and 37; App., *BC* 3, 74, 302; *RGDA* 4.

49. See Fasti Triumphales, *Inscr. Ital.* xiii, 1, 534–71.

50. See the Feriale Duranum, *Yale Class. Stud.* vii, 1940.

51. *Inscr. Ital.* 128f. and 144.

52. For the new imperial festivals and games, see A. Degrassi, *Inscr. Ital.* 368f.; 373–5; *Yale Class. Stud.* vii, 1940, 226–317, including epigraphic records of celebrations of the older festivals under the Empire.

53. *Yale Class. Stud.* vii, 1940, 182–7. Of the consecrated first-century emperors only Vespasian, Titus and Nerva are missing; but the record of celebrations in the last three months of the year (the time of Vespasian's and Titus' birthdays) does not survive on the papyrus.

54. *Inscr. Ital.* 237–62.

55. G. Wissowa, RK, 353f. (Isis); 317–27 (Magna Mater).

56. *Inscr. Ital.* 261 (Fasti of Philocalus); G. Wissowa, RK 365–8; *RE* iiiA, 907–12.

57. Macrob., *Sat.* 1, 16, 6; *Inscr. Ital.* 367.

58. *CT* 2, 8, 19; 2, 8, 22.

59. *Inscr. Ital.* 263–76 (Fasti Polemii Silvii); Aug., *Conf.* 6, 2; *Ep.* 29, 9f.; *RE* i, 1816f. (Amburbium); J. Carcopino, *Aspects mystiques de la Rome païenne*, Paris, 1942, 35ff. (Syracuse). See, generally, G. Wissowa, RK 95–102. On celebration of the Memorials of the Christian martyrs, Aug., *Conf.* 6, 2; *Ep.* 29, 9.

60. Cic., *Ad Att.* 14, 10, 1; 14, 14, 2 etc. See index to Tyrrell-Purser, *The Correspondence of M. Tullius Cicero*.

61. *Ad Att.* 5, 20, 5; 6, 1, 12; 7, 7, 3. TH 3, 78, on the army's fondness for the Saturnalia.

62. Cic., *De Legg.* 2, 29; Cato, *RR* 57; Col. 2, 21, 1–5. Cf. Virg., *Georg.* 1, 268–72.

63. Cic., *De Rep.* 1, 14; *De Or.* 1, 24; *Ad Q.f.* 3, 1, 1; *Ad Att.* 2, 1, 1; Juv. 11, 191; Plin., *Ep.* 9, 6. Cf. Hor., *Ep.* 1, 7, 75.

64. Pollution of holy days, Macrob. 1, 16, 9–12; Serv. ad Virg., *Georg.* 1, 268; Fest. 292 L; A. K. Michels, *O.c.* (n. 2), 71f. Varro, *LL* 6, 17–20. March 15th, Ovid, *Fast.* 3, 523–42. Quinquatrus, *Inscr. Ital.* 122f. 'Artificum Dies', Ovid, *Fast.* 3, 809–34; Plin., *NH* 35, 143. Merchants and Mercury, Ovid, *Fast.* 5, 663–92. Bakers, Lyd., *De Mens.* 4, 94. Flute-players, L 9, 30, 5–10; Fest. 134 L; Ovid, *Fast.* 6, 649–710; Varro, *LL* 6, 17. Bargees etc., *RE* xvi, 2531–3. Fishermen, Fest. 274f. L; Ovid, *Fast.* 6, 235–40. On the Saturnalia and Compitalia, see pp. 124–6.

65. On marked days, see Ovid, *Fast.* 1, 45–52; Macrob., *Sat.* 1, 16, 2f.; A. Degrassi, 331–7 with full references, and now A. K. Michels, *O.c.* (n. 2) 22–35; 173–90 who, mistrusting the interpretation 'fasti principio' (182f.), counts the 3 FP days as F, making the number of *dies fasti* in the Republic 42. Degrassi calculates 193 *dies comitiales* in the late Republic, Mrs. Michels 195.

66. *Inscr. Ital.* 331; Macrob., *Sat.* 1, 14, 12; Suet., *DA* 32, 2.

67. SHA, *MA* 10, 10.

68. Fest. 162L. See A. Degrassi, 332–4, 106 N or NP days; A. K. Michels, *O.c.* (n. 2), 35, 107 such days.

69. The question is discussed at length by A. K. Michels, *O.c.*, (n. 2) 69–83. See A. Degrassi 332–7 on the numbers of days of different type in the year. His figures for the Julian calendar are: F, 52; C, 191; N. 58; NP, 50; EN, 8; F.P., 3; Q.R.C.F., 2; Q.ST.D.F., 1; for the Republican calendar (with Mommsen's variants, *CIL* 1², 295f., in brackets): F, 39 (45); C, 193 (191); N, 58 (56); NP, 48 (52); EN, 11 (8); F.P., 3 (0); Q.R.C.F., 2 (2); Q.ST.D.F., 1 (1). Mrs. Michels' figures are: F, 42; C, 195; N, 58; NP, 49; EN, 8; *Fissi*, 3.

70. *TA* 14, 12, 1. Cf. Hor., *Car.* 2, 13, 1. See AG 4, 9, 5; 5, 17, 1; Non. 103L, for this late, popular and, Gellius thought, incorrect, use of *nefastus*.

71. For speculation on the date and nature of the Lex Pupia, *RE* xii, 2405; A. K. Michels, *O.c.* (n. 2) 42–5. Days of meeting, *RE*, Supplb. vi, 702f.; Th. Mommsen, *Staatsr.* iii, 2, 921–3. A list of

the dates of known meetings is given by C. Bardt, *Hermes* 1873, 14–27 and 1875, 317f.

72. Cic., *Ad Att.* 1, 14, 5.

73. Cic., *Ad Fam.* 8, 8, 5, dispensation given on Sept. 29th 51 B.C. for the following March.

74. *Discessus Senatus*, Cic., *Ad Fam.* 3, 9, 4; *Ad Att.* 12, 40, 3. *Res Prolatae*, *Ad Att.* 14, 5, 2; TA 2, 35, 1. In the Ciceronian period, except for the two years of public crisis, 44 and 43, there are no known meetings of the Senate between April 5th and May 15th. See Cic., *Ad Fam.* 1, 9, 8. The Conference of Luca, with hundreds of senators present, took place during this break in 56 B.C. On the holiday, see Schol. Bob. on Cic., *In Cur. et Clod.*, 88 Stangl.

75. TA 12, 23, 1; Th. Mommsen, *Staatsr.* iii, 2, 912f.

76. L. 3, 38, 6; Cic., *Phil.* 1, 12; *RE*, Supplb. vi, 700–3.

77. Cic., *Ad Fam.* 8, 8, 5.

78. Cic., *Ad Q.f.* 2, 1, 1.

79. Suet., *DA* 35, 3; CD 55, 3, 1; *Inscr. Ital.* 363.

80. Cic., *Pro Cael.* 1; *In Verr.* 1, 31; 2, 2, 130.

81. Cic., *Pro. Mur.* 28; Sen., *De Brev. Vit.* 7, 8 make this clear.

82. Plin., *Ep.* 8, 21, 2; *FIRA* 1, 7, 7 and 9 (*FIR* 10, 7 and 9); Cic., *Ad Att*, 1, 1, 2; Suet., *DA* 32, 3; cf. D. Cl. 23; *Galb.* 14, 3; *RE* 1, 332–4 (s.v. '*Actus Rerum*').

83. Cic., *In Verr.* 1, 31.

84. *Dig.* 2, 12, 1 and 3f.

85. *CT* 2, 8, 19; 2, 8, 24f.

Chapter III

1. L., *Per.* 59; Suet., *DA* 89, 2; AG 1, 6.

2. CD 56, 10, 3. On Augustus' legislation, see my *Roman Women*, 76f.

3. P. 36, 17, 5–10.

4. H. M. Last, 'Letter to N. H. Baynes, '*JRS* 1947, 152–6.

5. In his painstaking account of features of human generation at the beginning of book 7 of his *Natural Histories* the elder Pliny in-interests himself in women who had numbers of children (57–60), but not in women who had none, though he points to cases of infertile marriages of men and women like Augustus and Livia, each of whom had produced children in a different marriage (57).

In 34,166 he states that wearing something like lead corsets is a powerful check on aphrodisiac tendencies in men. That lead could be damaging to health was generally known. Pliny, *NH* 34,167 says that, when heated, its fumes should not be breathed in. Vitruvius 8, 6, 10f. remarks on the pallor of lead-workers and on the deposit of white lead (*cerussa*) in water from lead pipes and on the advantage, from the point of view both of health and taste, of getting water through earthenware pipes and of keeping it always in earthenware jars. See S. C. Gilfillan, *Bibliography*, p. 344.

6. See my *Roman Women*, 193f. For children of M. Aurelius, *RE* i, 2289. Julian, *CI* 10, 32, 24 (*CT* 12, 1, 55).

7. See *RE* x, 1282–4, s.v. '*Ius Liberorum.*'

8. *Dig.* 47, 11, 4.

9. Keith Hopkins, 'A Textual Emendation in a Fragment of Musonius Rufus', *CQ* 1965, 72–4; 'Contraception in the Roman Empire', *Comparative Studies in Society and History* 1965/6, 124–51.

10. R. Syme, 'Bastards in the Roman Aristocracy', *Proc. Am. Philos. Soc.* 1960, 323–7; Aug., *Conf.* 4, 2, 2.

11. Lucr. 4, 1268–77.

12. Hopkins, 'Contraception . . .' (n. 9 above), 142.

13. Petron., *Sat.* 116. It is harder to draw the same inference from '*Ad liberos suscipiendos*' in Plin., *Ep.* 2, 7, 5, *suscipere* not retaining the literal meaning of *tollere*. Apuleius has the story of a husband (in Greece) who, departing on a journey, instructed his pregnant wife to destroy her child if it should be a girl (*Met.* 10, 23).

14. Suet., *DA* 94, 3, on the authority of Julius Marathus (*RE* x, 669, no. 337).

15. App., *BC* 1, 20, 83; Plin., *Ep.* 7, 24, 3; Petron., *Sat.* 74. See my *Roman Women*, 204f.; 210.

16. CD 69, 20. See A. Watson, *The Law of Persons in the later Roman Republic*, Oxford, 1967, 82–90.

17. Suet., *Gram.* 7 (M. Antonius Gnipho); 21 (C. Melissus of Spoletium); W. L. Westermann, *The Slave Systems of Greek and Roman Antiquity*, Philadelphia, 1955, 86 and works there quoted. For Asia Minor, see A. Cameron, *Anatolian Studies presented to W. H. Buckler*, Manchester, 1939, 27–62; Plin., *Ep.* 10, 65f. For Egypt, *P. Oxy.* 1, 37f. etc. For N. Africa, e.g. *CIL* viii, 2394; 2396; 3002; 12879; 24687.

18. Twelve the minimum age for marrage, CD 54, 16, 7. Living together before twelve, *Dig.* 23, 2, 4; 24, 1, 32, 27; 48, 5, 14(13), 8; cf. Plut., *Numa* 26, 1–3—even from the age of seven, *CIL* vi, 21562; ix, 3710. Puberty of girls at fourteen, Macrob., *In Somn. Scip.* 1, 6, 71; at twelve, *Sat.* 7, 7, 6. Quintilian's wife had a child at thirteen, Friedlaender iv, 135; F. Vollmer, *Rhein. Mus.* 1891, 348. For the improbable view that marriages were frequently consummated before the girl's puberty, M. Durry, 'Le mariage des filles impubères à Rome', *CRAI* 1955, 84–91; 'Le mariage des filles impubères dans la Rome antique', *Rev. int. des Dr. de l'Ant.* 1955, 263–73; 'Sur le mariage romain', *Rev. int. des Dr. de l'Ant.* 1956, 227–43; 'Le mariage des filles impubères chez les anciens Romains', *Anthropos*, 1955, 432–4; K. M. Hopkins, 'The Age of Roman Girls at Marriage', *Population Studies*, 1965, 315 ff.

19. Plin., *Ep.* 8, 10.

20. See my *Roman Women*, 195f., with notes; Fronto, *De nep. amisso* ii, 1 (ii, 222 Loeb); *CIL* iii, 3572; Quint. 6, praef. 6; 10.

21. *FIRA* 24 (*FIR* 30), 56; Ulp. 16, 1a.

22. H. J. Leon, *The Jews of Ancient Rome*, Philadelphia, 1960, 229.

23. *CT* 11, 27, 1, A.D. 315; 5, 10, 1 (*CI* 4, 43, 2), A.D. 329.

24. *ILS* 977; 6509; 6675; 6818 (quoted in text); Plin. *Ep.* 7, 18; *Pan.*, 28; *Dig.* 34, 1, 14, 1; 35, 2, 89; H. Mattingly–E. A. Sydenham, *RIC* ii, 220; 240; 250; 259; 261; 277f.; 286f.; B. W Henderson, *Five Roman Emperors*, Cambridge, 1927, 214–24; F. C. Bourne, 'The Roman Alimentary Program and Italian Agriculture', *TAPA* 1960, 47–75; R. Duncan-Jones, 'The Purpose and Organization of the Alimenta', *PBSR* 1964, 123–46, an admirable and fully documented article. Cf. P. Garnsey, *Historia* 1968, 367–80.

25. Quint. 4, 2, 42, '*Natum filium sustuli, educavi, in adulescentiam perduxi*'; Macrob., *Sat.* 1, 16, 36; Suet., *Nero* 6, 2.

26. SHA, *MA* 9, 7–9 (confused); Apul, *Apol.* 89; F. Schulz, 'Roman Registers of Births and Birth Certificates', *JRS* 1942, 78–91; 1943, 55–64.

27. Sen., *Ep.* 12, 3; Macrob., *Sat.* 1, 11, 49.

28. Hor., *Sat.* 2, 3, 247, '*Plostello adiungere mures*'.

29. Dogs, Juv. 9, 61; Plin., *Ep.* 9, 12, 1. Birds, Petron., *Sat.* 46, '*In aves morbosus est*'; PLM (Petronius) iv, 43, 91. Regulus, Plin., *Ep.* 4, 2, 3.

30. Hor., *Sat.* 2, 3, 248, '*Equitare in harudine longa*'.

31. Pers., *Sat.* 3, 51; Hor., *Car.* 3, 24, 57.

32. Hor., *Sat.* 2, 3, 247 and 275.

33. Hor., *Car.* 3, 24, 58; *Sat.*, 2, 3, 171f. and 248; Pers., *Sat.* 3, 48f.; Mart. 5, 84, 1–3; 14, 18.

34. Macrob., *Sat.* 1, 7, 22.

35. Plut., *Cato mi.* 2, 6f.; SHA, *Gallieni ii* 4, 3; *SS* 1, 4; Epict., *Man.* 29, 3 (cf. D–S ii, 1587, fig. 3584); CD 41, 39, 4.

36. Sen., *Ep.* 24, 13.

37. Aug., *Conf.* 2, 4, 9; 2, 6, 12.

38. Plut., *Cato mai.* 20, 5; Tac., *Dial.* 28, 6; Quint. 1, 1, 6; Plut., *Sert.* 2, 1.

39. Cic., *Brut.* 79; Quint. 11, 2, 50; VM 9, 7, 6.

40. Aug., *Conf.* 1, 14, 23; Auson., *Comm. Prof. Burd.* 8; *Ep.* 22, 45–50; Marrou, 379–88. *CT* 13, 3, 11, regulation for appointment of a Greek *grammaticus* at Trier, A.D. 376.

41. Quint. 1, 1; Tac., *Dial.* 29, 1.

42. Plin., *NH* 7, 128, the highest sum ever paid for a slave; Suet., *Gram.* 3; *RE* xiii, 2095, no. 15.

43. So F. Muenzer, RE xiii, 892, s.v. 'M. Livius Salinator'. E. Fraenkel is sceptical, *RE*, Supplb. v, 598–607, s.v. 'Livius Andronicus'. See also Schanz-Hosius 1, 45f. The main sources are Hieron., *Chron.*, ann. 1830 (ii, 125p Schoene); Cic., *Brut.* 72f.; Suet., *Gram.* 1.

44. AG 15, 11, 1; Cic., *De Or.* 3, 93; Quint. 2, 4, 42; Suet., *Rhet.* 1; Hieron., *Chron.*, ann. 1938 (ii, 133 Schoene); Suet., *DJ* 42, 1; *DA* 42, 3; Oros. 7, 3, 6. They were rated below dancing girls, however, in the famine of A.D. 383 or 384, AM 14, 6, 19.

45. Plut., *Cat. mai.* 22f.; *Dig.* 50, 13, 1–6; Tac., *Agr.* 4, 4f.

46. Quint. 7, 1, 38; 7, 4, 39; *Decl.* 268; Tac., *Dial.* 5, 4f.; 8, 3; Sen., *Ep.* 88.

47. Plin., *Ep.* 3, 3, a boy educated at home until the final stage (rhetoric), and then sent to school; Quint. 1, 2.

48. Plut., *Cato mai.* 20, 4–7; Cic., *Ad Q. f.* 2, 4, 2; M. Aur., *Med.* 1, 4.

49. Plin., *Ep.* 2, 18; cf. 3, 3, 3 ff.; Quint. 1, 2, 3 and 16. ILS 7763, an elementary schoolmaster 'summa cum castitate in discipulos suos'. For this same emphasis on moral standards in enactments of fourth-century emperors, cf. *CT* 13, 3, 5f.

50. Suet., *D. Vesp.* 18; Juv. 7, 186f., 2000 sesterces per pupil per annum; Aug., *Conf.* 1, 16, 26, '*Legum supra mercedem salaria decernentium*'.

51. Plin., *Pan.* 47; SHA, *Hadr.* 16, 10; Aug., *Conf.* 5, 13, 23; H. Bardon, *Les Empereurs et les lettres latines d'Auguste à Hadrien*, Paris, 1940, 299–303.

52. Plin., *Pan.* 47; *Dig.* 50, 4, 18, 30; 27, 1, 6, 8f.

53. Cic., *De Rep.* 4, 3.

54. AG 16, 6, 1, '*Linguae Latinae litterator Roma a Brundisinis accersitus*'; Strabo 4, 181C; TA 3, 43; Eumenius, *Pro instaur. scholis*, *Pan. Lat.* (OCT) 9; T., *Agr.* 21, 3; Florus, *Virgilius orator an poeta*; Fronto, *Ad Amicos* 1, 7 (ii, 168 Loeb.).

55. McCrum-Woodhead 458; H. Herzog, 'Urkunden zur Hochschulpolitik der roem. Kaiser', *SitzB. Berlin* 1935, 967–1019; *Dig.* 50, 4, 18, 30; 27, 1, 6, 2f.

56. See Th. Haarhoff, *Schools of Gaul*, Oxford, 1920, 135–50.

57. Plin., *Ep.* 4, 13.

58. Apul., *Flor.* 18; Aug., *Conf.* 2, 3, 5.

59. [Lucian], *Amores* 44; Quint. 1, 1, 8 (cf. 1, 2, 10); Suet., *Gram.* 23 (Remmius Palaemon); Mart. 11, 39; Juv. 10, 117 (*capsarius*); Suet., *Nero* 36, 2; Hor., *Sat.* 1, 6, 71–82.

60. Sen., *Ep.* 88, 20; Quint. 1, 1, 15–18; Mart. 9, 68; Marrou, 389–99; Aug., *Conf.* 1, 13, 20. On elementary arithmetic, Hor., *AP* 325–30.

61. Aug., *Conf.* 1, 9, 14–13, 22; 1, 16, 26; Auson., *Ep.* 22, 24–34; L. 6, 25, 9.

62. Mart. 9, 68; 14, 223; *C. Gloss Lat.* 3, 645f. Cf. Aus., *Ep.* 13, 10, six hours teaching a day for the schoolmaster, and six hours rest.

63. Marrou, 400–11; Haarhoff, *O. c.* (n. 56), 52–68.

64. Quint. 1, 12, 13. On authors studied, see Aus., *Ep.* 22, 45–65; Marrou, 404–6. Terence, Aug., *Conf.* 1, 16, 26.

65. Marrou, 412–21; Haarhoff, *O.c.* (n. 56), 68–93.

66. Sen., *Controv.* 1, 5. Cf. Juv. 7, 158–70; Aug., *Conf.* 1, 17, 27.

67. Cic., *De Or.* 1, 53–7; 68f.; 3, 76–80 (Philosophy); 1, 166–200; *Orat.* 120 (Law); *De Or.* 1, 158f.; 201 *Orat.* 120 (History.)

68. Quint. 1, pr. 9–20; Tac., *Dial.* 28–35.

69. Schol., Juv. 1, 128; AG 13, 13, 1; Marrou, 418–21; C. Pharr, 'Roman Legal Education', *CJ* 1938/9, 257–70. Alfenus Varus, AG 7, 5, 1; *RE* i, 1472–4, no. 8.

70. *Dig.* 3, 1, 5 (cf. VM 8, 3).

71. *Dig., Const.* '*Omnem*' 9 and 11; *CT* 14, 9, 1 (tr. C. Pharr).

72. Sen., *Ep.* 88; Quint. 1, 4, 22; 2, 1, 1ff. (but cf. 3, 1, 3); Tac., *Dial.* 28ff., esp. 29, 4 and 30, 1; Petron., *Sat.* 3. On this subject, R. E. Burton, 'The Elective System in the Roman Schools', *CJ* 1920/1, 532–5; E. O. Nybakken, 'Progressive Education in the Roman Empire', *CJ* 1938/9, 38–42.

73. For criticism to this effect, cf. Sen., *Ep.* 106, 12; 108, 30–4; Petron., *Sat.* 1; Tac., *Dial.* 35; Juv. 7, 150–77. For a defence of Roman rhetorical education, see E. P. Parks, *The Roman Rhetorical Schools as a Preparation for the Courts under the early Empire,* Baltimore 1945, esp. 61–107.

74. C. Pharr, *O.c.* (n. 69).

75. Juv. 7, 178–88; Plut., *Mor.* 4B (*De lib. educ.*).

76. Tac., *Agr.* 21.

77. L. 26, 22, 15; Quint. 1, 1, 6.

78. Quint. 1, 2, 6–8; T., *Dial.* 29; Juv. 14.

79. CIL vi, 21846; 18324; 33929 (from Rome). See H.-I. Marrou, *ΜΟΥΕΙΚΟΣ ΑΝΗΡ*, Rome, 1964, esp. 197–207 for further examples.

80. Veg. 2, 9; cf. Haarhoff, *O.c.* (n. 56), 124–32.

81. Quinquatrus, Hor., *Ep.* 2, 2, 197f.; Ovid., *Fast.* 3, 829f.; Juv. 10, 114f.; Symmach., *Ep.* 5, 85. Summer, Mart. 10, 62.

82. Varro, *RR* 1, 17, 5; CN., *Att.* 13, 4. *Novicii*, Quint. 1, 12, 9; *Dig.* 21, 1, 65, 2.

83. Plin., *NH* 33, 135; TA 14, 43, 4; Petron., *Sat.* 37 and 47; ILS 2927.

84. CD 56, 27, 3; *CIL* vi, 6213–6640; W. L. Westermann, *The Slave Systems of Greek and Roman Antiquity,* Philadelphia, 1955, 88f.

85. J.E. Packer, 'Housing and Population in imperial Ostia and Rome', *JRS* 1967, 80–95, esp. 85 and 87; A. Mairui, *La Casa di Menandro,* Rome, 1933, 1, 186–8; 2, pl. 1, nos. 35–8; M. Rostovtzeff, *SEHRE* 565, n. 23; Plin., Ep. 2, 17, 9 and 22; 7, 27, 13; Westermann, *O.c.* (n. 84), 107.

86. Cic., *Pro Mil.* 59; *Part. Or.* 118; *Pro Deiot.* 3; *Dig.* 49, 14, 2, 6. State purchase, CD 55, 5, 4 (Augustus); TA 2, 30, 3; CD 57, 19, 2 (Tiberius). Torture, Cic., *Pro Cluent.* 176.

87. Cic., *Ad Fam.* 4, 12, 3; *S.C. Silanianum* (A.D. 10) and *S.C. Claudianum* (A.D. 57), *Dig.* 29, 5, esp. 29, 5, 19; Paul, *Sent.* 3, 5, 1–12; *TA* 13, 32, 1.

88. *TA* 14, 42–5.

89. Plin., *Ep.* 3, 14.

90. *Dig.* 29, 5, 1, 22; Plin., *Ep.* 8, 14, 12–25. Cf. *Dig.* 29, 5, 10, 1.

91. *TA* 14, 42–5.

92. *Dig.* 40, 8, 2; SHA, *Hadr.*, 18, 10; Gaius, *Inst.* 1, 53.

93. Sen., *De Ben.* 3, 28; *Ep.* 47 (picked up in Macrob., *Sat.* 1, 11, 7–16); Westermann, *O.c.* (n. 84), 113–7; E. J. Jonkers, 'De l'influence du Christianisme sur la législation relative à l'esclavage dans l'antiquité, '*Mnemosyne* 1934, 241–80.

94. Galen 5, 17–21K; Sen., *Ep.* 47; Petron., *Sat.* 67; 74.

95. VP 2, 67, 2; App., *BC* 4, 43, 179—48, 208. The story of Restio's slave is repeated by Macrob., *Sat.* 1, 11, 18–20. Cf. Sen., *De Ben.* 3, 23–7 on signal nobility of slaves in their masters' interest. Cf. J. Vogt, *Sklaverei und Humanität*, Wiesbaden, 1965, 83–96.

96. *TA* 15, 51 and 57.

97. Cic., *Ad Fam.* 16, 1–9; 11f.; Plin., *Ep.* 5, 19.

98. Hor., *Sat.* 2, 7; Cic., *Ad Fam.* 16, 16. On slavery in the Roman household, chapter 2 of R. H. Barrow, *Slavery in the Roman Empire*, London, 1928, is excellent.

99. Plut., *Cato mai.* 21, 7f.; *Crass.* 2, 7. Epictetus, *RE* vi, 126f., no. 3.

100. *ILS* 1825f. Infant geniuses, *ILS* 7755f. Teachers, *CIL* vi, 1052 (*A Capite Africae*); 7290; 9740. *Dig* 33, 7, 12, 32; Plin., *Ep.* 7, 27, 13; AM 26, 6, 15; 29, 3, 3. See *RE* xviii, 2204f., s.v. '*Paedagogiani*'; Herzog, *O.c.* (n. 55), 1015; C. A. Forbes, 'The Education and Training of Slaves in Antiquity', *TAPA* 1955, 321–60 and other works there quoted, p. 322, n. 6.

101. See J. A. Crook, *Law and Life of Rome*, London, 1967, 200–2.

102. Sen., *De Ben.* 3, 21; cf. *Dig.* 21, 1, 65, 2; 25, 1, 6.

103. Lex Fufia Caninia, Gaius, *Inst.* 1, 42–6; Ulp. 1, 24; Paul, *Sent.* 4, 14. Lex Aelia Sentia, Gaius, *Inst.* 1, 18; 38–43.

104. *SIG*[3], 543.

105. Stat., *Silv.* 3, 3; Mart. 7, 40; *RE* iii, 2670f., no. 31.

106. Petron., *Sat.* 45 and 126 (with J. P. Sullivan, *The 'Satyricon' of Petronius*, London, 1968, 119–22); Juv. 9; *TA* 12, 53, 1; Gaius,

Inst. 1, 84; P. R. C. Weaver, 'Gaius i, 84 and the *S.C. Claudianum*', *CR* 1964, 137–9; A. J. Crook, 'Gaius, *Institutes* i, 84–6', *CR* 1967, 7f. and *O.c.* (n. 101), 62.

107. Lucr. 3, 894–6; Juv. 14; Sen., *De Provid.* 2, 5. On married life from the woman's point of view, see my *Roman Women*, 173–223.

108. Plin., *Ep.* 9, 12.

109. SHA, *MA* 29, 10.

110. So Gaius, *Inst.* 1, 55.

111. L. 2, 41, 10; Sen., *De Clem.* 15.

112. Suet., *Tib.* 15, 2. On *peculium*, cf. L. 2, 41, 10.

113. F. H. Schulz, *Classical Roman Law*, Oxford, 1951, 227f.

114. VM 8, 6, 3; Plin., *Ep.* 4, 2, 2; *CT* 2, 8, 1; J. A. Crook, '*Patria Potestas*', CQ 1967, 113–22.

115. Cic., *Pro Cluent.* 141; *De Orat.* 2,224; *De Offic.* 1, 129; Plut., *Cato mai.* 20, 7f.

116. Macrob., *Sat.* 1, 16, 36.

117. Marriage at twelve, *CI* 5, 4, 24. Engagement, AG 4, 4; CD 54, 16, 7; 60, 5, 7; *Dig.* 23, 1, 14. Just., *Inst.* 1, 10, affinity, etc. Aug., *Conf.* 6, 13–15. See my *Roman Women*, 177–9.

118. *Dig.* 23, 1, 11f.; A Watson, *The Law of Persons in the later Roman Republic*, Oxford, 1967, 11–18.

119. Girls, Auson., *Ep.* 22 pr, quoting Ter., *Eun.* 313. Boys, Porphyrio and ps. Acron on Hor., *Sat.* 1, 2, 31f; Ter., *Hec.* 541–56. Cf. Cic., *Pro Cael.* 48 ff.; Aug., *Conf.* 2, 3, 5–8.

120. *Bulla*, Macrob., *Sat.* 1, 6, 9–14; *RE* iii, 1048–51.

121. Suet., *DA* 38, 2; Cic., *Ad Att.* 6, 1, 12; Suet., *C. Cal.* 10, 1. See *RE* viA, 1450–3, s.v. '*Tirocinium Fori*' for full refs.

122. Ovid., *Fast.* 3, 771–88. See A. Degrassi, 425f.

123. CD 55, 10, 2.

124. See J. A. Crook, *O.c.* (n. 101) 115–8.

125. See, on this question, K. M. Hopkins, *O.c.* (n. 18), with criticism of A. G. Harkness, ' Age at Marriage and at Death in the Roman Empire,' *TAPA* 1896, 35–72 and M. Bang, 'Das gewöhnliche Alter der Mädchen bei der Verlobung und Verheiratung' in Friedlaender iv, 133–41. See also n. 18 above. Alimentary inscriptions, *ILS* 6278; 6818.

126. Plut., Crass. 1, 1–3. Cf. J. A. Crook, CQ 1967, 117f.

127. Sen., *De Ben.* 1, 11f.; Mart. 8, 64; 9, 53; 10, 24, 29 and 87; Ovid., *Trist.* 3, 13; 5, 5; Censorin., *De Die Nat.*; *CT* 16, 10, 12; *RE* vii, 1143f.

128. *Dig.* 50, 16, 98. See p. 58.

129. Auson., *Parental.*; VM 2, 1, 8; Mart. 9, 54f.; Tertull., *De Idol.* 10; Ovid, *Fast.* 2, 533–68 and 617–38.

130. See *RE* xiii, 1648–51, s.v. '*Lucina*' (Latte); xiv, 2306–9, s.v. '*Matronalia*' (Weinstock) and esp. Plaut., *Mil. Glor.* 691; Hor, *Car.* 3, 8, 1; Mart. 5, 84, 11f.; Suet., *D. Vesp.* 19, 1; *Dig.* 24, 1, 31, 8. Entertainment of slaves, Macrob., *Sat.* 1, 12, 7; Lydus, *De Mens.* 3, 22.

131. Hor., *Ep.* 2, 2, 197f.; Symmach., *Ep.* 5, 85. See, further, p. 75.

132. Ovid, *Fast.* 4, 353–6; AG 2, 24, 2; 18, 2, 11; *Fast. Praen., Inscr. Ital.* xiii, 2, 126; Plaut., *Men.* 101; L. 10, 23, 1–10.

133. Fest., p. 460L; Plut., *QR* 100 and H. J. Rose, *The Roman Questions of Plutarch*, Oxford, 1924, p. 209.

134. Length of the holiday, Cic., *Ad Att.* 13, 52, 1; Suet., *C. Cal.* 17, 2; Mart. 4, 88, 2; 14, 72; Macrob., *Sat.* 1, 11, 50. Schools closed, Mart. 5, 84. The market, Schol. Juv. 6, 154. Presents, *RE* iiA, 2278, s.v. '*Sigillaria*'. Candles, Varro, *LL* 5, 64; Macrob., *Sat.* 1, 7, 32. Dolls, Sen, *Ep.* 12, 3. Other gifts, Mart. 4, 88; 7, 53; 14, 72 etc.; SHA, *Hadr.* 17, 3; *Aurel.* 50, 2. Money, Suet., *D. Cl.* 5.

135. Gaming, Mart. 5, 84; 14, 1. Dress, Mart. 14, 1 and 141. Slaves, Sen., *Ep.* 47, 14; Mart. 14, 79; Macrob., *Sat.* 1, 7, 26 and 37; 1, 24, 22f. See generally *RE* iiA, 201–11, s.v. '*Saturnalia*' (Nilsson).

136. Epict., *Diss.* 1, 25, 8; Sen., *Ep.* 47, 14; Lucian, *Saturn.* 2 and 4; T*A* 13, 15, 2f.

137. Mart. 5, 84.

138. Cato, *De Agr.* 5, 3; 57; Col. 11, 1, 19; *Inscr. Ital.* xiii, 2, 390f.

139. Tertull., *De Idol.* 10 and 14; Liban., *Orat.* 9; *Progymn.* 12, 5; M. P. Nilsson, 'Studien zur Vorgeschichte des Weihnachtsfestes', *Archiv. f. Religionsw.* 1918/9, 50–150 (*Opuscula Selecta*, 1, 1951, 214–311).

140. P. 6, 53–5; T*A* 3, 76.

141. *Lex. Col. Iul. Urs., FIRA* 1, 21 (*FIR* 28), 95; AG 16, 4, 3f.; *Novendialis Cena*, T*A* 6, 5,1; Porphyr. on Hor., *Epod.* 17, 48; Apul., *Met.* 9, 31.

142. Petron., *Sat.* 71; VM 7, 8, 5–9.

143. Cic., *In Verr.* 2, 1, 110; Gaius, *Inst.* 2, 224–7.

144. On the problem of the sum, see *RE* xii, 2418–20. The evidence is AG 6, 13 and Gaius, *Inst.* 2, 274 (*aeris*); ps-Asconius 247 Stangl (on Cic., *In Verr.* 2, 1, 104) and CD 56, 10, 2 (sesterces). Cf. Cic., *In Verr.* 2, 1, 104–14.

145. Cic., *De Fin.* 2, 55; Gaius, *Inst.* 2, 274.

146. Suet., *DA* 101, 2; Plin., *Ep.* 8, 18, 2; Petron., *Sat.* 71.

147. Plin., *Ep.* 8, 18 with S-W's notes.

148. VM 8, 2, 2; Tac., *Agr.* 43, 4 (Domitian co-heir of Agricola with widow and daughter). Cf. T*A* 14, 31, 1; 16, 11, 2 etc. As Mr. Oswyn Murray ingeniously points out to me, a will naming the Emperor among the legatees should have been safe from attack by a *delator*.

149. V.M. 7, 7, 6f.

150. Plin., *Ep.* 4, 2.

Chapter IV

1. Cic., *De Offic.* 1, 69; T*A* 4, 40, 8, 'reipublicae negotia'.

2. L. 21, 63, 3.

3. Plaut., *Trinumm.* 330–2.

4. Cic., *De Offic.* 2, 89.

5. Cic., *De Offic.* 1, 150f.

6. Plin., *NH* 29, 1–27; Suet., *Tib.* 68, 4.

7. Mart. 5, 9; Galen 10, 4f. K (*Meth. Med.* 1, 1); S. Reinach, s.v. '*medicus*', in D–S 3, esp. 1671b and 1674b; I. E. Drabkin, 'On Medical Education in Greece and Rome', *Bull. Hist. Med.* 15, 1944, 333–51; C. A. Forbes, 'The Education and Training of Slaves in Antiquity', *TAPA* 1955, esp. 343–53. Inscriptions, *ILS* 7786–7812.

8. See Marrou 401; 412f. (E.T. 284); Auson, *Grat. Act. pro Cons.* 7.

9. Cic., *Ad Fam.* 13, 6, 9 and 65; *Ad Att.* 11, 10, 1.

10. Cic., *Ad Fam.* 13 passim; *De Offic.* 1, 151; *De Senect.* 51–60; Petron., *Sat.* 48; 75ff.

11. Municipal offices, *FIRA* 1, 13 (*FIR* 18), 94 (cf. Cic., *Ad Fam.* 6, 18, 1 and *In Verr.* 2, 2, 122). Mart. 5, 56, 11; M. Rostovtzeff,

SEHRE, pl. iv; xxvi, 2; xxviii; xxx; xxxiii; R. Meiggs, *Ostia*, Oxford, 1960, pl. xxvii. Cf., especially, *ILS* 4851 (*mango*); 7457 (reaper); 7477; 7519; 7542; 7715. For the whole assortment, see *ILS* 7366–7817 and the index vol. iii, pp. 726–44. See F. M. de Robertis, *Lavoro e lavatori nel mondo romano*, Bari, 1963.

12. Petron., *Sat.* 29.

13. Cic., *De Div.* 2, 142; *Pro Planc.* 66; Suet., *DA* 45, 1; SHA, *MA* 15, 1.

14. *Curc.* 555f. Cf. *Truc.* 611, '*umbraticulus*', again a soldier's epithet for a civilian.

15. TA 13, 42, 4; 14, 53, 4; *Dial.* 5, 3; Quint. 1, 2, 18; 10, 5, 17; 11, 3, 26; 12, 3, 11f.; 12, 10, 15; Cic., *Pro. Mur.* 29 (quoted in the text); Dio Chrys., *Or.* 32, 20.

16. Cic., *Tusc. Disp.* 2, 11, 27; *De Legg.* 3, 14; Juv. 7, 173 (with Mayor's notes); Quint. 1, 2, 18, '*umbratica vita*'; Petron., *Sat.* 2, '*umbraticus doctor*'. '*Umbratilis miles*' in AM 18, 6, 2 is a chocolate soldier.

17. Cic., *De Offic.* 1, 69; Sen., *De Tranq. An.* 2, 3ff.; TA 4, 40, 8; TH 2, 86, '*Cornelius Fuscus . . ., . quietis cupidine senatorium ordinem exuerat*'.

18. Sen., *De Otio* 3, 3 (even Stoics conceded this); 8.

19. Sen., *De Vita Beat.* 7, 3; cf. Cic., *De Orat.* 3, 63f.

20. Sen., *De Otio* 6.

21. *De Offic.* 1, 71; *Ad Att.* 1, 17, 5.

22. TA 4, 40, 8, '*Insigni tranquillitate vitae, nullis rei publicae negotiis permixtos*'.

23. AV, *De Caes.* 37, 6f.

24. Tac., *Dial.* 5, 3. Cf. Ovid, *AA* 3, 541f.

25. *Ad Att.* 4, 18, 2; *Ad Q.f.* 3, 5, 4; *De Offic.* 2, 2–4; 3, 1–4.

26. *De Offic.* 2, 3.

27. Sall., *Cat.* 4, 1.

28. *De Senect.* 51–60.

29. Sall., *BJ* 4, 1ff.; Juv. 7, 105; Polyb. 12, 27.

30. Sen., *De Brev. Vit.* 14f. '*Humaniter vivere*', Cic., *Ad Fam.* 7, 1, 5.

31. The subject of the *NQ*. He had written an early work on the geography of Egypt. Cf. *Ep.* 79, where Lucilius is asked to climb

Etna, to report on whether the volcano is really shrinking in size; *De Otio* 5.

32. *De Brev. Vit.* 13, 1–9, '*Inane studium supervacua discendi*'; *Ep.* 88.

33. Quint. 12, 3, 12; Sen., *De Vit. Beat.* 21–3.

34. Cic., *De Offic*, 1, 155; *De Orat.* 3, 56–61; 72; Quint. 12, 1, 1; 12, 2, 4–10.

35. *Iners* or *segne otium*, Sall., *BJ* 4, 3; CN, *Att.* 15, 3; Sen., *De Ben.* 4, 13, 1; 7, 2, 2; *Ep.* 71, 15; 77, 15; 78, 26; 81, 2. *Inertia*, Hirt., *BG* 8, praef. 1. Habit-forming, Tac., *Agr.* 3, 1.

36. T*A* 12, 49, 1; Suet., *D.Cl.* 5.

37. T*A* 13, 42, 4. On Suillius, see p. 185.

38. Tac., *Agr.* 42, 5.

39. T*A* 3, 30; VP 2, 88, 2.

40. Sen., *Ep.* 83, 14f.; VP 2, 98, 3. For Piso, see *PIR²*, 'C', 289; Cossus, *PIR²*, 'C', 1380.

41. 'βίος μὴ σώφρων', Herod. 2, 6, 6. 'Pleasures unworthy of an educated man', Cic., *De Offic.* 2, 2.

42. See p. 208.

43. Plut., *Lucull.* 41, 4–7.

44. Cic., *Pro Sest.* 138f.; Ovid, *Ex Pont.* 2, 9, 61; Sen., *De Brev. Vit.* 7, 1f.; *De Otio* 7, 1; *Ep.* 55, 5 etc.

45. Cato, fr. 110 Jordan; Hor., *Sat.* 1, 3, 17f.; Cic., *De Fin.* 2, 8, 23; Sen., *Ep.* 122, 2f., 9ff.

46. Hor., *Car.* 3, 21, 23; Juv. 8, 9–12; Mart. 7, 10, 5; Plin., *NH* 14, 142; T*A* 16, 18, 1 (Petronius); SHA, *Elagab.* 28, 6; Sen., *Ep.* 122 (Buta and Papinius).

47. *ILS* 8157; *CIL* iii, 12274c; xiv, 914; Aug., *Conf.* 1, 18, 29; *ILS* 8626f.

48. *Lautitiae* is the word used *ad nauseam* by Petronius of Trimalchio's style of living: *Sat.* 21; 26, 31f.; 34; 47; 57; 65; 70; 73.

49. *Ep.* 55, 3ff.

50. *De Brev. Vit.* 12, 2–13, 9; cf. *Ep.* 88, 6–8; Petron., *Sat.* 50–2. Augustus' collection of *Corinthia*, Suet., *DA* 70, 2. Quizzes, Suet., *Tib.* 70, 3.

51. *De Brev. Vit.* 12, 5. Cf. *Ep.* 47, 5–8 and, on over-addiction to eating and drinking, *Cons. ad Marc.* 22, 2; *Ep.* 89, 22; 95, 18f. and 25; 110, 12f.

52. T. S. Jerome, *Aspects of the Study of Roman History*, New York–London, 1923, 79–107, esp. 98ff.

53. *RE* viA, 581–4, no. 7.

54. T*A* 4, 58, 1; *RE* iv, 131f., no. 14.

55. Suet., *Tib.* 43. Even Tacitus, though he avoids Suetonius' extravagance, writes, '*Occultiores in luxus et malum otium resolutus*', T*A* 4, 67, 5. No more sensible account of Tiberius' life on Capri exists than that of Norman Douglas, *Capri*, Florence, 1930, 136–142. The allegations made against Tiberius had been made earlier against Dionysius of Syracuse, Sen., *Cons. ad Marc.* 17, 5 (Seneca had evidently never heard the scandal about Tiberius). Cf. A*M* 21, 16, 6, '*Quod crimen, etiam si non invenit, malignitas fingit, in summarum licentia potestatum*'.

56. Quoted by A*G* 19, 10, 12. See, on the passage, J. M. André, *L'Otium dans la vie morale et intellectuelle romaine*, Paris, 1966, 17ff.; 22; 35f.; 40.

57. *De Brev. Vit.* 7, 6ff.; *Ep.* 104, 9.

58. Ovid, *Ex Pont.* 1, 5, 44; Hor., *Car.* 2, 16; Sen., *De Tranq. An.* 2, 6; 2, 9; *Ep.* 1, 1; 28, 1; 104, 13–15 and 17ff.

59. 3, 1057–67.

60. *De Tranq. An.* 2, 13.

61. Sen., *De Tranq. An.* 12, 2–4. Cf. Hor., *Ep.* 1, 11, 28, '*Strenua inertia*'; Sen, *De Brev. Vit.* 12; 16, 1ff, '*Dum nihil agunt, occupatos esse*'; Mart. 4, 78, 10; Manil. 5, 64–6.

62. Plut., *Mor.* 469E (*De Tranq. An.* 9).

63. See R. H. Barrow, *Plutarch and his Times*, London, 1967, 108–12.

64. Fronto, *De Bell. Parth.* 9 (ii, 28 Loeb); V*M* 8, 8, 1f.; Cic., *De Orat.* 2, 22–5. Cf. *Laus Pisonis*, *PLM* 1, 15, 190f.

65. Sen., *De Tranq. An.* 17, 7.

66. *Cons. ad Polyb.* 6, 4f; on his translations, 8, 2; 11, 5.

67. Aus., *Ep.* 10, 25–34.

68. See C. E. Boyd, *Public Libraries and Literary Culture in ancient Rome*, Chicago, 1915, esp. 1–20; 31–40; also entries in *TDAR*.

69. Plin., *Ep.* 1, 8; 7, 18, 2; *ILS* 2927; *Forschungen in Ephesos* v, 1, 1944, 'Die Bibliothek', with inscription no. 13 (p. 75); *ILS* 9362 (Timgad); M. R. Cagnat, 'Les Bibliothèques municipales dans l'empire romain', *MAI* xxxviii, 1, 1909, 1–26.

70. *Ad M. Caes.* iv, 5 (i, 178 Loeb). Cf. AG 19, 5, 4 (Tibur); SHA, *Aurel.* 1, 7.

71. AG 5, 21, 9; 11, 17, 1f.; 13, 20, 1; 16, 8, 1f.; Aug., *Conf.* 6, 3, 3.

72. Cic., *Ad Q.f.* 3, 5, 7. Translating, Plin., *Ep.* 7, 9, 2; Quint. 10, 2f.

73. AG 19, 8.

74. Suet., *DJ* 56, 5.

75. Plut., *Brut.* 4, 7f.

76. Cat. 29, 54, 57.

77. T*A* 1, 72, 4.

78. T*A* 4, 31, 1; 6, 9, 3; 6, 39, 1; 14, 48, 1.

79. Plin., *Ep.* 4, 14.

80. Plin., *Ep.* 5, 12, 1; 7, 9 and 17; 8, 3, 4, 15, 19 and 21; 9, 1, 4 and 25; 9, 26, 13; 9, 28, 3. Successful recital, Plin., *Ep.* 3, 18, 4. Defence of the practice, Plin., *Ep.* 5, 3. Disdain for it, Juv. 1, 1–21; Pers., *Sat.* 1; Plin., *Ep.* 1, 13, 4.

81. T*A* 14, 15; 16, 4; Suet., *Nero* 22–4; 49, 1; Suet., *D. Tit.* 3, 2; *Epit. de Caes.* 14, 2; 45, 5f.; AM 30, 9, 4; SHA, *MA* 4, 9.

82. Birds, Catull. 2f.; Sen., *Cons. ad Marc.* 12, 2; SHA, *AS* 41, 5–7. Dogs, VM 1, 5, 3; Sen., *Cons. ad Marc.* 12, 2; Mart. 1, 109; 11, 69; Petron., *Sat.* 64; Juv. 6, 654; *CIL* x, 659; J. M. C. Toynbee, *PBSR* 1948, 34–6. Lion, Juv. 7, 75ff. Monkeys, snakes etc., Plaut., *Mil. Glor.* 162; 179; *Merc.* 229–33; Mart. 7, 87; Suet., *Tib.* 72, 2. See Jennison, 126–36.

83. Catull. 2f.; Petron., *Sat.* 28f.; Plin., *NH* 10, 121–4; Jennison, 116–121.

84. For refs., see Jennison, 100–21.

85. Col. 8, 2, 5; Plut., *Mor.* 319F; Herod. 3, 10, 3; M. Aurel., *Med.* 1, 6.

86. Sen., *De Tranq. An.* 17, 4; Macrob., *Sat.* 3, 14, 5ff.; CD 37, 49, 3.

87. See p. 51 above; Suet., *Tib.* 42, 1; Plut., *Cato mi.* 6, 1–4; Sen., *De Tranq. An.* 17, 4; Plin., *Ep.* 3, 12.

88. *CIL* iv, 807, 'The Elephant' at Pompeii; iv, 581 (the haunt of the *Seribibi*); 1679. On the whole subject, see T. Kleberg, *Hôtels, restaurants et cabarets dans l'antiquité romaine*, Uppsala, 1957.

89. *ILS* 7477; Catull. 37, 1; Mart. 5, 84, 4f.; Fronto, *De Orat* 10 (ii, 110 Loeb); Auson., *Mosel.* 123f.; SHA, *AS* 49, 6. See refs. in Mayor's note on Juv. 11, 81. Inns and bars at Ostia, R. Meiggs,

Roman Ostia, Oxford, 1960, 428–30. Restaurant scene portrayed, G. E. Rizzo, *La Pittura Ellenistico-Romana*, Milan, 1929, tav. 198a.

90. Juv. 8, 158; 172–6; Hor., *Ep.* 1, 14, 21–5.

91. H. J. Rowell, *AJA* 1958, 123–5.

92. Suet., *Tib.* 34, 1; *Nero* 16, 2; CD 60, 6, 7; 62, 14, 2; 66, 10, 3; AM 28, 4, 3f.

93. SHA, *Hadr.* 16, 4. He had written a poem commiserating with Hadrian on his hard life, starting, '*Ego nolo Caesar esse*'. Hadrian replied, '*Ego nolo Florus esse*
 ambulare per tabernas
 latitare per popinas
 culices pati rotundas.'

94. E.g. Cic., *In Pis.* 13; *Phil.* 2, 77.

95. Nero, TA 13, 25; Suet., *Nero* 26, 1; Plin., *NH* 13, 126; SHA, *L. Ver.* 4, 6f. Cf. Juv. 3, 278–301.

96. Plaut., *Mil. Glor.* 164f.; Hor., *Car.* 3, 24, 58; Ovid, *Trist.* 2, 472. Saturnalia, Mart. 4, 14; 5, 84; 11, 6; 14, 1, 3. Betting on sports, *Dig.* 11, 5, 2.

97. Cic., *Phil.* 2, 56; Ps. Asc. on *Div.* 24, p. 194 St.

98. *Dig.* 11, 5, 1, 2.

99. Cic., *De Orat.* 3, 58; G. Charles-Picard, *La Civilisation de l'Afrique romaine*, Paris, 1959, pl. 43, opp. p. 275; Ovid, *Trist.* 2, 471–84; Suet., *D.Cl.* 33, 2. Suetonius' book, AG 9, 7, 3; Serv. ad *Aen.* 5, 602; J. Taillardat, *Suétone*, Paris, 1967, 27–43; 64–73; 149–74.

100. Juv. 1, 88–93; Plaut., *Curc.* 355f.; Mart. 4, 66, 16; 5, 30, 8.

101. Ovid, *AA* 2, 203–8; 3, 354–60; Prop. 2, 33B, 26.

102. Cic., *De Senect.* 58.

103. Mart. 5, 84; 14, 18; Pers. 3, 44–50.

104. Suet., *DA* 70, 2; 71, 2–4.

105. Suet., *C. Cal.* 41, 2; Sen., *Cons. ad Polyb.* 17, 4.

106. Suet., *D.Cl.* 5; 33, 2; Sen., *Apok.* 12; 15.

107. Mart. 4, 14, 8; 11, 6, 2; 14, 1, 3 etc. There were various other forms of dice-box, the *phimus* (Hor., *Sat.* 2, 7, 17) and the *pyrgus* or *turricula* (Mart. 14, 16). This last was 'stepped' or grooved on the inside, in a manner which should prevent manipulation of the throw. For illustrations of *tali*, dice and dice-box, see *British Museum Guide to the Exhibition illustrating Greek and Roman Life*,[2] 1920.

108. Cic., *De Fin.* 3, 16, 54.

109. Cic., *De Div.* 1, 23; 2, 48; 2, 121; Mart. 14, 14; Plaut., *Curc.* 359. See L. Becq de Fouquières, *Les Jeux des anciens*,[2] Paris, 1873, 329–59.

110. Plaut., *Curc.* 357; Prop. 4, 8, 45f.; Ovid, *AA* 2, 206; Pers. 3, 49. On numbers and names, Pollux 9, 99f.

111. Suet., *DA* 71, 2; Pers. 3, 48, '*Dexter senio*'.

112. L. Becq de Fouquières, *O.c.* (n. 109), 337f.

113. Pers. 3, 50; Mart. 4, 14, 9; Pollux 9, 103.

114. Mart. 4, 66, 15.

115. Non. 250, 22L; Ovid, *AA* 3, 363–6; *Trist.* 2, 475f. The game was brilliantly reconstructed by L. Becq de Fouquières, *O.c.* (n. 109 above), 357–83, on the basis of an epigram of Agathias describing a game of the emperor Zeno (474–91 A.D.). Cf. *AP* 9, 482; *CIL* iv, Suppl. 3494; *RE* v, 1794–6 (Mau). Pieces illustrated, *B.M. Guide* (n. 107), p. 206, fig. 245. See *PBSR* 1948, 33 for ivory *tesserae* from a child's sarcophagus on the *Via Appia* (inscribed with charioteers and race-horses) which could have been used for this game. On Scaevola, Cic., *De Orat.* 1, 217; Quint. 11, 2, 38. Cf. Auson., *Comm. Prof. Burd.* 1, 25–30.

116. *NSA* 1887, 396; illustrations, *B.M. Guide* (n. 107), p. 206, fig. 245.

117. Plaut., *Mil. Glor.* 74, 76 and 949. See *RE* xii, 980.

118. Mart. 14, 17, '*Calculus hac gemino discolor hoste perit*'.

119. Mart. 7, 72, 8. The main aids to the reconstruction of the game are the *Laus Pisonis*, *PLM* 1, 15, 190–208 and Isidore, *Origines* 18, 67. See L. Becq de Fouquières, *O.c.* (n. 109) 422–56; A. Tilley, 'Ludus Latrunculorum', *CR* 1892, 335f.; L. Traube, 'Zur lateinischen Anthologie', *Philologus* 1895, 132ff; *RE* xii, 980–4 (K. Schneider).

120. SHA, *Proculus* 13, 2.

121. See the lists in Ovid, *AA* 3, 3, 353–66 and *Trist.* 2, 471–484 with S. G. Owen's admirable notes on the latter passage, Oxford, 1924.

122. *PLM* iv, 132, pp. 119f. (*Carmina xii Sapientium*); Max Ihn, 'Römische Spieltafeln', *Bonner Studien*, Berlin, 1890, 223–239; Max Ihn, 'Delle Tavole lusorie Romane', *Röm. Mitt.* 1891, 208–20; Ch. Huelsen, 'Neue Inschriften', *Röm. Mitt.* 1904, 142–6.

123. Petron., *Sat.* 33. Pieces illustrated, *B.M. Guide* (n. 107), p. 197.

124. Mart. 14, 17; Sen., *Ep.* 117, 30, '*Tabula latruncularia*'.

125. AM 28, 4, 21 and 29f.

126. Schol. Juv. 5, 109 (C. Piso); Sen., *De Tranq. An.* 14, 7.

127. See above, pp. 16, 26.

128. Marrou, 431–4. See M. Rostowzew, *Römische Bleitesserae, Klio* beiheft. 3, 1905, esp. pp. 59–63; M. Della Corte, *Iuventus*, Arpino, 1924 and *NSA* 1939, 239–327 on the inscriptions and *graffiti* of the Grande Palestra by the Amphitheatre at Pompeii; S. L. Mohler, 'The *Iuvenes* and Roman Education', *TAPA* 1937, 442–79; *RE* x, 1357f. and Supplb. vii, 315f., s.v. '*Iuvenes*'; *ILS* 6212 (a girl member at Tusculum); 6264 (revival, after disappearance, of *Lusus Iuvenum* at Anagni); 2745; 6546; 6555; 6589; 6590 (*Magistri*); 6631; 6632 (*Curatores*); 6715 (*Sacerdos*). Curiously there is little evidence of the *Iuventus* at Ostia, Meiggs, 334.

129. Polyb. 31, 14 (Demetrius); 29 (Scipio).

130. Plut., *Cato mai.* 20, 6; *RGDA* 14, 2.

131. Ovid., *Fast.* 2, 365–8. This point is emphasized by Mohler, *O.c.* (n. 128) and is strikingly confirmed by the *graffiti* of the great palaestra at Pompeii, Della Corte, *NSA* 1939, 318–22.

132. Cic., *Pro Cael.* 11.

133. Strabo 5, 236C.

134. Plut., *Mar.* 34, 5ff.; *Cato mi.* 50, 1; Sen., *Ep.* 104, 33.

135. Veget. 1, 10. Exercises for army recruits (1, 9) were narrower in range and designed for direct practical use: route-marching, jumping, swimming. For Tiber-swimming, cf. Cic., *Pro Cael.* 36; Hor., *Car.* 1, 8, 8; 3, 12, 7; *Sat.* 2, 1, 7f.; Ovid, *AA* 3, 386. Swimming after exercise in the cool water of the Aqua Virgo, Ovid., *Trist.* 3, 12, 21f.; *AA* 3, 385; Sen., *Ep.* 83, 5.

136. *Car.* 3, 24, 54–7. Cf. 3, 6, 33–44.

137. Hor., *Sat.* 2, 2, 9–13. Ball, javelin, hoop, arms-training and riding listed as a male prerogative, Ovid, *AA* 3, 382–6.

138. *De Offic.* 1, 104.

139. This is not to be explained by the fact that Romans, like Greeks, rode without stirrups. Stirrups reached Europe from the East in the early eighth century.

140. On these sports and their devotees, see Hor., *Car.* 1, 8; Ovid., *Trist.* 3, 12, 19–24; Cic., *De Senect.* 58. Augustus, Suet., *DA* 45, 2. M. Aurelius, *Med* 7, 61; SHA, *MA* 4, 9; Fronto. *Ad M. Caes.* 2, 12, 1 (i, 150 Loeb). Gratian, Auson., *Grat. Act. pro Cons.* 14.

141. Suet., *DJ* 57 and 61; *DA* 83.

142. Suet., *DA* 43, 2; *CD* 54, 26. It is described by Virgil, *Aen.* 5, 545–574. See L. R. Taylor, '*Seviri Equitum Romanorum* and municipal *Seviri*', *JRS* 1924, 158–71.

143. On the holding of this title by successive princes of the imperial house, see Rostowzew, *O.c.* (n. 128), 71f. and *RE* xxii, 2296–2311, s.v. '*Princeps Iuventutis*'.

144. G. Bendinelli, 'Il Monumento sotterraneo di Porta Maggiore in Roma,' *Monumenti antichi* xxxi, 1926, 674–7, fig. 9 (p. 675) and tav. xv, xvii, xviii. Excellently reproduced photographs are to be found in *MAAR* 1924, pl. xli, xlii.

145. Veget. 1, 11; 2, 23. Compare stuffed sacks used to train modern soldiers in bayonet-fighting.

146. Petron., *Sat.* 29.

147. See above, n. 128, esp. Della Corte, *Iuventus*, for details.

148. *Ep.* 15, 2f.; cf. 88, 18. Cf. Mart. 14, 48, 2, '*Grandia qui vano colla labore facit*'.

149. *TA* 14, 20, 6; Quint. 1, 11, 15f.; 10, 1, 33; 11, 3, 26; 12, 10, 41; Celsus 1, 3. Cf. Claudius on Valerius Asiaticus, '*Et odi illud palaestricum prodigium*', *ILS* 212.

150. Cf. *CIL* iv, 1595 for the '*Serpentis ludus*', a complicated piece of riding by the *iuvenes* at Pompeii.

151. In Rome, Hor., *Ep.* 1, 18, 53f.; *AP* 379–81.

152. *CD* 66, 15, 2. Mohler, *O.c.* (n. 128), 445, n. 10 is certainly right against Rostowzew, *O.c.* (n. 128), 88 and Della Corte, *Iuventus* 17, in interpreting *CIL* xii, 533 as the epitaph of a young professional gladiator, not of a *iuvenis* proper, though perhaps a professional trainer of *iuvenes*.

153. *Encycl. Brit.*, s.v. 'Tournament'.

154. M. Della Corte, *NSA* 1939, 318f.

155. On the subject, see Marquardt 841–7; D–S, s.v. '*Pila*'. Illustrations, S. Reinach, *RPGR* 259, figs. 4 and 6, from Rome. See also n. 144 above.

156. Ovid., *Trist.* 2, 485f.; Galen, *De parvae pilae exercitio* (v, 899–910K), ed. J. Marquardt, 1879.

157. Galen v, 899–903K, 906–9K.

158. 9, 104–6. Cf. Eustathius, *Comm. ad Odyss.* 9, 376.

159. Mart. 4, 19, 6; 7, 32, 10; 7, 67, 4f.; 14, 48.

160. *Dig.* 9, 2, 52, 4.

161. Athen. 1, 14f—15a, tr. C. B. Gullick (Loeb).

162. See n. 156 above (J. Marquardt).

163. Sidon. Apoll., *Ep.* 2, 9, 4, '*Sphaeristarum contrastantium paria*'. This was, perhaps, the '*duplex pila*' of Lucil. 26, 641 M.

164. *De Benef.* 2, 17, 3–5. Cf. 2, 32, where he goes to the ball game for an analogy to '*beneficium*'.

165. Isid., *Orig.* 18, 69, 2. Cf., on *trigon*, Lucil. 1134–6 M.

166. *CIL* iv, 1936. *Pilicrepi*, Sen., *Ep.* 56, 1; *CIL* iv, 1147, 1905 and 1926.

167. Petron., *Sat.* 27.

168. Manil. 5, 157–73; *Laus Pisonis, PLM* 1, 15, 185, '*Nec tibi mobilitas minor est*'.

169. Macrob., *Sat.* 2, 6, 5.

170. Left-hand, Mart. 7, 72, 11; 14, 46; *MAAR* 1926, p. 675, fig. 5 (relief on ceiling of the underground basilica of the Porta Maggiore). See pl. 8b.

171. Petron., *Sat.* 27.

172. Mart. 12, 82, 3f.; 7, 72, 10.

173. Quint. 6, 3, 62, '*Sic petis tamquam Caesaris candidatus*'.

174. '*Tum isti qui ludunt datatim . . . . et datores et factores omnes*', Plaut., *Curc.* 296f. *Expulsim*, Varro ap. Non. 149L.

175. For a stone relief showing this game played by young girls, see L. Friedlaender, '*Fanciulli giuocanti*', *Ann. dell' Ist. di Corr. arch.* 1857, 142–6 and tav. d'agg. BC.

176. *Laus Pisonis* (n. 168), 185–7. I follow Marquardt's interpretation (n. 156), 843, n. 5.

177. Stat., *Silv.* 1, 5, 57f., '*Quid nunc strata solo referam tabulata crepantis/auditura pilas?*'

178. Plin., *Ep.* 2, 17, 12; 5, 6, 27.

179. *CIL* x, 7004. Cf. Vitruv. 5, 10, 1; Col. 1, 6, 2.

180. Suet., *D. Vesp.* 20.

181. *Paganica*, Mart. 7, 32; 14, 45. Invention of *follis*, Athen. 1, 14f.
Cf. Mart. 14, 47 (also 4, 19, 7; 7, 32, 7; 12, 82, 5, the sycophant
again); Suet., *DA* 83; Plin. *Ep.* 3, 1, 8; Cic., *De Senect.* 58.

182. Sen., *Ep.* 114, 4–8; 120, 19; Hor., *Sat.* 1, 5, 48; 2, 6, 49. Cf. 1, 6,
126 (*trigon*); SHA, *MA* 4, 9. Martial lists the ball-games in 7, 32,
'*Non pila, non follis, non te paganica thermis/praeparat ...... /non
harpasta vagus pulverulenta rapis.*'

183. Mart. 10, 86.

184. *ILS* 5173.

185. Hor., *AP* 379–81.

186. *Clava*, Cic., *De Senect.* 58. *Palaria*, Stat., *Silv.* 4 praef.; cf. Veget.
1, 11; 2, 23. Running and jumping, Sen., *Ep.* 15, 4. Wrestling,
Mart. 4, 19, 5; 7, 32, 9. Dumb-bells and weight-lifting, Sen.,
Ep. 15, 4; 56, 1; *ILS* 5174a, with Dessau's note. Exercise all day,
Sen., *De Tranq. An.* 3, 1.

187. L. Bernarbò Brea, *Musei e monumenti antiche in Sicilia*, Novara,
1958, 144. Cf. n. 175 above.

188. Mart. 7, 67, 4–8; Juv. 2, 53; 6, 246–67 and 431–33; CD 61, 17, 3
(A.D. 59); TA 15, 32 (A.D. 63); CD 66, 25, 1 (A.D. 80); 67, 8, 4
(A.D. 89); 75, 16, 1 (Septimius Severus). Ovid, *AA* 3, 381–6 shows
that in his time women did not take part in the tougher forms of
exercise and sport.

189. Mart. 1, 12; Juv. 7, 178–80, both on driving horses in porticoes
of private villas.

190. 5, 11, 1.

191. A. Maiuri, *NSA* 1939, 165–238 (Pompeii), esp. 195, on the date;
Ercolano, i nuovi scavi, Rome, 1958, 113–43.

Chapter V

1. Military service to forty-six, L. 43, 14, 6; up to fifty, L. 40, 26, 7;
42, 31, 4; 42, 33, 4; Sen., *De Brev. Vit.* 20, 4. Senate, Sen., *De
Brev. Vit.* 20, 4. For those over sixty in the Senate there were age-
barriers for certain functions, Sen. Rhet., *Controv.* 1, 8, 4 (sixty-
five); E–J 311, 112f. (seventy). Jury-service, *FIR* 10 (*FIRA* 1, 7), 13.

2. Lucian, *De Mort. Peregr.* 10; Cic., *Pro Rosc. Amer.* 100. For the
correct explanation, Ovid. *Fast.* 5, 633f.; Fest. 452L, quoting

Verrius Flaccus (against Varro, quoted by Non. 525, l. 23). See *RE* iiA, 2025f., s.v. '*Sexagenarii*'; L. R. Taylor, *Roman Voting Assemblies*, Michigan, 1966, 92 and 152, n. 18.

3. T*A* 14, 55, 2.

4. Stat., *Silv.* 3, 5; Strabo 5, 246C.

5. Quint. 2, 12, 12; 12, 11, 1–7.

6. Cf. Plin., *Ep.* 4, 24, 3; T*A* 4, 41, 4; *Agr.* 6, 3; 40, 4.

7. Sen., *De Brev. Vit.* 3, 5.

8. Hor., *Epod.* 2; *Sat.* 1, 1, 28–120; *Epist.* 2, 2, 145–8; Juv. 14, 107ff; 139, '*Crescit amor nummi quantum ipsa pecunia crevit*'; Sen., *Ep.* 17, 5, '*Nondum habeo quantum satis est*'; Mart. 5, 58, '*Cras te victurum, cras dicis, Postume, semper.*'

9. *De Brev. Vit.* 4.

10. Accession, Suet., *Tib.* 24, 2; Rhodes, 10, 2; Capri, T*A* 4, 41; 4, 57f.

11. Suet., *D.Cl.* 35, 2.

12. CD 68, 3, 1.

13. Lact., *De Mort. Persec.* 18f. In praise, Eutrop. 9, 16; AV, *De Caes.* 39, 48. Cabbages, *Epit. de Caes.* 39, 6. Dates, *RE* viiA, 2421, 2493. Piazza Armerina, H. P. L'Orange, *Symbol. Osl.* 1952 and 'Nuovo Contributo allo studio del Palazzo Erculio di Piazza Armerina', *Act. Inst. Rom. Norveg.* 1965, 65–101.

14. Lact., *De Mort. Persec.* 20, 3–5. Cf. Julian's threat of abdication to frighten his unruly troops in the East in A.D. 363, AM 24, 3, 7.

15. The expression is used three times by Cicero, *Pro. Sest.* 98; *De Orat.* 1, 1; *Ad Fam.* 1, 9, 21, and has raised an unnecessarily large cloud of scholarly dust, e.g. P. Boyancé, '*Cum Dignitate Otium*', REA 1941, 172–91; Ch. Wirszubski, 'Cicero's *Cum Dignitate Otium*: a Reconsideration', *JRS* 1954, 1–13; J. P. V. D. Balsdon, '*Auctoritas, Dignitas, Otium*', CQ 1960, 43–50.

16. See M. Gelzer, 'Die Nobilität der röm. Republik', *Ges. Schr.* 1, Wiesbaden, 1962, 17–135, esp. 39ff.

17. Cf. Cic., *Ad Att.* 9, 6A; 9, 9, 3; 9, 11A, 1 for the use of these words.

18. Livy, *Per.* 13; Cic., *De Senect.* 16; Plut., *Pyrrh.* 18, 8–19, 4; App., *Samn.* 10, 4f.

19. E.g. *Ad Fam.* 4, 4, 4; 9, 15, 4; 9, 17.

20. On Salinator, *RE* xiii, 891–9, no. 33. On the trials of the Scipios, H. H. Scullard, *Roman Politics 220–150 B.C.*, Oxford, 1951, 290–303.

21. L. Flamininus, see *RE* xxiv, 1040–7, no. 43. Census of 70, Ascon. 84C; Livy, *Per.* 98.

22. *FIR* 28 (*FIRA* 1, 21), cv, charter of the colony of Urso in Spain.

23. See *RE* 1A, 1919f.

24. Sources in *RE* i, 560.

25. CD 54, 15, 4–7.

26. See *RE* vi, 1683–5, s.v. '*Exilium*'. On Naples, Praeneste etc., L. 29, 21, 1; 43, 2, 10 (171 B.C.); Polyb. 6, 14, 8; Cic., *Pro Balb.* 28; *Pro Sulla* 17.

27. Pompey, Cic. *Ad Att.* 6, 1, 3; 6, 3, 5; Cicero, *Ad Att.* 11, 1, 2; *Ad Fam.* 5, 20, 9.

28. *Ad Fam.* 2, 12, 2, '*Omnis peregrinatio* (i.e. living abroad) . . . *obscura et sordidast iis quorum industria Romae potest inlustris esse*'. Cf. *Ad Att.* 5, 10, 3; 5, 11, 5; 6, 3, 2; *Ad Fam.* 2, 11, 1.

29. On Sittius, *RE* iiiA, 409–11, no. 3. *Ad Fam.* 5, 17 is a most interesting consolatory letter to him from Cicero.

30. On Rutilius, *RE* iA, 1269–80, n. 34.

31. Q. Metellus Numidicus attending lectures in Rhodes (100/99 B.C.), Plut., *Mar.* 29, 12; Livy, *Per.* 69. Q. Servilius Caepio, cos. 106, in Smyrna, Cic., *Pro Balb.* 28; L. Opimius, cos. 121, in Dyrrachium, Cic., *Pro Sest.* 140. P. Autronius Paetus, banished 62 B.C., in Epirus, Cic., *Ad Att.* 3, 7, 1. P. Rutilius Rufus in Mytilene, then Smyrna, CD fr. 97, 3f. Memmius in Athens, Cic., *Ad Fam.* 13, 1; *Ad Att.* 5, 11, 6.

32. C. Porcius Cato, cos. 114, in Tarraco, Cic., *Pro Balb.* 28. L. Cornelius Scipio Asiagenus, cos. 83, at Marseilles, Cic., *Pro Sest.* 7. Catiline, Sall. 34, 2. Milo, CD 40, 54, 3.

33. '*Hortorum amoenitas*', TA 16, 27, 2f.

34. TA 16, 22, 1.

35. Plin., *Ep.* 3, 7, 1–8. Cf. C. Galba, cos. A.D. 22, elder brother of the later emperor, who found himself pauperized, and so retired from Rome to the country, TA 6, 40, 3; Suet., Galb. 3, 4.

36. Plin., *Ep.* 7, 3 (see S–W ad loc.). The story of his later career is revealed by inscriptions, esp. *AE* 1950, 66 (Smallwood 193). See R. Syme, *Historia* 1960, 374–9.

37. CD 54, 18, 3; 60, 11, 8; TA 16, 27, 2f.; CD 77, 20.

38. BGU 611 (Smallwood 367), col. 3.

39. TH 4, 9.

40. CD 54, 35, 1; SHA, AS 16, 1; CT 6, 4, 9; RE Supplb. vi, 766f., s.v. 'Senatus'.

41. Sen., Ep. 36, 1; De Brev. Vit. 18; Plin., Ep. 3, 1, 12; 4, 23, 4.

42. TA 6, 40, 3.

43. Tac., Agr. 41f.; ILS 1011; RE iA, 2026–9 (no. 15).

44. TH 2, 86; 4, 80. He came from Toulouse (Suet., Vit. 18). If this man is the same as the M. Antonius Primus, also of Toulouse, to whom Martial dedicated epigrams, he enjoyed a long retirement in his native town (see PIR, 'A' 866). But A. E. Housman, CQ 1919, 75f., may be right in thinking they were different men.

45. TA 6, 29, 3. Cf. JC, BC 1, 4, 4, Caesar's allusion to the number of those who became his inimici when he associated himself with Pompey.

46. Whether they quarrelled over a ring at a sale (Plin., NH 33, 20) or for some more serious reason (E. Badian, SGRH 34–70).

47. TA 3, 12, 4. Cf. JC, BC 3, 16, 3, Bibulus' stress in the civil war on the fact that he had privatae inimicitiae as well as public with Caesar.

48. TA 3, 24.

49. TA 2, 70, 3; 6, 29, 1–4.

50. Suet., DA 66, 3; CD 54, 19, 6; 55, 7; TA 3, 30, 6f., comparing Sallustius Crispus and Maecenas, 'Speciem magis in amicitia principis quam vim tenuit'; 14, 53, 3.

51. TA 14, 52–6.

52. Plin., NH 19, 110.

53. SHA, Hadr. 11, 3; 15, 2.

54. SHA, Hadr. 24, 6.

55. TA 6, 30.

56. C. Turranius, Sen., De Brev. Vit. 20, 3; TA 11, 31, 1. Cf. PIR, 'T' 297; RE viiA, 1441f., no. 5. Father of Claudius Etruscus (we do not know his name), Stat., Silv. 3, 3, esp. 156–67; RE iii, 2670–2, no. 31.

57. Dig. 3, 2, 2; SHA, AS 32, 3.

58. Plin., Ep. 7, 25, 2ff.; ILS 6120.

59. Sen., *Ep.* 19, 5–9; 20, 8; 31, 9; *RE* xiii, 1645, no. 26.

60. Plin., *Pan.* 86f.

61. SHA, *Hadr.* 8, 7; 9, 3f.; *TA* 13, 14, 1.

62. Miriam T. Griffin, '*De Brevitate Vitae*', *JRS* 1962, 104–113, esp. 106f.

63. Plin., *Ep.* 4, 22; 6, 22 and 31; Juv. 4; SHA, *AS* 16. See, generally, A. J. Crook, *Consilium Principis*, Cambridge, 1955.

64. See the articles of Kleinfeller in *RE* on *Deportatio in insulam*, *Exilium* and *Relegatio*. On *relegatio*, Paul., *Sent. rec.* v, 15, 5; v, 22, 2; v. 28; *Dig.* 48, 22, 7. On the distinction between *deportatio* and *relegatio*, *Dig.* 48, 22, 14f.

65. *Dig.* 48, 22, 5 and 7; Suet., *DA* 45, 4.

66. *Dig.* 48, 22, 5; Suet., *D.Cl.* 23, 2.

67. *TA* 16, 9, 1.

68. Paul., *Sent. rec.* v, 17, 3; *Dig.* 48, 22, 14f.

69. *Dig.* 48, 19, 4; *TA* 1, 72, 4; 4, 21, 5.

70. List in *RE* iA, 564.

71. *TA* 3, 68f.; 4, 30, 1f.

72. VP 2, 100, 5; CD 55, 10, 14; Mart. 7, 44f.; *RE* xviii, 1907, no. 1. On Ovidius, see further, p. 243.

73. *TA* 15, 71, 7; SIG³ 811f. Cf. TH 1, 3, 1, '*Comitatae profugos liberos matres, secutae maritos in exilium coniuges*'.

74. Plin., *Ep.* 4, 11, 1–3.

75. CD 38, 18–29, esp. 28, 1.

76. Philo, *In Flacc.* 168.

77. See n. 75 above.

78. E.g. *Ad Fam.* 6, 6, 12. Cf. *Ad Fam.* 5, 17, 3, to P. Sittius in 57 B.C.

79. Plut., *Mor.* 603E–604C.

80. Suet., *C. Cal.* 28; Philo, *In Flacc.* 183ff.

81. CD 59, 3, 6; TH 1, 90; Plut., *Otho* 1; CD 68, 1, 2; *RE* xvii, 1920.

82. *TA* 4, 31, 5f.; 13, 42f.

83. *TA* 4, 13, 2; 4, 28–30.

84. Sources in *RE* xvi, 893f., no. 1. For his reflections on the acceptability of exile, even its opportunities of self-improvement, see Stob., *Anth.* 3, 748–57.

85. Sources in *RE* vi, 1995, no. 22 (Fannia); viii, 216–221, no. 3 (Helvidius). On the date of the expulsion of philosophers, S–W on Pliny, *Ep.* 3, 11.

86. Plin., *Ep.* 3, 11, 3; 7, 19; 9, 13, 3. See S–W on *Ep.* 3, 11, 3.

87. *RE* vi, 126–31, no. 3.

88. Expelled by Tiberius, T*A* 2, 32, 5; CD 57, 15, 7 (A.D. 16); by Claudius, T*A* 12, 52, 3 (A.D. 52); by Vitellius, T*H* 2, 62; Suet., *Vit.* 14, 4; by Vespasian in 70 A.D., CD 66, 9, 2. Cf. T*H* 1, 22, '*Mathematici ... genus hominum potentibus infidum, sperantibus fallax, quod in civitate nostra et vetabitur semper et retinebitur.*'

89. CD 60, 8, 5; T*A* 13, 42, 5; Schol. Juv. 5, 109; *RE* i, 2241f.

90. *Cons. ad Polyb.* 18, 9; *Cons. ad Helv.* passim, esp. 6 (para 5 of which is here quoted); 7f. and 10; *Octavia* 381–4. On Seneca's interest in natural science, see p. 139.

91. E.g. *Trist.* 1, 1. His offence, *Trist.* 2, 208f. To his wife, *Trist.* 1, 6; 3, 3; 4, 3; 5, 2; 5, 14; *Ex Pont.* 1, 4; 3, 1. Winter in Tomi, *Trist.* 3, 10; 5, 10; *Ex Pont.* 4, 14, 27f. Language of the inhabitants, *Trist.* 5, 7; 5, 10, 35–42. Learning to speak Getic, *Trist.* 5, 7, 55–60; 5, 12, 57f.; *Ex Pont.* 3, 2, 40. His poem in Getic, *Ex Pont.* 4, 13, 17–38. No books, *Trist.* 5, 12, 53. Nostalgia for home, *Ex Pont.* 1, 8.

92. Plin., *Ep.* 3, 1, 12.

93. Plin., *Ep.* 3, 7, 3.

94. Cic., *De Offic.* 1, 151; Ovid, *Trist.* 4, 8; AM 30, 2, 10.

95. Fronto, *Ad M. Caes.* ii, 11 (i, 140 Loeb); Sen., *Ep.* 86, 14–21.

96. Plin., *Ep.* 7, 25.

97. Plin., *Ep.* 3, 1.

98. Macrob., *Sat.* 1, 7, 3.

99. CD 69, 19; SHA, *Hadr.* 9, 5; *RE* ivA, 871ff.

100. On the various forms of discharge from the army, honourable and dishonourable, *Dig.* 3, 2, 2, 2. Cf. AM 16, 7, 1; 16, 11, 7; 24, 3, 2. An officer, of course, could be cashiered like a private soldier.

101. '*Ad Lares reverti*', ILS 2311. '*Digredi in otium*', AM 28, 4, 20; 28, 6, 25; Ovid, *Trist.* 4, 8, 21f.

102. *Aerarium militare*, RGDA 17, 2; Suet., *DA* 49, 2; CD 55, 25, 1–3. Terms of service, CD 55, 23, 1. Evidence of the *diplomata* for

terms of discharge of auxiliaries, *ILS* 1986–2010; 9052–60. See the important article of Géza Alföldy, 'Zur Beurteilung der Militärdiplome der Auxiliarsoldaten', *Historia* 1968, 215–27, showing that before Trajan auxiliaries did not regularly leave the service on receipt of their retirement benefits after twenty-five years. See also H. M. D. Parker, *The Roman Legions*², Cambridge, 1958, 212–47; G. L. Cheesman, *The Auxilia of the Roman Army*, Oxford, 1914, 31–6.

103. *FIRA* iii, 19 (2nd cent. A.D.); Herod. 3, 8, 5; P. M. Meyer, *Der röm. Konkubinat*, Leipzig, 1895, 93–116; H. Nesselhauf, *CIL* xvi, 154f.

104. Cf. stoppages from pay in military accounts, *P. Geneva* 1 (McCrum-Woodhead, 405), with Veget. 2, 20.

105. E.g. the men given '*castris*' for domicile, *ILS* 2483 (E–J 261).

106. *FIRA* iii, 19; *ILS* 9059 (McCrum-Woodhead 404) *ad fin.*

107. CD 53, 11, 5; TA 1, 17, 6 and 9. Corn allowance, Suet., *Nero* 10, 1; cf. *P. Geneva* 1 (n. 104 above); TA 15, 72, 1 and M. Durry, *Les Cohortes prétoriennes*, Paris, 1938, 269.

108. *ILS* 9059 (n. 106 above) *ad fin.* is exceptional, a legionary who receives legitimation for his three children (A.D. 94).

109. Juv. 14, 197; *CIL* viii, 2891; 3001 (died at 71; 48 years service); *ILS* 2034; 2649 (died at 64; 46 years service); 2653 (died at 70; 45 years service); H. Dessau, 'British Centurions', *JRS* 1912, 21–4; E. Birley, 'Promotions and Transfers in the Roman Army, ii, The Centurionate', *Carnuntum Jahrbuch* 1963/4, 21–32; G. Alföldy, *O.c.* (n. 102 above).

110. TA 14, 27, 3f.; *ILS* 2020. Cf. 2923, showing that Columella, the writer on agriculture, was an ex-officer of legion vi Ferrata (stationed in Syria) and died at Tarentum. He was conceivably involved in this settlement of veterans at Tarentum.

111. TA 14, 27, 1; 12, 32, 4; 14, 31, 5; TH 4, 64f.

112. *RE* xvi, 539–41, s.v. 'L. Munatius Gallus', no. 21; vA, 1235f., s.v. 'Thamugadi'; *ILS* 6841. *ILS* 6105, '*In coloniam deducti*' after 25 years service, from Deultum in Thrace, from the time of Domitian.

113. TA 1, 17, 5.

114. *ILS* 2267 records a soldier from a Rhine legion, discharged in A.D. 14 probably, who was handsomely treated by Nîmes (Nemausus), presumably his home town.

115. *ILS* 2648; 2652; 2687; 2689f.; 2693; 2726; 6254; 6266; 6285; 6536 (all Italian except 2652, from Emona); 6936 (Spain); 6995; 7004; 7025 (Gaul). Cf. A. R. Burn, *Past and Present* 1953, 5.

116. *ILS* 2472.

Chapter VI

1. *P. Oxy.* 14, 1647; 4, 725; *P. Fuad* 37; H. C. Youtie, 'The Heidelberg Festival Papyrus: a Reinterpretation', *Studies in Roman Economic and Social History in honour of Allan Chester Johnson*, Princeton, 1951, 178–208; Lucian, *De Parasito* 15.

2. List of Spas, *RE*, s.v. 'Aquae', ii, 294–307; Supplb. i, 113; iii, 136f.; Friedlaender i, 387f.; iii, 178. On sensationally curative waters, see Plin., *NH* 31, 1–20. (Compare the wonderful satire of Norman Douglas, *South Wind*, chapter 16.) See also index of *ILS*, p. 605. T*H* 1, 76, of Vicus Aquensis in Switzerland, '*Amoeno salubrium aquarum usu frequens*'. Cassiodor., *Var.* 10, 29, Aquae Bormiae (Bormio) in the Alps for gout; 11, 10, Mons Lactarius (Monte Lattaro) on the Sorrentine peninsula for tuberculosis.

3. L., *Per.* 61.

4. M. Rostovtzeff, *SEHRE*, pl. xxxv, 2 and note (medicinal spring of Umeri in Spain).

5. Mart. 1, 12, 2; Plin., *NH* 31, 10; Galen 11, 393K–20 kms. from Rome.

6. Varro, *LL* 9, 69.

7. Cf. Mart. 11, 82, 1 (of Sinuessa).

8. Cumae-Baiae (in repute from the early second century B.C., L. 41, 16, 3f.); Vitruv. 2, 6, 2; Celsus 2, 17, 1; CD 48, 51, 1f.

9. SHA, *Hadr.* 25, 5f.

10. T*A* 12, 66, 1 (cf. CD 60, 34, 4); T*H* 1, 72 (Tigellinus here, when forced to suicide); Plin., *NH* 31, 8; Mart. 11, 7, 11.

11. Hor., *Ep.* 1, 15, 2–9; Suet., *DA* 81, 1; CD 53, 30, 3f. Cf. Plin., *NH* 19, 128; 29, 6–10.

12. Plin., *NH* 24, 28; Plin., *Ep.* 5, 19, 7.

13. CN, *Att.* 14, 3; *RE*, Supplb. viii, 516 (cf. vi 2271f., s.v. 'Ficulea'). Cf. Suet., *D.Cl.* 5, 5, '*Modo in hortis et suburbana domo, modo in Campaniae secessu delitescens*'.

14. See P. Grimal, *Les Jardins romains*, Paris, 1943, esp. 113–75; 193–7; Georgina Masson, *Italian Gardens*, London, 1961, 11–31.

15. Hor., *Sat.* 1, 8, 14–16; Grimal, *O.c.* (n. 14), 152–5.

16. Cic., *Ad Att.* 15, 15, 2; Hor., *Sat.* 1, 9, 18; Legacy, Suet., *DJ* 83; TA 2, 41, 1; CD 44, 35, 3. Gardens of Caesar, Grimal, *O.c.* (n. 14), 121–3; of Agrippa, 193–6.

17. *Horti Sallustiani*, TA 13, 47, 3; *Luculliani*, Plut., *Lucull.* 39, 2; TA 11, 1, 1; 3, 2; 32, 1; 37, 1; Seneca's *horti*, TA 14, 52, 2; 53, 6; 54, 4; 55, 5.

18. Suet., *Nero* 31, 1f.; 39, 2; TA 15, 42, 1; TDAR 166–72, s.v. 'Aurea'; Axel Boethius, *The Golden House of Nero*, London, 1960.

19. TA 14, 53, 6; 15, 60, 7; Juv. 10, 16, '*Magnos Senecae praedivitis hortos*'.

20. Mart. 1, 12, 4.

21. Plin., *Ep.* 4, 2, 5.

22. *Ep.* 2, 17, 2.

23. July, Stat., *Silv.* 1, 3, 5f.; 4, 4, 12–29. August, Hor., *Ep.* 1, 7, 1–9. September, Hor., *Sat.* 2, 6, 18f.; *Ep.* 1, 16, 15f.; Juv. 4, 56f.; 6, 517f.

24. Laurels, Herod. 1, 12, 1f. Villas for convalescence, Cic., *Ad Fam.* 7, 26; Catull. 44; Sen., *De Ben.* 4, 12, 3, '*Salubritatis causa et aestivi secessus*'.

25. Herod. 2, 6, 3.

26. Stat., *Silv.* 1, 3, 1 (*glaciale*); Mart. 1, 12, 1; 4, 64, 32; Hor., *Car.* 1, 18, 2; 3, 4, 23.

27. Metellus' villa, Cic., *De Or.* 2, 263; *Ad Fam.* 12, 2, 1; *Phil.* 2, 42 and 109; 5, 19; CIL xiv, 3588. Augustus, Suet., *DA* 82, 1.

28. Vopiscus, Stat., *Silv.* 1, 3; CIL xiv, 4242; RE xiv, 1143f. On Roman residents at Tibur, Ella Bourne, *A Study of Tibur*, Wisconsin, 1916, 34–9.

29. SHA, *Hadr.* 23, 7; 26, 5; AV, *Caes.* 14, 5; H. Kähler, *Hadrian und seine Villa bei Tivoli*, Berlin, 1950; S. Aurigemma, *Villa Adriana*, Rome, 1961. There is a charming account, with splendid illustrations, by Georgina Masson, *O.c.* (n. 14), 21–5, and an extremely imaginative study by Eleanor Clark, *Rome and a Villa*, London, 1953.

30. See RE viiA, 1463–91, esp. 1484 and 1487–9 (list of well-known villa-owners).

31. Cic., *De Dom.* 62; *Ad Att.* 4, 2, 5 and 7: *Ad Q.f.* 2, 2, 1: Plin., *NH* 22, 12 (the villa once Sulla's). Scaurus, *NH* 36, 113–5.

32. Praeneste, Virg., *Aen.* 7, 682; Hor., *Car.* 3, 4, 23f.; Juv. 3, 190; 14, 88; Flor. 1, 5, 7. Lanuvium, Suet., *DA* 72, 2. Nomentum, CN, *Att.* 14, 3; Sen., *Ep.* 104, 1; Mart. 6, 43.

33. Plin., *NH* 14, 48–52, story of the successful Remmius Palaemon, whose land Seneca bought.

34. Pompey, Cic., *Ad Att.* 4, 11, 1; 7, 5, 3. Domitian, CD 67, 1, 2; Juv. 4, 145. Stat., *Silv.* 3, 1, 61–3.

35. Mart. 1, 105; 6, 43; 10, 48, 18–20; Hor., *Car.* 3, 16, 25–44; *Sat.* 2, 7, 118; *Ep.* 1, 14, 1–5.

36. Col., 1, 1, 18–20; Plin., *NH* 18, 43.

37. For moralizing about building on high or low ground, Sen., *Ep.* 51, 11f. On maritime villas generally, C. Gatti, 'Le Ville marittime italiche e africane', *Rend. Ist. Lomb.* 1957, 285–305.

38. Serv. ad *Aen.* 10, 184, Strabo 5, 225f. C, describing the coast, says nothing of its bad climate, which is largely inferred from Plin., *Ep.* 5, 6, 1f., '*gravis et pestilens ora Tuscorum*'. Etruscan wine, the best from Luna, Plin., *NH* 14, 68.

39. JC, *BC* 1, 34, 2.

40. Plin., *Ep.* 6, 31. See S–W ad loc., and S. Bastianelli, 'Centum Cellae' etc., *Italia Romana* s. 1, vol. xiv, 1954, 35f. M. Aurelius at Centum Cellae, Fronto, *Ad M. Caes.* iii, 20 (i, 172 Loeb).

41. Suet., *Nero* 5, 2. Other villas, Rutil. Nam. 1, 223f.

42. VM 8, 1, *damn* 7 (125 B.C.); Cic., *Pro Mil.* 54; *Ad Att.* 13, 50; Plin., *Ep.* 6, 10; Fronto, *De Fer. Als.* 2–4 (ii, 2–18 Loeb); *CIL* xi, 3720.

43. SHA, *AP* 1, 8; 12, 6; Fronto, *Ad M. Caes.* ii, 15 and 30; v, 7 (i, 154; 172; 196 Loeb.).

44. Strabo 5, 242C; Cic., *Ad Att.* 2, 8, 2, '*Cratera illum delicatum*'.

45. '*Stagnosum Liternum*', Sil. Ital. 6, 653f.; Sen., *Ep.* 86, 1–13; Plin., *NH* 14, 49; 16, 234. So Cato in the second century B.C. visited with respect the villa of M. Curius, the hero of the early third century, near Tusculum, Cic., *De Senect.* 55.

46. Plut., *C. Gracch.* 19; Cic., *De Or.* 2, 60; *Phil.* 2, 48.

47. Naples: '*Docta Parthenope*', Col. 10, 134. Cf. Stat., *Silv.* 5, 3, 104–29; 205ff.; AG 9, 15 and A. Rostagni, 'La Cultura letteraria

di Napoli antica', *Parol. d. Pass.* 1952, 344–57. On Puteoli, Ch. Picard, 'Pouzzoles et le paysage portuaire', *Latomus* 1959, 23–51; *RE* xxiii, 2036–60 (M. W. Frederiksen).

48. This and much other helpful knowledge about Campanian villas I owe to Mr. J. H. D'Arms of the University of Michigan, who most generously allowed me to read the typescript of his thesis on Campanian villas which, as *Romans on the Bay of Naples*, is to be published by the Harvard Unversity Press. Cf. G. Hahn, *Der Villenbesitz der röm. Grossen in Italien zur Zeit der Republik*, Diss. Bonn, 1922, 1–133.

49. CD 48, 36, 5.

50. Villas at Formiae and Tusculum possessed by 66 B.C., *Ad Att.* 1, 4, 3. At Arpinum, bequeathed by his father, who died in 64. At Pompeii, by 60 B.C., *Ad Att.* 1, 20, 1; 2, 1, 11. On Lucrine Lake (*Cumanum*), *Ad Q.f.* 2, 6 (5), 4; *Ad Att.* 4, 9, 1. At Puteoli, *Ad Att.* 14, 7, 1; *RE* xxiii, 2059; A. Annechino, 'Il Puteolanum di Cicerone', *Campania Romana* 1, 1938, 19–43. At Astura, *Ad Att.* 12, 19, 1. At Antium, sold, *Ad Att.* 13, 47a, 1. In 46 he had contemplated buying P. Sulla's villa at Naples, *Ad Fam.* 9, 15, 5. On Cicero's villas, see E. O. Schmidt, *Neue Jahrbücher f.d. klass. Altertum*, 1899, 328–355; 466–97.

51. Marius' villa at Misenum, Plut., *Mar.* 34, 3f. See J. H. D'Arms, 'The Campanian Villas of C. Marius and the Sullan Confiscations', *CQ* 1968, 185–8.

52. See J. H. D'Arms, 'Roman Campania: Two passages from Cicero's Correspondence', *AJP* 1967, 195–200.

53. Posilypon, Plin., *NH* 9, 167; CD 54, 23, 5; *RE* viiiA, 568–70, no. 8. Surrentum, *CIL* x, 691–713. Capri, *TA* 4, 67, 5; Suet., *DA* 92, 2; CD 52, 43, 2; Strabo 5, 248C. See A. Maiuri, 'La Villa augustea di 'Palazzo a mare' a Capri', *Campania Romana* 1, Naples, 1938, 115ff.

54. Plin., *NH* 9, 172; *TA* 14, 4, 3 and 5, 7; P. J. Bicknell, 'Agrippina's Villa at Bauli', *CR* 1963, 261f. On imperial villas generally, see O. Hirschfeld, 'Der Grundbesitz der röm. Kaiser in den ersten drei Jahrhunderten', *Klio* ii, 1902, 45–72; 284–315.

55. Sen., *Ep.* 55.

56. Domitia, *TA* 13, 21, 6; CD 61, 17, 2. Piso, *TA* 15, 52, 1f.

57. Strabo 5, 244f. C; CD 48, 50. See J. Beloch, *Campanien*, Breslau,

1890, 168–71; 194–202 with maps; H. Nissen, *Italische Landes-kunde*, Berlin, 1902, 727f.; C. G. Starr, *The Roman Imperial Navy*,² Cambridge, 1960, 14–17.

58. Destruction of Herculaneum, Mart. 4, 44. Government measures, CD 66, 24, 3f. Cf. Stat., *Silv.* 3, 5, 72–5; 104 ('*Stabiasque renatas*'); 4, 4, 78–86. *Via Domitiana*, Stat., *Silv.* 4, 3.

59. *MGH* xi, 1, xlvf.

60. Stat., *Silv.* 3, 1, 78–80 and 91–101; 2, 2, 52–9 and 30ff.

61. Baiae, Strabo 245C. Naples, Hor., *Epod.* 5, 43 ('*otiosa*'); Ovid, *Met.* 15, 711f.; Stat., *Silv.* 3, 5, 81–94; Strabo 246C; CD 55, 10, 9; Suet., *Nero* 20, 2. Costume, Cic., *Pro. Rab. Post.* 26f.; Suet., *DA* 98, 3; CD 60, 6, 2. Of the twelve known owners of villas in Naples itself, the only three consulars, L. Lucullus, L. Iulius Caesar and L. Domitius Ahenobarbus, were all somewhat Bohemian.

62. J. Day, 'Agriculture in the life of Pompeii', *Yale Class. Stud.* 1932, 177f.

63. Petron., *Sat.* 29f. Cf. Sen., *Ep.* 86, 7 on tasteless extravagance of freedmen's establishments.

64. Sen., *Ep.* 51, 12.

65. As is recorded by Plut., *Pomp.* 6, 1; VP 2, 29, 1. Cf. JC, *BC* 1, 15, 4; M. Gelzer, *Kl. Schr.*, Wiesbaden, 1962, 1, 95–7; R. Syme, *The Roman Revolution*, Oxford, 1939, 28.

66. Plut., *Cato mi.* 20, 2. Cf. Plut., *Cic.* 7, 2 on the large number of prominent men's estates bordering on the main roads of Italy.

67. JC, *BC* 1, 17, 4; 1, 34, 2.

68. *ILS* 212 (Smallwood 369), col. 2, ll. 1ff.; TA 3, 55, 4.

69. JC, *BC* 1, 15, 2. Cf. Plin., *Ep.* 5, 14, 9 to a friend, '*Campania tua*'; 7, 11, 5, '*Larius noster*'.

70. CD 52, 42, 6; TA 12, 23, 1.

71. Plin., *Ep.* 9, 7; cf. 3, 19, 1–4.

72. Plin., *Ep.* 5, 6.

73. Plin., *Ep.* 7, 30, 3; 9, 37; 10, 8, 5.

74. Plin., *Ep.* 6, 19, with S–W's notes. Marcus Aurelius perhaps reduced the proportion to a quarter, SHA, *MA* 11, 8. It is hard to know why Mommsen thought a third or a quarter only of the basic million sesterces which a senator needed to possess, *Staatsr.* ii, 2, 877 and 899f.

75. CD 76, 2,1.

76. The most complete literary accounts of villas are those of the younger Pliny, *Epp.* 2, 17 (his Laurentine villa) and 5, 6 (his villa at Tifernum) and of Sidonius Apollinaris, *Ep.* 2, 2. For modern literature see A. N. Sherwin-White, *The Letters of Pliny*, 186ff, and especially Georgina Masson, *O.c.* (n. 14), 11–31 and plates 1–18.

77. Pliny's Tuscan villa, *Ep.* 5, 6, 7f. and 14f.

78. Stat., *Silv.* 1, 3, 64–75; Plin., *Ep.* 4, 30.

79. *Cryptoporticus*, Plin., *Ep.* 2, 17, 16–19; 5, 6, 28–31. *Xysti*, Plin., *Ep.* 2, 17, 18–20; 5, 6, 16–19 and 23.

80. The plane an imported tree from Greece, Plin., *NH* 12, 6–13. 'Caelebs' etc., Hor., *Car.* 2, 15, 5f.; Virg., *Georg.* 4, 146; Mart. 3, 58, 3; Quint. 8, 3, 8.

81. On these trees in villas, Mart. 3, 58, 2f. and 46; Hor., *Car.* 2, 15, 9; Plin., *Ep.* 5, 6, 16–18, 27 and 35. Ivy, Plin., *Ep.* 5, 6, 32. Cherry, Plin., *NH* 15, 102–5.

82. Plin., *NH* 12, 13; Cic., *Ad Q.f.* 3, 1, 5.

83. Quint. 8, 3, 8; Paestum roses, Virg., *Georg.* 4, 119; Ovid, *Ex Pont.* 2, 4, 28; Mart. 4, 42, 10. List of Roman garden flowers and trees with full ancient references and modern names, P. Grimal, *O.c.* (n. 14), 497–501. Picture of boskage on the wall of Livia's dining-room at Prima Porta (now in Museo delle Terme), Grimal, pl. xx; G. Masson, *O.c.* (n. 14), pl. 3.

84. Sen., *Controv.* 5, 5. Cf. Hor., *Car.* 2, 18, 23–8; Sen., *Ep.* 90, 39; Juv. 14, 141–51.

85. See Cic., *In Verr.* ii, 4 (*De Signis*); *Ad Att.* 1, 3, 2; 1, 4, 3; 1, 8, 2; 1, 9, 2; 1, 10, 3; *Ad Fam.* 7, 23 (purchase of statues for Cicero); Juv. 4, 112; 7, 79f.

86. *Piscina* in villa of Q. Cicero, *Ad Att.* 3, 1, 3. Cf. Sen., *Ep.* 86, 6; Plin., *Ep.* 5, 6, 25. Heated pool, Plin., *Ep.* 2, 17, 11.

87. Mart. 3, 47; 3, 58, 48–50; Quint. 8, 3, 8.

88. Cic., *Ad Att.* 2, 9, 1; *Paradox. Stoic.* 5, 38; Varro, *RR* 3, 3, 10; 3, 17, 2–9 (esp. on Lucullus and Hortensius, on whom cf. Plin., *NH* 9, 170–2); Col. 8, 16f.; *RE* xx, 1783–5, s.v. 'Piscina'. The notorious fish-enthusiasts were M. Philippus, cos. 56 B.C., Hortensius and the two Luculli, Plin., *NH* 9, 170. Vedius Pollio,

Plin., *NH* 9, 77; Sen., *De Ira* 3, 40, 2; CD 54, 23, 2; *RE* viiiA, 568–70, no. 8.

89. Sergius Orata, VM 9, 1, 1; Plin., *NH* 9, 168f.; *RE* iiA, 1713, no. 33.

90. Philippus, Varro, *RR* 3, 3, 9; Col. 8, 16, 3. Lucullus, Varro, *RR* 3, 17, 9; Plut., *Lucull.* 39, 3; VP 2, 33, 4; Sen., *De Tranq. An.* 3, 7. Mockery of such fantasies, Hor., *Car.* 2, 18, 20ff.; 3, 24, 1–4; Varro, *RR* 3, 17, 2.

91. Quotation from G. Iacopi, *The Grotto of Tiberius*, E. T., Rome, 1967, 7 (see, for bibliography, p. 4); Georgina Masson, *O.c.* (n. 14), 27–9. Good pictures in G. Iacopi, *L'Antro di Tiberio a Sperlonga* (*I Monumenti Romani* iv), Rome, 1963.

92. Plin., *NH* 9, 170; Varro, *RR* 3, 2, 17 (forty thousand sesterces); Col. 8, 16, 4 (four hundred thousand).

93. Varro, *RR* 3, 17, 3; Plin., *NH* 9, 171; *RE* xiii, 1642–5, no. 25.

94. *Aviarium* at Q. Cicero's villa, Cic., *Ad Q.f.* 3, 1, 1. *Ornithon*, Varro, *RR* 3, 2, 2f.; 3, 3–11. On its management, Col. 8, 1–15. On its profit, Varro, *RR* 3, 2, 15. *Leporaria* etc., Varro *RR* 3, 3, 1f.; 3, 12–15; Col. 9, 1. Geese and *foie gras*, Plin., *NH* 10, 51f. *Vivaria*, Plin., *NH* 8, 211 (of fish, 9, 168 and 171).

95. Varro, *RR* 3, 16; Col. 9, 2–16.

96. See J. Lugli, *Forma Italiae* 1, 1, 2 (Circeii), Rome, 1928; P. Grimal, *O.c.* (n. 14), 109.

97. Trimalchio, n. 63 above; Mart. 3, 58.

98. Plin., *Ep.* 5, 6. Cf. n. 73 above.

99. Sen., *Ep.* 86, 5.

100. Cf. R. C. Carrington, 'Studies in the Campanian "Villae Rusticae"', *JRS* 1931, 110–30.

101. See p. 393, n. 13.

102. Hor., *Car.* 2, 18, 3–5; Juv. 7, 182f.; 14, 86–95; Sen., *Ep.* 86, 6; Plin., *NH* 36, 48–50.

103. Hor., *Car.* 2, 15; Quint. 8, 3, 8; Sen., *Ep.* 89, 21.

104. M. Rostovtzeff, *SEHRE*, pl. ix (murals from houses at Stabiae and Pompeii); Hor., *Car.* 2, 18, 20–2; 3, 1, 33–7, 'Contracta pisces aequora sentiunt'; 3, 24, 1–4. On Lucullus, n. 90 above.

105. Mart. 10, 62. See p. 106 above.

106. AG 9, 15, 1; 18, 5, 1 ('*feriae aestivae*'); 19, 5, 1.

107. Hor., *Ep.* 1, 7, 1–15; 1, 10, 15; *Car.* 2, 6, 9–24; Virg., *Georg.* 4, 116–48.

108. Hor., *Ep.* 1, 15.

109. Mart. 2, 48.

110. *Discessus*, Cic., *Ad Fam.* 3, 9, 3; *Ad Att.* 12, 40, 3. *Res prolatae*, *Ad Att.* 14, 5,2; *Ad Fam.* 1, 9, 8; *In Clod. et Cur.*, Schol. Bob. 88 St.

111. 74 B.C., Cic., *Pro Planc.* 65; 60 B.C., *Ad Att.* 1, 20, 1; 59 B.C., *Ad Att.* 2, 4–17 (esp. 2, 8, 2); 55 B.C., *Ad Att.* 4, 9–11; 54 B.C., *Ad Att.* 4, 14; *Ad Fam.* 7, 6.

112. Mart. 10, 30. Cf. Cic., *Ad Att.* 14, 16, 1, who may have kept a resident staff at his '*Cumanum*'.

113. See above, p. 106.

114. *Ad Fam.* 8, 9, 2. Elections in 51 B.C., *Ad Fam.* 8, 4, 1.

115. *Ad Q.f.* 3, 1, 1.

116. After Augustus, the praetors' responsibility, CD 54, 2, 3.

117. Sen., *Apok.* 7.

118. *FIR* 10 (*FIRA* 1, 7), 13 and 17 (domicile); 23 (availability at the time); 9 (Sept. 1st).

119. Cic., *De Orat.* 1, 24–9.

120. Plin., *Ep.* 10, 8, 5.

121. Senators, Suet., *DA* 35, 3; cf. Sen., *De Brev. Vit.* 7, 8. Courts, Suet., *DA* 32, 3; *Galb.* 14, 3.

122. Plin., *Ep.* 10, 8, 3, with S–W's notes; 9, 37, 5.

123. Ascon., *In Mil.* 31f. C.

124. Hor., *Sat.* 1, 5, 86. Cf. Hor., *Sat.* 2, 6, 42; Cic., *Pro Mil.* 28f. and 55. See D–S, s.v. '*rheda*'. Though Suetonius *DJ* 57 calls the hired carriage in which Caesar covered 100(R) miles in a day when on campaign a '*reda*', it must have been something far more like a *cisium*. Tiberius, using the public posting system after its introduction by Augustus, once travelled 200 miles in 24 hours, Plin., *NH* 7,84. Ausonius, *Ep.* 4, 5f.; 10, 13–15 implies that the *raeda* and the *petorritum* were more dangerous than a three-horse *cisium*.

125. '*Dormitoria*', Dig. 34, 2, 13.

126. Juv. 10, 19–21; Sen., *Ep.* 87, 2–4 and 7; 123, 7.

127. Hor., *Sat.* 1, 6, 107–9.

128. See p. 207.

129. Cic., *Pro Rosc. Am.* 19; *Phil.* 2, 77; Sen., *Ep.* 72, 2. See D–S, s.v. For illustrations, *NSA* 1939, 229, fig. 37 (Pompeii); A. Maiuri, *La Casa del Menandro*, Rome, 1932, 191–3 and fig. 88; E. Espérandieu, *Bas-reliefs de la Gaule romaine* 6, Paris, 1915, p. 57 (from Igel).

130. Plin., *Ep.* 2, 17, 2; Stat., *Silv.* 4, 3, 27–9.

131. Juv. 3, 242.

132. AG 10, 3, 5, quoting C. Gracchus.

133. Catull. 10, 14–20; Cic., *In Verr.* 2, 5, 27.

134. Suet., *DA* 82, 1; Cic., *Ad Att.* 12, 41, 1; 43, 2; 44, 3 etc.; Suet., *Tib.* 60; Lact., *De Mort. Persec.* 17, 3. On travel by litter, Sen., *Ep.* 15, 6.

135. Suet., *DA* 82; Hor., *Sat.* 1, 5, 27; CD 60, 21, 3.

136. The subject is fully treated by T. Kleberg, *Hôtels, restaurants et cabarets dans l'antiquité romaine*, Uppsala, 1957.

137. Kleberg, *O.c.* (n. 136), 31–6 (Pompeii); 44f. (Herculaneum); 45–8 (Ostia); A. Mau, *Pompeji in Leben und Kunst²*, Leipzig, 1908, 419f.; Anhang, 1913, 56 (E.T., *Pompeii, its Life and Art*, London, 1899, 392f.); H. T. Rowell, 'Satyricon 95–96', *CP* 1957, 217–22. Locking hotel doors, Petron., *Sat.* 94; Apul., *Met.* 1, 11 and 14.

138. *CIL* iv, 2145f.; 2155f.; 2159; Cic., *De Invent.* 2, 14.

139. Hor., *Sat.* 1, 5, 2–4. Cf. *Ep.* 1, 11, 12, 'caupona'; *Sat.* 1, 1, 29, 'perfidus caupo'.

140. Varro, *RR* 1, 2, 23.

141. *ILS* 7478.

142. Polyb. 2, 15, 4–6.

143. See Kleberg, *O.c.* (n. 136), 62.

144. Cf. Plin., *Ep.* 2, 17, 26, of his Laurentine villa, '*In vico balinea meritoria tria, magna commoditas si forte balineum domi . . . . . brevior mora calfacere dissuadeat*'.

145. Hor., *Sat.* 1, 5, 38.

146. *Ad Q.f.* 2, 6(5), 4; *Ad Fam.* 7, 18, 3; *Ad Att.* 12, 34, 1.

147. J. Carcopino, *The Secrets of Cicero's Correspondence*, London, 1951, 51–3.

148. *Ad Fam.* 7, 23, 3 (Terracina).

149. *Ad Att.* 10, 5, 3.

150. *Ad Att.* 11, 5, 2; cf. *Ad Fam.* 12, 20.

151. Cf. *Ad Att.* 14, 4, 1; 14, 20, 1.

152. Plin., *Ep.* 6, 14; 6, 20, 5 and 10; cf. 2, 17, 29; 3, 1; 7, 16, 2; Cic., *Ad Fam.* 9, 15, 5; *Top.* 1, 1; *De Offic.* 3, 58; Varro, *RR* 3, 2, 8; Symmach., *Ep.* 3, 23; 7, 15.

153. Plaut., *Mil. Glor.* 738–48; *Stich.* 347–57; Juv. 14, 59–67.

154. Plin., *Ep.* 1, 9, 4–6. *Lectiuncula*, Cic., *Ad Fam.* 7, 1, 1; cf. *Top.* 1, 1; Symmach., *Ep.* 3, 50.

155. Fronto, *De Fer. Als.* 3, 1 (ii, 4 Loeb).

156. Plin., *Ep.* 9, 36.

157. Plin., *Ep.* 7, 30, 5.

158. Plin., *Ep.* 9, 15, 3; cf. 7, 30, 3; 9, 36, 6; 5, 14, 8 with S–W's notes.

159. *Ep.* 3, 23, 1; 5, 78 (76).

160. SHA, *Hadr.* 2, 1, '*Venando usque ad reprehensionem studiosus*'; 20, 12f.; 26, 3. Hunting and fishing as country relaxations, *PLM* iv, Petronius 81.

161. Plin., *Ep.* 5, 6, 8 and 46; 5, 18, 2; 9, 10, 1; 9, 16, 1; 9, 36, 6 (on his estate in Tuscany); AM 28, 4, 18; Symmach., *Ep.* 1, 53 (47); 3, 23, 1; 5, 67; 7, 15; 8, 2; 9, 28 (26). Hunting is frequently depicted on stone reliefs and in mosaics, s.g. *SEHRE*, pl. lxxvii, 1.

162. Plin., *Pan.* 81, 1–3.

163. Auson., *Ep.* 14, 33–40 (scars); Sall., *Cat.* 4, 1; Valentinian, AM 29, 3, 3.

164. Symmach., *Ep.* 5, 68. Cf. Hor., *Car.* 3, 24, 54–8.

165. Symmach., *Ep.* 7, 35, 1.

166. Prop. 1, 11; 1, 12, 11; Sen., *Ep.* 51; Symmach., *Ep.* 8, 23.

167. On Lucrine Lake, Mart. 3, 20, 20; Stat., *Silv.* 4, 3, 113. On Como, Plin., *Ep.* 6, 24, 2. Off Formiae, Mart. 10, 30, 11–13. In Bay of Naples, Cic., *Ad Att.* 14, 16, 1; 16, 3, 6; Sen., *Ep.* 53, 1–5.

168. Hor., *Ep.* 1, 1, 92f.; *Car.* 2, 16, 21; 3, 1, 39.

169. Plin., *Pan.* 81, 4–82.

170. AM 28, 4, 18.

171. Plin., *Ep.* 2, 17, 11.

172. Suet., *C. Cal.* 54, 2.

173. Mart. 10, 30, 16–18; Plin., *Ep.* 9, 7, 4. Cf. Auson., *Mosella* 240–82 for a description of netting and fishing on the Moselle; also *Ep.* 14, 52–62 (at Médoc).

174. Cic., *De Offic.* 3, 58–60.

175. Plut., *Cato mi.* 10, 2; Strabo 14, 674C.

176. *TA* 2, 59–61.

177. L. 5, 8, 3; 33, 29, 4; 43, 11, 10.

178. L. 43, 14, 7.

179. *Dig.* 49, 16, 14 (Paulus); Quint. 7, 4, 14; Sen., *De Ira* 1, 18, 3–6.

180. Presumably only in the non-fighting season.

181. *TH* 1, 46; cf. 1, 58.

182. *TA* 1, 17, 6; 1, 35, 1 (A.D. 14).

183. See n. 181 above.

Chapter VII

1. *ILS* 2483 (E–J 261).

2. Plin., *NH* 5, 9f. (see *RE* xxi, 1455 on the date); P. 3, 48, 12, with Walbank's note.

3. P. 3, 58f.

4. Strabo 3, 144C; Plin., *NH* 2, 117f. (inadequate use of the new opportunities by geographers); Friedlaender i, 335.

5. *Acts* 27; Suet., *Terenti Vita* 5; *PIR²*, 'A' 1183; Jos., *Vit.* 15. Cf. Cic., *Ad Fam.* 16, 9, 1.

6. *Maccab.* 1, 8.

7. Plin., *Ep.* 10, 45f. Cf. 10, 120f. on the issue of a *diploma* for compassionate and not for official reasons at all. On the *cursus publicus*, see E. J. Holmberg, *Zur Geschichte des Cursus Publicus*, Uppsala, 1933, esp. 53–8.

8. SHA, *Pert.* 1, 5.

9. W. Riepl, *Das Nachrichtenwesen des Altertums*, Leipzig–Berlin, 1913, 129–57; Friedlaender i, 331–4 (E.T. i, 280–2).

10. Suet., *DJ* 57.

11. *VM* 5, 4, 3. Plin., *NH* 7, 84 must be wrong in saying that Tiberius was driving, not riding. On riding, W. Riepl, *O.c.* (n. 9), 147–52.

12. Riepl, *O.c.* (n. 9), 129–47, esp. 146; Friedlaender i, 333.

13. Sailing, Friedlaender i, 336–40 (E.T. i, 283–7). Start of sailing season, Hor., *Car.* 1, 4, 2. End of season, Plin., *NH* 2, 125. Cicero held up, *Ad Fam.* 16, 9, 1.

14. Plin., *NH* 19, 4 (Cadiz, Marseilles); Philostr., *Vit. Apoll. Tyan.* 7, 10 (Corinth-Puteoli); Arist., *Or.* 48, 65–8 Keil; Friedlaender i, 339.

15. Ovid, *Tr.* 1, 10, 9f.; 1, 11, 5f.; Propert. 3, 21, 19ff.; Galen 5, 18K.

16. Symmach., *Ep.* 8, 61; Plin., *Ep.* 10, 15, with S–W's notes. Cf. Cic., *Ad Fam.* 4, 12, 1; *RE* xiv, 859–63; *IGR* iv, 841.

17. Plin., *NH* 19, 3, voyage from Puteoli to Alexandria in nine days without strong winds a record. Fifteen-hundred-tonners, Lucian, *Navig.* 5f.; Friedlaender i, 425f. Numbers of passengers, Jos., *Vit.* 15; Ael. Arist., *Or.* 45, 155; *Acts* 27, 37 (276 passengers or alternatively on the reading of Codex Vaticanus, about 76).

18. Plin., *Ep.* 5, 19, 6f., with S–W's notes; Plin., *NH* 24, 28; 31, 63; Celsus 3, 22, 8; Galen 12, 191K.

19. Quintil. 4, 2, 41.

20. Sid. Apoll., *Ep.* 1, 5, 2; Cic., *De Offic.* 2, 64; Plin., *NH* 9, 26; *IGR* i, 674; Cic., *Ad Att.* 6, 1, 25 (cf. R. Syme, 'Who was Vedius Pollio?', *JRS* 1961, 23–30).

21. *Or.* 51 (27), 1–6 Keil.

22. Ravenna, Sid. Apoll., *Ep.* 1, 5, 5–8; Mart. 3, 56f.; *RE* viiA, 1320f. (for refs. to Tiro). Donat., *Vit. Virg.* 35 (51).

23. Cic., *De Legg.* 3, 18; Mommsen, *Staatsr.* ii, 1, 690ff.; Suet., *Tib.* 31, 1.

24. *CD* 52, 42, 6f.; 60, 25, 6; *TA* 12, 23, 1; Mommsen, *Staatsr.*, iii, 912f.

25. Propert. 3, 21, 29f.; Liban., *Ep.* 947. Nero, *CD* 63, 14, 3. On Strabo (cf. 2, 117C), G. W. Bowersock, *Augustus and the Greek World*, Oxford, 1965, 127, Cf. L. Waddy, *AJA* 1963, 296–300, who thinks Strabo did visit Athens.

26. Lost popularity of the oracle, Plut., *De Defect. Orac.*, e.g. 411Ef. Guides, *De Pyth. Orac.* 2 (*Mor.* 395A).

27. Sights, Strabo 14, 652C. Decorum, Dio Chrys., *Or.* 31, 157–63.

28. Paus. 7, 5; Propert. 1, 6, 31, '*Mollis Ionia*'.

29. On Alexandria, *AM* 22, 16, 7–13; Dio Chrys., *Or.* 32, 36; Strabo 17, 791–5 and 801C; André Bernard, *Alexandrie la grande*, Paris, 1966. On Carthage, Herod. 7, 6, 1.

30. *RE* xvi, 801–21. Hadrian, SHA, *Hadr.* 20, 2.

31. Strabo 17, 807C; Plin., *NH* 8, 185.

32. *RE* vA 1553–82, esp. 1580–2, s.v. 'Thebai'; xv, 648, s.v. 'Memnon'; *TA* 2, 61, 1 and Furneaux ad loc.; Strabo 17, 816C; Plin., *NH* 36, 58; Paus. 1, 42, 3; Dio Chrys., *Or.* 31, 92; Lucian, *Toxaris* 27.

33. *CIL* iii, 30–66 (cf. *ILS* 8759 a–g); *CIG* iii, 4719–61. See *CIL* iii, p. 968 for the possible date 205 A.D. for *CIL* iii, 52. See now A. and E. Bernard, *Les Inscriptions grecques et latines du Colosse de Memnon* (Inst. franç. d'Archéologie orientale, Bibliothèque d'Étude, tome 31, Cairo, 1960).

34. *CIG* iii, 4747.

35. SHA, *SS* 17, 3.

36. *TA* 2, 59. Edicts issued by him, E–J 320. C. Numonius Vala (*PIR*, 'N' 193) who cut a record of his presence at Philae in 2 B.C. (*ILS* 8758) was presumably not a senator at the time, or he had received a special permit.

37. Suet., *C. Cal.* 24, 2; 51, 1.

38. Nero and Egypt, Suet., *Nero* 19, 1; B. W. Henderson, *Life and Principate of the Emperor Nero*, London, 1903, 234f. Hadrian, SHA, *Hadr.* 13, 3; 14, 3.

39. *TA* 2, 53f.

40. *TA* 2, 59–61; Plin., *NH* 8, 185.

41. *TH* 2, 1–4; Suet., *D. Tit.* 5, 1–3.

42. SHA, *SS* 16, 9–17, 4; CD 75, 13, 1f.

43. Cic., *Ad Att.* 5, 10, 5.

44. L. 45, 27f. Cf. the tone of Horace, *Ep.* 1, 11.

45. See n. 33 above; *CIL* iii, 34 (centurion from Vienne).

46. Strabo 4, 181C.

47. Alexandria, Strabo 14, 673–5C (comparing Tarsus); Galen 2, 220K; AM 22, 16, 18 (quoted in text); Plut., *Ant.* 28, 3; Lucian, *Toxaris* 27. Berytus, Marrou 378.

48. Friends of the elder Cicero, *RE* viiA, 838; of the younger, Cic., *Ad Att.* 12, 32, 3; *RE* viii, 2339. Quint. 12, 6, 6f.

49. Ovid, *Tr.* 1, 2, 77f.; *Ex Pont.* 2, 10, 21–42; *Fast.* 6, 417–24. The dates are uncertain; see A. L. Wheeler, 'Topics from the life of Ovid', *AJP* 1925, 20–2.

50. Cic., *Ad Att.* 12, 32, 2; *Ad Fam.* 16, 21, 3; AG 18, 2.

51. *Ad Fam.* 16, 21. For other refs. to Cicero at Athens, *RE* viiA, 1284.

52. *Tusc. Disp.* 2, 34; 3, 53; 5, 77; *Ad Fam.* 12, 16, 2.

53. *Ad Fam.* 12, 16, 1f.; *Ad Att.* 6, 7, 2; JC, *BC* 3, 110, 6.

54. Catull. 46 and 31; Propert. 1, 6; Tibull. 1, 3, 1-3 and 55f.; 1, 7 (cf. F. Della Corte, 'Tibullo e l'Egitto', *Maia* 1966, 333-7). Persius, Suet., *Vita.* Seneca, *Cons. ad Helv.* 19, 4-7. Galerius, *RE* vii, 598.

55. Cic., *Pro Cael.* 73; Plut., *M. Brut.* 3; Cic., *Ad Att.* 6, 2, 7-9.

56. Cic., *In Verr.* 2, 2, 28f. (on Scipio and the selection of *comites* in general); Plut., *Lucull.* 34, CD 36, 14, 4 and Cic., *De Har. Resp.* 42 (Clodius). JC, *BG* 1, 39.

57. Sen., *Controv.* 9, 25, 1 (of L. Flamininus). Serv. ad Virg., *Aen.* 8, 688; Cic., *In Verr.* 2, 5, 30-4.

58. *TA* 3, 34, 12.

59. *TA* 3, 33, 1.

60. Suet., *D. Cl.* 2, 1 (cf. *CIL* xiii, p. 227); *TA* 1, 41, 3; 12, 27, 1; 2, 54, 1; *Agr.* 6, 3; 29, 1.

61. *TA* 2, 55, 5 (cf. 3, 33, 3); 1, 69, 1f.

62. *TA* 1, 40.

63. *TA* 3, 33f.

64. Sen., *Cons. ad Helv.* 19, 6.

65. Sall., *BJ* 21, 2; 26; JC, *BG* 7, 3, 1; 7, 55, 5; App., *Mith.* 22, 83-23, 91; Memnon, *FGH* 434, F. 22, 9.

66. Plut., *Cato mi.* 59-61; *Bell Afr.* 90, 3.

67. M. Rostovtzeff, *SEHHW* ii, 920-2; Th. Homolles, 'Les Romains à Delos', *BCH* 1884, 75-158; *RE* iv, 2493-6; *OGIS* 135 (127 B.C.).

68. *SEG* 9, 8, 1 (E-J 311); E-J 360a and b.

69. L. 43, 3, 1-4; App., *Iber.* 38, 153; J. Hatzfeld, *Les Trafiquants italiens dans l'Orient hellénique*, Paris, 1919; A. J. N. Wilson, *Emigration from Italy in the Republican Age of Rome*, Manchester, 1966.

70. E. Gabba, *Le Origini della guerra sociale*, Pavia, 1954, 81-9.

71. *IGR* i, 246; 249, 252f.; 279; 293; 299f.; 339; 373 etc.; Juv. 3, 62.

72. *OGIS* 595. Cf. C. Dubois, *Pouzzoles antique*, Paris, 1907, 83–110; R. Meiggs, *Roman Ostia*, Oxford, 1960, 214–6.

73. *FGH* 88, T. 1 and 4; *IGR* i, 233.

74. *IGR* i, 153; L. Moretti, *Iscrizioni agonistiche greche*, Rome, 1953; *IGR* i, 160–6; 444–9.

75. Plut., *De Defect. Orac., Mor.* 410Aff.; *IG* xiv, 2548; I. A. Richmond, *Antiquity* 1940, 193–5. Strabo 17, 816C; *RE* ivA, 81–5.

76. Florus, *Virgilius Orator an Poeta*.

77. Mart. 7, 44f.; 10, 44.

Chapter VIII

1. On these, see W. Warde Fowler, *The Roman Festivals of the Period of the Republic*, London, 1899; Degrassi 364–71.

2. Cf. Tertull., *De Spect.* 5.

3. See Degrassi 368f.

4. T*H* 4, 40.

5. Plin., *Ep.* 2, 1, 9; CD 68, 2, 3.

6. SHA, *MA* 10, 10.

7. On the Ludi, see Degrassi 372–6 and on the whole subject of this chapter, Friedlaender ii, 1–160; iv, 179–283 (E.T. ii, 1–130; iv, 148–270).

8. G.Wissowa, *RK* 125–8. On *ludi magni*, L. 27, 33, 8; L. R. Taylor, *TAPA* 1937, 296–8. Scipio, L. 28, 38, 14.

9. Ludi Apollinares, L. 25, 12, 8–15; 27, 23, 5–7; 37, 4, 4. For sources and details of the origin and development of these and the following games, see W. Warde Fowler, *O.c.* (n. 1 above) and Degrassi, under the particular dates at which the games were held.

10. Or from the 4th to the 18th. All depends on whether the sixteenth day which Antony added in 44 B.C. was the 4th, as Degrassi thinks, or the 19th, as Mommsen thought. The length, indeed, may not yet have been fifteen days at the beginning of the first century B.C. See Degrassi 507.

11. Plin., *NH* 2, 94.

12. Cic., Phil. 2, 110. See n. 10 above.

13. New imperial *ludi*, Degrassi 373–5. Parilia, Degrassi 443–5. Ludi Augustales, Degrassi 516.

14. VM 2, 10, 8. Cf. Tertull, *De Spect.* 17.

15. Cic., *De Legg.* 2, 38, '*Iam ludi publici sunt cavea circoque divisi*'.

16. Ovid., *Fast.* 4, 681–712 with J. G. Frazer's notes. W. Warde Fowler, *O.c.* (n. 1 above), 77–9 speculates on the origin of this ceremony.

17. Ovid., *Fast.* 5, 371–4; Mart. 8, 67, 4.

18. Cf. Tertull., *De Spect.* 6 for the distinction: '*A primordio bifariam ludi censebantur, sacri et funebres, id est deis nationum et mortuis*'. Suet., *Tib.* 34, 1, '*Ludorum ac munerum impensas*'.

19. See L. Malten, 'Leichenspiel und Totenkult', *Röm. Mitt.* 1923/4, 300–40, esp. 328.

20. Junius Pera, L., *Per.* 16; VM 2, 4, 7; *RE* x, 1026, n. 59. Metellus, Plut., *Coriol.* 11, 4; *Romul.* 10, 3.

21. L. 23, 30, 15.

22. L. 28, 21.

23. CD 37, 8, 1; Plin., *NH* 33, 53; Plut., *JC* 5, 9. For a list of recorded Republican gladiatorial shows, see *RE*, Supplb. iii, 760–4, s.v. '*Gladiatores*'.

24. Tertull., *De Spect.* 12.

25. L. 39, 42, 7–12; Plut., *Cato mai.* 17, 1–5; *Flam.* 18, 4–10.

26. Plut., *C. Gracch.* 12, 5f.

27. See L. R. Taylor, *TAPA* 1937, 299; *RE* vA, 600f.

28. The statement of Ennodius in his panegyric of Theoderic is convincingly refuted by G. Ville, *Mél. d'arch. et d'hist.* 1960, 305–7.

29. CD 44, 6, 2; 47, 40, 6.

30. *RGDA* 22, 1, with Gagé's notes. The dates of seven of these shows are attested: 29, 28, 16, 12, 7 and 2 B.C. and A.D. 6.

31. CD 66, 25; Suet., *D. Tit.* 7, 3.

32. Trajan, CD 68, 15, 1; *Fast. Ost., Inscr. Ital.* xiii, 1, 198–201. See A. Degrassi ad loc., 227f. Hadrian, *Inscr. Ital.* xiii, 1, 202f.

33. CD 54, 2, 3f. Regulation stiffened by Tiberius, Suet., *Tib.* 34, 1; relaxed by Gaius, CD 59, 14, 3.

34. *Inscr. Ital.* xiii, 2, 237–62: December 2, 4–6, 8, 19–21, 23, 24.

35. *CT* 2, 8, 19; 2, 8, 22.

36. Degrassi 372.

37. *CT* 15, 12, 1 (in A.D. 325); *CI* 11, 44 (43).

38. *RE*, Supplb. iii, 771f. In East, *CI* 11, 44 (43); Euseb., *Vit. Const.*
4, 25; Liban., *Orat.* 1, 5. St. Almachius, Theodoret, *HE* 5, 26.
On the whole question of the end of gladiatorial fighting and
wild beast fighting and St. Almachius in particular, see G. Ville,
'Les Jeux de gladiateurs dans l'empire chrétien', *Mél. d'arch. et
d'hist.* 1960, 273–335, esp. 326–9; André Chastagnol, *Le Sénat
romain sous le règne d'Odoacre*, Bonn, 1966, 61f.

39. Cassiod., *Var.* 5, 42.

40. Salvian, *Gub. Dei* 6, 10f.; A. H. M. Jones, *The Later Roman Empire*
977f., with notes; R. Browning, *CR* 1965, 339; Cassiod., *Var.*
1, 20; 2, 9; 3, 39 and 51; Procop., *Bell. Goth.* 7, 37, 4 (Totila).

41. Varro, *LL.* 5, 153.

42. L. 8, 20, 2 (329 B.C.); 41, 27, 6 (174 B.C.); CD 49, 43, 2 (Agrippa).
On the ornaments of the *spina*, Tertull., *De Spect.* 8; Cassiod.,
Var. 3, 51. Mosaic pictures of racing in the Circus, G. V. Gentili,
La Villa Erculia di Piazza Armerina, I mosaici figurati, Rome, 1964,
fig. 3 and tav. ix; P. Wuilleumier, *Lyon, métropole des Gaules*,
Paris, 1953, pl. viii; G. Charles-Picard, *La Civilisation de l'Afrique
romaine*, Paris, 1959, pl. 44, opp. p. 306 (late 2nd cent.). For the
Circus generally, see *TDAR*, s.v. See also *Arch. Aelian.* 1885,
133–7 and n. 43 below.

43. *TDAR* 116. Arcades clearly visible on a coin of Trajan, H. Mat-
tingly-E. A. Sydenham, *RIC* ii, 284, no. 571, pl. x, 187. For a
description of the Circus, DH, *AR* 3, 68.

44. On the Circus Vaticanus and Stadium Domitiani, see *TDAR*.
For ancient evidence and a photograph of the latter, see D. R.
Dudley, *Urbs Roma*, London, 1967, 184f. and pl. 57.

45. L., *Per.* 48; App., *BC* 1, 28, 125, misdating badly; Oros. 4, 21, 4.
Cf. VP 1, 15, 3; Aug., *CD* 1, 31.

46. VM 2, 4, 2. Cf. TA 14, 20, 2f.; Plaut., *Amphitr.*, prol. 65 etc.

47. See L. R. Taylor, *Roman Voting Assemblies*, Michigan, 1966,
29–32. Cf. Cic., *Pro Flacc.* 16; VM 2, 2, 5; Auson., *Ludus Sept.
Sap.* 19–41.

48. TA 14, 20, 2f.; AG 10, 1, 7; Tertull., *De Spect.* 10.

49. Cic., *De Har. Resp.* 24; Quint. 3, 8, 28f. See J. A. Hanson, *The
Roman Theater-Temples*, Princeton, 1959, 9–26.

50. Plut., *Pomp.* 42, 8f. For ancient evidence about and illustrations of
the site of this theatre, sec D. R. Dudley, *O.c.* (n. 44), 180–4 and
pl. 55f.

51. *RE* iv, 1268–71, no. 70; *TDAR* 513; F. W. Shipley, *MAAR* 1931, 37f.

52. Julius Caesar, Suet., *DJ* 44, 1; CD 43, 49, 2. Augustus, *RGDA* 21, 1; Suet., *DA* 29, 4; CD 53, 30, 5; 54, 26, 1; F. W. Shipley, *O.c.* (n. 51), 50 and 52. For other ancient evidence about, and photograph of, this theatre, see D. R. Dudley, *O.c.* (n. 44), 178–80 and pl. 54.

53. *ILS* 5627; R. Étienne, *La Vie quotidienne à Pompéi*, Paris, 1966, 425–33.

54. Plin., *NH* 8, 21; DH, *AR* 3, 68, 2; Suet., *DJ* 39, 2; Jennison 156.

55. Plin., *NH* 36, 116–20; *RE* i, 1960, s.v. 'Amphitheatrum'; W. Beare, *The Roman Stage²*, London, 1955, 162.

56. CD 51, 23, 1; *TA* 3, 72, 3. Destruction in A.D. 64, CD 62, 18, 2.

57. *TA* 13, 31, 1; Plin., *NH* 16,200; Suet., *Nero* 12, 1; Calp. Sic. 7, 23f.

58. Suet., *D. Tit.* 7, 3; CD 66, 25.

59. VM 2, 4, 6; Plin., *NH* 19, 23; AM 14, 6, 25 (wrongly dated); *RE* xiii, 2088.

60. Prop. 3, 18, 13; CD 53, 31, 3; Plin., *NH* 19, 23f.

61. Prop. 4, 1, 15; Ovid., *AA* 1, 103; M. Bieber, *The History of the Greek and Roman Theater²*, Princeton, 1961, 179f. Sailors, SHA, *Commod.* 15, 6.

62. Suet., *C. Cal.* 26, 5; Mart. 12, 29, 16.

63. Lucr. 6, 109–11, tr. W. H. D. Rowse (Loeb); Prop. 3, 18, 13, 'Fluitantia vela'; 4, 1, 14, 'Sinuosa vela'; Mart. 9, 38, 6; 11, 21, 6; 14, 28f.

64. Lucr. 4, 75–83, tr. Rowse (see n. 63).

65. CD 63, 6, 2; Plin., *NH* 19, 24.

66. Ovid., *AA* 1, 103f.; Lucr. 2, 416f.; Prop. 4, 1, 16; Lucan, *Phars.* 9, 808f.; Mart. 3, 65, 2; 5, 25. 7f.; 11, 8, 2; Plin., *NH* 21, 33; Fronto, *De Eloqu.* 1, 12 (ii, 64 Loeb).

67. Mart. 9, 38, 5, of a juggler.

68. Ovid., *Tr.* 2, 501, 'Girls and boys, married men and women, see the most disgusting of mimes'.

69. Tickets, Bieber, *O.c.* (n. 61 above), p. 246, figs. 811–6.

70. Cic., *Ad Q.f.* 3, 1, 1. Cf. *Ad Att.* 2, 1, 5; *Pro Mur.* 67; 72.

71. Ovid, *Amor.* 3, 2; *Tr.* 2, 283f.; Juv. 11, 201f.

72. L. R. Taylor, *Studies in honour of Gilbert Norwood*, Toronto, 1952, 153, n. 13, disputes this view. Cf. Suet., *DA* 44, 2f.

73. Plut., *Sulla* 35, 5–11.

74. Suet., *DA* 44, 2f.; CD 58, 2, 4 (where Livia's remark is set in an implausible context).

75. Suet., *Nero* 12, 4.

76. *TDAR* 9f.; Calp. Sic., *Ecl.* 7, 26f. (proximity of the *pullati* to the women's seats in Nero's amphitheatre); Sen., *De Tranq. An.* 11, 8; Cic., *De Senect.* 48.

77. Suet., *DA* 45, 1; *Nero* 12, 2.

78. VM 2, 4, 3; CD 55, 22, 4; 60, 7, 3f.; Suet., *D. Cl.* 21, 3.

79. Justin 43, 5, 10 (special privileges of Massiliots); Jos., *AJ* 14, 210.

80. Suet., *DA* 44, 1.

81. TA 13, 54, 3–6; Suet., *D. Cl.* 25, 4 (the same story told of Claudius' principate).

82. Plut., *Cic.* 13, 2–4; Plin., *NH* 7, 117.

83. Plin., *NH* 8, 21; TA 15, 32, 2, with Furneaux's note.

84. TA 6, 3, 1–3.

85. *CIL* vi, 32098 a–i, l, m; Henzen, *Acta Fratr. Arv.* cvif. See Ch. Huelsen, 'Il Posto degli Arvali nel Colosseo e la capacità dei teatri di Roma antica', *Bull. Comunale di Roma* 1894, 312–324; H. Jordan–Ch. Huelsen, *Topographie der Stadt Rom im Altertum* 1, 3, Berlin, 1907, 292–8; A. Chastagnol, *O.c.* (n. 38), 24–6.

86. Cic., *Ad Att.* 2, 1, 5.

87. Suet., *DA* 44, 2; *CIL* vi, 32098 c, [pra]etext[atis]; d, [paedagogis p]uer[orum.]

88. Cic., *Pro. Mur.* 73; Suet., *DA* 44, 3; TA 4, 16, 6.

89. Plin., *NH* 37, 64.

90. Mommsen, *Staatsr.* ii, 1, 517–22. Cf. Cic., *In Verr.* 2, 5, 36. Ludi Victoriae Sullae, *RE*, Supplb. v, 628f.

91. Fulvius Nobilior, L. 39, 5, 6–10; 39, 22, 1–3. Gracchus, 40, 44, 10f.

92. Cic., *De Offic* 2, 57 (uncritical).

93. L. 7, 2, 13.

94. Suet., *DJ* 10, 1.

95. See *MRR* for refs.

96. CD 54, 2, 3f.

97. TA 1, 15, 5.

98. T. *Agr.* 6, 4; Plin., *Ep.* 7, 11, 4.

99. *Fast. Amit. min.*, under dates 4 September, 4 November, 6 July and 13 October respectively, *Inscr. Ital.* xiii, 2, 201–12.

100. CD 54, 17, 4; Mart. 10, 41, 5; Friedlaender ii, 11.

101. SHA, *Hadr.* 3, 8; Fronto, *Ad L. Ver.* 2, 7, 5 (ii, 154 Loeb.).

102. Zosim. 2, 38, 4; Olympiodor. ap. Phot., *Bibl.* 80 (*FHG* 4, 67f, 44).

103. P. 31, 28, 6.

104. Cic., *Ad Q.f.* 3, 6 (8), 6; *Pro Mil.* 95.

105. TH 2, 95; *Dig.* 35, 1, 36.

106. TA 11, 22, 3; 13, 5, 1; Suet., *D.Cl.* 24, 2; *Domit.* 4, 1; SHA, *AS* 43, 3; Degrassi 533f.

107. Cic., *Pro Sest.* 106.

108. Cic., *Ad Fam.* 7, 1, 1; Hor., *Sat.* 1, 10, 38; *AP* 386–9.

109. Cic., *Ad Att.* 2, 19, 3.

110. See F. F. Abbott, 'The Theatre as a Factor in Roman Politics under the Republic', *TAPA* 1907, 49–56.

111. Jos., *AJ* 19, 24f.; *TH* 1, 72; Tertull., *De Spect.* 16.

112. Cic., *Ad Q.f.* 2, 3, 2 (56 B.C.); TA 1, 16, 4f.; *Dig.* 48, 19, 28, 3.

113. Piazza Armerina, G. V. Gentili, *O.c.* (n. 42), tav. x; *Tunisia, Ancient Mosaics* (Unesco World Art Series), 1962, pl. 28; Degrassi 373.

114. Herod. 1, 12, 5; CD 72, 13. On popular demonstrations between A.D. 180 and 238, see C. R. Whittaker, 'The Revolt of Papirius Dionysius', *Historia* 1964, 348–69.

115. Cassiod., *Var.* 1, 32.

116. *Dig.* 1, 12, 1, 12; TA 1, 77, 2; 13, 28, 1.

117. TA 1, 77, 1, a tribune of the praetorian guard because the City Prefecture, with command of the urban cohorts, was not yet established; 4, 14, 4; 13, 24; 13, 25, 4.

118. Suet., *DA* 45, 1.

119. Plin., *Pan.* 51, 3–5.

120. Fronto, *Princ. Hist.* 17 (ii, 216 Loeb); Juv. 10, 78–81; Jos., *AJ* 19, 130. Cf. Dio Chrys., *Or.* 32, 31, of Alexandrians at the time of Trajan.

121. J. Carcopino, *Daily Life in ancient Rome*, London, 1941, 210. Estimates of the population of Rome in the early Empire vary on one side or other of the figure of a million; see W. J. Oates, 'The Population of Rome', *CJ* 1934, 101–16.

122. Mart. 12, 57, 13.

123. These figures are derived from the impressive article of Ch. Huelsen (n. 85 above), whose findings are universally accepted, but the compulsive inferences are not drawn from them. See Jordan-Huelsen, *O.c.* (n. 85), 515f., 519f. and 528 (theatres); 297 (Colosseum). I am most grateful to Mr. P. A. Brunt and to Mr. Oswyn Murray for allowing me to seek their concurrence with what I have written on this topic.

124. Hor., *Sat.* 2, 6, 44; Tac., *Dial.* 29, 3.

125. Dio Chrys., *Or.* 32, 45; Cic., *Ad Fam.* 7, 1; MA, *Med.* 6, 46; Sen., *Ep.* 7.

126. Sen., *De Provid.* 2, 8f.; 4, 4 (a brave *murmillo*—but also '*militares viri gloriantur vulneribus*'); *De Tranq. An.* 11, 4f. Cf. Cic., *Pro Mil.* 92; *Tusc. Disp.* 2, 41; Plin., *Pan.* 33, 1; AG 12, 5, 13.

127. Sen., *Ep.* 22, 1; *De Ira* 1, 11, 2.

128. Aug., *Conf.* 6, 7, 11–8, 13.

129. *Ad Q.f.* 3, 5, 7. Cf. Tac., *Dial.* 2–4 on the writing of plays for recitation and publication at the end of the 1st century A.D.

130. For details, see M. Schanz–C. Hosius, *Geschichte der röm. Literatur*,[4] Munich, 1959, 1, 44–150.

131. Quint. 10, 1, 97; Hor., *Ep.* 2, 1, 55–7; A. Klotz, *Scaenicorum Romanorum Fragmenta* 1, Munich, 1953.

132. On Plautus, see Schanz–Hosius, *O.c.* (n. 130), 1, 55–86. On his humour, J.-P. Cèbe, *La Caricature et la parodie dans le monde romain antique*, Paris, 1966.

133. Hor., *AP* 270–3; Quint. 10, 1, 99f. On Terence, Schanz–Hosius, *O.c.* (n. 130), 1, 103–24.

134. *Phorm.*, prol. 30–3; *Hec.*, prol. 33–42. See W. M. Lindsay, *CQ* 1931, 144f. on the translation of '*pugilum gloria*'.

135. The *praetexta*, with the *togata*, was praised by Horace, *AP* 285–8. See *RE* xxii, 1569–75, s.v. '*Praetexta*'; viA, 1998–2001, s.v. '*Tragoedia*' and viA, 1660–2, s.v. '*Togata*'. *Togata* sub-divided into *praetexta* (tragic) and *tabernaria* (comic). See Festus 480, 12L.

136. Nonius 7, 756, 17L (*Ambracia*); AG 9, 14, 13; Cic., *De Div.* 1, 44f. (quotation from Accius' *Brutus*).

137. Ps.-Acron on Hor., *AP* 288, '*Praetextae et togatae*'. Pomponius Secundus, Quint. 10, 1, 98 (cf. TA 11, 13, 1; Plin., *Ep.* 7, 17, 11); Schanz–Hosius, *O.c.* (n. 130), 2, 475f. Balbus, Cic., *Ad Fam.* 10, 32, 3. The surviving *Octavia*, written probably by a pupil of Seneca, is a *praetexta*.

138. Hor., *Ep.* 1, 182–213; Cic., *Ad Fam.* 7, 1, 2.

139. *Amphitr.*, 51–5.

140. Schanz–Hosius, *O.c.* (n. 130), 1, 142; *RE* i, 708–10, Afranius, no. 5; Quint. 10, 1, 100.

141. Cic., *Pro Sest.* 118; Suet., *Nero* 11, 2.

142. Cic., *De Offic.* 1, 114 (Rupilius); *Pro Sest.* 120–3; *Ad Fam.* 7, 1, 2; *Ad Att.* 16, 2, 3; 16, 5, 1 etc. See Tenney Frank, 'The Decline of Roman Tragedy,' *CJ* 1916, 176–87, esp. 177f. for list of recorded revivals.

143. CD 63, 9, 4–6; Suet., *Nero* 21, 3.

144. See D. S. Robertson, 'The Authenticity and Date of Lucian, *De Saltatione*', *Essays to W. Ridgeway*, Cambridge, 1913, 180–5; L. Robert, *Hermes* 1930, 120f.

145. L. 7, 2, 4; TA 14, 21, 2.

146. Luc., *De Salt.* 34; L. Robert, 'Pantomimen im griechischen Orient', *Hermes* 1930, 106–22; *RE* xviii, 2, 834–69.

147. Women, Schol. Juv. 11, 162; *ILS* 5260. Pantomimi, *ILS* 5182–8.

148. Luc., *De Salt.* 66f., 'one body, many souls'.

149. Luc., *De Salt.* 35f.; 75.

150. Talking with the hands, Luc., *De Salt.* 63; Quint. 11, 3, 85; Cassiod., *Var.* 1, 20, 5. Cf. Kaibel, *Epigr. Gr.* 608, from Rome; Sen., *Ep.* 121, 6. The prince from Pontus, Luc., *De Salt.* 64.

151. Luc., *De Salt.* 30; 80; *RE* xviii, 2, 854–6.

152. Vast and extensive repertoires, Luc., *De Salt.* 35–59; Sid. Apoll., *Car.* 23, 263–99; *RE* xviii, 2, 847–9.

153. Luc., *De Salt.* 37.

154. Luc., *De Salt.* 61.

155. Luc., *De Salt.* 80.

156. Luc., *De Salt.* 83.

157. *Or.* 32.

158. Luc., *De Salt.* 72, tr. H. W. and F. G. Fowler.

159. Lib., *Or.* 64, esp. 42–9; 119.

160. Luc., *De Salt.* 76.

161. Macrob., *Sat.* 2, 7, 12–16.

162. Sen., *NQ* 7, 32, 3.

163. For surviving fragments and ancient evidence on mimes, see M. Bonaria, *Mimorum Romanorum Fragmenta*, Genoa, 1955/6 and *Romani Mimi*, Rome, 1965.

164. Cic., *Phil.* 2, 65; Sen., *Ep.* 114, 6; Suet., *C. Cal.* 57, 4.

165. *Faba*, Cic., *Ad Att.* 1, 16, 13; Sen., *Apok.* 9, 3. On the significance of *Faba* and other titles, *RE* xv, 1745f.

166. Ovid., *Tr.* 497–500.

167. VM 2, 6, 7.

168. Min. Fel., *Oct.* 37, 12; Cyprian, *De Spect.* 4; *RE* xv, 1755–7; Aug., *Conf.* 3, 2.

169. Cic., *Ad Att.* 14, 2, 1; 14, 3, 2; *Ad Fam.* 7, 11, 2.

170. Macrob., *Sat.* 2, 7, 11.

171. E.g. *Ep.* 8, 9; 94, 28 and 43; 108, 9 and 11; *Cons. ad Marc.* 9, 5; *De Tranq. An.* 11, 8. The 734 surviving aphorisims attributed to Syrus are to be found in J. W. and A. M. Duff, *Minor Latin Poets* (Loeb, 1961), 3–111.

172. On all this, *RE* xv, 1747f. *Archimimi, ILS* 2178f.; 5208–5209a. *Archimima,* 5211f. *Stupidi,* 2178f.; 5224.

173. Quint. 6, 3, 29.

174. On which see *RE* ii, 1914–21 (F. Marx); W. Beare, *O.c.* (n. 55), 127–38; P. Frassinetti, *Fabula Atellana*, Genoa, 1953 and, on its Samnite origins, E. T. Salmon, *Samnium and the Samnites*, Cambridge, 1967, 119–23.

175. Cic., *Ad Fam.* 7, 1, 3; *TA* 4, 14, 4; Strabo 5, 233C.

176. Juv. 6, 71; Schol. Juv. 3, 175; *ILS* 2179.

177. Cic., *Ad Fam.* 9, 16, 7.

178. L. 7, 2, 12; VM 2, 4, 4.

179. VM 2, 5, 4; Festus 238L.

180. Quint. 6, 3, 47. Surviving fragments are to be found in P. Frassinetti, *Fabularum Atellanarum Fragmenta*, Turin, 1955; *Atellanae Fabulae*, Rome, 1967.

181. *ILS* 5219.

182. *RE* ii, 1918 gives a list of known titles.

183. Macrob., *Sat.* 1, 10, 3f.; Petron., *Sat.* 53.

184. Suet., *Tib.* 45; *C. Cal.* 27, 4; *Nero* 39; *Galba* 13; TA 4, 14, 4.

185. Cic., *Pro Arch.* 10; CN Praef. 5; L. 24, 24, 3; Tac., *Dial.* 10, 5; Cic., *De Offic.* 1, 150.

186. So Tenney Frank, 'The Status of Actors at Rome', *CP* 1931, 11–20, criticized by W. M. Green, *CP* 1933, 301–4. See B. Warnecke, 'Die bürgerliche Stellung der Schauspieler im alten Rom', *Neue Jahrb. f.d. klass. Alt.* 1914, 95–109 and *RE* viii, 2116–28, s.v. 'Histrio'.

187. L. 7, 2, 12 (written c. 25 B.C.); VM 2, 4, 4.

188. *Dig.* 3, 2, 2, 5, quoting jurists of 1st cent. A.D.; *FIR* 18 (*FIRA* 13), 123.

189. *Dig.* 23, 2, 44 pr.

190. Suet., *DA* 45, 3.

191. TA 1, 77.

192. Suet., *Tib.* 37, 2. Obviously not all actors, as TA 4, 14, 4 and CD 59, 2, 5 imply.

193. TA 13, 25, 4. Cf. 14, 21, 7.

194. Plin., *Pan.* 46, 2f.

195. Macrob., *Sat.* 3, 14, 6–8.

196. Sall., *Cat.* 25, 2; CD 53, 31, 3; 54, 2, 5; 55, 10, 11; 61, 17, 3; AG 20, 4.

197. Sen., *NQ* 7, 32, 3.

198. Schol. Juv. 7, 243; SHA, *MA* 11, 4. Cf. Sen., *Ep.* 80, 7.

199. TA 1, 77, 5, 'De modo lucaris'.

200. Cic., *Pro Rosc. Com.* 23.

201. Sen., *Cons. ad Helv.* 12, 6.

202. Plin., *NH* 7, 129; Cic., *Pro Rosc. Com.* 23, where 600,000 sesterces must be the right figure; Macrob., *Sat.* 3, 14, 13.

203. Macrob., *Sat.* 3, 14, 14.

204. Suet., *Vit. Terent.* 2.

205. Quint. 10, 1, 98; Tac., *Dial.* 12, 6; *RE* viiiA, 413.

206. *Pro Rosc. Com.* 27–31; *Dig.* 32, 73, 3.

207. E.g. *ILS* 5182, with Dessau's note; 5184–95; 5206; Suet., *Tib.* 47; CD 57, 11, 6; *Dig.* 40, 9, 17.

208. Petron., *Sat.* 53; AG 20, 4; SHA, *AS* 34, 2; *Dig.* 21, 1, 34. Ummidia Quadratilla, Plin., *Ep.* 7, 24, 4–7; *ILS* 5628 (building of amphitheatre and theatre at Casinum); 5183 (one of her *pantomimi*); R. Syme, *Historia* 1968, 75–8.

209. AM 14, 6, 19f.; Tertull., *De Spect.* 22.

210. *ILS* 5186; 5188f.; 5191; 5193–5; 5233, mostly from the 2nd cent. A.D.

211. Festus 438, 19–27; Mart. 9, 28, 9; *ILS* 5186; 5189; 5193f.; 5196; 5200f.; 5209a; 5275. On the 170 B.C. visit, P. 30, 22. See A. Müller, 'Die Parasiti Apollinis,' *Philol.* 1904, 342–61.

212. Galen 14, 630–3K. There were precedents for such a diagnosis; cf. Plut., *Demetr.* 38, 4; App., *Syr.* 59, 312; Lucian, *De Dea Syr.* 17f.

213. On Roscius, *RE* iA, 1123–5, no. 16; Cic., *Pro Quinct.* 78; *Pro Rosc. Com.* 17 and 23; *De Nat. Deor.* 1, 79; *De Orat.* 3, 221; Quint. 11, 3, 111; Macrob., *Sat.* 3, 14, 13.

214. *Pro Sest.* 120–3 and Schol Bob. *ad loc.*, 136f. St.

215. D. Laberius, *RE* xii, 246–8, no. 3. Publilius Syrus, *RE* xxiii, 1920–8, no. 28. For the episode described, see Cic., *Ad Fam.* 12, 18, 2; AG 8, 15; Macrob., *Sat.* 2, 7, 2–11 (quoting the prologue); Suet., *DJ* 39 (erroneous); Sen., *Controv.* 7, 3, 9; E. Hoffmann, *Rhein. Mus.* 1884, 471–6 (the best explanation of what happened).

216. CD 54, 17, 5; Macrob., *Sat.* 2, 7, 12–19; Suet., *DA* 45, 4. See articles in *RE*, esp. on Pylades, xxiii, 2082f., no. 2.

217. Suet., *C. Cal.* 36, 1; 55, 1; 57, 4; CD 60, 22, 3–5; 60, 28, 3–5; *TA* 11, 4, 1f. and 36, 1–3. If he is the Ti. Iulius Mnester of *ILS* 5181, he was manumitted by Tiberius.

218. *ILS* 5181a; *TA* 13, 19–21; 13, 27, 7; *Dig.* 12, 4, 3, 5; CD 63, 18, 1; Suet., *Nero* 54.

219. CD 68, 10, 2; *ILS* 5185; *PIR*[2], 'A' 1590; *RE* xxiii, 2083, nos. 3f.

220. She was notorious, even if Procop., *Anecd.* 9 is not wholly true. *CI* 5, 4, 23 is a statute of Justinian altering the law so as to legalize the marriage.

221. Quint. 11, 3, 178–80.

222. Diod., 37, 12, tr. F. R. Walton (Loeb).

223. Plin., *NH* 7, 184f.

224. Flautist, *ILS* 5239; Petron., *Sat.* 53; AG 20, 4. Horn-players and trumpeters, Juv. 10, 214; Petron., *Sat.* 53. Cithara-players, *ILS* 5245; Suet., *Domit.* 4, 4. Vocal soloists, *ILS* 5231f. Chorus-singers, *ILS* 5232; 5234ff. *Citharoedi*, *ILS* 5242–4; Suet., *Domit.* 4, 4.

225. *Magister odariarius*, *ILS* 5229.

226. Suet., *Nero* 20, 1.

227. TA 16, 5, 5; Suet., *Vesp.* 4, 4 (in Greece).

228. Main sources, TA 14, 14–16 (A.D. 59); 15, 33 (Naples in 64); 16, 4f. (Rome in 65); Suet., *Nero* 20ff.; CD 63, 9–19 (in Greece).

229. Suet., *Nero* 20, 1 (but cf. Plin., *NH* 34, 166); TA 15, 39, 3; 16, 4, 2f.

230. Suet., *Nero* 49, 1.

231. TA 14, 15, 8f.; Suet., *Nero* 20, 3.

232. TA 14, 15, 7.

233. Juv. 8, 211–30; CD 63, 9.

234. Acrobats, Petron., *Sat.* 53. Conjurers, Sen., *Ep.* 45, 8. Jugglers, Mart. 9, 38; Manil. 5, 168–71; Quint. 10, 7, 11 (quoted). Puppets, Hor., *Sat.* 2, 7, 82. The prodigious boy, Suet., *DA* 43, 3.

235. AG 18, 5, 2.

236. Boxing and wrestling, Hor., *Ep.* 2, 1, 186; Ovid., *Tr.* 4, 6, 31f.; Suet., *DA* 45, 2; *C. Cal.* 18, 1; *Nero* 45, 1.

237. *Mos. et Rom. Legg. Coll.* 11, 7, 4 (*FIRA* ii, 572); Tertull., *De Spect.* 19.

238. TA 12, 56, 5; Suet., *D. Cl.* 21, 6; CD 60, 33, 3.

239. Cf. CD 43, 23, 4 (Julius Caesar in 46 B.C.).

240. Execution of *noxii* as a feature of shows, *ILS* 5063; 'debita noxae mancipia', [Quint.], *Decl.* 9, 5. Conditions of purchase and time limit, *ILS* 5163, 58 (S.C. of A.D. 177/80); *Mos. et Rom. Legg. Coll.*, see n. 237; Paul., *Sent.* 5, 17, 2(3); Mommsen, *Eph. Epig.* 7, 1892, 407ff. (*Ges. Schr.* 8, 521f.).

241. Sen., *Ep.* 7, 3ff.

242. Paul., *Sent.* 5, 17, 2(3); 5, 23, 4 (*FIRA* ii, 405, 408); *Mos. et Rom. Legg. Coll.*, see n. 237; Tertull., *De Spect.* 19; Mommsen, *Ges. Schr.* 8, 523f.

243. Spartacus, App., *BC* I, 116, 539; Florus 2, 8, 8; Plut., *Crass.* 8, 2; Suet., *Vitell.* 12; SHA, *Hadr.* 18, 8; *Dig.* 11, 4, 5.

244. Acro on Hor., *Sat.* 2, 7, 59, 'Qui se vendunt ludo (gladiatorio) auctorati vocantur'.

245. Cic., *Ad Fam.* 10, 32, 3; Suet., *C. Cal.* 27, 2.

246. L. 28, 21, 2; Hor., *Ep.* 1, 18, 36; Sen., *Ep.* 99, 13; Juv. 8, 199–210; 11, 5–8 and 20.

247. *ILS* 5163, 62; CD 72, 19, 3.

248. Quint. 8, 5, 12.

249. Sen., *De Provid.* 4, 4.

250. Suet., *DJ* 39, 1; CD 43, 23, 5 (knights allowed to fight by Julius Caesar); CD 48, 43, 3 (senators forbidden in 38 B.C.); Suet., *DA* 43, 3 and CD 56, 25, 7f. (knights allowed by Augustus until forbidden by senate); Suet., *Tib.* 35 and CD 57, 14, 3f. (Tiberius); CD 59, 10, 1–4 (Gaius); TA 14, 14, 6 and Suet., Nero 12 (knights encouraged by Nero); TH 2, 62 (prohibition by Vitellius); SHA., *Commod.* 12, 10f. and CD 72, 19 (Commodus).

251. CD 57, 14, 3.

252. Women gladiators, TA 15, 32, 3; Suet., *Domit.* 4, 1; Stat., *Silv.* 1, 6, 51–6; Mart., *Lib. Spect.* 6; Juv. 6, 246–67. Cf. Nic. Damasc., *FGH* 90, F. 78; Petron., *Sat.* 45 (mulier essedaria); CD 75, 16, 1 (Sept. Severus); L. Robert, *Les Gladiateurs dans l'Orient grec*, Paris, 1940, 188, no. 184 and pl. xii.

253. *ILS* 5107.

254. Hor., *Sat.* 2, 7, 58; Sen., *Ep.* 37, 1; *Apok.* 9; Petron., *Sat.* 117. See Mommsen, *Ges. Schr.* 3, 9, n. 4.

255. Suet., *D. Cl.* 21, 5; Mart. 5, 24 (Hermes, Helius, Advolans). See L. Robert, *O.c.* (n. 252), 297.

256. *ILS* 5083, 5083a.

257. *Familia gladiatoria*, *ILS* 5060; 6296. *Familia gladiatoria speciosa, nobilis, gloriosa*, Cic., *Pro. Sest.* 134. *Familia lanisticia*, Petron., *Sat.* 45. List of members of, *ILS* 5083f.

258. Strabo 5, 250C. Nic. Damasc., *FGH* 90, F. 78 tells a similar story of Romans in the Republic. There were two or three bouts, he says, and they were fights to the death.

259. Faustus Sulla buying up gladiators in 63 B.C. in Naples for funeral games in memory of his father given in 60, Cic., *Pro*

Sull. 53–5; CD 37, 51, 4. Clodius uses his brother's for rioting in 57 B.C., Cic., *Pro Sest.* 78; CD 39, 7, 2. Vatinius' gladiators (or *bestiarii*), Cic., *Pro Sest.* 132–5. C. Cato's in 56, Cic., *Ad Q.f.* 2, 5, 3 (2, 4, 5). Milo's, CD 39, 8, 1; Cic., *De Offic.* 2, 58. See A. W. Lintott, *Violence in Republican Rome*, Oxford, 1968, 83–5.

260. 65 B.C., Suet., *DJ* 10, 2. 63 B.C., Sall., *Cat.* 30, 7; Cic., *Pro Sest.* 133. 49 B.C., Cic., *Ad Att.* 7, 14, 2; JC, *BC* 1, 14, 4f.

261. 105 B.C., VM 2, 3, 2. In Rome under Augustus, Suet., *DA* 42; CD 55, 26, 1. At Capua, Plut., *Crass.* 8, 2; JC, *BC* 1, 14, 4; Cic., *Ad Att.* 7, 14, 2.

262. Pompeii, *CIL* iv, 4280–4423 (at least twelve schools in the late Republic and early Empire); A. Mau, *Pompeii*², Leipzig, 1908, 164–70 (E.T. London, 1902, 157–64); Venafrum, *CIL* x, 4920; Venusia, *ILS* 5083f.; Augustodunum in Gaul, TA 3, 43, 4; Miletus, *CIG* 2889; Thasos, *CIG* 2164; Alexandria, *ILS* 1397. Cf. L. Robert, *O.c.* (n. 252), 124f.

263. Cic., *Ad Att.* 4, 4a, 2; 4, 8, 2 (56 B.C.).

264. Plut., *JC* 32, 4; Suet., *DJ* 31, 1.

265. Suet., *DA* 42, 3; CD 55, 26, 1; 59, 14.

266. *ILS* 1396 (for western provinces); 1412 (Italy); 9014 (Italy and Danube provinces); 1397 (Egypt); Mommsen, *Staatsr.* ii, 2, 1070–2.

267. *Procurator ludi matutini*, *ILS* 1420; 1428; 1437. *Procurator ludi magni*, *ILS* 1338; 1420.

268. TA 11, 35, 7; Plin., *NH* 11, 245, C. Caesaris ludus.

269. Suet., *Domit.* 4, 1, 'E suo ludo'; *ILS* 5126, a *paegniarius* of the Ludus Magnus who lived to ninety-nine; Mommsen, *O.c.* (n. 266); *Hermes* 1886, 274; Jordan–Huelsen, *O.c.* (n. 85) 1, 298–300; Plin., *Pan.* 54, 4, Senate consulted 'de ampliando numero gladiatorum' under Domitian (to whom the Chronographer of A.D. 354—Mommsen, *MGH*, *Chron. Min.* 1, 146—ascribes all four schools). Illustrations, E. Nash, *PDAR* ii, 24–6 and A. M. Colini–L. Cozza, *Ludus Magnus*, Rome, 1962. Accommodation: H–G. Pflaum, *Les Carrières procuratoriennes équestres* ..., Paris, 1960, 215.

270. Friedlaender ii, 65f. Also, perhaps, in Spain, for Gaul and Spain, at Barcelona, *CIL* ii, 4519.

271. Classed with pimps, Sen., *Controv.* 10, 4 (33), 11; Sen., *Ep.* 87, 15 (and rich); Juv. 6, 216; *ILS* 6085, 123. Cf. *ILS* 5163, 37. Caesar and training, Suet., *DJ* 26, 3. The inscriptions of *lanistae* (*ILS* 5151; *CIL* vi, 10171; 10200) are to be taken as forgeries: see Mommsen on *CIL* x, 1733 and Ch. Huelsen, *Röm. Mitt.* 1895, 293–6. *Lanista* appears on an otherwise unintelligible Pompeian *graffito*, *CIL* iv, 4865. *Negotiator familiae gladiatoriae*, *CIL* xii, 727.

272. Doctors, Scrib. Larg. 101; Plin., *NH* 26, 135; Galen, xiii, 599–602; xviii, 2, 56f. K; Sen., *Cons. ad Helv.* 3, 1; *ILS* 5119; 5152. *Unctor* and *manicarius*, *ILS* 5084. *A veste glad.*, *ILS* 5160. Cf. Suet., *Domit.* 4, 1. *Praepositus armamentario*, *ILS* 5153. Spartacus, Plut., *Crass.* 8, 3.

273. Veget., *Epit. Rei Mil.* 1, 11; 2, 23; Juv. 6, 247; Sen., *Ep.* 18, 8. *Primus palus*, *ILS* 5100; 5114f.; *CIG* 2663; *IG* xiv, 1832; SHA, *Commod.* 15, 8. *Secundus palus*, *CIG* 3765. See Friedlaender, E. T. iv, 170f. for a different explanation.

274. For details of the different types of gladiator (at least sixteen) see Friedlaender iv, 258–67, F. Drexel (E.T. iv, 171–81); *RE*, Supplb. iii, 777f. Cf. the list of gladiators in *ILS* 5083f. (Venusia). A spectator's criticism, when a Myrmillo lumbered after a Retiarius, Quint. 6, 3, 6.

275. Juv. 8, 199–210; Artemid., *Oneirocrit.* 2, 32.

276. *ILS* 5091f.; 5099; 5103; 5116; 9341f.

277. *ILS* 5128–32. See Friedlaender, E. T. iv, 170f. It is now agreed that what were once considered *tesserae gladiatoriae* (Friedlaender, E. T. iv, 168–70) have nothing at all to do with gladiators: see M. Cary, *JRS* 1923, 110–3; *RE*, s.v. 'Nummularius', xvii, 1415–55 (R. Herzog).

278. Plut., *JC* 42, 4; SHA, *Commod.* 11, 11; Apul., *Apol.* 98. *Decretoria arma*, Sen., *Ep.* 117, 25; Quint. 10, 5, 20. On the Ludus Magnus, see Colini–Cozza, *O.c.* (n. 269), esp. pp. 37 and 57 (illustrations).

279. Tirones, *ILS* 5083f.; 5088; Suet., *DJ* 26, 3; Mommsen, *Hermes* 1886, 267f. Veterani, *ILS* 5084; 5092.

280. [Quint.] *Decl.* 9, 21; Mau, *O.c.* (n. 262), 167–70 (E.T. 154–8).

281. Prop. 4, 8, 25, 'immundae saginae'; [Quint.] *Decl.* 9, 5, 'gravior omni fame sagina'; TH 2, 88, 'gladiatoria sagina'; Plin., *NH* 18, 72, 'hordearii'; 36, 203; Schol. Juv. 11, 20.

282. *ILS* 5089; 5093; 5124; 5126; *AE* 1960, 139; L. Robert, *O.c.* (n. 252), 306.

283. Sen., *De Ira* 2, 8, 2; Quint. 2, 17, 33.

284. A. Mau, *O.c.* (n. 262), 168 (E.T. 161f.); L. Robert, *O.c.* (n. 252), 21f.; 86; 182; 187; 269; 306f. On Nemesis, *RE* xvi, 2372f.; A. v. Premerstein, 'Nemesis und ihre Bedeutung für die Agone', *Philol.* 1894, 400–415; H. Volkmann, 'Studien zum Nemesiskult', *Archiv. f. Religionswiss.* xxvi, 1928, 296–321; xxxi, 1934, 73f.; *ILS* 5121. *Deceptus* is a stock euphemism for 'killed', *ILS* 5111, '*Fato deceptus, non ab homine*'; 5112; 5121f.

285. Celadus and Crescens, *ILS* 5142, a–c (see A. Mau, *O.c.* (n. 262), 229, E.T. 226). Married gladiators, *ILS* 5090 (died at 38, after 18 fights); 5095; 5097; 5098 (died at 35, won 20 victories); 5100; 5104 (died at 45, one son); 5107 (died at 21, in the school 4 years, 5 fights); 5112; 5115 (married at 15, 2 daughters, died at 22 after 13 fights); 5120–3; *AE* 1960, 140 (died at 30, fought 15 times). The gladiator with four sons, Suet., *D. Cl.* 21, 5. *Ludia*, Juv. 6, 104 (cf. Mart. 5, 24, 10). Eppia, Juv. 6, 82–113; see my *Roman Women* 280f.; Petron., *Sat.* 126. Curtius Rufus, *TA* 11, 21, 1. Nymphidius, Plut., *Galba* 9.

286. *Munerarius*, Quint. 8, 3, 34; *ILS* 5081; 5123. Contracts, Gaius, *Inst.* 3, 146; *ILS* 5163, 29–37, reading, '*Summo ac famoso gladiatori*'.

287. Suet., *Tib.* 7, 1; L. 44, 31, 15.

288. *ILS* 5143; 5145f.

289. Plut, *Mor.* 1099B; Tertull., *Apol.* 42, 5; Symmach., *Ep.* 2, 46.

290. [Quint.], *Dec.* 9, 6.

291. [Quint.], *Decl.* 9. Cf. Calp. Flacc., *Decl.* 52 for a similar theme— the unredeemed prisoner of pirates, sold to a gladiatorial school.

292. Sen., *De Ira* 2, 2, 4 (quoted); *Ep.* 7, 3–5; 95, 33. Claudius, Suet., *D.Cl.* 34, 2; CD 60, 13, 4. Tertull., *De Spect.* 21; Apul., *Met.* 4, 13; Mommsen, *Ges. Schr.* 8, 521–3.

293. Suet., *C.Cal.* 26, 5; Stat., *Silv.* 1, 6, 51–64 (Domitian, quoted); CD 71, 29, 3 (M. Aurelius); *ILS* 5163, 63, '*Is quoque qui senior atque inabilior . . .*'; A. Degrassi, *Inscr. Ital.* xiii, 1, 228; CIL ii, 5523. *Paegniarii*, *ILS* 5084; 5126.

294. *Prolusio*, Cic., *De Orat.* 2, 317; 325. Abuse, Lucil. iii, 117 ('Rhinoceros'); iv, 153–8 Marx. *Decretoria, pugnatoria arma*, Sen. *Ep.* 117, 25; Suet., *C. Cal.* 54, 1. Music, [Quint.], *Decl.* 9, 6, '*Sonabant*

clangore ferali tubae'; *ILS* 5150. Illustrations, S. Aurigemma, *I Mosaici di Zliten*, Milan, 1926, 151–4; 163.

295. *CIL* iv, 1182; 1421f.; 2508; S. Aurigemma, *O.c.* (n. 294), 149–72.

296. Quint. 2, 11, 2; Auson., *Technopaegnion* 12, 3, 'Quis mirmilloni contenditur? aequimanus Thraex.'; Suet., *C. Cal.* 32, 2; 55, 2; *D.Cl.* 34, 1; *D. Tit.* 8, 2; *Domit.* 10, 1; Mart. 9, 68, 8; 14, 213.

297. Mart., *Lib. Spect.* 29 (quoted). '*Stans missus*', *ILS* 5088; 5106; 5113; 5133; 5135; Sen., *Ep.* 92, 26. For '*Ad digitum pugnare*', cf. Quint. 8, 5, 20.

298. Ter., *Andr.* 83; Plaut., *Most.* 715; *Rud.* 1143; Virg., *Aen.* 12, 296; Sen., *De Const. Sap.* 16, 2.

299. Appeal, Sen., *Ep.* 37, 2; 117, 7; Suet., *DA* 45, 3. Pictures, S, Aurigemma, *O.c.* (n. 294), 150f.; 155; 159. Merciful gladiators. [Quint.], *Decl.* 9, 18; CD 77, 19, 3; *ILS* 5115.

300. '*Pollicem vertere*', Juv. 3, 36. '*Pollicem premere*', Plin., *NH* 18, 25. Handkerchiefs, Mart. 12, 29, 7f. Sen., *De Ira*, 1, 2, 4; *ILS* 5134, '*Missos, missos, iugula, iugula*'; Suet., *DJ* 26, 3; Ovid, *Ex Pont.* 2, 8, 53f. Contrast Juv. 3, 36f.

301. Cic., *Tusc. Disp.* 2, 41; *Pro Sest.* 80; Sen., *Ep.* 30, 8; *De Tranq. An.* 11, 4. Cartoons of such deaths, *CIL* iv, 8055f. (Pompeii).

302. Sen., *Ep.* 93, 12. *Palma*, Suet., *C.Cal.* 32, 2; *ILS* 5098. Crowns, 5087; 5102; 5120 etc. Prize money, Suet., *D. Cl.* 21, 5; *ILS* 5163 45f; Mommsen, *Ges. Schr.* 8, 528. *Sandapila*, S. Aurigemma, *O.c.* (n. 294), 162–5.

303. Wounded, S. Aurigemma, *O.c.* (n. 294), 159; *ILS* 5119, 'In medicina decessit'; Galen, *O.c.* (n. 272). Flogging, Petron., *Sat.* 45. Keen to fight again, Ovid, *Trist*, 2, 17; *Ex Pont.* 1, 5, 37f.

304. *ILS* 5143; *Mart.* 5, 24, 8.

305. Suet., *C. Cal.* 38, 4; CD 59, 14, 1–4; Mommsen, *Ges. Schr.* 8, 526, n. 5.

306. *ILS* 5088 (twice a day); CD 77, 6, 2 (Caracalla); *ILS* 5090; 5107; 5112–5; 5121f.; L. Robert, *O.c.* (n. 252), 294.

307. Petron., *Sat.* 45, tr. W. Arrowsmith. Eleven pairs, eleven killed, *ILS* 5062. Eighty-eight victories, *CIL* iv, 2387. Over thirty fights or victories, *ILS* 5094; 5096; 5113; *CIL* iv, 4870.

308. Lucil. iv, 149–58 Marx (cf. C. Cichorius, *Untersuch. zu Lucil.* 262–4); Cic., *De Opt. Gen. Or.* 17; *Tusc. Disp.* 4, 48; *Ad Q. f.* 3, 4, 2; Hor., *Sat.* 2, 7, 97; Mart. 5, 24.

309. *ILS* 5086; 5088; 5095f.; 5138. See L. Robert, *O.c.* (n. 252), 287–292 (against Mommsen's and Dessau's interpretation).

310. Tert., *De Spect.* 21; Suet., *Tib.* 7, 1.

311. In this section I am happy to acknowledge my great debt to an Oxford scholar, the late George Jennison of the Zoological Gardens, Belle Vue, Manchester, not only for his fascinating book, *Animals for Show and Pleasure in Ancient Rome*, Manchester, 1937 but also for conversation and correspondence which I had with him in connexion with a book which, if he had not died, we might have combined in writing.

312. Elephants, Varro, *LL.* 7, 39; Sen., *De Brev. Vit.* 13, 3; Plin., *NH* 8, 16; Eutrop. 2, 8. Ostriches, Plaut, *Persa* 199. Leopards (called *pantherae*, later *pardi*), Plaut., *Poen.* 1011f. (see Jennison 183–7 on the identification of this animal and *MRR* 1, 423, n. 6 on rules against import). Lions, L. 39, 22, 2. Hippopotamus, Plin., *NH* 8, 95f. Rhinoceros, lynx, Plin., *NH* 8, 70f., cf. Lucil. iii, 118 Marx (CD 51, 22, 5 gives 29 B.C. as the date of the first exhibition of a hippopotamus and rhinoceros). Giraffe, Plin., *NH* 8, 69; CD 43, 23, 1f. Tiger, Plin., *NH* 8, 65; Suet., *DA* 43, 4 (cf. CD 54, 9, 8, gift of tigers from India to Augustus in 20 B.C.). Polar bears, Calp. Sic., *Ecl.* 7, 65f. (probably under Nero; yet it is strange, in that case, that the elder Pliny did not know of polar bears, Jennison 70f.; 188f.).

313. SHA, *Gord.* iii, 33, 1–3.

314. Varro, *RR* 3, 13.

315. Cats, Jennison 129 (cf. Sen., *Ep.* 121, 19; Plin., *NH* 10, 202). Alexandria, Jennison 28–30. *Vivaria*, Jennison 126–36. Cornificius, CD 49, 7, 6. Imperial elephant-herd, Ael., *Nat. An.* 2, 11; Juv. 12, 102–10; *ILS* 1578. Julius Caesar's triumph, Suet., *DJ* 37, 2; CD 43, 22, 1. Nero's Golden House, Suet., *Nero* 31, 1.

316. Cic., *Ad Fam.* 2, 11, 2; 8, 2, 2; 8, 4, 5; 8, 6, 5, 8, 8, 10; 8, 9, 3; *Ad Att.* 6, 1, 21; Plut., *Cic.* 36, 6.

317. Symmach., *Ep.* 4, 12; 7, 59; 7, 122.

318. Plin., *NH* 8, 65; Mart. 9, 57, 10; Suet., *DA* 43, 4. Androcles, AG 5, 14, 30. Elagabalus, SHA, *Elag.* 21, 1.

319. Plut., *Mor.* 973E (*De Sollert. An.* 19).

320. Monkeys, Juv. 5, 153–5; Aelian, *Nat. An.* 5, 26. Crocodiles, Strabo 17, 814f.C; cf. *RE* vA, 536f.

321. Training, Plut. *Mor.* 968C (*De Sollert. An.* 12); same story in Plin., *NH* 8, 6. Variety of tricks, Plin., *NH* 8, 4–6; Aelian, *Nat. An.* 2, 11; Sen., *Ep.* 85, 41. Tightrope-walking, CD 61, 17, 2 (A.D. 59); Sen., *Ep.* 85, 41; Plin., *NH* 8, 6. Dancing, Mart. 1, 104, 9f.

322. Lions, Mart. 1, 6, 14, 22, 48 and 104. Cf. Stat., *Silv.* 2, 5. Bears, J. M. C. Toynbee, *PBSR* 1948, 36, pl. x, figs. 29f. Seals, Plin., *NH* 9, 41.

323. L. 39, 22, 2; 44, 18, 8.

324. Crassus–Scaevola, Plin., *NH* 8, 53; Cic., *De Offic.* 2, 57; *In Verr.* 2, 4, 133. Sulla, Plin., *NH* 8, 53; Sen., *De Brev. Vit.* 13, 6. Scaurus, Plin., *NH* 8, 64.

325. Plin., *NH* 8, 19.

326. Lions and leopards, Plin., *NH* 8, 53 and 64. Elephants, CD 39, 38; Plin., *NH* 8, 20f.; Sen., *De Brev. Vit.* 13. Cf. Cic., *Ad Fam.* 7, 1, 3.

327. Cassiod., *Var.* 10, 30 (K. Theodahad to Honorius). On elephants and moon-cult, A. Passerini, *Athenaeum* 1953, 142–9.

328. Jennison 56f.

329. Plin., *NH* 8, 22 (sixty men to each elephant); Suet., *DJ* 39, 3; App., *BC* 2, 102, 423; CD 43, 23, 3.

330. Plin., *NH* 8, 182. Cf. Suet., *D.Cl.* 21, 3.

331. CD 53, 27, 6.

332. Augustus, *RG* 22, 3. Titus, CD 66, 25, 1; Suet., *D.Tit.* 7, 3. Trajan, CD 68, 15, 1. Hadrian showed 1,000 beasts in Athens, *Vita* 19, 3. For Gordian, see *Vita* 3, 6.

333. VM 2, 7, 13f.; L., *Per.* 51; *Pan. Lat.* xii (ix), 23; Strabo 6, 273C.

334. S. Aurigemma, *O.c.* (n. 294), 182–4; Cic., *Ad Fam.* 10, 32, 3; Petron., *Sat.* 45.

335. AG 5, 14, 29; SHA, *Carac.* 1, 5.

336. Suet., *Nero* 31, 1; *ILS* 399; 5055; 5062; 5159 etc.

337. Mart., *Lib. Spect.* 17–19; 22; S. Aurigemma, *O.c.* (n. 294), 180–97.

338. J. B. Ward Perkins and J. M. C. Toynbee, 'The Hunting Baths at Lepcis Magna', *Archaeologia* 1949, 166–95, esp. 181 (quoted) and pl. xliif.

339. Sen., *Ep.* 70, 20; cf. MA, *Med.* 10, 8, 2; Mart., *Lib. Spect.* 15, 22 and 27. Enfranchisement, Fronto, *Ad M. Caes.* 1, 8, 2 (i, 118f. Loeb). On the Lex Petronia, *Dig.* 48, 8, 11, 2; *RE* xii, 2401.

340. Sen., *De Ben.* 2, 19, 1.

341. Suet., *Tib.* 72, 2; CD 72, 18, 1; Juv. 1, 22f. Commodus, Herod. 1, 15, 5f. (quoted).

342. SHA, *Prob.* 19, 2f. (planting of a forest in the Circus Maximus); Calp. Sic., *Ecl.* 7, 70–3.

343. Plin., *NH* 8, 21; Suet., *DJ* 39, 2; DH, *AR* 3, 68, 2.

344. Calp. Sic., *Ecl.* 7, 48–53. For details, see Jennison 154–64.

345. Liban., *Ep.* 1399; Plut., *Mor.* 965Af.; Cic., *Ad Fam.* 7, 1, 3. *Graffito*, CIL iv, 8017. From the first publication of the Tunisian mosaic (discovered in 1953) by G. Charles-Picard in *CRAI* 1954, 418–24 to his article in *Bull. arch.* 1957, 106–13 and his book, *La Civilisation de l'Afrique romaine*, Paris, 1959, 242–4; 348 it has received a variety of different interpretations; see above pp. 351f.

346. Plin., *NH* 8, 27 and 32–5.

347. Jennison 95–7; Symmach., *Ep.* 4, 58 and 60; 7, 48 (horses); 2, 77 (Irish wolfhounds); 2, 76; 7, 121; 9, 132 and 142 (bears); 2, 76; 9, 117 (lions and leopards); 9, 141; 6, 43 (crocodiles). For these and other animals, see L. Poinssot and P. Quoniam, 'Bêtes d'amphithéâtre sur trois mosaiques du Bardo', *Karthago* 1951/2, 129–65.

348. Jennison 140–9; J. Aymard, *Essai sur les chasses romaines*, Paris, 1951. Piazza Armerina mosaics, G. V. Gentili, *O.c.* (n. 42), tav. xx.

349. Jennison 149–53; G. V. Gentili, *O.c.* (n. 42), fig. 5, tav. xxvi, xxvii, xxviii (embarkation of ostriches, rhinoceros, tiger, bison, antelope, elephant).

350. Plin., *NH* 36, 40; Plut., *Brut.* 8, 6f.

351. *Dig.* 39, 4, 16, 7.

352. ILS 5158 (*adiutor ad feras*); 5159 (*praepositus herbariarum*); Suet., *C.Cal.* 27, 1; Symmach., *Ep.* 6, 43; Apul., *Met.* 4, 13f.

353. CIL vi, 130; Procop., *Bell. Goth.* 1, 22, 10; Jennison 174–6.

354. Release in amphitheatre, AM 28, 1, 10; Jennison 159–61; straw dummies (*pilae*), Mart., *Lib. Spect.* 9, 4; 19, 2; 2, 43, 5f.

355. Jennison 167f.; Sen., *Ep.* 85, 41.

356. T., *Dial.* 29, 3; MA, *Med.* 1, 5.

357. Tertull., *De Spect.* 9; Plin., *NH* 7, 186.

358. CD 55, 10, 5.

359. J. Marquardt–G. Wissowa, *Rom. Staatsv.* iii,[2] 517–20.

360. Marquardt–Wissowa 521, n. 3.

361. *Dominus et agitator, ILS* 5296f.; Plin., *NH* 10, 71; Suet., *Nero* 22, 2.

362. Marquardt–Wissowa 520–3; *ILS* 5285, with Dessau's notes.

363. *Medicus, ILS* 5310, 5313; *doctor* (trainer), 5298; *conditor* (store-keeper), 5295, 5305f., 5313; *hortator*, 5307; *succonditor*, 5313; *tentor*, 5313; *sutor*, 5313; *cellarius*, 5309, 5313; *morator*, 5313. Suet., *C.Cal.* 55, 2; Marquardt–Wissowa 520–2.

364. Plin., *NH* 8, 162; Col. 6, 29, 4.

365. Spain, Mart. 14, 199; Symmach., *Ep.* 4, 7; 58 (*'dives equini pecoris Hispania'*); 60; 63; 5, 82f.; 7, 48; 82; 105f.; 9, 18–25; *CIL* vi, 10053.

366. *PBSR* 1948, pl. iv, fig. 9.

367. Schol. Juv. 1, 155; *RE* xvii, 2056–61.

368. CD 61, 6, 1–3.

369. *ILS* 5299; 5300, *'bigarius infans'*, both fascinating epitaphs in verse. Mosaic of *bigae, PBSR* 1948, pl. i, fig. 2.

370. *ILS* 5286–8. On *trigae*, see DH, *AR* 7, 73, 2.

371. *ILS* 5288; DH, *AR* 7, 73, 3. See Friedlaender iv, 183 (F. Drexel) (E.T. iv, 152); R. M. Geer, *TAPA* 1935, 211, n. 15 on *apobatai*.

372. Cassiod., *Var.* 3, 51, 4.

373. On the start, Ovid, *Am.* 3, 2, 65 and 77–80; Sid. Apoll., *Car.* 23, 318–41, largely based on Stat., *Theb.* 6, 389–409. Napkin, Juv. 11, 193–5; Suet., *Nero* 22, 2; Tertull., *De Spect.* 16; Cassiod., *Var.* 3, 51, 9.

374. CD 49, 43, 2.

375. Ovid, *Am.* 3, 2, 69f., an unskilful turn (too wide).

376. Sen., *Ep.* 30, 13; Sid. Apoll., *Car.* 23, 371f., *'Stringis quadriiugos et arte summa/in gyrum bene septimum reservas.'*

377. Sid. Apoll., *Car.* 23, 339–427.

378. *ILS* 5291a; 5293; 5307f.

379. *ILS* 5287f. See Friedlaender iv, 189 (E.T. iv, 157f.).

28

380. *ILS* 5287, 10f. See A. Elter, *Rhein. Mus.* 1886, 535ff.; Friedlaender iv, 191 (E.T. iv, 159f.).

381. *A carceribus ad calcem*, Cic., *De Senect.* 83; Sen., *Ep.* 108, 32; Plin., *NH* 35, 199. *Ad albatum* etc., *ILS* 5287, 9; Friedlaender iv, 190 (E.T. iv, 158f.).

382. Plin., *NH* 8, 160.

383. *ILS* 5278; 5283f.; 5288, 3; Ovid., *Am.* 3, 2, 73–8; Sen., *Controv.* 1, 3, 10; Friedlaender iv, 182f. (E.T. iv, 151).

384. Mart. 6, 46; 11, 33.

385. Doping, AM 26, 3, 3; 28, 1, 27; 28, 4, 25. Spells, *ILS* 8753 (quoted); Cassiod., *Var.* 3, 51, 2f. See A. Audollent, *Defixionum Tabellae*, Paris, 1904; *CI* 9, 18, 9.

386. Cf. Henzen, *Acta Fratr. Arv.* 36–9 for prizes at the *ludi* of the Arvales; Suet., *Nero* 5, 2.

387. Cassiod., *Var.* 3, 51, 10; Serv. ad Virg., *Georg.* 3, 18; CD 59, 7, 2f.; Suet., *Nero* 22, 2; Marquardt–Wissowa 515, n. 2; Degrassi 373f.

388. Plin., *Ep.* 9, 6; cf. Cassiod., *Var.* 3, 51, 12f.

389. Suet., *Vit.* 7, 1; 14, 3; CD 77, 10, 1; Mart. 6, 46.

390. CD 59, 14, 6; 63, 6, 3; 72, 17, 1; 73, 4, 1; 79, 14, 1; Suet., *C.Cal.* 55, 2; *Ner*, 22; SHA, *L.Ver.* 4, 7; 6, 3; Petron., *Sat.* 70.

391. Juv. 11, 197–201; cf. Cassiod., *Var.* 3, 51, 11.

392. AM 28, 4, 11 and 29–31, '*Cupitorum spes omnis Circus est maximus.*'

393. Refs. in Marquardt–Wissowa 523, n. 6. Cf. Galen's story, x, 478K, that enthusiasts gauged a horse's fitness by examination of its dung.

394. Petron., *Sat.* 70; Ovid, *AA* 1, 167; Mart. 11, 1, 15; Juv. 11, 201f.; Tertull., *De Spect.* 16.

395. Ovid, *Am.* 3, 2; Juv. 11, 201f.

396. Plin., *NH* 10, 71.

397. Tertull., De Spect. 22. Granting of freedom, *Dig.* 40, 9, 17; CD 69, 16, 3. Relations with emperors, Suet., *C.Cal.* 55, 2; CD 77, 1, 2. Scorpus, Mart. 10, 50 and 53.

398. Mart. 10, 74, 6; Juv. 7, 112–4.

399. *ILS* 5288.

400. *ILS* 5285.

401. *ILS* 5287; *CIL* xiv, 2884. For the details of all these racing records, see Friedlaender iv, 179–96 (E.T. iv, 148–64).

402. CD 62, 15, 1.

403. Suet., *DJ* 39, 2; L. 44, 9, 3f.; *BMC, R. Rep.* i, 301–3 and 549f.; ii, 288f.; pl. xxxvii, 10–12; liv, 22f.; xciv, 8f.; Cic., *Pro Mur.* 57; Varro, *RR* 2, 7, 15; *ILS* 5050, 154; Henzen, *Act. Frat. Arv.* 36; *RE* v, 255–9, s.v. *'Desultor'; Bull de la soc. nat. des antiquaires de France*, 1961, 117–20. Cf. Sen., *Suas.* 1, 7; Ovid, *Am.* 1, 3, 15.

404. *Mél. d'arch. et d'hist.* 1886, 327f., pl. ix; Sil. Ital., *Pun.* 10, 467–71; Manil., *Astr.* 5, 85–9.

405. Running, DH, *AR* 7, 73, 3; CD 60, 23, 5; Plin., *NH* 7, 84. Boxing and wrestling, DH, *AR* 7, 73, 3; Suet., *DA* 45, 2; *C.Cal.* 18, 1; Hor., *Ep.* 2, 1, 186.

406. Suet., *DA* 18, 2; CD 51, 1, 2; Strabo 7, 325C.

407. Friedlaender ii, 145f.; iv, 281 (E.T. ii, 117–9; iv, 263f.). On the Italika at Naples, Suet., *DA* 98, 5; Strabo 5, 246C; CD 55, 10, 9; *IG* xiv, 748 (43rd celebration, A.D. 170); 754f.; W. Dittenberger–K. Purgold, *Die Inschriften von Olympia*, Berlin, 1896, no. 56 (reproduced in *Par. d. Passato* 1952, 406ff); R. M. Geer, 'The Greek Games at Naples,' *TAPA* 1935, 208–221. On Greek games generally in Rome and the Empire, Friedlaender ii, 145–60; iv, 276–83 (E.T. ii, 117–30; iv, 263–70). Cf. Plin, *Ep.* 10, 75, a legacy which might be applied to the creation of quinquennial games, *Traiani*, in Pontus in honour of Trajan.

408. Schol. Juv. 4, 53.

409. Main sources, T*A* 14, 20f.; Suet., *Nero* 12, 3f.; CD 61, 21, 1f.; coins, H. Mattingly–E. A. Sydenham, *RIC* i, 171–4, *Certamen quinquennale Romae constitutum; RE* xvii, 42–8, s.v. *'Neronia'*.

410. T*A* 14, 22, 1.

411. T*A* 16, 4f.; Suet., *Nero* 21; CD 62, 29, 1.

412. Censorin., *De die nat.* 18, 15; Suet., *Dom.* 4, 4; Mart. 4, 1, 6; 4, 54, 1; 9, 23, 5; Juv. 6, 387f.; *RE* iii, 1527–9; Friedlaender ii, 147f. (E.T. ii, 120f.; iv, 264–8).

413. Kaibel, *Epigr. Gr.* 618 (*ILS* 5177); Stat., *Silv.* 3, 5, 31–3; 5, 3, 225–7.

414. *ILS* 5178.

415. *ILS* 5288, 15f. (2nd cent. A.D.); Herod. 8, 8, 3; *CI* 10, 53; AV, *Caes.* 27, 7; *RE* xvii, 46f. On the history of the Agon Capitolinus, see Friedlaender ii, 148f.; iv, 276–80 (E.T. iv, 264–8).

416. Suet., *DJ* 39, 1; *C.Cal.* 58, 1; *Nero* 12, 1; SHA, *Hadr.* 19, 8 etc.

417. See, on this whole subject, *RE* xiii, 2059–67, s.v. *'Lusus Troiae'* (K. Schneider). A. Alföldi, *Early Rome and the Latins*, 281–3 disagrees.

418. Plut., *Cato mi.* 3, 1f. See my article, 'Sulla Felix', *JRS* 1951, 1–10.

419. CD 48, 20, 2; 49, 43, 3; 51, 22, 4.

420. *Aen.* 5, 545–603.

421. CD 54, 26, 1; 55, 10, 6; Suet., *DA* 43, 2. Galen xiv, 212K is the only later reference to such activity.

422. Marquardt–Wissowa 527.

423. App., *BC* 2, 102, 423; Suet., *D.Cl.* 21, 6.

424. Julius, CD 43, 23, 4; 45, 17, 8. Augustus, *RG* 23; VP 2, 100, 2; Suet., *DA* 43, 1, *Caesarum nemus*; TA 14, 15, 3, *navale stagnum*. Vestiges in Cassius Dio's time, CD 55, 10, 7. See *TDAR*, s.v.

425. Suet., *Domit.* 4, 2.

426. 46 B.C., Suet., *DJ* 39, 4. 2 B.C., *RG* 23; CD 55, 10, 7. A.D. 52, TA 12, 56; Suet., *D.Cl.* 21, 6; CD 60, 33, 3f. Nero, Suet. *Nero* 12, 1; CD 61, 9, 5. Titus, Suet., *D.Tit.* 7, 3; Mart., *Lib. Spect.* 24–6 and 28; CD 66, 25, 3f. On the representation of Actium, Hor., *Ep.* 1, 18, 59–64.

427. *RG* 23; TA 12, 56, 2; Friedlaender ii, 92–4 (E.T. ii, 74–6).

428. *FIR* 28 (*FIRA* 1, 21; *ILS* 6087), 70f. (magistrates) and 128 (*magistri*).

429. *ILS* 5053, 4. Cf. R. Étienne, *O.c.* (n. 53), 434. On *Catervarii*, cf. *ILS* 5176 and Suet., *DA* 45.

430. Capua, *CIL* 1, 2², 675–8, pp. 518f. Antium, Cic., *Ad Att.* 2, 8, 2. Fundi etc., *ILS* 6281; 6333; 6451; 6295.

431. *CIL* xi, 5820.

432. *FIR* 28 (see n. 428 above), 128.

433. TA 13, 49, *vulgarissimum senatus consultum*; Plin., *Pan* 54, 4.

434. Asiarchs, *ILS* 5081; *IGR* iv, 156; Galen xiii, 599–601; xviii, 567K. See Mommsen, *Ges. Schr.* 8, 517, n. 6 for further references to shows by Asiarchs. Cf. *ILS* 5079 (Baetica).

435. *ILS* 5163, 59–61; 9340.

436. Theveste, *ILS* 6838; Apul., *Met.* 10, 18.

437. *ILS* 5163, 14–18. See J. H. Oliver, R. E. A. Palmer, 'Minutes of an Act of the Roman Senate,' *Hesperia* 1955, 320–49, pointing out that money was to be saved by the cheap supply of men condemned to death (*noxii*), and that an immediate consequence may have been the massacre of Christians at Lugdunum in A.D. 177. P. Keresztes, 'The Massacre at Lyons in 177 A.D.', *Historia*, 1967, 75–86, disagrees.

438. *ILS* 5062; 5092; 5163, 39–42. On formal imperial approval, Mommsen, *Ges. Schr.* 8, 513 and n. 3.

439. Cic., *Pro Sull.* 54. Though not fully legal in the case of Roman citizens until the time of Nerva and Hadrian (see S–W on Plin., *Ep.* 10, 75), such legacies to communities were evidently effective earlier.

440. *ILS* 5064.

441. *ILS* 5065. Cf. *XIL* viii, 9092.

442. Plin., *Ep.* 10, 75.

443. Hor., *Sat.* 2, 3, 84–7; Suet., *Tib.* 37, 3.

444. Plin., *Ep.* 1, 8, 9–13.

445. Petron., *Sat.* 45.

446. *CIL* v, 8664 (Concordia); xi, 6377 (Pisaurum); ix, 1175 (Aeclanum).

447. *ILAfr.* 390. See, for full details, R. Duncan-Jones, *PBSR* 1962, 96f.; 1965, 270. On Iguvium, see n. 431 above.

448. *ILS* 411. See R. Duncan-Jones, *PBSR* 1962, 111, n. 145.

449. Suet., *Vit.* 12; Juv. 3, 34–40. Fidenae, *TA* 4, 62f. (50,000 casualties); Suet., *Tib.* 40 (over 20,000 killed). The Chronographer of A.D. 354 (see *MGH*, Chron. Min., ed. Th. Mommsen, 1, 145) gives less sensational figures (4,205 killed). Cf. Suet., *DA* 43, 5 for fear even at Rome that such temporary structures might collapse.

450. *ILS* 5163, 29f.; Mommsen, *Ges. Schr.* 8, 512. In Mart. 5, 24, 9, *locarii* presumably means men who charged for seats.

451. *TH* 2, 67; 2, 21; *ILS* 5628. On Ummidia Quadratilla, see n. 208 above.

452. For a list of known Italian and provincial theatres, see Friedlaender iv, 243–57.

453. Aug., *Conf.* 3, 2, 2–4.

454. For a list of known Italian and provincial amphitheatres, see Friedlaender iv, 205–40 (E.T. iv, 193–255); M. Grant, *Gladiators*, London, 1967, 85–8.

455. Plin., *Ep.* 10, 39.

456. Alexandria, Strabo 17, 795C. Racing at Trier, M. Bös, 'Spielsteine als Rennpferde,' *Bonn. Jahrb.* 1955/6, 178–83. List of known circuses in the Empire, *RE* iii, 2584f.; Friedlaender iv, 240–2, seventeen in the western provinces and N. Africa.

457. *ILS* 5053, 4.

458. P. Wuilleumier, *O.c.* (n. 42), 63–71.

459. *Athletae* at Pompeii, CIL iv, 7989; 7993.

460. R. Étienne, *O.c.* (n. 53), 436.

461. L. 41, 20, 10–13.

462. Athens and Corinth, Dio Chrys., *Or.* 31, 121; Philostr., *Vit. Apoll. Tyan.* 4, 22. Liban., *Or.* 35, 4 and 13f.; 48, 6f. Cf. L. Robert, *O.c.* (n. 252).

463. Jennison 165–73; *ILS* 5053–5; 5059–62; 5063a. On Numidian bears and African boars, Jennison 49f., arguing that Plin., *NH* 8, 228 is wrong in denying their existence.

464. Plin., *Ep.* 6, 34; Apul., *Met.* 4, 13f.

465. Plin., *Ep.* 10, 118, *certamina iselastica*, with S–W's notes. Vienne, Plin., *Ep.* 4, 22. See Friedlaender iv, 281–3; L. Moretti, *Iscrizioni agonistiche greche*, Rome, 1953, 165–9, on women competitors.

466. Dio Chrys., *Or.* 32; Liban., *Or.* 64, 79–82; L. Robert, *O.c.* (n. 252).

467. *P. Oxy.* iii, 413.

468. *CIL* iv, 1183; 1185f; 3881f.; 3884; 7992; 7994f.

469. *CIL* iv, 1989.

470. *CIL* iv, 2508.

471. *ILS* 5186; 5189; 5193f.; 5196; 5200; 5209a; 5275.

472. Suet., *DA* 44, 1. Local dignitaries at Urso, *FIR* 18 (*FIRA* 21), 125–7.

473. R. Étienne, *O.c.* (n. 53), 429, fig. 41; A. Mau, *Pompeji in Leben und Kunst*, Leipzig, 1908, 223f. (E.T. 213–5).

474. *ILS* 2178f. See Th. Mommsen, 'Schauspieleninschriften,' *Hermes*, 1871, 303–8.

475. Fronto, *Princ. Hist.* 17 (ii, 214–6 Loeb.).

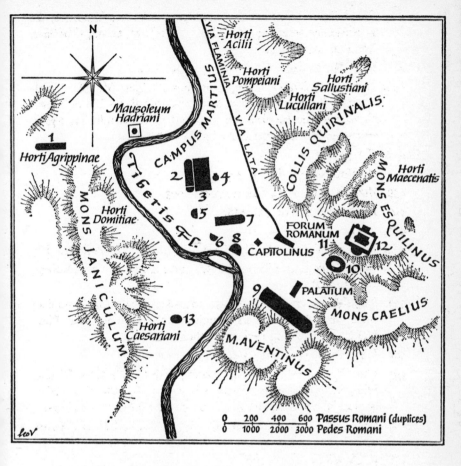

KEY TO PLAN OF ROME

1 Circus of Gaius and Nero	8 Theatre of Marcellus
2 Stadium of Domitian (Piazza Navona)	9 Circus Maximus
3 Thermae of Nero	10 Amphitheatrum Flavium (Colosseum)
4 Pantheon	11 Site of Golden House of Nero
5 Theatre of Pompey	12 Baths of Trajan
6 Theatre of Balbus	13 Naumachia of Augustus
7 Circus Flaminius	

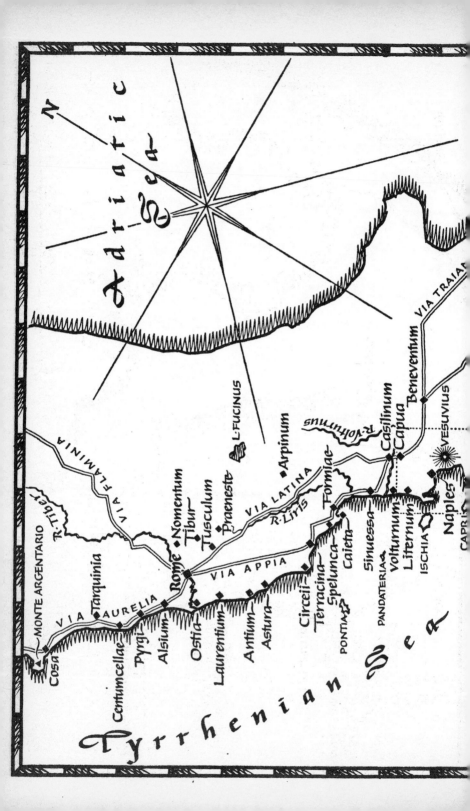

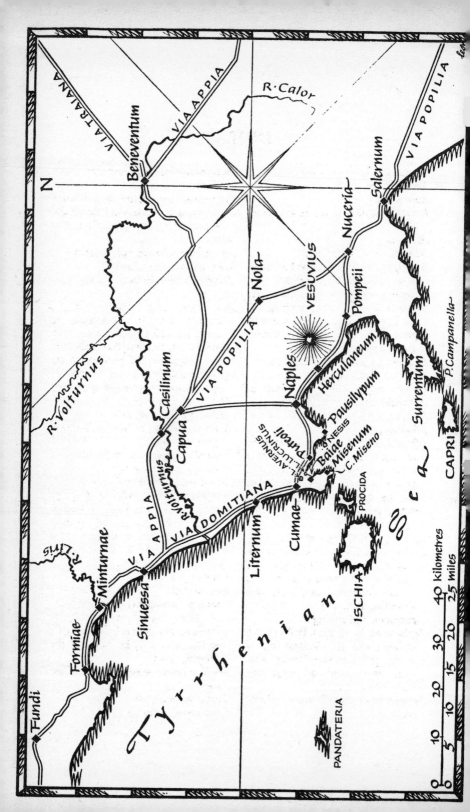

INDEX

Kate Page-Smith